MATTHEW, JAMES, AND DIDACHE

Society of Biblical Literature

Symposium Series

Victor H. Matthews
Series Editor

Number 45

MATTHEW, JAMES, AND DIDACHE

MATTHEW, JAMES, AND DIDACHE:

THREE RELATED DOCUMENTS
IN THEIR JEWISH AND CHRISTIAN SETTINGS

Edited by

Huub van de Sandt

and

Jürgen K. Zangenberg

Society of Biblical Literature

Atlanta

MATTHEW, JAMES, AND DIDACHE

Library of Congress Cataloging-in-Publication Data

Matthew, James, and Didache : three related documents in their Jewish and Christian setting / edited by Huub van de Sandt and Jürgen Zangenberg.
    p. cm. — (Society of Biblical Literature symposium series ; no. 45)
    Proceedings of a conference held Apr. 12-13, 2007 at the University of Tilburg, the Netherlands.
    Includes bibliographical references (p.   ) and indexes.
    ISBN 978-1-58983-358-6 (paper binding : alk. paper)
    1. Bible. N.T. Matthew—Criticism, interpretation, etc.—Congresses. 2. Bible. N.T. James—Criticism, interpretation, etc.—Congresses. 3. Didache—Criticism, interpretation, etc.—Congresses. 4. Christianity and other religions—Judaism—Congresses. 5. Judaism—Relations—Christianity—Congresses. I. Sandt, Hubertus Waltherus Maria van de, 1946- II. Zangenberg, Jürgen.
    BS2575.52.M39 2008
    226.2'06—dc22

                                                                    2008027162

15 14 13 12 11 10 09 08 07   5 4 3 2 1

Printed in the United States of America on acid-free, recycled paper conforming to ANSI/NISO Z39.48-1992 (R1997) and ISO 9706:1994 standards for paper permanence.

CONTENTS

PART 4. INTERPRETING TORAH

PART 5. OBSERVING RITUALS

ABBREVIATIONS

1. PRIMARY SOURCES: ANCIENT TEXTS

'Abod. Zar.	*'Abodah Zarah*
Acts Paul	*Acts of Paul*
Apoc. Mos.	*Apocalypse of Moses*
Apos. Con.	*Apostolic Constitutions*
b	Bavli (Babylonian Talmud)
2 Bar.	*2 Baruch* (Syriac Apocalypse)
Barn.	*Barnabas*
B. Bat.	*Baba Batra*
B. Meṣi'a	*Baba Meṣi'a*
B. Qam.	*Baba Qamma*
Ber.	*Berakot*
CD	Cairo Genizah copy of the Damascus Document
1–2 Clem.	*1–2 Clement*
Diogn.	*Diognetus*
1 En.	*1 Enoch* (Ethiopic Apocalypse)
2 En.	*2 Enoch* (Slavonic Apocalypse)
Giṭ.	*Giṭṭin*
Gos. Pet.	*Gospel of Peter*
Gos. Thom.	*Gospel of Thomas*
H	Codex Hierosolymitanus 54
Ḥag.	*Ḥagigah*
Herm. *Vis.*	Sheperd of Hermas, *Vision*
Herm. *Sim.*	Sheperd of Hermas, *Similitude*
Hor.	*Horayot*
Ḥul.	*Ḥullin*
Ketub.	*Ketubbot*
Kidd.	*Kiddušin*
L.A.E.	*Life of Adam and Eve*
Let. Aris.	*Letter of Aristeas*
m	Mishnah
Meg.	*Megillah*
Mek.	*Mekilta*

Menaḥ.	Menaḥot
Naz.	Nazir
Ned.	Nedarim
Ps.-Phoc.	Pseudo-Phocylides
Pss. Sol.	Psalms of Solomon
1QM	Milḥamah *or* War Scroll
1QS	Serek Hayaḥad *or* Rule of the Community
4QpIsaᵃ	4QIsaiah Pesherᵃ
4QpPsᵃ	4QPsalms Pesherᵃ
11QTemp	11QTemple Scroll
Roš Haš.	*Roš Haššanah*
Šabb.	*Šabbat*
Sanh.	Sanhedrin
Sib. Or.	Sibylline Oracles
t	Tosefta
Ta'an.	Ta'anit
T. 12 Patr.	Testaments of the Twelve Patriarchs
T. Ash.	Testament of Asher
T. Benj.	Testament of Benjamin
T. Dan	Testament of San
T. Iss.	Testament of Issachar
T. Jos.	Testament of Joseph
T. Jud.	Testament of Judah
T. Zeb.	Testament of Zebulun
y	Yerushalmi (Palestinian Talmud)
Yebam.	Yebamot

2. Secondary Sources:
Journals, Periodicals, Major Reference Works, and Series

AB	Anchor Bible
ABD	Anchor Bible Dictionary.
ABR	*Australian Biblical Review*
ABRL	Anchor Bible Reference Library
AGJU	Arbeiten zur Geschichte des antiken Judentums und des Urchristentums
AJSR	*Association for Jewish Studies Review*
ALGHJ	Arbeiten zur Literatur und Geschichte des hellenistischen Judentums
AnBib	Analecta biblica
ANRW	*Aufstieg und Niedergang der römischen Welt.* Part 2, *Principat,* 26.1. Edited by W. Haase and H. Temporini. New York: de Gruyter, 1992.

ANTZ	Arbeiten zur neutestamentlichen Theologie und Zeit-geschichte
ATR	*Australasian Theological Review*
AUSS	*Andrews University Seminary Studies*
BAR	*Biblical Archaeology Review*
BBR	*Bulletin for Biblical Research*
BETL	Bibliotheca ephemeridum theologicarum lovaniensium
BEvT	Beiträge zur evangelischen Theologie
BFCT	Beiträge zur Förderung christlicher Theologie
BHT	Beiträge zur historischen Theologie
Bib	*Biblica*
BibInt	*Biblical Interpretation*
BSac	*Bulletin de la Société d'archéologie copte*
BTB	*Biblical Theology Bulletin*
BWA(N)T	Beiträge zur Wissenschaft vom Alten (und Neuen) Testament
BZ	*Biblische Zeitschrift*
BZAW	Beihefte zur Zeitschrift für die alttestamentliche Wissenschaft
BZNW	Beihefte zur Zeitschrift für die neutestamentliche Wissenschaft
BZRGG	Beihefte zur Zeitschrift für Religions- und Geistesgeschichte
CBQ	*Catholic Biblical Quarterly*
ClQ	*Classical Quarterly*
CNT	Commentaire du Nouveau Testament
ConBNT	Coniectanea neotestamentica or Coniectanea biblica: New Testament Series
CRINT	Compendia rerum iudaicarum ad Novum Testamentum
CSHJ	Chicago Studies in the History of Judaism
DJD	Discoveries in the Judaean Desert
Ebib	Etudes bibliques
EKKNT	Evangelisch-katholischer Kommentar zum Neuen Testament
Enc	*Encounter*
EncJud	*Encyclopaedia Judaica. 16 vols. Jerusalem, 1972*
ExpTim	*Expository Times*
FB	Forschung zur Bibel
FRLANT	Forschungen zur Religion und Literatur des Alten und Neuen Testaments

GNT	Grundrisse zum Neuen Testament
HeyJ	*Heythrop Journal*
HNT	Handbuch zum Neuen Testament
HTKNT	Herders theologischer Kommentar zum Neuen Testament
HTR	*Harvard Theological Review*
HUCA	*Hebrew Union College Annual*
HvTSt	*Hervormde teologiese studies*
ICC	International Critical Commentary
JAAR	*Journal of the American Academy of Religion*
JBL	*Journal of Biblical Literature*
JECS	*Journal of Early Christian Studies*
JESHO	*Journal of the Economic and Social History of the Orient*
JJS	*Journal of Jewish Studies*
JNES	*Journal of Near Eastern Studies*
JQR	*Jewish Quarterly Review*
JSJ	*Journal for the Study of Judaism in the Persian, Hellenistic, and Roman Periods*
JSJSup	Journal for the Study of Judaism in the Persian, Hellenistic, and Roman Periods: Supplement Series
JSNT	*Journal for the Study of the New Testament*
JSNTSup	Journal for the Study of the New Testament: Supplement Series
JSOTSup	Journal for the Study of the Old Testament: Supplement Series
JSPSup	Journal for the Study of the Pseudepigrapha: Supplement Series
JTS	*Journal of Theological Studies*
Jud	*Judaica*
KBL	Koehler, L., and W. Baumgartner, *Lexicon in Veteris Testamenti libros*. 2nd ed. Leiden, 1958
KEK	Kritisch-exegetischer Kommentar über das Neue Testament (Meyer-Kommentar)
LCL	Loeb Classical Library
LEC	Library of Early Christianity
L&N	*Greek-English Lexicon of the New Testament: Based on Semantic Domains*. Edited by J. P. Louw and E. A. Nida. 2nd ed. New York, 1989
LNTS	Library of New Testament Studies
LSJ	Liddell, H.G., R. Scott, H.S. Jones, and R. McKenzie, *A Greek-English Lexicon*. 9th ed. with revised supplement. Oxford, 1996

LUÅ	Lunds universitets årsskrift
MdB	*Le Monde de la Bible*
NBf	*New Blackfrairs*
Neot	*Neotestamentica*
NICNT	New International Commentary on the New Testament
NIGTC	New International Greek Testament Commentary
NovT	*Novum Testamentum*
NovTSup	Novum Testamentum Supplements
NTAbh	Neutestamentliche Abhandlungen
NTOA	Novum Testamentum et Orbis Antiquus
NTS	*New Testament Studies*
NTTS	New Testament Tools and Studies
OBO	Orbis biblicus et orientalis
ÖTK	Ökumenischer Taschenbuch-Kommentar
PFLUS	Publications de la Faculté des lettres de l'université de Strasbourg
QD	Quaestiones disputatae
RB	*Revue biblique*
REJ	*Revue des études juives*
RHR	*Revue de l'histoire des religions*
RNT	Regensburger Neues Testament
SANT	Studien zum Alten und Neuen Testaments
SBL	Society of Biblical Literature
SBLDS	Society of Biblical Literature Dissertation Series
SBLSBS	Society of Biblical Literature Sources for Biblical Study
SBLSP	Society of Biblical Literature Seminar Papers
SBLSymS	Society of Biblical Literature Symposium Series
SBS	Stuttgarter Bibelstudien
SC	Sources chrétiennes
ScrHier	Scripta hierosolymitana
SE	*Studia evangelica*
SemeiaSt	Semeia Studies
SJLA	*Studies in Judaism in Late Antiquity*
SJT	*Scottish Journal of Theology*
SNTSMS	Society for New Testament Studies Monograph Series
SNTSU	Studien zum Neuen Testament und seiner Umwelt
SP	Sacra pagina
SR	*Studies in Religion*
STDJ	Studies on the Texts of the Desert of Judah
StPB	Studia post-biblica
StPatr	Studia patristica

SUNT	Studien zur Umwelt des Neuen Testaments
TANZ	Texte und Arbeiten zum neutestamentlichen Zeitalter
TDNT	Theological Dictionary of the New Testament
ThH	Théologie historique
THKNT	Theologischer Handkommentar zum Neuen Testament
TLZ	*Theologische Literaturzeitung*
TNTC	Tyndale New Testament Commentaries
TRE	*Theologische Realenzyklopädie*
TSAJ	Texte und Studien zum antiken Judentum
TU	Texte und Untersuchungen
TZ	*Theologische Zeitschrift*
VC	*Vigiliae christianae*
VCSup	Vigiliae christianae Supplements
WBC	Word Biblical Commentary
WMANT	Wissenschaftliche Monographien zum Alten und Neuen Testament
WUNT	Wissenschaftliche Untersuchungen zum Neuen Testament
ZAC	*Zeitschrift für Antikes Christentum/Journal of Ancient Christianity*
ZAW	*Zeitschrift für die alttestamentliche Wissenschaft*
ZBK	Zürcher Bibelkommentare
ZKG	*Zeitschrift für Kirchengeschichte*
ZNW	*Zeitschrift für die neutestamentliche Wissenschaft und die Kunde der älteren Kirche*
ZTK	*Zeitschrift für Theologie und Kirche*

INTRODUCTION

Huub van de Sandt and Jürgen K. Zangenberg

On April 12 and 13, 2007, an international conference on Matthew, James, and the Didache in their historical, social, and religious settings was held at the University of Tilburg in the Netherlands. This meeting represents the continuation of a research process initiated with a conference held at Tilburg in April 2003 whose main concern was to exchange ideas on the possible common environment of two early Christian writings, Matthew and the Didache. The proceedings of that conference were edited by Huub van de Sandt and published as *Matthew and the Didache: Two Documents from the Same Jewish-Christian Milieu?* (Assen: Van Gorcum, 2005).

The subject of the 2007 meeting broadened the scope of the 2003 conference to include the Letter of James as well. It is commonly accepted that Matthew and James share important features, and the same holds true for Matthew and the Didache and—perhaps to a lesser degree—for James and the Didache. The agreements and common perspectives within Matthew, James, and the Didache may be accounted for by theories of sources or traditions the authors used, or more generally their common Jewish-Christian background. The likelihood that the relationship between the three writings is one of literary dependence seems negligible however.

Matthew, James, and the Didache are writings that most certainly span the worlds of Judaism and Christianity. As far as we can tell, the vast majority of Jewish Christians continued to observe the whole law, taking for granted that they were still obliged to do so. The three documents could reflect various stages in the development of a network of communities that shared basic theological assumptions and expressions, or they may represent contemporaneous strands or different regional forms of the same wider phenomenon we now call Jewish Christianity. Of particular importance for the reconstruction of the religious and social milieu of the communities behind Matthew, James, and the Didache are issues such as the observance of Jewish law and elements of Jewish piety. We believe that in addition to the Pauline and Johannine "schools," Matthew, James, and the Didache represent a third important religious milieu within earliest Christianity, which is characterized by its distinct connections to a particular ethical stream of contemporary Jewish tradition. This is so even if cohesion between these three documents is less distinct and constituted differently compared to the Pauline and Johannine corpora and would certainly not exclude possible affinities to other early Christian documents. This is why we prefer the somewhat more vague term "milieu" to the sociologically more definitive "school" with all its problems, assumptions, and implications. The ultimate aim of this conference was to explore ways to identify topics common to these three documents, discuss possible implications for a reconstruction of their sociological background and make attempts to describe this "milieu."

This volume contains the papers presented at the 2007 meeting in Tilburg. Each paper focuses on individual aspects of the interrelationship between the Gospel of Matthew, the Letter of James, and the Didache. Their authors are scholars of the New Testament, Second Temple Judaism, the History of Liturgy and Patristics. Instead of looking at Matthew and James as a subject of study belonging to the New Testament only and instead of considering the Didache as pertaining to Patristics alone, each author was asked to place his or her individual topic in the wider context of Jewish and Christian religious history.

The seventeen papers included in this volume are arranged in five sections. The first section, "Methods and Milieus," deals with the social context of each of the three documents, Matthew, James, and the Didache, in an integrative perspective. The issue at stake is the vexing problem of reconstruction. To what extent do these texts help us trace their own roots and histories? How can we move from the literary world of texts to the social, or "real," world to which Matthew, James, and the Didache belonged? In the opening article David Sim examines the social and religious milieu of Matthew and his intended readers. He joins the fairly well-established consensus about Antioch as the place where the Gospel was written sometime after 70 c.e. The question of the social and religious setting of Matthew is then put in a broader perspective, taking up the question of the relationship between Matthew's community and the Jewish world. Did Matthew's group still identify itself as part of the Jewish world, or had it broken ties with its Jewish heritage, and if yes, in what respect? Matthean scholarship is divided over this issue. Yet what is often missing in discussions of the social setting of this Gospel is a careful assessment of the relationship of the Matthean community with the Gentile world, the Roman Imperial context, and other Christian groups.

Oda Wischmeyer explores the social and religious milieu of James. She begins with brief reflections on the term milieu and ways to specify its relevant parameters. Applying these parameters to James's text, a religious and literary Christian milieu emerges whose religious culture is shaped by the Septuagint in its early Christian ethical interpretation. The addressees must also have been acquainted with Jewish and Christian traditions (oral as well as textual) and were generally interested in literature that combines religion and ethics.

Jürgen Zangenberg takes up the same issue with respect to the Didache. He approaches the question with several caveats that seem especially appropriate in the case of Didache. The first of these is the general murkiness of all relationships between a text and what we call "milieu." While texts contain elements that can be used to reconstruct its social and ideological background, they are never comprehensive or direct enough to be taken as simple "reflections" of a supposed "milieu." Didache's character as an anonymous and composite document needs to be taken into account by anyone attempting to reconstruct its cultural and sociological background. After a step-by-step analysis of crucial passages and their relationship to other Jewish and early Christian traditions, Zangenberg comes to the tentative conclusion that the Didache "came from anywhere in the Greek-speaking (eastern) Mediterranean, that it was deeply rooted in Judaism and shows striking similarities with Matthew and—to a lesser but still significant degree—with James, and all three might very well have come from a common 'milieu'" (p. 69).

The second section, "Conflicts and Contacts," presents three studies of Matthew, James, and the Didache in their socio-historical settings. These contributions focus on disputes between and competition among other early Christian groups and on how contact and conflict with the "outside" world were regulated. After a brief survey of the general problems involved in textual interpretation, Magnus Zetterholm turns to the specific problems of texts that cannot be located in time or space with any precision, written by authors who cannot be identified, directed to communities unknown to us. These issues have by no means been resolved. As a way out of the dilemma, Zetterholm pursues a hypothetical-deductive model in which relatively well-founded conjectures regarding the origin and development of the texts are used as theoretical assumptions. This approach is suggested as a point of departure for investigating Matthew and the Didache. Both writings are taken to reflect historical developments in the relations between Jews and non-Jews within the Jesus-believing movement in Antioch. The conclusion is that both Matthew and the Didache should be seen as two different ways of dealing with the problem of alleged moral impurity among non-Jews.

Peter Tomson outlines a rough framework of Jewish history in the Roman Empire between 50 and 150 c.e. The series of Jewish wars against Rome in the late-first and early-second centuries imply that profound transformations had taken place within Judaism. The extent of these transformations has recently become a much-debated subject. One may distinguish two approaches to the period between 66 and 135 c.e.: the "classical" approach represented by Gedalyahu Alon and Shmuel Safrai and a modern one embodied by Seth Schwartz in particular. Tomson emphasizes the ideological and military power of the Jews in the ultimate collision with Rome, the important role of rabbinic leadership in this conflict and the growing confrontation between Jews, Judaeo-Christians, and Gentile Christians in the period under discussion. This historical background directly affects the interpretation of the three writings. For Tomson, Matthew and the Didache reflect social tensions between each of these communities and the Pharisees, even a clash between these communities and Jewish society as a whole. And it is also possible to read the Letter of James under the assumption that certain Jewish Christian groups had come under fire from competing Gentile Christian quarters.

Joseph Verheyden addresses how these three documents have figured in discussions about how to define what is usually called "Jewish Christianity." He points out that all definitions are hampered by the very fragmentary character of available sources (literary as well as archaeological) and often blurred by academic debates about overarching historical or dogmatic issues. The criteria by which ideological and behavioral phenomena are considered "Judaeo-Christian" often remains unclear. The debate is a healthy reminder that neither Judaism nor Christianity were monolithic entities. For Verheyden the only reasonable consequence is to choose a broad definition. He concludes: "There is no standard definition of Jewish Christianity and there never was. There are only ways and forms of being a Jewish Christian and we have only a very limited access to them. Perhaps then the real challenge is not to focus on what holds the evidence together, but rather fully to recognize that the evidence is of necessity and by definition diverse because of the nature of the phenomenon itself" (p. 128). What then does all that mean for the interpretation of Matthew, James, and the Didache? Following Gunnar Garleff, Verheyden sees these three documents as an attempt to shape early Christian identity by forming ethos, ritus, and community structure in close contact and often also conflict with Judaism. Nevertheless, an analysis of these three documents raises further questions, above all about "the limits of this apparently quite flexible concept of Jewish Christianity" (p. 135).

Four other topics are treated in the third section on "Community and Identity." How did the communities behind Matthew, James, and the Didache shape their identity both ideologically and structurally? What factors contributed to that process? In this section's first paper, Jonathan Draper carefully examines six leadership roles found in the three texts: prophet, teacher, apostle, bishop, deacon and elder. In the course of his analysis, he compares these roles in Matthew, Didache, James and other early Christian texts. While the Didache and Matthew do show significant affinities, James clearly stands apart and fits instead into an environment better characterized by "wisdom than charisma." Yet the comparison displays some overlap as well since "all three writings appear concerned about false leaders who seek to exploit the community financially, as well as to give false teaching, and all three see the lifestyle of the leader as the appropriate test of authenticity" (p. 176).

Wim Weren analyzes the semantics of how each of the three documents constructed individual images of the ideal community. He explores three topics: how the community is referred to, the community's relationship to God and Jesus, and the concept of perfection (*teleios*). In Matthew both the local community and the totality of such communities is referred to as *ekklesia*. For Weren the concept has a polemic connotation over against other Jewish groups and communities. In James and the Didache the term *ekklesia* is associated with diaspora and symbolizes the hope that Christian communities will participate in a united Israel. With respect to the second topic, James and the Didache focus prominently on God, whereas Matthew elaborates the community's close relationship to Jesus. The adjective *teleios* represents the third theme, a term describing ideal behavior in each of the three documents (on this topic see also Jens Schröter in this volume). In Matthew, James, and the Didache, *teleios* expresses full observance of the Torah. Yet the Didache takes a position of its own and opens up the community to members who are not "perfect."

In their analyses of Matthew, James, and the Didache commentators time and again have treated "poor" and "pious" as parallel concepts. John Kloppenborg puts this assumption to the test. Are the poor, the exploited and destitute underclasses to be equated with the pious? Was poverty a religiously charged concept? The paper examines the historical and conceptual basis for this notion of poverty and finds that in biblical and later Judaean literature those in a state of poverty were not thought to be privileged by virtue of their poverty. Kloppenborg then focuses on the Didache, Matthew, and James. Although Did. 3:7–4:4 is often taken to reflect the belief typical of the "piety of the poor," the passage shows no trace of poverty. Matthew too has relatively little to say about the poor or poverty. His concern is not primarily with the poor but with the households of the Jesus movement. At first sight one might think that James firmly identifies with the poor against the rich via the traditional piety-poverty link. However he does not show solidarity with the plight of the poor and still less equates the poor with believers. He uses the common rhetorical topos of rich and poor only in order to expose inequalities already generally lamented in Greco-Roman society.

Jens Schröter explores the Jesus (or synoptic) traditions in Matthew, James, and the Didache. The concept of "perfection" is central to his paper (on this topic also see Wim Weren's article in this volume). This element presents itself prominently in all three writings and functions as an interpretive key for the Jesus traditions found there. However each of the three documents deals with this topic in a noticeably different way. In James, Jesus traditions are used side by side with quotations from Scripture or other Jewish and early Christian traditions in order to develop the idea of wisdom as the way to perfection. There is no trace at all that James knew these traditions as specifically connected to Jesus. An important feature in Matthew is the presentation of Jesus's ethical teachings, which brings traditional Jewish commandments to their completion. Traditions are regarded valid only if interpreted from Jesus's radicalized perspective. In the Didache the "entire yoke of the Lord" (6:2) is important. The notion entails all commandments of the *sectio evangelica* (Did. 1:3b–2:1), which must be kept in order to achieve perfection. The presence of the Jesus traditions in these Didache instructions and even more in its teaching of liturgical and eschatological matters serves to help develop a "Christian" in contrast to a "Jewish" identity.

The fourth section, "Interpreting Torah," investigates the exposition of the Torah, halakic discussion, and moral imperatives with regard to Matthew, James, and the Didache. J. Andrew Overman observes that over the last twenty years scholarship concerned with formative Christianity and Judaism has emphasized the diversity within so-called Judaisms and early Christianities. However this new approach raised problems of how to distinguish between Jews, Christians, and Jewish Christians (on this issue also see Joseph Verheyden's article in the present volume). Overman's observation is particularly relevant for the study of such seemingly related documents as Matthew, James, and the Didache. Matthew focuses on the competition between his community and another closely related group of Jewish leaders and retainers. Matthew believes his community and their application of the Torah is much better suited to guide the local population by urging them to get along with Roman provincial authorities. The Didache is a manual for a community that is well on the way to being organized; it focuses above all on internal issues and behavior. James represents a type of Judaism that found certain Greek philosophical notions quite compatible with Jewish history and whatever Jesus came to accomplish. It is only their usage of a shared Two Ways ethical tradition that requires us to relate the documents to one another.

Matthias Konradt concentrates on the command to love one's neighbor which is based on Lev 19:18 and is found three times in Matthew's Gospel (5:43; 19:19; 22:39). In Matthew the command has developed in two directions. By referring to outsiders—even enemies—the love command transcends the boundaries of the local community. Moreover, it involves the social perspective of merciful care for the poor. The love command in Jas 2:8 is based upon the Hebrew Scriptures. It is quoted in a context rejecting partiality toward rich people. As in Matthew, it features prominently, functions as a summary of God's will, and implies charitable love. Didache 1:2 associates the two precepts occurring in Lev 19:18 (to love man) and Deut 6:5 (to love God) with the proclamation of the Golden Rule as a summary of the whole Torah. In this respect the Didache reveals a strong affinity with the Matthean Gospel, which also takes the double-love commandment and the Golden Rule as summary statements of the law (Matt 22:37–40 and 7:12). There is also a resemblance among the three documents, Matthew, James, and the Didache (that is the pre-Didache recension in Did. 1:1–3a; 2:2–6:1), in as much as they evidence a similar relation of the love command and the Decalogue. The affinities between Matthew and the Didache in these and other respects demonstrate that in some way the material derived from a common tradition. The Didache may represent a later stage in the development of the type of "Christianity" reflected in Matthew. Of course, there are close connections between Matthew and James too, but this affinity cannot be equated with the close relationship between Matthew and the Didache.

Patrick Hartin shows how James, Matthew, and the Didache reflect a similar ethos and ethical perspective, the first of which he believes to be the earliest of the three. The ethical admonitions in these documents are the boundary markers expressing the identity (ethos) of the members of the respective communities. The admonitions examined in this paper are "being perfect," the imitation of God rather than the imitation of Jesus, the double mindedness and the double-love command. Having considered these ethical perspectives, Hartin then briefly examines the relationship of the three documents to the ethos and ethics of other traditions and other Christian literature from the same period. He pays special attention to the Sayings Source Q, the form of the Two Ways in the Letter of Barnabas, the letters of Paul and the Gospel of John. He argues that in their own way all three documents express the understanding that faith must be articulated through action. Their identity and perspective clearly assigns them to a common, developing milieu that was still at home within the social and ideological context of Israel. The different stages in the development of this milieu are reflected in the successive documents: James (middle of the 60s), Matthew (early 80s) and the Didache (90s through 120s).

Huub van de Sandt argues that the commonalities of perspective with regard to the law in Matthew and James is the result of their common use of a section of the Jewish Two Ways which is best preserved in Did. 3:1–6. He first demonstrates that theme and terminology in the teknon section of Did. 3:1–6 betray close affinities with materials collected and preserved in the pious milieu of the early Hasidic Sages. This specific ethical stream within early rabbinic Judaism is probably the concrete life situation of the teknon passage. Van de Sandt then draws attention to the Matthean Antitheses and James's Letter. Matthew and James used traditional materials identical or similar to those transmitted in Two Ways 3:1–6 when respectively formulating the Antitheses (5:17–48) of the Sermon on the Mount and creating specific segments of James's letter (1:13–21; 2:8–11 and 4:1–4). The ethical code passed on in the Antitheses and in James—both imposing higher standards for the halakic way of life—finds its best explanation in light of Did. 3:1–6 and Hasidic tradition. This traditional type of instruction does not provide us with a full understanding of Matthew's Antitheses or the Letter of James however. The argument in the latter writings is more rigorous than is the line of reasoning in the Two Ways. Matthew and James independently represent a further development and radicalization of the warnings in Did. 3:1–6.

A conference on the relationship between Matthew, James, and the Didache would not be complete without considering how each document envisioned ritual observance. The fifth and last section of the book is therefore dedicated to this issue. In the first of the section's three papers, Alistair Stewart-Sykes analyzes the close relationship between paraenesis and baptism in Matthew, James, and the Didache. Employing the key term *apokuesis logo aletheias*, Stewart-Sykes first examines the character of paraenesis (especially in James) and asks "whether the paraenetic content of James is meant to recall instruction given before baptism

as a means of restoring the hearers to their baptismal resolve through reminding them of their initial incorporation into James's group" (p. 347). He then
examines baptism in Matthew, James and Didache, emphasizing the strong connection between paraenesis and baptism all three documents express in detail
despite their differences.

In the second paper of this section Martin Vahrenhorst presents a case study
of a topic that was particularly vexing for many early-first-century Christians as
well as Jews, the prohibition against taking oaths. This was a matter of intense
Jewish debate since it concerned the question how the name of God could be
protected from being profaned in the process of swearing. "Almost all Jewish
sources," Vahrenhorst asserts, "deal with it and even non-Jewish sources reveal
a strong interest in it" (p. 365). Examining how this controversial issue is treated
in each of the three documents can help better place them within the context
of contemporaneous Jewish discussions. Vahrenhorst sees Matthew and James
deeply connected to the Jewish debate.

Last but not least, Boris Repschinski deals with purity, one of the crucial
defining notions of Second Temple Judaism and a concept not only based upon
Scripture but also on (often controversial) supplemental halakic traditions. After
analyzing a number of relevant passages in Matthew, James, and the Didache,
Repschinski comes to the conclusion that while each document shows a very
peculiar approach to the topic (Didache and James largely ignoring it), they all
share a certain tendency to reinterpret purity issues in ethical or christological
terms and use them as a means to define one's own identity against competing
Judaism. While Matthew remains closest to Jewish tradition, he also delegiti-
mizes purity traditions by taking up impulses from the early Jesus tradition.

The papers presented at this conference clearly demonstrate both the promise and problems of an approach that takes Matthew, James, and the Didache as
related documents and reads them as distinctly Judaeo-Christian voices in their
Jewish and Christian contexts. Apart from presenting many exegetical details
and illuminating insights, the articles demonstrate that it is more difficult than
ever to distinguish between "Jewish" and "Christian" because they were sociologically and theologically too closely related and—in different respects—in *statu
nascendi*. Theological affinities, common topics, accepted practices, and similar
linguistic habits connect Matthew, James, and the Didache. The articles in this
book invite a closer examination of the repercussions these assumptions have
both for the interpretation of each individual document and for the construction of a framework for understanding early Christianity in general. It would be
a misunderstanding, however, were this connection to be described uncritically
at the cost of linguistic, social, and theological dissimilarities between these three
texts or by excluding other documents that share individual elements—such as
1 Peter with James.

The broad range of methodological approaches and research interests represented by the authors in this book amply demonstrates that the topic raised

by the 2007 Tilburg Conference is tackled with utmost care and simplifications are avoided. The discussion is far from finished, of course. Neither the book as a whole nor any individual contribution claims to have had the last word on this matter. Further research is certainly necessary on, for example, the relationship between the milieu represented by these three documents (and others?) to voices that are clearly not part of it and the representation of the non-Jewish and non-Christian outside world in general. On the basis of the results of the 2007 Tilburg Conference, it seems likely that these questions will not be resolved by simple answers and compact concepts that lump the three documents together indiscriminately. Instead we can expect that research in such a direction might also demonstrate that Matthew, James, and the Didache kept their own profile within a common milieu that represents only one multivocal voice in the disparate choir of early Christianity.

We would like to extend our heart-felt gratitude to all who have contributed to bringing this book to light. We first thank all the colleagues who devoted their time and expertise to make the conference and this proceedings volume possible with their written and oral contributions. We are further indebted to the Faculty of Humanities at Tilburg University (above all the Department of Religious Studies and Theology) and the Royal Dutch Academy of Sciences (KNAW) for generously making all necessary personal and financial resources available to launch the conference. It is a pleasure to thank the staff of SBL, especially Victor Matthews, Bob Buller, and Leigh Andersen for skillfully guiding this book through its various stages of development from conceptualization to publication. Substantial assistance was rendered by John Flanagan (Leiden) and David Lee (Amsterdam) who helped improve the English of a number of articles. Last but not least, we are indebted to Ms. Nathalie Bastiaansen (Tilburg) for her contribution to the process of editing and preparing the final text.

We initially invited Wiard Popkes to present a paper at the conference. Despite his increasingly severe illness, Wiard Popkes was quick to respond and promised a paper on "Initiation and Celebration: Rites and Religious Practices in James, Matthew, and the Didache." Not much later, however, we received the sad message from his son that Wiard Popkes had passed away on January 2, 2007. The editors and all contributors to the Tilburg conference deeply regret the loss of such a fine scholar. Through his erudition and his ability to read texts in their historical and theological context, Wiard Popkes has deeply influenced New Testament scholarship over a long period and especially stimulated the interpretation of the Letter of James. There were many occasions during the conference when his work was cited and his personal presence was greatly missed. In the name of all the participants and with deep gratitude and respect we dedicate this volume to his memory.

Part 1
Methods and Milieus

RECONSTRUCTING THE SOCIAL AND RELIGIOUS MILIEU OF MATTHEW: METHODS, SOURCES, AND POSSIBLE RESULTS

David C. Sim

The social and religious milieu of Matthew[1] has been the dominant theme in Matthean scholarship over the last two decades or so. Interest in this fascinating issue shows no sign of waning soon; in fact, it appears to be intensifying as scholarly discourse becomes polarized on a number of fundamental questions. In this study I wish to examine a number of issues that are directly pertinent to this theme. The first concerns whether or not it is permissible even to engage this subject. The challenge to the consensus view of "the Matthean community" by Richard Bauckham and others has the potential to bring to an abrupt halt all inquiry into the Gospel's social and religious contexts. The evidence suggests, however, that the attack by Bauckham has not won the day.

Following this preliminary discussion, I will move to the question of the Gospel's date. Because most scholars date the Gospel in the same general period, this is not an issue that significantly occupies scholarly attention. Yet, as I will argue, there may well be grounds for dating Matthew some decades later. If this policy were to be entertained or even accepted, it would impact in important

---

1. For the sake of convenience and with due reference to convention, I use the term "Matthew" to denote both the Gospel and its author. I agree with the scholarly consensus that the author of this Gospel was not the disciple Matthew. The only serious and sustained attempt in recent times to demonstrate that he was this disciple has come from Robert Gundry, who has tried to substantiate the tradition transmitted by Papias that is preserved in the writings of Eusebius (*Hist. eccl.* 3.39.3–16). See Robert H. Gundry, *Matthew: A Commentary on His Handbook for a Mixed Community under Persecution* (2nd ed.; Grand Rapids: Eerdmans, 1994), 609–22 and, more recently, "The Apostolically Johannine Pre-Papian Tradition concerning the Gospels of Mark and Matthew," in *The Old Is Better: New Testament Essays in Support of Traditional Interpretations* (ed. R. H. Gundry; WUNT 178; Tübingen: Mohr Siebeck, 2005), 49–73. For a critique of Gundry's arguments, see David C. Sim, "The Gospel of Matthew, John the Elder and the Papias Tradition: A Response to R. H. Gundry," *Hervormde Teologiese Studies* 63 (2007): 283–99.

ways how we perceive the social and religious settings of this document. Another matter that requires attention is the location of the Gospel. The consensus view that it was composed in Antioch has come under challenge from those who suggest a Galilean provenance. The credentials of this alternative hypothesis have rather inexplicably not been tested fully in the scholarly arena, but I will attempt to demonstrate that it suffers from serious weaknesses. Related to the question of the Gospel's location is the issue of whether it is possible to write a history of the Matthean community. This is certainly possible if that community is situated in Antioch because we know a lot about the history of the Christian movement in that particular city, but it becomes more difficult if the Gospel is located elsewhere. I will also examine another method of reconstructing the history of the evangelist's group, one that uses the layers of tradition in the Gospel itself, and conclude that this approach faces serious difficulties.

In terms of the social and religious milieu of Matthew's community, the point will be made that scholars have largely focused on its Jewish setting and that opinions are sharply divided on this question. But the Jewish context for this Gospel, while doubtless important, is simply one of its settings, and scholars need to broaden the discussion to take these other contexts into account. A start has been made on the Roman imperial context of the Gospel, but much more needs to be done in terms of its Christian setting and its relationship with the Gentile world.

1. THE GOSPEL FOR ALL CHRISTIANS OR FOR THE MATTHEAN COMMUNITY?

Up until a decade or so ago, it was common practice to assume that Matthew was the spokesperson for a particular Christian community, and that he had written his Gospel and edited his sources to address the particular needs of that group. Working with that assumption, it was a short step from noting the peculiar themes and emphases in the Gospel to reconstructing the social and religious setting of the addressees. But the certainty associated with this approach came to an abrupt end when Richard Bauckham called the underlying assumption into question and argued to the contrary that all of the Gospels were written for much broader Christian readerships, possibly all Christians in fact.[2] Bauckham's work was potentially explosive for scholarly reconstructions of any Gospel community because it denied that the evangelists had composed their Gospels to meet the needs of their home communities. For Bauckham there were no Gospel communities at all. Therefore all reconstructions of the social setting of Matthew's group,

---

2. Richard Bauckham, "For Whom Were Gospels Written?," in *The Gospels for All Christians: Rethinking the Gospel Audiences* (ed. R. Bauckham; Grand Rapids: Eerdmans, 1998), 9–48. The other contributions in this volume attempted to support Bauckham's hypothesis by examining related themes.

for example, were based upon a false assumption and were to be rejected as a scholarly fiction.

Bauckham's study had an immediate and influential impact, especially in more conservative scholarly circles, but it was not long before the inevitable challenges to it saw the light of day.[3] The debate initiated by Bauckham continues to engage the attention of scholars,[4] although the intensity of the initial exchanges has arguably lessened over time. But even though this issue has not yet been resolved, it is true to say that Bauckham's work has not had a major impact on studies of the Gospel communities. In the specific case of the Matthean community, the fact that a number of doctoral dissertations on this theme have recently been published testifies that the new generation of Matthean scholars has sided with Bauckham's critics. The study of the religious and social milieu of this Gospel and its underlying community, despite the critics of this approach, can be deemed legitimate.

2. Date

I want to begin the discussion of this theme with an issue that is usually taken as a given, the date of Matthew's Gospel. This is a matter of fundamental importance because the date of any given text directly governs the manner in which we understand its background and the context(s) in which it took shape. The vast majority of scholars continue to date Matthew in the 80s or the 90s, that is, in the decades following the Jewish revolt against Rome.[5] That the Gospel was written after this conflict is based largely on two arguments.[6] First, the evangelist used Mark as a major source, and that Gospel was composed in the late 60s or the early 70s. Secondly, in his heavily redacted version of the parable of the wedding feast (Matt 22:1–10), Matthew reveals his knowledge of the destruction of Jerusalem

---

3. See in particular, Philip F. Esler, "Community and Gospel in Early Christianity: A Response to Richard Bauckham's *Gospels for All Christians*," *SJT* 51 (1998): 235–48; David C. Sim, "The Gospels for All Christians? A Response to Richard Bauckham," *JSNT* 24 (2001): 3–27; Wendy E. Sproston North, "John for Readers of Mark? A Response to Richard Bauckham's Proposal," *JSNT* 25 (2003): 449–68, and Margaret Mitchell, "Patristic Counter-Evidence to the Claim that 'The Gospels Were Written for All Christians,'" *NTS* 51 (2005): 36–79.

4. For a full survey of the debate up to 2004, see Edward W. Klink, "The Gospel Community Debate: State of the Question," *Currents in Biblical Research* 3 (2004): 60–85.

5. There are occasional attempts to demonstrate an earlier date prior to 70 c.e. In more recent times, see Gundry, *Matthew: A Commentary on His Handbook*, 599–609; Richard T. France, *Matthew: Evangelist and Teacher* (Exeter: Paternoster, 1989), 82–91, and John L. Nolland, *The Gospel of Matthew: A Commentary on the Greek Text* (NIGTC; Grand Rapids: Eerdmans, 2005), 14–17.

6. See the detailed discussion of these arguments in David C. Sim, *The Gospel of Matthew and Christian Judaism: The History and Social Setting of the Matthean Community* (Studies of the New Testament and Its World; Edinburgh: T&T Clark, 1998), 31–40.

(verse 7). The evidence that Matthew must be given a date no later than the first century is derived from the letters of Ignatius of Antioch. Ignatius shows some familiarity with the written Gospel, and his epistles can be dated to the first or second decade of the second century.

All of these arguments require some comment. The Gospel of Mark provides no unambiguous clues as to its date, despite the ingenious scholarly reconstructions that attempt to link Mark's apocalyptic discourse with the Jewish war, and some Marcan scholars have argued that this Gospel belongs to a much earlier period.[7] The witness of Matt 22:7, which does seem to be a direct reference to the destruction of Jerusalem, poses a further problem of its own that is not usually acknowledged. If Matthew composed his Gospel relatively soon after the Jewish war and saw fit to refer to the fate of Jerusalem in this text, then why does he include only this single allegorical reference to this event? It is instructive to compare this allusion to Luke's much more clear statements about the destruction of Jerusalem and the Temple. In the unique material of Luke 19:41–44, Jesus weeps when he approaches Jerusalem as he foresees the siege and destruction of the city. A little later Luke refers again to the siege and desolation of Jerusalem in his redaction of Mark (Luke 21:20; see Mark 13:14). Luke's great interest in the Jewish war remains puzzling given that this Gospel was probably written somewhere in Greece and was therefore far removed from the arena of the conflict. By the same token, Matthew's comparative disinterest is striking if, as most Matthean scholars accept, Matthew was located much closer to the war zone.

But we may pursue this point a little further. Most Matthean scholars argue that in one way or another the Jewish conflict with Rome and its disastrous aftermath radically affected the evangelist and his readers. It is commonly accepted that Matthew's Christian group came into conflict with the leaders of formative Judaism after the Jewish revolt when a struggle for power ensued within the Jewish community. Other scholars have suggested that Matthew's group underwent a fundamental change because of the influx of refugees after the war. Yet others have made a case that this community suffered persecution by Gentiles as a direct result of the Jewish war, while another view maintains that the evangelist hardened his view against Roman imperialism in the light of Roman excesses both during and after the conflict. Almost all Matthean scholars, therefore, would argue that the events of 66–70 had a dramatic and lasting impact on the Matthean community.

Yet, despite the supposedly crucial consequences of these events, the evangelist was content to refer to them on a single occasion and even then in an allegorical way. One cannot escape this difficulty by claiming that there are further references to the Jewish war in the apocalyptic discourse of chapters 24–25.

---

7. See James G. Crossley, *The Date of Mark's Gospel: Insight from the Law in Earliest Christianity* (JSNTSup 266; London: T&T Clark, 2004), who dates Mark to the mid-40s at the latest.

As with all material of this nature, it is open to a variety of interpretations, and it is true to say that most scholars apply parts of this material to the Jewish revolt on the grounds that they assume beforehand that Matthew is post-70. If it were presumed instead that Matthew was a pre-war document, other interpretations of this material would be adopted. So the problem remains. Scholars who argue that Matthew wrote after the revolt and that his community was heavily influenced by these events are required to explain why he says so little about it.

One way to avoid the difficulty would be to date the Gospel somewhat later than we currently do. A date in the early decades of the second century, when memories of the terrible events of 66–70 C.E. were receding, might explain the evangelist's failure to emphasize these events. Needless to say, any attempt to posit a later date would seem to be precluded by the evidence of Ignatius of Antioch who, on the accepted chronology, refers to the written text of Matthew at precisely this time. But this response may not be as convincing as it first seems. Ignatian studies have undergone a major development in recent times, and Matthean scholars must take this into account.

Some years ago a debate exploded between those scholars who accepted the traditional view that Ignatius should be dated to the time of the emperor Trajan, and those who argued that the letters were in fact pseudonymous and should be dated to the 160s or the 170s. Reinhard M. Hübner has argued that the epistles were written in the name of Ignatius by a follower of Noetus of Smyrna around the years 165–175 C.E. in order to combat the growing threat of Gnosticism.[8] In a similar vein Thomas Lechner has claimed that the Ignatian corpus was written in this period as a direct response to the heretical notions of Valentinus.[9] Replies to these views were quick to appear, and all of them criticized the claim of pseudonymity and/or the late dating of the Ignatian letters.[10] While there is no necessity here to enter into the details of this debate, it is legitimate to ask what affect it might have on the reconstruction of Matthew's social setting. If it could be shown that the Ignatian epistles were indeed later than the reign of Trajan, and even one critic of Hübner and Lechner concedes that they have established this much,[11]

---

8. Reinhard M. Hübner, "Thesen zur Echtheit und Datierung der sieben Briefe des Ignatius von Antiochien," *ZAC* 1 (1997): 44–72.

9. Thomas Lechner, *Ignatius Adversus Valentinianos? Chronologische und theologiegeschichtliche Studien zu den Briefen des Ignatius von Antiochen* (VCSup 47; Leiden: Brill, 1999).

10. For responses to Hübner, see Andreas Lindemann, "Antwort auf die Thesen zur Echtheit und Datierung der sieben Briefe des Ignatius von Antiochien," *ZAC* 1 (1997): 185–94; Georg Schöllgen, "Die Ignatianen als pseudepigraphisches Briefcorpus: Anmerkung zu den Thesen von Reinhard M. Hübner," *ZAC* 2 (1998): 16–25; Mark J. Edwards, "Ignatius and the Second Century: An Answer to R. Hübner," *ZAC* 2 (1998): 214–26, and Hermann J. Vogt, "Bemerkungen zur Echtheit der Ignatiusbriefe," *ZAC* 3 (1999): 50–63. For a rejoinder to Lechner, see the review of his book by A. Lindemann, *ZAC* 6 (2002): 157–61.

11. See Lindemann, "Antwort auf die Thesen zur Echtheit," 193–94.

then there is no reason to set the latest date for the Gospel in the first century; it might be the case that it was written in the early part of the second century. Such a view would have a considerable impact on the setting of the Matthean community in many ways. I shall mention some of these in due course, but it is pertinent to discuss one now.

That Matthew's Gospel, especially the material openly critical of the scribes and Pharisees, reflects a conflict with formative Judaism is a well-established opinion in the field. This view, however, becomes progressively less likely the earlier we date the Gospel. Many decades ago, it was accepted that the transition from Pharisaism to an authoritative and powerful rabbinic Judaism took place almost immediately after the Jewish war. The Pharisees, under the leadership of Johanan ben Zakkai, managed to fill the power vacuum left by the revolt, and to force their own brand of Judaism on the remainder of the Jewish population. This was the view of William D. Davies in his seminal work on the Sermon on the Mount. In a long and detailed discussion of the Matthean Sermon and the Pharisaic developments at Yavneh, Davies concluded that the Sermon on the Mount was the Christian answer to Yavneh.[12] On this view we can date Matthew with confidence to the 80s or the 90s because this proto-rabbinism emerged and established its authority very soon after the war.

But the problem with this line of argument is that we now know, thanks in large measure to the pioneering work of Jacob Neusner, that this developmental process from Pharisaism to rabbinic Judaism was much more complex and took much longer to achieve than was earlier thought. Neusner coined the term "formative Judaism" to describe the complicated and lengthy transitional phase between the pre-war Pharisees and the much later Judaism of the rabbis.[13] In the light of Neusner's work, which has largely been accepted, it is not so easy to see Matthew's community, on the consensus dating, in conflict with the proponents of formative Judaism. Would the scribes and Pharisees, two of the leading groups of formative Judaism, have been sufficiently powerful and influential by the 80s or the 90s to have caused the problems for Matthew's group that we identify in the Gospel? In sociological parlance, could an embryonic or even fledgling formative Judaism have constituted the "parent body" with which the sectarian Matthean community was in dispute? The difficulty remains even if Matthew is located in the heartland of formative Judaism, Galilee, and it becomes progres-

---

12. William D. Davies, *The Setting of the Sermon on the Mount* (Cambridge: Cambridge University Press, 1964), 256–315. In his later commentary on Matthew, in association with Dale C. Allison, Davies presented the same thesis, though in an abridged form. See William D. Davies and Dale C. Allison, *A Critical and Exegetical Commentary on the Gospel according to Saint Matthew* (3 vols; ICC; Edinburgh: T&T Clark, 1988, 1991, 1997), 1:133–38.

13. Neusner has presented his views in a multitude of publications. A concise summary of his overall position is found in Jacob Neusner, "The Formation of Rabbinic Judaism: Yavneh from A.D. 70–100," *ANRW* 19.2:3–42.

sively more problematic the further Matthew is placed beyond that location. To his credit, William D. Davies noted the problem that Neusner's work created, and he responded by continuing to argue that formative Judaism in Yavneh was a sufficiently cohesive and authoritative movement by the 90s.[14] Unlike Davies, however, many other scholars have not really addressed this issue at all. Their work has proceeded largely on the assumption that formative Judaism had achieved some degree of cohesion and authority by that time, albeit with the cautions and qualifications necessitated by the work of Neusner.[15]

Yet this problem can be overcome to a large extent by dating the Gospel to a later time. A date for Matthew and his community some decades later in the second century would allow a much longer period for the establishment of formative Judaism as a cohesive and dominant force in the evangelist's setting. In raising this point I am not calling for an immediate redating of Matthew to the 120s or the 130s. That proposition may itself contain serious flaws. What I am suggesting is that Matthean scholarship may need to revisit the question of the Gospel's date. If the evidence that constrained us to a first-century dating (the date of the epistles of Ignatius) is now itself in doubt, then we may at least entertain the notion that Matthew too may be later than previously considered. A later date would certainly be more consistent with the evidence of the conflict between the Matthean community and formative Judaism, and it would open up further possibilities in terms of the social and religious setting of the Gospel.

3. Location

The location of the Gospel is also of major importance in terms of reconstructing the social and religious milieu of the evangelist and his underlying community. By contrast with the dating of the Gospel, there is no agreement at all on its provenance. As is well known, Matthean scholars have been especially

---

14. See Davies and Allison, *Critical and Exegetical Commentary*, 3:692–704.

15. See especially J. Andrew Overman, *Matthew's Gospel and Formative Judaism: The Social World of the Matthean Community* (Minneapolis: Fortress, 1990); Anthony J. Saldarini, *Matthew's Christian-Jewish Community* (CSHJ; Chicago, Ill.: University of Chicago Press, 1994); Boris Repschinski, *The Controversy Stories in the Gospel of Matthew: Their Redaction, Form and Relevance for the Relationship Between the Matthean Community and Formative Judaism* (FRLANT 189; Göttingen: Vandenhoeck & Ruprecht, 2000) and, most recently, Anthony O. Ewherido, *Matthew's Gospel and Judaism in the Late First Century C.E.: The Evidence from Matthew's Chapter on Parables (Matthew 13:1–52)* (SBL 91; New York: Lang, 2006). Similar views are found in, amongst others, Sim, *Gospel of Matthew and Christian Judaism*, 109–50; Graham N. Stanton, *A Gospel for a New People: Studies in Matthew* (Edinburgh: T&T Clark, 1992), 144–45; Daniel J. Harrington, *The Gospel of Matthew* (SP 1; Collegeville, Minn.: Liturgical, 1991), 14–16; Craig S. Keener, *A Commentary on the Gospel of Matthew* (Grand Rapids: Eerdmans, 1999), 46–48, and Aaron M. Gale, *Redefining Ancient Borders: The Jewish Scribal Framework of Matthew's Gospel* (London: T&T Clark, 2005), 15–30.

creative in proposing possible locations for this Gospel. Among these suggestions, we find Alexandria,[16] Caesarea Maritima,[17] Caesarea Philippi,[18] Transjordan,[19] Damascus,[20] Phoenicia,[21] and Edessa.[22] None of these suggestions, however, has gained wide support. In the current climate, there are only two favored locations. The first is Antioch on the Orontes, the capital of the Roman province of Syria and one of the largest metropolises in the Roman Empire. The second is the general region of Galilee, with some advocates offering a more precise location of either Sepphoris or Tiberias.

The Antiochene hypothesis was first presented by Burnett H. Streeter in his classic study of the origins of the four Gospels,[23] and it quickly attracted support. By the 1980s it had firmly established itself as the consensus view,[24] and it still enjoys this prominent position in current Matthean scholarship.[25] The

16. Samuel G. F. Brandon, *The Fall of Jerusalem and the Christian Church: A Study of the Effects of the Jewish Overthrow of A.D. 70 on Christianity* (London: SPCK, 1951), 217–43, and Sjef van Tilborg, *The Jewish Leaders in Matthew* (Leiden: Brill, 1972), 172.

17. Benedict Viviano, "Where Was the Gospel according to St. Matthew Written?" *CBQ* 41 (1979): 533–46.

18. Georg Künzel, *Studien zum Gemeindeverständnis des Matthäus-Evangeliums* (Calwer Theologische Monographien A/10; Stuttgart: Calwer, 1978), 251.

19. H. Dixon Slingerland, "The Transjordanian Origin of Matthew's Gospel," *JSNT* 3 (1979): 18–28.

20. Joachim Gnilka, *Das Matthäusevangelium* (2 vols; HTKNT 1; Freiburg: Herder, 1986, 1988), 2:515, and Petri Luomanen, *Entering the Kingdom of Heaven: A Study on the Structure of Matthew's View of Salvation* (WUNT 2/101; Tübingen: Mohr Siebeck, 1998), 275–76.

21. George D. Kilpatrick, *The Origins of the Gospel according to St. Matthew* (Oxford: Clarendon, 1946), 130–34.

22. Benjamin W. Bacon, *Studies in Matthew* (London: Constable, 1930), 15–23; J. Spencer Kennard, "The Place of Origin of Matthew's Gospel," *ATR* 31 (1949): 243–46, and Robert E. Osborne, "The Provenance of Matthew's Gospel," *SR* 3 (1973): 220–35.

23. Burnett H. Streeter, *The Four Gospels: A Study of Origins* (London: Macmillan, 1924), 500–523.

24. See the discussion in John P. Meier, "Antioch," in Raymond E. Brown and John P. Meier, *Antioch and Rome: New Testament Cradles of Catholic Christianity* (New York: Paulist, 1983), 22–26. See too Davies and Allison, *Critical and Exegetical Commentary*, 1:143–47, though these authors are more tentative.

25. Although acknowledging different degrees of probability in their opinions, proponents of this view in the last dozen years or so include Sim, *Gospel of Matthew and Christian Judaism*, 53–62; Gundry, *Matthew: A Commentary on His Handbook*, 609; Keener, *A Commentary on the Gospel of Matthew*, 41–42; Ewherido, *Matthew's Gospel and Judaism*, 11; Donald A. Hagner, *Matthew* (2 vols; WBC 33A–B; Dallas: Word Books, 1993–1996), 1:lxxv; Donald Senior, *The Gospel of Matthew* (Interpreting Biblical Texts; Nashville, Tenn.: Abingdon, 1997), 82; Warren Carter, *Matthew and Empire: Initial Explorations* (Harrisburg, Pa.: Trinity Press International, 2001), 36–37; Michelle Slee, *The Church in Antioch in the First Century C.E.: Communion and Conflict* (JSNTSup 244; London: Sheffield Academic Press, 2003), 118–22, and Ulrich Luz, *Matthew 1–7* (Hermeneia; Minneapolis: Fortress, 2007), 56–58.

arguments in favor of Antioch are well known and can be mentioned briefly. The internal evidence of the Gospel itself suggests that it was written in a large eastern urban center where Greek was the major language. This city contained a substantial Jewish population in addition to the Gentile majority, and it was not directly involved in the Jewish war. Many cities of course satisfy these criteria, but what points to Antioch to the exclusion of other possibilities are the following. Peter is prominent in the Gospel and he was an important figure in the church of Antioch (Gal 2:11–14) and the first citation of this Gospel appears in the letters of Ignatius of Antioch.[26]

The major weakness of the Antiochene hypothesis is that this location seems too far away to have been the site of the conflict between Matthew's Christian Jewish group and formative Judaism. Since the scribes and Pharisees were based in Galilee, it is much more likely that the Gospel was composed either in Galilee or nearby. At first glance this is a forceful and compelling argument, and it must be acknowledged that it causes some difficulty for the Antiochene hypothesis. But it is not conclusive or definitive. If it can be demonstrated or at least rendered plausible that those people who were responsible for the emergence of formative Judaism in Galilee were also present in Antioch, then the difficulty is considerably reduced. I have argued previously that it is certainly possible that Pharisees were found in Antioch prior to the Jewish war, and probable that they were there after the conflict when many refugees fled their homeland to find a new life in Diasporan Jewish centers.[27] Moreover, if we postulate a later date for the Gospel, then this increases the likelihood of Antioch for the Gospel's location. Such a revision would allow for the consolidation of formative Judaism in Galilee and its expansion into other Jewish communities.

We may now move to the alternative hypothesis that Matthew was composed in Galilee. This possibility was first raised by J. Andrew Overman,[28] and has attracted some support in the ensuing years.[29] The strongest argument in favor of this thesis is the Matthean community's conflict with formative Judaism. Since the latter movement was based in Galilee, we should expect that Matthew's

---

26. The issue of the date of the Ignatian corpus, as discussed above, does not radically affect this point. A later date for the letters of Ignatius may be offset by a later date for the Gospel, in which case it is still important that the Bishop of Antioch was the first to cite the Gospel.

27. Sim, *Gospel of Matthew and Christian Judaism*, 60–61.

28. Overman, *Matthew's Gospel and Formative Judaism*, 158–59. Overman later restated his views in his *Church and Community in Crisis: The Gospel According to Matthew* (The New Testament in Context; Valley Forge, Pa.: Trinity Press International, 1996), 16–19.

29. Harrington, *The Gospel of Matthew*, 9–10; Anthony J. Saldarini, "The Gospel of Matthew and Jewish-Christian Conflict in the Galilee," in *The Galilee in Late Antiquity* (ed. L. I. Levine; Cambridge, Mass.: Harvard University Press, 1992), 26–27, and Paul Hertig, "Geographical Marginality in the Matthean Journey of Jesus," *SBL Seminar Papers, 1999* (SBLSP 36; Atlanta: SBL, 1999), 479. The most detailed defense of this position has come from Aaron M. Gale, *Redefining Ancient Borders*, 41–63.

Christian group was located here as well.[30] A second argument that is often proposed is that Matthew emphasizes Galilee in his Gospel narrative. He knows the region well and basically limits the mission of Jesus to Galilee (and to Capernaum in particular). This reflects the actual setting of the evangelist and his community.[31] Related to this is Matthew's depiction of the Pharisees. They are essentially restricted to Galilee, and the debates between them and Jesus also reflect the conflict between them and Matthew's group in Galilee.[32]

In terms of a more specific location, Anthony J. Saldarini contends that it must have been a large city and he suggests Sepphoris, Tiberias, Capernaum, and Bethsaida as possibilities.[33] Overman speculates that the Gospel was written in a city that was large enough to contain a court. Since the seat of the Sanhedrin was located at different stages in both Tiberias and Sepphoris, these cities are the most likely candidates, and Overman leans more towards the latter.[34] Sepphoris is also the preferred location of Aaron M. Gale, who provides more information about this city.[35] Gale notes that Sepphoris was the largest city in Galilee and was wealthy and cosmopolitan. Its population was largely Jewish and its Jewish residents were rather conservative. For Gale the location of the Gospel in the city of Sepphoris is entirely consistent with what we can reconstruct of the Matthean community and its conflict with formative Judaism.

To my knowledge the Galilean hypothesis has never really been subjected to intense scrutiny or to a detailed critique. While this is a task that needs to be done, all that can be offered here are some brief responses to the arguments in favor of this location. The contention that Galilee is dictated by the conflict with formative Judaism is in and of itself a reasonably strong argument but, as Overman concedes,[36] it cannot stand alone. It requires additional support, and it is here that the hypothesis begins to unravel. While it is certainly true that Matthew restricts the mission of Jesus to Galilee, is it feasible to maintain that he does so because his community resides there? Surely it is more likely that he does so because of his view that the mission of Jesus was restricted to the people of Israel

---

30. So Overman, *Matthew's Gospel and Formative Judaism*, 158; idem, *Church and Community in Crisis*, 17–18; Gale, *Redefining Ancient Borders*, 51–52; Saldarini, "Gospel of Matthew and Jewish-Christian Conflict," 27, and Harrington, *The Gospel of Matthew*, 10.

31. Overman, *Matthew's Gospel and Formative Judaism*, 159 and idem, *Church and Community in Crisis*, 17. See too Gale, *Redefining Ancient Borders*, 56–57; Saldarini, "Gospel of Matthew and Jewish-Christian Conflict," 26–27, and Hertig, ""Geographical Marginality in the Matthean Journey of Jesus," 479.

32. Overman, *Matthew's Gospel and Formative Judaism*, 159, and Gale, *Redefining Ancient Borders*, 57.

33. Saldarini, "Gospel of Matthew, and Jewish-Christian Conflict," 27.

34. Overman, *Matthew's Gospel and Formative Judaism*, 159, and idem, *Church and Community in Crisis*, 17–19.

35. Gale, *Redefining Ancient Borders*, 57–63.

36. Overman, *Matthew's Gospel and Formative Judaism*, 158.

(10:5–6; 15:24). The limitation of this mission to the Jews necessitated a restriction of his travels to Jewish territory. We can add to this the additional point that, if the Gospel was written in either Tiberias or Sepphoris, why is neither city mentioned in the text? It seems odd that Matthew would emphasize the general region of Galilee but avoid mentioning his own city. This would be all the more remarkable had the historical Jesus visited these cities, as Gale suggests as a distinct possibility.[37]

With regard to the Pharisees in the Gospel narrative, it is simply not the case that their conflict with Jesus is restricted to Galilee. They appear as a major opposition to Jesus when he is in Jerusalem, especially when he is in the temple (21:23–24:1). Jesus tells the parable of the wicked tenants (21:33–43) and the chief priests and the Pharisees believe he is speaking about them (21:45). The parable of the wedding feast that follows (22:1–10) is directed at them as well, and the Pharisees then plot how to trap Jesus (22:15). After Jesus silences the Sadducees, the Pharisees again test him (22:34–35). Jesus then asks them about the relationship between David and the Christ (22:41–46). Then, while still in the temple, Jesus delivers his stinging polemical attack on the Pharisees (23:1–39). Finally, it is the Pharisees along with the chief priests who approach Pilate to request that a guard be placed over the tomb of Jesus (27:62–66). The evidence is clear. The Pharisees are not a Galilean movement in Matthew's narrative, nor is their conflict with Jesus restricted to that region. It is significant that Overman and Gale overlook almost all of these passages. While they do acknowledge that Matt 27:62–66 is an exception to the usual depiction of the Pharisees as residents of Galilee,[38] they are inexplicably silent on the remaining passages.[39] We may conclude then that none of the supplementary arguments supports a Galilean provenance.

Let us now consider the other side of the coin. What are the arguments that testify against a Galilean location for Matthew? There are many. The first is the issue of language. It is widely acknowledged that the major language of Galilee was Aramaic. This was the language of Jesus and his disciples. We would therefore expect a Gospel from Galilee to be written in Aramaic, but Matthew was written in Greek and was based upon Greek sources.[40] Aaron M. Gale attempts to dilute the importance of this objection by pointing out from inscriptional and numismatic evidence that Greek was also spoken and read in Galilee.[41] He claims "It

---

37. Gale, *Redefining Ancient Borders*, 57.

38. Overman, *Matthew's Gospel and Formative Judaism*, 156 n. 13. See too Gale, *Redefining Ancient Borders*, 57.

39. It is no surprise that Anthony J. Saldarini does not propose this argument, since he is well aware that the scribes and Pharisees oppose Jesus in both Galilee and Jerusalem. See Saldarini, *Matthew's Christian-Jewish Community*, 44.

40. Meier, "Antioch," 18–19, and Davies and Allison, *Critical and Exegetical Commentary*, 1:140.

41. Gale, *Redefining Ancient Borders*, 49–51.

is not true that Aramaic was the *only* language spoken throughout Palestine,"[42] and concludes that "The idea that *only* Aramaic was spoken and written in Galilee is false."[43] It is clear from these quotations that Gale has not fairly represented the argument of his opponents. No one has ever claimed that Aramaic was the sole language of Galilee and that Greek was never used there. There is, as Gale demonstrates, plenty of evidence to the contrary. But establishing the presence of Greek in Galilee does not necessarily lead to the conclusion that the Greek Gospel of Matthew was written there. The point stands that Aramaic was the dominant language of the region, even if it was not the sole language. Given that it was the language of Jesus, we should expect that a Christian community hailing from the same area as him would have written an account of his mission in the language that Jesus himself used.

The Jewish war presents a second and even greater difficulty for the Galilean hypothesis. The Jewish homeland, including Galilee, suffered greatly at the hands of the Roman army as it reconquered the territory it had lost. Whole cities and towns were destroyed and depopulated. In the aftermath of such a disastrous conflict, is it likely that a Christian community would have had the resources or even the will to compose a long and complex text such as Matthew?[44] It might be said in reply that the destruction that affected so much of Galilee did not apply to Sepphoris, which sided with the Romans and therefore was spared the vengeance of the imperial army. But Sepphoris did not escape the conflict completely unscathed. Josephus reports that at the beginning of the war he heard that the citizens of Sepphoris had approached the Romans for protection. He then led his Galilean forces in a major assault on the city. The Galilean soldiers were so intent on destroying Sepphoris utterly that Josephus was forced to trick them into retreating, but not before they had inflicted significant damage (*Life* 373–380; *War* 2.645–646). Neither Overman nor Gale addresses this difficulty.

Moreover, the Jewish war is significant in another way. A Galilean Matthean community in Sepphoris or elsewhere must have witnessed firsthand the disastrous and devastating effects of the conflict. But if this was the case, why do the war and its aftermath not occupy more the attention of the evangelist? As noted above, there is but a single allegorical reference to the destruction of Jerusalem in this Gospel. Matthew's comparative lack of interest in the war is more consistent with a location that was somewhat removed from the arena of conflict.[45] This point too receives no mention in any of the studies by the advocates of the Galilean hypothesis. This objection could be obviated to some extent if it were argued that Matthew was composed at some point in the second century, since we would

---

42. Ibid., 49 (emphasis added).

43. Ibid., 51 (emphasis added).

44. Meier, "Antioch," 18.

45. Davies and Allison, *Critical and Exegetical Commentary*, 1:140–41.

not expect a Gospel far removed in time from the conflict to focus much attention on it.

The view that the Gospel of Matthew was written in Galilee does not therefore stand up to close examination. Its advocates need to present more and better evidence in its favor in addition to the primary argument that Galilee is suggested by the conflict with formative Judaism. Further, they need to engage and counter the difficulties that their view involves. Until this is done, it is doubtful whether the Galilean hypothesis will ever seriously threaten its Antiochene rival.

4. The History of the Matthean Community

One consequence of locating Matthew in Antioch is that it allows the possibility of reconstructing the history of the evangelist's community. We know a good deal about the Christian movement in Antioch both before the time of the Gospel and in the period following its composition. This enables us not merely to describe the social and religious settings of the Matthean community at the time the Gospel was composed, but to plot all the social and historical forces that shaped his particular church over many decades. However, arriving at some sort of consensus on what that history was like is much more difficult. It is interesting to note that the two major reconstructions of the Matthean community in its Antiochene context offer completely different accounts.

In his important discussion of the Antiochene church,[46] John P. Meier argued that the Christian community was founded by the Hellenists and later included Paul. After the dispute in Antioch between James and Paul on the status of the Gentile Christians, Peter played a moderating role between the liberal and conservative factions of the church. This moderating Petrine influence is found in the Gospel of Matthew a generation later. The evangelist also desired to bring together the different factions in his church by synthesizing the liberal and conservative sources at his disposal. In the next generation we find Ignatius of Antioch who also faced extremist groups, docetists, and judaizers, and who brought together a number of disparate sources to advance his own mediating position. Meier's reconstruction can be compared with my own, which differs from it in almost every respect.[47] The original church in Antioch that the Hellenists founded was indeed "Law-free," but James managed to impose the Torah on all members of the Antiochene church. The Matthean community of next generation was the heir to this "Law-observant" Christian tradition initiated by James and overseen by Peter. The Pauline church of Ignatius of Antioch was not directly related to the Matthean community, but had an independent origin. And

---

46. Meier, "Antioch," 12–86.

47. Sim, *Gospel of Matthew and Christian Judaism*, *passim*. For a similar view, though differing on some major points, see Slee, *The Church in Antioch, passim*.

there is good evidence in the Ignatian epistles that Matthew's Christian Jewish group was in conflict with the church of Ignatius.

Even though Meier and I understand the history of the Antiochene Christian community and the place of Matthew within that history quite differently, we are in agreement on one fundamental point. Any reconstruction of the Matthean community in Antioch necessitates as well a reconstruction of the history of the Antiochene church. This must be done so that the interpretation of the Matthean community is consistent with the events that happened previously in Antioch and those that transpired later. In other words, the reconstructed community must make sense within its local Antiochene setting. The absence of this methodological necessity means that the suggested interpretation of the Matthean community has no checks or balances and no firm historical anchor. In my opinion many reconstructions of the Matthean community in Antioch suffer from this deficiency in so far as the Christian group reconstructed from the Gospel is often alien to the history of the Christian movement in that city. It looks nothing like it should in the light of earlier events, and nothing like it should in the light of later events.

In making this point, I wish to comment on an alternative approach to understanding the history of the evangelist's community. Some scholars accept that we can reconstruct the history of this community not by identifying its city of origin and proceeding from there, but by stratifying different parts of the Gospel and using this material to plot a coherent historical sequence. A recent attempt to do this is that of Wim Weren.[48] Weren begins by noting the tension between the older and newer layers in the Gospel and, while conceding the hypothetical nature of his enterprise, distinguishes three phases in the history of Matthew's community. The first is the pre–70 period when the members of this group still considered themselves to be within the Jewish community. The second phase concerns the period between 70 and 80 and reflects the losing conflict with the Pharisees. In the third period, between 80 and 90, these Jewish Christians came into contact with other Christian groups who had included Gentiles in their number. Matthew writes during this time and reflects a community that had become alienated from its Jewish roots.

This method seems to me to be fraught with considerable difficulties. While it can be acknowledged that Matthew's Gospel contains layers of material from different periods, ranging from the time of Jesus to the time of Matthew himself, I remain unconvinced that we can move from this observation to a realistic reconstruction of the Matthean community's history, especially when the time-frames are so short. Even Weren has to acknowledge that there is considerable overlap

---

48. Wim Weren, "The History and Social Setting of the Matthean Community," in *Matthew and the Didache: Two Documents From the Same Jewish-Christian Milieu?* (ed. H. van de Sandt; Assen: Van Gorcum, 2005), 51–62.

between the second and third phases, and that Matthew as the redactor seems to have been active during both periods.[49] Weren's analysis also draws too rigid a distinction between tradition and redaction. We know from Matthew's redaction of Mark that he altered or omitted sections he did not like, so why does the evangelist retain some earlier traditions, the anti-Gentile statements for example, when in Weren's view he was keen to recruit Gentiles? Finally, Weren's reconstruction involves a complex scenario whereby the original Matthean community began life in lower Galilee and later moved to upper Galilee and southern Syria. But why need we posit this? Why could not the Matthean community in Antioch or elsewhere have come into possession of Galilean traditions just as it inherited Roman traditions from Mark? More needs to be done to demonstrate that the provenance of some early Gospel traditions reflects the location of Matthew's group in an earlier phase.

All in all I remain unconvinced that only the text of the Gospel itself is a sufficient resource for reconstructing the history of the evangelist's community. A better approach is to determine if possible the location of the Gospel, and to use the available information to reconstruct its prior and later history.

5. The Social and Religious Milieu

When Matthean scholars have considered the question of the social and religious milieu of Matthew, they have usually focused on a single issue, the Jewish context of the Gospel and its community. The attention here has been primarily on the conflict with formative Judaism, and Matthean scholarship owes a large debt to the early work of William D. Davies and to the later works of Overman, Saldarini, and Stanton. These later scholars in particular have shown how the methods of social-scientific criticism have proved an invaluable resource in delineating the precise relationship between the evangelist's group and the larger Jewish body with which it was in dispute. It is now common to view the Matthean community as a sect or deviant group in opposition to its more powerful rival, though of course there is no agreement on what this actually entails. For Overman and Saldarini, this community constitutes a sect within Judaism, while for Stanton it is a sect outside the borders of the Jewish faith, and I shall say more about this divergence of opinion shortly. But whatever their differences in detail, these scholars and others as well have demonstrated that much light can be shed on the social setting of this community by the careful application of sociological principles. The real impact of the social sciences in this field can be measured by the fact that the terms "sect," "parent body," "legitimation," "conflict theory," "deviance association," "symbolic universe," and many other sociological terms are now firmly established in the lexicon of Matthean scholars.

---

49. Ibid., 52–53.

The acknowledgment that there was a conflict between formative Judaism and Matthew's group inevitably raises a further question: What was the relationship between this Christian community and the religion of Judaism? Did Matthew's group still identify itself as a part of the Jewish world, in which case the conflict with formative Judaism was an internal Jewish debate? Or had it broken in some definitive sense with its Jewish heritage so the conflict was in reality one between Christianity and Judaism? As we all know, Matthean scholarship is much divided over this issue. One side are those who see the evangelist's group as a minority and distinctive type of Judaism,[50] and on the other side are those who argue that it had rejected the Jewish faith and can therefore be described as a type of Christianity.[51] The issues involved in this important debate are too diverse and too complicated to be addressed here, but they involve matters such as our understanding of first-century Judaism, the role of the Torah in the Matthean community, the number and the status of any Gentiles in that community, the use of the term "the church" in the Gospel, and the evangelist's high Christology. This debate, which has dominated studies of this Gospel for nearly two decades, is far from resolution and will continue to command the attention of scholars.

Yet, as important as this question is, it would be a mistake to confine the social setting of Matthew's community to this single theme. The Gospel of Matthew took shape in a complex world and we should expect the setting of the Gospel to reflect this complexity. One such aspect of the evangelist's milieu that has recently and correctly come to prominence is its Roman imperial context. The evangelist and his community lived in a world dominated by the might and power of Rome,

---

50. See Overman, *Matthew's Gospel and Formative Judaism*, *passim*; Saldarini, *Matthew's Christian-Jewish Community*, *passim*; Davies and Allison, *Critical and Exegetical Commentary*, 3:692–704; Sim, *Gospel of Matthew and Christian Judaism*, 12–27, 109–63; Repschinski, *Controversy Stories*, 343–49; Daniel J. Harrington, "Matthew's Gospel: Pastoral Problems and Possibilities," in *The Gospel of Matthew in Current Study* (ed. D. E. Aune; Grand Rapids: Eerdmans, 2001), 66–69, and more tentatively Alan F. Segal, "Matthew's Jewish Voice," in *Social History of the Matthean Community: Cross-Disciplinary Approaches* (ed. D. L. Balch; Minneapolis: Fortress, 1991), 36–37.

51. So Stanton, *A Gospel for a New People*, 113–45; Luz, *Matthew 1–7*, 52–56; Ewherido, *Matthew's Gospel and Judaism*, 20–26; Weren, "Matthean Community," 53, 58; Robert H. Gundry, "A Responsive Evaluation of the Social History of the Matthean Community in Roman Syria," in Balch, ed., *Social History of the Matthean Community*, 62–67; Douglas R. A. Hare, "How Jewish is the Gospel of Matthew?," *CBQ* 62 (2000): 264–77; John K. Riches, *Conflicting Mythologies: Identity Formation in the Gospels of Mark and Matthew* (Studies of the New Testament and Its World; Edinburgh: T&T Clark, 2000), 202–25; Donald A. Hagner, "Matthew: Apostate, Reformer, Revolutionary?," *NTS* 49 (2003): 193–209; idem, "Matthew: Christian Judaism or Jewish Christianity?," in *The Face of New Testament Studies: A Survey of Recent Research* (ed. Scot McKnight and Grant R. Osborne; Grand Rapids: Baker, 2004), 263–82, and Paul Foster, *Community, Law and Mission in Matthew's Gospel* (WUNT 2/177; Tübingen: Mohr Siebeck, 2004), *passim*. Petri Luomanen can also be included in this category, though he is more tentative on this issue. See his *Entering the Kingdom of Heaven*, 263–65.

and this reality dominates his Gospel narrative; Jesus after all lived under Roman occupation and was executed by Roman soldiers at the express command of the local Roman governor. The first scholar to draw our attention to the importance of the Roman context of Matthew was Warren Carter, who was critical of earlier scholarship for ignoring such an obvious setting for the Gospel.[52] Carter argued, amongst other things, that the evangelist disputed Rome's imperial claims and presented Jesus as totally opposed to Roman arrogance, power and exploitation, as well as its idolatrous imperial theology. In reading Matthew in this way, Carter offered fresh interpretations of certain Matthean passages. While Carter perhaps at times overemphasizes the Roman setting for Matthew, there is still no doubting the importance of his work. He has opened up a whole new area of research that awaits further fruitful exploration.[53]

But it would be wrong to stop at this point. The social and religious setting of the Gospel encompasses much more than its Jewish and Roman contexts. Other neglected features that require serious scholarly attention are the relationship between Matthew's community and the Gentile world, and the place of this community within its broader Christian context.[54] Let us briefly examine these subjects in turn.

In earlier scholarship it was simply accepted without question that Matthew was a pro-Gentile Gospel. The evangelist depicted the Gentiles favorably in his narrative, he embraced a universalistic outlook, and the Matthean community was engaged in a Gentile mission that the risen Christ had commanded (28:16–20). This mission demanded baptism and not circumcision as the rite of initiation (28:19).[55] In the 1990s, however, other views began to surface, particularly from those scholars who emphasized the thoroughly Jewish nature of the Gospel and its community. J. Andrew Overman, for example, contended that the Matthean community probably contained only a few Gentiles, though he conceded that it was beginning to turn to the Gentile world.[56] For his part, Anthony J. Saldarini argued that the Gentile characters in Matthew's narrative are peripheral, and the emphasis remains throughout his story on the Jews and Jewish matters. Like

---

52. See Warren Carter, *Matthew and the Margins: A Sociopolitical and Religious Reading* (Maryknoll, N.Y.; Orbis, 2000), 36–43, and especially, idem, *Matthew and Empire, passim.*

53. One attempt to build upon the work of Carter is the collection of essays in John K. Riches and David C. Sim, eds., *The Gospel of Matthew in Its Roman Imperial Context* (JSNTSup 276; London: T&T Clark, 2005).

54. See the discussion of the necessity of these issues in David C. Sim, "The Social Setting of the Matthean Community: New Paths for an Old Journey," *Hervormde Teologiese Studies* 57 (2001): 268–80.

55. The most detailed statement of this position is that of Guido Tisera, *Universalism according to the Gospel of Matthew* (European University Studies 23/482; Frankfurt: Peter Lang, 1993).

56. Overman, *Matthew's Gospel and Formative Judaism*, 157–58.

Overman, Saldarini also accepted that the evangelist's community was in the process of widening its missionary endeavors to include the Gentiles.[57]

In a long article I published on this very theme, I tried to take the discussion in new directions.[58] To this end I questioned much of the prevailing scholarly consensus on the subject of the place of the Gentiles in the Gospel and in the Matthean community. The major points I made were that the evangelist did not depict all Gentiles positively in his narrative, that scholars have not taken seriously the anti-Gentile statements in the Gospel (5:46–47; 6:7–8, 31–32; 7:6; 18:15–17), that Matthew's community had probably been persecuted by Gentiles at the time of the Jewish war, that it was not certain this community was engaged in a comprehensive Gentile mission, and that any Gentiles in the evangelist's group would have been circumcised (if male) and obedient to the Torah. This rather different account of the Gentile question evoked a good many responses, which tended to criticize my arguments and make a case for the traditional understanding of this issue.[59]

There are many complex themes involved in this debate, but it seems to me that scholars need to attend to a number of central questions. Did the Matthean community experience Gentile persecution, and, if so, under what circumstances? How does this persecution affect our understanding of this community's mission to the Gentiles? But the most important question of all concerns the nature of any Gentile mission. Were the Gentiles in the Matthean community expected to observe the Mosaic Law, or were they exempt from this requirement? This question depends upon where one places the emphasis on two key Matthean texts. Matthew 5:17–19 appears to demand obedience to all of the Torah by followers of Jesus, yet the risen Christ mentions baptism and not circumcision in his commission to the disciples to evangelize all the nations (28:19). Is the necessity of circumcision assumed for Gentile converts in this concluding pericope, or is it now replaced by baptism? The debate continues on this issue.[60]

---

57. Saldarini, *Matthew's Christian-Jewish Community*, 68–83.

58. David C. Sim, "The Gospel of Matthew and the Gentiles," *JSNT* 57 (1995): 19–48. The arguments in that article were developed and refined in my *Matthew and Christian Judaism*, 215–56. Other studies of mine that relate to this general theme include "The 'Confession' of the Soldiers in Matthew 27:54," *HeyJ* 34 (1993): 501–24, and "The Magi: Gentiles or Jews?," *Hervormde Teologiese Studies* 55 (1999): 980–1000.

59. See especially, Donald Senior, "Between Two Worlds: Gentile and Jewish Christians in Matthew's Gospel," *CBQ* 61 (1999): 1–23, and Brendan Byrne, "The Messiah in Whose Name 'The Gentiles Will Hope' (Matt 13:21): Gentile Inclusion As an Essential Element of Matthew's Christology," *ABR* 50 (2002): 55–73. The Byrne article is followed by my response to it; David C. Sim, "Matthew and the Gentiles: A Response to Brendan Byrne," *ABR* 50 (2002): 74–79. For a different approach to the whole question, see Warren Carter, "Matthew and the Gentiles: Individual Conversion and/or Systemic Transformation?" *JSNT* 26 (2004): 259–82.

60. For the view that circumcision and Law-observance is assumed in this text, see Sim, *Gospel of Matthew and Christian Judaism*, 247–54. In agreement is Slee, *The Church in Antioch,*

In the past Matthean scholars have devoted too much attention to the question of whether the Great Commission advocates the Gentile mission at the expense of the Jewish mission, but it is now generally agreed that both missions are enjoined. We need therefore to move forward to examine the nature of each mission in practical terms. Was observance of the Torah expected of Jewish converts alone or was it integral to both missions? If obedience to the Mosaic Law was expected of Jews but not of Gentiles, how would such a mission be conducted by the same community? Where are the parallels in the early Christian movement of the same community conducting two such diverse missions?

This point brings us to the issue of Matthew and the broader Christian world. Just as the Matthean community did not live in a vacuum vis-à-vis the Jewish world, the Roman world and the Gentile world, so too did it not live in a vacuum within the movement of believers in Jesus. The Matthean Christian (Jewish) tradition existed alongside other forms of the Christian tradition, and it is reasonable to ask what Matthew would have thought of these alternative Christian groups. For example, what would the evangelist have made of Paul and his version of the gospel? Does Matthew's narrative about Jesus contain information about this issue? For the most part, Matthean scholars have tended to avoid these questions.[61] They often note that Matthew is non-Pauline, but they are content to leave the matter there. But this position is hardly satisfactory. Paul was a well-known and controversial figure in the early decades of the Christian movement, and his writings were probably widely distributed when Matthew composed his Gospel. Matthew was clearly non-Pauline, but he must have had some opinions about Paul, either positive or negative, and it is entirely legitimate to look for these in his Gospel.

I have argued in a number of publications that the evangelist, who accepted that both Jewish and Gentile followers of Jesus needed to observe the Torah in its entirety, stood diametrically opposed to the theological tradition of Paul, and that he saw fit to air his views within the context of his narrative.[62] I do not wish to repeat any of that discussion here. What I wish to highlight is that this matter requires serious and immediate attention in the field. Matthean scholars can no longer ignore the evangelist's Christian context. One way or another Matthew must be placed within the broader Christian movement, and his relationship with the Pauline tradition and other Christian traditions must be investigated. Until

---

140–42. The alternative position is best represented by Riches, *Conflicting Mythologies*, 216–22.

61. See the review of scholarly literature dealing with Matthew and Paul in David C. Sim, "Matthew's Anti-Paulinism: A Neglected Feature of Matthean Studies," *Hervormde Teologiese Studies* 58 (2002): 767–83.

62. In addition to the article cited in the previous note, see Sim, *Gospel of Matthew and Christian Judaism*, 188–211, and David C. Sim, "Matthew 7.21–23: Further Evidence of Its Anti-Pauline Perspective," *NTS* 53 (2007): 325–43.

this is done, no scholar can claim that they have considered or reconstructed the totality of the social and religious setting of this Gospel.

6. Results

In this study I have attempted to raise some pertinent issues in terms of the social and religious milieu of Matthew's community. One matter that needs to be revisited is that of the Gospel's date. Since there may be no valid reason to restrict Matthew to the late-first century C.E., it might pay dividends to explore the possibility that the Gospel could be some decades later than we currently believe. As I have tried to show, a later dating seems to be more consistent with some of the social settings that have been postulated for Matthew's group. On the important question of provenance, the location of the Gospel in Antioch on the Orontes is still the most probable hypothesis. The Galilean alternative seems to me to suffer from a number of serious weaknesses. There is very little in the Gospel itself that points to a Galilean provenance, and there are real problems created by considerations external to the text. The location of the Gospel may or may not afford the opportunity to write a history of the Matthean community. This is certainly possible if the Antiochene hypothesis is accepted, and it may be the case for other suggested locations. But if we are to reconstruct such a history, then a firm grounding in a given provenance is necessary. I remain unconvinced that simply the text itself with no real external factors considered provides sufficient reliable evidence for such an undertaking.

Finally, the scholarly study of the Matthean community has yielded firm results. There is little doubt that the most obvious setting of this community is the conflict with formative Judaism, though there is little agreement over the implications that follow from this. The precise relationship between Matthew's Christian group and the religion of Judaism is still to be resolved. But more too needs to be done on other issues. We have made a start on the Gospel's Roman setting, but the question of the Gentiles in this community needs more concrete discussion. On what basis were they converted, and what was their status within this group? And where do we situate the Matthean community within the general Christian movement? What did Matthew think of alternative Christian traditions, and was he in conflict with them? We may conclude that, while much important work has been done in reconstructing the social and religious milieu of Matthew, there is still much to occupy our attention in the years to come.

Reconstructing the Social and Religious Milieu of James: Methods, Sources, and Possible Results

Oda Wischmeyer

1. Definitions of the Term "Milieu"

Let me begin with some reflections about the term "milieu." The term does not belong to the well-known vocabulary in historical studies or historical theory.[1] "Milieu" was introduced in the nineteenth century by Hippolyte Taine, who used it in connection with his theory of the sociology of art, which he thought to some degree to be based on science.[2] In his work "Histoire de la Littérature Anglaise" Taine uses the three terms of race, milieu, and moment "as the three principal motives or conditioning factors that lie behind any work or art. . . . By 'milieu' he meant the circumstances or environment that modified the inherited racial disposition" while "race" is defined as "the inherited disposition or temperament that persists stubbornly over thousands of years."[3] The term was sharpened and differentiated in subsequent discussion of social history and sociology. A helpful definition reads: "Unter M(ilieu)s versteht man . . . soz(iale) Einheiten, die durch die Koinzidenz einer Reihe von Strukturmerkmalen, wie Religion, regionale Tradition, wirtschaftl(iche) Lage, kulturelle Orientierung u(nd) schichtenspezif(ische) Zusammensetzung der intermediären Gruppen, gekennzeichnet sind. M(ilieu)s als gesellschaftl(iche) Großgruppen weisen Gemeinsamkeiten insbes(ondere) in drei Dimensionen auf: geteilte Standards der Sinnkonstruktion, der Werte und Normen; ein gemeinsames Netzwerk v(on) Institutionen . . . u(nd) geteilte Ritualisierungen des Alltags- und Festtags-Lebens." This definition is especially useful for our inquiry about the milieu of James because it names a number of crucial

---

1. It does not appear as lemma in, e.g., "Grundbegriffe der Geschichte," "Der Neue Pauly," and other standard encyclopaedias.

2. Hippolyte Taine, *Philosophie de l'art*. (2 vols.; Paris: Hachette, 1881).

3. "Art. 'Race, Milieu, and Moment'," in *The New Encyclopaedia Britannica. Micropaedia*, 7:368.

parameters: ideas of religion and ethics, values and behavior, and circumstances of life shared by the group to which the author belonged. These parameters provide elements of the milieu that influenced his convictions and the literature he wrote.

2. What is Social Milieu? (Considerations on Method 1)

The underlying assumption for asking such a question is that there indeed was something like a homogeneous or uniform milieu whose traces we are able to recover from the letter of James and that might enable us to reconstruct the social milieu of the community to which the author belonged and for which he wrote. Furthermore, the question suggests that we are indeed able to identify a certain group connected to this milieu. With Malina, one might assume that this group is a fictive kin group of a certain number[4] of persons, who define themselves by belonging to this group.[5]

Methodologically, the basis for all attempts to reconstruct James's milieu is a thorough analysis of the vocabulary the letter uses to describe groups, and of the way it addresses its readers. We have to consider whether and how the group or problems of the group or of groups in general do feature in the letter. In this respect, we especially have to discuss the beginning of the letter (1:1) and the figures of speech used in addressing the readers in the wider corpus of the letter.

A second issue is the question how the author depicts or touches the social milieu. Is it one distinct milieu of a single group, or are different sceneries mentioned? Does the author differentiate within the group or the groups? Are there indications of structures, of hierarchies and leadership functions, or of struggle within or among groups? Are there parties or subgroups? How can we define the author's place in the scenario? What about meetings and rites? What about mutual help and solidarity? Finally, are there traces of a collective identity, so that we might be able to reconstruct an in-group to which the author belongs or for or against whom the author writes his letter?

3. Observations on the Social Milieu (Sources 1)

Following terms are important indicators of the author's understanding of the group to whom he wrote his letter:
- Twelve tribes in the dispersion (διασπορά, only in 1:1)[6]
- (My) (beloved) brothers (1:2 and more often)

---

4. See Bruce J. Malina, *The New Testament World: Insights from Cultural Anthropology* (3rd ed.; Louisville, Ky.: Westminster John Knox, 2001), 214–17.

5. Malina, *New Testament World*, 214–17.

6. See 1 Peter 1:1.

- Your assembly (συναγωγή, 2:2)
- A brother or a sister (2:15)[7]
- Anyone among you (5:13 and elsewhere, notice 5:19)
- Assembly (ἐκκλησία, 5:14)
- To confess sins to each other and pray for each other (5:16, cf. 5:19)

The author's vocabulary in addressing his audience does not provide much evidence of the group he belonged to or was addressing. The author and his literary audience are connected with each other, and he addresses them with terminology taken from metaphorical kinship, but at the same time also as teacher with a teacher's authority (1:16 μὴ πλανᾶσθε; 1:19 ἴστε; 2:5 ἀκούσατε; 2:20 θέλεις δὲ γνῶναι; 2:22 βλέπεις; 2:24 ὁρᾶτε; and elsewhere, particularly 3:1–2). He writes from a certain position of distance: it is "your" assembly and "your" problems (2:2; particularly 4:1–5:6).

The author's vocabulary for special groups within the above-mentioned brotherhood is partly rather general, partly more specific, but mostly has the function of a literary figure:

- Orphans and widows (1:27)
- The poor and the rich (chapter 2 and elsewhere)
- Teachers (3:1, note the following "we" which makes clear that the author puts himself into this special group of teachers which he wants to remain a very small one)
- Traders (4:13–17, metaphorically expressed and addressed)
- The rich (5:1–6, see above)
- The elders of the assembly (5:14)

On the whole, we only find a limited section of aspects connected to the author's social world, and of his conceptions concerning the social world around him and his addressees. The author's perception of the social world is rather poor and simple. It is not an issue that is in the focus of his interest, nor is structures, hierarchies and authorities in the community. Only πρεσβύτεροι are mentioned. This is certainly too little evidence to speculate about real hierarchies in the community.

We only find two sentences in which the author refers to "wars" and "battles" among the addressees: 4:1 and (only as an allusion) 4:11 as well as 5:9. 4:1 belongs to a specific ethical discourse[8] and, in opposition to 1 Corinthians, the passage does not reflect actual parties or conflicts within a specific Christian community. The fictitious discourse in 2:14–19 and the subsequent ethical-theological

---

7. It is interesting that the author refers to "sisters" concerning support and subsidy, but constantly addresses only "brothers."

8. See Christoph Burchard, *Der Jakobusbrief* (HNT 15/1. Tübingen: Mohr Siebeck, 2000), 165–66.

διδαχή of 2:20–26, which is written as diatribe,[9] throw some light on the conflict that took place within or between the Christian groups the author addresses. The author apparently is particulary interested in general ethical issues and notices and blames different διδαχαί over these issues.

In general, the author himself as well as his addressees belongs to the city-milieu (4:13–17).[10] But there is no sign of particular "Lokalkolorit" in James,[11] and we do not have any indications either about where the author lived[12] or about the location of the addressees.[13] The metaphors taken from nature (1:11) or rural milieu (3:12; 5:4, 7) are part of the rhetoric strategies to express ethical concerns. The author likes to sketch different social milieus, but uses popular rhetorical instruments of simplification, exaggeration, and opposition (e.g. "poor and rich"). Both milieus are depicted in the literary scene in chapter 2. The traders seem to belong to the group of the "rich" as we learn from the literary scene of chapter 4. The farmer belongs to the group of the "poor" within this special social logic. It is obvious that the author is not interested in the real social milieus as an independent issue, but only uses imaginary social milieus illustratively within the literary strategy of his general ethical discourse.

The letter contains a number of interesting references to community gatherings and rituals. I already mentioned the brief literary scene in chapter 2, which documents that social differences play an important role in an imaginary gathering where the higher ranking person can expect to be honored in a special way.[14] The social rank in this literary situation results from the wealth a person displays through jewels and garments as well as from the rank the person is granted by the assembly. In chapter 5 the author gives some advice on ritual practices of the group (anointing). For him, the community should be a place of mutual consolation and spiritual help. The passage is a good example of how important ethical admonition is for the author.

---

9. See Oda Wischmeyer, "Römer 2.1–24 als Teil der Gerichtsrede des Paulus gegen die Menschheit," *NTS* 52 (2006): 356–76.

10. See Ekkehard W. Stegemann and Wolfgang Stegemann, *Urchristliche Sozialgeschichte: Die Anfänge im Judentum und die Christusgemeinden in der mediterranen Welt* (2nd ed.; Stuttgart: Kohlhammer, 1997), 219–305; Burchard, *Jakobusbrief*, 6.

11. Burchard, *Jakobusbrief*, 7.

12. Ibid.; nor is Jerusalem ever mentioned.

13. The "twelve tribes in the diaspora" is an ecumenical address that refers to the whole *Imperium Romanum*.

14. See Malina, *New Testament World*, 27–57.

4. What is Religious Milieu? (Considerations on Method 2)

Contemporary theory is very cautious in defining religion.[15] If we define religion from a functional perspective we can ask questions that help us in reconstructing the religious system of a specific author and his addressees. Gerd Theissen's threefold conception of religion is based on a semiotic understanding of religion ("Die urchristliche Religion als autonome Zeichenwelt"[16]), which then continues to an analysis of important theological ("*Mythos* und Geschichte"[17]) and *ethical* concerns in early Christianity, as well as of central *rites*.

On the basis of this theoretical framework, we should begin by looking for something like a valid and perhaps homogeneous theory of explaining the κόσμος in terms of *myths* or historical narratives, which also generates a construction of ethical values combined with the general explanation of the world and the destiny of mankind.[18] We have to look for ideas of gods, goddesses or deities, for the salvation of mankind or of special groups, for *rites* as well as for ritual and ethical advice. So far the issues concern the general function of religion.

There is a second issue that is more closely related to our text, namely, the question of where the letter positions itself in the wider range of contemporary religions.[19] What should his readers think about the author's religion? Which religion is he teaching in this letter? And does he teach "religion" at all? Or does he only mention some religious identity markers in order to point out to his

---

15. See Hubert Cancik and Burkhard Gladigow "Introduction," in *Handbuch religionswissenschaftlicher Grundbegriffe* (eds. H. Cancik, B. Gladigow and M. Laubscher; 5 vols.; Stuttgart: Kohlhammer, 1988–2001), 1:19–40; Günther Kehrer, "Definitionen der Religion," in *Handbuch religionswissenschaftlicher Grundbegriffe* (eds. H. Cancik, B. Gladigow and M. Laubscher), 4:418–25; Hans-Josef Klauck, *Die Religiöse Umwelt des Urchristentums* (2 vols.; Stuttgart: Kohlhammer, 1995–6), 1:13–26.

16. Gerd Theissen, *Die Religion der ersten Christen* (3rd ed.; Darmstadt: WBG, 2003), 225–82.

17. Ibid., 47–100.

18. Ibid., 30, gives an overview over the connection between general explanations of the κόσμος and ethical norms.

19. See Klauck, *Religiöse Umwelt*, 1:19–26; Ulrich Berner, "Moderner und antiker Religionsbegriff," in *Neues Testament und Antike Kultur* (ed. K. Erlemann et al.; 2nd ed.; 5 vols.; Neukirchen-Vluyn; Neukirchener Verlag: 2004 – 2007), 1:13–21: Religion "erfüllt die Funktion, dem Menschen Normen für das Leben zu geben und Trost für das Sterben; die Erfüllung dieser Funktion wird ermöglicht oder zumindest unterstützt durch Institutionen, die einen Rahmen für rituelle Erfahrungen bieten; die Normen werden durch den Bezug auf Gesetze begründet, die höher sind als die von Menschen gemachten, und der Trost wird zumeist durch den Bezug auf einen Bereich gegeben, der über das irdische Leben hinausgeht" (ibid., 16). Transl.: "Religion works by giving people standards for living and consolation for dying. These functions are supported by institutions with ritual structure. Norms are founded by reference to laws higher than those made by men, and consolation is given by referring to a world going beyond mortal life."

audience his religious focus, or to accentuate the religion that unites him with his audience, before he starts on his proper subject? This includes a short discussion of the main issue and the main purpose of the letter.

Particularly we will have to observe allusions to Judaism, to *ethical* schools, and to Christianity, and discuss the importance of those allusions within the literary concept of the letter as a whole.

5. Observations on the Religious Milieu (Sources 2)

Concerning myth(s) we only find individual myth-based metaphors or personifications, all more-or-less clearly echoing Old Testament themes:
- The "birth" of sin (1:14s, cf. the mythological language in Rom 7)
- God "bears" the Christians by the word of truth (1:18)
- Wisdom "from above" (3:17; ἄνωθεν)
- Struggle between living according to God or according to the κόσμος or the διάβολος (4:4–10).

Sometimes we can observe that the author uses metaphoric or mythical language including personifications when he writes about the law and the last judgment (2:8–13 law; 2:19 demons; 3:6 γέεννα; 3:15 σοφία δαιμονιώδης; 5:1–6 ἐσχάται ἡμέραι).[20] We may conclude that there is no evidence of pagan mythological thinking or allusions in the letter of James. Mythical elements in his language relate to Septuagint phrases.

The author is quite clear on monotheism and on God's attributes:[21]
- πατὴρ τῶν φώτων (1:17)
- God is not tempted, he does not tempt anyone (1:13)
- God chooses the poor (2:5)
- God and father (1:27)
- εἷς ἐστιν ὁ θεός (2:19; cf. 4:12 "one is the eternal lawgiver and judge").
- In 5:4 God is called with a title, taken from the Septuagint: κύριος σαβαώθ

In short: God is good, he is One. He is to be thought of as residing in an atmosphere of ethical perfection that is expressed by images of heaven (above, light, glory). God is the father of mankind and cares for human affairs. He is the guarantor of law, of justice, of ethics, and of the final punishment. In spite of the fact that the author does not emphasize the Jewish perspective, the reader of the letter may well understand that the author has the God of Israel in mind (e.g., 5:4).

---

20. See Wiard Popkes, *Der Brief des Jakobus* (THKNT 14; Leipzig: Evangelische Verlags-anstalt, 2001), 22–26.

21. See ibid., 23, and Hubert Frankemölle, *Der Brief des Jakobus* (ÖTK 17/1–2; Gütersloh: Gütersloher Verlagshaus, 1994), 2:367–87.

There are some additional remarks on Jesus Christ that are well known and broadly discussed[22] in scholarly literature:

- κύριος τῆς δόξης
- Judge (1:1 and 2:1; 5:9; cf. 2:7 and 4:15)

I agree with Wiard Popkes who points out that there is no explicit christology in the letter of James: "Eine Christologie entfaltet Jak(obus) nicht eigens. Sie ist weitgehend Teil der Gotteslehre."[23] But we have to consider what this statement means with regard to our quest for the author's religious milieu. It seems to me that christology is not an issue for the author nor for his audience. Given the clear difference to, for example, the letters of John, we can assume that James does not suspect any christological αἵρεσις among his audience. On the other hand both the author and his addressees are Christians. There is no need for the author to emphasize this religious affiliation.

The use of the Septuagint is much more important for the reconstruction of the religious milieu of James than christology. The Septuagint is the pre-text of the letter, the author expects his readers to know the Septuagint, and both the author as well as his addressees, consider the Septuagint as "scripture."[24] Both use the Septuagint first and foremost as a collection of moral examples:

- Abraham and Rahab (2:21–25)
- The prophets (5:10)[25]
- Job (5:11)[26]

The use of the Septuagint does not have the function of recommending Judaism to the addressees, nor does it act as boundary marker against other religions. The Septuagint simply is the religious, ethical, and cultural canonical book for the Christian community to which the author and his audience belong. The Septuagint remains "the book" for James's religious community.

Concerning religious *rites*, we can concentrate on chapter 5, because chapter 2 only confirms that the addressees of the letter are accustomed to come together in assemblies, that at least some of them seat there, and that there are more and less honorable seats to use. Chapter 5 gives us some insight into religious practices of the group the letter addresses. The members of the group (ἐκκλησία) pray, especially in case of illness.[27] The social context of prayer is not necessarily the assembly together with the πρεσβύτεροι, but the spiritual community of individual members of the group, and their mutual responsibility and sympathy. Even the confession of sins is left to each individual member of the group. There

---

22. See Popkes, *Brief des Jakobus*, 23; Frankemölle, *Brief des Jakobus*, 376–87.

23. Popkes, *Brief des Jakobus*, 23.

24. Ibid., 27–29.

25. Ὑπόδειγμα.

26. Note the phrases "you have heard" and "you know," which assume the biblical characters to be known.

27. Popkes, *Brief des Jakobus*, 337–39.

is only one religious rite reserved for the πρεσβύτεροι, namely the unction of the infirm. This rite is only attested at one other place in early Christianity (Mark 6:13).[28] In spite of such a notably flat or perhaps even non-existent hierarchic structure we can understand the group as being an in-group with a distinct religious-ethical boundary: "to keep oneself unstained from the world" (1:27).

The short text of 1:26–27 demonstrates the author's *ethical* perspective. He redefines worship (θρησκεία) in a moral sense in two directions: first by relating θρησκεία to speech ethics,[29] alms, and supply; second by spiritualizing it as a kind of ethical purity. The author writes for an audience that wants to get ethical advice by means of apostolic letters written and authorized by leading apostles of Jerusalem, and at the same time is familiar with the Septuagint, and this means with Jewish ethics. The author does not use the ethical authority of Jesus.[30]

6. Tentative Results

Our observations showed that neither the social nor the religious milieus are key topics of the letter. Instead, it is obvious that the main concern of James is ethics, namely, ethics transmitted in the literary form of a letter.

Our particular interest focused on the social and religious milieu of the letter. In the *salutatio* we are presented with a group the author teaches in ethics. He addresses a group that shows a definite religious bias and whose members are in close contact with each other. It is a group that holds meetings and that understands itself as a union of individuals who at the same time belong to a group and bear responsibility for each other. To some degree it can be stated that the author has an elitist position in relation to the group, introducing himself as "brother" but also as "teacher." He addresses his readers as the "twelve tribes in the διασπορά," which is a literary address with a twofold setting, namely,, a Jewish and a Christian one. "Diese *salutatio* schafft eine fiktionale, besser literarische Leserschaft, des Näheren handelt es sich um eine theologisch-ekklesiologische Binnenadresse. Mit Hilfe der Briefadresse . . . schafft sich der Autor ein Publikum

28. Burchard, *Jakobusbrief*, 210 (cf. *Apoc. Mos.* 9.3 and *L.A.E.* 36.2; 40–41). See also Sigurd Kaiser, *Krankenheilung: Untersuchungen zu Form, Sprache, traditionsgeschichtlichem Hintergrund und Aussage von Yak 5,13–18* (WMANT 112; Neukirchen-Vluyn: Neukirchener Verlag, 2006).

29. See William R. Baker, *Personal-Speech Ethics in the Epistle of James* (WUNT 2/68; Tübingen: Mohr Siebeck, 1995).

30. This fact remains a problem for scholars who give reasons "of an early dating for this letter" and relate the letter in close proximity to James, the brother of Jesus. See Luke T. Johnson, *The Letter of James* (AB 37A; New York: Doubleday, 1995), 118; see the whole introduction (1–164).

als Ansprechpartner."[31] The addressees are expected to understand the religious allusion to Israel as well as to Christianity, and especially to the Jesus tradition. The salutation is a very specific one and only to be understood by an in-group public that is used to read religious literature and is acquainted with Jewish as well as with Christian texts and that knows about the differences. By using the pseudepigraphic name, the author transmits his ethical advice to Jesus and to the Judaeo-Christian community of Jerusalem[32] before the Judean war as well as to the high religious and moral authority of James himself.[33]

In conclusion, on the one hand we can observe a Christian author who teaches ethics that derives basically from the Septuagint in the interpretation of early Christian theologians,[34] and on the other hand we assume a basically Christian readership that knows the Septuagint to a greater or lesser extent and is interested in reading further and perhaps more 'modern' ethical texts. We find ourselves at the roots of a kind of ethical literature that is written by Christian teachers who claim authority by means of pseudepigraphy. Later on they will write in their own name, like Justin or Clement of Alexandria. In short, we may gain a view into a rather urban, religious, and literary milieu that combines religion and ethics, in which people like to read literature of the quality of a treatise and in which Christian authors do not yet dare to use their own name but bind themselves and their writings to the Jesus or the Pauline tradition. The ethical impact of this tradition increased in the last decades of the first century, generating different literary genres, such as the longer synoptic Gospels of Matthew and Luke[35] as well as the Pastorals.

---

31. Oda Wischmeyer, "Beobachtungen zu Kommunikation und Gliederung des Jakobusbriefes," in *Das Gesetz im frühen Judentum und im Neuen Testament* (ed. D. Sänger and M. Konradt; NTOA 57; Göttingen: Vandenhoeck & Ruprecht, 2006), 320.

32. This term has no denominational meaning: cf. Burchard, *Jakobusbrief*, 5 (the author was "kein Judenchrist").

33. Cf. the analogous process in the other Catholic letters concerning Peter and Jude.

34. Cf. 2:8–11 to Pauline texts and gospel texts. Cf. Popkes, *Brief des Jakobus*, 155–57.

35. The literary milieu to which James and his addressees also belong is reconstructed in the volume of R. Bauckham, ed., *The Gospels for All Christians: Rethinking the Gospel Audiences* (Edinburgh: T&T Clark, 1998). The contributions concentrate on the gospels, but at the end of the first century we may assume a Christian reading audience that was interested in narratives (gospels) as well as in moral treatises (letters) as we learn from 2 Pet 1:16–21.

Reconstructing the Social and Religious Milieu of the Didache: Observations and Possible Results

Jürgen K. Zangenberg

1. Approaching the Question

If we want to examine the milieu of a given text, we are faced with a complex of difficult questions.[1] I perceive "milieu" as a particular cultural setting, evidenced by language, style, and content of a text. "Milieu" is effective in a particular communicative process, describing a "location" in a social, religious, and also topographical sense. While language might be the medium to construct and maintain a milieu, to offer orientation to members of that milieu, create cohesion among them, draw boundaries, express belonging and desires, and target elements that need to be changed, there are always factors in the milieu that are not part of written or spoken language. "Milieu" entails actions and location; milieu "happens" as well as requiring a place in time and space. All these factors can certainly be made an object of language by making them a topic in texts and debates, but that is not necessarily a one-to-one reflection. Texts never are simply a mirror of a given milieu, never offer a complete representation of all or even most elements of the milieu they are part of. Texts always select, emphasize, ignore, and alter elements of that milieu in order to fulfill their intended purpose. A milieu, consequently, never only "rests" in texts alone, nor is it only present by means of language. There *is*, however, a certain correspondence between milieu and the language used in texts originating from it ("jargon"), and it is certainly possible to assign texts to a common milieu by identifying overlaps in content, especially in the way the content ("traditions") is presented through style and language.

Milieu is broader than a group. "Milieu" means a group or related groups *plus* their context, and *in relation* to their context. Didache, for example, was written in and by a particular group, but this group might only be part of a wider network

---

1. See also Oda Wischmeyer's article in this volume.

and belong together with other groups to a larger milieu. Milieu, in fact, is a *relational* term. If more than a single group exists within a milieu, these groups can be expected to be in intensive communication with each other and with the given social, practical, and intellectual environment they inhabit. These groups would share common expressions and interpretations of their milieu, but not necessarily use these common traditions in an identical manner nor in unison. Different accents, even fierce competition and conflict might be the result.

What does all that mean for the study of Didache? Ever since its first publication at the end of the nineteenth century, Didache has attracted scholars because of its—in many ways—unique form and content. The question of how Didache fits into the intellectual and geographic landscape of early Christianity, has played an especially important role. To put it differently: What, many asked, was the didachist's milieu?

And yet, despite much effort and a lot of new insights, overall "progress" was small.[2] One almost gets the impression that Didache systematically escaped all attempts to pin down its social and ideological context, define its place of origin or help identify a region where it might originally have circulated. I can only agree with Clayton N. Jefford who, at the beginning of a very constructive article on "The Milieu of Matthew, the Didache, and Ignatius of Antioch," exclaimed: "There is likely no greater issue that remains within modern research on the Didache about which is less known and more is assumed than (. . .) the question of the provenance of the text."[3] The prevailing insecurity is certainly to a large extent a result of Didache's character: while Didache, on the one hand, deals with a number of issues in unparalleled detail, such as ethics, baptism, a communal meal, and itinerant functionaries, the text also is, on the other hand, awkwardly unspecific and vague when it comes to pinning these details down on our virtual map of early Christian texts and their communities. Despite its apparent concreteness, Didache shares the *selective* character that texts have in relation to the milieu they belong to.

The other difficulty lies in the fact that too little is known about how far New Testament and early post-New Testament literature were connected to a particular region and how such a connection could be demonstrated. This, of course, is a result of the general vagueness of many texts about where precisely they origi-

---

2. See, for example, Gunnar Garleff, *Urchristliche Identität in Matthäusevangelium, Didache und Jakobusbrief* (Beiträge zum Verstehen der Bibel 9; Münster: LIT, 2004), 89 who states that research is "insgesamt nicht weit über das Hypothetische hinausgelangt" ("in general not reached far beyond the hypothetical")

3. Clayton N. Jefford, "The Milieu of Matthew, the Didache, and Ignatius of Antioch: Agreements and Differences," in *Matthew and the Didache: Two Documents from the Same Jewish-Christian Milieu?* (ed. H. van de Sandt; Assen: Van Gorcum, 2005), 35. On Jefford's own suggestion—shared with others—that Matthew, Didache, and the *Corpus Ignatianum* originate from Antioch, see below.

nated or where they were supposed to be read. The Pauline literature only is a welcome exception to this rule. The debate over how the seemingly so explicit information on the recipients of 1 Peter and James should be interpreted is a good example. Other texts, such as the Gospels and some of the New Testament letters, do not give any explicit indication at all about where they were written and for whom. Sometimes early post-New Testament texts help fill some gaps in the record by referring to traditions and speculations about authors and contexts, but often they rise more questions than they answer. A most notable example is Papias of Hierapolis whose opinions are notoriously controversial. Wherever even that information is lacking, we are fully dependent upon implicit and indirect allusions picked from the texts themselves (language, vocabulary, the way that traditions are used). Didache belongs to precisely that category of texts.

After von Harnack's pioneering edition, two places or regions have been proposed as Didache's original context, namely, Egypt and Syria/Palestine.[4] A significant number of scholars have recently made a strong case for Antioch, but others have called for caution.[5] In my paper I do not want to discuss this hypothesis directly, nor do I want to propose an alternative location for the "community of the Didache." I rather want to go one step back and look at Didache from a distance to critically assess the clues the text provides about its origin and context.

---

4. I only name as examples Klaus Wengst, *Didache (Apostellehre), Barnabasbrief, Zweiter Klemensbrief, Schrift an Diognet* (Schriften des Urchristentums 2; Darmstadt: Wissenschaftliche Buchgesellschaft, 1984), 61–63 (rural place in Syria); Kurt Niederwimmer, *Die Didache* (Kommentar zu den Apostolischen Vätern 1; Göttingen: Vandenhoeck & Ruprecht, 1989), 78–79 (Syria/Palestine, but rather not Antioch); Georg Schöllgen, *Didache: Zwölf-Apostel-Lehre* and Wilhelm Geerlings, *Traditio Apostolica: Apostolische Überlieferung* (Fontes Christiani 1; Freiburg: Herder, 1991), 84–85 (any city in Syria/Palestine rather than Egypt, but evidence is tentative); Adolf Adam, "Erwägungen zur Herkunft der Didache," *ZKG* 68 (1957): 1–47 (Pella as "hypothetische Vermutung," p. 47). All these studies offer ample references. Georg Schöllgen, "Die Didache: Ein frühes Zeugnis für Landgemeinden?" *ZNW* 76 (1985): 140–43 rejects the idea that Didache came from a rural environment (against Wengst, *Didache (Apostellehre)*, 33–34 and 61–63). Symptomatic for the weak ground on which all these assumptions are moving is especially von Harnack who has repeatedly revised his opinion.

5. Apart from Jefford, "Milieu of Matthew, the Didache, and Ignatius" I only want to point to John P. Meier, "Antioch" in Raymond E. Brown and John P. Meier, *Antioch and Rome: New Testament Cradles of Catholic Christianity* (New York: Paulist Press, 1983), 12–86; Michelle Slee, *The Church in Antioch in the First Century CE: Communion and Conflict* (JSNTSup 244; London: Sheffield Academic Press, 2003); Magnus Zetterholm, *The Formation of Christianity in Antioch: A Social-Scientific Approach to the Separation between Judaism and Christianity* (Routledge Early Church Monographs; London: Routledge, 2003) and the article by Magnus Zetterholm in this volume (with more references). Bas ter Haar Romeny, "Hypotheses on the Development of Judaism and Christianity in Syria in the Period after 70 C.E." in van de Sandt, ed., *Matthew and the Didache*, 13–33, however, is rightly cautious and suggests Didache and Matthew "were written somewhere in each other's neighbourhood, closer to Palestine, perhaps even in Galilea."

I will certainly offer more questions and second thoughts than answers. I hope that my *Schritt zurück* is no *Rückschritt*, but helps to see a bit clearer why no real progress was, in fact *could not*, be made with regard to our question.

2. DIDACHE'S CHARACTER

There are a couple of major obstacles that are not easy to overcome for anybody attempting to identify Didache's social and religious milieu precisely:

2.1. ANONYMITY

Many difficulties arise from the fact that Didache's original title is lost, if it had one at all.[6] I am well aware of the fact that such a statement sounds awkward to many, but I am indeed more sceptical about this issue than most colleagues. Unfortunately, manuscript tradition cannot help us retrieve a reliable candidate for an original title. P. Oxy. XV 1782, our oldest but very fragmentary witness from the end of the fourth century, only starts with Did. 1:3 and breaks off shortly thereafter, and our most important text Codex Hierosolymitanus 54 ("H") is often unreliable and contains many disputed readings.[7] Above all, it offers two titles, a short one διδαχὴ τῶν δώδεκα ἀποστόλων written in a separate line, and a long one διδαχὴ κυρίου διὰ τῶν δώδεκα ἀποστόλων τοῖς ἔθνεσιν which is graphically presented in such a way that it is likely the copyist considered it already part of the text.[8] This duplication has long been an issue of debate with arguments put forward in favor of the originality of the shorter or the longer version (now predominately accepted).[9] I think H clearly shows the intention of the copyist at least of this manuscript to document variant titles he found in his *Vorlagen* and also his decision to adopt the shorter one as "title" of the text and relegate the longer one to a secondary position as "incipit." None of these titles, however, need be authentic.[10] Vielhauer's suggestion that the text might initially have circulated without a title at all[11] should not be dismissed too quickly with reference to the textual tradition which only seemingly offers the choice of *alternative* titles.

---

6. For a different opinion on the title see Garleff, *Urchristliche Identität in Matthäusevangelium*, 111–17. Aaron Milavec, *The Didache: Faith, Hope and Life of the Earliest Christian Communities 50–70 C.E.* (New York: Newman, 2003) also doubts that Didache originally had a title, but on the basis of different observations than the ones proposed here.

7. On these witnesses see, for example, Niederwimmer, *Die Didache*, 33–39.

8. Niederwimmer, *Die Didache*, 81.

9. Schöllgen, *Didache: Zwölf-Apostel-Lehre*, 25–26; Jean-Paul Audet, *La Didachè: Instructions des Apôtres* (Paris: Gabalda, 1958), 91–103.

10. Wengst, *Didache (Apostellehre)*, 15; Niederwimmer, *Die Didache*, 81–82.

11. Philipp Vielhauer, *Geschichte der urchristlichen Literatur: Einleitung in das Neue Testament, die Apokryphen und die Apostolischen Väter* (Berlin: de Gruyter, 1981), 722–25; Willy

There still is the option that initially there was *no* title at all, a feature Didache would then share with many other ancient writings including, for example, the Gospels. Above all, Niederwimmer rightly asks if the title mentioned in the *testimonia* does indeed refer to the Didache in particular and not in a more general way to any paraenetic text in the form of a Two Ways Tractate.[12] This is certainly a good point!

What does that mean? Schöllgen is certainly right that the text implies strong authority,[13] but whoever wrote it remained anonymous and "borrowed" authority from the "sources" and instructions it propagates: insight in right and wrong ways, the Lord and scripture. This authority does not require to be expressed in a title. Moreover, the way that ἀπόστολος is used in Didache is not prominent enough to warrant an exclusive connection of its authority with this particular group of community leaders. To ascribe exclusive "apostolic" authorship to this text (as well as to others, see "Apostolic Traditions") makes more sense in a later period when internal authority was no longer considered sufficient, and Didache finally received its title.[14] *Precisely when* this happened remains unclear. It does not seem too far fetched to assume that the phrase διδαχὴ τῶν ἀποστόλων from Acts 2:42 was instrumental in this process.

It is often claimed that Clement of Alexandria already knew (a version of) Didache, but he quotes Did. 3:5 as γραφή without naming a specific title (*Strom.* 1 [20] 100.4). Strictly speaking, Clement only attests that the authority of the tradition he refers to was regarded as highly as that of Scripture itself, but it remains entirely hypothetical that Clement actually quotes from a work similar to what we now know as Didache.[15]

The first to quote from "teachings of the apostles" (in fact, from a Latin translation entitled *Doctrinae apostolorum*) is Pseudo-Cyprian's *Adversus aleatores* (around 300).[16] The fact that phrases from Did. 14:2 and 15:3 are combined and employed in a passage also containing quotations from 1 Cor merely shows how freely such paraenetic passages could be combined with each other (see also above on Clement). We do not know if Ps.-Cyprian quotes from a different version of Didache, or if he just combined and altered as appropriate what he received from general tradition. But if Ps.-Cyprian indeed quoted from a version of Didache, its alleged apostolic character seems to have encouraged him to juxtapose Didache traditions with Pauline ones whose apostolic authority had long been established.

Rordorf and André Tuilier, *La Doctrine des Douze Apôtres (Didachè)* (SC 248; Paris: Cerf, 1978), 13–17.

12. Niederwimmer, *Die Didache*, 81–82.

13. Schöllgen, *Didache: Zwölf-Apostel-Lehre*, 17–21 and 26.

14. Bentley Layton, "The Sources, Date and Transmission of *Didache* 1.3b–2.1," *HTR* 61 (1968): 382 speaks of "a clear example of archaism" with regard to the title.

15. Niederwimmer, *Die Didache*, 19–20.

16. Ibid., 21–22.

In that case, Ps.-Cyprian is our oldest witness that Didache (or versions of it) has gained "apostolic" status, that is, by the year 300. Where and how that process had begun is impossible to say. What we can say is that some time before 300 some users of Didache assumed that its implicit and explicit authority, as well as its apparently encyclopedic character could only mean that it was "apostolic." But this is more a statement about the text's authority around 300 than about its origins. All other witnesses (e.g., Eusebius, Canon Lists) presuppose that status and have nothing to contribute to the question of *how* Didache's apostolicity came about. But I have no doubt that the "apostolic" character helped Didache to survive. Given its transitional and composite character (see below under 2.2. and 2.3.), we could well be inclined to speculate that Didache might never have been handed down further if it had not been declared "apostolic." The dim manuscript tradition, however, is a result of the fact that—in the course of time—Didache had been superseded and replaced by more comprehensive and more "orthodox" "church orders."

Since it lacks an original title, we do not know how the author himself wanted to have his work understood and see it used.[17] A title cannot help us in defining Didache's milieu, instead we have to approach that question on the basis of the form and content of the text alone.

2.2. Didache and "Authorship"

Before we move on to the question of "authorship," we have to address another *caveat*. Speaking of an "author" might itself be problematic. "Author" implies intentionality, functionality, purpose, communication, and meaning. But *did* Didache have an author, and if yes, in what respect? No author is named for Didache; it is anonymous like most early Christian texts. Nor does early Christian tradition supply one, which is the case with many anonymous early Christian texts. Of course, even the Didache as we have it today must have been composed and written down by someone, but it is doubtful if Didache had an author in the way, for example, that Paul authored his letter to the Romans. In ancient literature, collections of ethical, behavioral, and "liturgical" instructions are often anonymous. I would put Didache next to texts like the *Tabula Cebetis*, the *Sentences of Sextus* or even the document represented by the various versions of 1QS and 4QS. Rainer Hirsch-Luipold rightly described the *Tabula Cebetis* as a "Sam-

---

17. Rordorf and Tuilier, *La Doctrine des Douze Apôtres (Didachè)*, 16–17: "Tout compte fait, les deux titres qui nous sont parvenus dans la tradition manuscrite ne peuvent nous éclairer sur les origines de l'ouvrage, son genre littéraire ou ses destinataires; et c'est dans le texte lui-même qu'il faut chercher la réponse à ces questions;" Niederwimmer, *Die Didache*, 82: "Man darf den Titel διδαχὴ (bzw. Διδαχαὶ) τῶν ἀποστόλων in keinem Fall als Leseanweisung verstehen. Er ist . . . ein nachträgliches Etikett, dessen Hinweis auf die ἀπόστολοι für die Schrift selbst ohne Bedeutung bleibt."

melbecken unterschiedlicher . . . Traditionen"[18] which escapes clear classification, a definition that fits Didache's character nicely.

With respect to such texts, Didache's "authorship" is of a very limited nature. Such texts grow out of the need of the communities that use them or meet the demands of a quite anonymous *Sitz im Leben* (teaching, moral adhortation). In those contexts it makes sense that Didache is not transmitted under an individual's name, but under the authority of a collective.

Having such paraenetical and constitutional writings in mind, one might perhaps go one step further and ask if there ever existed a standard *text* of Didache at all. Texts like Didache, as well as similar traditions behind or alongside it, were always open to be edited, transplanted, supplemented, updated, or rewritten into new forms and compositions. It is very unfortunate that our scant manuscript tradition does not allow us to take a deeper glimpse into the history that led to the Didache text as we have it today. We must consider the possibility that the Didache text as we have it today only represents a moment in time in a longer development of instructional tradition. Didache 10:8 might be just such an addition.[19] A relatively unstable text as evidenced in the manuscript tradition[20] as well as rewritings and adoptions of material presented in Didache in later texts such as the 7th book of the *Apostolic Constitutions* demonstrates that catalogues of that kind are always in *statu transformandi*.[21]

---

18. Rainer Hirsch-Luipold, in *Die Bildtafel des Kebes: Allegorie des Lebens* (ed. R. Hirsch-Luipold et al.; SAPERE 8; Darmstadt: Wissenschaftliche Buchgesellschaft, 2005), 23. On its alleged author see the considerations of Heinz-Günther Nesselrath, ibid., 38–48. It should be noted that *Tabula Cebetis* represents a pagan version of the Two Ways motif.

19. The thanksgiving on the unguent in 10:8 is lacking in Hierosolymitanus, but is present in a Coptic translation and in later church orders just after instructions on the Eucharist. Did H leave the passage out? On the problem see Wengst, *Didache (Apostellehre)*, 57–59 (possibly part of the original Didache); Niederwimmer, *Die Didache*, 205–9 (early addition to Didache text). See also Huub van de Sandt, "The Egyptian Background of the 'Ointment' Prayer in the Eucharistic Rite of the Didache (10:8)," in *The Wisdom of Egypt: Jewish, Early Christian, and Gnostic Essays* (ed. G. H. van Kooten and A. Hilhorst; Ancient Judaism and Early Christianity 59; Leiden: Brill 2005), 227–45.

20. A particularly interesting case on the fluctuality of the Didache text is the so-called *Sectio evangelica* in Did. 1:3b–2:1. Since Did. 1:3b–2:1 is attested in P. Oxy. XV 1782, it cannot be considered a later addition to Didache as often assumed (see Niederwimmer, *Die Didache*, 37; differently Wengst, *Didache (Apostellehre)*, 20: "Interpolation in den Text der Didache"), but should be seen as an "insertion into the christianized Two Ways tradition" (thus John S. Kloppenborg, "The Use of the Synoptics or Q in *Did.* 1:3b–2:1," in van de Sandt, ed., *Matthew and the Didache*, 129) and therefore belongs to the "pre-history" of Didache as we have it now. Layton, "The Sources, Date and Transmission of *Didache* 1.3b–2.1," 382 speaks about "a cloud of uncertainty as to what constituted the 'original' *Didache*."

21. On the adaptation of Didache in *Apos. Con.* 7 see Niederwimmer, *Die Didache*, 45–47.

2.3. Didache as Composite Text

Didache's great potential for researching its "milieu" lies in the fact that it attests to literary forms (above all the Two Ways Instruction), community structures (functionaries, hospitality) and practices (baptism, communal meal) in one single document that are usually only known from different contexts in early Christian literature. Didache claims normativity, while other texts are descriptive or far less comprehensive. Research in recent years has made it plausible that Didache is a composite text combining elements that each have their own history and not necessarily the same functional context. This, of course, adds to our problems.

It is worth examining to what extent the diversity of elements within Didache does or does not suggest a diversity of milieus or diversities within the milieu Didache belongs to. In any case, Didache's composite nature requires us to differentiate between its various parts. Not all parts necessarily function on the same level and with the same purpose. I am not saying that the components I am about to discuss necessarily are *Traditionsstücke* (some of them actually are), I only note that they differ in function, intention, and content. Functionally, the question of whether a particular passage has been adopted as a *Traditionsstück* or not seems of little relevance since even *Traditionsstücke* are integrated into the present context as it is and it is in such a way that Didache is directed to and received by its audience.

We find sections in Didache that seem less intended to regulate actual behavior than to reemphasize and reassure the common ground of the audience. The doctrines of the Two Ways seems to be one such case (1:1–6:3) and the apocalyptic teaching another (16:1–8).

Intensive research on the Two Ways passage has made clear that Didache incorporates ethical material that has close parallels with early Jewish paraenesis using dual forms of the "way" imagery ("good"/"evil," "light"/"darkness," "death"/"life" or "broad"/"narrow;" see, for example, Deut 30:15–20; Jer 31:8; 21:8–10; Prov 12:28 (LXX); Sir 15:11–17; 1QS III, 18–IV, 26; Ps.-Phoc. 5–79). While terminology and content of the Didache version certainly comes from a Jewish background, the Two Ways (or a similar binary) structure of admonition in general is by far not confined to it, but has parallels in popular pagan philosophy (cf. Hesiod, *Op.* 287–292; Xenophon, *Mem.* 2.120–130; *Tabula Cebetis* and many others). Such imagery has enjoyed wide-spread use in paraenetical texts as it is very suitable for comprehensive and fundamental catalogues of "virtues" and "vices." It is adaptable to various contexts, easy to understand and remember, and the bipolar structure can be fleshed out with details at will and is open to combination with other formula-like sequences (see, e.g., the τέκνον-sayings in Did. 3:1–6). It is not surprising, therefore, that Didache is not the only example of a Christian text incorporating such exhortations (the closest parallel being *Barn.* 18:1–20:2; but cf. also Matt 7:13–14). Even if Huub van de Sandt and David

Flusser might go too far in reconstructing the *Wortlaut* of a Jewish "Two Ways" document with the help of Didache and Barnabas, there can be no doubt that Did. 1:1–6:3 incorporates material that comes from a Jewish background.[22]

Didache in its present form, however, is a Christian text. What type of audience, therefore, does the Two Ways passage target in its Didache context and why? If the Two Ways passage was addressed to members of the Didache group, it seems unlikely that it had an immediate interventive purpose. It can be assumed that community members were well familiar with the regulations and not actively engaged in committing the crimes targeted in the list.[23] Some scholars, therefore, see the Two Ways passage as admonition to outsiders to bring up their behavior to the community's standard and as part of pre-baptismal catechesis (7:1).[24] That may well be the case. Didache 11:1 suggests that similar traditions were used as criteria to judge unknown Christians who sought a place in the community —a very different function and a different audience! If Did. 7:1 and 11:1 are seen together, it becomes clear that the Two Ways teaching defined the group's identity in general, is the basis of their identity as Christians, and could be applied to various purposes ranging from instructing Gentiles before baptism over reassuring one's own fold to testing unknown Christians of their orthodoxy. More on that topic will follow below.

Other paraenetic passages are more concrete and regulate details of practices whose general structure and overall motivation remains undisputed and unchanged. That is especially the case in 7:1–10:7 where the didachist addresses central elements of communal behavior such as baptism, fasting, prayer and the communal meal. It can be assumed that these practices have the same fundamental importance to construct identity and coherence of the community as the ethical norms expressed in 1:1–6:3. While 1:1–6:3 mostly reassure the community, 7:1–10:7 in fact regulate, but by intervening only in detail, they implicitly stabilize all issues that are not specifically addressed. It is interesting to see that in the series of practices, the most "global" regulations concern baptism, while instructions on fasting, prayer, and communal meals concern practical details

---

22. Huub van de Sandt and David Flusser, *The Didache: Its Jewish Sources and Its Place in Early Judaism and Christianity* (CRINT 3/5; Assen: Van Gorcum, 2002), 1–190. Also see Niederwimmer, *Die Didache*, 83–88; Peter Tomson, "The Halakhic Evidence of Didache 8 and Matthew 6 and the Didache Community's Relationship to Judaism" in van de Sandt, ed., *Matthew and the Didache*, 131–41. Skeptic about the role of *T. 12 Patr.* and the possibility to reconstruct a Greek Two Ways scheme are Marinus de Jonge, "The Testaments of the Twelve Patriarchs and the 'Two Ways,'" in *Biblical Traditions in Transmission* (JSJSup 111; ed. C. Hempel and J. M. Lieu; Leiden: Brill 2006), 179–94 and Kari Syreeni, "The Sermon on the Mount and the Two Ways Teaching," in van de Sandt, ed., *Matthew and the Didache*, 92–94.

23. I agree with Wengst, *Didache (Apostellehre)*, 23 who says that Didache mostly reiterates what "schon weitgehend geübte Praxis war" in his community.

24. See, e.g., Syreeni, "Sermon on the Mount," 89 with caution.

(fasting), new content (prayer), or new interpretive elements (communal meal). Only in chapter 7:1–4, Didache regulates both structural (what has to happen at baptism, what after it?), practical (what can we do if we have no ὕδωρ ζῶν?), and interpretive elements (baptizing εἰς τὸ ὄνομα τοῦ πατρὸς καὶ τοῦ υἱοῦ καὶ τοῦ ἁγίου πνεύματος).

The passage on the communal gathering on the κυριακὴ τοῦ κυρίου (chapter 14) shows a similar general character as the regulations on baptism (chapter 7). Here, too, crucial elements are named (breaking of bread, thanksgiving, confession of sins), special instructions given (14:2) and all is placed within an interpretive framework (14:3). The fact that instructions about prayers at and access to communal meals (εὐχαριστία, in 9:1–10:7) are not given in conjunction with regulations on the κυριακὴ τοῦ κυρίου (in 14) might at first sight seem somewhat awkward. It makes, in fact, sense if the Didache community knew communal meals outside gatherings on κυριακὴ τοῦ κυρίου (thanksgiving being the connecting principle, whereas θυσία and confession of sins were specially emphasized κυριακὴ τοῦ κυρίου). It also places the following instructions on ἐπίσκοποι and διάκονοι in their proper liturgical context as having their prime purpose as "overseer" and "servants" at the κυριακὴ τοῦ κυρίου gatherings of local communities, and differentiates them from other functionaries who are either itinerant (chs. 11–13 ἀπόστολοι and προφῆται) or are not explicitly connected to a particular way of life and locale (διδάσκαλοι and to a certain extent perhaps also προφῆται, see 15:1). It might also indicate a difference in ritual. The presence of functionaries at the meals on a κυριακὴ τοῦ κυρίου indicates that these meals have a higher significance for the community as a whole (here the entire community gathers in semi-public context, therefore mutual forgiveness is an issue), whereas the meals presupposed in 9:1–10:7 could be celebrated in smaller groups or in the family, needed no "officials," but had their community-related significance only via the proper εὐχαριστία and through the exclusion of outsiders.

The difference in handling these rites (baptism and celebration on a κυριακὴ τοῦ κυρίου over against fasting, prayer and "simple" meals) is a telling indication not about the importance of each rite for the community as reflected in Didache—they were all important—but rather about the familiarity with each rite that the didachist could expect among the members of his community and about their cultural context. It suggests that baptism and the κυριακὴ τοῦ κυρίου-celebration were relatively new practices for the Didache community, while the other three could easily be continued only after a couple of necessary elements had been altered and adapted to the new Christian identity of the group.

A third type of passages aims at fundamentally reforming limited, but important elements of communal practice (11:1–13:7). Here, Didache's regulations aim at clearly defined persons in clearly defined situations and give very explicit instructions in a very casuistic style (generalizing πᾶς signals the normative character of the passage, whereas ἐάν "whenever" and εἰ "in case" indicate the goal to be comprehensive and set its internal structure). Different criteria are named on which the recommended practice should be based and consequences of certain behavior are described. Here, it seems, urgent problems are being dealt with on a very pragmatic level.

Summarizing, we thus may argue, then, that in Didache quite specific and *ad hoc* regulations go hand in hand with more fundamental passages that almost appear unrelated to a particular community and its situation. It is clear that each of these passages makes its own contribution to our quest for Didache's social and religious background (more on that below). While 11:1–13:7 can tell us very precisely how Didache's situation and behavior triggered the "author's" intervention and therefore opens fascinating windows into elements of early Christian life, 1:1–6:1 is on a different level, speaks in a much more general way, and does not seem to have targeted particular misbehavior. The density of "argumentation" is a helpful criterion: the more signs of actual argumentation, dissuasion and persuasion one can identify, the closer the passage seems to be to "real life" and "real issues."

Despite its suggestive encyclopedic appearance as a composite text and its normative intentions, Didache has more of an *ad hoc* text about it than many might expect, and the question arises how comprehensive the text actually is for the *entire* life and milieu of its community. Didache is not a *Kirchenordnung* in a general sense, it is no "encyclopedia of early Christian life," of a certain period or even perhaps a certain region. The "author" selected some topics and neglected others, he adopted and adapted traditions, and all that without giving *reasons* for *why* he mentions this and ignores the other. Neither is Didache a *Bestandsaufnahme* of all or even the most important practices of its community, nor does it offer a complete or nearly complete list of deviant positions or practices of its opponents. I think recent scholarship has, under the lasting influence of von Harnack's enthusiasm, overestimated Didache's comprehensive nature.[25]

That insight is not entirely new, of course. Many scholars have already emphasized the fact that Didache does not present an exposition of Christian doctrine (or even parts of it), such as giving a rationale for baptism or communal meal, nor does it refer to any narratives about Jesus and his followers. Nieder-

---

25. Garleff, *Urchristliche Identität in Matthäusevangelium*, 94–97; Adolf von Harnack, *Lehre der Zwölf Apostel nebst Untersuchungen zur ältesten Geschichte der Kirchenverfassung und des Kirchenrechts* (TU 2/1; 2nd ed.; Leipzig: Hinrichs, 1893), 36 writes: "Je mehr man sich [in Didache] vertieft, desto deutlicher gewahrt man, dass ihr Verf. in seinem Sinne wirklich Alles erschöpft hat, was in einen kurzen evangelisch-apostolischen Leitfaden für das christliche Leben des Einzelnen (im täglichen Verkehr der Gemeinde) hineingehört." Similar, Milavec, *Didache*, ix: In contrast to Paul or Acts, "The Didache . . . offers a full-blown description of nearly every aspect of community life." Or: "No document in the Christian Scriptures is as descriptive, as organized, and as comprehensive as the *Didache* when it comes to offering evidence about the community that lies behind the text" (ibid., xxv).

wimmer rightly rejects the view that Didache is a "work of theology," but he might go too far if he calls Didache only a "Reglement für die kirchliche Praxis, ein Handbuch für die kirchliche Moral, das kirchliche Ritual und die kirchliche Disziplin."[26] The fact that Didache is composite and practically oriented does not mean Didache has no theology, or that the community behind Didache was not interested in giving their behavior a rationale. The problem lies on a different level. Though quite prosaic and sometime haphazard, Didache's decisions and recommendations are certainly based on theological choices and imply doctrinal positions, but its paraenetic character and composite nature often prevented the "author" to express detailed theological motivations for recommended behavior which poses no small obstacle for anyone who wants to reconstruct Didache's milieu.[27]

It lies in the character of Didache as composite text, that it will be much easier to identify parallels to single elements within it than to the entire text itself.

3. Constructive Approach

But what can we positively say after all these *caveats*? What information in the text can we use as basis for reconstructing Didache's social and religious context? The common method of reconstructing the Didache's social and religious background is to look at the most prominent elements and their ideological and social origin. We cautiously follow that approach.

3.1. The "Two Ways Schema" (1:1–6:1)

As indicated above, David Flusser and Huub van de Sandt have intensively discussed the role of the Two Ways Schema for defining Didache's religious background and intentions. With regard to the material presented, it indeed seems beyond doubt that the schema employed in Did. 1:1–6:1 is of Jewish origin. The passage is full of Old Testament material and the Christian patina is only superficial. But such and similar lists of ethical regulations are also widely known from

---

26. Niederwimmer, *Die Didache*, 13.

27. Ibid., 13 including note 8 rightly warned: "Es wäre töricht, die vollständigen Lehranschauungen des Didachisten aus der Didache erheben zu wollen. Natürlich gibt es en passant und zuweilen implizit einiges, das die Lehrmeinungen des Didachisten (bzw. seiner Quellen) deutlich macht; aber es wäre verkehrt, daraus eine 'Theologie' des Didachisten konstruieren zu wollen. Die Lehranschauungen des Didachisten dürfen nicht auf das reduziert werden, was sich en passant und implizit aus seiner Schrift ergibt. Das ist grundsätzlich auch ein Vorbehalt gegenüber allen Versuchen, die 'Theologie' der Didache zu bestimmen und gegen andere (z. B. Mt. oder Paulus) abzuheben. . . . Solche Versuche verstoßen gegen die Regel, die es verbietet, Texte mit verschiedenem Reflexionsniveau unmittelbar miteinander zu vergleichen. "

popular pagan literature. Even *materialiter* there are many parallels (including the Golden Rule). Two Ways passages usually are composed of smaller units, show a tendency towards agglutination, and are open for adaptation and alteration.[28] The fact that an originally Jewish ethical "canon" forms the basis of Didache's teachings not only indicates the close connection of the didachist to Jewish paraenetical traditions, but also demonstrates how similar the practical behavior of his community must have been to that of Jews. There is in fact almost no way to distinguish "Jewish" from "Christian" apart from the context in which the Two Ways-scheme is placed in Didache. For Marinus de Jonge Didache is an "interesting case of incorporation and assimilation of traditional material" "that may be Jewish and Christian in a Christian document."[29]

3.2. Instructions on Communal Practice (8:1–10:7 and 14)

This impression can be confirmed by observing Didache's regulations on fasting (8:1), prayer (8:2–3), and even the communal meal (9:1–10:7). Many scholars have already pointed out that all three rituals are—despite some obvious Christian peculiarities—grounded in Jewish theology and practices. One particularly instructive issue is fasting, which many scholars count among regular Jewish religious practice.[30] The didachist only requires to change the days on which his community is to fast (Wednesday and Friday instead of Monday and Thursday). Peter Tomson refers to Epiphanius, *Pan.* II 15.1 who confirms that Monday and Thursday were common Jewish fasting days according to the Rabbis, probably even before 135.[31] A recent study on markets in Roman Palestine by Ben-Zion Rosenfeld and Joseph Menirav largely confirms Tomson's findings. Rosenfeld and Menirav discuss a couple of rabbinic texts that demonstrate that Monday and Thursday were indeed periodic market days in large towns and cities (e.g., *m. Ketub.* 1:1; *m. Meg.* 1:1).[32] Markets were not only occasions for economic activities, but were very important social events fostering cohesion and communication within a community. They provided the context for gatherings of the court and communal services with Torah readings, prayers in the synagogue. Rosenfeld and Menirav further emphasize that large town and

---

28. Niederwimmer, *Die Didache*, 55–58; Schöllgen, *Didache: Zwölf-Apostel-Lehre*, 27–41.

29. De Jonge, "Testaments of Twelve Patriarchs," 185, 194. De Jonge sees close parallels between the incorporation and use of the Two Ways Scheme in Didache and the *T. 12 Patr.* (esp. *T. Ash.*).

30. Tomson, "Halakhic Evidence of Didache 8," 135–37.

31. Ibid., 135.

32. On markets in ancient Palestine, see Ben-Zion Rosenfeld and Joseph Menirav, *Markets and Marketing in Roman Palestine* (JSJSup 99; Leiden: Brill, 2005), 43–45, 215. Unfortunately, Rosenfeld and Menirav do not explicitly discuss Didache. I thank my colleague Johannes Tromp for directing my attention to this valuable book.

city markets should not be confused with village markets, which notably took place on Fridays. Both market days did not overlap, because they fulfilled different functions: "Villagers could thus take advantage of the business potential of the city on Mondays and Thursdays, and then on Fridays, offer the rest of their goods for sale in the village market, along with the goods which they had purchased in the city."[33] Reading Rosenfeld and Menirav, one gets the strong impression that both market systems were in a delicate and useful balance, so why play one out against the other as in Didache? And why is Wednesday mentioned when it does not play a role in these rabbinic discussions? And finally why talk about fasting in this context?

Lets us start with the last point. Fasting, first of all, has a strong religious significance. It is a practice that regulates social contacts by temporarily suspending the opportunity to practice table fellowship. By refusing to eat, people send out a signal to others (e.g., in times of mourning about their status, or as a sign of their piety, cf. Matt 6:16–18). If people fast at the same time, they unite and want to be perceived by outsiders as manifestly belonging together.[34] By regulating that rite, Didache intends to secure that his group distinguishes itself from others who pursue the same practice but in a different way. By prohibiting members of his community to take part in such an occasion, Didache has very effectively cut them off from their social and religious matrix, but without requiring them to abandon an important element of common pious practice in general. As fasting is not simply a private matter, but has public implications, the Didache community's new practice would have been noticeable for everybody.

But fasting is not only a religious issue; it has economic implications, too. Fasting means to refuse consumption of food, something that is understandably *not* desired at market days, because it reduces food demand and sends prices down. It is remarkable that one passage in *m. Ta'an.* 2:9 explicitly makes that point: "They do not decree a fast for the community in the first instance for a Thursday, so as not to disturb market prices."[35] The continuation of the passage demonstrates that there was a controversial discussion among Jewish authorities about fasting on periodic city market days. There seems to have been a conflict between economic interests and the religious aspects of market days as days of communal gatherings in which some people might have fasted to underline their religious observance. Is Didache taking part in this discussion? Many exegetes have assumed that fasting on Monday and Thursday was a common and positive thing (which it certainly was), and concluded that the rejection of such a practice is a sign that Didache breaks the ties with its social and religious context.

---

33. Rosenfeld and Menirav, *Markets and Marketing in Roman Palestine*, 44.
34. Thus Niederwimmer, *Die Didache*, 166–67.
35. Rosenfeld and Menirav, *Markets and Marketing in Roman Palestine*, 44.

If I understand *m. Ta'an.* 2:9 correctly, it is just the opposite. Fasting on Monday and Thursday was not desired by those who depended on smoothly functioning city markets. Was that the motivation behind Didache's rejecting of Monday and Thursday as fasting days? If yes, one could argue that Didache actually takes the standpoint of a city-dweller who benefits from booming market days when villagers flock into the city to buy and sell and therefore does not want to jeopardize prices by announcing a fast. That might indeed be a plausible solution, even more so because Didache does not reject fasting as such, but keeps it as a religious practice—and moves it to two days, one of which, Friday, we know was one of the traditional market days in villages. On *these* market days, as Rosenfeld and Menirav show,[36] only villagers would come together to exchange their products largely among themselves. City dwellers would hardly participate in village market days because they only get into contact with traders from villages as the latter entered the cities—on Mondays and Thursdays. If that path is correct, Didache would reject fasting days *in order to* keep in contact with the interests of the urban community its congregation lives in, *not* to break with it. Didache further would promote its piety *at the cost of* contacts with villagers (who would above all be named ὑποκριταί).

There is only one problem: while this scenario can explain why Didache rejects Monday and Thursday and prefers Friday, it cannot explain why Wednesday is required as second fasting day. The text itself is silent on that question, so we can only speculate. It may well be that Didache refers to an unknown local practice of fasting also on Wednesdays; it can also be that Didache invents that second day of fasting as a parallel to the two days it rejected. Or Jaubert was on the right track referring to a hypothetical Jewish practice to use Wednesday, Friday, and Sunday as fast days, now adopted by the didachist who at the same time of course had to leave out Sunday because this day has gained a completely new purpose as κυριακὴ τοῦ κυρίου (chapter 14).[37] Be that as it may, the issue certainly needs further exploration. What is evident is that Didache, both with respect to the option it rejects and the option it prefers, entirely moves *within* the confines of Jewish debates. It is true that fasting regulates communality and that Didache intends to do exactly that, but I do not think it regulates communality at the cost of contact with Jews in general.

---

36. Ibid., 41–43. One should note that the only specifically Palestinian element in this debate is that we hear about it in Palestinian sources. The market day system itself was a common feature of the Roman Empire (*ibid.*, 44).

37. Annie Jaubert, "Jésus et le calendrier de Qumrân," *NTS* 7 (1960/61): 1–30. I agree with Tomson, "Halakhic Evidence of Didache 8," 136 and Marcello Del Verme, *Didache and Judaism: Jewish Roots of an Ancient Christian-Jewish Work* (New York: T&T Clark, 2004), 178–80 that this suggestion should be taken more seriously. Niederwimmer, *Die Didache*, 167 n. 16, however, finds Jaubert's suggestion "sehr unwahrscheinlich."

It is an interesting question (which I cannot pursue further here) how far the order to fast on days different from the ὑποκριταί structurally equals the instruction not to let unbaptized people take part in εὐχαριστίαι ὑμῶν (9:5, see below). In any case, being baptized becomes the only decisive criterion for sharing community and fellowship; it restricts "any form of commensality, of eating and drinking with Christians."[38] If the same group is addressed in 8:2 and 9:5, the message is simple: when we cannot eat with you (see 9:5) we cannot *not* eat with you either. If not, the general intention of Didache's rulings is still evident: Through these measures the didachist is able to create boundaries on the basis of a widely unquestioned common ground of practices. He forms identity by emphasizing boundaries *and* continuing to move on common ground. I find it problematic, therefore, to take Didache's instruction as step in a "Ablösungsprozess von der Mutterreligion."[39] Didache might simply have opted for a different form of Judaism than that he encountered in person of the ὑποκριταί, different through certain practical innovations and different through the belief in Christ. Here, perhaps, lies the most important element of Didache's milieu. We will have to get back to this later.

The second issue that finds the didachist's attention is prayer. This, too, is an important expression of Jewish piety. A common Jewish substratum is not only present in the instruction to pray τρὶς τῆς ἡμέρας (8:3, see Dan 6:11), but also in the style and contents of the prayer the didachist recommends.[40] Does the didachist quote the prayer word for word because his recipients did not know it? That is not unlikely,[41] even more so if one considers the very close similarity with the Matthean version of the Lord's Prayer (Matt 6:9–13 over against the shorter Q-version in Luke 11:2–4)[42] and the explicit introduction to the prayer with οὕτως προσεύχεσθε. In any case, the didachist sees this prayer as coming directly from the κύριος and his εὐαγγέλιον. While Did. 8:2 should not be pressed too hard and be taken to indicate that Didache is dependent upon Matthew, it

---

38. Gerard Rouwhorst, "Didache 9–10: A Litmus Test for the Research on Early Christian Liturgy Eucharist," in van de Sandt, ed., *Matthew and the Didache*, 148.

39. Thus Schöllgen, *Didache: Zwölf-Apostel-Lehre*, 47, although Schöllgen repeatedly and rightly emphasizes that Didache largely continues Jewish practices. This apparent contradiction in Schöllgen's description suggests a serious terminological dilemma when describing the "Judaism" evident in Didache, since our perspective and consequently most of our labels are formulated *post factum*, and thus anachronistic. For a different view see Jonathan A. Draper, "Do the Didache and Matthew Reflect an 'Irrevocable Parting of the Ways' with Judaism?" in van de Sandt, ed., *Matthew and the Didache*, 217–41.

40. On the Jewish character of the Lord's Prayer see, e.g., Ulrich Luz, *Das Evangelium nach Matthäus: Mt 1–7* (EKKNT 1/1; Zürich: Benziger, 1985), 332–53.

41. Wengst, *Didache (Apostellehre)*, 79 n. 68 rejects that idea and refers to Didache's character as "Kirchenordnung, die Regularien und Formulare bietet."

42. Tomson, "Halakhic Evidence of Didache 8," 134–35 on the Lord's Prayer and Didache's closeness to Matthew.

demonstrates that Didache taps early Christian traditions as resources that are also present in Matthew. By quoting the Lord's Prayer, Didache standardizes Christian prayer and replaces other formulae that might have been spoken in the didachist's community before, while the structure of praying three times a day is explicitly reiterated and retained. As in the case of fasting, Didache seems not to have left "Jewish tradition" or "Judaism" as such, but chose for one Jewish option instead of another.[43] Unlike in the case of fasting, however, the alternative prayer he recommends comes from early Christian tradition, but its stance is still deeply connected to Judaism.

It is notable that fasting and prayer are also discussed in Matt 6:5–18, although in reverse order. While Matthew's discussion of prayer is quite similar to that in Didache ("wrong" practice should be replaced by adopting the Lord's Prayer), the passage on fasting follows a different path. While in Matthew all effort is made to see Christians fast ἐν τῷ κρυφαίῳ, because if they do otherwise and attract attention they will already have received their reward (Matt 6:16–18), Didache points in a different direction and rather limits contacts with Jews who also fast.

The third element of Jewish piety mentioned in Matt (6:1–4), namely, alms-giving, is not part of Didache's list, but is mentioned in passing at the end of the paraenetic section in a very general, affirmative way (15:4). Interestingly enough, ἐλεημοσύναι appear also in a tripartite combination with εὐχαί and—generaliz-ing—πᾶσαι αἱ πράξεις to which certainly also the νηστεῖαι from 8:1 belong. Here, too, the εὐαγγέλιον τοῦ κυρίου ἡμῶν is named as authority and orientation.

In addition to the three cardinal practices of Jewish piety, Didache also deals with what is called εὐχαριστίαι (9:1–10:7). It is clear that these εὐχαριστίαι have their context in meals. A separate εὐχαριστία is mentioned for the cup/drinking (9:2, ποτήριον) and one for the bread/eating (9:3–4, κλάσμα). The text does not say that the meals in which the εὐχαριστίαι featured had a specifically sacramental context (see above on the relation of 9:1–10:7 to chapter 14), nor do the prayers imply any reference to Jesus's Last Supper.[44] Even if one would not want to see a direct relationship with Hellenistic symposia in particular, as Matthias Klinghard proposes,[45] one should, on the other hand, not underestimate the fact that the institution narrative is lacking *as well as* all other references to the Last Supper and death of Jesus.[46] A comparison of Didache's prayers with the Matthean "eucha-ristic" tradition (Matt 26:26–29) does not help to explain Didache's practice and

43. Ibid., 137–39.

44. I therefore refrain from calling this meal "Eucharist" to avoid anachronistic and alien connotations. For a different view on Did. 9–10 see Rouwhorst, "Didache 9–10," 143–56.

45. Matthias Klinghardt, *Gemeinschaftsmahl und Mahlgemeinschaft: Soziologie und Litur-gie frühchristlicher Mahlfeiern* (TANZ 13; Tübingen: Francke, 1996).

46. Here I criticize Rouwhorst, "Didache 9–10," 146–47, but I agree with him that Did. 9–10 makes "no clear distinction . . . between what we would tend to call a 'normal' meal and

is therefore futile. But even outside of a "sacramental framework," these prayers clearly have a "liturgical" function: they structure and interpret eating practices. But instead of commemorating Jesus's death, they celebrate God's power as δεσπότης παντοκράτωρ of all creation and especially as giver of bread and wine, the staple ingredients of any meal, and as savior through Jesus τοῦ παιδός σου (9:2; 10:2), and present the ἐκκλησία as God's property (σου ἡ ἐκκλησία in 9:4). Thematically and structurally these prayers are analogous to Jewish meal prayers,[47] and consequently the passage 9:1–10:6 has the same function as 8:2, namely, to replace liturgical formulae that are not considered any longer to be appropriate expressions of the new faith that Didache's audience belongs to.

The fact that the didachist's opponents are called ὑποκριταί in 8:1 and 2 and κύνες in 9:5 does not contradict the closeness of the Didache community to the practices of its opponents. On the contrary, it shows that the conflict was fought out with great determination using common polemical labels and on the basis of a wide common ground. Both ὑποκριταί and κύων also connect Didache with Matthew's jargon to address competitors who—on the basis of language and content of the dispute—can likely be defined as close to Pharisaic/pre-rabbinic circles.[48] Didache certainly is a Christian text, but the Christianity it propagates very much remains within the common practices of Jewish piety: fasting, prayer, meal practice and almsgiving are continued within a new interpretive framework. By using such terminology, the Didache community perceives itself as, to take Marcello Del Verme's words, "different" but not "separate" from Judaism.[49] Apart from the perseverance of common structures of behavior, Didache also shows a clear intention to separate socially from the pharisaically inspired matrix. It does not suggest that Didache intended to leave Judaism as such, or in fact had done so.

3.3. Community Structures and Communication (11:1–13:7 plus 15:1–3)

The character of Did. 11:1–13:7 and 15:1–3 is quite different, and compared with the character of regulations the issues dealt with in the previous chapters

---

the Eucharist," apart from the fact that I would not want to call the meal in Did. 9–10 "Eucharist" at all.

47. Klinghardt, *Gemeinschaftsmahl und Mahlgemeinschaft*, 407–27; Rouwhorst, "Didache 9–10," 149 both righly emphasizing the characteristic blending of Jewish and Christian elements.

48. See Tomson, "Halakhic Evidence," 139–41; Draper, "Irrevocable Parting of the Ways," 230–36; see also Del Verme, *Didache and Judaism*, 143–88; Jürgen Zangenberg, "A Conflict Among Brothers: Who were the *hypokritai* in Matthew?," in *Festschrift for Sean Freyne* (ed. M. Daly Denton, B. McGing and Z. Rodgers; Leiden: Brill, forthcoming). See also with a different purpose Huub van de Sandt, "'Do Not Give What Is Holy to the Dogs' (Did 9:5d and Matt 7:6a): The Eucharistic Food of the Didache in Its Jewish Purity Setting," *VC* 56 (2002): 223–46.

49. Del Verme, *Didache and Judaism*, 85.

7–10, it is remarkably specific and detailed. Wengst might well be right in saying that the didachist reacts to acute problems here and that the level of individual innovative intervention is higher than elsewhere.[50]

The passage documents that the community has local functionaries in the form of διδάσκαλοι and προφῆται, who base their role on expertise (teachers) and charisma (prophets). Prophets, whose activities are described in much more detail and contours than those of teachers, are already mentioned in 10:7: they may give thanks as often as they wish. Many more characteristics are mentioned in 11:7–12. First of all, they are inspired by the Spirit; they are independent and may not be judged by the community. Prophets are allowed to teach (διδάσκειν), a clear parallel to the διδάσκαλοι. Another parallel is that prophets and teachers did not have to work, but were supported by the congregations among which they lived (13:1–7).

The limits of this privilege are mentioned in 11:9, 12: prophets (and teachers, too?) are not allowed to require food directly or ask for money for themselves in return for their service. Such behavior (τρόποι) is not consistent with their gift and indicates that they are liars (on incongruent lifestyle as a criterion for ψευδοπροφῆται see Matt 7:15–23). Although prophets appear to be mobile, they seem to stay longer in a given community than ἀπόστολοι (13:1 καθῆσθαι and 13:4 ἐὰν μὴ ἔχητε προφήτην instead of 11:4 ἐρχόμενος πρὸς ὑμᾶς). Their models are the prophets of old (οἱ ἀρχαῖοι προφῆται, 11:11), and according to 13:3, prophets explicitly take the place of High Priests (ἀρχιερεῖς), to which the community obviously did not feel connected anymore. The Didache community copied priests in several respects: it is explicitly said that it is the prophets present in the community who are now the recipients of regular material support, called by the traditional term "first offering" (ἀπαρχή).[51] Less explicit, but still somewhat telling is the privilege of unlimited thanksgiving, because it is well conceivable that the Didache community regarded its prayers (and especially the ones uttered by the prophets) as a form of sacrifice (see θυσία in 14:2!). One should also not forget that High Priests not only sacrificed, but gave *torah*, and were considered to have the gift of prophecy.[52]

The consequences of these shifts are significant. It is obvious that community institutions, at least one as central as the prophets, replaced the temple and its prescriptions. No offerings were sent to the temple anymore, no priests were

---

50. Wengst, *Didache (Apostellehre)*, 23.

51. On the ἀπαρχή see Del Verme, *Didache and Judaism*, 188–220.

52. On (High) priests and prophecy see Oliver Gussmann, "Das Priesterverständnis des Flavius Josephus" (Ph.D. diss., Universität Erlangen-Nürnberg, 2007), 263–70; Marinus de Jonge and Johannes Tromp, "Jacob's Son Levi in the Old Testament Pseudepigrapha and Related Literature," in *Biblical Figures Outside the Bible* (ed. M. E. Stone and T. A. Bergen; Harrisburg, Pa.: Trinity Press International, 1998), 203–36; David E. Aune, *Prophecy in Early Christianity and the Ancient Mediterranean World* (Grand Rapids: Eerdmans, 1983), 138–44.

necessary since the community pursued a non-sacrificial cult whose only sacrifices were prayers spoken during the celebration on the κυριακὴ κυρίου (Did. 14:1–3). That does not mean that the group considered itself "less" holy or that they thought their piety is of a lesser quality. On the contrary, the warning not to practice table fellowship with unbaptized outsiders (9:5) makes it clear that new boundaries between "in" and "out" are being drawn. Baptism and appropriate behavior has replaced circumcision as a criterion for belonging to the group, and participation in the community meal has substituted for taking part in the sacrificial cult in the temple. It is notable that Didache does not mention purity regulations in contexts that regulate admission or exclusion to the cultic community and social contacts, but we cannot be sure if that means that the Didache group had already abandoned purity observance—remembering that absence of evidence is not evidence of absence. But even if we leave the issue of purity aside, one is tempted to ask if Didache's position might still be called "Jewish," at least in this respect?[53]

In effect all these regulations taken together would indeed have made maintaining relations with Jews extremely difficult. But this does not negate the fact that Didache still has structural and behavioral parallels and similarities with Judaism (see above). Some of the innovations might have been triggered through new situations, such as was the case, in my view, with prophets taking the place of priests. If Didache was written after 70 (which I take as the most plausible hypothesis), the destruction of the temple would of course have left a vacuum that many other Jewish communities, not only the earliest Christians, would have had to fill in various respects. The urge to do so would certainly have been big, and it would make sense if a community rooted so deeply in Judaism as the one behind Didache decided to boost a traditional, highly respected institution such as the prophets to fill the gap. In that respect, the replacement of the temple would not signal a "break" with Judaism, but rather demonstrate one attempt among others to reorganize life without it. If Didache can be shown to reflect a deliberate decision to leave the temple *before* it was destroyed and form substitute institutions, matters would be quite different and it would be more difficult to describe the Didache group as still being within the confines of Judaism. Acknowledging the many other elements of Jewish piety and theology, I am still inclined to favor the former option, but the latter should not be dismissed out of hand.

Finally, there are also elements in Didache, inherited from very early Christian tradition, that are potentially explosive: baptism in place of circumcision or the inclusion of Christological elements into liturgical formulae. Thus, the question is not how and to what extent Didache might be called "Jewish," the fact

---

53. Huub van de Sandt rightly asked this question when we were discussing this paper. He indeed has a point, especially when we consider how Ed P. Sanders defines "common Judaism" in his *Judaism: Practice and Belief 63 BCE – 66 CE* (London: SCM Press, 1992).

is that Didache represents a type of Christianity that to a very large degree still defines itself by using Jewish theologumena and following Jewish practices. Not before long, this—to us—rather ambiguous and contradictory position came under pressure from both sides, reconstituting Judaism and increasingly "Gentile" Christianity. Didache, however, belongs to a time that still had room for hybridity within both Judaism and Christianity.

The role and character of the ἀπόστολοι is much less clear (11:3–6). Didache says little about their activities and characteristics apart from the fact that they are intinerant. No particular theological connotation nor programmatic profile is discernible. Their parallel listing with προφήται under the heading "teaching" is certainly suggestive,[54] but no traditional models as in 11:11 and 13:3 are employed in connection with them. Were the ἀπόστολοι that Didache deals with only envoys from other Christian communities? By what authority did they claim to wander, teach, and be hosted? The temptation to supply all these details from other, more explicit Christian texts (especially Paul or Luke who have a very distinct understanding of apostleship) is strong, but all that remains hypothetical. Didache seems only interested in regulating contacts with ἀπόστολοι from outside. It is the same apostles who come and after a short stay need to leave and move on. This makes it unlikely that these ἀπόστολοι are simply messengers holding contact between different communities comparable to the rabbinic שלי׳ח. Nowhere does Didache mention ἀπόστολοι dispatched from its own community to others, nor do they turn up in the discussion of bishops and deacons (15:1–2), so that one can seriously ask if the Didache community had "own" ἀπόστολοι in its fold at all. The methods to deal with ἀπόστολοι are harsh, but not unjust: they are only to receive a minimum of hospitality and support (see 13:2). Obviously, abuse of Christian morale was too serious to show more generosity (cf. 13:5 χριστέμπορος with Lucian, Peregr. 13). It is not for reasons of voluntary isolation or a particular Nischenexistenz that foreign ἀπόστολοι are kept at some distance. The same criteria are used to judge the apostles' practical behaviors that are also taken to assess prophets (no asking for money, only minimum support). This does not indicate that the community was suspicious of outsiders per se. On the contrary, although the Didache community has clear theological criteria against anybody coming from outside (11:1–2; 12:1–5) and having a permanent function (15:1), it is open and accessible. Its community structure neither prevents nor hampers outside contacts; foreigners who can support themselves can stay (13:3–4).

The real innovation, however, is the didachist's recommendation to choose ἐπίσκοποι and διάκονοι in 15:1—a combination of titles that we also find in Phil 1:1. Two observations, at first contradicting each other, make it likely that

---

54. It is notable that in Did. 11:1–2 the more general participle and verb are used, while Did. 13:2; 15:1–2 use the apparently more formal διδάσκαλος.

ἐπίσκοποι and διάκονοι are new functions. On the one hand, the didachist emphasizes that ἐπίσκοποι and διάκονοι perform the same services as the long-established προφῆται and διδάσκαλοι (15:1). On the other hand, he shows a strong interest in seeing them promoted to the same high level of respect as the former: apparently they still lack such honor (τετιμημένοι, 15:2). Why that doubling of functionaries if they do the same as prophets and teachers? Perhaps because they have, apart from teaching and prophesying, additional, different tasks that the didachist does not explicitly mention, but which become evident if one looks at the context. There can be little doubt that ἐπίσκοποι and διάκονοι fulfill a particular function at the communal gatherings on the κυριακή τοῦ κυρίου (14:1–3). In Christian literature διάκονοι often appear in connection with communal meals (cf. Acts 6:1–7), and ἐπίσκοποι in many communities function as leaders or preside over special ceremonies. Ἐπίσκοποι especially betrays some Hellenistic connotations. The term used for the appointment rite (χειροτονήσατε) and the criteria used to describe them and the function in the context of communal meals very much resemble what we can read in contemporary literature of the late-first/early-second century C.E. (cf., e.g., Ign. *Trall.* 3.2; 1 Tim 3:3). But instead of being directly dependent upon each other, these texts draw from similar sources and make similar developments transparent.[55]

It is perhaps striking that we do not find a trace of the perhaps most common Jewish functionary, the elder (πρεσβύτερος), a title that also enjoyed widespread use in early Christianity (e.g., Acts 11:30; 14:23; 15:2, 4, 22–3; Jas 5:14). It is well possible that Didache speaks of διδάσκαλοι where other texts name πρεσβύτεροι, (the authority to teach and advise often being connected to age), but we do not have positive evidence of such a usage in Didache. The lack of this title, though perhaps not its function, again underscores the relative independence of Didache's community structure.

4. Putting Didache on the Intellectual Map of Early Christianity

It is time to combine these observations and draw some conclusions about the "milieu" that Didache might have been part of, fully aware of the *caveats* discussed above and also fully aware of the fact that many scholars have already scrutinized potential similarities and dissimilarities between Didache and other early Christian texts, above all Matthew, the Synoptic tradition, James, but also Paul, Ignatius, or the Johannine circle.

Before we begin to compare Didache with other New Testament texts, we have to reiterate an observation made above: Didache is witness for a type of Christianity that was deeply rooted in Judaism. Material for liturgical formulae,

---

55. Wengst, *Didache (Apostellehre)*, 42–43. On the background of these instructions see Jürgen Roloff, *Der erste Brief an Timotheus* (EKKNT 15; Zürich: Benziger, 1988), 148–89.

ethical teachings, and for formulating the role and designation of early Christian functionaries is—although Christianized—deeply influenced by Judaism.[56] In contrast to Matthew, who directly attacks the "Pharisees" and therefore helps to put his opponents at least on an imaginary map, Didache only uses a label to identify his targets. Indirect evidence, however, might nevertheless help grasp the contours and also tentatively point to Pharisaic circles with which Didache struggled, although that should not exclude other groups as well. I find it quite likely that—despite all polemics—the didachist might have considered his group as still being "Jewish" and not "outside" even though they clearly adhered to Christian traditions. Marcello Del Verme pointedly speaks about "cohabitation."[57] Here, I see the biggest common feature between Matthew and Didache: "neither community is external to Israel."[58] Bas ter Haar Romeny aptly describes the milieu to which I also would assign Didache: "even after 70 C.E. there were people in the larger area of Palestine and Syria who in terms of kinship and religious background would have defined themselves as Jews, but differed from the rabbinic interpretation of the law and had come to believe that Jesus brought salvation. . . . Here, there are no grounds for assuming a separate Jewish sect of Jewish-Christian group with its own elaborate theology."[59]

At the same time, Didache is a document of "alienation." Although I am unable to judge if Didache and Matthew indeed "represent *different stages* in the process of alienation from Israel"[60] nor if Matthew and Didache internally show traces of a development from a Jewish to a predominately Gentile document,[61] there are clear indications of conflict. Despite a wide common theological basis with Jewish circles, Didache seems very strict about enforcing a clear separation in table-fellowship and other rituals such as fasting. The adherence to the specifically *Christian* interpretation of the Jewish heritage seems to have made practical cohabitation with unbaptized non-believers (in their majority certainly Jews) increasingly problematic. This awkward relation between separation and continuity reminds me of rabbinic warnings against Samaritan blessings because they "bless by Gerizim," which was probably the only unique element that dis-

---

56. Del Verme, *Didache and Judaism*, 75–76 rightly sums up the evidence: "As a matter of fact, some institutions present in the *Didache* appear to be a mere adaptation or transposition to the new Christian environment of institutions typically Jewish."

57. Ibid., 77–78.

58. Draper, "Irrevocable Parting of the Ways," 239. See also Del Verme, *Didache and Judaism*, 87, who refuses to talk about an irreversible "parting of ways" and instead writes: "The picture emerging from the *Didache* is that of a community internally marred by divisions but not yet broken off from the coeval Judaism(s)" (ibid., 85).

59. Ter Haar Romeny, "Hypotheses on the Development of Judaism and Christianity," 32.

60. Draper, "Irrevocable Parting of the Ways," 239 (italics mine).

61. So Huub van de Sandt in our discussion over Didache or Wim Weren, "The History and Social Setting of the Matthean Community," in van de Sandt, ed., *Matthew and the Didache*, 51–62.

tinguished a "Samaritan" meal from a common Jewish one.[62] But this element has the potential to receive unparalleled attention and to function almost to wipe out all common ground. I therefore find it likely that it was not the integration of Gentiles that created the problems,[63] but the increasing integration of the christological confession into communal expressions of piety as a consequence of belonging to the group of baptized.

In terms of contents, the only manifest connection between Didache and New Testament writings concerns the Synoptic tradition, first and foremost Matthew, but nowhere is it necessary to assume a direct literary dependence. Didache participates in a pool of ethical teachings that are widely adopted in other Christian texts without being dependent on each other. It particularly shows influence from a pool of Jesus-*logia* that also was tapped by the Synoptics (including an archaic attitude towards *logia* as the highest source of authority). Above that, Didache shares many literary forms and ideological elements with the redactional basis of Matthew. That does not mean, however, that Didache considered Matthew as the sole source of authority. When Didache quotes from the εὐαγγέλιον to regulate the life and behavior of his audience (Did. 8:2; 11:3; 15:3–4), it most likely does not refer to a gospel book in particular, but aims at words of the living Lord.[64]

Garleff is right when he prefers to speak about "situative soziokulturelle Kontexte" to describe Didache's theological profile among other early Christian writings rather than to look exclusively at literary relationships or concepts of intertextuality.[65] Just as Matthew is not "the" gospel that provides Didache with its theological foundation, Didache does not simply offer the practical application of what Matthew presents in narrative form. The profound similarities between Didache and Matthew, of course, leave room for differences and contrasts, e.g., in the use of the Old Testament (in Didache mostly indirect adaptations, in Matthew frequent use), the role and behavior of early Christian functionaries (Didache is much more detailed than Matthew), or the character and connotations of early Christian meals (Didache obviously differentiates between a common community meal and a particular meal, but never refers to Jesus's Last Supper like

---

62. See the texts in Jürgen Zangenberg, ΣΑΜΑΡΕΙΑ: *Antike Quellen zur Geschichte und Kultur der Samaritaner in deutscher Übersetzung* (TANZ 15; Tübingen: Francke, 1994), 150–52.

63. Didache certainly knows former Gentiles among its flock (see 6:1–3), but they were integrated on the basis of "a minimum of cultic purity to enable them to share table fellowship with Israelites" (Draper, "Irrevocable Parting of the Ways," 240). They were, however, not circumcised, but baptized, which did not change their status in the eyes of observant Jews and traditional Jewish-Christians who may have formed a large contingent of the milieu to which Didache belongs.

64. Niederwimmer, *Die Didache*, 71–77; also see the article by Schröter in this volume.

65. Garleff, *Urchristliche Identität in Matthäusevangelium*, 90.

Matthew). Aware of both similarities *and* differences, I concur with Clayton Jefford and assume that Matthew and Didache have indeed "drawn from the same
store house of material" and could well have come from the same community.[66]
The relationship to Paul is a bit more complicated, as Didache seems to contradict seemingly "Pauline" tenets without referring to them directly (6:2–3).
Matthew and James are also supposed to pursue an anti-Pauline agenda, but I see
no direct references from one side to the other.[67] It is true that Didache knows
a communal meal with clearly christological implications (Christ as "medium"
through which God's blessings are mediated towards the community, see meal
prayers connected with Jesus as παῖς and διά), but without references to the death
of Jesus (Did. 9:1–10:7). That seems very odd if Didache should indeed have been
influenced by or been in contact with Pauline theology, for whom the reference
to the *death* of Jesus ὑπὲρ ὑμῶν was fundamental for the character of the communal meal and its proper practice (1 Cor 10:14–11:1 and 11:17–34). Of course,
lacking explicit evidence we cannot know if the breaking of bread on the κυριακὴ
κυρίου referred to in 14:1–3 had such sacramental undertones, but the passage
at least connects different theologumena with the event: prayer as καθαρὰ θυσία
to celebrate God, the great king of all nations. The instruction to refrain from
sacrificial meat because it is λατρεία θεῶν νεκρῶν (Did. 6:3) at least tendentially
contradicts the more liberal and community-oriented solution proposed by Paul
(1 Cor 10:23–11:1) and better fits warnings from a Jewish perspective against
sympathizers or God-fearers.[68] The situation is similar with respect to baptism:
Paul and Didache know the institution, but differ in its practice and motivation.
While, for Paul, baptism is strictly connected to Christ (1 Cor 1; Rom 6), Didache
uses a triadic formula that is also found in Matt 28:19.

Other, non-content-related issues, such as elements of community structure
(e.g., the important role of apostles and charismatics such as in 1 Cor) and the
high mobility between communities, do indeed look "Pauline," but Didache and
Paul are not dependent upon each other but rather share common structures.
The fact that ἀπόστολοι and charismatic προφῆται also appear in Corinth does
not tell us much about the Didache, as long as we do not know more about Jewish
and non-Jewish community structures, which have varied considerably from
place to place. The same might apply to the fact that Paul directed his letter to the
Philippians to the "holy in Jesus Christ who are in Philippi" σὺν ἐπίσκοποις καὶ
διάκονοις, a combination very similar to Did. 15:1. Unlike Didache, Paul does

---

66. Jefford, "Milieu of Matthew, the Didache, and Ignatius," 41 plus the discussion on pp.
39–42.

67. See Jürgen Zangenberg, "Matthew and James," in *Matthew and His Contemporaries*
(ed. D. Sim and B. Repschinski; LNTS 333. London: Continuum, 2008), 104–22 with references. For a different view see the article by David Sim in this volume.

68. Wengst, *Didache (Apostellehre)*, 96.

not seem to have introduced that institution to Philippi, but in the end we do not know where the didachist got these concepts from. Despite all occasional similarities, I agree in the end with S. E. Johnson who writes: "The Didache is not necessarily anti-Pauline, but it is certainly non-Pauline,"[69] even if the didachist might actually not have known whom he was contradicting.

Apart from similarities to Matthew and the Synoptic tradition, Didache shows a very peculiar independence from almost all we know from other Christian literature. I see no indication that Didache knew the Johannine tradition. The few similarities with Ignatius can be explained on the basis of common, but independent, use of early Christian motifs. With the Letter of James, however, the situation seems to be different. Didache and James show a couple of similarities. Both, for example, have a positive attitude towards the law. James 1:25; 2:8–12; and 4:11–12 call the law "law of freedom," and speak of the "perfect" and the "royal law." Didache 6:1–2 warns against leaving the path τῆς διδαχῆς that, in the form of the Two Ways tractate, includes many precepts taken from the Torah and calls to keep the entire yoke of the Lord (βαστάσαι ὅλον τὸν ζυγὸν τοῦ κυρίου) in order to be "perfect" (τέλειος ἔσῃ). Matthew uses similar vocabulary (11:29–30). Although referring to "bearing the yoke" is a common Jewish and Christian way to circumscribe devotion to the law, connecting it with the aim of perfection is only common to James, Didache, and Matthew.[70] Patrick Hartin sums up his observations: "These three texts speak to groups with a common ethos, a common vision, but at different moments in time."[71] I agree with Hartin that these groups emerged "from a common milieu whereby the members continue to view themselves as firmly rooted within the house of Israel," but I am not sure if it is really possible to recognize "different stages of communities."[72] Another element of that milieu was the creative adaptation of the Jesus sayings traditions.[73] The fact that Jas 5:14 (ἐλαῖον) and Did. 10:8 (μύρον) both attest the important role of oil in Christian communities does not necessary point to a particularly close connection between these two writings. Not only is oil also mentioned in Mark 6:13 as means of healing (paralleling Jas 5:14), even more important is the uncertain textcritical status of Did. 10:8 which may well be a later addition.[74]

In general, however, allusions to New Testament texts are superficial at best. Didache seems to be a quite independent witness of early Judeo-Christian tradition that is most closely—if at all—related to the same milieu as Matthew (and

---

69. In Niederwimmer, *Die Didache*, 73, n. 43.

70. On these topics see the contributions by Hartin and Weren in this volume.

71. Hartin, p. 297 in this volume.

72. Ibid.

73. Here see the articles by Schröter, Kloppenborg, and Hartin in this volume.

74. See above note 19.

perhaps James). It is interesting to see that all communication and interaction within and among early Christian communities through itinerant messengers (of which Didache is itself a telling witness), has at least for a certain period not led to a standardization and leveling out of theological and structural differences.

According to Niederwimmer, who is careful not to overstretch the evidence, the Jewish-Christian character of Didache's sources does not contribute much to localize Didache.[75] He sees reasons to consider Syria as well as Egypt, with a slight preference towards Syria, but in the end rules out a megalopolis like Antioch. Others, such as Slee, Zetterholm, or Jefford, plead for Antioch. Antioch is, on the one hand, big enough to function as a haven for different Christian circles, which would explain both contacts with Matthew and differences to Ignatius. Antioch is close enough to Palestine to warrant some familiarity with the Jesus tradition, but it is far enough away to give room for obvious differences. On the other hand, Didache's distinctly non-Pauline character and the uncertain relationship with Ignatius make it very hard to reconcile the document with an Antiochene setting.[76] Of course, different groups, even different "milieus" could have been present in a city like Antioch, but where are the arguments that help exclude all other options? Likewise, the arguments that are usually invoked to promote Syria in general (the closeness to Matthew, the lack of water according to Did. 7:2 and the collection of crops from the mountains Did. 9:4) are too unspecific to *prefer* Syria over against any other candidate in the eastern Mediterranean. All these observations are only based on the fact that the text does not directly contradict them. What we lack is *positive* evidence, but that we will hardly ever get. From what Didache tells us directly, we can only conclude that the text came from anywhere in the Greek-speaking (eastern) Mediterranean, that it was deeply rooted in Judaism and shows striking similarities with Matthew and—to a lesser but still significant degree—with James, and all three might very well have come from a common "milieu." Speaking of a "common milieu" helps avoid to assign the texts to a common "group," which would indeed take us farther than the evidence allows.

I stop here. I have less to offer than a conclusion. My paper raised questions and came forward with observations and more or less plausible hypotheses. I leave it up future discussion what can stand and what not.

---

75. Niederwimmer, *Die Didache*, 79.

76. I must admit that I remain skeptical about explaining common features between Didache and Ignatius by postulating Didache was known to Ignatius (Jefford, "Milieu of Matthew, the Didache, and Ignatius," 44–47 is symptomatically vague), even more skeptical about the assumption that the lack of explicit references should be seen as the result of a deliberate attempt to avoid reference to it on the part of Ignatius. That is too close to circular reasoning.

PART 2
CONFLICTS AND CONTACTS

The Didache, Matthew, James—and Paul: Reconstructing Historical Developments in Antioch

Magnus Zetterholm

1. The Web of Uncertainties

Historical disciplines are, of course, completely dependent on different kinds of sources in order to produce plausible historical reconstructions. In the field of New Testament Studies, the predominant source is ancient texts of various genres and in order to derive historical information from them, scholars have to engage in the delicate process of interpreting the texts. This task, however, involves a multitude of rather complicated issues, many of which are dependent on circumstances outside the text.

A key factor in trying to understand the message of a given text is to locate it correctly in time and space in order to acquire a general understanding of the text's social and historical setting. In addition, a whole range of cultural features, rhetorical strategies, and philological aspects have to be understood properly if we, even on a theoretical level, can profess to have understood a text in the way the author intended.[1] But the major problem when using ancient texts in order to understand a complex scenario or to comprehend the theology of a certain

---

1. Some would, of course, claim this to be theoretically unfeasible and from certain points of departure this is certainly true; see, e.g., Stanley Fish, *Is There a Text in This Class? The Authority of Interpretive Communities* (Cambridge, Mass.: Harvard University Press, 1980); William K. Wimsatt and Monroe C. Beardsley "The Intentional Fallacy," in *The Verbal Icon* (ed. W. K. Wimsatt; New York: Noonday Press, 1966 [1954]), 3–18. See also the discussion in Anthony C. Thiselton, *New Horizons in Hermeneutics: The Theory and Practice of Transforming Biblical Reading* (Grand Rapids: Zondervan, 1992), 515–50. However, the prospect of a general possibility of intra-personal communication through texts, even ancient ones, is a necessary assumption in every historical work and must simply be taken for granted. If we really believe it to be theoretically impossible to access the original (or close to the original) meaning in a text, we would accordingly have to close down every history department.

author is that we often lack relevant information about crucial factors related to the text, such as authorship, dating, geographical location, communication situation, and addressees. With regard to the four canonical gospels, for instance, it is evident that they were written by people of whom we know virtually nothing, and we really have no reliable information about the contexts in which they were produced or for what purpose.

However, even when we are reasonably certain about the authorship of a given text and its geographical location, there might still be many issues that cannot be settled. As for Paul, an increasingly important complex of problems concerns his relationship to the Torah and to Judaism in general. Scholars, who traditionally have found an almost absolute opposition between Paul and Judaism, have during recent decades been profoundly challenged by those who argue that Paul remained faithful to the Torah, but believed that non-Jews should refrain from involving themselves in Torah observance.[2] Since the same texts have given rise both to the idea that Paul opposed Judaism and that he lived and died as a Torah-observant Jew, it is obvious that Paul is being read from different perspectives. It is not a far-fetched conjecture that a general anti-Jewish theological paradigm has influenced the way scholars have understood Paul's letters.[3] Thus, the idea of a fundamental distinction between Judaism and Christianity has not emerged from a "neutral" or "objective" reading of Paul but has rather been the normal point of departure when interpreting him and when determining the causes for the conflicts within the early Jesus movement.

This dominant paradigm has also affected terminology in a way that has not promoted analytical precision. The labels "Christian" and "Christianity" when used to describe religious groups during the first century C.E. are hardly neutral notions, but rather theological concepts, and often convey certain theological ideas of how Jews and non-Jews are believed to have related to each other within the early Jesus movement. To define Paul as a "Christian" strongly implies that he was no longer "Jewish"; to speak of the early Jesus movement as "Christianity" implies a homogeneous movement, with a common ideology and a common ritual behavior—in reality a "third race."[4] This perspective on the early Jesus movement is not the result of an unprejudiced study, but of a certain reading from a certain theological perspective. In reality, there are numerous other ways

---

2. See overview in John G. Gager, *Reinventing Paul* (Oxford: Oxford University Press, 2000), 21–75.

3. As an introduction see Ed P. Sanders, *Paul and Palestinian Judaism: A Comparison of Patterns of Religion* (Minneapolis: Fortress, 1977), 1–59, and the overview in Gager, *Reinventing Paul*, 21–42.

4. Ed P. Sanders, *Paul, the Law, and the Jewish People* (Minneapolis: Fortress, 1985), 171–79.

of picturing the relationship between Jews and non-Jews within the early Jesus movement.[5]

It is important to recognize that this general uncertainty and ambiguity with regard to rather fundamental issues within the field of New Testament Studies reflects the normal situation. Authorship is a complex matter. The communication situation is often quite unclear, as is dating and the redaction history of many texts. As scholars, we are consciously or unconsciously influenced by centuries of theologically motivated interpretations and a confessionally determined terminology. Conventional wisdom does, of course, to a certain extent, represent the collected results of centuries of painstaking research, but has quite often developed into an overarching scientific paradigm that determines the outcome of a specific investigation even before it has been carried out.

2. In Quest of Certainty

The situation described above is certainly relevant when it comes to the Didache, James, and Matthew, which are all characterized by numerous isagogic problems. We cannot be sure when and where these documents were written or by whom. With regard to these texts, we are all trapped in a situation where we lack an Archimedian *charistiōn* that would enable us to move the whole earth. We should not rule out the possibility of finding evidence that could bring more clarity to the historical setting of these documents, but it may be wise not to expect too much in this regard. Perhaps it is more realistic to try to find the most efficient methodological strategy for using these documents without being absolutely certain of their geographical location, dating, or specific communication situation.

In this respect, the approach suggested by the Norwegian philosopher Dagfinn Føllesdal may prove helpful. Føllesdal has argued for the applicability of the hypothetico-deductive method also within the humanities.[6] This method, which is used primarily within the natural sciences, suggests that a theory is systematized using hypotheses. "Theory," in this instance, is understood to be a number of opinions whose relationship has been made explicit, while a hypothesis is a statement we do not know is true, but which we nonetheless use to make deductions in order to test the hypothesis. As such, a hypothetico-deductive system is a form of axiomatic system, but instead of using certain axioms considered

---

5. On the "terminological fallacy" see Donald H. Akenson, *Saint Saul: A Skeleton Key to the Historical Jesus* (Oxford: Oxford University Press, 2000), 55–67.

6. Dagfinn Føllesdal, "Hermeneutics and the Hypothetico-Deductive Method," in *Readings in the Philosophy of Social Science* (ed. M. Martyn and L. C. McIntyre; Cambridge, Mass.: MIT Press, 1994), 233–45; Dagfinn Føllesdal et al., *Argumentasjonsteori, språk og vitenskapsfilosofi* (4th ed.; Oslo: Universitetsforlaget, 1986), 45–130.

to be true, as in Aristotelian or Euclidian philosophy, a hypothetico-deductive system uses hypotheses that are not confirmed as true. In fact, one reason for using hypotheses in a hypothetico-deductive system is precisely to determine the extent to which they can be verified. But while the consequences in a proper axiomatic system of the Euclidian kind are justified through deduction from the true axioms, verification in a hypothetico-deductive system works the other way around: the hypotheses are verified if the consequences deduced from them correspond to "our experiences and with our other well-supported beliefs."[7]

This means that coherence is a key factor in the verification process. A specific hypothesis is thus, to some extent, verified on the basis of how well it fits into the whole reconstruction and how well the reconstruction corresponds to our general experience. It is important to note, however, that even if all consequences derived from a hypothetico-deductive system should correspond to our experience, this does not prove that a given hypothesis is completely verified, since it is possible that other hypotheses may lead to the same result.[8] Thus, the results that we reach using a hypothetico-deductive method are always tentative and heuristic; they are, among other things, completely dependent on the hypotheses we are using, and there are always other possible solutions to consider.

Despite this, it seems to me that the hypothetico-deductive method as presented by Føllesdal is a promising approach, for instance, when trying to figure out the geographical location of a certain text. In Føllesdal's view, the hermeneutic method is, in fact, the hypothetico-deductive method applied to meaningful material such as texts and works of art.[9] Thus, it is especially well-suited for interpreting sources in order to understand complex scenarios. Furthermore, an awareness of the fact that we are using a hypothetico-deductive method may enable us to formalize our investigations in a way that facilitates interaction with other scholars. One benefit of such open systems is that it is easy to exchange one hypothesis for another and see how the whole reconstruction is affected. By clearly identifying our hypotheses and by presenting them as such, the prospect of intersubjective testability increases, and it is easier for other scholars to criticize and develop our scholarly efforts.

When criticizing our own, or the historical reconstructions of others who use hypothetico-deductive systems, it is important to distinguish between two levels of critique. On the one hand, there may be reasons to question the basic hypotheses used in the reconstruction. We may not agree with some scholars' view of authorship and dating of, for instance, the Pastoral Letters. We may understand Paul's chronology or the correlation between his letters and Acts differently. Recent research may have provided us with new arguments for changing

---

7. Føllesdal, "Hermeneutics and the Hypothetico-Deductive Method," 234.

8. Ibid., 234.

9. Ibid., 233.

a specific hypothesis. These are, of course, common reasons for wanting to re-examine a certain issue. On the other hand, we may be in perfect agreement on every basic hypothesis, but still find the internal coherence deficient. Thus, while there may be nothing wrong, in our opinion, with the assumptions of a certain study, we may find that the author is drawing the wrong conclusions or making assertions that cannot be justified.

Focusing now on the Didache and Matthew, I will attempt to demonstrate the benefits of using the hypothetico-deductive method in creating rather complex historical reconstructions and illustrate how such an openly constructed presentation may serve as a point of departure for further reflection.

3. A Test Case: Draper on Troublesome Apostles

As we have seen, the geographical location for the composition both of the Didache and the Gospel of Matthew are veiled in obscurity. However, in a highly interesting article from 1991, "Torah and Troublesome Apostles in the Didache Community," Jonathan Draper provides a reconstruction, which is an excellent example of the use of a hypothetico-deductive system. Draper uses some very specific hypotheses about circumstances that certainly are not known to us. From these, he makes certain deductions that provide us with information, which of course is totally dependent on the correctness of his assumptions, but neverthe-less constitutes a coherent historical reconstruction. I would like to use Draper's study as an example of the use of a hypothetico-deductive approach and show how such a method can provide us with highly plausible results, which can be used as a point of departure for further reflection thanks to the methodological openness of the system.

Draper suggests that the correlation between the Didache and the Gospel of Matthew, which has been a much-discussed issue in the research on the Didache,[10] should be understood not primarily as a one-way literary depen-dence, but as a dialectic relationship in which the two documents influence each other. The reason for this, according to Draper, is that they emerged in the same community, namely, the one in Antioch.[11] By assuming a particular geographical location for these two documents, Draper is able to relate them to a very spe-cific historical context, which may explain some important features in both texts. Even though Antioch has been suggested as a likely location for the Didache

---

10. For overview and references see Jonathan A. Draper, "The Didache in Modern Research: An Overview," in *The Didache in Modern Research* (ed. J. A. Draper; AGJU 37; Leiden: Brill, 1996), 16–19; John S. Kloppenborg, "Didache 1. 1–6. 1: James, Matthew, and the Torah," in *Trajectories through the New Testament and the Apostolic Fathers* (ed. A. Gregory and C. Tuckett; Oxford: Oxford University Press, 2005), 193–94.

11. Jonathan A. Draper, "Torah and Troublesome Apostles in the Didache Community," *NTS* 33 (1991): 355.

and for Matthew,[12] scholars are not in complete agreement on this, and other locations are certainly possible.[13] But by attaching a specific location to these documents, Draper is making a case for Antioch as the location of Didache and Matthew through the internal coherence of his reconstruction. Thus, the basic hypothesis that Matthew and the Didache originated and developed in Antioch is, to some extent, confirmed by the same analysis that used this result as a point of departure.

Draper begins his article by analyzing the form and redaction of Did. 11:1–6 and argues that it is likely that 11:1–2 represents a later redaction that modifies the earlier instruction on apostles in 11:3–6, which, like the other sections of instructions, are introduced with the formula περὶ δέ.[14] The fact that 11:1–2 lacks such an introductory formula suggests that the verses are a later addition; in fact, they represent an intermediate phase in the development of the text, at a time when the view of some apostles may have constituted a threat to the community.[15] This brings in the relationship between the Didache and Matthew.

According to Draper, the Didache draws from the same traditions as Matthew, although it cannot be said to be dependent on Matthew in its present form. But since they both evolved within the same community, it is possible that the Didache lies behind the composition of parts of Matthew. Draper believes this to be true for the section on the abiding validity of the Torah in Matt 5:17–20. A close comparison of Did. 11:1–2 and Matt 5:17–20 shows far-reaching similarities, which, according to Draper, indicate some kind of literary relationship. The use of the rather uncommon word καταλῦσαι in Did. 11:2,[16] which can be shown

---

12. See the discussions of Antioch as a possible location for Matthew in William D. Davies and Dale C. Allison, *A Critical and Exegetical Commentary on the Gospel According to Saint Matthew: Matthew 1–7* (Edinburgh: T&T Clark, 2004 [1991]), 143–47 and David C. Sim, *The Gospel of Matthew and Christian Judaism: The History and Social Setting of the Matthean Community* (Edinburgh: T&T Clark, 1998), 40–62. See also Clayton N. Jefford, "Social Locators as a Bridge between the Didache and Matthew," in *Trajectories through the New Testament and the Apostolic Fathers* (ed. A. Gregory and C. Tuckett; Oxford: Oxford University Press, 2005), 256–64, who argues for Antioch as the location for both Didache and Matthew.

13. As for the Didache, see, e.g., Raymond E. Brown and John P. Meier, *Antioch and Rome: New Testament Cradles of Catholic Christianity* (New York: Paulist Press, 1983), 83–84; Huub van de Sandt and David Flusser, *The Didache: Its Jewish Sources and Its Place in Early Judaism and Christianity* (CRINT 3/5; Assen: Van Gorcum, 2002), 52, who argue for a rural location. See also J. Andrew Overman, *Matthew's Gospel and Formative Judaism: The Social World of the Matthean Community* (Minneapolis: Fortress, 1990), 158–59, who suggests a Galilean city as the most likely location for the Gospel of Matthew. See also Jürgen Zangenberg's article in this volume.

14. See Did. 6:3; 7:1; 9:1, 3.

15. Draper, "Torah and Troublesome Apostles" 348–54.

16. Cf. Matt 5:17: καταλῦσαι τὸν νόμον.

to function as a technical term for undermining the Torah,[17] and the word δικαιοσύνη, also in 11:2,[18] which in Matt 5:20 and 6:1 introduces and concludes a section of legal interpretation, suggest that Did. 11:1–2 is also connected to problems concerning the validity of the Torah. Both texts seem to describe someone who "breaks one of the least of these commandments, and teaches others to do the same" (Matt 5:19).[19] In fact, Draper argues that the same historical situation lies behind both texts. But while Did. 11:1–2 has the form of instruction, that indicates a setting in the life of the community, Matt 5:17–20 primarily reflects a later development when the dispute over the Torah was a past debate, yet still detectible in the final redaction of the text. Draper states that "Matthew represents a development of the material by means of theological reflection, and its authority is guaranteed by setting it on the lips of Jesus himself."[20]

This statement is due to another basic assumption in Draper's study, namely, that "it is more likely that teachings emerge out of the concrete life-situations of a community in a rudimentary and unattractive form, and are later developed and refined theologically into a consistent whole."[21] This is indeed very likely, but it is important to note that Draper's view of the relationship between the Didache and Matthew is largely dependent on this postulation from the world outside the text.

In Did. 6:1–3 Draper finds additional clues to the historical context, for instance, the reference to "the yoke of the Lord (τὸν ζυγὸν τοῦ κυρίου)" in 6:2, and the instruction on food (βρώσεως) in 6:3, which clearly allude to the context of "idol worship" and what Draper refers to as "Jewish ritual food laws."[22] Thus, Draper finds no reason to doubt that the subtitle of the Jerusalem manuscript of the Didache "The teaching of the Lord through the twelve apostles to the Gentiles (Διδαχὴ κυρίου διὰ τῶν δώδεκα ἀποστόλων τοῖς ἔθνεσιν)," should be taken literally. In Draper's view, the Didache community remains within the realm of Torah-observant, Jesus-believing Jews who advocate Torah observance also for non-Jews.[23] While aware of the problems for non-Jews in the taking on the "whole yoke of the Lord (ὅλον τὸν ζυγὸν τοῦ κυρίου)" (Did. 6:2), the Didache community expects non-Jews eventually to become Jews and thus be found "perfect."[24]

Draper's idea of placing both the Didache and Matthew in the same community in Antioch makes it possible for him to connect these texts to another significant event in the history of the early Jesus movement, namely, the inci-

---

17. Draper refers to 2 Macc 2:22; Josephus, *Ant.* 16.36, *War* 2.393, 4.382; Philo, *Spec.* 3.182.

18. Cf. Matt 3:15; 5:6, 10, 20; 6:1, 33; 21:32.

19. Bible translations are from the NRSV unless otherwise indicated.

20. Draper, "Torah and Troublesome Apostles," 359.

21. Ibid., 350.

22. Ibid., 362.

23. Ibid., 362.

24. Ibid., 368–69.

dent in Antioch (Gal 2:11–14). The threat that the Didache community faces and that is reflected in Did. 6:1–2; 11:1–2; 16:1–2, and Matt 5:17–20 is, according to Draper, directly connected to Paul and to the incident in Antioch. Paul is the false apostle who advocates abolition of the Torah; he is the one who once was "welcomed as the Lord (δεχθήτω ὡς κύριος)" (Did. 11:4), but who has turned away and now teaches something different (ὁ διδάσκων στραφεὶς διδάσκῃ ἄλλην διδαχήν)" (Did. 11:2). Compared to Matthew, the Didache reflects an earlier phase when the conflict was more acute. Matthew 5:17–20 reflects the same clash but reveals, at the same time, signs of the beginning of rapprochement. In Matt 5:19 the one who "breaks one of the least of these commandments, and teaches others to do the same" will certainly be called "least in the kingdom of heaven (ἐλάχιστος κληθήσεται ἐν τῇ βασιλείᾳ τῶν οὐρανῶν)," but evidently still belongs to the in-group. The Didache, on the other hand, instructs the community to exclude a false teacher (μὴ αὐτοῦ ἀκούσητε; Did.11:2).

To sum up, by employing what must be considered a hypothetico-deductive method, Draper presents a scenario that appears rather plausible. Using certain assumptions as hypotheses, he is able to create a coherent reconstruction of how the Didache and Matthew may relate to each other, and he also suggests possibilities concerning the historical development behind the text. It is important to note that without these assumptions, this study would not have come into existence. However, while we still do not know whether the Didache and Matthew should be located in Antioch or at some other location, Draper's study shows that the hypothesis that both documents stem from the same milieu is fully compatible with a number of circumstances that are known to us, for instance, specific wordings in the texts and the rather uncontroversial fact that a conflict between Paul and Peter took place in Antioch.

Thus, by presenting a reconstruction that exhibits a high degree of internal coherence, I would say that the plausibility that the Didache and Matthew originated in Antioch has increased somewhat. This does not mean that Draper now has proven an Antiochean origin. Other locations and developments are still fully possible (assuming an origin in Egypt, for instance, would certainly lead to a significant change in Draper's reconstruction), but the fact that all these circumstances can be related to each other without excessive exegetical creativity undeniably functions as some sort of verification. However, even though the hypothesis of Antioch as the geographical setting of the Didache and Matthew has been verified to some extent, I would like to question some of Draper's other assumptions in an attempt to demonstrate that the "Antioch hypothesis" may fit into several scenarios.

4. The Troublesome Apostle—A Modified Suggestion

We noted above that it is important to distinguish between two levels of critique when engaging in the process of interacting with historical reconstructions that use a hypothetico-deductive approach. Firstly, there may be cause to criticize the general internal coherence of a specific study. Perhaps an author draws incorrect conclusions from his or her assumptions or stretches the interpretation of certain texts more than is really possible. In general, Draper's study is characterized by a high degree of coherence, which is why its result should be taken seriously. There are, nonetheless, some details in the study that could be viewed differently. For instance, Draper's statement that the wording of Did. 11:1–2 and Matt 5:17–20 is so close that one should assume a literary relationship could be questioned.[25] Both texts certainly use the same words (διδαχή, καταλῦσαι, δικαιοσύνη), but hardly in a way that must imply a literary dependence. This admittedly minor objection is, however, one example of a certain deduction that could be viewed differently.

I would now like to turn to the second level of critique and use Draper's suggestion that the Didache and Matthew should be localized in Antioch, but adopt a different set of hypotheses. This will result in a somewhat different way of relating the Didache and Matthew to the historical development of the community in Antioch. My basic hypothesis is that the main problem within the early Jesus movement probably had very little, if anything, to do with Jewish views of the validity of the Torah for Jesus-believing Jews, but rather concerned the relations between Jews and non-Jews within the movement. I will take my point of departure in Draper's interpretation of the Antioch incident and the issue of "ritual impurity."

Draper claims that the primary issue of the Antioch incident concerned the observation of food laws and the fear of becoming ritually impure.[26] I find this unlikely for several reasons. The purity laws in the Hebrew Bible regulated when it was permissible to contact the divine sphere.[27] But as Jonathan Klawans has argued, impurity was quite a normal state; it usually had natural causes and was generally not considered sinful.[28] Sexual intercourse, childbirth and genital

---

25. Ibid., 356.

26. That the main problem concerned food and ritual purity is a very common view; see, e.g., Hans D. Betz, *Galatians: A Commentary on Paul's Letter to the Churches in Galatia* (Philadelphia: Fortress, 1979), 104, 108; James D. G. Dunn, "The Incident at Antioch (Gal. 2:11–18)," *JSNT* 18 (1983): 31; Philip F. Esler, *Community and Gospel in Luke-Acts: The Social and Political Motivations of Lucan Theology* (SNTSMS 57; Cambridge: Cambridge University Press, 1987), 71–109; Philip F. Esler, "Making and Breaking an Agreement Mediterranean Style: A New Reading of Galatians 2:1–14," *BibInt* 3 (1995): 285–314; Ronald Y. K. Fung, *The Epistle to the Galatians* (Grand Rapids: Eerdmans, 1988), 110–11.

27. Ed P. Sanders, *Judaism: Practice and Belief 63 BCE–66 CE* (London: SCM Press, 1994), 214–22; Peter J. Tomson, *"If This Be from Heaven . . .": Jesus and the New Testament Authors in Their Relationship to Judaism* (The Biblical Seminar 76; Sheffield: Sheffield Academic Press, 2001), 94–98.

28. Jonathan Klawans, *Impurity and Sin in Ancient Judaism* (Oxford: Oxford University Press, 2000), 23. The only exceptions from the general rule that impurity of this kind was not

discharges, among other things, made it impossible for the individual to come in contact with sancta, which meant, in practical terms, that he or she was not allowed to enter the temple. This impure status, however, was by no means permanent and by performing certain purification rituals involving immersion in water and with the passage of time the individual could again become pure.[29]

With regard to the food laws in Lev 11 and Deut 14:3–21, it is evident that "unclean" should be understood, first and foremost, as "forbidden." In Lev 11 it is explicitly stated that some animals are not to be eaten—they are to be regarded as "unclean." In addition, touching dead animals, both those forbidden and those permitted for consumption, would render the individual "unclean" (Lev 11:24–28, 39–40). But it seems clear that eating meat from a forbidden, "unclean" animal does not create the same kind of impurity. A person carrying away a domestic animal that may have died from natural causes would contract the kind of impurity that would prevent him or her from entering the temple. But a person eating a forbidden animal would be guilty of sin and as such be in need of forgiveness, which presupposes a pure status in relation to the sacred. Even though the same word (טמא), is used for both these kinds of impurities it is obvious that there is a fundamental difference.[30] In this respect Klawans' distinction between "ritual" and "moral" impurity may prove helpful.

Klawans argues that Lev 11–15 and Num 19 deal with a contagious but impermanent defilement that primarily is related to the cultic status of the individual. This kind of impurity, which Klawans refers to as "ritual impurity," is, as we noted above, unavoidable, not sinful and impermanent.[31] Ritual impurity, however, is to be distinguished from "moral impurity," which results from what is defined as immoral acts, mainly sexual sins (Lev 18:24–30), idolatry (Lev 19:31; 20:1–3), and bloodshed (Num 35:33–34). Thus, while ritual impurity is not the result of any sinful act, moral impurity is the direct result of grave sin. But, unlike some forms of ritual impurity, moral impurity is not associated with contact-contagion and does not affect the ritual status of the individual.[32]

The ideology behind (moral) impurity caused by sexual sins is clearly expressed in Lev 18:24–30, which also contains the significant detail that these regulations also apply to "the alien who resides among you (והגר הגר בתוככם)" (Lev 18:26). This, of course, raises the question of the extent to which ritual purity applied even to non-Jews. Christine Hayes has convincingly argued that the ritual purity laws of Lev 12–15 did not apply to non-Jews during biblical

---

considered sinful is when an individual refuses to purify him- or herself from corpse impurity, and if someone entered the sancta or came into contact with holy food while in an impure state; see Klawans, ibid., 25.

29. Sanders, *Judaism: Practice and Belief*, 222–29.
30. Tomson, *If This be from Heaven*, 98.
31. Klawans, *Impurity and Sin in Ancient Judaism*, 22–26.
32. Ibid., 26–31.

times or during the Second Temple period. According to Hayes, purity and holiness should be understood as covenantal notions, which means that non-Jews, by definition, were exempted from the ritual purity regulations and were not considered intrinsically impure "nor derivatively (i.e., rendered impure) by the sources of ritual impurity detailed in Lev 12–15."[33]

But whereas ritual impurity did not apply to non-Jews, moral impurity did, as is evident from Lev 18:26.[34] I would assume that this, and not the fear of contracting ritual impurity, is the ideological context of the Antioch incident. It is important to note that Gal 2:11–14 never mentions food but rather hints at issues surrounding table fellowship as the decisive point of disagreement. In 2:12 Paul writes:

> for until certain people came from James, he [Peter] used to eat with the Gentiles (μετὰ τῶν ἐθνῶν συνήσθιεν). But after they came, he drew back (ὑπέστελλεν) and kept himself separate (ἀφώριζεν ἑαυτόν) for fear of the circumcision faction (φοβούμενος τοὺς ἐκ περιτομῆς).

What is emphasized here is clearly commensality, not the food itself.[35] It is unlikely, for several reasons, that the Jewish Jesus-believing community in Antioch had abandoned the food laws.[36] This supposition rests on the assumption that Paul believed that the Torah had lost its validity even for Jews. But this idea no longer stands unchallenged and it is fully possible to work from the assumption that Paul considered Jewish Torah observance to be entirely compatible with faith in Jesus as the Messiah of Israel in a Jewish context. As I have argued elsewhere, from a sociological point of view, it is most likely that the first non-Jewish adherents to the Jesus movement in Antioch were recruited from non-Jews who already were associated with a Jewish community in Antioch, before its members came in contact with the idea that Jesus of Nazareth was the Messiah of Israel.[37] Non-Jewish interest in Judaism during the first century C.E.

---

33. Christine E. Hayes, *Gentile Impurities and Jewish Identities: Intermarriage and Conversion from the Bible to the Talmud* (Oxford: Oxford University Press, 2002), 21. See also Jonathan Klawans, "Notions of Gentile Impurity in Ancient Judaism," *AJSR* 20 (1995): 290.

34. For an extensive discussion of moral impurity as applying to non-Jews see Hayes, *Gentile Impurities and Jewish Identities*, 19–67.

35. Mark D. Nanos, "What Was at Stake in Peter's 'Eating with Gentiles' at Antioch?" in *The Galatians Debate: Contemporary Issues in Rhetorical and Historical Interpretation* (ed. M. D. Nanos; Peabody, Mass.: Hendrickson, 2002), 282–318.

36. Magnus Zetterholm, *The Formation of Christianity in Antioch: A Social-Scientific Approach to the Separation between Judaism and Christianity* (Routledge Early Church Monographs; London: Routledge, 2003), 160–61; Magnus Zetterholm, "Purity and Anger: Gentiles and Idolatry in Antioch," *Interdisciplinary Journal of Research on Religion* 1 (2005): 16.

37. Magnus Zetterholm, "Paul and the Missing Messiah," in *The Messiah: In Early Judaism and Christianity* (ed. M. Zetterholm; Minneapolis: Fortress, 2007), 43–46.

is well attested and seems to have included a partial adaptation to a Jewish life-style,[38] including eating Jewish food.[39] The first non-Jewish adherents to the Jesus movement were accordingly already used to being guests in a Jewish milieu and had adapted to a Jewish lifestyle. Thus, the problem in Antioch had nothing to do with food, ritual purity, or Jewish fear of becoming impure by contact.

According to Acts, it was discussions within the Antiochean community about the soteriological status of non-Jews within the movement that led to the apostolic council. "Certain individuals" and "believers who belonged to the sect of the Pharisees" (Acts 15:1, 5) suggested that non-Jews first should convert to Judaism before they could be saved through faith in Jesus. It is reasonable to assume that one reason for this position was the assumed morally impure status of the non-Jewish adherents to the movement.

Jews in general seem to have accepted that non-Jews, even those who participated in the activities of the synagogues, were also involved in what, from a Jewish perspective, was regarded as "idolatry." This tolerant view was probably a result of the socio-political system of the Greco-Roman city-states: with the exception of Jews, every inhabitant had to participate in the official religion of the city and failure to do so could have severe consequences. Thus, it is even possible that Jews encouraged non-Jewish guests to continue expressing loyalty towards the official religion since accusations of having led non-Jews astray could also affect Jewish privileges.[40] Within the Jesus movement, however, the soteriological status of non-Jews made such tolerance impossible. As covenantal partners who were guaranteed a place in the world to come on the same grounds as Jews and were thus socially more closely connected to the Jewish community, non-Jews could no longer be involved in dubious cults that risked influencing even Jewish Jesus-believers. From this perspective, the solution of turning Jesus-believing non-Jews into Jesus-believing Jews seems like an efficient way of guaranteeing a morally pure status for the whole community. As Jews, former non-Jewish Jesus-believers would be obligated to observe the Torah, which, if observed properly, would provide effective protection against moral contamination. This solution would also provide the former Jesus-believing non-Jew with a legally accepted way of avoiding participation in the official religion.

As is clear from Acts 15:7–21, and hinted at in Gal 2:1–10, the apostolic council reached another decision: non-Jews should remain non-Jews, and should

---

38. See, e.g., Shaye J. D. Cohen, "Respect for Judaism by Gentiles According to Josephus," *HTR* 80 (1987): 409–30; Michele Murray, *Playing a Jewish Game: Gentile Christian Judaizing in the First and Second Centuries CE* (Studies in Christianity and Judaism 13; Waterloo, Ont.: Wilfred Laurier University Press, 2004), 11–27.

39. See, for example, Josephus, *Ag. Ap.* 2.282; Juvenal, *Sat.* 14.96–99.

40. Dieter Mitternacht, "Foolish Galatians? A Recipient-Oriented Assessment of Paul's Letter," in Nanos, ed., *Galatians Debate*, 408–32: 431–32; Mark D. Nanos, *The Irony of Galatians: Pauls' Letter in First Century Context* (Philadelphia: Fortress, 2001), 257–71.

not observe the Torah, but should submit to the apostolic decree, presumably to avoid moral impurity. It is interesting to note that the apostolic decree (Acts 15:20), seems to deal precisely with at least two aspects that were especially connected to moral impurity in Jewish tradition, namely, idolatry (τῶν ἀλισγημάτων τῶν εἰδώλων) and sexual immorality (τῆς πορνείας).[41] This is another indication that the main problem in Antioch concerned the alleged moral impurity of non-Jews and not the food.

In Gal 2:7–9, Paul states that he and James were in agreement about the decision reached in Jerusalem: "they gave to Barnabas and me the right hand of fellowship." I would assume that this also includes the implementation of the apostolic decree,[42] which probably represents a general Jewish halakah on how to deal with non-Jewish guests in the synagogues of the Diaspora.[43] Still, shortly after this agreement, emissaries from James appear in Antioch advocating circumcision of the non-Jews,[44] which seems to contradict the decision reached at the apostolic council.[45] However, if we accept the idea that Paul implemented the apostolic decree in Antioch, and that there was nothing wrong with the food from a Jewish standpoint, the fact that James seems to have changed his mind could still become intelligible against the background of a general Jewish view of moral impurity thus shared by both James and Paul.

It is important to note that even Paul seems quite concerned with the purity status of the non-Jewish adherents to the Jesus movement. In 1 Cor 6:9–11 he alludes to two major categories of sinful behavior that, according to Leviticus, would defile a person: idolatry and sexual immorality, that is to say, precisely what

---

41. Cf. Acts 15:29; 21:25. On the relation between Lev 17–18 and the apostolic decree, see now Terrance Callan, "The Background of the Apostolic Decree (Acts 15:20, 29; 21:25)," *CBQ* 55 (1993): 284–97.

42. Zetterholm, *Formation of Christianity in Antioch*, 143–49. See also John C. Hurd, *The Origin of 1 Corinthians* (Macon, Ga.: Mercer University Press, 1983 [1965]), 259–62; Mark D. Nanos, *The Mystery of Romans: The Jewish Context of Paul's Letter* (Minneapolis: Fortress), 50–56; van de Sandt and Flusser, *The Didache: Its Jewish Sources*, 259–60. Cf. Sim, *Gospel of Matthew and Christian Judaism*, 90–91.

43. Draper, "Torah and Troublesome Apostles," 363; David Flusser, "Paul's Jewish-Christian Opponents in the Didache," in *Gilgul: Essays on Transformation, Revolution and Permanence in the History of Religions* (ed. S. Shaked et al.; Leiden: Brill, 1987), 72–73; van de Sandt and Flusser, *The Didache: Its Jewish Sources*, 251–52; Zetterholm, *Formation of Christianity in Antioch*, 146.

44. Even though this is not the only possible interpretation of Gal 2:12 (see Nanos, *Irony of Galatians*, 152–54; Nanos, "What Was at Stake in Peter's 'Eating with Gentiles'," 285–92; Zetterholm, "Purity and Anger," 17–18) this seems to be the most natural one. Peter fears "the circumcision faction (τοὺς ἐκ περιτομῆς)" and there seems to be an emphasized casual connection between Peter's withdrawal from table fellowship with the non-Jews and the arrival of "certain people from James": πρὸ τοῦ γὰρ ἐλθεῖν τινας ἀπὸ Ἰακώβου ... ὅτε δὲ ἦλθον. See also Sim, *Gospel of Matthew and Christian Judaism*, 93.

45. Cf. Esler, "Making and Breaking an Agreement," 285–314.

the apostolic decree seems to deal with. Some of the non-Jewish Jesus believers in Corinth were once guilty of these offenses, but now, Paul states, they have been "washed" (ἀπελούσασθε), "sanctified" (ἡγιάσθητε), and "justified" (ἐδικαιώθητε) "in the name of the Lord Jesus Christ and in the Spirit of our God" (1 Cor 6:11).[46] This "purity language" indicates that Paul believed he had found a way of dealing with the "moral impurity" of Jesus believing non-Jews apart from the Torah,[47] which means that, in Paul's mind, the major obstacle for social interaction between Jews and non-Jews within the Jesus movement had been effectively removed. Jesus-believing non-Jews could now be considered "holy" and "pure" and this is very likely to have affected, for instance, commensality. It may, for instance, be the case that the non-Jews within the Antiochean community were entrusted with handling food and wine in a way that was not typical of an "ordinary" Jewish community or that seating was organized in a way that departed from the standard conventions.[48]

Thus, while James may have been in perfect agreement with Paul on the mission to the non-Jews, and on preserving their ethnic identity, he may not have foreseen the social consequences. From his perspective, non-Jews were still to be considered potential idolaters, mainly due to their socio-politically motivated involvement in Greco-Roman religion, which may have been hard for any non-Jew to completely refrain from. Thus, according to James, and in spite of Paul's efforts to turn morally impure non-Jews into purified worshippers of the God of Israel, intimate contact between Jews and non-Jews still constituted a threat to the moral purity of the whole community. In this situation, where close social relations between Jews and non-Jews already existed, James may have come to the conclusion that this could only continue if the non-Jews were turned into Jews. Thus, from these assumptions, the rationale behind James's course of action in Antioch was his rejection of Paul's way of dealing with the moral impurity problem.

If the Didache reflects this crisis within the Antiochean community, it indicates that the community chose another strategy and returned to the praxis with regard to relations between Jews and non-Jews that existed before it was influenced by messianic ideas. It should be noted that the Didache nowhere indicates that non-Jewish males should undergo circumcision. It does, however, state that non-Jews are expected to observe the Torah, at least in part. According to Draper, the Jesus-believing Jews of the Didache community expected non-Jews eventually to become Jews and through this become "perfect" (τέλειος ἔσῃ; Did. 6:2). This is, of course a possible scenario, but not the only one. It is perhaps even more plausible that Did. 6:2 provides a hint of how some Jewish communities

---

46. See also 1 Cor 1:2; 3:17; 6:1–2, 19; 7:14; Phil 1:10; 2:14; 4:21; 1 Thess 4:3, 7.
47. Zetterholm, "Purity and Anger," 11–12.
48. Nanos, "What Was at Stake in Peter's 'Eating with Gentiles'," 316.

may have related to non-Jews in general,[49] because one reason for non-Jewish involvement in the Torah, seems to have been *that Jews actually encouraged non-Jews to engage in Torah observance.*

As Stanley Stowers has argued, the Torah was frequently presented as a way of achieving the Greco-Roman ideal of "self-mastery" (ἐγκράτεια).[50] Both Philo and Josephus claim that the Torah has influenced the non-Jewish nations. In *Spec.* 2.62, Philo states that "thousands of schools" (διδασκαλεῖα), which most certainly means "synagogues,"[51] stand open in every city in order to proclaim the virtues of Judaism. In *Spec.* 2.163, he explains the mission of the Jewish people to serve as priests to the nations of the world with regard to "purification offerings" (τοῖς ἀγνευτικοῖς καθαρσίοις). Josephus (*Ag. Ap.* 2.282) also mentions that there is "not one city, Greek or barbarian, nor a single nation, to which our custom of abstaining from work on the seventh day has not spread . . . and many of our prohibitions in the matter of food are not observed."[52] Stowers concludes that "Jewish teachers encouraged Gentiles to learn applicable moral teachings and practices from the law of Moses."[53]

Interestingly enough, this "universalistic" tendency has its counterpart in somewhat later rabbinic discussions. Marc Hirshman has drawn attention to the fact that some Tannaitic texts clearly picture non-Jewish involvement in the Torah as something positive. According to Hirshman, in the early Tannaitic period a school of thought existed that actually believed that the Torah was intended for all peoples.[54] In the *Mekilta de R. Yishmael*, for instance, it is stated that the Torah was given, not in the Land of Israel, but in the "wilderness publicly and openly, in a place that is free for all, everyone wishing to accept it, could come and except it" (*Bahodesh* 1).[55] In a similar way, *Sipra* to Lev 18:1–5, presents the idea that a non-Jew who observes the Torah is like the high priest. The text motivates this idea by stating that Lev 18:5 ("You shall keep my statutes and

49. Cf., however, Flusser, "Jewish-Christian Opponents," 85–86.

50. Stanley K. Stowers, *A Rereading of Romans: Justice, Jews and Gentiles* (New Haven, Conn.: Yale University Press, 1994), 58–65.

51. Donald D. Binder, *Into the Temple Courts: The Place of the Synagogue in the Second Temple Period* (SBLDS 169; Atlanta: Society of Biblical Literature, 1999), 133–35; Lee I. Levine, *The Ancient Synagogue: The First Thousand Years* (New Haven, Conn.: Yale University Press, 2000), 82–83.

52. *Josephus* (trans. H. St. J. Thackeray; *et al.* 10 vols. LCL; Cambridge: Harvard University Press, 1926–1965).

53. Stowers, *Rereading of Romans*, 65.

54. Marc Hirshman, "Rabbinic Universalism in the Second and Third Centuries," *HTR* 93 (2000): 102.

55. Trans. by Jacob Z. Lauterbach, *Mekhilta de-Rabbi Ishmael: A Critical Edition on the Basis of the MSS and Early Editions with an English Translation, Introduction and Notes*, 3 vols. Philadelphia: Jewish Publication Society, 1976 [1933–1935].

my ordinances; by doing so a person (האדם) shall live; I am the Lord")[56] does not specify that only priests, Levites or Israelites are intended *but all humankind*. The midrash ends with a citation from Isa 26:2: "Open the gates, so that the righteous nation that keeps faith may enter in." The important point in these, and other examples mentioned by Hirshman, is that this school of thought, which seems to be associated with R. Yishmael, encouraged missionizing and proselytizing but also welcomed non-Jews who were involved in Torah observance but who did not convert to Judaism.[57]

This ideological background is usually not taken into consideration when discussing relations between Jews and non-Jews within the early Jesus movement, but in my view, constitutes an important aspect. If non-Jews actually were encouraged to observe the Torah without any demands of becoming Jews, the function of Did. 6:2–3 as a reaction to the Antioch incident becomes rather different than what is usually assumed. The text clearly encourages non-Jews to get involved in Torah observance: "if you are able to bear the whole yoke of the Lord (ὅλον τὸν ζυγὸν τοῦ κυρίου), you will be perfect. But if you are not able, then do what you can." It is difficult to deny the allusion of the statement about "the yoke of the Lord" to Matt 11:28–30 where the word ζυγός clearly refers to the Torah. This is also the most likely reference in Did. 6:2.[58]

Considering the fact that several sources, both Roman and Jewish, attest to non-Jewish involvement in Torah observance, and that some Jewish sources indicate the presence of a Jewish ideology that favored such behavior, I would assume that Did. 6:2 reveals that the community in Antioch returned to the model for interaction between Jews and non-Jews that existed before the idea of Jesus as the Messiah of Israel was introduced, or rather, before Paul arrived in Antioch.[59] Thus, the community essentially rejected the standpoint of both Paul and James and once again allowed non-Jews to partake in worshipping the God of Israel through observing the Torah, yet without demanding conversion to Judaism.[60]

---

56. My translation.

57. Hirshman, "Rabbinic Universalism," 102–3. See also Flusser, "Paul's Jewish-Christian Opponents," 82–83, and van de Sandt and Flusser, *The Didache: Its Jewish Sources*, 264–69, who draw similar conclusions.

58. See Davies and Allison, *Matthew 8–18*, 289–90; Draper, "Torah and Troublesome Apostles," 364; van de Sandt and Flusser, *The Didache: Its Jewish Sources*, 240–41. Cf., however, Aaron Milavec, "When, Why, and for Whom Was the Didache Created? Insights into the Social and Historical Setting of the Didache Communities," in *Matthew and the Didache: Two Documents from the Same Jewish-Christian Milieu?* (ed. H. van de Sandt; Assen: Van Gorcum, 2005), 73–75.

59. Thus, I hardly believe Sim to be right in stating that the "overwhelming success of the mission which Luke reports in 11:21" can be explained by the "Hellenists' negative stance on the Torah" and that the "mission to the Gentiles was law-free"; see Sim, *Gospel of Matthew and Christian Judaism*, 73.

60. Cf. ibid., 300.

By stressing those aspects of "idolatry" that would constitute the most acute problem with regard to moral impurity—consummation of food offered to "idols" (Did. 6:3)—the Antiochean community was able to uphold an acceptable level of moral purity that enabled safe social interaction between Jews and non-Jews within the community.

It is not a far-fetched assumption that the non-Jews in the community felt relieved by this decision. Contrary to what is usually assumed, the sources indicate that non-Jews wanted to express their allegiance to the God of Israel through the Torah. Judging from the highly rhetorical discourses in Paul's letters, it seems as if he had a hard time convincing non-Jewish Jesus-believers to refrain from imitating a Jewish way of relating to God.[61] If the critique of the apostle who once was welcomed "as if he were the Lord" (Did. 11:4) but to whom one no longer should listen (Did. 11:2) refers to Paul, it may very well be the case that the non-Jews of the community concurred in this critique.

Thus, after Paul's ideological defeat in connection with the arrival of "certain people from James," the Jesus-believing Jews of the community returned to their previous praxis with regard to non-Jews. But the Gospel of Matthew could be seen as evidence of a further development within the same community. In the aftermath of the Jewish war, when increasingly involved in a conflict with the emerging formative Judaism and at the same time being persecuted by the non-Jewish majority society, the Jewish identity of the community was accentuated to such a degree that non-Jews no longer had a place in the life of the community.[62] Thus, in reality the community finally adopted James's view from the Antioch incident and demanded conversion to Judaism from those non-Jews who still may have been present. This radicalization may have been the trigger off that eventually led to the emergence of the non-Jewish movement, which in the beginning of the second century was led by Ignatius of Antioch.[63] In this context

---

61. There are several ways of understanding the reasons for Paul's position that non-Jews were prevented both from becoming Jews and from observing the Torah. With regard to Paul's idea of preserving the ethnic identity of non-Jewish adherents to the Jesus movement, Nanos has argued that Paul's rationale was that the "oneness" of God would be compromised if humanity was saved only as Jews; see Nanos, *Mystery of Romans*, 184. I have argued elsewhere that the reason why Paul so vigorously opposed non-Jewish involvement in the Torah can be found in intra-Jewish discussions on the applicability of the Torah for the nations; see Zetterholm, "Paul and the Missing Messiah," 46–48; also Flusser, "Paul's Jewish-Christian Opponents," 84–85.

62. See Overman, *Matthew's Gospel and Formative Judaism*; Anthony J. Saldarini, *Matthew's Christian-Jewish Community* (Chicago: Chicago University Press, 1994); Sim, *Gospel of Matthew and Christian Judaism*.

63. Cf. Jefford, "Social Locators as a Bridge," 258–64, who relates the Didache and the Gospel of Matthew to the historical development in a somewhat different way. Jefford suggests that the Didache can be seen as a reaction to an increasing non-Jewish influence within the Jesus movement, which eventually led to the Ignatian church around the turn of the century. In

and in a distorted way, Paul's ideas would again become a salient feature but then, of course, his soteriological universalism was turned into its opposite and Torah observance and Jewish identity ceased to be relevant in every way.

5. Conclusion

The development that has been outlined here, and which is the result of the use of the hypothetico-deductive method, suggests that the main problem within the early, predominantly Jewish, Jesus movement was the relation to the non-Jews. Contrary to what is often assumed, I doubt that the question of the validity of the Torah for Jews constituted a major problem within the movement. I would assume that everybody, even Paul, agreed that faith in Jesus as the Messiah of Israel did not fundamentally change a Jewish person's relation to the Torah, while there exist different suggestions on how non-Jews should relate to God's foremost gift to the Jewish people. This clearly calls for a shift in focus from different attempts to define "Jewish-Christianity" to emphasizing different models for understanding "Gentile-Christianity."

By exchanging some of Draper's hypotheses, I have been able to present a rather different scenario. The different strategies that various parts of this rather complex messianic movement developed with regard to non-Jews can all be seen as attempts to handle the problem of the moral impurity of the non-Jew and it seems that there existed at least three options: 1) in accordance with a universalistic tendency within first-century Judaism, the Didache encouraged non-Jews to partake in Torah observance while preserving a non-Jewish ethnic identity, 2) according to Paul, who probably was influenced by an ideology that considered the Torah to be the exclusive property of the Jewish people, non-Jews should refrain from Torah observance, and remain non-Jews, 3) according to the Gospel of Matthew, non-Jews no longer had a place in the movement that considered Jesus, the Messiah, the foremost teacher of the Torah.

Thus, if the Didache and the Gospel of Matthew really emerged in the same community in Antioch, where also Paul had been active, they could both be seen as two different ways of dealing with the problem of the alleged moral impurity among non-Jews and as reactions to Paul, who may have been seen as such a troublesome apostle that his model for interaction between Jews and non-Jews had to be completely rejected.

---

fact, Jefford's interpretation of the historical development and the one suggested in this essay do not necessarily exclude each other. Given the fact that many texts often function within several ideological frameworks during different periods, it is perhaps possible to consider these scenarios as complementing one another.

Transformations of Post-70 Judaism: Scholarly Reconstructions and Their Implications for our Perception of Matthew, Didache, and James

Peter J. Tomson

Crucial to nascent Christianity was its relationship to Judaism, either in its positive significance of "mother religion" or in the more negative one of "rival sister," and the social implications of this familial imagery are very much in place. The evolution of the relationship may even be seen as a major component in the development of Christian identity. There are two sides to this: the developments within the early Christian movement itself, and the evolution of Judaism as a whole. This is also true of the genesis of early Christian documents in the bosom of specific communities.

Therefore, studying Matthew, Didache, and James in their relationship to Judaism also requires a fair understanding of Jewish history in the Roman Empire during their time of origin, that is, the late-first and early-second century C.E. It was a period dominated by the series of wars fought by the Jews against Rome between 66 and 135, and most specialists would agree that this must imply that profound transformation processes took place. What transformations these are, however, and what significant social entities could have been involved in them is the subject of intense discussion.[1]

In order for us to be able to say sensible things about the historical setting of our three documents, we have no choice but to engage in the discussion and to ponder which elements in it are worth retaining. In addition to the general questions about historical interpretation, we shall see that biography plays a significant role. Historians are themselves part of history and, while playing their allotted role, are subject to shifts in perspective engendered by changes in contemporaneous geopolitics. Such shifts could either illuminate or obscure developments in the ancient period they are studying. It will only be later gen-

---

1. I am indebted to my colleague Joshua Schwartz for important comments and suggestions. The positions taken are mine, however, including any errors.

erations who are in a position to judge,[2] but meanwhile we must try to make the best of it and keep a watchful eye on the way the interference between biography and historiography works out.

Let us start out, however, from the basics of historiography.

1. INTERPRETATION

There are occasions where it is necessary to remind ourselves again that historiography is based on interpretation and nothing but interpretation. The present paper is such an occasion as it deals with a discussion between historiographers on the formative period of rabbinic Judaism, which—coincidence or not[3]—was also the period in which main New Testament writings took shape.

A common interpretation is that events surrounding the destruction of the Jerusalem Temple in 70 C.E. reduced Jewish existence to one drawn-out, tragic exile.[4] With strong theological judgments added, this is not unlike the image of Jewish history embedded in the Church history of Eusebius of Caesarea, which practically gained canonical status in Christian historical consciousness. In this view, the Roman war and the ensuing exile were God's punishment of the Jews for their rejection of Jesus as Messiah.[5] After the two further abortive revolts against the Romans under Trajan and Hadrian,[6] the Jews effectively disappear from ecclesiastical history, except in the guise of Judaeo-Christians, Judaizers, or other heterodox phenomena. In the meantime, as Eusebius made sure to inform us, the writings of the New Testament as well as some of the so-called Apostolic

---

2. See the refreshing remarks by Tal Ilan, below at n. 53.

3. It is difficult to view the rise to prominence in the Church of Matthew and John as completely detached from the anti-Jewish polemics of precisely these two Gospels, see Peter J. Tomson, "The New Testament Canon as the Embodiment of Evolving Christian Attitudes to the Jews," in *Canonization and De-Canonization, Papers presented to the International Conference of the Leiden Institute for the Study of Religions (LISOR) held at Leiden 9–10 januari 1997* (ed. A. van der Kooij and K. van der Toorn; Leiden: Brill, 1998), 107–31.

4. Similarly, Benjamin Isaac and Aharon Oppenheimer, "The Revolt of Bar Kokhba: Ideology and Modern Scholarship," *JJS* 36 (1985): 33–34, adding the modern repetition of this conception in handbooks of Christian, especially Protestant scholars; see also Oppenheimer's opening chapter in *The Bar Kokhva-Revolt* (ed. Aharon Oppenheimer; Jerusalem: Zalman Shazar Center, 1980), 9–10 (Hebrew).

5. Eusebius, *Hist. eccl.* 3.5–9 brings excerpts from Josephus's *Jewish War* prefaced with tendentious quotes from the New Testament and Eusebian historiosophics.

6. *Hist. eccl.* 4.2, reports from "historians of the Greeks" about the wars between Jews and "Greeks" under Trajan; and 4.6, the report from Ariston of Pella on the Bar Kokhba war epilogued with the continuation of Eusebius's episcopal chronography in which it is said that Hadrian made Jerusalem into a Roman town *after* the war, and that henceforth non-Jewish bishops officiated. This overview suggests Eusebius's chronology of Hadrian's building project and decrees is also biased by the author's theological anti-Judaism.

Fathers had been created, but without any clear interaction with Jews or Juda-ism. As the Caesarean church father saw it, Christianity was not only superior to, but also *ab ovo* separate from Judaism.[7] Hence, Jewish history and thought cannot possibly have a positive relevance.[8] The obvious fact that this is an utterly polemical reading of history does little to counteract its massive influence.

The point is, this influence also made its way to Jewish chronographers and historians. It is formally correct to describe much of Jewish existence in history as "exile," meaning that it has been devoid of independent statehood and of residence in the ancestral Land.[9] From that point on, however, all is interpre-tation. One would say that such ages of prosperity as experienced by the Jews in Hellenistic Alexandria or in late-antique Babylonia do not at all justify the depressing model of interpretation that Salo Baron has irreparably exposed as "the lachrymose view of Jewish history."[10] Yet Baron had reason enough for his anti-lachrymogenic revision. Heinrich Graetz, the nineteenth-century father of modern Jewish historiography, did consider the period we are dealing with as "eine Leidens- und Gelehrtengeschichte" ("a history of suffering and of schol-ars").[11]

But neither is early Christian history the continuous crescendo of truth triumphant that Eusebius wants us to believe. Walter Bauer made the sobering point in his watershed *Rechtgläubigkeit und Ketzerei im ältesten Christentum* (1934; trans. *Orthodoxy and Heresy in Earliest Christianity*): what later was to become "orthodoxy," at an earlier stage was one rival sect among others. Anyone who sees the use of crossing borders between New Testament and patristic schol-arship would also value the insight that the Apostle Paul would quite probably

---

7. See the way the introduction jumps from Joshua to Jesus (fittingly, both called Ἰησούς), *Hist. eccl.* 1.2–3.

8. Eusebius does quote Philo and Josephus, but, especially in the latter case, hardly in a positive light (above n. 5). See Heinz Schreckenberg, "Josephus in Early Christian Literature and Medieval Christian Art," in *Jewish Historiography and Iconography in Early and Medieval Christianity* (ed. H. Schreckenberg and K. Schubert; CRINT 3/2; Assen: Van Gorcum, 1992), 63–71.

9. See "The Elements of Exile" in Gedalyahu Alon, *The Jews in Their Land in the Talmudic Age* (2 vols.; Jerusalem: Magnes, 1980–84), 1:4–17. In ibid., 3, Alon indicates that rabbinic sages also spoke in terms of exile. However, as shown among others by Isaiah Gafni, "The Status of Eretz Israel in Reality and in Jewish Consciousness following the Bar-Kokhva Uprising," in *The Bar-Kokhva Revolt: A New Approach* (ed. A. Oppenheimer and U. Rappaport; Jerusalem: Yad Izhak Ben Zvi, 1984), 224–32, this is the case only from the Usha generation onwards.

10. Michael Stanislawski, "Salo Wittmayer Baron: Demystifying Jewish History," n.p. [cited April 6, 2007], online: http://www.columbia.edu/cu/alumni/Magazine/Winter2005/llbaron.html, locates the phrase in Salo W. Baron's article "Ghetto and Emancipation: Shall We Revise the Traditional View?," *The Menorah Journal* 14 (1928): 515–26.

11. As quoted by Stanislawski (see previous note) and also, in the translation by Gershon Levy, in the preface of Alon, *Jews in Their Land*, 1.

have stood condemned for subordinationism had he been involved in the Christological debates of the fourth century.[12]

The crucial work of interpretation is done in the first place in the choice and use of sources. As to sources, the important additions to those available in the nineteenth century are the manuscripts discovered in the Cairo Geniza and at Qumran. For a correct perspective, it is important to note that in addition to Aramaic and Greek, most of the new discoveries are in Hebrew and invite us to reconstitute considerable parts of culture expressed in that more typically "Jewish"[13] language that were no longer on record. Lachrymose or not, history, and certainly Jewish history, is always also the tale of quantities of source material gone lost.[14]

Thus, the task ever ahead of us is to create a coherent imaginary world using the familiar categories of material: archaeology and epigraphy; pagan Greek and Latin sources; Graeco-Jewish sources; Qumran documents typical of the desert community; early Christian sources; classical rabbinic literature and such "fringes" as targumic, mystical, and prayer texts.

Most of the discussion we are engaged in deals with the interpretation of classical rabbinic and early Christian literature, and this is hardly a coincidence. As distinct from the other categories, these concern writings proper to the two rival religious traditions that survived from our period, embodying a sense of community, of identity, and of "historical justification" if not apology on both the Jewish and the Christian side. Because most scholars who get drawn into the discussion are motivated by values emanating from either tradition, they must somehow deal with the relationship to the "other" one. This is one area where biography tends to get involved. It is also what makes the discussion we are head to toe engaged in so complex—and so fascinating.

The contentious questions are not new. These are some of them: Who were the Pharisees before 70 and how important were they in Jewish society? Who were the rabbis after 70 and how important were they? How does one assess the use of rabbinic literature in this connection? How reliable are the early Christian sources?

---

12. See 1 Cor 15:23–28; cf. 11:3. Incidentally, the same subordination of Christ under God is echoed in Jude 25 and may be viewed as "orthodox" for the earlier period, a possibility Athanasius would never admit, of course.

13. Although of course Hebrew by origin is a Canaanite, West Semitic, language, and in no way typically "Jewish."

14. There is more at play here than sheer loss of material. The almost total loss of Graeco-Jewish sources, which is most likely due to demographic changes that befell the Greek-speaking Jews, has not prevented scholars across the board from getting highly interested in "Hellenistic Judaism." We possess only what the Church Fathers chose to preserve, notably Eusebius, and this channel of preservation apparently engenders predilection. It is not the same with the lost Hebraic-Jewish sources.

But neither is it our task merely to repeat well-known questions. Drawing in the novel evidence from Qumran and the Geniza, we must reread our sources and try to accommodate them in a synthesis that does justice to the complex realities of the age we are interested in. We cannot pretend to do so from scratch, however, and we will begin with a major synthesis that was created in the mid-twentieth century and has remained on the agenda ever since.

A final preliminary remark is in place. Historiography is interpretation, and this always involves considerations of likelihood and margins of uncertainty. One who cannot live with such margins and is afraid to choose between greater and smaller probabilities will be ill at ease as a historian. This is because a "synthetic" approach is needed. If we want to describe, for example, the setting of an early Christian document in relation to Judaism, we must view Jewish and Christian sources together; we cannot study them in comfortable isolation. Of course, we must analyze the sources and their development through adequate literary methods. At the risk of losing its historical relevance, however, such analysis cannot be separated from the synthetical approach and must be practically simultaneous. Rudolf Bultmann, one of the founders of form criticism, a related New Testament discipline that figures prominently in what follows, spoke of a "hermeneutical circle": we must analyze our sources in a historical perspective, but our historical synthesis is based on the same sources.[15] Without the support of external sources, form-critical study of the Gospels has consequently remained rather unsuccessful.[16]

2. ALON's SYNTHESIS

In 1925, a young Zionist intellectual from Bielorussia named Gedaliah Rogoznitzky, having completed a yeshiva in neighboring Lithuania and a year at a rabbinical seminary in more westward Berlin, learned of the founding of the Hebrew University in Jerusalem. He decided to move to Palestine, changed his surname into Alon (also transliterated Allon), and registered for courses in the departments of Classics and Jewish Studies at Mount Scopus. He was there to stay, a brilliant student among the first to graduate in 1931 and subsequently teaching Jewish history until his sudden death in 1950. At that point, he had not yet finished his dissertation, which at Hebrew University was half a life's work in those years, but he had begun to set out his innovative approach in a series of

---

15. Rudolf Bultmann, *Die Geschichte der synoptischen Tradition* (9th ed.; Göttingen: Vandenhoeck & Ruprecht, 1979), 5.

16. Craig A. Evans, "Source, Form and Redaction Criticism: The 'Traditional' Methods of Synoptic Interpretation," in *Approaches to New Testament Study* (ed. S. E. Porter and D. Tombs; Sheffield: Sheffield Academic Press, 1995), 17–45: with the *Vorlage* in Mark, the tradition units contained in Matthew and Luke are easier to grasp than those in Mark itself, which lack external support.

studies, published especially in Hebrew in *Tarbiz*, the leading scholarly journal edited by J. N. Epstein, a main pillar of critical rabbinic scholarship and one of Alon's primary teachers. The articles were published by his colleagues and students, notably Shmuel Safrai, and most of them were subsequently translated into English (*Jews, Judaism and the Classical World*, 1977). Also gathered up and, where necessary, reconstructed from the students' notes was his course on early Jewish history, "edited," as the very conscientious translator said, as *The Jews in Their Land in the Talmudic Age* (1980–84).[17]

Alon mustered the range of sources from archaeology, via Greek and Latin literary sources including Roman military records, to rabbinic, patristic, and Byzantine literature, and put this vast learning to use with a creative imagination and a talent for historical synthesis.[18] A socio-political outlook was one of his methodological assets.[19] Alon was well aware of the import of the early Christian sources for Jewish history, and one of his innovations was his readiness to find halakah in them, even in such a glaringly anti-Jewish writing as the Epistle of Barnabas.[20] He had discovered that halakah, especially when combined with economic and political information and supported by archaeological data, is a historical source of great sociological significance. In this way, for example, he approached the thorny subjects of the purity laws and of the "impurity of Gentiles" in ancient Jewish law, searching for their background and development in a socio-historical perspective.[21]

---

17. See Gershon Levy's own foreword in Alon, *Jews in Their Land*, 1:vii–xiii. At p. xi he indicates himself as the "editor" who "presumed" to reorganize the division of the book. In vol. 2:v–xii, Levi published a more personal preface, reviewing also the discussion on "Alon the historian." See also Shmuel Safrai, "Allon, Gedalya," *EncJud* 2:654–65.

18. See Safrai's introduction to Gedalyahu Alon, *Jews, Judaism and the Classical World* (Jerusalem: Magnes, 1977).

19. The article "Sociological Method in the Study of the Halacha," *Tarbiz* 10 (1938–39): 241–82 (Hebrew) is a highly critical review of the presumed "sociological method" used simplistically in Louis Finkelstein, *Akiba: Scholar, Saint and Martyr* (New York: Covici Friede, 1936). Alon does not at all want to discard the "sociological method" for the study of the halakah: "On the contrary: it does have the potential to bring us in various ways closer to the truth. We may even say that the (halakic) tradition itself contains explicit examples to prove this" (282, my translation). I am not aware, though, that he offered methodological elaboration on the point. Jacob Neusner, *A Life of Rabban Yohanan ben Zakkai c. 1–80 C.E.* (1st ed.; StPB 6; Leiden: Brill, 1962), 10–11, n. 3 takes good notice of Alon's criticism, but says he follows Finkelstein where possible.

20. Gedalyahu Alon, "The Halakah in the Epistle of Barnabas," *Tarbiz* 11 (1939–40): 23–38, 223 (Hebrew); idem, "The Halakah in the Teaching of the Twelve Apostles," *Tarbiz* 11 (1939–40): 127–45 (Hebrew).

21. See the chapters "The Levitical Uncleanness of Gentiles" and "The Bounds of the Laws of Levitical Cleanness," in Alon, *Jews, Judaism and the Classical World*, 146–89 and 190–234 respectively. Critical discussion is mainly with Emil Schürer and Alfred Büchler.

Armed with these tools and with a clear, analytical sense of purpose, Alon set out to rewrite post-70 Jewish history. He consciously aimed at a departure from the prevailing Jewish histories of "'suffering and scholars" and the "lachrymose view" they incorporate.[22] The task first of all involved defining the period, a well-known problem for historians. It is of course nothing but interpretation, but even so it expresses the particular interest that the historian had better state openly.[23] In the energetic Jerusalem-based Jewish university, we may assume, there were courses on Second Temple Judaism and Medieval Jewish history, but it also seemed obvious to offer a course on the history of the Jews in Palestine between the destruction of the Temple and the Arab conquest. How must one name this period, if not "the post-70 period of Jewish exile"? Alon takes an interesting experimental approach, asking: "*How much* exile?" Complete "exile" would be constituted by the progressive subtraction of the following six elements of statehood: demographical mass, territory, internal governance, authority over exile communities, and military power. In sum, Alon defines the period as one of *transition*, from previous independent Jewish statehood to eventual complete exile.[24]

This definition reflects the modern conception of history as a socio-political process, while zooming in on the specifics of Jewish history. Another definition is also used, however, especially in the title of the book: "The Talmudic Age," or in the original Hebrew edition "The Period of Mishna and Talmud." The title was apparently chosen by the editors, though it could have been the one by which the course was known at the time.[25] It expresses a different, seemingly more idealistic interest, one that would also favor speaking, among other periods, of "the Biblical Age."[26] By way of comparison, a history of earliest Christianity would be titled "A History of the New Testament Age," thus misleadingly applying a much later category of canonized literature to a period in which this literature was still in its formative stages at best.

---

22. See above n. 11.

23. Alon, *Jews in Their Land*, 1:18–19.

24. Alon, *Jews in Their Land*, 1:3–38. He subdivides this in the Tannaitic period ending with the death of the last Severan emperor in 235; the Amoraic period till the abolition of the Jewish Patriarchate in 420; and the Byzantine period till the Arab conquest in 636.

25. The text of the book at p. 1 speaks of "the era that created (in the Hebrew: laid the foundations of) Talmudic Judaism," by that term meaning the Judaism of the age that followed. The confusion actually suggests the definition Alon wanted to avoid: the post-70 period as the one of "scholars and suffering."

26. "The Era of the Mishnah and Talmud (70–640)" is also the title of Safrai's contribution in the six-part *History of the Jewish People*, edited by H. H. Ben-Sasson (London: Weidenfeld and Nicholson, 1976), the English translation of the Hebrew work, which, under the popular title of *ha-historia ha-aduma* (by the color of its jacket), was obligatory literature for history and literature students in Jerusalem in the 1970s and 1980s. The ancient Israelite period, however, is titled here "The Period of the First Temple, the Babylonian Exile and the Restoration."

There is, however, a major historians' dilemma here, the choice being between focusing on the general developments conditioning Jewish history or on the factors making it Jewish. Arthur Hertzberg has classically formulated this "paradoxical truth" while referring to the history of Zionism: "For the general historian, Zionism is not easy to deal with because it is too 'Jewish,' the Jewish historian finds it hard to define because it is too general."[27] Incidentally, the relevant volume of the *Cambridge History of Judaism* carries a title that embraces both sides of the dilemma: *The Late Roman-Rabbinic Period*.[28]

Following his concept of a "transition period," Alon proceeds to unroll post-70 Jewish history. The destruction of the Temple meant the loss not only of "a house of prayer" but also of an impressive center of identity, authority, and financial power, as well as a range of institutions and procedures connected with it. Furthermore, the Roman occupation of Judaea had huge consequences in terms of economy and land ownership, and there was also mention of persecution, apostasy, and collaboration with the occupiers. Finally, Judaea was made into a Roman province, involving a more direct tax-raising system as well as the permanent garrison of the Tenth Legion, the Fretensis, at Jerusalem.[29] It was in this setting that the leadership of Johanan ben Zakkai and of Gamliel the Younger must be assessed. Talmudic tradition attributes Johanan with reformulating Judaism on a new, spiritual basis, a conception that is also found in modern historiography. Again, Alon insists on pragmatic history and pursues the following questions: What was the political status of Yavneh, Johanan's administrative center? What was the position of Johanan in internal politics? What results can be attributed to him in the public domain? For Alon, an important political element is that Johanan distinctly belonged to those Jews who preferred to compromise with the Romans all along.[30]

---

27. *The Zionist Idea: A Historical Analysis and Reader* (repr.; New York: Atheneum, 1973), 20.

28. See Steven T. Katz, ed. *The Late Roman-Rabbinic Period* (vol. 4 of *The Cambridge History of Judaism*; ed. W. D. Davies and L. Finkelstein; Cambridge: Cambridge University Press, 2006).

29. Alon, *Jews in Their Land*, 1:41–85.

30. A cruder picture is given in Alon's 1935 *Zion* article (originally a lecture, apparently), "The Attitude of the Pharisees to Roman Rule and the House of Herod," *ScrHier* 7 (1961): 53–78 (Hebrew); repr. in his *Jews, Judaism*, 18–47. After Agrippa's death, he interestingly posits (pp. 45–46) two novel religio-political attitudes to have arisen alongside the traditional Pharisaic attitude of "realistic nationalism": zealot nationalism (epitomized by זכריה בן אבקולס, according to *b. Giṭ* 56a, identified by Alon with Ζαχαρία υἱὸς Ἀμφικάλλει in Josephus, *War* 4.4.1 = 4.225) and total submission to Rome (seen in Hanina the Deputy High Priest and, hesitatingly, even in Johanan ben Zakkai (ibid., 44), but essentially from the Usha period onwards). The attitude of "realistic nationalism" was still shown in Akiba and his comrades when supporting Bar Kokhba, but it declined after the defeat. The article reads as an epitome of Alon's entire work and is especially important for the explicit emphasis on Pharisaic pluralism. This

The ensuing period of Gamliel the Younger is similarly approached. Alon sees this as the real period of reconstruction, and significantly, he looks for the underlying power basis. With his sharp political eye, he recognizes the import of the rabbinic reports that Gamliel "went to get permission (*reshut*) from the Governor in Syria."[31] Along with a number of related reports, this is reason for Alon to establish that Gamliel succeeded in obtaining political and administrative recognition from the Romans, also setting up a system of civil servants and creating liaisons with the Roman judicial system. This came down to a relative restoration of Jewish autonomy under Roman occupation. As to the time when this change came about, Alon carefully estimates it involved a series of events starting with local acceptance and ending with official recognition acquired during the journeys to Rome of which rabbinic tradition informs us. It could only come to full deployment, however, after the Flavian dynasty ended with Domitian's murder in 96 C.E.[32]

After a number of pages that analyze the local economic and administrative basis of this relative Jewish self-government,[33] Alon turns to its central institutions, the Sanhedrin and the Patriarchate, and their judicial power. He establishes that, until the abolition of the Patriarchate, the Jews existed in the land "as an ethnos, a socially and nationally distinct group with certain rights to administer its own internal affairs."[34] With these powers, Gamliel and his colleagues ran affairs even in diaspora communities, notably the important calendar affairs and financial contributions. Also, a series of *takkanot* or reformative measures were issued, ranging from adaptations of priestly levies and purity rules to a new Passover liturgy, a decision about the biblical canon, and the introduction of the

---

must be brought to bear on such unwarranted statements as "From the days of the Hasmoneans and onwards the Pharisees constituted the vast majority of the nation (*Ant.* 13.15.5, etc.), and, hence, generally speaking, we have to regard the history of Jewry in our period, in all spheres, as also reflecting the history of the Pharisees" (ibid., 22). See the criticism specifically on this article by Tal Ilan, "The Attraction of Aristocratic Women to Pharisaism During the Second Temple Period," *HTR* 88 (1995): 2.

31. Alon, *Jews in Their Land*, 1:121; in the Hebrew original (*Toledot ha-Yehudim be-Erets-Yisrael bi-tekufat ha-Mishna weha-Talmud* [Tel-Aviv: Hakibbutz Hameuchad, repr. 1967–1970], 1:71) is says שהלך ליטול רשות מהגמון שבסוריה (*b. B. Qam.* 38a; *y. B. Qam.* 4, 4b; *Sipre Deut* 344).

32. For further consideration see Shmuel Safrai, "The Travels of the Sages of Yavne to Rome," in *Sefer zikkaron li-Shlomo Navon* (ed. R. Bonfil *et al.*; Jerusalem: Mosad Shlomo Meir/ Mosad Raphael Cantoni, 1978), 151–61 (Hebrew); repr. in *In Times of Temple and Mishnah: Studies in Jewish History. Collected Studies* (ed. S. Safrai; 2 vols.; Jerusalem: Magnes Press, 1994; repr. 1996), 2:365–81.

33. Chapters 7–9, in the Hebrew chapter 5, which was wholly restored by S. Safrai from his own notes taken during Alon's lectures; see the preface by Ezra Zion Melamed to vol. 1 of Alon, *Jews in Their Land.*

34. Alon, *Jews in Their Land*, 1:206.

birkat ha-minim, a deprecation of heretics in the main prayer of eighteen benedictions.[35] With historical acumen, Alon realized the significance of Gamliel's
measures against the Christians, taking in relevant information from rabbinic
and patristic sources as well as recently discovered Geniza texts. In his estimation,
the various groups of Jewish Christians were effectively removed from the Jewish
people.[36] It is of great importance for our discussion that in Alon's analysis not
only did these measures have decisive social consequences for Christian-Jewish
and for inner-Christian and inner-Jewish relations, but they also were connected
with Gamliel's Roman power base.

Alon calculates that Gamliel must have died before 115 C.E., the year when
the "war under Trajan" broke out among the Jews in Cyrenaica and Egypt. It
lasted till 117 and in Alon's history, which after all is about ancient Palestinian
Jewry, it figures only in relation to the question whether Palestinian Jews were
involved. The answer is that this was marginally the case in the so-called "war of
Quietus," which hardly left a trace.[37]

By contrast, the war that broke out in Judaea under Hadrian seventeen years
later proved a turning point in Palestinian Jewish history. The Bar Kokhba war
(132–135) involved an incredible effort on the Jewish side. By Alon's detailed
count—and it is not inappropriate here also to recognize the commissioned
officer in the Jewish defense force, the Hagana[38]—the revolt kept twelve or thir-
teen Roman legions plus auxiliary troops engaged for three and a half years, as
compared with the three or four legions during the first Roman war. The war
ended, however, with the massacre at Beitar and the destruction of Judaea, and
it brought about a deep moral crisis. The causes for this poorly documented war
are far from evident. Alon concludes that they lay in the Hellenizing politics of
Hadrian, which—here agreeing with Emil Schürer—involved a ban on genital
mutilation including circumcision but was not aimed as such against the Jews.[39]
Alon also estimates that not only R. Akiba, but also the Patriarchal family and the
high court, and as a result a majority of rabbinic sages supported the war effort.[40]

---

35. Alon assumes the eighteen obligatory daily benedictions to have existed before Gam-
liel. Cf. however Shmuel Safrai, "Gathering in the Synagogues on Festivals, Sabbaths and
Weekdays," *BAR International Series* 499 (1989): 7–15; Ezra Fleischer, "On the Beginnings of
Obligatory Jewish Prayer," *Tarbiz* 59 (1989–90): 397–441.

36. G. Levy made the section on the Judaeo-Christians into a separate chapter entitled
"Jewish Christians: The Parting of the Ways" (in Alon, *Jews in Their Land*, 2:288). More mark-
edly, the Hebrew version (ibid., 179) calls this דיחוים של המינים מכלל האומה, "the removal
of the *minim* . . . from the Jewish people." This is in fact what seems implied in the term
ἀποσυνάγωγος in the Gospel of John; see below.

37. See the conclusion in Alon, *Jews in Their Land*, 2:426–27.

38. See Levy in his preface to Alon, *Jews in Their Land*, 2:x.

39. Alon, *Jews in Their Land*, 2:583–91.

40. Ibid., 2:618–32.

After the defeat, the Romans punished the Jews by closing law courts, forbidding religious gatherings, and prohibiting another number of sensitive ritual commandments.[41] Furthermore, "as a result of the Bar Kokhba war, the legal basis for Jewish autonomy ceased to exist."[42] Many fled the country or abandoned Jewish tradition. Also, many moved to the north: "We may describe the second half of the second century as a demographic turning point, when the center of gravity of the Jewish population in Palestine shifted northwards, to Galilee."[43] For decades to come, thus Alon, Jewish life in Palestine maintained a low profile.

It was only under the more favorable reign of the Severi (193–235) that a measure of Jewish autonomy in Palestine returned. At the same time, the rabbinic leadership showed a more submissive attitude to the occupiers. In Alon's formulation, "the long drawn-out, stubborn refusal of the Jews to come to any kind of terms with Roman rule had been weakened by the defeat in the Bar Kokhba war."[44] The decimated and "Romanized" Jewish community, while living in the Land of Israel, now experienced a greater measure of "exile" than ever before.

3. Followers and Opponents

It is fair to say that for a long time Alon's synthesis was accepted as a basis for further research by a majority of Israeli historians and archaeologists.[45] The publication of his collected works was realized by his former students, first and foremost Shmuel Safrai, who later became professor of Jewish history at the Hebrew University. Safrai's own research, based on exhaustive study of the rabbinic sources and a constant watch of archaeological results, in many ways consisted in supplementing and refining Alon's synthesis, and he also conveyed this approach to his students.[46] When in 1980 Aharon Oppenheimer, a former student of Safrai's and professor at Tel Aviv University, published a reader on the Bar Kokhba war in Hebrew, he chose the relevant chapter from Alon's history for an opening chapter.[47] It is also clear that Alon's influence extends well beyond

---

41. Ibid., 2:632–37.

42. Ibid., 2:648.

43. Ibid., 2:645.

44. Ibid., 2:698.

45. See Seth Schwartz, *Imperialism and Jewish Society, 200 B.C.E. to 640 C.E.* (Princeton: Princeton University Press, 2001), 5–6.

46. See esp. Shmuel Safrai, "Further Observations on the Problem of the Status and Activities of Rabban Yohanan ben Zakkai after the destruction [of the temple]," in *Sefer zikkaron le-Gedalyahu Alon* (ed. M. Dorman, S. Safrai and M. Stern; Tel-Aviv: Hakibutz Hameuchad, 1970), 203–26 (Hebrew); repr. in S. Safrai, ed., *In Times of Temple and Mishnah*, 2:341–64 and idem, "Travels of the Sages of Yavne."

47. Aharon Oppenheimer, ed., *The Bar-Kokhva Revolt* (Jerusalem: Zalman Shazar Center, 1980), 23–56 = Alon, *Jews in Their Land*, 2:592–637 (see also below). Similarly, Isaac and

Israeli scholarship. As Safrai put it in his preface to the 1977 English edition of Alon's collected studies, "During the past few decades, anybody who has read any literature in English investigating the Jewish history of those centuries [i.e., the Roman period] has been influenced by Gedalyahu Alon, whether the reader recognized the fact or not,"[48] and, one might wish to add, whether the reader agreed with him, or not.

There has always been criticism as well, as there ought to be in scholarship. Unsurprisingly, North American Jewish scholars sometimes find Alon a "Zionist" historiographer. For one, Jacob Neusner, in his remake of *A Life of Rabban Yohanan ben Zakkai* of 1970, counted Alon among "Israeli revisionist [i.e., right-wing Zionist] historians" whose "tendency in general is to treat Yohanan [ben Zakkai] as a traitor, a quisling" because of his flight from beleaguered Jerusalem.[49] Curiously, these pronouncements, which do little justice to Alon, were added in the "complete revision" of a study dating from 1962. Neusner added: "It is pure anachronism to make judgements about first-century events and people in the light of twentieth-century values and ideals. That does not mean anyone can be free of anachronism who proposes to study history. But it does mean we have to criticize our judgments and to recognize our own presuppositions."[50] The reference to contemporary circumstances suggests that the world-wide tensions generated by the Six Day War in 1967 contributed to Neusner's sudden change of perspective. The first edition, which is to be counted among the richly footnoted early work of Neusner's, is still unambiguous in its esteem for Alon.[51]

The main difference between both editions is in the historical account being made "entirely separate" from the "form-critical" analysis of the sources, which was now simultaneously made available in Neusner's *Development of a Legend*. The method of analysis, which took inspiration from Neusner's teacher Morton Smith in borrowing from form-critical Gospel study and was to become central in Neusner's subsequent work, knowingly considers each source in isolation: "The complex relationships between one rabbinic document and another are not

---

Oppenheimer, "Bar Kokhba Revolt," 37: "G. Alon laid the foundations of the modern study of the period of the Mishnah and the Talmud through critical examination of talmudic literature."

48. See Safrai's introduction to Alon's work, above n. 18.

49. Jacob Neusner, *A Life of Rabban Yohanan ben Zakkai, ca. 1–80 c.e.* (2nd ed.; Leiden: Brill, 1970), 147 and 243–45, quoted by Levy in his preface to Alon, *Jews in Their Land*, 2: ix–xi.

50. Neusner, *A Life of Rabban Yohanan ben Zakkai*, 2nd ed., 245.

51. J. N. ["Y. N."] Epstein is also duly mentioned. Similarly, Neusner's valuable study on "The Fellowship of the Second Jewish Commonwealth" of 1960 goes along with Alon's analysis of ancient purity laws. The positive references to Alon have remained in *A Life of Rabban Yohanan*, 2nd ed., now yielding an ambiguous result, and disappear from Neusner's subsequent work.

under study here".[52] There is an inherent contradiction here, since form criticism builds on Synoptic studies and by nature implies a comparative or synthetic approach of the sources, not atomization. Also, as observed at the beginning, external sources such as archaeological ones are essential in setting up an interpretive framework. In addition, as we have seen, form criticism from the start has been conscious of the necessary interrelation between source analysis and historical synthesis. We shall also see that a similar method of "atomistic" analysis was to be adopted by Peter Schäfer, and that it was criticized by Seth Schwartz.

With comprehensive insight and a refreshing touch of humor, Tal Ilan, while in 1995 engaging in a discussion about the Pharisees, critically set off Neusner's "Diaspora" viewpoint from Alon's "Zionist" approach. Implementing Neusner's theoretical insight that no historian is free from "anachronistic" presuppositions, she also wrote: "I am certain that I too can be placed on the Pharisee research chart by someone standing further away from the present discussion and in command of a better view of the discipline."[53]

More recently, sophisticated methodological objections against Alon were advanced by Seth Schwartz of the Jewish Theological Seminary in New York. Under the title *Imperialism and Jewish Society 200 B.C.E. to 640 C.E.*, Schwartz wrote a prize-winning monograph with the ambition of offering an alternative to Alon's synthesis. Although in my view there are some misunderstandings, the endeavor is convincing in large parts and deserves to be taken very seriously. In Schwartz's view, Alon belonged to the type of Jewish historians who "are writing from deep inside some sort of romantic nationalist ideology, nowadays usually Zionism."[54] As did other Zionist historians of the first generation, Alon would have "argued that the Jews had always constituted what amounted to a nation, even in periods when they lacked political self-determination, mainly because Judaism always had a national component at its center." And because of this "powerful national sensibility," "the Jews were always devoted to Judaism."[55] Schwartz terms this approach the typically Israeli "field of Jewish history in the 'Talmud period'" of which he considers Alon to be the founder,[56] illustrating

---

52. The foreword of Jacob Neusner's *Development of a Legend: Studies on the Traditions Concerning Yohanan ben Zakkai* (StPB 16. Leiden: Brill, 1970), xi mentions Neusner's teacher, Morton Smith, who stressed that the study of parallels in rabbinic literature must be approached in a similar way as the synoptic study of the Gospels. The foreword of *A Life of Rabban Yohanan ben Zakkai*, 2nd ed., refers to Vincent Taylor's *Formation of the Gospel Tradition*.

53. Ilan, "The Attraction of Aristocratic Women," 5–6.

54. See Schwartz, *Imperialism and Jewish Society*, 5, tending to caricature, 111: "Alon . . . always ascribed to the rabbis absolutely as much power and popularity as the most romantically sentimental reading of rabbinic literature would allow."

55. The criticism is to the point especially in view of the article referred to in n. 30 above.

56. Schwartz, *Imperialism and Jewish Society*, 6 n. 8 and p. 7.

this by quoting the long phrase that concludes Alon's preface: "We shall begin our study by regarding the [Talmudic] age as a continuation of the Second Commonwealth."[57] Possibly misled by the translation, Schwartz overlooks Alon's critical discussion of the problem of naming the period a few pages further on and does not recognize that indeed the title given by the editors to this "problematic book"[58] is ill-suited to Alon's own approach.

Methodologically, Schwartz thinks this view presupposes "an unusually close connection between the prescriptions of the rabbis . . . and the Jews' behavior." It involves a "hermeneutics of goodwill" in which, in contrast to the "hermeneutics of suspicion now widespread among non-Israeli scholars," it is thought the rabbis are nothing but "the distillation of the Jewish national will." According to this "rabbinocentric" model, which Alon's followers apply less critically than he did himself, "rabbinic prescriptions could be used to *describe* Jewish life," and "rabbinic disagreements were thought to reflect deeper social and political conflicts among the Jews." As the one massive objection to this model, Schwartz adduces the archaeological and epigraphic material gathered and interpreted by Erwin R. Goodenough in his *Jewish Symbols in the Greco-Roman Period* with the conclusion that "the rabbis did not control Jewish life." Judging by archaeology, most Jews of the period practiced "a profoundly hellenized, mystical, platonic version of Judaism" as exemplified by Philo of Alexandria.[59] On the basis of a similar critical insight, thus Schwartz, Jacob Neusner first conceived his theory of the rabbinic documents not as "repositories of tradition" reflecting reality but as ideologically motivated "selections of material" attempting to construct reality. Schwartz embraces this emphasis of the early work of Neusner, who "*historicized* rabbinic literature and reduced it to an artifact of a society in which it was in fact marginal." However Schwartz thinks that in his later work, Neusner has allowed these salutary methodological caveats to rigidify into positivist "orthodoxies," maintaining that all attributions of traditions to named rabbis are false and that

---

57. Schwartz, *Imperialism and Jewish Society*, 6 quoting Alon, *Jews in Their Land,* 1:2. The translation has: "Later on we shall outline some criteria for evaluating the fundamental aspects of life in those times. But it should be stated at the outset that we shall begin our study by regarding...." But more correctly translated, the Hebrew states, "Further on at the beginning of the introduction, some important criteria shall be outlined as to the fundamental definition of our period. *Initially* (מתחילה), we must consider it as a continuation of the Second Temple period." See Gedalyahu Alon, *Toledot ha-Yehudim be-Erets-Yisrael bi-tekufat ha-Mishna weha-Talmud* (Tel Aviv: Hakibbutz Hameuchad, 1967–70), 1:1, emphasis in original. Alon obviously means the six subtractive criteria he mentions on p. 4 in order to define how much exile there is in the period under discussion; see n. 24 above.

58. Schwartz, *Imperialism and Jewish Society*, 7 n. 10.

59. But see Erwin R. Goodenough's *An Introduction to Philo Judaeus* (2nd ed.: Oxford: Blackwell, 1962), in which he attached much more importance to Philo's Jewish specificity than in earlier work; see Peter J. Tomson, *Paul and the Jewish Law: Halakha in the Letters of the Apostle to the Gentiles* (CRINT 3/1; Assen: Van Gorcum, 1990), 40–42.

every rabbinic work is *per se* the expression of a distinct ideology. In Schwartz's calculation, the rabbinic texts were shared by a couple of thousand people and by consequence must have a basic coherence, for which reason "an atomistic reading" of them is "most problematic of all."[60]

In his preface to the second volume of Alon's history, the translator, Gershon Levy, takes issue with the objection of Alon's "Zionist" bias. No historian is free from subjective interests, and the historian Alon was "a Jew living in his ancestral homeland, writing about his people's past experiences and traditions not as a stranger, but from within." To that extent he was a "Zionist" historian, "but in the final analysis his work must be judged by the evidence he adduces, and the reasoning he employs."[61] Basically, that is a healthy approach.

Following Karl Popper's widely shared theory,[62] science and scholarship advance by setting up imaginative theories, bombarding them with observed facts (in our branch, source evidence), and then taking stock of what has remained standing. Without the "leap of imagination," no new theories are born; without the falsifiability by observable facts, they do not become scientific. In that sense, Alon's experimental approach to the problem of defining our period can be viewed as truly scientific. He put up the theory of the period as one of transition from "national statehood," of which the destruction of the Temple was an important turning point, to the situation of "exile," and then went looking at what the sources tell us to contradict that theory, or in other words, where less autonomy is indicated than was theorized. His "Zionist" bias motivated him in finding as much evidence of Jewish autonomy as he could find; his conscientiousness as a scholar ought to have prevented him from maintaining theories that are contradicted by the sources. In order to assess the outcome, let us review the approach of Alon's major recent critic.

4. The Synthesis of Seth Schwartz

The ambition of Seth Schwartz, as the opening paragraph of his extremely clearly written book states, is:

(to trace) the impact of different types of foreign domination on the inner structure of ancient Jewish society, primarily in Palestine. It argues that a loosely centralized, ideologically complex society came into existence by the second century B.C.E., collapsed in the wake of the Destruction and the imposition of direct Roman rule after 70 C.E., and reformed starting in the fourth century,

---

60. Schwartz, *Imperialism and Jewish Society*, 8–12.

61. Levy in Alon, *Jews in Their Land*, 2:xi.

62. For a helpful overview see Stephen Thornton, "Karl Popper," Internet Stanford Encyclopedia of Philosophy, n.p. [cited 6 June 2007]. Online: http://plato.stanford.edu/entries/popper/.

centered now on the synagogue and the local religious community, in part as a response to the christianization of the Roman Empire.[63]

Schwartz' ambition is not unlike Alon's, only the perspective is opposite: where Alon tends to observe Judaism from the interior and to look for signs of autonomy, Schwartz observes it from the outside and looks for the impact made by external forces. This epistemological constellation is not without merits. I will come back to this.

Developing the opening paragraph just quoted, Schwartz's book is in three parts. The first part describes the making of Second Temple Judaism and its central institutions, Torah and Temple, in the framework of successive empires: Persian, Hellenistic, and Roman (539 B.C.E.–70 C.E.). The idea is that the imperial support for these institutions made for the integration of the Jews in society. Until the last part of the period, Roman governance was fairly non-interventional, though less so than the preceding empires.

The author's own description of the second part deserves being quoted at some length:

> The second part of the book concerns the period from 135 C.E. to 350 . . . when the Jews were under the direct rule of the relatively centralizing pagan Roman state. . . .
>   I suggest that under the combined impact of the Destruction and the failure of the two revolts, the deconstitution of the Jewish "nation," and the annexation of Palestine by an empire at the height of its power and prosperity, Judaism shattered. . . . For most Jews, Judaism may have been little more than a vestigial identity, bits and pieces of which they were happy to incorporate into a religious and cultural system that was essentially Graeco-Roman and pagan.[64]

Judging from archaeological and epigraphic evidence, Schwartz observes that the Jews did not distinguish themselves from others in this period and that they largely shared the motifs and values of surrounding Graeco-Roman paganism. Yet this was also the period in which some of the main literary texts of the rabbis were created. In a sense, these were two worlds apart.

The third part of the book is about the Christianized empire, 350–640. As evidenced by archaeology, it was only in that period that synagogues began to be built in any quantity; it was also the period of continued literary production by the rabbis. Apparently the two worlds somehow merged, and Schwartz's explanation is that it was rivalry with the Christianized state that brought them together and caused a "Judaization" of the Palestinian Jews.

---

63. Schwartz, *Imperialism and Jewish Society*, 1.
64. Ibid., 15.

Before saying anything else, I want to state that I find this an impressive book, in its erudition, its methodology, and its theoretical elucidation. I agree with the historian of Rome, Fergus Millar, who, in an important review article titled "Transformations of Judaism under Graeco-Roman Rule" (I saw this title long after I had posted mine), wrote that the book is "not only a salutary challenge," but also "a very significant step forward in the study of this period."[65] I think Schwartz has an important point especially for the third to sixth centuries, while I have doubts as to the earlier period.

What occurred to me at once is the practical absence of the two great Jewish wars against the Romans and of the intervening period of Yavne, 70–132. Where is Rabban Johanan ben Zakkai, where is the regime of Rabban Gamliel? In his review article, Fergus Millar also notes the curious absence of the Yavne period.[66] Furthermore, Millar points out bodies of evidence that are not covered by Schwartz's approach and that must cause his theory to be adapted. I join Millar in reviewing evidence that needs to be taken account of, adding some of my own observations and formulations.

1. Unlike Alon, Schwartz does not take in the evidence of the Gospels and of the fierce late-first-century conflict with the "Pharisees" (Matthew) or with the "Jews" (John). The contrast with the much more subdued picture emerging from Mark and the more socially specific account of Luke make the evidence of Matthew and John the more compelling.[67] The Pharisees must have succeeded in causing a lot of trouble for the Christians in Palestine and Asia Minor and apparently even in ousting them from the Jewish community, because that is how I think we must translate the unique word ἀποσυνάγωγος used in John 9:22, 12:42 and 16:2.[68]

---

65. Fergus G. B. Millar, "Transformations of Judaism under Graeco-Roman Rule: Responses to Seth Schwartz's *Imperialism and Jewish Society* (2001)," *JJS* 57 (2006): 139–58. The review was made on the occasion of the paperback edition, the hardback having slid off the *JJS* desk unnoticed.

66. Millar, "Transformations of Judaism," 142: "an odd omission"; 144: "Three . . . missing chapters (the First Revolt, the Inter-War Period, and the Second Revolt)."

67. For an overview see Peter J. Tomson, *"If This be from Heaven": Jesus and the New Testament Authors in Their Relationship to Judaism* (trans. J. Dyk; The Biblical Seminar 76; Sheffield: Sheffield Academic Press, 2001), chapters 5–7. For detailed studies see idem, "'Jews' in the Gospel of John as Compared with the Palestinian Talmud, the Synoptics and Some New Testament Apocrypha," in *Anti-Judaism and the Fourth Gospel: Papers of the Leuven Colloquium, 2000* (ed. R. Bieringer *et al.*; Jewish and Christian Heritage Series 1; Assen: Van Gorcum, 2001), 301–40 and idem, "Das Matthäusevangelium im Wandel der Horizonte: vom »Hause Israels« (10,6) zu »allen Völkern« (28,19)," in *Judaistik und Neutestamentliche Wissenschaft* (ed. L. Doering *et al.*; FRLANT; Göttingen: VandenHoeck & Ruprecht, forthcoming).

68. See Tomson, "The Wars against Rome, the Rise of Rabbinic Judaism and of Apostolic Gentile Christianity, and the Judaeo-Christians: Elements for a Synthesis," in *The Image of the*

2. Schwartz does not take into account the archaeological evidence confirming the large spread and the enormous intensity of the Bar Kokhba war, that is, the elaborate underground structures that were excavated in the hills of Judaea and even in Galilee and that agree remarkably with the account of Dio Cassius.[69] Alon of course could not yet dispose of the Judaean excavations that were done in the 1970s and 1980s and seem to confirm his account.

3. Schwartz does not take in the evidence (but Millar points out that some of it became available only after his book appeared) about fifth-century synagogues in which Graeco-Roman pagan motifs seem to merge with literary motifs from rabbinic tradition, thus confirming the complex coexistence with Byzantine culture. This seems to corroborate what earlier scholarship had supposed, namely, that rabbinic tradition had been developing all along and now was ready to step in and fill in the gaps left available for the new "rabbinic culture." Millar correctly points out the bi- or even trilingual culture of the mixed pagan-Jewish cities and villages of Byzantine Palestine. Years ago, Moshe Herr concluded that indeed in fifth and sixth century C.E. midrashic works, the influence of "Hellenization"—meaning the intrusion of Greek vocabulary in rabbinic parlance—is most in evidence.[70] All this throws illuminating light on the importance of the preceding periods of latency and of "post-70 transition."

4. Schwartz does not take in the modern study of the Mishna founded by Alon's teacher J. N. Epstein that is the starting point for anything done in the field in Israeli academic circles. The evidence of the Mishna is brought up by Millar, but in my view he is too skeptical about the possibility of dating the process of redaction and final editing. The development of the Mishnaic tradition as tradition-critically pioneered by Epstein testifies to the creative development of rabbinic tradition during the period of latency and of underground survival after the Bar Kokhba war. This analysis must of course not be done in "literary" isolation but, as exemplified by Epstein, presupposes being integrated in a thoroughly historical approach.

Judaeo-Christians in Early Jewish and Christian Literature (ed. P. J. Tomson and D. Lambers-Petry; WUNT 158; Tübingen: Mohr Siebeck 2003), 14–18.

69. See Amos Kloner, "Hideout-Complexes from the Period of Bar-Kokhva in the Judean Plain," in *The Bar-Kokhva Revolt: A New Approach* (ed. A. Oppenheimer and U. Rappaport; Jerusalem: Yad Izhak Ben Zvi, 1984), 153–71; Amos Kloner and and Boas Zissu, "Hiding Complexes in Judaea: An Archaeological and Geographical Update on the Area of the Bar Kokhba Revolt," in *The Bar Kokhba War Reconsidered: New Perspectives on the Second Jewish Revolt against Rome* (ed. P. Schäfer; TSAJ 100; Tübingen: Mohr Siebeck, 2003), 181–216; Yuval Shahar, "The Underground Hideouts in Galilee and Their Historical Meaning," in *The Bar Kokhba War Reconsidered,* 217–40.

70. Moshe D. Herr, "Ha-hellenismus veha-Yehudim be-Erets Yisrael." *Eshkolot* n.s. 3 (1977–78): 20–27.

We can speculate as to what may have induced a sophisticated author like Schwartz to such oversights. As concerns the Bar Kokhba war, at any rate, he has amended them, as we will see when reviewing his 2006 overview of the period. If Schwartz felt impressed by the methodological problems surrounding the Bar Kokhba war as raised especially by Peter Schäfer (see next section), he has explicitly criticized the "atomistic" method adopted by Neusner and Schäfer.[71] Even so, Schwartz seems to share the wariness vis-à-vis "rabbinocentric" approaches strongly voiced by Schäfer. One could also wonder, as Tal Ilan did in the case of Jacob Neusner, to what extent Schwartz's Diaspora-based Jewish standpoint could condition his views on early Jewish history.[72] But however one turns it, the fact is that Schwartz's synthesis, valuable as it is, does not take account of a certain amount of evidence and needs to be amended.

Coming back to the growth of scholarly knowledge as theorized by Popper, I propose to consider Alon's viewpoint as one vantage point whence to observe the Judaism of 70–135, and Schwartz's as another, complementary one. Schwartz's entirely convincing approach is, starting from the Persian period, to look for the impact of empire; it involves an outside perspective in which Jewish phenomena are interpreted in Graeco-Roman terms. No less coherently, Alon's ambition is, in continuity with the Second Temple period, to look for the expression of Jewish motifs; it involves an inside perspective in which elements from Graeco-Roman culture are interpreted in Jewish terms. What "leaps of imagination" does either perspective yield? And do these survive the confrontation with the range of available sources? Such an epistemological constellation reminds me of the debate between Adolf von Harnack and Theodor Zahn over (coincidental or not) the formation of the New Testament canon. Where von Harnack stressed the impact of Christian polemics with adversaries, Zahn underlined the internal dynamics of community reading. When studying the subject I had to conclude that both perspectives combined produce the best starting point for studying such a complex process.[73]

5. Discussion about the Bar Kokhba War

The synthesis presented by Alon is very much at stake in the intense debate about the Bar Kokhba war, which we noted was effectively omitted in Schwartz's endeavor along with the entire Yavne period. The debate has been going on for

---

71. See n. 60.

72. For Ilan, see at n. 53 above. It is advisable not to adopt the language of "revisionist" (Schwartz) as against "traditional history" (Alon) as does Michael Satlow in his review of Schwartz; see "A History of the Jews or Judaism? On Seth Schwartz's *Imperialism and Jewish Society, 200 B.C.E. to 640 C.E.*," *JQR* 95 (2005): 157. Neusner called Alon "revisionist," see n. 49.

73. See Tomson, "New Testament Canon."

the last thirty years, and much of it has evolved around ideological motives at play in interpreting the evidence, especially the rabbinic part. Likewise, and increasingly so, the import of the recent archaeological excavations has been brought to bear on the discussion. Several collections of studies were published, and the subject is prominent in a recent handbook. Major questions debated include the scale of the war effort, the amount of support for it among the people, and the involvement of the rabbis.

An early contribution was made by G. S. Aleksandrov, "The Role of 'Aqiba in the Bar Kokhba Rebellion." In his view, there is no proof that a majority of rabbis supported the rebellion, nor that Akiba was a leader or organizer, though possibly his eschatological mysticism did make him a supporter. In rejecting Alon's hypotheses, Aleksandrov is much more decisive than Alon was while presenting them. Originally written in Russian, the paper was brought into the discussion by Jacob Neusner who published an English translation in his *Eliezer ben Hyrcanus*.[74]

In 1976, Shimon Appelbaum published his *Prolegomena to the Study of the Second Jewish Revolt* in the supplementary series of the British Archaeological Reports. The tactical strength of the Roman forces receives minute attention, the conclusion being that at a later phase of the war seven complete legions were involved, plus ample auxiliaries; the calculated total numbered at least 74,000 troops. Appelbaum included a tactical comparison with the Roman campaign against the Welsh and concluded that as opposed to that episode, the campaign in Judaea reflected "the decision of the Roman government to exterminate the Jewish population of the Judaean massif."[75] The core of the revolt was in the peasantry, which had become embittered by the Roman land policy after 70, and direct causes lay in Hadrian's Hellenizing program.

The discussion gained full speed with Aharon Oppenheimer's reader, *The Bar-Kokhva Revolt* (1980, in Hebrew). The revolt has been much neglected in scholarship, the editor states, not only because of the paucity of sources but also because of the ingrained idea that the Jews disappeared from political history in 70 C.E. A major cause for the novel interest in the revolt was the publication of the Bar Kokhba letters.[76] As noted above, Oppenheimer, a main player in the debate, chose the pertinent pages from Alon's history for an opening chapter because

---

74. Originally published in 1973 in Russian and simultaneously in *REJ*: G. S. Aleksandrov, "The Role of 'Aqiba in the Bar Kokhba Rebellion," in *Eliezer ben Hyrcanus: The Tradition and the Man* (2 vols.; ed. J. Neusner; SJLA 3–4; Leiden: Brill, 1973), 2:422–36, also in *REJ* 132 (1973): 65–77.

75. Shimon Appelbaum, *Prolegomena to the Study of the Second Jewish Revolt (A.D. 132–135)* (BAR 7; Oxford: British Archaeological Reports, 1976), 52.

76. Aharon Oppenheimer, ed., *The Bar-Kokhva Revolt* (Jerusalem: Zalman Shazar Center, 1980), 9–10 (introduction).

they embody "a general survey of the revolt and of the problems it poses."[77] Valuable studies dating as far back as 1897 (Büchler on Samaritan participation in the revolt) and 1923–24 (Carol or Carroll on the archaeological remains at Bettar, called *Khirbet al-Yahud* in local Arab) drew attention.

Another major partner in the discussion has been Peter Schäfer. His 1981 collection of studies in German, *Der Bar Kochba-Aufstand*, consists of elaborate analyses of literary sources pertaining to major aspects of the revolt. The introduction explains that these analyses are aimed at "destroying common clichés and naïve prejudices." Alon is mentioned furtively; it is stated that his approach is "similar to the one of Yeivin, but more critical." Schäfer is explicit: "The method is one of rigorous and 'atomistic' source criticism."[78] As did Neusner in his *Development of a Legend*, Schäfer proceeds to analyze the sources one by one, probing each isolated case for its measure of historical reliability, but unlike Neusner, no attempt at a synthesis ensues.

That was precisely where Oppenheimer criticized Schäfer in his 1983 review. While agreeing that the groundwork done is very useful for a new synthesis, the reviewer thinks the atomistic approach tends to negate the historical value of the sources. "For each subject the book deals with, the sources are broken down into their components, each of which is treated in isolation. . . . Because of the nature of talmudic literature, historical details are cited in it only incidentally. The aim of talmudic literature is not historiographical. . . . The possibility of utilizing it for historical research depends largely on combining various sources from different works."[79] Also, the archaeological sources are hardly taken into account.

Next to appear was a collection of "new research papers"[80] edited by Aharon Oppenheimer and Uriel Rappaport, *The Bar-Kokhva Revolt: A New Approach* (1984). Among other interesting studies, Dalia Ben-Haim Trifon, studying "aspects of internal politics," doubts the reliability of rabbinic reports on the support from the rabbis including R. Akiba for the revolt. Aharon Oppenheimer investigates Jewish rituals practiced by Bar Kokhba as witnessed by his correspondence; not only do these exude a "nationalistic flavor," they also agree with rabbinic halakah. Amos Kloner reports on the numerous subterranean "hideout complexes" in the Judaean hills that had recently come to attention and that seem

---

77. Ibid., 7 (foreword).

78. Peter Schäfer, *Der Bar Kochba-Aufstand: Studien zum zweiten jüdischen Krieg gegen Rom* (Tübingen: Mohr Siebeck, 1981), Introduction, 5–6. See the criticism by Seth Schwartz, see n. 60.

79. Aharon Oppenheimer, Review of P. Schäfer, *Der Bar Kokhba Aufstand: Studien zum zweiten jüdischen Krieg gegen Rom, JSJ* 14 (1983): 218. Similarly, Isaac and Oppenheimer, "Bar Kokhba Revolt," 38: the method that "dissects talmudic sources into their component parts and studies each source separately" has the "fundamental weakness that it fails to consider the sources in combination," sometimes leading to worse conjecture than the method criticized.

80. Thus the subtitle in the Hebrew: מחקרים חדשים.

to confirm Dio Cassius's report on the guerilla methods used by the Jewish rebels. Following a survey by Ze'ev Safrai, the evidence on extinction of Jewish settlement in various regions of the Land of Israel testifies to the extent of the Bar Kokhba war, most of all in Judaea. Joshua Schwartz, to be sure, concludes that Jewish settlement in post-war Judaea did not become completely extinct. Furthermore, Isaiah Gafni finds that only following the Bar Kokhba revolt do rabbinic traditions evidence an emphasis on living in the Land and against Diaspora life.

An important attempt at defusing the ideological motivations behind the debate was made by Benjamin Isaac and Aharon Oppenheimer.[81] Whereas certain historians identified fully with the Roman point of view, others, among whom were Yeivin and Alon, identified with the Jewish viewpoint. More balanced approaches are also noted. The need for a sober and critical assessment of the sources is obvious. It was, however, "G. Alon [who] laid the foundations of the modern study of the period of the Mishnah and the Talmud through critical examination of talmudic literature." Schäfer's method is again criticized because it "dissects talmudic sources into their component parts and . . . fails to consider the sources in combination, and this sometimes results in conjecture that is no better founded than that which it criticized in the first place." Also, "the most substantial contribution to our information on the revolt has been made by archaeological exploration, epigraphy, and numismatics."[82]

In 2003, Peter Schäfer rejoined with *The Bar Kokhba War Reconsidered*, a collection of papers read at a 2001 Princeton conference. The editor agrees that recent developments, especially in archaeology, justify a *status quaestionis*. Oppenheimer and Isaac participated along with many others, including archaeologists Amos Kloner and Hanan Eshel. Schäfer opens with a paper on "Bar Kokhba and the Rabbis," stating for his aim to refute the concern of "most Jewish Studies scholars . . . with placing the revolt firmly within the emerging rabbinic movement of post-70 Judaism." In spite of the criticisms, Schäfer persists in his "atomistic" method, taking the sources on the revolt one by one. On that basis, he doubts the historicity of R. Akiba's support for the revolt and the rabbinic basis of Bar Kokhba's law observance—would he not rather have followed "pre-70 and non-rabbinic models"? Similarly, the reputed desecration by the rebels of idolatrous motifs on pagan utensils "might as well be the result of significant tear and wear." Having thus pulverized most of the evidence pertaining to the rabbinic tradition, Schäfer wants "to turn the tables" and "ask what kind of Judaism emerges if we rely above all on the primary sources. . . . It has become increas-

---

81. In their essay, "The Revolt of Bar Kokhba," 33–60. See also the sober study by Harry Sysling, "De Bar-Kochba opstand, historie en legende," *Ter herkenning* 14 (1986): 165–76.
82. Isaac and Oppenheimer, "The Revolt of Bar Kokhba," 36–38.

ingly clear . . . that there was not much of a rabbinic movement during the period under discussion."[83]

At the time of writing, the debate stands at the positions outlined in volume 4 of the *Cambridge History of Judaism* of 2006. Seth Schwartz, in the opening chapter on "Political, Social, and Economic Life in the Land of Israel, 66 – c. 235," starts out by highlighting the centrifugal movement in the aftermath of the Great War and the way in which "the norms of the Graeco-Roman city partly supplemented and partly replaced . . . native norms as the cultural ideal." As to the ensuing Bar Kokhba revolt, the importance of archaeological discoveries is acknowledged, while stressing the inscrutable nature and course of the revolt. Archaeology confirms reports in Dio Cassius and in patristic and rabbinic literature and warrants the conclusion, "The Bar Kokhba revolt seems to have been a mass uprising concentrated in Judaea." Shimon ben Kosiba, "apparently a pious Jew," was "its single leader (but) may never have succeeded in controlling it fully." It is uncertain if the rabbis operated as a group and "unknown what the views of individual rabbis aside from Rabbi Akiba might have been." While the question of the exact timing and scope of Hadrian's decrees must be left unsolved, the demographic shift to Galilee comes in full view from the fourth century onwards. We can conclude that Schwartz, writing for this assignment, has admitted the apparent importance of the Bar Kokhba war. He has remained sceptical, however, on the involvement of the rabbis. His whole summary of the Yavne period, including the wars, reflects an exclusively outside perspective. As to the choice of sources, the import of early Christian documents is not felt.

In the same volume, Bar Ilan archaeologist Hanan Eshel summarizes the archaeological evidence on the Bar Kokhba revolt, evaluating it in the light of the literary documents. He ends up not far from the summary by Benjamin Isaac and Aharon Oppenheimer, twenty years earlier. The numerous subterranean structures in Judaea confirm Dio Cassius' information on large-scale preparations by the Jews. The letters of Bar Kokhba show him, the sole leader, to have set up an elaborate administrative system, though the command structure remains unclear. The insurgents are seen as "strictly observing Jewish law" in such details as the Sabbath, the sabbatical year, and the defacing of deities portrayed on pagan utensils as prescribed in the Mishna (*m. 'Abod. Zar.* 4:5). In order to quench the insurrection, the Romans had to muster up elements from ten or eleven legions plus auxiliary units and apparently "perceived the uprising as a genuine threat to their empire."

---

83. The last phrase summarizes Catherine Hezser's study, *The Social Structure of the Rabbinic Movement in Roman Palestine* (TSAJ 66; Tübingen: Mohr Siebeck, 1997), a *Habilitationsschrift* prepared under Schäfer's direction. However, Hezser's own conclusions are more cautious.

6. Conclusion: Positioning Matthew, Didache, and James
between 50 and 150 c.e.

On balance, we may conclude that Alon's theory of the years 70–135 c.e. in Jewish history as part of a "transition period" from a situation of independent statehood to one of subjection and political insignificance has been vindicated, certainly if we frame it in the larger "imperial" outlook advocated by Schwartz. The pulverization of rabbinic evidence as propagated by Peter Schäfer cannot contribute to a historical reconstruction, almost *per definitionem*; a synthetic approach following the lead of archaeological and literary evidence is called for. Nor is Seth Schwartz's underrating of the inside perspective and his consequent scepticism as to the rabbinic sources for the Yavne period satisfying. Certainly, the various indications of apostasy and defection in the period may not be neglected; the challenges facing the Jewish leadership must have been legion, including those presented by the Christians. Indeed, the strong pressure from the rabbinic leadership felt in the early Christian sources is an important piece of the puzzle. Finally, there is the archaeological and other external evidence on the circumstances of the Bar Kokhba war. Judging from the system of underground caves and passageways, large preparations were made, and the Romans apparently needed to mobilize an exceptionally large part of their military potential. If we combine all of this evidence, Alon's depiction of the transition period as one in which political resilience coupled with religious devotion characterized a large proportion of Jews becomes not at all unlikely. The exact share the rabbis had in this ideological motivation is unclear, but many of them must have been somewhere near its center of gravity.

The Bar Kokhba war represents the ultimate and most violent confrontation of the Jews with the Roman Empire. It was not just its military power they opposed in this final showdown, but its ideology. The spirit of independence and non-submission with which the Jews had repeatedly responded to the assertion of absolute and quasi-divine power seems to have irritated the Romans quite a lot. In reaction, ideological motives seem to have played a role in their military strategy.[84] In other words, the ideological and military power of the Jews was

---

84. See Shimon Appelbaum, *Prolegomena to the Study of the Second Jewish Revolt (A.D. 132–135)* (British Archaeological Reports. Supplementary Series 7; Oxford: British Archaeological Reports, 1976), 2–5; Martin Goodman, "Trajan and the Origins of the Bar Kokhba War," in P. Schäfer, ed., *Bar Kokhba War Reconsidered,* 23–29, as also the important remarks *à propos* the work of James Rives in Seth Schwartz, "Political, Social, and Economic Life in the Land of Israel, 66 – c. 235," in *The Late Roman-Rabbinic Period* (ed. S. T. Katz; vol. 4 of *The Cambridge History of Judaism,* ed. W. D. Davies and L. Finkelstein; Cambridge: Cambridge University Press, 2006), 30. Having studied Roman military strategy extensively, Adrian Goldsworthy, *Roman Warfare* (The Cassell History of Warfare; London: Cassell, 2000; repr., London, Phoenix, 2007), 81–82, 148–49 explains that, while the Romans could impossibly tolerate even subdued insurgence, the

in ultimate collision with that of Rome, and more than ever we need both the "inside" and the "outside" perspective to study this part of Jewish history. The impression of massive Jewish resistance against the ruthless superpower, contrasting with the absence of any comparable phenomenon for the next eighteen centuries to come, is not easy to imagine for someone brought up with twentieth-century Western civility. Nor is the atmosphere of total defeat, starvation, and mass killings in the caves and at the last stronghold that seem to be echoed in the gloomy reports of rabbinic literature. It also seems that since this tragic episode, the rabbinic concept of *kiddush ha-Shem* or "sanctification of the name" took the meaning of "Jewish martyrdom."[85]

In turn, this atmosphere enhances the likelihood of a significant yet certainly not unanimous involvement of the "rabbis"[86] in the revolt and, conversely, of a relative popular acceptance of their guidance in the years preceding. It is well imaginable that the massive pressure of the Roman war machine in collision with the stubborn resistance of the Jews worked towards amalgamating the latter into a single whole and drove the rabbis to their ideological center. Ben Kosiba's acclamation as Messiah seems a fact, quite probably also under the influence of the atmosphere of extreme polarization and looming defeat, and the dissent of rabbis like Johanan ben Torta, if historical, must have required great spiritual independence.[87] This again highlights patristic evidence of a deadly conflict between Jews and Christians having built up in the meantime and now culminating in the requirement of allegiance to this Messiah and "denial" of theirs—or else "cruel punishment."[88]

Indeed, an aspect of the *interbellum* that deserves to be taken more seriously than it has been to date concerns the growing confrontation between Jews, Judaeo-Christians, and Gentile Christians. As we saw, Alon did devote considerable space to it. Probably dating from just before the war,[89] the so-called Epistle of Barnabas with its blatant anti-Judaism may be perceived as a counterpart of the reported rabbinic measures against the *minim* and their "books," which might

---

Jews were "exceptional" in their religiously motivated "sense of national identity and culture."

85. See Shmuel Safrai, "Martyrdom in the Teachings of the Tannaim" in *Sjaloom. Ter nagedachtenis van Mgr. Dr. A.C. Ramselaar* (ed. Th.C. de Kruijf and H. van de Sandt; Arnhem: Folkertsma Stichting voor Talmudica, 1983), 145–64.

86. For the likelihood of the honorific use of this appellation by this time see below, n. 108.

87. *Y. Ta'an.* 4, 68d; *Eikha Rab.* 2,4. Significantly, Johanan ben Torta is also known for his "prophetic" saying on the destruction of Shilo and the First and Second Temple, *t. Menah* 13:12; *b. Yoma* 9a; *Exod Rab.* 40:1; *Num Rab.* 7:10.

88. Justin, *1Apology* 31.6, καὶ γὰρ ἐν τῷ νῦν γεγενημένῳ Ἰουδαϊκῷ πολέμῳ Βαρχοχέβας, ὁ τῆς Ἰουδαίων ἀποστάσεως ἀρχηγέτη, Χριστιανοὺς μόνους [the exclusiveness is doubtful in view of rabbinic reports] εἰς τιμωρίας δεινάς, εἰ μὴ ἀρνοιντο Ἰησοῦν τὸν Χριστόν καὶ βλασφημοῖεν, ἐκέλευεν ἀπάγεσθαι. With minute variations, the report is cited by Eusebius, *Hist. eccl.* 4.8.4.

89. See Prostmeier, *Barnabasbrief*, 111–19.

well have included Christians by this time. The echo of Jewish measures against Christians in the Gospel of John enhances this possibility.[90] The use made in Pseudo-Barnabas of a halakic text in Greek as uncovered by Alon illuminates the polemical orientation of the work.[91] Furthermore, the epistles written in this period to various Asia Minor churches by the bishop of Antioch, Ignatius, testify to a fierce competition between Gentile and Jewish Christians.[92] The social conflict between Jews and Gentile Christians that crystallized out of this muddle was vigorous and could well have been guided and motivated by the rabbis.

Going back in time another step, it is then reasonable to accept the likelihood that Rabban Gamliel's measures against the Judaeo-Christians somehow had to do with the Eighteen Benedictions. Combining the rabbinic and early Christian evidence is crucial here.[93] If in addition we accept Alon's theory of the support of the Roman authorities secured by Gamliel, the rabbinic decrees against the Christians gain political weight as they coincide with similar phenomena in Rome. While anti-Jewish sentiment is evidenced under Domitian (81–96 c.e.),[94] there are also distinct reports on Roman police investigations in this period against Judaeo-Christians of Davidic descent, relatives of Jesus suspected of harboring messianic ambitions.[95] Needless to say, these were also the years when the major Gospels embodying the developing Christian sense of identity took final form, and their evidence is essential. The explicit Davidic emphasis of the beginning of Matthew is revealing in this context.[96]

The period immediately preceding the Great War of 66–70 is also important for the evidence of rising Jewish-Gentile tensions, for example, as reflected in the

---

90. T. Šabb. 13:5 and parallels. See Dan Jaffé, *Le judaïsme et l'avènement du christianisme: orthodoxie et hétérodoxie dans la littérature talmudique Ier-IIe siècle* (Patrimoines: Judaïsme; Paris: Cerf, 2005), 237–312. For the important term ἀποσυνάγωγος see n. 68.

91. See above n. 20.

92. Ignatius, *Magn.* 10.3; *Philad.* 5.6; *Smyrn.* 1.2 still displays the Apostolic ecclesiology.

93. See the endeavor made in Tomson, "Wars against Rome."

94. John M. G. Barclay, *Jews in the Mediterranean Diaspora from Alexander to Trajan (323 BCE – 117 C)* (Edinburgh: T&T Clark, 1996), 306–19. See also J. Andrew Overman, "The First Revolt and Flavian Politics" in *The First Jewish revolt: Achaeology, History, and Ideology* (ed. A. M. Berlin and J. A. Overman; London: Routledge, 2002), 213–20.

95. See discussion by E. Mary Smallwood, *The Jews under Roman Rule. From Pompey to Diocletian: A Study in Political Relations* (SJLA 20; Leiden: Brill, 1976; repr., 1981), 351–52; Appelbaum, *Prolegomena to the Study of the Second Jewish Revolt*, 2.

96. Matt 1:1–18, esp. in comparison with Ruth 4:18–22. Jesus's Davidic lineage (e.g., the phrase ἐκ σπέρματος Δαυίδ) is stressed in Apostolic and sub-apostolic literature (e.g., Rom 1:3; 2 Tim 2:8; Rev 5:5; Did. 9:2; Ignatius, *Eph.* 18.2 *et passim*), subsequently seems to decline, except for Origen, but is again strongly evidenced in fourth-century literature.

letters of Paul.[97] Though tense,[98] Christian-Jewish relations were still fundamentally open, as is seen in the sympathy of the Pharisees for James, the brother of Jesus who was lynched at the behest of the Sadducean high priest in 62 C.E.[99]

A rough framework of Jewish history between 50 and 150 C.E. having thus been established, we may now proceed and consider the genesis of our three documents in the perspective of evolving Christian relations with Judaism.

7. MATTHEW

Many scholars will agree that on top of its obvious Judaeo-Christian layer involving a range of expressions remarkably close to rabbinic literature,[100] Matthew underwent a redaction process reflecting a fierce conflict with the "Pharisees" or "scribes and Pharisees" as a class and as an apparently important social group.[101] This must represent just about the last redactional layer. In turn, the evidence embodied in this redactional layer makes the Gospel of Matthew into a very important source for the historiography of the period.

In addition, some have pointed out the indications that more than a mere conflict with the Pharisaic leaders seems involved: a clash with the Jewish community as a whole looms large. Involved are passages like the one announcing to the upper priests and Pharisees: "The kingdom shall be taken from you and given to another people (ἔθνος) which will bring the fruits of it" (Matt 21:43), or the episode of the guard at the tomb requested by the Pharisees and upper priests and their lie about the theft of Jesus's body (27:62–66; 28:11–15). The story, which may be seen as the beginning of a development resulting in a series of anti-Jewish apocryphal Gospels and also involving Jewish anti-Christian narratives,[102] points to thoroughly deteriorated Christian–Jewish relations. The severe conflict of Judaeo-Christians with "'rabbinic" Jews seems at this precise point to have been

---

97. See the overview in Peter J. Tomson, "'Die Täter des Gesetzes werden gerechtfertigt werden' (Röm 2,13); Zu einer adäquaten Perspektive für den Römerbrief," in *Lutherische und neue Paulusperspektive: Beiträge zu einem Schlüsselproblem der gegenwärtigen exegetischen Diskussion* (ed. M. Bachmann; WUNT 182; Tübingen: Mohr Siebeck, 2005), 215–20.

98. See Rom 15:31, ἵνα ῥυσθῶ ἀπὸ τῶν ἀπειθούντων ἐν τῇ Ἰουδαίᾳ.

99. Josephus, *Ant.* 20.200, a passage considered authentic by most.

100. Most conspicuously, βασιλεία τῶν οὐρανῶν (only in Matthew, *passim*) in parallel to מלכות שמים.

101. J. Andrew Overman, *Matthew's Gospel and Formative Judaism: The Social World of the Matthean Community* (Minneapolis: Fortress, 1990) contains a clear discussion of the conflict with "formative Judaism," a phrase coined by J. Neusner.

102. See the Gospels of Nicodemus, of Peter, and of Pilate. For some elaboration, see Tomson, "'Jews' in the Gospel of John," 330–39. On early Jewish anti-Christian polemics including the *toledot Yeshu* see Samuel Krauss and William Horbury, eds., *The Jewish-Christian from the Earliest Times to 1789* (TSAJ 56; Tübingen: Mohr Siebeck, 1995), 5–13.

spilling over into an all out confrontation between a no-longer Jewish church and Judaism.

As to the final date of Matthew, this brings us to the measures of Rabban Gamliel around the turn of the century. For a location, we must look for an area with intensive Jewish-Gentile interactions. Moreover the soldierly language of the tomb guard story could well be reflective of a Roman garrison town; it reminds us of the positive interest in Pilate and his wife (27:19–25) and the seemingly crude anti-Jewish revision of the story of the centurion of Capernaum (8:5–13).[103] This would fit with the long-standing argument for Antioch as a likely candidate, especially in view of the conflict with Judaeo-Christians reflected in the Epistles of Ignatius and of the close interaction with Antioch's large Jewish community at the time.[104] Alternatively, there are no indications against a location somewhere in Roman Palestine either; one could think of Caesarea.[105]

8. DIDACHE

The Didache's proximity to Matthew by cultural background, tradition, and apparently also social milieu, is well-known, but there are important differences. One concerns the absence of indications of a conflict with the Pharisees—apart, that is, from chapter 8, which appears to have been inserted into the largely non-polemical book of ritual that runs from chapter 7 through 15 and treats of Baptism, the Eucharist, hospitality towards "apostles" and prophets, and other community matters. Links with Judaeo-Christian and Jewish tradition have been argued on solid grounds;[106] ties with the "apostolic preaching tradition" evidenced in the synoptic tradition and in Paul could be added.[107] Nor should we

---

103. Κουστωδία Matt 27:65–66; 28:11; see J. Andrew Overman, *Church and Community in Crisis: The Gospel According to Matthew* (The NT in Context; Valley Forge, Pa.: Trinity, 1996), 400 and Tomson, "Matthäusevangelium im Wandel."

104. See Magnus Zetterholm, *The Formation of Christianity in Antioch: A Social-Scientific Approach to the Separation Between Judaism and Christianity* (London: Routledge, 2003), esp. chapter 5, "Politics and Persecution."

105. See Overman, *Church and Community in Crisis*, 16–19; idem, *Matthew's Gospel and Formative Judaism*, 158–59: Galilee (Tiberias, Capernaum, or Sepphoris). The post-70 garrison of the X Legio Fretensis near Jerusalem would not yet have built up sufficient social interaction with local Jews. Caesarea, however, could fit (Acts 10:1), as could Capernaum (Luke 7:1).

106. Huub van de Sandt and David Flusser, *The Didache: Its Jewish Sources and Its Place in Early Judaism and Christianity* (CRINT 3/5; Assen: Van Gorcum, 2002); Marcello Del Verme, *Didache and Judaism: Jewish Roots of an Ancient Christian-Jewish Work* (London: T&T Clark, 2004).

107. Compare Did. 11–13 with the complex described in Tomson, *Paul and the Jewish Law*, 125–31; also with 1 Thess 4:9–12; 2 Thess 3:7–13 and see Peter J. Tomson, "Paul's Practical Instruction in 1 Thess 4:1–12 Read in a Hellenistic and a Jewish Perspective," in *Not in the*

forget the apocalypse in chapter 16, which is linked to the "synoptic apocalypse" yet has independent features.[108]

Chapter 8 deals with fasting and praying "unlike the hypocrites." It is reminiscent of Matt 6:1–18, which similarly stresses almsgiving, prayer, and fasting "unlike the hypocrites." At the previous Tilburg conference, I argued that the halakic substratum of these passages in combination seems to point to the institution by Rabban Gamliel of the daily prayer of Eighteen Benedictions.[109] As I said, this is the sole passage in the Didache that testifies to the conflict with the Pharisees or "rabbis," as they would probably have been called by this time.[110] In sum, the document gives much less of an impression of having been worked over in a polemical atmosphere than Matthew.

The question is how to interpret these observations. As to a dating relative to Jewish developments, one could hypothesize that the Didache just did not undergo a thorough revision similar to Matthew's. This could be because a "book of ritual" embodied less of an ideological investment and required less updating. However, we know too little of the *Sitz im Leben* (a term fully in place here) of a "gospel" as compared with this "book of ritual" to really understand this. What was a gospel used for? Could it be that the Didache was left alone at a somewhat earlier stage than Matthew, with just the one insertion in chapter 8 having been made? It is difficult to make out.

I do not see further clues to the background of the document. The Didache could well be of Antiochian origin as well, though the oft-adduced picturesque argument of the mountainous regions in Syria as an ideal area for wandering prophets sounds unconvincing to my urbanized ears. Is there anything against Caesarea for an option?

9. James

The Epistle of James betrays no evidence of social tension between Jews and Gentiles in any way comparable to Matthew or even the Didache. A general ques-

---

Word Alone: The First Epistle to the Thessalonians (ed. M. D. Hooker; Monographic Series of "Benedictina" 15; Rome: "Benedictina" Publishing, 2003), 120–24.

108. Del Verme, *Didache and Judaism*, 254. But see Jos Verheyden in "Eschatology in the Didache and the Gospel of Matthew," in *Matthew and the Didache; Two Documents from the Same Jewish-Christian Milieu?* (ed. H. van de Sandt; Assen: Van Gorcum, 2005), 193–215.

109. Peter J. Tomson, "The Halakhic Evidence of Didache 8 and Matthew 6 and the Didache Community's Relationship to Judaism," in H. van de Sandt, ed., *Matthew and the Didache*, 131–41.

110. See Matt 23:8. The evolution of the title "rabbi" requires further study in light of the historiographical discussions here reviewed. See meanwhile the considered discussion by Overman, *Matthew's Gospel and Formative Judaism*, 44–48, 122–24, 145–46. See also Hezser, *Social Structure of the Rabbinic Movement*.

tion then is: Does this indicate that a similar conflict had not yet arisen at the time of writing, or, alternatively, that it has already lost its interest? The second option would bring us in the comfortable position of dating the Epistle late and taking it for a sub-apostolic pseudepigraphon, a purely literary creation free from awkward social entanglements. The very absence of "historical color" would seem to suggest as much.

As soon as we focus, however, on the topic of the law, which is pervasive in James, relations between Jews and non-Jews appear to be involved. This need not imply the justly criticized method of reading James on Pauline terms.[111] Rather, it may mean opening our eyes to common themes existing between James and, especially, Romans, even of the same terminology of "hearers" and "doers of the law" being used (ἀκροαταί, ποιηταὶ νόμου).[112] Romans is notable for its attention to the interests of Judaeo-Christians, most visibly in Rom 3:1–2; 9:4–5; 11:25. The same can be observed in James, as in the address to the "twelve tribes in the diaspora"; the stress on the "perfect royal law of freedom", νόμος τέλειος [βασιλικός] τῆς ἐλευθερίας and the emphasis on "no faith without works". Moreover, in both cases popular philosophic shareware of Stoic vintage and the related use of the diatribe form can be observed.[113]

These similarities with Romans, when added to the absence of an acute social conflict, rather point to a situation similar to the one Paul was facing. An important passage in this connection is Gal 2:1–10, where in his polemics with the "Judaizers" over the forced circumcision of Gentile Christians (Gal 2:14; 6:13) the Apostle adduces the apostolic agreement reached by himself and Barnabas with James, John, and Peter. Otherwise, Paul reminds us, "one who has himself circumcized is obliged to keep the whole law" (ὅλον τὸν νόμον, Gal 5:3, and see the same phrase in Jas 2:10). All this is in keeping with the "apostolic rule" Paul quotes in 1 Cor 7:18–19: those called either when circumcised or "having a foreskin" should remain as they are. Except that in the atmosphere of growing tension between Jews and Gentiles, Paul has to plead for the rights of Gentile Christians in Galatians, and of Jewish Christians in Romans.

It is entirely possible to read the definitely non-Pauline letter of James in the same light. "James" is addressing the "twelve tribes in the diaspora" and telling them that "faith without works is dead" and that they must by all means stick to "the royal law of freedom." As in the case of Romans, this context would suppose Jewish Christians to have come under fire, especially from Gentile Christian quarters. But there is a difference in audience. While Paul is explicitly addressing the

---

111. Richard J. Bauckham, *James: Wisdom of James, Disciple of Jesus the Sage* (New Testament Readings; London: Routledge, 1999), 113–20.

112. Rom 2:13; Jas 2:22–23, 25; 4:11. See Tomson, "Täter des Gesetzes," 203–7.

113. See especially the commentary by Martin Dibelius.

Gentile Christians in Rome (11:13) with an appeal for tolerance, James addresses the Jewish Christians in order to encourage them in their specific calling.

On this interpretation, there is no real evidence against a dating of James to around 60.[114] Nor is "James the brother of the Lord" (Gal 1:19; see Josephus, *Ant.* 20.200) an unlikely author at all; the riddle of the evasive structure of the letter combined with a perfect command of Greek really is a question of secondary order.

Apart from such speculations, James also contains material that points to traditions in common with Matthew. I fail, however, to see convincing similarities on the redactional level. The achieved style of Graeco-Judaeo-Christian wisdom makes one think of a higher social milieu than the soldierly Matthew. Some chique Judaeo-Christian colonnade or "stoa" may be thought of, in some provincial capital. Caesarea again? Or, indeed, a place like "Solomon's portico" in pre-66 Jerusalem (Acts 5:12)?

---

114. See considerations by Bauckham, *James: Wisdom of James*, 11–25.

Jewish Christianity, a State of Affairs: Affinities and Differences with Respect to Matthew, James, and the Didache

Joseph Verheyden

The Gospel of Matthew, the Letter of James, and the Didache have all three most probably been produced by Christians of Jewish descent and represent (some of) the views and thoughts, hopes and expectations these groups cherished and wished to promote and divulge. Taking this commonly accepted position as my starting point, I will make two comments.

1. On Defining Jewish Christianity

The first one is about defining Jewish Christianity. This looks hopeless. It is the kind of question many of us would probably rather prefer to avoid being asked because it proves to be so complex and difficult a task to answer it. Yet not a few scholars have tried their hand at it and by doing so, one could say, have shown my reticence to be fully justified.[1] In reviewing the extensive literature on this topic and the broad scale of positions that have been argued, readers could be tempted to settle for one of three possible conclusions. Either the specialists just do not know, or Jewish Christianity is what you make of it, or even there is no such thing as Jewish Christianity. Personally I do not think the third one is true.

---

1. Literature on Jewish Christianity in general has increased exponentially in the past decades. To wit, I just cite two collective works that have appeared recently, both of them featuring ample bibliographies, and both also containing essays on the issue of how to define the phenomenon: Oskar Skarsaune and Reidar Hvalvik, eds., *Jewish Believers in Jesus: The Early Centuries* (Peabody, Mass.: Hendrickson, 2007), with contributions by O. Skarsaune, "Jewish Believers in Jesus in Antiquity: Problems of Definition, Method, and Sources," 3–21 and James Carleton Paget, "The Definition of the Terms *Jewish Christian* and *Jewish Christianity* in the History of Research," 22–52; and Matt Jackson-McCabe, ed., *Jewish Christianity Reconsidered: Rethinking Ancient Groups and Texts* (Minneapolis: Fortress, 2007), with an essay by the editor entitled "What's in a Name? The Problem of 'Jewish Christianity'," 7–38.

There simply is too much independent evidence in and after the New Testament of Christians looking for ways to find a balance between their Jewish origins and their current life as members of a newly established or developing religious community. The other two conclusions would be quite understandable, but perhaps it is not all weeping and gnashing of teeth. It is not necessary for our purpose to add one more survey to the many that have been written on this problem. Rather I just want to formulate a couple of comments.

1. First a word about the material. Basically there are two kinds of evidence, literary and archaeological. All too often discussion of the latter has been polarized by the views of maximalists versus minimalists. The first, represented most prominently by the Franciscan school of Jerusalem, tend to have a very (too?) optimistic view of the amount of evidence that can still be recovered and of our ability to assure its Jewish-Christian origins.[2] The other side is much more (or again, too?) critical and would allow for only a few remnants to be assigned confidently to Jewish-Christian settlements.[3] Suffice it to say that nothing of this material can in any way be linked directly to the communities of Matthew, James, or the didachist.

Part of the literary evidence is secondhand only. It is the information that can be culled from the comments of the Fathers and that for obvious reasons is to be handled with great care. But there is also some firsthand evidence. Some of this has been preserved in the form of a small number of excerpts cited by later authors who are as a rule highly suspicious of their content, yet do not hesitate to speak of "gospels" in this respect (the Gospel of the Ebionites and the Gospel of the Nazoraeans). These gospels pose their own problems of identification and interpretation.[4] Some more material can be found in a number of other writ-

---

2. Prominent members of this school are B. Bagatti, its "founder," E. Testa, and F. Manns. From their many publications, see esp. Bellarmino Bagatti, *The Church from the Circumcision: History and Archaeology of the Judaeo-Christians* (trans. Eugene Hoade; Publications of the Studium Biblicum Franciscanum. Smaller Series 2; Jerusalem: Franciscan Printing Press, 1971); Frédéric Manns, *L'Israel de Dieu: Essais sur le christianisme primitif* (Studium Biblicum Franciscanum Analecta 42; Jerusalem: Franciscan Printing Press, 1996); and the collection of essays by the same author, *Le Judéo-christianisme, mémoire ou prophétie?* (ThH 112: Paris: Beauchesne, 2000). The archaeological evidence is also discussed at length, but somewhat more critically, by Simon C. Mimouni, *Le judéo-christianisme ancien: Essais historiques* (Paris: Cerf, 1998), 337–473.

3. See above all the, at times very critical, assessment by Joan E. Taylor, *Christians and Holy Places: The Myth of Jewish Christian Origins* (Oxford: Clarendon, 1993).

4. For a collection of relevant material on these so-called Jewish-Christian gospels from Patristic (and later) sources see Albertus F. J. Klijn and Gerrit J. Reinink, eds., *Patristic Evidence for Jewish-Christian Sects* (NovTSup 36; Leiden: Brill, 1973); Albertus F. J. Klijn, *Jewish-Christian Gospel Tradition* (VCSup 17; Leiden: Brill, 1992). Compare now also Oskar Skarsaune, "The Ebionites" and Wolfram Kinzig, "The Nazoraeans," in *Jewish Believers in Jesus* (ed. O. Skarsaune and R. Hvalvik), 419–62 and 463–87.

ings of various genres (e.g., the Pseudo-Clementine literature), in which have been incorporated older writings and traditions that are most difficult to unearth again. But fortunately with such writings as Matthew's gospel, James's letter, and the Didache we also possess quite substantial and even complete documents of Jewish-Christian origin, and this of a very early period.

However there is a double problem. These documents are not mentioned in patristic sources dealing with Jewish-Christian groups and they are often only somewhat marginally present in much of the modern discussion and research on Jewish Christianity. The former can readily be explained. The Fathers evidently regarded Jewish Christianity as a heterodox movement and were intent on cutting off any possible link with the earliest, in their opinion orthodox, communities of the first century. The second observation is more difficult to handle, but it is nevertheless what one finds in the literature. To give only a few examples. All three of these documents are understandably missing in Marcel Simon's classical study *Verus Israel*, which focuses on later developments within Jewish Christianity only.[5] Simon Mimouni in his monograph on Jewish Christianity does mention Matthew and Didache, but not James, and the former two are apparently not really considered to be major exponents of the history of Jewish Christianity.[6] In his survey of Jewish Christianity in *The Cambridge History of Judaism*, James Carleton Paget reserves a place for Matthew and James, but not for Didache.[7]

But in a sense the secondary role these documents are given in recent surveys on the history of Jewish Christianity is also quite understandable. Two of them—James and Didache—were apparently not known or almost not received in later Jewish Christianity, nor for that in the rest of the Church. And the one document that has left its traces in later so-called Jewish-Christian texts and milieus was obviously not capable of offering by itself the kind of support and solutions these groups needed and were looking for. They made use of Matthew in composing their own gospels,[8] but apparently this gospel could not claim any sort of supremacy over these other writings, and it certainly did not reach the kind of status it held quite soon in many "orthodox" Gentile-Christian circles throughout the second century. The latter may explain the relative lack of success

---

5. *Verus Israel: A Study of the Relations between Christians and Jews in the Roman Empire C.E. 135–425* (Oxford: Oxford University Press, 1986); trans. of *Verus Israel: Etude sur les relations entre chrétiens et juifs dans l'empire romain (135–425)* (2nd ed.; Paris: Boccard, 1983).

6. See his *Le judéo-christianisme ancien*.

7. "Jewish Christianity," in *The Cambridge History of Judaism* (4 vols.; ed. W. Horbury, W. D. Davies, J. Sturdy; Cambridge: Cambridge University Press, 1999), 3:731–75.

8. For evidence of this with regard to the Gospel of the Ebionites, see, e.g., Joseph Verheyden, "Epiphanius on the Ebionites," in *The Image of the Judaeo-Christians in Ancient Jewish and Christian Literature* (ed. P. J. Tomson and D. Lambers-Petry; WUNT 158; Tübingen: Mohr Siebeck, 2003), 182–208.

of Matthew among later Jewish-Christian groups, but it is also in itself significant for assessing the "Jewish-Christian" character of Matthew's gospel. It seems it was deemed to be insufficiently "Jewish-Christian" by some to become their voice and standard bearer, yet sufficiently open or manageable to be received by others who had distantiated themselves from such Jewish-Christian groups. The latter move may have strengthened whatever reservations there might have existed about Matthew within certain Christian communities of Jewish descent.

2. Second, the criteria and characteristics. Scholars have increasingly become aware of how difficult it is to establish general criteria and categories taking into account the great variety of opinions and positions that is echoed in the material and that apparently is itself a major characteristic of ancient Jewish Christianity. As a result one can observe, on the one hand, a growing dissatisfaction with attempts to identify "Jewish Christianity" as one or even the distinctive force and phenomenon within or of early Christianity and, on the other hand, a growing concern somehow to validate the evident diversity. Thus, Jean Daniélou's *Théologie du Judéo-christianisme* is now widely criticized for its all-embracing claims, labeling all of early Christian theology as "Jewish-Christian."[9] It is the kind of critique one can read in many a survey.[10] As yet it has not been countered by the efforts of the Jerusalem Franciscans to throw in the archaeological evidence.

But there is more. It is not only that there never has existed "one" Jewish Christianity, but even the search for one overarching criterion or category that would (more or less) hold together the various forms and groups of "Jewish-Christians" has become problematic. In the same surveys I just mentioned, one will find that Simon's "ethnic" definition (a Jewish-Christian is a Christian of Jewish descent who in one way or another wants to remain true to his roots) has now largely been abandoned because this factor was played out in different ways by different groups and in part also because it does not take into account the presence of "judaizing" tendencies among what apparently are non-Jewish groups.[11] Definitions that are solely based on matters of "doctrine" or "praxis"

---

9. *The Theology of Jewish Christianity*; London: Darton, Longman & Todd, 1964); trans. of *Théologie du judéo-christianisme* (Tournai: Desclée, 1958).

10. See, e.g., Jean-Daniel Kaestli, "Où en est le débat sur le judéo-christianisme?," in *Le déchirement: Juifs et chrétiens au premier siècle* (ed. D. Marguerat; MdB 32; Genève: Labor et Fides, 1996), 244–46: "En conclusion, la catégorie introduite par Daniélou est à abandonner. Elle est abstraite, sans relation avec des groupes historiques déterminés, basée sur des oppositions artificielles" (ibid., 246). See Carleton Paget, "Definition of the Terms *Jewish Christian* and *Jewish Christianity*," 737–39; Mimouni, *Le judéo-christianisme ancien*, 42–45 and 326–31; and most recently, Jackson-McCabe, "What's in a Name," 23–27.

11. Kaestli, "Où en est le débat," 248–50. Carleton Paget, "Definition of the Terms *Jewish Christian* and *Jewish Christianity*," 733–34: "To accept a purely ethnic definition of Jewish Christianity is not really to define anything meaningful at all" (ibid., 734), with reference to Georg Strecker, "Judenchristentum," in *TRE* 17: 311.

meet with the same kind of problems.[12] The Church Fathers in any case never tried to narrow the issue to just one of these aspects.[13]

The sole way out of the impasse, it seems, is to go for a definition that is broad enough somehow to include several or all of the features just mentioned. It is this kind of definition that is proposed by Mimouni: "Le judéo-christian-isme ancien est une formulation récente désignant des juifs qui ont reconnu la messianité de Jésus, qui ont reconnu ou n'ont pas reconnu la divinité du Christ, mais qui tous continuent à observer Torah."[14] This is a workable approach on account that one acknowledges, first, that "Jewish Christianity" is thus of neces-sity defined in terms of "varieties" or "specimens" and that one better speak of "Jewish Christianities," second, that it is best not taken to be a complete cata-logue of all the qualifications one must meet to be labeled a Jewish-Christian, and, finally, that after all it very much remains a modern scholarly construct.

Carleton Paget favors a similar approach when pleading for a definition that is "sufficiently narrow to refer to something we can call an entity, and sufficiently broad or open-ended to take account of a range of evidence, almost all of which is literary."[15] And it is something of this kind, indeed a flexible and functional definition, that is argued for by Petri Luomanen when proposing "to replace one-sided definitions with the study of indicators of Jewish-Christian profiles. This approach focuses on several issues that have had key roles in early-Jewish-Chris-tian communities."[16] Luomanen lists several of these "indicators."[17] So there are many ways to be or present oneself as a Jewish-Christian, but not all should be traveled through. A variety of characteristics is what the sources show, but they do not tell us that there was an "absolute" list.

3. Third, and building on the previous. For modern scholars, then, defin-ing forms of "Jewish Christianity" is not only about identifying characteristics

---

12. For a critique of the latter, see among others, Carleton Paget, "Definition of the Terms *Jewish Christian* and *Jewish Christianity,*" 744–46; Jackson-McCabe, "What's in a Name," 32–34.

13. See Carleton Paget, who observes with regard to the latter of these two: "After all, it is clear that when heresiologists came to discuss groups that clearly adopted Jewish practices, they often also discussed their theological opinions" ("Definition of the Terms *Jewish Christian* and *Jewish Christianity,*" 736).

14. *Le judéo-christianisme ancien*, 70; the chapter is a revised version of his "Pour une définition nouvelle du judéo-christianisme ancien," *NTS* 38 (1992): 161–86.

15. "Definition of the Terms *Jewish Christian* and *Jewish Christianity,*" 740.

16. "Where Did Another Rich Man Come From? The Jewish-Christian Profile of the Story about a Rich Man in the 'Gospel of the Hebrews' (Origen, *Comm. in Matth.* 15.14)," in *VC* 57 (2003): 268.

17. Ibid., 268–69: observing "Jewish practices"; adhering to "Jewish ideas"; the pedigree of the group; the role of Jesus in its worshipping and ideology; the status of baptism in the name of Jesus; and the function of all these features in shaping the identity of the group as border markers over against "those outside."

or establishing criteria, but rather, and perhaps even more so, about describing and assessing how a certain, open, set of concerns and interests, doctrinal and practical ones, was dealt with and accommodated by various groups in various ways in and while acknowledging Jesus Christ and interpreting his message, and how these concerns and interests in turn have shaped the thought and life of these Christians and their appreciation of other Christians ("Pauline" Christians) and of their Jewish neighbors. It is a matter of assessing how these groups were handling their own heritage. And this in turn was a matter of finding a balance between the old and the new, of giving a place to the belief in Jesus within the framework of Jewish religious tradition. But it was not only about balance, it was also a matter of gradations, and in the end, of "orthodoxy." Upholding (aspects of) Torah obviously was a core issue among Jewish Christians, but they did so in different ways. In a similar way, criticising Paul can be a primary or a less important activity and goal among different groups. Some of these groups would end up on the "wrong side," others would prove able to find their place in the "Great Church."[18] Hence, it is not just what is said that counts and should be looked into, but also, as far as possible, how, why, and when this is said. All these aspects and factors taken together will determine the degree of "Jewish Christianity" of a text and of the group that speaks through and unfortunately also hides behind it. In a word, there is no standard definition of Jewish Christianity and there never was. There are only ways and forms of being a Jewish Christian and we have only a very limited access to them. Perhaps then the real challenge is not to focus on what holds the evidence together, but rather to recognize fully that the evidence is of necessity and by definition diverse because of the nature of the phenomenon itself.

2. MATTHEW, JAMES AND THE DIDACHE AS JEWISH-CHRISTIAN DOCUMENTS

My second comment has more directly to do with Matthew, James, and the Didache, and specifically with the question of how the identity markers that can be found in these documents can reveal us something about the self-identification of these groups or communities as Jewish Christians. I have chosen to focus on the recent monograph by Gunnar Garleff that has the double advantage that it precisely deals with the issue of identity in all three of these documents and that it offers for this purpose a model for analyzing how these communities have

---

18. Most recently, this aspect has been emphasized by Skarsaune when arguing for a distinction between those Jews who came to believe in Jesus but "at the same time continued a wholly Jewish way of life" and those who finally "chose to become more or less 'orthodox' Christians within mixed communities" ("Jewish Believers in Jesus in Antiquity," 4). The former Skarsaune proposes to call "Jewish Christians," as defined by Mimouni, but for the latter he prefers the phrase "Jewish believers in Jesus." The distinction is interesting and obviously also reflects something of what actually did happen.

described and established their identity as a group ("collective identity") through the texts they produced.[19]

Garleff distinguishes three categories and six criteria for identifying aspects of this collective identity.[20] Two of these criteria are formal ones. They have to do with indicators of continuity and differentiation, with how a group or community creates a link with its own past and roots and how it also demarcates its present situation from that past. Three other criteria are described as the means by which the group expresses its identity. These are labeled by Garleff the "Story" (he uses the English word), the "Ethos," and the "Ritus." The first is not just about the choice for a literary genre, but also about how the group handles the story of Jesus in expressing its identity. The second and third are about the norms and values the group cultivates and lives by and about the praxis it has developed for building its community life as a separate group and for allowing possible candidates to join the group. A category or level that Garleff distinguishes has to do with how the group organizes itself as a community, that is, with issues of hierarchisation and with the critical reflection upon it.[21]

Garleff is not specifically interested in demonstrating the Jewish-Christian character of any of the documents he is studying. However, one should realize that while the criteria he mentions probably do not all carry the same weight in bringing out the Jewish-Christian identity of a particular writing or community, they all can and even must be interpreted in light of that specific situation. "Being a Jewish Christian," or for that, "a Jewish believer in Jesus," is not just one factor among others, but rather the one overall component that holds together all these different identity markers and that rules the way these are handled. This is true for all criteria, even for the last one. The whole issue of gradually developing separate and autonomous forms of organiszation and hierarchization obviously is put in a totally different perspective when undertaken by Gentile Christians or by Jews claiming to be or have become Christians, acting within the orbit and traditions of their own "native" religion, or trying to break away from it and thereby consciously challenging the established order with its structures and its hierarchy, which they had belonged to or had believed in so far.

Garleff shows that the three documents, while all relying on the same set of criteria, apparently display a great variety and diversity in formulating and handling these criteria.[22] The central question, as I see it, is then to establish to what extent these differences reflect not just different ways of expressing

---

19. *Urchristliche Identität in Matthäusevangelium, Didache und Jakobusbrief* (Beiträge zum Verstehen der Bibel 9; Münster: LIT, 2004).

20. This framework is developed and described in detail in the second chapter of his book (ibid., 26–47).

21. See the table in ibid., 47, at the end of his second chapter.

22. See the table in ibid., 325.

the same identity, but maybe also different identities. One should of course be extremely careful in drawing firm conclusions from these differences for distinguishing between the various groups that produced these documents, let alone for reconstructing a "history of Jewish Christianity" in this early period. Yet the differences are real and should be accounted for in defining each of these three documents. This is obviously true for the way each community positions itself with regard to its Jewish roots and demarcates itself from "the others," but also for what it has to tell about its own organization, as well as for the means it has chosen to mediate its identity, which is the most complex, some might say weakest, part of Garleff's model.

I begin with the first category and will focus on the differentiation. Matthew is generally recognized to be singled out from the two other documents by its strong and sustained polemics against representatives of the Jewish religious authorities. These polemics are part and parcel of Matthew's story of Jesus. They are found both in discourse and in narrative material, in various forms and genres. They cannot be dismissed as echoes of a distant past or of intra-Christian disputes. The nature and vehemence of the polemics also shows that the links are still very close, or rather, that the wounds are still fresh. The break is still very much on the minds and in the hearts of Matthew's readers.[23] No such kind of harsh polemics is found in Didache or James. In the Didache "the others" are Jews, as in Matthew, but they really have already become "others," members of a clearly distinct religious community from which one has separated and wants to remain separated. They are occasionally referred to in order to illustrate the difference, not to explain how this came about, as this is still very much the case in Matthew.[24] In James "the others" even have taken a completely different identity. They are not Jews but fellow Christians. But these remain relatively marginal and indeed rather shadowy figures that are not further identified beyond the cipher of the "rich brothers."[25]

---

23. Or, as Garleff puts it with reference to Matt 23, "Durch die narrative Verknüpfung mit der Konfliktgeschichte Jesu und den gleichzeitigen Gegenwartsbezug (Mt 8–12) wird die Weherede zur Ätiologie der Trennung der mt Gemeinde vom formativen Judentum. Sie verarbeitet somit die neue Existenz ausserhalb des Synagogenverbandes" (*Urchristliche Identität in Matthäusevangelium*, 75).

24. Garleff recognizes the first element in this description (the otherness) when observing, with reference to a keyword in addressing the others that figures in Matthew and in Didache alike, "Als Fazit kann hinsichtlich des Stichwortes ὑποκριταί festgehalten werden, dass sich die Didache in Did 8,1f von anderen jüdischen Gruppen abgrenzt" (ibid., 123), but he does not develop the second one.

25. The experience of difference is explicitated in two ways, through the diaspora motif and through that of "the wealthy." Garleff points out that the contours of these opponents of the author of the letter can be somewhat delineated by contrasting James's critique to Paul's way of handling matters of hierarchy within the context of the house church: "PsJakobus' Kritik am Patronat ist total, er will eine andere Gemeindestruktur, in der die Egalität höher gestellt ist

As for the means by which this sense of identity is shaped, and keeping to the categories proposed by Garleff, one has again to admit that there are obvious differences between Matthew, Didache, and James. The difference is not just about a mere shift in emphasis from "Story" (Matthew) to "Ritus" (Didache) to "Ethos" (James) in selecting the primary means for expressing the collective identity of the group. The choice for "Story," "Ritus," or "Ethos" can be paraphrased as a choice for either a descriptive, a prescriptive, or a combination of a reflective-admonitory approach to the question. It further appears that Matthew by opting for the "Story" component has better succeeded in integrating the other two components than have Didache or James. Garleff rightly characterizes Matthew as an "inclusive story." Matthew constructs the identity of his community by telling its story through that of Jesus and his disciples. The other aspects are made an integral part of that story. Garleff shows how this works for the "Ethos" component, which is being formulated or developed, sometimes even somewhat artificially, as part of the "Story" of Jesus's ministry.[26] But the same is true also for the "Ritus" component that Garleff says is lacking in Matthew. One could maybe speak of a "rituelles Defizit" with regard to James, where this component is basically reduced to a somewhat marginal note on praying for the sick (4:13), but that is definitely too strong a label with regard to Matthew. Prescripts for Christian behavior on fasting or prayer, on the common meal, and on baptism occur also in Matthew. These prescriptions are by no means marginal, but they are integrated in the story, respectively as the subject of Jesus's teaching or as part of his controversies with the scribes and Pharisees, as a dramatic event in his life, and as a commandment of the risen Lord at the very end and climax of the Gospel.

The "Ethos" and "Ritus" the Matthean community keeps and propagates and identifies with are founded in Jesus Christ. Neither the didachist nor James can or wish to make such a claim. The former knows the story of Jesus as told by Matthew and occasionally alludes to and borrows from it, and James naturally assumes it, but it does not play that decisive a role in shaping the identity of the community as it does in the Gospel of Matthew. It would seem then that Matthew's option for the "Story" component as its primary means for communicating its identity makes all the difference.

A similar kind of difference also exists between Didache and James. The didachist's interest in "christianizing" ethical teaching and ritual praxis that has

---

als die Hierarchie, damit stellt er sich der urchristlichen Entwicklung und auch Paulus entgegen" (ibid., 269).

26. See his analysis of the Sermon on the Mount and the comments on Matt 5:17–20 and the antitheses: "Entsprechend der Positionierung des Textes [i.e., 5:17–20] in der Komposition der Jesusgeschichte ist es bezeichnend, dass Jesus sich hier selbst in Opposition zu diesen beiden Gruppen bringt, denen er im Evangelium bis dahin noch nicht als handelnde Person begegnet ist" (ibid., 68).

its origins in Jewish tradition results in making the teaching of the community as formulated and passed on by Didache the sole norm and source of authority. In the end it is the Didache itself that prescribes how Christians should behave and live.[27] For James, by contrast, it is the Law, here rebaptized as the "Law of freedom," that is still claimed to regulate the life of the community.[28] In short, the preference for one means over another involves moving away from Torah as the primary or even the sole normative instance towards Jesus, and even towards the community (and/or its leaders).

A word finally on the issue of the organization of the community. In each of the documents there appears to exist a strong connotation between the way difference is created and the views it holds on developing community structures. This is again particularly clear in Matthew, which promotes egalitarian tendencies and is openly critical of hierarchical structures. The two obviously go together. They are combined and developed in some detail as part of the controversy with the scribes and Pharisees when contesting their claims and privileges and offering the "Christian" way as the better alternative (23:8–12). But it is precisely the ongoing controversy that forces the community also to look for ways to organize itself as an autonomous and independent entity.[29] Similar links can also be found in the Didache and in James's letter. If "the others" are no longer seen as "opponents" but as members of another movement, as in the Didache, the community has to come to terms with the issue of how to organize itself as an

---

27. Garleff illustrates this on the basis of the phrase κατὰ τὴν ἐντολήν, of which he concludes: "die Formel selbst (lässt) keine Rückschlussmöglichkeiten auf eine Detailstory zu. Sie zeigt jedoch, wie der Didachist seine ethischen Anweisungen verstanden wissen will: Sie sind Gebote" (ibid., 150).

28. This reinterpretation of the concept of "Law of freedom" is made most obvious in a section such as 2:8–12, but it is also at the background of 2:14–26. "Der Jakobusbrief warnt vor einem Heilsautomatismus, der den Christen zu einer zu schnellen Heilsgewissheit verleitet. Darum setzt er dem Hören des Wortes der Wahrheit das Tun des Gesetzes der Freiheit entgegen und mahnt zur ganzheitlichen christlichen Existenz, die zur vollkommenen Identität werden soll. Der kontroverstheologische Akzent liegt darin, dass Jakobus eine klare Unterscheidung oder gar Trennung von Evangelium und Gesetz nicht kennt, vielmehr sind sie für ihn das eine verbindliche und kontinuierliche Wort Gottes" (ibid., 284).

29. Garleff seems to be aware of the tension there potentially is in Matthew between criticism on the one hand, and the interest in and need for forms of hierarchisation on the other (ibid., 76–77: "Dagegen gibt es aber auch Hinweise, dass das MtEv dies sesshaften Sympathisantengruppen als Ortsgemeinden stärken will. Die Übertragung der Binde- und Lösegewalt an Kollektive in Mt 18,18 kann als solches Signal gelesen werden. Auch die Existenz von Schriftgelehrten in der Gemeinde deutet darauf hin. Aber anders als in der späteren Didache propagiert das MtEv für die ortsfeste Gemeinde noch keine eigenen Ämter, die auf eine Hierarchie hindeuten"), but he looks upon it as developments that are linked to the missionary activity of the community rather than as a consequence of a struggle to overcome the gradually deteriorating relations with the synagogue and its leaders.

autonomous entity with its own structures and ministries.[30] James, for his part, shows an interest in forms of collective leadership that may echo a critique of, or at least some reticence about, certain inclinations towards a more centralized form of organization in (some of) the communities he is addressing.[31] But after all this may be a more ambivalent case, for the Letter at the same time also contains a critical note of more independent-minded communities that need to be "reminded" or maybe even "corrected" on this point by someone who presents himself in a way as the spokesperson of some kind of "central authority," a position that is not without significance when pretending to address "the Church in the Dispersion." *Magistri non sunt multiplicandi*!

The evidence from second-century "heretical" Jewish-Christian groups shows that there are significant differences among these groups that modern scholars nevertheless have tried to bring together under the one label of "Jewish Christians." The evidence from Matthew, Didache, and James seems to confirm this picture. At the risk of overgeneralizing, I would summarize the differences as follows. As I understand it, Matthew's community has already pulled out of the Jewish world in which it originally had taken form. It claims it has not given up the Law, only it believes it has found the definite key to read and interpret it.[32] As a matter of fact, the dispute over the authority for interpreting the Law and the break that resulted from it were the very reason why this gospel was written. The Gospel of Matthew tells the story of a drama that at the same time is an attempt at healing the trauma it caused for the community and maybe also for

---

30. And the Didache itself is proof that is was all but an easy task. The list of "ministers" runs from teachers to bishops and deacons, but it also includes the more debatable categories of apostles-missionaries and the apparently even more controversial one of the prophets (see ibid., 189–98), which makes it rather more difficult correctly to assess the subject and the limits of the "fraternal correction" that is mentioned in 15:4. Garleff refers to the latter at the end of the section, almost symbolically, as if a corrective to the impression of hierarchization that might have been created by the interest in ministries in what had preceded: "In Summa lässt sich für die Didache nicht feststellen, dass sie von einer wie auch immer zu beschreibenden Gemeinde-hierarchie ausgeht. . . . Für eine egalitäre Gemeindestruktur spricht nicht zuletzt die correctio fraterna in Did 15,4" (ibid., 199). But can we be so sure that this rule really was or could still be applied to all members of the community once the movement towards hierarchization had begun? The latter must in any case have had some effect on the way the principle of 15:4 could still function or be appealed to.

31. So Garleff who thinks this view is expressed in a double way, through the importance given to forms of collective leadership and through the efforts of the author of the letter to describe and present himself as a member of such a body. "Überblickt man die beiden Signale zur Gemeindeorganisation im Jak, so ist festzustellen, dass der Verfasser sowohl in 3,1 als auch in 5,14 Kollektive nennt. Ein einzelnes herausragendes Leitungsamt oder nur eine einzelne "Amts"-Person ist nicht im Blick" (ibid., 315).

32. On this hotly debated issue, see now the fine analysis by Paul Foster, *Community, Law and Mission in Matthew's Gospel* (WUNT 2/177; Tübingen: Mohr Siebeck, 2004).

fellow Jewish Christians. The future it offers and the solution it proposes was not new—the mission outside of Israel did not start with Matthew—but it was a new move for his community, one that needed to be explained and that inevitably would further consolidate the break with its Jewish neighbors. Matthew's was a Jewish-Christian community before the break, and he made sure it could go on considering itself this way afterwards if it wished, even when "turning to the Gentiles." The Law has not been put out of force but has been "fulfilled" in the teaching of Jesus, which eventually means it can now even also be "obeyed" by non-Jewish converts.

The Didache apparently has left this trauma behind. It focuses on the internal life and organization of the community and only occasionally refers to those former co-religionists who now have become strangers that are only invoked to mirror, in a negative way, the rules and prescriptions the didachist wants to promote. Its shows no particular concern about saving the status of the Law, but by recuperating or relying so heavily on the ethical teaching and religious practices of Jewish tradition, it fully proves how much it still values its past, and so again there are good reasons for labeling Didache "Jewish-Christian."

James obviously does not question the status of the Law but rather reflects on its commandments for what the Law itself has to say. He shows no particular interest in the struggle for authority, for who can decide on the correct interpretation of Torah, a matter that is central to Matthew. "The others" are not prominently present and they are not to be found among fellow Jews, but among such groups and individuals that apparently are following other leaders and experimenting with other forms of community building. James is not crudely polemical and he certainly does not openly oppose any mission to the Gentiles. But the way he serenely and consistently opts for "the Law of freedom" as his guide and focus again very much makes his letter a "Jewish-Christian" document.

In short, Matthew describes the process that led to the transformation of his community and finds in it the remedy for the crisis it caused. The didachist lives in this transformed community and starts building it according to its own rules and principles and its own rituals, thereby heavily relying on its own past. James is aware that there are some "others" who could be said to have been "transformed," but it is not the kind of solution that appeals to its author or that he seeks to promote. There apparently are indeed many ways and various "degrees" of being "Jewish Christian."

This conclusion raises two further questions. The first one has to do with the label "Jewish Christian." Does this really mean anything, or is it an empty box? And if it still makes sense to speak of Jewish Christians with regard to Matthew's Gospel, the Didache, and James's Letter alike, what is it that holds them together and might link them to other such groups? The answer is probably not to be found in matters of ethics, or ritual and praxis, nor in doctrine, but in the way these various groups and communities are positioning themselves in relation to the Judaism they originated from, hence in what Garleff calls the formal criteria. What these groups have in common is, negatively, that they do not outrightly reject their Jewish roots and religious heritage, nor do they even struggle to free themselves from it, but, positively, rather try to "master" their past and keep it functioning as well as possible within the new reality that is installed with and by Jesus and that they also fully recognize as such. Further what holds them together is a sense for the dramatic, or for tragedy if you wish. This can be exemplified in many ways. One can easily imagine it must have been regarded as quite a statement, both from a Christian and from a Jewish side, when the Didache so emphatically christianizes prayers that it most probably took over from the liturgical praxis of its own Jewish past. A same kind of ambiguity speaks from the attempts one finds in these documents at emphasising the links with Israel, Garleff's first formal criterion. These attempts cannot be understood adequately and fully as a mere act of provocation or appropriation of Jewish tradition. But they could readily be understood as such by the synagogue. Is it a sign of confidence that a group goes on to "work" with or tries to "integrate" elements of the tradition it was gradually leaving behind, or is it not rather a somewhat desperate attempt at connecting the new present with the past by interpreting one's own situation as an ongoing process rather than as a break? The truth, and the tragedy of Jewish Christianity as a whole, probably is that it could well be the one and the other depending on which side was commenting on it.

My second question has to do with the limits of this apparently quite flexible concept of Jewish Christianity. What the Church Fathers report on "Jewish-Christian" groups of a later time gives the impression that some at least had wandered so far away from each other that they must have regarded the others as complete strangers. Would the same already be true also for Matthew, James, and the didachist, and for their communities? Were the groups who produced these documents still on speaking terms, and would they still have appreciated each other's efforts in marking out their identity. It would seem that this was after all still the case for the Didache with regard to Matthew, especially if one accepts that the former was familiar with that gospel, as I think it was, even when it was dealing with "other" but "related" matters of Jewish tradition. I am somewhat more skeptical whether this would also apply for James, but am tempted to answer the question positively, if only because he does not appear to have explicitly rejected one potentially dividing issue, namely, the mission to the Gentiles.

PART 3
COMMUNITY AND IDENTITY

Apostles, Teachers, and Evangelists:
Stability and Movement of Functionaries in Matthew, James, and the Didache

Jonathan A. Draper

One of the longest running debates in the study of the New Testament and the Apostolic Fathers since the Reformation has been the matter of ecclesiastical functionaries in the early church and their relation to modern church polity. From its first publication in 1883, the existence side by side in the same text of apostles, prophets, teachers, bishops and deacons in the Didache ensured that it would be the subject of controversy. Adolf von Harnack's famous argument for the emergence of "early Catholicization" in *Die Mission und Ausbreitung des Christentums in den ersten drei Jahrhunderten,* first published in 1902, arose out of the findings of his 1884 commentary, *Die Lehre der zwölf Apostel,*[1] and made the instructions of the Didache the center point of his reconstruction. Gerd Theissen's influential study, *Soziologie der Jesus Bewegung* (1977), essentially presents the same picture.[2] The missing piece of the puzzle for Von Harnack was provided by Did. 15:1–2, where it appeared to him that bishops and deacons are in the process of replacing (apostles), prophets, and teachers, so that charismatic ministry is being replaced by hierarchical functionaries in the emerging Catholic church. On this reasoning, the titles apostles, prophets, and teachers belong together in a scarcely differentiated way so that Heinrich Kraft puts it as follows: "Like the apostolate, the charismatic teaching office is also a special instance of

---

1. Adolf von Harnack, *Die Lehre der zwölf Apostel nebst Untersuchungen zur ältesten Geschichte der Kirchenverfassung und des Kirchenrechts* (TU 2/1–2; Leipzig: Hinrichs, 1884).

2. First published in English as *Sociology of Early Palestinian Christianity* (trans. J. Bowden; Philadelphia: Fortress, 1978; British ed., *The First Followers of Jesus: A Sociological Analysis of Early Christianity* (London: SCM Press, 1978). For an attempt to trace the history of this influence and to present an alternative hypothesis, see Jonathan A. Draper, "Weber, Theissen, and 'Wandering Charismatics' in the Didache," *JECS* 6 (1998): 541–76.

the prophetic office."[3] He is followed in this by H. A. Stempel,[4] who finds the teacher to be the predominant form of charismatic official in the local community. However, the evidence has proved slippery and certainly there is a need for a reevaluation of the evidence, particularly in the light of the emerging recognition that the Didache, like Matthew's Gospel and the Epistle of James, should be read together against a Jewish Christian or Christian Jewish background.[5] This paper is an attempt to read the evidence again, with an eye on the particular issue of the identity and nature of the respective leadership provided by "wandering charismatics" and the officials in the "settled local communities" that supported them.

The word "charismatic" emerges from the foundational work in the field of sociology by Max Weber, which was published posthumously in 1922 as *Wirtschaft und Gesellschaft: Grundriss der verstehenden Soziologie*.[6] It constituted a key principle in his theory of the three forms of legitimate leadership: traditional, charismatic, and legal-rational. In his understanding, times of crisis throw up a new kind of leader "not like other men," who owes his authority simply to an inner quality manifesting aspects of the numinous. After the death of the charismatic leader, a process of "routinization of charisma" replaces this initial personal charismatic leadership with an institutional leadership. The difficulty in using this language and this model of Weber in the study of the Didache is that Weber was himself influenced by Adolf von Harnack's thesis of "early Catholicization," which, as we have seen, was itself based on his interpretation of the Didache.[7] In this study we will use the term, if at all, in its narrow sense as referring to leadership, which is understood by the leader and the community in which s/he exercises leadership as authority that is unmediated since it springs directly from the inspiration of the Holy Spirit.

-----

3. Heinrich Kraft, "Die Anfänge des geistliches Amtes," *TLZ* 100 (1975): 93; cited in Hermann-A. Stempel, "Der Lehrer in der 'Lehre der Zwölf Apostel'," *VC* 34 (1980): 209–17.

4. Ibid., 209–17.

5. See Jonathan A. Draper, "The Holy Vine of David made known to the Gentiles through God's servant Jesus: 'Christian Judaism' in the Didache," in *Jewish Christianity Reconsidered: Rethinking Ancient Groups and Texts* (ed. M. A. Jackson-MacCabe; Minneapolis: Fortress, 2007), 257–83. Note especially here the major work of Huub van de Sandt and David Flusser, *The Didache: Its Jewish Sources and its Place in Early Judaism and Christianity* (CRINT 3/5; Assen: Van Gorcum, 2002). A recent study by Gunnar Garleff (*Urchristliche Identität in Matthäusevangelium, Didache und Jakobusbrief* [Beiträge zum Verstehen der Bibel 9; Münster: Lit Verlag, 2004]) has contributed significantly to this process with his attempt to plot the development of early Christian identity in a trajectory across Matthew, Didache, and James utilizing social-scientific methodology.

6. The English translation was published as *Economy and Society: An Outline of Interpretive Sociology* (ed. G. Roth and C. Wittich; trans. Ephraim Fischoff; Berkeley and Los Angeles: University of California Press, 1978).

7. Draper, "Weber, Theissen, and 'Wandering Charismatics,'" 541–76.

A second and related problem concerns the epithet "wandering," which is often combined with the "charismatics" in discussions of early Christianity. The terminology relates again to Weber's understanding that the charismatic leader bursts on the scene, unencumbered by tradition, property, family, and material concerns. However, not all travel, even in the pursuit of religious goals, is itinerant. It may be undertaken on a temporary basis with the intention of returning to normal life after the completion of the journey. Here, a distinction will be made between permanent itinerant travel and temporary purposive travel. Further, Weber understood the itinerant phase as limited to the lifetime of the charismatic leader, while the leader's death is followed by a period of "routinization" in which the leader's followers settle.

A final difficulty relates to the use of the term "functionary," which is also not without its problems, since it brings to mind some kind of formal position in a community, when the function could be exercised spontaneously by a number of persons as need arises. Here we will use "functionary" to describe a person who holds a recognized position in the community related to a particular task or "function," whether they are paid or not and whether they are formally "ordained" and appointed to that position or not.

1. Settled and Wandering Functionaries in Matthew's Gospel

1.1. Introduction

It goes without saying that Matthew's Gospel is no Church Order or Manual of Discipline, but a narrative standing in the tradition of, and in partial dependence on, Mark. Therefore any information about the church and its functionaries in Matthew's own time and situation has to be inferred from his redaction of Mark and "Q" and by his (re)arrangement of his source material in the narrative. It describes itself as a "Book of the Genealogy of Jesus Christ, Son of David, Son of Abraham." This marks it out already as a text with a dual orientation, first towards the covenant people, the Israel on whose throne God had declared a son of David would sit for ever, but on the other hand also towards the Gentiles who would receive a blessing through Abraham, "father of multitudes of nations/Gentiles" (πατὴρ πλήθους ἐθνῶν, Gen 17:4; see Rom 4:13–25). The narrative signal of Matthew's opening is confirmed by the concluding commission to the eleven disciples to go to all nations. So it is not surprising that it is difficult to obtain a clear picture of the kind of social and leadership structures prevailing in Matthew's community, which stands at an historical crossroads for Jewish Christianity in relation to the Gentile mission, as Ulrich Luz has argued.[8] Fol-

---

8. Ulrich Luz, *Matthew 1–7: A Continental Commentary* (Minneapolis: Fortress, 1989), 84–87.

lowing Luz's insistence on an interpretation of Matthew that "looks through the window" to take account of the historical circumstances and community that produced it,[9] Garleff has rightly argued that story is one medium for the identity construction of the community in which it is narrated, both in reflecting and creating norms.[10] It provides signals of both continuity and of change, and this applies to its representation of leadership as much as to other issues.

1.2. The Disciples and Mobility of Functionaries in Matthew

It is striking that, as has often been noted, Matthew broadens the geographical scope of Jesus's proclamation of the good news at the beginning of his ministry beyond what he found in Mark: firstly by the reference from Isa 9:1–2 to Galilee as "Galilee of the Gentiles," which brings great light to "those who dwell in the region and shadow of death" (4:12–16); secondly by the substitution of εἰς ὅλην τὴν Συρίαν (4:24) for Mark's εἰς ὅλην τὴν περίχωρον τῆς Γαλιλαίας (1:28) to describe the extent to which Jesus's reputation had spread; thirdly by the addition of a description of the crowds who followed Jesus, which includes those from the wider region, including areas normally (but not necessarily) associated with Gentiles, καὶ ἠκολούθησαν αὐτῷ ὄχλοι πολλοὶ ἀπὸ τῆς Γαλιλαίας καὶ Δεκαπόλεως καὶ Ἱεροσολύμων καὶ Ἰουδαίας καὶ πέραν τοῦ Ἰορδάνου (4:25). This broad context extending from Judaea and Perea up to Syria[11] provides the setting for the delivery of Jesus's authoritative teaching in the Sermon on the Mount, which Matthew inserts between Mark 1:28 and 29 to serve as the foundation of the new Christian community. I have argued elsewhere that this summary of Jesus's teaching found in "Q" sets the basic catechetical teaching of the community on the lips of Jesus.[12] In Matthew, significantly, the teaching is given by

---

9. Ulrich Luz, *Matthew in History: Interpretation, Influence, and Effects* (Minneapolis: Fortress, 1994), 24, 41.

10. Garleff, *Urchristliche Identität in Matthäusevangelium*, 48.

11. While there is widespread agreement on the likelihood of Syria as the place of origin for Matthew's Gospel, there is less agreement on the precise location (see Luz, *Matthew 1–7*, 90–92). However, an increasing number of scholars have come to support Syrian Antioch as the community that produced it and have attempted to tabulate and interpret the relationship between the various texts that emerge from that city. For further discussions see John P. Meier, "Antioch," in Raymond E. Brown and John P. Meier, *Antioch and Rome: New Testament Cradles of Catholic Christianity* (New York: Paulist Press, 1983), 12–86; David C. Sim, *The Gospel of Matthew and Christian Judaism: The History and Social Setting of the Matthean Community* (Studies of the New Testament and Its World; Edinburgh: T&T Clark, 1998), 53–107; Michelle Slee, *The Church in Antioch in the First Century C.E.: Communion and Conflict* (JSNTSup 244; London: T&T Clark, 2003).

12. Jonathan A. Draper, "The Genesis and Narrative Thrust of the Paraenesis in the Sermon on the Mount," *JSNT* 75 (1999): 25–48; see Alan Garrow, *The Gospel of Matthew's Dependence on the Didache* (JSNTSup 254; London: T&T Clark, 2004). For a use of the tradition

Jesus to the disciples (καθίσαντος αὐτοῦ προσῆλθαν αὐτῷ οἱ μαθηταὶ αὐτοῦ καὶ ἀνοίξας τὸ στόμα αὐτοῦ ἐδίδασκεν αὐτοὺς λέγων—of whom only Peter, Andrew, James, and John have been mentioned thus far by Matthew) in the presence of these great crowds (ἰδὼν δὲ τοὺς ὄχλους), symbolizing the mission of Matthew's community. The presence or absence of the crowd is a significant marker for Matthew's redaction, beyond what is found in Mark, not only in the Sermon on the Mount, but also, importantly, in the two feeding narratives of Matthew, where the role of the disciples as intermediaries is formulaic and moves beyond the simple function of sharing out what Jesus provides:

Matt 14:19 καὶ κλάσας ἔδωκεν τοῖς μαθηταῖς τοὺς ἄρτους, οἱ δὲ μαθηταὶ τοῖς ὄχλοις.
Matt 15:36 καὶ ἐδίδου τοῖς μαθηταῖς, οἱ δὲ μαθηταὶ τοῖς ὄχλοις.
Mark 6:41 καὶ ἐδίδου τοῖς μαθηταῖς [αὐτοῦ] ἵνα παρατιθῶσιν αὐτοῖς
Luke 9:16 καὶ ἐδίδου τοῖς μαθηταῖς παραθεῖναι τῷ ὄχλῳ.

The crowds represent those who are attracted to the gospel, Jews and Gentiles together, while the disciples represent those charged with mediating the teaching and ministry of Jesus to them after the resurrection.[13]

Matthew's redaction of the "Q" material he had to hand in the macarisms of the Sermon on the Mount provides clues to his and his community's self-consciousness, as has been often noted. Most striking in terms of this study is the sudden shift from the third person address in the first eight blessings, which provide a kind of universal ethic (where Luke has the second person plural), to the second person plural in 5:11, which promises blessing in the face of persecution and calumny. In what is clearly a redactional touch, Matthew applies the "Q" saying—that "their" fathers persecuted the prophets also—pointedly to his own community, and the disciples in particular, as the locus of prophecy in his own day. The prophets of the Hebrew Scriptures are the predecessors of the disciples of Jesus and their successors: οὕτως γὰρ ἐδίωξαν τοὺς προφήτας τοὺς πρὸ ὑμῶν (Matt 5:12).

---

in Luke, see Jonathan A. Draper, "Jesus' 'Covenantal Discourse' on the Plain (Luke 6:12–7:17) as Oral Performance: Pointers to 'Q' as Multiple Oral Performance," in *Oral Performance, Popular Tradition, and Hidden Transcript in Q* (ed. R. A. Horsley; SemeiaSt 60; Atlanta: Society of Biblical Literature, 2006), 71–98. Luz (*Matthew 1–7*, 214) notes the "foundational character" of the Sermon on the Mount, but understands this in a theological sense, where I am arguing that it is foundational in a sociological sense and has a specific setting in life as catechesis of converts to the Christian way. I suggest that this explains its particular characteristics (binary opposites, exposition of the ethical commandments of the Decalogue and so on).

13. Anthony J. Saldarini, *Matthew's Christian-Jewish Community* (CSHJ; Chicago: University of Chicago Press, 1994), 37–40, has also noted the importance of the crowds in Matthew's narration. He understands them as referring to those attracted by Jesus within Israel, where I would emphasize the importance of signals that they come from Gentiles as well.

As we have noted, the teaching is addressed through the disciples to the crowds. The implication of this signal switch seems to me to be that the disciples may be understood to be standing in continuity with the prophets in their mission to those represented by the crowds, which inevitably brings persecution.[14] This signal would need to find confirmation in the rest of the text before it could be considered significant. However, we should note here that in line with what is already signaled in the opening words of the Gospel, the sudden switch to second person plural is heightened by two parabolic sayings that have their nuclei in Markan sayings but are given a new direction by their combination with each other and with what precedes. The mission of the disciples in continuity with the prophets "who were before you" is on the one hand directed towards the people of Israel as "salt of the land" (ὑμεῖς ἐστε τὸ ἅλας τῆς γῆς, 5:13) and on the other hand directed towards the Gentiles as "light of the world" (ὑμεῖς ἐστε τὸ φῶς τοῦ κόσμου, 5:14). We have already heard in Matthew that Jesus goes to the "land" of Zebulun and the "land" of Naphthali in order that the Gentiles may receive "the great light" that takes them out of the shadow of death. It is no wonder, then, that Jesus's teaching in the Sermon on the Mount continues with a discussion of the Torah and its continuing validity in the "greater righteousness" Jesus requires of his followers, which is described as "being perfect" (5:17–48). Both words δικαιοσύνη and τέλειος are key identity markers for Matthew's community as for that of the Didache, as we shall see.[15]

If, at the beginning of the Sermon on the Mount, the disciples are characterized as true prophets standing in succession to the prophets before them, then at the end of the Sermon on the Mount, the false prophets "who come to you" are described in considerable detail (7:15–23):

> Beware of false prophets, who come to you in sheep's clothing but inwardly are ravenous wolves. You will know them by their fruits. Are grapes gathered from thorns, or figs from thistles? In the same way, every good tree bears good fruit, but the bad tree bears bad fruit. A good tree cannot bear bad fruit, nor can a bad tree bear good fruit. Every tree that does not bear good fruit is cut down and thrown into the fire. Thus you will know them by their fruits. Not everyone who says to me, "Lord, Lord," will enter the kingdom of heaven, but only the one who does the will of my Father in heaven.
>
> On that day many will say to me, "Lord, Lord, did we not prophesy in your name, and cast out demons in your name, and do many deeds of power in your

---

14. On this much debated switch of person, see Luz, *Matthew 1–7*, 242; Hans Dieter Betz, *The Sermon on the Mount: A Commentary on the Sermon on the Mount, including the Sermon on the Plain (Matthew 5:3–7:27 and Luke 6:20–49)* (Hermeneia; Minneapolis: Fortress, 1995), 147.

15. Georg Strecker, *Der Weg der Gerechtigkeit: Untersuchung zur Theologie des Matthäus* (3rd ed.; FRLANT 82; Göttingen: Vandenhoeck & Ruprecht, 1971). See Draper, "Genesis and Narrative Thrust of the Paraenesis."

name?" Then I will declare to them, "I never knew you; go away from me, you evildoers" (All biblical references are to the NRSV).

The situation is clearly in mind here in which some prophets come to the community from outside it and prove to be false prophets. The description of the prophets in terms of sheep and wolves is important, since sheep are used already to describe Israel in the Old Testament (e.g., Jer 13:17; Isa 40:11; Ezek 34:31; Hos 4:16; Mic 7:14; Zech 10:3; Pss 79:13; 95:7; 100:3) and in Intertestamental literature (e.g., *1 En.* 90.20–27; *Ps. Sol.* 17.40), and subsequently to describe members of the new community called into being by Jesus in the gospels and consistently in early Christian literature (e.g., *Herm. Vis.* 5; *Herm. Sim.* 10.1). These prophets never were genuine members of the community, but were all along predators from outside only disguised as members, "wolves in sheep's clothing." The second important information on these persons, seemingly well-known in the life of Matthew's community, is that they cannot be tested on the basis of what they say but only on the basis of what they do. The test is their lifestyle, and the image of the necessary connection between a particular tree and its particular fruit is framed by an emphatic *inclusio*:

ἀπὸ τῶν καρπῶν αὐτῶν ἐπιγνώσεσθε αὐτούς (7:16)
ἄρα γε ἀπὸ τῶν καρπῶν αὐτῶν ἐπιγνώσεσθε αὐτούς (7:20).

In this Matthew heightens and extends the "Q" saying found also in Luke 6:43–44 though without the saying concerning the "treasure of the heart" found in Luke 6:45 (which is probably "Q," since it is found in *Gos. Thom.* 45). We are not told in Matthew why the prophets cannot be tested on the basis of what they say, but only on the basis of what they do. In the background though, inevitably, stands Deut 18:18–22, which poses the problem sharply and provides the basis for all subsequent discussion of false prophets in the rabbinic texts and in Qumran (11QTemp 61:1–4):

I will raise up for them a prophet like you from among their own people; I will put my words in the mouth of the prophet, who shall speak to them everything that I command. Anyone who does not heed the words that the prophet shall speak in my name, I myself will hold accountable. But any prophet who speaks in the name of other gods, or who presumes to speak in my name a word that I have not commanded the prophet to speak—that prophet shall die. You may say to yourself, "How can we recognize a word that the LORD has not spoken?" If a prophet speaks in the name of the LORD but the thing does not take place or prove true, it is a word that the LORD has not spoken. The prophet has spoken it presumptuously; do not be frightened by it.

The problem is that a true prophet receives words directly from the Lord and so cannot be challenged, but not all people who claim to speak the Lord's words are actually true prophets. It is not entirely clear what is meant by "does not take place or prove true" in the Hebrew text (ולא־יהיה הדבר ולא יבוא הוא הדבר) or in the Septuagint (καὶ μὴ γένηται τὸ ῥῆμα καὶ μὴ συμβῇ τοῦτο τὸ ῥῆμα). In the text given in "Q" the actualization of the prophetic word that proves it to be true or false is interpreted in terms of its results in the lifestyle of the person concerned.

Further information is given in Matthew's account concerning these false prophets who come to the community from outside: they claim to be believers, who address Jesus as "Lord" and they will say on the day of judgment that they prophesied, cast out demons and worked deeds of power in the name of Jesus: πολλοὶ ἐροῦσίν μοι ἐν ἐκείνῃ τῇ ἡμέρᾳ· κύριε κύριε, οὐ τῷ σῷ ὀνόματι ἐπροφητεύσαμεν, καὶ τῷ σῷ ὀνόματι δαιμόνια ἐξεβάλομεν, καὶ τῷ σῷ ὀνόματι δυνάμεις πολλὰς ἐποιήσαμεν; (7:22). It is striking that the number of those who will make this claim on the day of judgment is "many" (πολλοί). Clearly this is a problematic area for the community Matthew represents. However, none of their displays of power will save them because of their evil fruit, which is described in the words of Ps 6:9 (LXX) as οἱ ἐργαζόμενοι τὴν ἀνομίαν. Significantly, Jesus slips again into the second person plural mode of address: οὐδέποτε ἔγνων ὑμᾶς (7:23). Again, it should be noted that ἀνομία is a key identity marker in Matthew representing the opposite of the τέλειος/δικαιοσύνη complex (7:23; 14:21; 23:28; 24:12), as well as in the Didache, as we will see. In the last days many false prophets will arise and lead people astray, while ἀνομία will increase (24:11–12). The saying concerning the lifestyle of the prophet is concluded by instruction in the third person again, i.e., no longer to the disciples only but to "everyone" that they should not only hear but also do the words of Jesus in the face of the storm that is coming, in the parable of the House built on the Rock or the Sand taken from "Q" (= Luke 7:24–27). The switch from third person to second person in the macarisms at the beginning of the discourse is matched chiastically by the switch from the second person to the third person at the end of the Sermon on the Mount. The mode switch is thus a significant indicator of a change of reference from community members in general to leaders. Moreover, in the narrative context of the Sermon on the Mount, it seems that the nature of the leadership connected by Matthew with the disciples is described in terms associated with prophecy. Prophets are presumably unknown personally to the community since they come from outside it, and are thus characterized by mobility.

There is no doubt that discipleship is a key concept for Matthew. This was established in detail already by Günther Bornkamm in his groundbreaking study of the Stilling of the Storm in Matt 8:23–27.[16] However, the account of the Stilling of the Storm begins again with a great crowd around and the disciples within the circle, which, as we have seen, is characteristic of Matthew's composition, so

---

16. Günther Bornkamm, "The Stilling of the Storm in Matthew" in *Tradition and Interpretation in Matthew* (ed. G. Bornkamm, G. Barth and H. J. Held; London: SCM, 1963), 52–57.

that it may be addressed to the narrower circle of those engaged in the mission to the nations rather and not necessarily to all those who accept the kingdom proclaimed by Jesus. In this narrative, a scribe who seeks to follow Jesus, addressing him as "teacher" (διδάσκαλε), is rebuffed by Jesus with a description of the homelessness and possessionless lifestyle of the Son of Man (8:20). A disciple, addressing him as "Lord" (κύριε), requests to be allowed to stay with his father (one must take the request to bury his father as a request to stay within the household), but is firmly instructed to leave home and follow Jesus on the road (8:21–22). Since the crowds are in the background on the bank while the disciples "follow" Jesus into the boat and storm, this homeless lifestyle does in some way seem to reflect Matthew's expectation of whoever his community views as the successors of the disciples in their own day. This fits with what we have observed about the lifestyle of the false prophets who come to the community from outside and it seems not unreasonable to assume that it characterizes also the lifestyle of the true prophets to which the Sermon on the Mount points. It is confirmed by Matthew's redaction of Markan material in chapter 19. In the context of a discussion on divorce, Jesus refers to an inner circle of those who do not marry but make themselves eunuchs for the sake of the kingdom:

His disciples said to him, "If such is the case of a man with his wife, it is better not to marry." But he said to them, "Not everyone can accept this teaching (οὐ πάντες χωροῦσιν τὸν λόγον), but only those to whom it is given. For there are eunuchs who have been so from birth, and there are eunuchs who have been made eunuchs by others, and there are eunuchs who have made themselves eunuchs for the sake of the kingdom of heaven. Let anyone accept this who can (ὁ δυνάμενος χωρεῖν χωρείτω)" (19:11–12).

The language of "accepting what one is able to accept" in this connection is important as we shall see for the Didache also, where the general ethic is based on the principle, "Do what you are able to do" (6:2–3). The same tendency to limit what is general in Mark to an inner group of those who are able can be seen in Matthew's redaction of the discussion between Jesus and the disciples after the story of the Rich Young Man (19:16–22). Jesus responds to Peter's question about the reward for leaving everything to follow him with an eschatological promise, which Matthew draws from "Q" (see Luke 22:30), that the disciples will sit on twelve thrones judging the twelve tribes of Israel, and certainly they will receive the hundred-fold reward promised also in Mark, but no mention is made of "in this time" (19:28–29). The reward here is limited to the Twelve, i.e., to those who serve in the role of apostles in the commission of Jesus to convert the nations given at the end of the Gospel, and no longer to all Christians.

We should also note that the title διδάσκαλος for Jesus has a negative connotation for Matthew, as we saw already in 8:20, whereas it was an appropriate title for addressing Jesus in Mark. This is matched by the prohibition of the use of the title ῥαββί for community leaders in Matthew 23:7–8, on the basis of equality in the kingdom with Jesus as the only teacher: ὑμεῖς δὲ μὴ κληθῆτε ῥαββί· εἷς γάρ ἐστιν ὑμῶν ὁ διδάσκαλος, πάντες δὲ ὑμεῖς ἀδελφοί ἐστε. The only disciple to use the title "rabbi" to address Jesus is Judas on the night he betrays him, addressing him this way twice (26:25, 49). The basis for the aversion to the title is its use by the party of the scribes and the Pharisees, who are reported to love honor and not to do what they teach:

> The scribes and the Pharisees sit on Moses' seat (ἐπὶ τῆς Μωϋσέως καθέδρας ἐκάθισαν). Therefore, do whatever they teach (εἴπωσιν) you and follow it; but do not do as they do, for they do not practice what they teach. (23:2–3)

We should note again both the presence of and distinction between crowds and disciples as addressees in 23:1. Matthew accepts the authority of the teacher of the law: the problem is not with teaching[17] and interpretation of the Torah *per se*, but only the gap between saying and doing, which we have already observed is a key to discerning the false prophet. This matches the oblique but approving reference to the role of the scribe in 13:52: "And he said to them, 'Therefore every scribe who has been trained for the kingdom of heaven is like the master of a household who brings out of his treasure what is new and what is old.'" Jesus addresses the disciples only in this statement, having "left" the crowd (13:36), and it is his response to the declaration of the disciples that they have understood his teaching: "'Have you understood all this?' They answered, 'Yes.'" (13:51). So despite the prohibition of the title "rabbi," the disciple is expected to exercise the role of the scribe by learning, understanding, and teaching the words of Jesus, even "adding to it" something new, it seems.[18]

The importance of the *task* of teaching for Matthew's community is highlighted by its presence at the conclusion to the gospel, where the eleven remaining disciples are charged with the mission to "all nations," i.e., to the Gentiles (as well as to the Jews?), baptizing them and "teaching them to obey everything that I have commanded you" (28:20). This command to undertake a mission to the Gentiles stands parallel and in something of a paradoxical tension with the instructions in 10:5: "Go nowhere among the Gentiles, and enter no town of the Samaritans, but go rather to the lost sheep of the house of Israel." However, this tension characterizes the gospel from beginning to end: it seeks to hold in tension the temporally prior address of Jesus to his own people with the subsequent experience of the Gentile mission. At the time of the composition of the gospel the community would seem to be fundamentally reconciled to and oriented towards the universal mission to all people, without sacrificing its continuity with its Jewish roots or its claims to represent true continuity with Israel.

---

17. Although the word used is εἴπωσιν rather than διδάσκειν.
18. See "adding to righteousness" in Did. 11:2.

So far, it seems that the disciples represent in some way the leadership of the new community[19] faced with the mission to both Jews and Gentiles represented by the crowds that accompany Jesus. As such, they reflect a task that appears to include both prophecy and teaching. The third role they are specifically given by Jesus is that of apostle. This title is used only once, namely, when Jesus calls the Twelve and names them apostles at the beginning of their mission to "the lost sheep of Israel" in 10:4. Jesus's calling of apostles is said by Matt 9:36–38 to be a response to the need of the crowds, who are designated as "sheep," code language usually reserved for community members.[20] So the meaning of "apostle" may extend beyond that of mission to that of leadership within the new community:

> When he saw the crowds, he had compassion for them, because they were harassed and helpless, like sheep without a shepherd. Then he said to his disciples, "The harvest is plentiful, but the laborers are few; therefore ask the Lord of the harvest to send out laborers into his harvest."

What is specific to the task of the apostle is made clear from the outset, namely, delegated authority: ἔδωκεν αὐτοῖς ἐξουσίαν (10:1). The task of the *shaliaḥ* in Jewish culture is a legal function of representation, in which decisions made by the representative are deemed legally binding on the one who sends: "A person's apostle is as him/herself" (*m. Ber.* 5:5; *b. Ned.* 72b; *b. Kidd.* 41b; *b. Ḥag.* 10b; *b. Naz.* 12b; *b. B. Meṣiʿa* 96a; *b. Menaḥ* 93b; *Mek. Ex.* 12:4 [5a], 6 [7a]).[21] It is in the nature of such delegated authority that it is temporary: it is only valid for and during the exercise of the task in hand. So an embassy to Rome, a finan-

---

19. Though without minimizing the egalitarian claims of 23:7–8.

20. For this reason, I do not agree with Ulrich Luz's contention (*Matthew in History*, 41), that "there seems to be no difference between the 'historical' term *apostle* and the 'transparent' term *disciple*," so that all the followers of Jesus, without distinction are called to the same lifestyle. It seems to me that the text signals a reference to *leadership* rather than general members of the community, whom Matthew designates as *ekklesia*.

21. The Jewish community in Palestine or Jerusalem sent rabbis to the Diaspora as "apostles" of the Great Sanhedrin for various purposes: to regulate the calendar (Akiba in *m. Yebam.* 16:7, R. Meir in *t. Meg.* 2:5) and to declare the beginning of the new month (*m. Roš Haš.* 1:3, 14; 2:2). According to *y. Ḥag.* 1,76c, 31–32, Patriarch Juda II (ca. 250 C.E.) sent three rabbis to Palestine to appoint teachers. The important feature of the Jewish apostles is that they were appointed for a specific task, and only until the completion of that task did they have their plenary function. They were not missionaries nor necessarily even teachers, although rabbis seem usually to have been chosen for religious delegations. Hospitality towards such *talmidim hakhamim* was enjoined as especially meritorious (*b. Ber.* 10b; *b. Sanh.* 92a). They were not regular officers of the community, yet they must have been a common feature of life in the Diaspora, keeping communities in touch with one another and with the center of Jewish religious life in Palestine. Strict rules are laid down for the "poor travelling from place to place" (*m. Pe'ah* 8:7; *t. Pe'ah* 4:8; *y. Pe'ah* 8, 21a). These "poor" were not necessarily only wandering destitutes or beggars, because the same rules apply to anyone needing support on a journey.

cial negotiation or a marriage contract or some other such legal function lies in the background. The mission of the Twelve/ Seventy in the gospels as "apostles" would have had this sense. In Mark, in fact, this is most clearly expressed: they "go out" (6:12) and then "gather together to Jesus and report back" on their mission (6:30).[22] However, in Matthew this aspect of the role of the apostle is tempered at the end of the gospel, where Jesus says he has received authority (ἐδόθη μοι πᾶσα ἐξουσία ἐν οὐρανῷ καὶ ἐπὶ τῆς γῆς, 28:18) and now delegates it to them (πορευθέντες οὖν, 28:19). Since Jesus now leaves them, there can be no return in this age to the one who sent them, and in fact the continuing nature of the delegated authority is emphasized by his presence with them to the close of the age. In this way, for Matthew, the name he is given at the beginning of the gospel is thus confirmed and validated: he is "God with us." So the description of the sending of the Twelve in Matt 10, which combines Markan and "Q" material, has a clear relevance to the continuing role of the disciples after Jesus's resurrection. Jesus sends them out and gives them instructions (10:5). The extended instructions then follow without any further reference to the mission or return, simply, "Now when Jesus had finished instructing his twelve disciples, he went on from there to teach and proclaim his message in their cities."

The concept of the office of apostle underlies the woe pronounced against the scribes and Pharisees in 23:29–39 also. Here, the latter are accused of standing in line with their ancestors who murdered the prophets, since they now persecute those whom Jesus sends:

> Therefore I send (ἀποστέλλω) you prophets, sages, and scribes (προφήτας καὶ σοφοὺς καὶ γραμματεῖς), some of whom you will kill and crucify, and some you will flog in your synagogues and pursue from town to town, so that upon you may come all the righteous blood shed on earth, from the blood of righteous Abel to the blood of Zechariah son of Barachiah, whom you murdered between the sanctuary and the altar. Truly I tell you, all this will come upon this generation. Jerusalem, Jerusalem, the city that kills the prophets and stones those who are sent to it! (verses 34–37).

Yet the ones sent as Jesus's apostles are named as "prophets, sages, and scribes" and not "apostles." This is a highly significant indication that an apostle is not viewed by Matthew as a separate office, but rather a function of representation. The offices in view are primarily conceived as prophets, since just as the scribes and the Pharisees stand in the line of the murderers of the prophets, so those who are Jesus's apostles stand in the line of the prophets of old, as we have already seen. Yet beside the office of prophet stand the two "wisdom" or teaching offices

---

22. See Jonathan A. Draper, "Wandering Radicalism or Purposeful Activity? Jesus and the Sending of Messengers in Mark 6:6–56," *Neot* 29 (1995): 187–207, where I am concerned more with discerning the role of the "historical Jesus."

of "sages and scribes." It is not clear whether three functionaries are really in view or whether this is a threefold elaboration of the same office. In any case, these ones whom Jesus sends are envisaged as moving from town to town under the pressure of persecution, which again speaks against them being a settled local ministry.

The instructions to the Twelve seem remarkably similar in reverse to what the false prophets claim to have done: prophecy, exorcism and acts of power (7:22). Jesus gives them "authority over unclean spirits, to cast them out, and to cure every disease and every sickness (10:1). Again in 10:7–8, "Proclaim the good news, 'The kingdom of heaven has come near.' Cure the sick, raise the dead, cleanse the lepers, cast out demons." So it would seem that what we have already observed about Matthew's portrait of the disciples as community leaders is still true: they seem remarkably like true prophets as opposed to false prophets, both known by their fruits whether good or bad. The reference to sheep and wolves in 10:16 seems to confirm this. Whereas the false prophets appear to be sheep coming into the community, they are actually wolves in disguise. On the other hand, the true prophets are sheep by nature, sent out into an environment where the false leaders of the people are dangerous wolves and predators. A further mark of the instructions to the apostles is that they will speak in the Spirit when they are brought before judges and rulers: οὐ γὰρ ὑμεῖς ἐστε οἱ λαλοῦντες ἀλλὰ τὸ πνεῦμα τοῦ πατρὸς ὑμῶν τὸ λαλοῦν ἐν ὑμῖν (10:20; see Mark 13:11). At this point Luke, reflecting the "Q" emphasis on wisdom rather than prophecy, only says that this will be an opportunity to witness and Jesus promises, "for I will give you words and a wisdom (ἐγὼ γὰρ δώσω ὑμῖν στόμα καὶ σοφίαν) that none of your opponents will be able to withstand or contradict." (21:15). So it is no surprise that the words about "blasphemy against the Holy Spirit" in Matthew occur in the context of the repetition of the saying about "knowing a tree by its fruit," which also characterized the discussion of true and false prophets in the Sermon on the Mount:

> Therefore I tell you, people will be forgiven for every sin and blasphemy, but blasphemy against the Spirit will not be forgiven. Whoever speaks a word against the Son of Man will be forgiven, but whoever speaks against the Holy Spirit will not be forgiven, either in this age or in the age to come. "Either make the tree good, and its fruit good; or make the tree bad, and its fruit bad; for the tree is known by its fruit" (12:31–33).

However people may have responded to Jesus, to silence his delegated representatives when they are speaking in the Spirit is the unforgivable sin of blasphemy against the Holy Spirit. Behind this lies Deut 18:15–22, as we have already shown. Those who silence the prophet God has sent will answer to God: "And whoever will not listen to my words that he shall speak in my name, I myself will require it of him" (Deut 18:19).

What we have already seen concerning the life of the disciple of Jesus in 8:20–22 is confirmed in the instructions given to the apostles in 10:8–42. Since this is well-known, we need do no more than sketch them here.[23] They are to go without taking money or supplies but are to depend on the hospitality of the householders who accept their mission:

> Take no gold, or silver, or copper in your belts, no bag for your journey, or two tunics, or sandals, or a staff; for laborers deserve their food. Whatever town or village you enter, find out who in it is worthy, and stay there until you leave. As you enter the house, greet it. If the house is worthy, let your peace come upon it; but if it is not worthy, let your peace return to you. If anyone will not welcome you or listen to your words, shake off the dust from your feet as you leave that house or town. Truly I tell you, it will be more tolerable for the land of Sodom and Gomorrah on the day of Judgment than for that town (10:9–15).

There is no word here of a restriction on how long the apostles may stay before moving on, only that they have a right to support and that their stay is only temporary—since they are apostles—but there is a note of eschatological urgency that impels them in the face of the day of judgment that is coming. They are expected to be fleeing from one town to the next to give their message of the breaking in of the kingdom in the face of persecution. Their presence is a blessing to those who do receive them, since their peace comes upon the house. So the picture of the apostles is one of traveling prophetic figures who proclaim the breaking in of the kingdom with eschatological urgency, in the face of persecution, who heal the sick and cast out demons and do works of power.

The sayings cluster (10:40–42) that concludes the instructions to the apostles is highly significant for our purposes:

> Whoever welcomes you welcomes me,
>   and whoever welcomes me welcomes the one who sent me.
> Whoever welcomes a prophet in the name of a prophet
>   will receive a prophet's reward;
> And whoever welcomes a righteous person in the name of a righteous person
>   will receive the reward of the righteous;
> And whoever gives even a cup of cold water to one of these little ones
>   in the name of a disciple
>   —truly I tell you,
> none of these will lose their reward.

---

23. For a discussion of this passage see Jonathan A. Draper, "First Fruits and the Support of Prophets, Teachers and the Poor in Didache 13 in Relation to New Testament Parallels" in *Trajectories through he New Testament and the Apostolic Fathers* (ed. A. Gregory; Oxford: Oxford University Press, 2005), 223–43.

We have already seen that the key aspect of an apostle is representation, not just delegation, but plenipotentiary authority. So here, those who welcome the ones Jesus sends will be welcoming Jesus and the One who sent him. But the promise to the settled householders who welcome and provide for the apostles whom Jesus sends is that they will receive the same blessing as the apostles. It is not clear whether three different offices or functions are in mind with "prophet," "righteous person" and "little one" or whether this is a triplet describing the same figure. Probably they all describe the same role, given the repeated occurrence of prophetic terminology in references to the role of the disciples.

To summarize: Matthew appears to identify the task of the disciples very closely with the role of prophets, standing in the tradition of prophecy in the Old Testament. Prophetic words, uttered in the Spirit, healing, exorcism, and deeds of power characterize their ministry and indeed mirror the claims of false prophets visiting the communities. The disciples are called apostles only when they are described as "sent by Jesus," but Matthew does not narrate the return of the apostles, whereas Mark and Luke (on both the sending of the Twelve and the Seventy) specifically mention the return and report back to Jesus after the sending out. This matches the open-ended commission to the eleven to undertake a mission to all nations at the end of Matthew on which Jesus would accompany them spiritually. While the role of the prophet predominates in the description of apostles, alongside them Matthew mentions "sages and scribes," but it is not clear whether these are to be understood as mobile in the same way as the apostle-prophet role.

1.3. The Settled Communities and Local Functionaries in Matthew

This summary of the data in Matthew would not, of course, be complete without a sideways glance at the pronouncement of Jesus to Peter after his confession at Caesarea Philippi in 16:18–19:

> And Jesus answered him, "Blessed are you, Simon son of Jonah! For flesh and blood has not revealed this to you, but my Father in heaven. And I tell you, you are Peter, and on this rock I will build my church, and the gates of Hades will not prevail against it. I will give you the keys of the kingdom of heaven, and whatever you bind on earth will be bound in heaven, and whatever you loose on earth will be loosed in heaven."

The most interesting thing here is that the promise that the church will be built on Peter as a rock is a response to a word of prophecy: Peter has spoken the words of the Father, not his own. So the authority is both a delegated authority from Jesus and hence apostolic, and the authority derived from speaking in the Spirit and so prophetic. I am not, of course, using these terms in the sense they have been given in the long debate over church hierarchies, but in the technical

sense in which they have emerged in our analysis. The choice of Peter is significant and no doubt relates to debates between Matthew's community and rival
communities in the early Christian movement. It signals their consciousness of
being directed to a mission simultaneously as salt to the people of Israel and as
light to the Gentiles. The imagery of "building" and "foundation stone" seems to
introduce an element of fixity or stability more consonant with resident communities than with wandering individuals. It is significant then that Peter, one of the
disciple-prophet-apostle figures we saw described in the first section, is understood as the foundation of a more settled entity. I have already indicated that the
motif of Jesus and commissioning and teaching the disciples in the presence or
absence of the crowds has already introduced an element corresponding to this
"wandering"/"settled" divide.

However, it cannot really be taken as evidence for the emergence of a fixed
local hierarchy, since the same terminology of binding and loosing is given to the
whole church in 18:14–20, where the importance of each of "these little ones" is
emphasized:

> So it is not the will of your Father in heaven that one of these little ones should
> be lost. If another member of the church sins against you, go and point out
> the fault when the two of you are alone. If the member listens to you, you have
> regained that one. But if you are not listened to, take one or two others along
> with you, so that every word may be confirmed by the evidence of two or three
> witnesses. If the member refuses to listen to them, tell it to the church; and if the
> offender refuses to listen even to the church, let such a one be to you as a Gentile
> and a tax collector. Truly I tell you, whatever you bind on earth will be bound in
> heaven, and whatever you loose on earth will be loosed in heaven. Again, truly I
> tell you, if two of you agree on earth about anything you ask, it will be done for
> you by my Father in heaven. For where two or three are gathered in my name, I
> am there among them.

Besides this, Matthew seems to emphasize the concept of "service," so that the
most important title in the community is held to be that of "servant" in contrast
to the authority structures of the Gentile rulers:

> But Jesus called them to him and said, "You know that the rulers of the Gen-
> tiles lord it over them, and their great ones are tyrants over them. It will not be
> so among you; but whoever wishes to be great among you must be your serv-
> ant (διάκονος), and whoever wishes to be first among you must be your slave
> (δοῦλος); just as the Son of Man came not to be served but to serve, and to give
> his life a ransom for many" (20:26–28).

The same preference for the title "servant/ deacon" comes in 23:11–12: ὁ δὲ
μείζων ὑμῶν ἔσται ὑμῶν διάκονος ὅστις δὲ ὑψώσει ἑαυτὸν ταπεινωθήσεται καὶ
ὅστις ταπεινώσει ἑαυτὸν ὑψωθήσεται. Of course, it cannot be concluded from
this that the word "servant/ deacon" designates an actual office in the commu-

nity, but it also does not speak against it. Otherwise, Matthew's Gospel provides no evidence for the kinds of officials mentioned in the Didache, such as a college of bishops and deacons, or in the Epistle of James, such as teachers and elders.

2. Settled and Wandering Functionaries in the Didache

2.1. Apostles

The problem of the status and role of functionaries in the Didache is already given by its title(s). While the text was widely known and quoted in antiquity under the title ΔΙΔΑΧΗ ΤΩΝ [ΔΩΔΕΚΑ] ΑΠΟΣΤΟΛΩΝ, it is not clear whether this refers to the Two Ways source incorporated into Did. 1–6 or to the full text as we now have it.[24] The Jerusalem Manuscript (H 54), our only complete text of the Didache first discovered by Archbishop Bryennios and published by him in 1883, begins the text proper with the longer title or perhaps *incipit*, Διδαχὴ κυρίου διὰ τῶν δώδεκα ἀποστόλων τοῖς ἔθνεσιν. The problem of the two titles has long exercised the minds of scholars and no agreement has been reached on how it is to be solved. However, it seems very likely that the longer title, as Rordorf and Tuilier have argued,[25] is associated with the redaction that inserted the Jesus tradition (1:3b–2:1) into the Two Ways source (whose beginning seems to cohere with the "long title" τούτων δὲ τῶν λόγων ἡ διδαχή ἐστιν αὕτη) and that inserted a series of references to the "gospel" into the text as a whole (8:2; 11:3; 15:3; 15:4). In terms of our topic in this paper, we can observe that the teaching is not described thereby as the "teaching of the apostles," but rather "the teaching of the Lord."[26] The apostles are the intermediaries, the delegated representatives of the Lord who are the tradents of the teaching of Jesus. This is important, since it relates directly to the situation depicted by the commission of Jesus to the eleven (!) at the end of Matthew (28:16–20) to go to all nations to make disciples, bap-

---

24. Witnesses to the various forms of the short title include Athanasius, Ps.-Athanasius, Nicephorus, Eusebius, Rufinus, and Pseudo-Cyprian. For a summary of the evidence see Niederwimmer, *Die Didache*, 4–6.

25. Willy Rordorf and André Tuilier, *La Doctrine des Douze Apôtres (Didachè)*; (2nd ed.; SC 248 bis; Paris: Cerf, 1998), 16.

26. Garrow (*Matthew's Dependence on the Didache*, 48–249) sees here a confirmation of his redaction critical argument for a dependence of Matthew on the Didache, in that he considers the gospel writer taking what he found before him as "teaching of the Lord" and setting it on the lips of Jesus. Garleff (*Urchristliche Identität in Matthäusevangelium*, 115) also argues for the security of the "long title" in the text and points to the importance of its attribution to the Lord rather than to the apostles.

tize and teach them all he had taught them, rather than to the "teaching of the apostles" suggested by Acts 2:42.[27]

On the other hand, this attribution of both teaching and mission to the apostles at the beginning of the Didache raises questions about the use of the name in 11:4–6, since there is no mention of the "Twelve" in this passage. Instead the instructions seem to envisage a larger group of mobile apostles. While the expression δεχθήτω ὡς κύριος seems to align itself with the concept of delegated authority of an apostle of Jesus, apostles here do not seem to be given any explicit role in the community. The concern in the instructions seems to be instead to protect the community against exploitation by "apostles" who come from outside and try to stay for long periods or obtain money for themselves. In response to this, the instructions limit the stay of the apostles to one day (11:4). On the following day they should leave with enough bread to last them to their next port of call (11:6). If they cannot travel on the very next day, perhaps because it is the Sabbath when travel is forbidden or perhaps out of sickness, they may stay a second day, but if they stay a third day, they are false prophets (11:5). Likewise, if they ask for money they are false prophets (11:6). If this were enforced, then it is hard to see in what way apostles could exercise any mission or any authority or even any leadership role in local communities. They would be always traveling.

It seems more likely to me that these instructions of apostles form a part of an early hospitality code for the community, together with instructions on the reception of travelers in general in 12:1–5, which has been edited by the insertion of material on prophets in 11:7–8.[28] There seems nothing in the nature of polemic nor anything contentious about the instructions on apostles, such as can be found in the instructions on prophets. Those Christians traveling on official business, representing communities elsewhere, and passing through this community, would be apostles from a wider group than the Twelve (see Andronicus and Junia in Rom 16:7). Paul seems to envisage apostles as a group (e.g., 1 Cor 12:28–29). Hospitality for them was absolutely essential for the development of the Christian movement, as indeed for any ancient group. They would often be unknown to the local community and carry letters of identification setting out where they come from and where they are going.[29] However, in the absence of any ability to check up on their credentials (such as is available today by telephone or e-mail), the possibilities for abuse were obvious. Major figures such

---

27. This has been argued again by Garleff (see previous footnote). However, it should be noted that the conceptions in Matthew and Luke are not unrelated, particularly if, as I would argue, the linking of authoritative teaching with the apostles derives from "Q" independently in Matthew, Luke, and Didache.

28. The kind of instruction found also in rabbinic writings concerning the "wandering poor," as we have shown in n. 21 above.

29. Such a letter of introduction for such an apostle is contained in *y. Ḥag.* 1,76d, 3–4: "Lo we send a great man as our envoy equal to ourselves until he come."

as Peter and Paul might not need letters, but even Paul is aware of the need to provide credentials and the problems associated with having no letter of authority from Jerusalem! Whether or not it happened historically, the manner of the sending of Judas Barsabbas and Silas along with Paul and Barnabas in Acts 15:22–35 provides the model for such an embassy where a letter would provide the authorization from a recognized authority to stay longer in a place. Where such a delegation was passing through to another place, e.g., Barsabbas, Silas, Paul and Barnabas en route to Antioch from Jerusalem would need to stay overnight along the route, then this would be covered only in a general way. With this we could compare 3 John 6, which seems to be a surviving example of such a letter: "You will do well to send them on their journey in a matter worthy of God." In such a case delegated apostles would only be allowed to stay one night on their journey, or else they prove that they are not really in earnest and so can be designated "false prophets" (ψευδοπροφήτης 11:5, 6).

The problem in understanding the text really hinges around this. If false apostles can be called false prophets, does this mean that true apostles are really true prophets? The problem is intensified by the coupling together of apostles and prophets in the section marker: Περὶ δὲ τῶν ἀποστόλων καὶ προφητῶν κατὰ τὸ δόγμα τοῦ εὐαγγελίου οὕτω ποιήσατε (11:3). I have argued at length that this is a redactional development of an original brief instruction entitled: Περὶ δὲ τῶν ἀποστόλων οὕτω ποιήσατε, following the model of the *peri de* section markers in the rest of the text, which elsewhere occur in this simple form with a single subject (6:3; 7:1; [7:4]; 9:1; [10:1]; [10:8]). The current form of the text at the very least signals the presence of a contentious issue since it refers to an authority that the community regards as definitive, the "ordinance of the Gospel" (κατὰ τὸ δόγμα τοῦ εὐαγγελίου). References to "the Gospel" seem to come from the latest redactional layer of the text (e.g., chapters 8 and 15). Are the apostles of necessity "charismatic" figures, that is, endowed by the Holy Spirit for a special task, ranged alongside the "charismatic" prophets, or are they simply delegates for a time?[30] The evidence is ambiguous, to say the least.

I would like to sidestep for the moment the question of original form and its redaction and concede that, on the basis of the final form of the text, the apostles are understood as connected with the prophets in some way. Not all apostles, then, would necessarily have been prophets, but perhaps prophets coming from outside the community would have fitted in the category of apostles, those arriving and claiming to be delegated representatives of the Lord and so to be received "as the Lord." Both apostles (πᾶς δὲ ἀπόστολος ἐρχόμενος πρὸς ὑμᾶς, 11:4) and prophets (πᾶς δὲ προφήτης ἀληθινὸς θέλων καθῆσθαι πρὸς ὑμᾶς, 13:1) came from outside the community and claimed to be sent by the Lord. Some apostles claimed, it would appear, also to be prophets and to speak in the Spirit. It was

---

30. See Draper, "Weber, Theissen and the Wandering Charismatics."

fundamental to the role of an apostle to be on the Lord's business, representing one community on a commission to another, and they could usually be authenticated by producing a letter or else they could require the person to move on as quickly as possible. A visit from an apostle would be a temporary one, even if someone were to arrive on a special embassy to *this* community, with covering letter and acceptable credentials for a *specific* task that might take longer.[31] But what if the person claimed, like Paul, to have been commissioned by Jesus in person and to be speaking in the Spirit of God? Would they need letters? This is where the problem really lies, since Deut 18:18–22 commands obedience to the word God puts in the mouth of the prophet and forbids that the prophet be silenced. Clearly prophets were arriving in the community(ies) of the Didache often enough for this to need regulating. The regulation agrees in essence with what is found in Matthew concerning false and true prophets.

2.2. Prophets

The prophet may not be tested or judged, since God's word is in his mouth and it would be blasphemy to contradict God's word (11:7). Interestingly, the phrase "blasphemy against the holy Spirit" found in Matthew is not found here, but only the warning that testing or judging the prophet speaking in the Spirit constitutes a sin that cannot be forgiven: πᾶσα γὰρ ἁμαρτία ἀφεθήσεται· αὕτη δὲ ἡ ἁμαρτία οὐκ ἀφεθήσεται.

Matthew 12:31–32
πᾶσα ἁμαρτία καὶ βλασφημία
ἀφεθήσεται τοῖς ἀνθρώποις
ἡ δὲ τοῦ πνεύματος βλασφημία
οὐκ ἀφεθήσεται.
καὶ ὃς ἐὰν εἴπῃ λόγον κατὰ τοῦ υἱοῦ τοῦ
ἀνθρώπου ἀφεθήσεται αὐτῷ ὃς δ' ἂν
εἴπῃ κατὰ τοῦ πνεύματος τοῦ ἁγίου, οὐκ
ἀφεθήσεται αὐτῷ οὔτε ἐν τούτῳ τῷ
αἰῶνι οὔτε ἐν τῷ μέλλοντι.

Didache 11:7b
πᾶσα γὰρ ἁμαρτία
ἀφεθήσεται
αὕτη δὲ ἡ ἁμαρτία
οὐκ ἀφεθήσεται

Similarity in concept and difference in wording is characteristic of the relationship between Matthew and Didache. The saying in Matthew is given by Jesus in response to the claim of the Pharisees that Jesus casts out demons by Beelzebul (12:24), so that they fall under the condemnation of Deut 18:19, "whoever will not listen to my words that he shall speak in my name, I myself will require it of

---

31. I am only raising this as a possibility, but the system would have to allow for some occasions when mutual business might take longer than an evening.

him." Matthew follows this with a repetition of the saying concerning knowing a tree by its fruits. The Pharisees cannot concede that the words Jesus has spoken prophetically "have come to pass" (Deuteronomy's test of the true prophet) and then argue that he has done it by Beelzebul. This is the force of the ἤ … ἤ construction in Matt 12:33: ἢ ποιήσατε τὸ δένδρον καλὸν καὶ τὸν καρπὸν αὐτοῦ καλόν, ἢ ποιήσατε τὸ δένδρον σαπρὸν καὶ τὸν καρπὸν αὐτοῦ σαπρόν· ἐκ γὰρ τοῦ καρποῦ τὸ δένδρον γινώσκεται. Here the wording in the Didache sounds like a proverbial saying, but it is also followed by a verification, namely, that the prophet's words must come to pass through the "ways of the Lord" (τοὺς τρόπους κυρίου) test. While these sayings derive from a common tradition, they do not seem to provide grounds for asserting a direct literary relationship, unless such a relationship has already been established on other grounds.

In any case, in the Didache, if no prophet speaking in the Spirit may be silenced, then not everyone who "speaks in the Spirit" is a true prophet, but only the prophet who has the "ways" or "lifestyle" of the Lord. The parallel way in which "speaking in the Spirit" is used here of the utterances of both the true prophet and the false prophet is interesting, even perplexing. It must indicate some kind of community praxis, in which there is no outward way of distinguishing the utterances formally. Only the outcome of the prophecy in terms of whether the prophet has the "ways of the Lord" (ἀλλ᾿ ἐὰν ἔχῃ τοὺς τρόπους κυρίου, 11:8b) can enable the community to know. It is significant that the metaphor of the tree and its fruit, which follows this saying in Matthew, is not used, but rather compatibility with "the ways of the Lord." Throughout the Didache there is ambivalence as to whether κύριος refers to Jesus or to the Lord God.[32] The usual assumption is that it refers here to Jesus's own lifestyle and this seems to be likely but not certain, depending on whether this is older *halakic* material. Τρόπος, especially in the plural, seems to refer primarily to the behavior or habits of a person,[33] but could perhaps refer to the "ways of God." Certainly, in its use in Matt 12:33 the tree-fruit test must relate to the Lord God vindicating the prophecy of Jesus by fulfillment. And in the use of the same tree-fruit test in 7:21 the fruit image elaborates on the meaning of "doing the will of my Father who is in heaven."

Having the "lifestyle/ways of the Lord" is then more closely defined by four units in 11:9–12:

A. καὶ πᾶς προφήτης ὁρίζων τράπεζαν ἐν πνεύματι

---

32. Aaron Milavec, *The Didache: Faith, Hope, and Life of the Earliest Christian Communities, 50–70 C.E* (New York: Newman, 2003), insists it always refers to the Lord God, but this seems to be unsustainable in the light of the reference to the "Gospel of the Lord." It is more likely that it fluctuates in usage of the text.

33. See LSJ s.v. III.

οὐ φάγεται ἀπ' αὐτῆς
    εἰ δὲ μήγε ψευδοπροφήτης ἐστί.

B. πᾶς δὲ προφήτης διδάσκων τὴν ἀλήθειαν
    εἰ ἃ διδάσκει οὐ ποιεῖ, ψευδοπροφήτης ἐστί

C. πᾶς δὲ προφήτης δεδοκιμασμένος ἀληθινός
    ποιῶν εἰς μυστήριον κοσμικὸν ἐκκλησίας
    μὴ διδάσκων δὲ ποιεῖν ὅσα αὐτὸς ποιεῖ
        οὐ κριθήσεται ἐφ' ὑμῶν·
            μετὰ θεοῦ γὰρ ἔχει τὴν κρίσιν·
                ὡσαύτως γὰρ ἐποίησαν καὶ οἱ ἀρχαῖοι προφῆται.

D. ὃς δ' ἂν εἴπῃ ἐν πνεύματι·
    δός μοι ἀργύρια ἢ ἕτερά τινα
        οὐκ ἀκούσεσθε αὐτοῦ
    ἐὰν δὲ περὶ ἄλλων ὑστερούντων εἴπῃ δοῦναι
    μηδεὶς αὐτὸν κρινέτω.

The first and last units (A and D) concern situations in which the prophet gains some kind of material advantage by his or her prophecy. In the first case (A) he may not order a meal for him/herself and then eat it. It has been suggested that "ordering a table" relates to convening a eucharistic celebration, since prophets are specifically allowed to "give thanks/ eucharistize as they wish" (10:7).[34] Aaron Milavec suggests, on the basis of Jewish practice in *b. Ber.* 48a–b, that the prohibition on the prophet eating from the table he orders would also prohibit him from presiding at the Eucharist, thus effectively neutralizing this privilege.[35] Probably the difference is more apparent than real, if every community Eucharist would have been a full meal as suggested by μετὰ δὲ τὸ ἐμπλησθῆναι (10:1) and conversely every full meal of the community would require a Eucharistia. In the last case (D), asking for money is forbidden unless it is for another person in need. This matches the prohibition on apostles asking for money in 10:6.

The two middle units (B and C) relate to issues of teaching. The first requires the prophet to do as he or she says, or be exposed as a false prophet. The second clearly reflects a controversial matter in the community because of its length and complexity. It is only permitted to a prophet who has already proved to be a genuine prophet (δεδοκιμασμένος ἀληθινός), presumably on the basis of his or her lifestyle. It must refer to some behavior (ποιῶν) of the prophet that would

---

34. See Jean-Paul Audet, *La Didachè: Instructions des apôtres* (Ebib; Paris: J. Gabalda, 1958), 450.
35. Milavec, *Didache: Faith, Hope, and Life*, 464–66.

be scandalous in anyone else but was acceptable for a prophet since it was the mark of Old Testament prophets also. It enacts in some some symbolic way (μυστήριον) a "mystery of the church in the world" by which the heavenly or eschatological reality of the church's existence is portrayed in temporal terms.[36] Much has been made of the idea of a "spiritual marriage" of a prophet and a prophetess, traveling together in an ascetic relationship. This was suggested already by Von Harnack[37] and has had an enduring appeal to scholars.[38] It is certainly possible, but has problems in that only tested and proven prophets might enact such a mystery, and a prophet arriving with a prophetess from outside the community would not be tested and proven until he and she had passed the lifestyle test. Likewise, the Didache does not show the marks of an ascetic text, unless one interprets another difficult text, namely, the "whole yoke of the Lord" and "concerning food" passages in 6:2–3 as referring to ascetic behavior. In any case, there is no concrete evidence for such a practice in the text itself, but it has to be inferred from external references.

If the prophets are understood as coming from outside the community in 11:6–12, the true prophets are allowed, unlike the apostles, to settle in the community in 13:1. If prophets are prohibited from asking for a table and eating from it in 11:9 on pain of being declared false prophets, then they are granted the right to food (ἄξιός ἐστι τῆς τροφῆς αὐτοῦ) from the community if they do settle. If they were prohibited from asking for money in 11:12, they now have a right in 13:3–7 not just to the first fruits of the community, but also to money and clothing and every other possession, at the discretion of the community member (ὡς ἄν σοι δόξῃ, 13:7). This is described as being κατὰ τὴν ἐντολήν, in my opinion a reference to an interpretation of the Old Testament laws concerning first fruits.[39] The contrast between chapters 11 and 13 seems to me to be so great that it indicates a redaction of an earlier tradition, at a time when prophets have obtained an increased importance in the community. This importance is highlighted in 15:1–2, where they clearly have such a high status and honor that the bishops and deacons are in danger of being despised in comparison with them. Again,

---

36. Only the Jerusalem Manuscript of the *Didache* has the word μυστήριον, which is absent from the Coptic and Ethiopic texts, though this may have been because the expression was not understood.

37. Von Harnack, *Lehre der zwölf Apostel*, 44–47.

38. See especially Georg Kretschmar, "Ein Beitrag zur Frage nach dem Ursprung frühchristlicher Askese," *ZTK* 61 (1964): 27–67. He is followed by Kurt Niederwimmer, "An Examination of the Development of Itinerant Radicalism in the Environment and Tradition of the *Didache*," in *The Didache in Modern Research* (ed. J. A. Draper; AGJU 37; Leiden: Brill, 1996), 321–39, who provides a discussion of the nature and origin of the practice of *syzygy*. See also Niederwimmer, *Die Didache*, 179–82.

39. Draper, "First Fruits and the Support of Prophets."

this appears to represent a redactional development within the overall text of the Didache, in a time of transition.

In 16:3, the community is warned, "For in the last days false prophets and corruptors will be multiplied and sheep will be turned into wolves and love will be turned into hatred." The couplet οἱ ψευδοπροφῆται καὶ οἱ φθορεῖς seems to be a hendiadys that refers to the same persons. In view of the use of "false prophets" to describe false apostles in 11:6, it could refer to those claiming to be either apostles or prophets. However, in this warning, it is not a matter of exploitation of the community for financial reward, but of false teaching "contrary to the law" (ἀνομία 16:4), which leads to division, quarrels, and betrayal:

Matt 7:15–16:
Προσέχετε ἀπὸ τῶν ψευδοπροφητῶν, οἵτινες ἔρχονται πρὸς ὑμᾶς ἐν ἐνδύμασιν προβάτων, ἔσωθεν δέ εἰσιν λύκοι ἅρπαγες. ἀπὸ τῶν καρπῶν αὐτῶν ἐπιγνώσεσθε αὐτούς.

Did. 16:3:
ἐν γὰρ ταῖς ἐσχάταις ἡμέραις πληθυνθήσονται οἱ ψευδοπροφῆται καὶ οἱ φθορεῖς καὶ στραφήσονται τὰ πρόβατα εἰς λύκους καὶ ἡ ἀγάπη στραφήσεται εἰς μῖσος.

Such people are aligning themselves to the "world deceiver." It is significant that these "false prophets" are not "wolves disguised as sheep" who come to the community from outside, as in Matt 7:15, but instead "sheep who have turned into wolves," those from inside the community who have turned against it.

2.3. TEACHERS

Of particular significance is that, in both chapters 13 and 15, the mention of the prophets is accompanied by references to teachers, indicating that in some sense they are coupled together in the consciousness of the community. No mention is made of apostles in either chapter. This seems to signal changed community relations both with the outside and in its own internal arrangements. It also raises the question of the teacher as a community functionary: is the teacher a "charismatic" and is the teacher a settled community figure or an itinerant? A further permutation of the question relates to the connection between the *function* of teaching, expressed in a verbal form, and the *office* of a teacher, expressed as a noun. It is significant, in other words, that the apostles are never mentioned together with the teachers, while the teachers are only mentioned together with the prophets. It would seem that apostles are not a significant office within the community in the Didache, while prophets and teachers are and both qualify for support from the community. If this represents the final redactional layer of the text, then it must signal a shift in emphasis from outside to inside, from mobile to stable. It could also signal a shift from "non-charismatic" to "charismatic" leadership within the community as opposed to outside it.

If we examine the first of the two occurrences of the title "teacher" in 13:2, then we learn that the teacher has to be verified for his or her genuineness before qualifying for support; s/he must be ἀληθινός. Secondly, no mention is made here of settling as in the case of the prophet. The instruction leaves open the question of whether the teacher comes from inside or outside the community. Thirdly, the instruction on teachers adds ὥσπερ ὁ ἐργάτης as a qualification to ἄξιος. This may indicate that, while it is his or her utterances in the Spirit that qualify the prophet for support, it is his or her *work* that qualifies the teacher. In other words, it is not a "charismatic" office as such, if by that is meant Spirit-directed. After this teachers fall out of the instructions on tithing in 13:3–7 and only the prophet is in view.

In the second occurrence of the title "teacher" in 15:1–2, nothing at all is given away about their work, except that they are linked with the prophets and share the performance (λειτουργοῦσι) of their "public duty" or "ministry" (τὴν λειτουργίαν). For this they receive along with the prophets the honor appropriate to those engaging in public duty (οἱ τετιμημένοι), which threatens to leave the bishops and deacons despised (μὴ οὖν ὑπερίδητε αὐτούς). Nevertheless, the bishops and deacons are described as sharing the same λειτουργία as the prophets and teachers. This is intended to indicate, I think, that all of the leaders of the community have the same obligation to public service (for instance gifts of money, public buildings, public work) for the good of the community, as would be expected of all those aspiring to public office in the ancient Graeco-Roman world, for which they receive honor. I do not think that the reference is to leadership of public worship described as "liturgy" in our modern sense—leadership of public worship is an aspect of "honor" rather than an aspect of "liturgy."

Otherwise, there are two functional appearances of teaching, which may or may not be carried out by leaders designated as "teachers." The first is the obvious one, that the foundational section of the Didache consists of διδαχή and so requires people who teach it. Such people are nowhere named, but they are mentioned in at least one place in 4:1–2:

Τέκνον μου τοῦ λαλοῦντός σοι τὸν λόγον τοῦ θεοῦ μνησθήσῃ νυκτὸς καὶ ἡμέρας τιμήσεις δὲ αὐτὸν ὡς κύριον· ὅθεν γὰρ ἡ κυριότης λαλεῖται ἐκεῖ κύριός ἐστιν. ἐκζητήσεις δὲ καθ' ἡμέραν τὰ πρόσωπα τῶν ἁγίων ἵνα ἐπαναπαῇς τοῖς λόγοις αὐτῶν.

Yet the principle here is that of representation: the one sent is as the one who sent him or her. So when the things of the Lord are spoken by those authorized to speak them, the Lord is there. This is closer to the function of the apostle than the teacher. Nevertheless, it is a teaching role and a substantial one: if the saints are to meet every day, this would make substantial demands on the one teaching, demands which would preclude the person from gainful employment. This would explain why the teacher is granted the right to support on the basis of being an ἐργάτης. It would also explain why they receive the same τιμή as the prophets, though their honour derives from *what* they teach and not *how* they derive it (from the tradition and not from the Spirit as in the case of the prophets). In any case, the continuing tradition of the Two Ways in the *Apostolic Church Order* makes it clear that teaching "the things of the Lord" should be regarded as a work requiring material support, and this seems to me to underlie the practice of the Didache also:

> You shall honour him as much as you are able from your sweat and from the labour of your hands. If the Lord through him has made you worthy to be given spiritual food and drink and eternal life, much the more should you bring him corruptible and temporary food. "For the workman is worthy of his hire" and "You shall not muzzle a threshing ox" and "Nobody plants a vine and does not eat the fruit of it."[40]

Echoes of this ethos are found also in *Barn.* 19:9–10, where a series of sayings on giving are linked by, "You shall love as the apple of your eye everyone who speaks the word of the Lord to you." The *Life of Shenudi* also gives a graphic representation of the kind of teaching role played by the Two Ways, where the Abbot Vita performs what he received from Abbot Shenudi:

> Listen attentively to me all of you when I begin and speak of the wonders and the miracles which God has worked by the hand of our pure father, the blessed Abba Shenudi, which I have seen with my own eyes, I, Visa, his son and his disciple, signs which my holy father has told me, that he has given to me through his pure mouth, without deception or trickery. And what I tell you is only a little (of what he has done). And surely he always used to teach and say, "The way is easy and the path twofold, one of life and the other of death." (my translation)[41]

As in the *Apostolic Constitutions* and the *Fides CCCXVIII Patrum / Syntagma Doctrinae*, the bare bones of the Two Ways provide the framework for the inter-

---

40. Alistair Stewart-Sykes, *The Apostolic Church Order: The Greek Text with Introduction, Translation and Annotation* (Early Christian Studies 10; Strathfield, Australia: Centre for Early Christian Studies, 2006), 107–8.

41. Text is taken from Émile C. Amélineau, *Monuments pour servir à l'histoire de l'Égypte chrétienne aux IVe, Ve, VIe et VIIe siècles* (Mémoires publiés par les membres de la mission archéologique du Caire 4; Paris: Leroux, 1895), 2:285–96. My translation is based on the French text of Amélineau, but corrected against the Arabic text with the kind assistance of Professor Gerhard van Gelder of the Oriental Faculty in Oxford.

pretive additions of the particular teacher.[42] However, all of these sayings are found in the Two Ways teaching used by the Didache as a source, so it is hard to draw anything more than the general conclusion that it continued an existing attitude or praxis towards support for the teacher.

A final contentious context in which the teaching function is mentioned is 11:1–2. Here it is clearly a case of a person coming from outside the community and teaching (ὃς ἂν οὖν ἐλθὼν διδάξῃ), who represents both promise and peril for the community. The community is instructed to test the teacher on the basis of his or her teaching against the material contained in the instructions so far: ταῦτα πάντα τὰ προειρημένα.[43] Anyone who "turns around" and teaches in such a way as to "break down" or "destroy" must be shunned: ἐὰν δὲ αὐτὸς ὁ διδάσκων στραφεὶς διδάσκῃ ἄλλην διδαχὴν εἰς τὸ καταλῦσαι μὴ αὐτοῦ ἀκούσητε (11:2). I have argued that this demonstrates a consciousness of schism and doctrinal conflict, probably over the question of Torah.[44] Only the person who "adds to righteousness" should be accepted ὡς κύριον. Interestingly, again, is the use of representational language proper to the apostolic function. The whole section clearly relates to Matt 5:17–20, since the concepts of breaking down true and false teaching and adding to righteousness occur in both texts.[45]

Stempel takes 11:1–2 in combination with 11:3–6 as evidence for the existence of wandering *teachers*. Even if the existence of the office of the teacher cannot be proven, he regards the function of the teacher at least as the primary role ("eine primäre Tätigkeit") in the community.[46] I have argued that the representational language (ὡς κύριον) makes it more likely that this is a redaction of the instructions on apostles that follow. In any case, the language is reminiscent of the reference to the increase of "false prophets" (those who came as apostles include false prophets according to 11:5, 6) in the last days in 16:3, where the same language of "turning" is used twice (καὶ στραφήσονται τὰ πρόβατα εἰς λύκους καὶ ἡ ἀγάπη στραφήσεται εἰς μῖσος), together with the sheep and wolves imagery employed in Matthew also for apostles and prophets. Hence, I am inclined to take the reference in 11:1–2 as a reference to apostles and/or to the prophets with

---

42. Jonathan Draper, "Vice Catalogues as Oral-Mnemonic Cues: A Comparative Study of the Two Ways Tradition in the Didache and Parallels from the Perspective of Oral Tradition," in *Jesus, the Voice, and the Text: Beyond the Oral and the Written Gospel* (ed. T. Thatcher; Waco, Tex.: Baylor University Press, 2008).

43. This echoes the warning against false teaching in 6:1: ὅρα μή τίς σε πλανήσῃ ἀπὸ ταύτης τῆς ὁδοῦ τῆς διδαχῆς ἐπεὶ παρεκτὸς θεοῦ σε διδάσκει. Baptism is likewise made conditional on the teaching contained in chapters 1–6: ταῦτα πάντα προειπόντες βαπτίσατε (7:1).

44. Jonathan A. Draper, "Torah and Troublesome Apostles in the Didache Community," in Draper, ed., *The Didache in Modern Research*, 340–63; published previously in *NovT* 33 (1991): 347–72.

45. See Draper, "Torah and Troublesome Apostles"; idem, "Genesis and Narrative Thrust of the Paraenesis."

46. Stempel, "Der Lehrer in der 'Lehre der Zwölf Apostel'," 215.

whom they are associated in 11:3. There is thus no certain evidence for "wandering teachers," and the need to teach the Two Ways, at least, suggests that there were already resident teachers who might be honored "as the Lord" for teaching "the things of the Lord," and who would receive some kind of support, either from the people they teach (as was the practice it seems in the Two Ways source), or from the community. Having said that, it must, of course be acknowledged that an apostle and a prophet might each be teachers as well, but that would not be their defining characteristic.

2.4. BISHOPS AND DEACONS

The final pair of functionaries that appear in the Didache are "bishops and deacons," mentioned merely together and only in 15:1–2. The same qualifications for office are given for both. So beyond what is contained in their titles we learn nothing to distinguish the one from the other. Nevertheless the titles are indicative: the bishop is an overseer with some kind of responsibility for exercising control; the deacon is a servant to the community with some practical role in the life of the community.

The bishop and deacon are both appointed by the community either by a laying on of hands (ordination) or by raising of hands (election). It is difficult to know which. Either way, it is the community that recognizes and appoints. They are not charismatic figures in the sense of receiving their office from God or the Spirit. Naturally, therefore, they are described as liable to testing by the community (δεδοκιμασμένους) to which they are accountable (15:1). Further qualities required of these two functionaries also speak much of what is expected of them. In the first place they are required to be "mild" or "gentle" (πραΰς). In other words, their role is to keep the peace among members of the community in which quarreling is frowned on and viewed as defiling the "pure sacrifice" of the community Eucharist. In the second place, they are required to be financially generous (ἀφιλαργύρους, 15:1). As I understand the situation, the bishops and deacons would be patrons of the community, men and women of social standing in the wider community and of sufficient wealth and property that they could host the eucharistic meal (and much later build churches) and further the work of the community.[47] In return they would receive the honor due to patrons. The difficulty seen in Did. 15 is that they are not receiving honor but instead contempt in comparison with the prophets and teachers. I do not see the bishops and deacons as emerging early catholic figures of the routinization of charisma,

---

47. This is how the local synagogues in the Diaspora were organized, as inscriptions show (see also Rom 16:23: "Gaius, who is host to me and to the whole church, greets you. Erastus, the city treasurer, and our brother Quartus, greet you").

but as figures from the earliest communities like the "overseer" or *mebaqqer* in the Dead Sea Scrolls.

It is not the position of the bishops and deacons, which is surprising and calls for comment, but the position of the prophets and teachers. The fact that these figures are mentioned coming from outside the community (at least in the case of prophets) and as receiving special honor above the local patrons, would already signal that there is trouble. I have suggested[48] that the war in Palestine in 68–70 c.e. fundamentally changed the situation for the communities, in that Jerusalem was no longer the center of authority and also in that Jewish-Christian refugees from Palestine would have started arriving in large numbers seeking to settle in new places. Some of these may have had first-hand knowledge of the teaching of Jesus found in the so-called "Q" tradition, beyond what was available to the local community teachers and other functionaries. They would have attracted admiration and honor, which undermined the position of the patrons of the community and so endangered its stability.

In conclusion, then, the bishops and deacons are settled figures of the local community, responsible for contributing material and social assets to the community, with the role of oversight and service. They are patrons of the community who have the resources to assist the community and homes large enough to meet in: finance, influence in the wider community which might serve to protect the community and enhance its status in the wider society, education and administrative competence. The possession of their resources depended, of course, on their being settled and influential members of the wider local society. In return for their public contribution of resources, such functionaries receive honor, a prized commodity in the ancient world. Their ascribed honor, however, would be challenged by the acquired honor of charismatic figures, whose resources came directly from God and were not allowed to be tested.

3. Settled and Wandering Functionaries in the Epistle of James

The genre of the Epistle of James has remained at the center of studies of this work, since Martin Dibelius[49] argued that the work consisted of paraenesis, ethical commonplaces that had no particular order or structure and no

---

48. See Jonathan A. Draper, "Social Ambiguity and the Production of Text: Prophets, Teachers, Bishops, and Deacons and the Development of the Jesus Tradition in the Community of the *Didache*," in *The Didache in Context: Essays on its Text, History, and Transmission* (ed. C. N. Jefford; NovTSup 77; Leiden: Brill, 1995), 284–312; see also Draper, "Weber, Theissen, and 'Wandering Charismatics,'" 541–76. This idea is taken up also, at length, by Milavec, *Didache: Faith, Hope, and Life*, 462–90.

49. Martin Dibelius and Hans Conzelmann, *The Pastoral Epistles: A Commentary on the Pastoral Epistles* (trans. P. Buttolph and A. Yarbro; Hermeneia; Philadelphia: Fortress, 1972). See Raymond A. Martin, *James* (Minneapolis: Augsburg, 1982).

discernible *tendenz*. Recent studies have moved away from his form-critical approach towards seeing a far more coherent purpose and structure than Dibelius allowed.[50] However, the Epistle of James gives little away about the nature of its community officials. Only elders and teachers are specifically mentioned. Prophets and prophecy occur only once and then apparently with reference to the prophets of the Hebrew Scriptures as examples of patience in suffering in 5:10. Even if the reference were taken to be to Christian prophets, which is unlikely, it would tell us little except that the historical time of their active ministry was over since it is couched in the Aorist tense. This makes it unlikely that prophets were active in the community either inside it or from outside. However, as we shall see, there are aspects of the role of the teacher that touch on the typology of the prophet.

Apostles are never mentioned in James, but the office is implied by the letter. James, whoever the person may be behind the use of the name, sends a letter to another community or communities among the Jewish Diaspora in which he, or the persona he has adopted, clearly has a recognized authority. He would have to send the letter with a delegated messenger who would be his apostle, speaking with the authority of the one who sent him, clarifying the message and taking the response of the community back with him to the author. Such letters could not circulate independently of messengers, arriving anonymously through the post as they might today. However, it is significant that James does not himself claim to be an *apostle* of Jesus; instead he designates himself simply "James, of God and of the Lord Jesus Christ slave" (1:1). Paul designates himself "Paul slave of Christ Jesus called apostle" alongside his claim to have been designated as Christ's apostle by a special calling and set apart for the gospel of God in Rom 1:1 (see Phil 1:1). The emphatic structure of the self-designation in James calls for comment. It may indicate that he considers such apostleship of the Lord to have been designated only to the Twelve, or it may be that his intention is polemical, in which case he is consciously adopting the role of the classical *eiron*.[51] Then calling himself simply a "slave" and making no other claims to be an apostle is designed to puncture the pretences of others who make inflated claims that he and those who support him would consider illegitimate. In any case, the designation is not simply an imita-

---

50. E.g., Patrick J. Hartin, *James and the Q Sayings of Jesus* (JSNTSup 47; Sheffield: JSOT, 1991); Wiard Popkes, "James and Paraenesis Reconsidered" in *Texts and Contexts: Biblical Texts in their Textual and Situational Contexts* (ed. T. Fornberg and D. Hellholm; Oslo: Scandinavian University Press, 1995), 535–61; David H. Edgar, *Has God not Chosen the Poor? The Social Setting of the Epistle of James* (JSNTSup 206; Sheffield: Sheffield Academic Press, 2001).

51. See Aristotle, *Eth.nic.* 4.7.14–17. For summaries of the use of irony in classical literature, as this applies to biblical texts, see Douglas C. Muecke, *The Compass of Irony* (London: Methuen, 1969); Edwin M. Good, *Irony in the Old Testament* (Sheffield: Almond, 1981); Jakob Jónsson, *Humour and Irony in the New Testament: Illuminated by Parallels in Talmud and Midrash* (BZRGG 28; Leiden: Brill, 1985).

tion of Paul and seems to recall the designation *ebed YHWH* in Old Testament references to the great prophets and teachers in Israel's past. It also carries with it the claim that as a faithful servant of God and his designated messiah Jesus, James's teaching carries their authority.[52]

The role of teacher seems to be pronounced in this short Epistle.[53] Following the well-known discussion of the relationship between faith and works, where some are arguing, it would seem, for salvation by faith alone. James counters that faith apart from works is dead and continues with instructions concerning teachers, in which he makes it clear that he himself is a teacher: "we who teach will receive (λημψόμεθα) greater judgment." It seems likely that there is a connection between the discussion on faith and works and his warning about teachers. Some teachers then appear to the author to be giving false teaching on this matter, which is causing dissension in the church, since after the instruction on teaching James asks in 4:1, "What causes quarrels and dissensions among you?" The key passage on teachers is found in 3:1–18:

> Not many of you should become teachers (διδάσκαλοι), my brothers and sisters, for you know that we who teach will be judged with greater strictness (μεῖζον κρίμα λημψόμεθα). For all of us make many mistakes. Anyone who makes no mistakes in speaking is perfect (τέλειος), able to keep the whole body (καὶ ὅλον τὸ σῶμα) in check with a bridle. If we put bits into the mouths of horses to make them obey us, we guide their whole bodies. Or look at ships: though they are so large that it takes strong winds to drive them, yet they are guided by a very small rudder wherever the will of the pilot directs. So also the tongue is a small member, yet it boasts of great exploits. How great a forest is set ablaze by a small fire! And the tongue is a fire. The tongue is placed among our members as a world of iniquity; it stains the whole body, sets on fire the cycle of nature, and is itself set on fire by hell. For every species of beast and bird, of reptile and sea creature, can be tamed and has been tamed by the human species, but no one can tame the tongue—a restless evil, full of deadly poison.
>
> With it we bless the Lord and Father, and with it we curse those who are made in the likeness of God. From the same mouth come blessing and cursing. My brothers and sisters, this ought not to be so. Does a spring pour forth from the same opening both fresh and brackish water? Can a fig tree, my brothers and sisters, yield olives, or a grapevine figs? No more can salt water yield fresh.

---

52. See the discussion in Edgar, *Has God not Chosen the Poor?*, 44–50.

53. Following Dibelius it became common to see James as a rather arbitrary and incoherent collection of traditional material on the form-critical basis that this was the nature of paraenesis. However, more recent work has begun to discover a distinctive over-arching world view in the text, an alternative Christian viewpoint in which the messiah is not a savior by virtue of his death and resurrection but a messiah who will return to "effect a violent purge of 'the wicked' and the restoration of Israel's twelve-tribe kingdom" (see Matt Jackson-McCabe, "The Messiah Jesus in the Mythic World of James," *JBL* 122 [2003]: 706). It is not irrelevant to our investigation that the same Christology and world view dominates the Didache.

> Who is wise and understanding (σοφὸς καὶ ἐπιστήμων) among you? Show by your good life that your works are done with gentleness born of wisdom (σοφίας). But if you have bitter envy and selfish ambition in your hearts, do not be boastful and false to the truth. Such wisdom (σοφία) does not come down from above, but is earthly, unspiritual, devilish. For where there is envy and selfish ambition, there will also be disorder and wickedness of every kind. But the wisdom (σοφία) from above is first pure, then peaceable, gentle, willing to yield, full of mercy and good fruits, without a trace of partiality or hypocrisy. And a harvest of righteousness (δικαιοσύνης) is sown in peace for those who make peace.

The danger with the teacher is that his teaching can guide the whole body: just as the bit in a horse's mouth or the rudder of a boat, his tongue can guide the community the way s/he wants to. It can be poisonous, inflammatory, and harmful because of its eloquence. For this reason the teacher will be severely judged.

Interestingly, there is no reference here to a specific body of accepted teaching that the teacher transmits and against which the teacher could be judged. However, the emphasis on wisdom signals that the author stands in a particular tradition of wisdom teaching within Israel,[54] and the reference to the "harvest of righteousness" (see 1:20; 2:23) carries the connotation of fulfilling the requirements of the Torah as interpreted by the Christian community, as in Matthew and the Didache, in view of the frequent occurrence of νόμος in James (1:25; 2:8–13; 4:11–12). So too does the use of τέλειος, which has a key role also in Matthew and the Didache as we have seen, referring to fulfilment of Torah ("the whole yoke of the Lord" in Did. 6:2).

It is significant that what comes out of the teacher's mouth is judged in as much as it should be blessing not curses, like fresh water and edible fruit rather than like brackish water and inappropriate fruit. The language is reminiscent of Matthew's criteria for judging the prophet, but, significantly, the "fruit" envisaged by James is applied not to lifestyle but to what comes from the "tongue." Nevertheless it is not ultimately the content of the teaching on which they are judged but on the basis of their lifestyle ("show by your good life, etc."). The hallmark

---

54. As Hartin, *James and the Q Sayings of Jesus*, 63 rightly points out, "Wisdom admonitions concentrate attention on the teaching element." The wisdom instruction in James focuses firstly on the lifestyle appropriate for the believer here and now, and secondly on the eschatological promise for right conduct. Hartin provides an excellent discussion of the wisdom teaching and its relation to Q, but this *content* of the teaching is not really relevant to our discussion in this paper. Hartin's insistence on both present and future aspects of wisdom is taken even further by Todd C. Penner, *The Epistle of James and Eschatology: Re-reading an Ancient Christian Letter* (JSNTSup 121; Sheffield: Sheffield Academic Press, 1996) who emphasizes the eschatological framework as determining the direction of the wisdom instruction. Matthew and the Didache have similar tensions between wisdom instruction and eschatological orientation, which suggest that wisdom and eschatology are not opposites but complementary.

of the true teacher, true wisdom, is equivalent to a life of purity, peacefulness, gentleness, mercy, sincerity and so on, which are described as the "harvest of righteousness" (3:18)—in other words the lifestyle of the teacher, the criterion also in Matthew and the Didache.

Since the content of the teaching may be tested against the yardstick of blessing God or cursing the neighbor, it probably does not have charismatic prophetic speech in mind.[55] It is seen as equivalent to wisdom and not to revelation, which is mediated by the Spirit. Nevertheless, it is interesting that the criterion against which the teacher will be judged is lifestyle as in the case of prophets in the Didache and Matthew.

It could be said that the Epistle itself provides an exemplar of the teaching offered by the teachers addressed in James, since its author includes himself among them in the "we" of James 3:1. Massey Shepherd[56] long ago pointed out that the letter seems to be structured around a central macarism in 1:25, and that it stands closely parallel to Matthew's Sermon on the Mount (both the "Q" and the "M" traditions), though sometimes closer to the wording of Luke. Shepherd[57] notes the same phenomenon in Ignatius and the Didache, and argues for a dependence of these, together with James, on Matthew. However, given that the parallels are to "Q" and are never exactly parallel in any of these writings, it seems possible that all four writings reflect a widespread and well-known catechetical tradition, that may even pre-date the Jesus tradition in some respect and reflect Hasidic teaching traditions.[58]

If chapter four is understood as continuing the discussion of teachers, then the "asking and not receiving" relates to their request for financial or material resources from the community. They are understood as wanting the money for the wrong reasons "to spend on [their] passions." This is incompatible with the lifestyle that is a "harvest of righteousness," which is here also linked with the indwelling of the Spirit:

> (4:4) Adulterers! Do you not know that friendship with the world is enmity with God? Therefore whoever wishes to be a friend of the world becomes an enemy of God. 5 Or do you suppose that it is for nothing that the scripture says, "God yearns jealously for the spirit that he has made to dwell in us"?

---

55. Though one should note Paul's test in 1 Cor 12:3: "Therefore I want you to understand that no one speaking by the Spirit of God ever says 'Let Jesus be cursed!' and no one can say 'Jesus is Lord' except by the Holy Spirit."

56. Massey H. Shepherd, "The Epistle of James and the Gospel of Matthew," *JBL* 75 (1956) 42.

57. Ibid., 48.

58. Van de Sandt and Flusser, *The Didache: Its Jewish Sources*, 193–237.

It seems that James imagines a certain asceticism as necessary for the indwelling of the Holy Spirit, and therefore for "speaking in the Spirit." Yet the message of the teachers cannot be equated with prophetic speech, since the whole point of the passage is that teachers should control their tongues like a rudder to steer a ship, rather than allow the Spirit to speak freely through them. There would seem to be no question of λαλοῦν ἐν πνεύματι. However, all of this is somewhat obliquely stated. At best we can say that teachers are the main functionaries who emerge in the epistle and that they are viewed rather ambivalently. They are liable to give wrong teaching, to cause controversy and to be greedy in their appropriation of community resources. They will be judged on their lifestyle as well as the content of their teaching. The content of the teaching provided by the author of the epistle appears to draw on conventional Jewish and Hellenistic wisdom themes.

The only other recognizable functionaries in the Epistle of James are the body of the elders. In this well-known passage, James instructs the sick person to call together the elders, thus indicating an acknowledged group in the community with authority especially over prayer and ministry. They would then, necessarily, be resident and settled in local communities:

> Are any among you sick? They should call for the elders of the church (πρεσβυτέρους τῆς ἐκκλησίας) and have them pray over them, anointing them with oil in the name of the Lord. The prayer of faith will save the sick, and the Lord will raise them up; and anyone who has committed sins will be forgiven. Therefore confess your sins to one another, and pray for one another, so that you may be healed. The prayer of the righteous is powerful and effective. Elijah was a human being like us, and he prayed fervently that it might not rain, and for three years and six months it did not rain on the earth. Then he prayed again, and the heaven gave rain and the earth yielded its harvest (5:14–18).

James H. Ropes[59] gives many rabbinic parallels to the idea of prayer over the sick by a righteous man or rabbi (e.g., *b. Ned.* 39b; *b. B. Bat.* 116a). Indeed a group of four rabbis go to pray for R. Eliezer (*b. Sanh.* 101a). Nevertheless, it is difficult to determine whether the "elders" constitute an officially defined body of functionaries or simply the senior members of the community. It is likely that synagogue organization in the Diaspora would have had a group recognized as "elders," since the later rabbinic texts (e.g., *b. Meg.* 23b) require a group of at least ten or *minyan* to constitute a legal assembly. While the quorum may have been a later innovation since it is not uniformly practiced, it seems to me to reflect an earlier understanding that a synagogue is constituted and organized by a group of elders.

---

59. *A Critical and Exegetical Commentary on the Epistle of St. James* (ICC; Edinburgh: T&T Clark, 1916), 304.

Oil was a widely recognized medium for healing in the ancient world.[60] Prayer and anointing with oil sound like a reference to liturgical and ritual practice rather than charismatic acts of power in the Spirit. Faith and righteousness, together with the invocation of the "Name of the Lord," are the source of the prayer's effectiveness. It is interesting, however, that their ministry is compared with that of the prophet Elijah engaged in a charismatic and miraculous exercise of power. On the other hand, Elijah's common humanity is emphasized and not his special charismatic endowment (Ἠλίας ἄνθρωπος ἦν ὁμοιοπαθὴς ἡμῖν). It is the faith and righteousness of the elders that is effective and not their possession of the Spirit. In any case, the exercise of healing power by the elders perhaps implies activity under the control of the community rather than deeds of power by charismatic figures, since they do not take the initiative but are called in (προσκαλεσάσθω, 5:14).

In most respects, then, it may be said that James does not fit easily in the same frame of reference with regard to functionaries as Matthew and the Didache, who do share a common framework. There are apostles bringing messages from the outside, from a recognized figure of authority, real or pretended—whether or not this letter comes from the historical James of Jerusalem or not cannot ever be proved or disproved. Apart from that, there are powerful resident teachers who direct the affairs of the community like a horse's bit or a ship's rudder. Then there are settled elders in the community, who are righteous, full of faith, and may in some respects be compared with the prophet Elijah "as a human being with a nature like theirs."

4. Conclusion

The wealth and complexity of the data from the three texts is difficult to bring into any neat and coherent pattern for the purposes of comparison. However, there are commonalities and connections as well as differences. The Didache and Matthew express a more clearly comparable set of figures and relations, where charismatic figures are portrayed as active and regarded with mixed feelings, while James seems to fit in an environment more closely related to wisdom than to charisma. Nevertheless, there are points of agreement between all three writings as well.

In both Didache and Matthew, apostles are associated with prophets in some way. In Matthew, Jesus's authentic disciples are sent by Jesus and so are his apostles but they also carry on the role of the true prophets in Israel who went before them, while false prophets also claim to be sent by the Lord to prophesy, perform exorcisms and do miracles in his name and hence claim to be apostles in the sense of bearing delegated authority. In Didache false apostles are called "false proph-

---

60. See ibid., 305–7 for examples.

ets." In both texts these figures seem to be mobile, coming into the community from outside and, while highly honored, they are also feared as potentially dangerous (wolves masquerading as sheep in Matthew or sheep turned into wolves in Didache). The danger seems to be associated with anti-nomism. They engage in acts of power and live a hard and dangerous life. Hospitality should be extended to them but they may not ask for money. They speak in the Spirit and may only be tested by their lifestyle, which should match that of their Lord. Their teaching and lifestyle must be consistent. According to Didache, prophets may settle in the community and must be supported by it. Apostles, on the other hand, in keeping with their nature as delegated representatives on a temporary mission, may not settle or even linger in the community. In Matthew, alternatively, apostles are sent by the risen Lord on a permanent mission to make disciples of all nations. They may even be the foundations of the church (if Jesus's designation of Peter as the rock on which he will build the church is allowed as an example rather than a one-time designation of authority). Both texts also associate prophets with teachers (at least in Matt 23:34 "sages and scribes" are "sent" by Jesus along with the prophets, while in the Didache teachers are named alongside the prophets in chapters 11:3, 13:1–2 and 15:1–2).

While James mentions neither, this profile of the apostles and prophets in Matthew and Didache matches the description of the teachers in the Epistle of James in significant although indirect ways. In the first place, while prophets are nowhere explicitly mentioned as active in James's community, the teachers' role is associated with God's Spirit "that he has made to dwell in us" in 4:4 (if teachers are still in mind at this point). What is different is the insistence in James that the teachers should be in control of what they say, since the tongue is like a horse's bit or a ship's rudder (3:2–5). In Did. 11:7, on the other hand, "speaking in the Spirit" is not to be controlled, though nothing is said about whether the prophet him/ herself is personally in control of what is being said. Nothing *requires* that the "speaking in the Spirit" is ecstatic speech or glossolalia. Secondly, the specific problem that is incompatible with the indwelling of God's Spirit in James is a desire to get (money) to spend on their material desires (4:1–3), just as it is for apostles and prophets in Did. 11:6, 12 and seemingly in Matt 10:9. Further, and most significantly, the teachers must be tested by their lifestyle in Jas 3:10–12, as in Did. 11:8 and Matt 7:15–23.

Both Didache and Matthew (with reservations about the use of the title) value teachers and associate them with the maintenance of traditional teaching (Two Ways, Torah). In both texts, the content of the authoritative teaching that is set on the lips of Jesus and entrusted to the apostles largely consists of "Q" tradition (the Sermon on the Mount in Matt 5–7 given by Jesus to the apostles in the presence of the mixed crowds of Jews and Gentiles, and the material inserted into the Two Ways in Did. 1:3–6 under the rubric "teaching of the Lord through the apostles to the Gentiles"). Moreover, in both texts nothing must be taken away from what has been passed on, though it may be added to: Did. 11:1–2 allows "adding to righteousness," which Matthew also allows in terms of "greater righteousness" than the Pharisees. Matthew affirms the kind of teaching authority accorded to the scribes and Pharisees but not their lifestyle.

Teachers ("sages and scribes") may be "sent" by Jesus and so perhaps be temporarily mobile as apostles, but they seem to be settled in the communities. In Didache it appears that at least some teachers (or "teaching functionaries") must be located within settled communities, since the daily meeting of the teacher with catechumens in the Didache would require continuity, and Matthew can associate the role of teaching with "a seat." On the other hand, the community of the Didache is warned in 11:1–2 against those who *come and teach* another teaching (function as teachers) to destroy the teaching they have already received. In both Matt 5–7, 28:20 and the "second title" of the Didache, as well as the Two Ways generally, the content of the teaching is associated with "the Lord," while the teaching activity itself is associated with catechesis ("making disciples"). James seems to envisage teachers as settled local functionaries, indeed the most important functionaries in the community, but little is said concerning the body of teaching they present, beyond what is contained in the letter coming from one who is himself a teacher. His teaching is coming from outside the community and anyone delegated to bring the letter to the community would also be functioning as a teacher. Like Matthew and the Didache, James has, as has often been noted, important links with "Q" tradition.

The (Twelve/ Eleven) Apostles may be sent "by the Lord" with authority to teach the Gentiles in Matthew and the Didache. However the word is also used in the latter, it seems, to designate routine representatives passing through on an embassy who may not stay longer than one or at most two days. In addition, we have seen that the Didache associates apostles and prophets in 11:3 and describes false apostles as "false prophets." Similarly, the role of the apostles in Matthew's story of the sending of the Twelve is (inversely) close to that of (false) prophets. James does not mention prophets or apostles. He does not even explicitly claim apostolic authority for himself, preferring the designation "servant/ slave of God and the Lord Jesus Christ." However, as we have noted, the sending of a letter would necessitate the delegation of authority to an "apostle" who could support the written text with verbal explanation and elaboration. Significantly, James does not address his letter to "all nations," but instead to "the twelve tribes scattered throughout the world." It is a moot point whether this represents a limitation of mission to Jews only, or whether the twelve tribes represent the new Israel in a supersessionist sense.

Bishops, deacons, and elders are nowhere in sight in Matthew, and neither are any other settled community functionaries. This may be to do with the nature of the gospel as narrative of the period of Jesus's ministry. In any case, the commission to Peter to be the rock on which the church will be built points in the direction of emerging settled leadership. Didache, as we have seen, knows of bishops and deacons whose qualities are not "charismatic" in the sense in which we have used the word, nor itinerant, since they are elected/appointed by the community and not designated by the Spirit. Their qualities match those one would expect in patrons who would serve (*leitourgia*) the community and receive honor in exchange: humility, generosity, truthfulness, being tried and tested. These qualities are under threat from the service of the prophets (who seem to come from outside and settle in the community) and teachers, who are receiving the honor due to the local patrons of the community. James knows teachers who seem to be the leading settled functionaries of the community, but also knows local "elders of the church" who form a body and can be called to prayer of "faith" and to anoint the sick with oil. This, however, seems to me less a "liturgical act" of a designated functionary class than the formal assembly of the senior members of the community, who would have the responsibility for its governance. They may be compared with the prophet Elijah, but only as a righteous man who was "human like us" and whose prayer was effective.

In sum, this study has shown the extent to which the conditions and relations in Matthew and Didache overlap, in a way that could not be explained by literary borrowing, but rather from their origin in a common milieu of mission and ministry. While Matthew does not speak of the bishops and deacons who appear briefly in the Didache as under threat from the prestige of prophets and teachers, his gospel does envisage the foundation of a "church" and other signs of the emergence of settled community relations. Otherwise, apostles, prophets, and teachers loom large on the horizon of both texts. Teachers and elders appear to provide a settled leadership in the community addressed by James, while the letter and its author provide some evidence of a continuing exchange of leadership and teaching beyond the local community that would require apostolic delegations in the general sense. All three writings appear concerned about false leaders who seek to exploit the community financially, as well as to give false teaching, and all three see the lifestyle of the leader as the appropriate test of authenticity.

THE IDEAL COMMUNITY ACCORDING TO MATTHEW, JAMES, AND THE DIDACHE

Wim J. C. Weren

The Gospel according to Matthew, the Letter of James, and the Didache originate from local religious communities that were Jewish-Christian in nature. Their contemporary situation was characterized by the fact that they—each in their own way—were looking for an identity of their own and a joint ethos that bound the members of these communities together and simultaneously differentiated them from other Jewish and pagan groups in their environment. The communities were aware of the tension between their own ideals and the complex daily reality. Their course was not only determined by developments within their own circle, but also by strategic choices and developments in other groups they felt related to and by groups that they saw as their rivals or even as their direct opponents.

In this contribution, I will explore what images of the ideal community in Matthew, James and the Didache played a role in this process. I will present the results of a semantic analysis of three topics: a) the way in which the community refers to itself; b) the community's relationship to God and Jesus; and c) the concept of perfection.

The following lexemes are central: ἐκκλησία, θεός, Ἰησοῦς Χριστός, and τέλειος. I will explore what connotations these terms acquire because, within the document in which they occur, they are incorporated into a wider semantic field that also includes words that derive from the same root or that are related to each other with respect to their meaning. This semantic field also contains contrasting concepts and antonyms.[1] In this semantic analysis, I will assume that a text is not an isolated phenomenon, but operates in a communicative context and has

---

1. See Hubert Frankemölle, "Das semantische Netz des Jakobusbriefes. Zur Einheit eines umstrittenen Briefes," *BZ* 34 (1990): 174. Louw and Nida's lexicon, in which the New Testament vocabulary is grouped in semantic fields, is a helpful tool: Johannes P. Louw and Eugene A. Nida, eds., *Greek-English Lexicon of the New Testament Based on Semantic Domains* (2 vols.; 2nd ed.; New York: United Bible Societies, 1989).

a pragmatic function. At the end of this contribution, I will try to synthesize the results and determine how the perceptions of the ideal community that emerge from Matthew, James, and the Didache relate to each other.

1. Ἐκκλησία AS A TERM WITH WHICH THE COMMUNITY REFERS TO ITSELF

Matthew, James, and the Didache have in common that the Christian community is referred to as ἐκκλησία. In non-biblical Greek, this term is applied to a congregation of people who belong to a particular group, especially a socio-political society. In the Septuagint, ἐκκλησία is the translation of קהל ("assembly, convocation of the people [especially of Israel]")[2] and refers to the congregation of Israel as a nation or religious community. In addition to ἐκκλησία, the term συναγωγή is also attested in the Septuagint. There it sometimes also reflects קהל but usually עדה ("congregation [of Israel]").[3] Therefore, ἐκκλησία and συναγωγή in the Septuagint can, to a certain extent, be considered synonyms occurring side by side without any conflict of meaning.

1.1. MATTHEW

In Matthew, ἐκκλησία occurs three times. Matthew is the only evangelist who uses this word. In 18:17, he brings ἐκκλησία in connection with the assembly of a local Christian group taking disciplinary measures against a member who is a threat to the community. The assembly protects the cohesion of the group and clearly distinguishes itself from outsiders, who are referred to as "tax collectors" and "Gentiles." In 16:18, ἐκκλησία is applied to all the Christian communities together. In translations, the difference is usually signaled by the use of the term "church." It is explicitly referred to as the church of Jesus, which is based on its faith in him as the Son of God. Within this universal community, Peter has the power to keep the Torah alive by taking decisions on what is allowed and what is forbidden. In doing so, he must take Jesus's interpretation of the Law as a point of departure, and not the teachings of the scribes and the Pharisees (16:12; 23:13).

The word ἐκκλησία thus indicates a community of like-minded people that considers itself to be an intra-Jewish group and therefore distinct from the Gentiles but also from other Jewish groups who do not perceive Jesus as the focus of their faith and actions.

In contrast to the Septuagint, Matthew creates a distinction between ἐκκλησία and συναγωγή. The term ἐκκλησία is reserved for the disciples of Jesus, and συναγωγή is used exclusively for local centers of Jewish religious life which,

---

2. KBL, 829.

3. KBL, 682–83.

in his time, was strongly dominated by the Pharisaic movement; the relations of his own communities with this movement were strained.

The situation depicted here can further be specified on the basis of some terms used in Matthew for socio-religious groups and classes of people:

• The terms λαός and οἶκος Ἰσραήλ both indicate the people of Israel as a nation and as a religious community (on the basis of Old Testament עם, λαός has the connotation of "people of God"). Matthew observes a particular distinction between the people and its leaders. Whereas the leaders are hostile to Jesus, there is a close relationship between Jesus and the people: he must save his people from their sins (1:21), he is the shepherd of his people Israel (2:6), he is a light that has dawned on the people who sat in darkness (4:16), and his ministry is primarily aimed at the lost sheep from the house of Israel (15:24; see also 10:5–6). Even after "the people as a whole" (πᾶς ὁ λαός), incited by the chief priests and the elders, has declared before Pilate that it takes the responsibility for the execution of Jesus (27:25), the chief priests and the elders continue to fear that the people will be receptive to the message of his disciples that he has risen from the dead (27:64). The use of these terms thus indicates that Matthew's community shows an openness for the people of Israel and that the gospel of Matthew does not offer any grounds for the idea, which later came to prevail, that the Christian community saw itself as the new Israel.[4]

• In 8:11–12, the expression "the children of the kingdom" is still an honorary title or a prerogative of the people of Israel, but in 13:38, this epithet is transferred to Jesus's disciples. This does not imply that the community saw itself as the circle of people in which the kingdom of heaven had been fully realized[5] and which would therefore be sure of eschatological salvation.[6] Rather, the community is aware of being a corpus mixtum and realizes that a separation of the good and the bad can only be made on the basis of ethical criteria at the final judgment.

---

4. Often Matt 21:43 is taken as evidence that the Matthean community saw itself as the nation that replaced the rejected Israel. However, the statement in this verse is aimed against the Pharisees (see 21:45) and must not be read as a condemnation of the entire Jewish people. The very vague term "people" does not necessarily refer to a people other than Israel, nor must that people be identified with the church or with the Gentiles; if that had been the case, Matthew would have chosen the term ἐκκλησία or τὰ ἔθνη. See Wim J. C. Weren, "The Use of Isaiah 5,1–7 in the Parable of the Tenants (Mark 12,1–12; Matthew 21,33–46)," *Bib* 79 (1998): 1–26.

5. For an opposing view, see Henry Wansbrough, "The New Israel: The Community of Matthew and the Community of Qumran," *SNTSU*. Serie A/25 (2000): 8–22.

6. For an opposing view, see Petri Luomanen, "*Corpus Mixtum*: An Appropriate Description of Matthew's Community?" *JBL* 117 (1998): 469–80. This article is critically discussed by Robert H. Gundry, "In Defense of the Church in Matthew as a *Corpus Mixtum*," *ZNW* 91 (2000): 153–65.

1.2. JAMES

The term ἐκκλησία is also used by James, but only once (5:14), in a passage in which the elders of the community pronounce a prayer over a sick person and anoint him with oil with the hoped-for effect that the Lord will cure the sick person. The elders here play a role in healing the sick, whereas in Matt 10:8 such a role is reserved for the twelve apostles. In Jas 5:14, ἐκκλησία refers to a local Christian group.

In 2:2, συναγωγὴ ὑμῶν is mentioned, the only time that συναγωγή occurs in this letter. Given the possessive pronoun, the word συναγωγή is used here for an assembly of a Christian community and is synonymous with ἐκκλησία as used in 5:14. The use of these two terms as synonyms also occurs in the Septuagint, but not in Matthew.

Text-critically, it is disputed whether συναγωγή in 2:2 is accompanied by the definite article. If this is the case, the emphasis is on the συναγωγή as a building; if not, the term refers to an assembly of the community members.[7] It is beyond the scope of this paper to speculate on the possibility that the Christian group gathers in a local synagogue that is also used by other Jewish groups. However, it is clear that the use of συναγωγή does not raise the slightest suggestion of a polemic attitude towards Jewish groups challenging the Christian community's right to exist.

In the prescript (1:1), the addressees of the letter are described as "the twelve tribes in Dispersion." What image does this characterization create of the communities to whom this letter was directed? In answering this question, I will focus on the composing parts of the description used. "Dispersion" can be interpreted metaphorically (the Christian communities are living "in foreign parts" since their true homeland is the heavenly kingdom; see Phil 3:20; Heb 11:13; 1 Pet 1:1, 17; 2:11), but also literally (the addressees live in Dispersion, in areas outside Palestine, among non-Jews; see John 7:35, where the Dispersion is a geographical reference). I prefer the second option. Within this interpretation, the term Dispersion contributes to a further specification of James's readers: it refers to followers of Jesus who thought their Jewishness essential to their identity, irrespective of their ethnic origin. Following many Old Testament and early Jewish texts, the author of the letter sees the Dispersion as a situation that is far from ideal and, with this term, evokes hopes of a future restoration of the one Israel.[8]

This image is confirmed by his referring to "the twelve tribes." The first meaning of this term is the people of Israel as the physical descendants of the

---

7. See Luke T. Johnson, *The Letter of James* (AB 37A; New York: Doubleday 1995), 221–22.

8. See Donald J. Verseput, "Genre and Story: The Community Setting of the Epistle of James," *CBQ* 62 (2000): 99–101.

twelve sons of Jacob. As a result of the spreading of the people over areas out-side the country of Israel, the term also became charged with the hope that God would reunite this people. In some eschatological texts (e.g., Matt 19:28 // Luke 22:30; Rev 7:4–8; 21:12), this reunification does not take place until the end of time. By calling his readers "the twelve tribes in the Dispersion," the author tells them that they belong to the one Israel, if not physically, at least in a spiritual sense. Because this letter further focuses on the internal problems of the commu-nity and treats these issues without raising disputes with Jewish groups outside the community, the readers possibly included those who had no trouble linking their faith in God and/or Jesus with their belonging to the one Israel.[9]

1.3. DIDACHE

In the Didache, ἐκκλησία occurs four times. In 4:14 ("in the assembly [ἐν ἐκκλησίᾳ] you shall confess your faults"), a meeting in a local house-church is meant, probably for joint prayer (ἐπὶ προσευχήν), which requires a clear con-science. In 11:11, ἐκκλησία occurs in a statement on a prophet who acts in a way that is incompatible with what he teaches to others. On the basis of the criterion formulated in 11:10, a prophet who does not practice what he preaches should be considered a false prophet. In 11:11, however, an exception is made to this rule. There are also prophets who will be judged by God alone, not by the community. It is suggested that the prophet in question does not do less than what he asks others to do, but in fact more. In the light of 6:2, it is likely that this extra effort consists of bearing the entire yoke of the Lord. That such a prophet may not be disqualified appears from the positive descriptions in 11:11: he is "proved true and acts on behalf of the earthly mystery of the church." Ἐκκλησία here refers to the church everywhere in the world. Apart from the local community, ἐκκλησία thus also refers to the universal church, in both the Didache and in Matthew.

The term further appears in two eucharistic prayers to God:

9:4 "May your church be gathered into your kingdom from the ends of the earth."

10:5 "Be mindful, Lord, of your church, to preserve it from all evil, and to per-fect it in your love. And, once it is sanctified, gather it from the four winds, into the kingdom which you have prepared for it."

In these prayers, the church of God (see σου) throughout the world is meant. The words of the prayer in 9:4 are repeated almost literally in 10:5, but this second

---

9. For an opposing view, see Sophie Laws, "Epistle of James," ABD 3:623, where the twelve tribes in the Diaspora are seen as the ideal description of the community in its role of the new, true Israel in the world.

prayer contains two new elements: a) the church is not yet perfect, it must be protected from evil by God and has not yet been fully sanctified; b) nonetheless, God has prepared his kingdom for it. As concerns contents, these prayers are related to Jewish prayers before and after meals in which God is asked to reunite Israel. There is also a connection with James's hope that the Christian communities living in the Dispersion will participate in this united Israel. In the Didache, the term ἐκκλησία does not have the connotation, encountered in Matthew, of contrast with the wider Jewish community or certain movements within it.

A certain awareness of the own distinct identity is expressed with the term Χριστιανός in 12:4. This word is used in the context of warnings against profiteers who do not work themselves but live off the community, and may have been chosen to contrast with χριστέμπορος in 12:5 ("someone who is trading on Christ").

1.4. Conclusion

The analysis of ἐκκλησία in Matthew, James, and the Didache shows that this term is used to refer to separate house-churches as well as to the totality of such communities, the universal church. In Matthew, the concept has a polemic connotation and is used to emphasize the contrast with other Jewish groups to which the Matthean communities felt related but whose claim of being the authentic guardians of Israel's heritage they disputed. Matthew held the view that this position pre-eminently belongs to his own communities. The dispersion of the communities to areas where Jews are a minority is central in James and the Didache. Within that situation, the emphasis is on the future restoration of the one Israel, which, also for the Christian communities, is both a comfort and a challenge.

2. The community in its relationship to God and Jesus

2.1. Matthew

In his attempt to give the community an own identity, Matthew emphasizes that it must not be led by human precepts (15:9; see also 16:17,23)—of which he accuses Jesus's opponents—but must be guided by the God-given revelation conveyed by Jesus (11:25–27; 16:17). The power to understand this revelation and know the secrets of the kingdom (13:11) is also a gift of God.

The community has been planted by God (15:13), its members are "children of God" (5:10, 45), and they consider God to be their only Father (23:9). Their ultimate goal is also with God: theirs shall be the kingdom (5:3, 10) and as "children of the kingdom" (13:38) the righteous will shine like the sun in the kingdom of their Father (13:43; see also 25:34), on the condition that they attune their actions to the ethical requirements bound up with the road that leads to life (e.g., 6:33; 7:13–14).

The community is also bound to Jesus. The church is his church (16:18); its members are the good seed sown by the Son of Man (13:37) and they must perceive Jesus's words (7:24–25) and the belief that he is the Messiah, the Son of the living God (16:16–17), as the foundation on which their community is built.

In the gospel according to Matthew, whose literary genre is related to the biographies from the Greco-Roman world, Jesus is the main character of the story. He is almost continuously surrounded by his disciples.[10] Although occasionally "the twelve disciples" are mentioned (10:1; 11:1; 20:37), the group of disciples cannot be limited to twelve persons, as is shown, in addition to a few broad descriptions of the group of disciples (5:48; 12:50; 16:24), by the fact that μανθάνω ("to learn") and μαθητεύω, verbs related to μαθητής, indicate that becoming a disciple is a possibility that is open to a larger group of people.[11]

The meaning of μαθητής is co-determined by the frequent combination with διδάσκαλος. Jesus's disciples have one teacher and they all are his students (23:8). They must not only be loyal to Jesus's teachings, but also have a deep personal relationship with him that they value so highly that it even takes precedence over

---

10. Μαθητής only occurs in the New Testament in the Gospels and in Acts (a total of 262 times; 72 times in Matt, 46 times in Mark, 37 times in Luke, 78 times in John, and 28 times in Acts). The general meaning of μαθητής is "learner, pupil, apprentice" (LSJ, 1072). See also Walter Bauer, *Griechisch-deutsches Wörterbuch zu den Schriften des Neuen Testaments und der frühchristlichen Literatur* (6th ed.; Berlin: de Gruyter, 1988), cols. 985–86: "1. d. Lehrling, d. Schüler; 2. d. Jünger, d. Anhänger [. . .] oft m. Angabe dessen, dem man anhängt, meist im Gen." The term μαθητής is gender-neutral and can refer to a man as well as to a woman. Greek also has the terms μαθήτρια and μαθητρίς to refer to female disciples (e.g., Acts 9:36; Gos. Pet. 12.50; Acts Paul 2.9).

The Hebrew equivalent of μαθητής is תלמיד (in Aramaic: תלמידא), a substantive that is derived from the verb למד. In the Hebrew Bible, תלמיד only occurs in 1 Chr 25:8. Μαθητής does not appear in the generally accepted text traditions of the Septuagint. However, this word does occur in three alternative readings, witnessed by A, with an obscure meaning (Jer 13:21; 20:11; 26:9). In the Septuagint, the Hebrew term used in 1 Chr 25:8 is reflected by the participle μανθανόντες.

The term תלמיד is quite common in the rabbinical literature, in which a disciple is someone who is taught by a rabbi and who is initiated by his master into the Written and Oral Torah. In the learning process, the emphasis is on the development of a loyal attitude towards the Torah, not on the personal relationship with the teacher. A student can join subsequent masters and, when fully qualified, he can become a teacher himself. The profile of the תלמיד in the rabbinical literature is related to that of the student in the philosopher's schools in the Hellenistic world.

11. The substantive μαθητής is connected to the μαθ-stem verbs μανθάνω ("to learn, to acquire a habit of / to be accustomed to / to perceive / to understand") and μαθητεύω ("to be a follower or a disciple of someone"), the transitive meaning of which is "to cause someone to become a disciple or a follower."

family relationships and that they take their cue from him as the example for their own actions (they endure everything "for his sake," they act "in his name"). They are therefore not to be called "rabbi" (23:8) and they are not to follow other teachers such as the Pharisees and the Sadducees, whose teachings are rejected as wicked (16:12). When—fully taught—they themselves start to teach, they will continue to be bound by Jesus's teachings (5:19; 28:20) and must resist the ambition to develop into leaders of their own school with their own teachings.

That the disciples are reported in Matthew as having little faith, troubled by doubt, does not make them unfit for the task to continue Jesus's mission. Although the Pharisees fear that the disciples are capable of even worse deception than Jesus (27:63–64), according to the evangelist, there is not the slightest risk that they will disseminate deviant doctrines. This danger is simply non-existent because God has given them the ability to understand what Jesus is telling them and to know the secrets of the kingdom (13:11, 51; 16:12; 17:13). During their worldwide mission trips, they can moreover be ensured that Jesus, who is also called Emmanuel (1:23), will remain bound to them (28:20).

In Matthew, Jesus is thus the heart of the community. Matthew's concept of the community is strongly colored by the way in which he portrays Jesus.[12]

2.2. JAMES

The close relationship between God and the community is such a frequent subject in James's letter that Frankemölle is of the opinion that the entire letter is theocentrically oriented: "Gottes Handeln auf die Menschen hin bildet Maßstab und Ermöglichung für das von Jakobus angezielte neue Handeln der Christen, ebenso ist Gottes Sein vorgegebenes Ideal für menschliches Sein."[13] This assertion is based on a large number of textual data, a few of which I will mention here. The author assumes that his readers believe that there is only one God (2:19), who is also the only lawgiver and judge (4:12). To this one God, he gives the titles of "Lord" (1:7; 3:9; 4:15; 5:4, 10, 11, 15) and "Father" (1:17, 27; 3:9). The communities originate from God: he has chosen the addressees (2:5), he has planted his word in them (1:21), and he bestows the wisdom from above (1:5; 3:15, 17) and grace (4:6). The eschatological salvation is also in his hands: he has promised the crown of life to those who love him (1:12) and he is able to save and destroy (4:12). He is already bestowing this life on the members of the community, who are the first fruits among his creatures and thus have a special status (1:18). The communities must therefore submit to God (4:7–8) and choose the friendship with God over friendship with the world; in doing so, they follow in

---

12. See Wim J. C. Weren, *De broeders van de Mensenzoon: Mt 25,31–46 als toegang tot de eschatologie van Matteüs* (Amsterdam: Bolland, 1979), 188–94.

13. Frankemölle, "Das semantische Netz," 182.

the track of Abraham, who is God's friend and their father. They must not be carried away by their own desires, as a result of which they fall prey to all kinds of temptations, which are not of God's making (1:13–18). Two ways emerge here, one of which leads to life and the other to death (see Matt 7:13–14 and particularly the doctrine of the Two Ways in the Didache).

The author pays relatively little attention to the figure of Jesus. In 1:1, he calls himself "a servant of God and of the Lord Jesus Christ." The double proper name "Jesus Christ" also occurs in 2:1, again accompanied by the title of "Lord." This title is also applied to Jesus—without his name being mentioned—in 5:7, 8, 14 in connection with his coming in the eschatological age. In total, Jesus's name is only mentioned twice. This is remarkable since the letter contains many statements that show a striking correspondence to words, which, in Matthew or Q or in other collections such as the Gospel of Thomas, are spoken by Jesus. In the letter, the words are not explicitly attributed to Jesus. The author presents these words as if they are his own. This may be connected to the fact that the idea that Jesus should be the only teacher is totally missing here. In fact, many teachers are mentioned, and the author seems to count himself among them, given the use of the first person plural in 3:1. James also reflects the idea that the members of the community are the bearers of a special knowledge, which they owe to God, but which is conveyed by teachers who are active in the community.

2.3. Didache

The author of the Didache is also fully convinced of the close tie between God and the community. Not only is the community in his hand, he is also the Creator of the world, the almighty Lord (δεσπότης παντοκράτωρ), who has made all things and who provides mankind with food and drink (10:3; see also 1:2). Within this broad orientation on all mankind, the community occupies a special place, because it moreover is provided by God with spiritual food and drink and eternal life. The statement in 10:2 shows a connection with Matt 11:25: God has made his holy name to dwell in the hearts of the faithful and has granted them revelation through his servant Jesus. Thus, the community is a bearer of special knowledge that opens the way to eternal life. According to 4:9–10, the community is convinced that it was called into existence by God and that it is inspired by his Spirit. God is not influenced by someone's social status. The community consists of men and women from various social strata, but they are now united by their joint focus on the fear of the Lord and their hope in the same God. The social differences within the community are leveled on the basis of the idea of the one God who is above all.

The name "Jesus" is mentioned in 9:2, 3 and 10:2, always in combination with the epithet "your servant" (παῖς σου), with which David is also referred to. In 9:4, the name "Jesus Christ" is part of a doxology addressed to God. As in

James, "Lord" is used to refer to both God and Jesus.[14] In the phrase "to bear the entire yoke of the Lord" (6:2), "the Lord" probably refers to God and to doing his will, which is to be found in the Torah.

The relationship between the community and Jesus is further clarified along three lines:

- Unlike James, the Didache sometimes explicitly attributes a statement to Jesus (9:5: "the Lord has said") or refers to "his gospel" (8:2; 15:4) or "the gospel" (11:3; 15:3).
- Activities like baptism (9:5) or missionary work (12:1) happen "in the name of the Lord," and office-bearers in the community, like bishops and deacons, must be worthy of the Lord (15:1); the addressees must receive itinerant teachers and apostles "as the Lord" (11:2, 4), but they must beware of prophets who do not reflect the ways of the Lord (11:8).
- The community's eagerly looking forward to eschatological salvation is expressed in the eucharistic prayers and, in the final chapter, which is often seen as an appendix, is linked to the eagerly awaited coming of Jesus (16:1, 7, 8).

2.4. CONCLUSION

In each of the three documents, the community's profile contains a focus on God and Jesus. In James and the Didache, the focus on God is very prominent, whereas, in Matthew, the close relationship to Jesus is elaborated. In each of the three documents, this relationship is the source of special knowledge, which enables the community to find the way to eternal life and to distinguish itself from surrounding groups.

3. THE CONCEPT OF PERFECTION

The adjective τέλειος occurs nineteen times in the New Testament; in Matthew we find this term three times (5:48 [twice]; 19:21), and in James five times (1:4 [twice], 17, 25; 3:2). The word also appears in the Didache (1:4; 6:2). In each of the three documents, this term is used to describe the ideal behavior of the community. The word has a broad lexical meaning. It indicates that something or someone is complete, without defect, and in that sense perfect.[15] Sometimes the term means full-grown, mature; τέλειος specifically indicates that someone is

---

14. In the Didache, "the Lord" refers to God in 4:1 [twice]; 4:12, 13; 10:5; 14:3 [twice]; to Jesus in 8:2; 9:5 [twice]; 10:6; 11:2, 4, 8; 12:1; 14:1; 15:1, 4; 16:1, 7, 8; see also μαραναθά in 10:6.
15. LSJ, 1769–70.

ethically perfect.[16] In some places in the Septuagint, τέλειος reflects תמים ("complete, intact, incontestable, blameless") and expresses unconditional devotion to God and not to the idols.[17] God himself is never called perfect, but his work, his word, and his law are perfect.[18]

In this paragraph, I will discuss how the general meanings of τέλειος are semantically colored in Matthew, James, and the Didache, also in light of the wider semantic field in which the word occurs there.

3.1. MATTHEW

In 5:48, Jesus calls on his disciples to be perfect as (or: because) their heavenly Father is perfect. This appeal is an allusion to God's appeal to Israel in Lev 19:2[19] and forms the conclusion to the six antitheses (5:21–47), in particular the sixth of that series (5:43–47). That God is perfect means, according to 5:45, that he takes care of all people without distinguishing between the good and the evil or between the righteous and the unrighteous. In this way, he is an example on which the community members must model themselves: they must try to become children of God (5:9). What they must do to achieve this is expressed in the opening sentence of the sixth antithesis on the basis of the commandment of love from Lev 19:18 (ἀγαπήσεις τὸν πλησίον σου, here without the addition ὡς σεαυτόν), to which is linked the statement that one should hate one's enemy. This addition, of which there is no known parallel in Scripture or in early Jewish literature, creates an antithesis within 5:43 between "neighbor" in the sense of fellow believer, and "enemy" in the sense of a person from outside the community of faith. This more limited meaning of πλησίον contrasts sharply with Lev 19, where loving one's neighbor also includes loving the alien (compare Lev 19:18 with 19:34). In his comment on the thesis from 5:43, Jesus chooses the same broadening approach that can be found in Lev 19. His listeners must not limit the concept of πλησίον to those whom they love (5:46; see also 5:47: "their brothers and sisters") but must also treat outsiders as their brothers and sisters, also if they are hostile to the community. In principle, this means that the community must break down the walls that separate them from other groups. The love towards the neighbor is free from all discrimination and requires equal treatment of insiders and outsiders. The Christian community's ethos thus defined is said to go far beyond that of the "tax collectors" and the "Gentiles" (περισσόν = "beyond the customary

---

16. L&N 1:746: "perfect in the sense of not lacking any moral quality"; Bauer, *Wörterbuch*, col.1614: "auf sittl. Gebiet volkommen."

17. KBL, 1031–32; see also Gerhard Delling, "τέλειος," *TWNT* 8:68–89.

18. Luke L. Cheung, *The Genre, Composition and Hermeneutics of James* (Paternoster Biblical and Theological Monographs; Carlisle: Paternoster, 2003), 181, n. 22.

19. See also Deut 18:13 in the version of the Septuagint: τέλειος ἐσῃ ἐναντίον κυρίου τοῦ θεοῦ σου.

measure"). Whether this does justice to these groups' own norms and values is a question that is not addressed in this text. The community's inside perspective determines its view of the outsiders.

Within the Sermon on the Mount, the appeal in 5:48 to be perfect is related to 5:20 where Jesus demands a righteousness that differs qualitatively from the righteousness of the scribes and the Pharisees (περισσεύσῃ πλεῖον in 5:20 parallels περισσόν in 5:47). While 5:43–47 is focused on the difference between the community and the world of the Gentiles, in 5:20 the difference with (other) Jewish groups is at the forefront. This is probably a polemic against the allegation voiced by these groups that Jesus is deficient in observing God's Torah. Matthew's community turns this allegation around: not they but the others are deficient. Only the exceptional righteousness to be practiced by the disciples gives access to the kingdom of heaven. This suggests that access to the kingdom is denied to the scribes and the Pharisees. The disciples' exceptional righteousness implies that they must abide by Jesus's interpretation of the Torah. His explanation of the Law is characterized by the following principles: a) the Torah, which expresses God's will, must be maintained fully, to the smallest detail; b) within the Torah, there is a certain hierarchy of values; minor commandments can be distinguished from the weighty ones, but that minor commandments are less important does not mean that they are unimportant;[20] c) whoever neglects the minor commandments will be allotted a lower position in the kingdom of heaven. The sanction in 5:19 (a lower position in the kingdom of heaven) does not correspond to the much weightier one mentioned in 5:20 (no access to the kingdom). The deficiency of the scribes and the Pharisees therefore cannot be that they ignore the minor commandments. This is confirmed in 23:23 where, on the basis of an example (paying tithes), they are said to observe such matters of the Law strictly. Jesus's reproach is that, as a result of their fixation on the minor matters of the Law, they fail to observe the fundamental values of the Torah, such as justice, mercy, and faith. Jesus's disciples do allow themselves to be inspired by these fundamental values. They do not limit the Torah to these fundamental values, but consider them as guidelines for their interpretation and observance of the other provisions of the Law. Thus, they do the one without failing to do the other.

Being perfect, therefore, means to be faithful to the Torah as interpreted by Jesus regarding contents and intention. The way in which Jesus opens up the

---

20. David C. Sim, *The Gospel of Matthew and Christian Judaism: The History and Social Setting of the Matthean Community* (Studies of the New Testament and Its World; Edinburgh: T&T Clark, 1998), 132.

Torah enables a way of life that can be characterized as "perfect," but which is out of reach if people are led by the opinions of rival Jewish groups.[21]

The term τέλειος further occurs in the story of the rich young man (19:16–22). The correspondence between 19:17 ("if you wish to enter into life") and 19:21 ("if you wish to be perfect") suggests that this is a case of Zweistufenethik: whoever wishes to enter into the life must observe the commandments (summarized on the basis of Exod 20:12–16 and Lev 19:18), but who wishes to be perfect, must meet extra requirements (selling one's possessions, giving the proceeds to the poor, and following Jesus). Konradt has rightly pointed out that being perfect is not a second, supplementary track but—as in 5:17–20—consists of putting the Torah into practice, as interpreted by the Matthean Jesus, who perceives the second table of the Decalogue and the commandment of love as the perspective that brings the intention of all other provisions of the Torah to light. Applied to the specific context of the young man, this yields the following conclusion. In his particular situation, the commandment "love your neighbor as yourself" implies that he must sell his possessions and give the proceeds to the poor. His statement that he has observed all commandments focuses on quantity, not on quality. He is not deficient because he has overlooked this or that commandment but because—like the scribes and the Pharisees—he does not fulfill the Torah on the basis of the fundamental norms emphasized by Jesus. Konradt summarizes his view of 19:16–22 as follows: "Nachfolge und Befolgung der Tora im Sinne und auf der Basis ihres von Jesus eröffneten Verständnisses sind für Matthäus zwei Seiten derselben Medaille."[22]

We can now formulate the meaning of τέλειος in Matthew as follows: being perfect implies that the community abides fully by the Torah as the central Jewish identity characteristic and is thereby led by the interpretation given by Jesus rather than that given by the Pharisees.[23] Matthew expects that this perfect life will have a positive effect on the community's Jewish and Gentile environment (5:13–16).[24]

---

21. Martin Meiser, "Volkommenheit in Qumran und im Matthäusevangelium," in *Kirche und Volk Gottes* (ed. M. Karrer et al.; Neukirchen-Vluyn: Neukirchener Verlag, 2000), 203: the scribes and the Pharisees are depicted as "negatives Gegenbild der Jünger." Matthias Konradt, "Die volkommene Erfüllung der Tora und der Konflikt mit den Pharisäern im Matthäusevangelium," in *Das Gesetz im frühen Judentum und im Neuen Testament* (ed. D. Sänger et al.; NTOA 57; Göttingen: Vandenhoeck & Ruprecht, 2006), 152, refers to "die abgrenzende Identitätsstiftende Funktion des Volkommenheitsethos im Kontext von Gruppenkonflikte."

22. Ibid., 141.

23. Ibid., 152: "Bei Matthäus ist die durch Jesus ermöglichte volkommene Erfüllung des Willen Gottes, die die Gemeinde gegenüber der pharizäischen Variante jüdischen Lebens als die wahre Sachwalterin des theologischen Erbes Israels auszeichnen soll."

24. Meiser, "Volkommenheit in Qumran," 204.

3.2. JAMES

In James, τέλειος is a key word that is connected to other important terms in the letter, such as ἔργον (1:4; 2:22), νόμος (1:25) and σοφία (1:5, 17).[25] Τέλειος here belongs to a word group that also includes other τελ-root words[26] and a number of terms whose meaning at least partly overlaps with τέλειος.[27] This word group is contrasted in this letter with another group containing words that indicate that someone has a double attitude, such as δίψυχος, "double-minded" or "double-souled" (1:8; 4:8), ἀκατάστατος (1:8, "unstable"), and ἀκαταστασία (3:16, "disorder").[28]

The author values the contents of the first word group positively and the second negatively. He uses a taxonomy that is determined by a certain knowledge and perception of reality, as is shown by his repeated use of words connected to "knowledge." The principal word reflecting this is "wisdom," but more terms indicate that he departs from a certain knowledge of reality that springs from a fundamental and undivided focus on God and leads to life.[29] He frequently draws his readers' attention to what they know and urges them to devote themselves to God without any compromise and to abandon the attitude that is rooted in the inclination to follow one's own desires and that inevitably leads to death.[30]

---

25. See the combination of τελειόω and ἔργον (2:22), νόμος (1:25; see the combination of τελέω and νόμος in 2:8 and the syntagm ὅλος ὁ νόμος in 2:10), and σοφία (1:5, 17). See Josef Zmijewski, "Christliche 'Volkommenheit': Erwägungen zur Theologie des Jakobusbriefes," SNTSU, Serie A/ 5 (1980): 73.

26. For example, ἀποτελέω (1:15), τελέω (2:8), τελειόω (2:22), and τέλος (5:11).

27. This series also includes ὅλος, "whole" (2:10; 3:2, 3, 6), ὁλόκληρος, "complete in every part" (1:4), ἐν μηδενὶ λειπόμενος, "falling short in nothing" (1:4) and ἁπλῶς, "generously" (1:5). Cheung, Genre, Composition and Hermeneutics of James, 177, extends this series with καθαρός, ἀμίαντος, ἄμεμπτος, ἄσπιλος and words with the root ἁπλο- or δικαι-.

28. Studies on perfection in James: Martin Klein, "Ein volkommenes Werk": Volkommenheit, Gesetz und Gericht als theologische Themen des Jakobusbriefes (BWANT 139; Stuttgart: Kohlhammer, 1995); Patrick J. Hartin, "Call to Be Perfect Through Suffering (James 1,2–4): The Concept of Perfection in the Epistle of James and the Sermon on the Mount," Bib 77 (1996): 477–92; idem, A Spirituality of Perfection: Faith in Action in the Letter of James (Collegeville, Minn.: Liturgical Press, 1999); Matt A. Jackson-McCabe, Logos and Law in the Letter of James: The Law of Nature, the Law of Moses, and the Law of Freedom (NovTSup 100; Leiden: Brill, 2001).

29. In James, the following words belong to the semantic domain of /knowing/: ἐπίσταμαι (4:14) and ἐπιστήμων (3:13), γινώσκω (1:3; 2:20; 5:20), οἶδα (1:19; 3:1; 4:4, 17) and οἴομαι (1:7). Knowledge is aimed at wisdom and truth (σοφία in 1:3; 2:20; 5:20; σοφός in 3:13; ἀλήθεια in 1:18; 3:14; 5:19).

30. Mark E. Taylor, "Recent Scholarship on the Structure of James," Currents in Biblical Research 3 (2004): 102: "one purpose attempted by the author is to convince the implied reader to adopt a certain 'system of convictions' . . . regarding how to perceive and order the realm of human experience."

From the worldview of the author, the contemporary socio-religious situation of the readers is far from ideal: he depicts them as people who are deficient where faith coupled with an impeccable way of life is concerned. This deficiency does not only touch upon the personal integrity of the community members, but also injures the cohesion within the group.

Right at the beginning of the letter, perfection is presented as the goal of Christian existence. Given this goal, the temptations that every believer is confronted with can be perceived positively. They have an educational value and form a decisive stage on the road to perfection. According to James, successfully resisting the temptations leads to steadfastness, steadfastness leads to a flawless life, to a faith that shines out in good deeds, and this leads to perfection (1:3–4). Perfection is thus a growing process. Its culmination is not reached until the eschatological age, with the coming of the Lord, when those who held out in times of trouble will receive "the crown of life" (1:12). The faithful cannot complete the road to perfection through their own efforts; they draw strength from the wisdom and mercy that God bestows when they ask God for them in their prayers.

There is an alternative way, which is diametrically opposed to the way to life or salvation. This way also has different stages, and temptations also form the crucial test. People end up in this way if they do not allow themselves to be led by the wisdom given by God, but by their own desires. Such people will not be able to stand their ground in times of trouble, but become inconstant and fall into sin, and once sin is fully grown, it breeds death (1:14–15).[31] The author cuts short the idea that God, who enables people to complete the way to life successfully, also stands at the beginning of the way to death. In contrast to ideas already prevailing in Scripture (for example, in Gen 22:1; Num 14:20–24), he argues that God does not cause the temptations. He thus throws the imperfect upon their own resources, liberty, and responsibility.

Does the dichotomy of these two ways bear witness to a deterministic view of reality? In James, this is not the case. The author takes it as a matter of course that all community members stumble many times (3:2), but they can confess their sins to each other and thus obtain forgiveness (5:15–16). It is therefore possible to abandon the way to death and strike into the way of life. The opposite is also possible: people can stray from the way of life and lapse into sin and the way to death. In other words, it is not guaranteed beforehand that the faithful will achieve ultimate salvation, nor is it certain that sinners will persevere in wickedness. This dynamic view is the pendant of Matthew's view that the community is a corpus mixtum and cannot be identified with the community of salvation at the end of time.

---

31. The way of the imperfect is described with a verb from the τελ-root, viz., ἀποτελέω: even imperfection is "perfect"!

The two ways contrast sharply and are made concrete in different ways in the rest of the letter. In the table below, this is elucidated on the basis of some antithetical statements.

THE WAY OF THE PERFECT	THE WAY OF THE DOUBLE-MINDED
faith → temptations → steadfastness → life	desires → temptations → sin → death
synergy of listening to the word and acting on it (1:22)	listening to the word but failing to act on it (1:23)
synergy of faith and works (2:22)	faith without works (2:14–17) or works without faith (2:18–26)
observing and fulfilling the perfect law of liberty (2:8, 10)	observing one commandment and breaking another (2:11)
solidarity with others, especially the poor (1:27)	partiality and discrimination: respecting the rich and despising the poor (2:2–7)
knowing how to bridle one's tongue and thereby the whole body (3:2)	speaking with a double tongue (1:26; 3:9–10)
allowing oneself to be led by the wisdom given by God (1:5)	allowing oneself to be led by earthly wisdom, which is unspiritual and devilish (3:15)
the God-given wisdom goes hand in hand with a virtuous life (3:13–18)	earthly knowledge goes hand in hand with a life full of sin (3:14–15)
friendship with God and enmity with the world (4:4)	friendship with the world and enmity with God (4:4)

Is there a link in James—as there is in Matthew—between being perfect and keeping the Torah, and if so, what does the author understand by the Torah? Is the whole Torah meant, down to the smallest detail, or does he reduce the organic whole to a few fundamental provisions, such as the love commandment and the second table of the Decalogue? To be able to answer this question, we must find out how νόμος ("torah" or "law") functions in this document.

This term occurs ten times in the letter (1:25; five times in 2:8–12 and four times in 4:11). In the first chapter "the word of truth" (1:18) gradually passes into "the perfect law" (1:25). Like wisdom, that word is a gift of God, who has planted the word (with baptism?) in the members of the community and has thus given them the new status as the first fruits among his creatures. This new position has practical consequences: they must not only listen to the word, but also act on it. After a comparison with someone who glances at himself in a mirror, this exhortation is taken up again, but "the word" is replaced by "the perfect law." This suggests that the word of God can be identified with the Torah. This does not preclude that the "word of truth" also concerns the Christian message, but, in the opinion of the author, this message does not in any way conflict with the law.

The relationship between the word of God and the law is confirmed by 2:11, where two quotations from the Decalogue are introduced with the remark that the person who spoke the one commandment also spoke the other (ὁ γὰρ εἰπών … εἶπεν καί); that nobody other than God could be meant here appears from 4:12, where it is said that God is the only lawgiver.

The content of "the perfect law" is shown in 2:1-13, where the author raises the concrete problem of community members showing bias by looking up to a wealthy person and looking down on a beggar. This behavior is criticized with a choice of arguments: it is incompatible with the faith in Jesus Christ (2:1) and with his message (cf. 2:5 with, e.g., Luke 6:20); it is inconsistent with the way in which God himself treats the poor (2:5); it is impossible to understand why the members of the community fawn upon the wealthy because they themselves are treated badly by the rich (2:6b-7).

What is crucial here is that favoritism infringes the law. This may need some explanation. Johnson has pointed out that 2:1 and especially 2:9 contains allusions to Lev 19:15 in the version of the Septuagint.[32] In the Septuagint, this verse reads as follows: οὐ ποιήσετε ἄδικον ἐν κρίσει· οὐ λήμψῃ πρόσωπον πτωχοῦ οὐδὲ θαυμάσεις πρόσωπον δυνάστου, ἐν δικαιοσύνῃ κρινεῖς τὸν πλησίον σου. The intertextual relation between the two documents is shown clearly by the fact that λαμβάνω πρόσωπον in Lev 19:15 corresponds to προσωπολημψία in Jas 2:1 and with προσωπολημπτέω in 2:9. The following arguments can be added to this:

- in both cases, there is a poor man (πτωχός in Lev 19:15 and Jas 2:2, 3, 5, 6);
- λαμβάνω πρόσωπον (in the Septuagint a translation of Hebrew נשׂא פנים) is echoed by ἐπιβλέπω in Jas 2:3;
- in both cases, terms connected with the administration of justice play a role (Lev 19:15: κρίσις and κρίνω; in Jas 2:4 διακρίνω and κριταί);
- both in Leviticus and in James, impartiality is needed in two directions, both towards a poor man and towards a powerful man.[33]

32. Johnson, *The Letter of James*, 221 and 231; see especially 228: "the very term *prosopolempsia* (2:1) is [...] a word choice that deliberately echoes Lev 19:15." See also: Luke T. Johnson, "The Use of Leviticus 19 in the Letter of James," *JBL* 101 (1982): 391-401.

33. This latter aspect is emphasized by Gerd Theißen, "Nächstenliebe und Egalität: Jak 2,1-13 als Höhepunkt urchristlicher Ethik," in *Der Jakobusbrief: Beiträge zur Rehabilitierung der "strohernen Epistel"* (ed. P. von Gemünden et al.; Beiträge zum Verstehen der Bibel 3; Münster: Lit, 2003), 120-42; in this study, he argues that New Testament ethics culminate in James's

Apart from correspondences, we also come across an important difference: the addressees of the letter do exactly the opposite of what is prohibited in Lev 19:15 (they despise the poor) and are led by conventional opinions about honor and shame, while Lev 19:15 wants to keep the administration of justice free from these socially and culturally accepted codes. The author reproaches the community for its inconsistent attitude, which is directly opposed to its ethos as described in 2:5–7.

The case presented in 2:2–4 forms the background to observations about the royal law in 2:8–13. The central verse here is verse 10, in which the author advances the thesis that wanting to fulfill "the whole law" implies that each separate provision must be observed (see also Matt 5:19). The law is an organic whole and all these individual provisions are equally important. According to Keith,[34] this general principle is explained in 2:11 on the basis of two quotations from the second table of Decalogue ("you shall not commit adultery" and "you shall not murder").[35] These two examples clarify that whoever infringes one provision breaks the whole law. One cannot observe one provision and ignore another. In 2:11, the unity of the law is inferred from the fact that the words of the Decalogue all originate from God and that there is only one lawgiver.

How does this observation on the unity of the Torah relate to the two antithetically parallel statements in 2:8–9? According to Keith, the general rule from verse 10 is applied here to the contemporary situation of the addressees.[36] The syntagm "the whole law" of verse 10 corresponds to "the royal law" in verse 8. The particles μέντοι . . . δὲ signal a sharp contrast between the statement in verse 8 and that in verse 9 ("if you *really* fulfill the royal law . . ., *but* if you show partiality'). Or in different words: "if you really fulfilled the royal law . . ., but you do not since you are guilty of partiality."[37] That the addressees, according to the author, do not meet the ideal depicted in verse 8 is shown by the fact, mentioned in verse 9, that they do not treat everybody in the same way. He thus accuses them of a selective observance of the Torah.

In concreto, the addressees drive a wedge between two provisions from Lev 19. These two provisions are the commandment from Lev 19:18, cited in verse 8, to love one's neighbor as oneself and the commandment from Lev 19:15 to treat

---

letter: "Kein neutestamentlicher Autor hat so eindeutig wie er das Liebesgebot als Verpflichtung zur Gleichbehandlung verstanden und es gleichzeitig relativ offen für Außenstehende formuliert" (120–21).

34. Pierre Keith, "La citation de Lv 19,18b en Jc 2,1–13," in *The Catholic Epistles and the Tradition* (ed. J. Schlosser; BETL 176; Leuven: Peeters, 2004), 243–45.

35. This order (committing adultery and murdering) also occurs in Deut 5:17–18 in the Septuagint; Luke 18:20; Rom 13:9; the reversed order in the masoretic text and in Mark 10:19 and parallels; Matt 5: 21, 27; Did. 2:2.

36. Keith, "La citation de Lv 19,18b," 246.

37. Theißen, "Nächstenliebe und Egalität, " 128.

all neighbors equally, to which Jas 2:9 alludes. They assume that the "royal law" coincides with Lev 19:18 and isolate this provision from the commandment in Lev 19:15. The author tries to induce his readers to abandon this opinion and to replace it by his own view, which can be described as follows:

- the "royal law" does not coincide with the love commandment but comprises "the whole law" (verse 10);
- the love commandment is the summa of the whole law, namely, in the sense that this commandment presents a norm that is central to the fulfilling of all other norms of the law;[38]
- the love commandment implies that every person is treated equally;
- the two provisions from Leviticus, which have the term "neighbor" in common, must be understood in conjunction;[39]
- the concept of "neighbor" then acquires a broad and open meaning, whereas it would be arbitrarily restricted if the love commandment is isolated from the commandment to treat everybody equally.

In the framework of this study into the concept of perfection, we can now conclude that, in James, the way of perfection means that the whole law is fulfilled in every respect. That is why he calls the (whole) law perfect and royal.[40]

James's interpretation corresponds to that of Matthew,[41] although a few differences in emphasis can be observed. Matthew is abundantly clear that ritual prescriptions are not exempted; in James, this is not explicitly mentioned, but neither is it excluded.[42] James emphasizes, more strongly than Matthew, that striving to be perfect is not only a task of the individual Christian but also has consequences for the life of the community as a whole. Matthew gives the Christian idea of perfection a profile of its own by contrasting it with the opinions of groups outside the community (tax collectors and Gentiles, the scribes and the Pharisees) which, in his view, are deficient. James, on the other hand, takes a stand against the alternative view held within the community itself that fulfilling the perfect law would merely come down to obeying the love commandment.[43]

---

38. Theißen, "Nächstenliebe und Egalität," 135: "Gehandelt werden soll nach der Norm, die sich in einer bestimmten Schriftstelle findet: nach dem Liebesgebot."

39. According to Keith, "La citation de Lv 19,18b," 239, the two statements must be combined on the basis of the hermeneutical rule known as *gezerah shawah*.

40. According to Theißen, "Nächstenliebe und Egalität," 132–34, the phrase "royal law" can refer to the quality of the law itself, to the quality of the lawgiver, and to the quality of those who keep this law. He argues in favor of a combination of these three possibilities.

41. The same results are to be found in Benedict T. Viviano, "La Loi parfaite de liberté: Jacques 1,25 et la Loi," in Schlosser, ed., *Catholic Epistles and the Tradition*, 213–26; Keith, "La citation de Lv 19,18b," 235–37.

42. Viviano, "La Loi parfaite de liberté," 221.

43. It is remarkable that many exegetes support the same reduction and argue that James wants to contrast the perfect (Christian) law of the love commandment and the Mosaic law.

3.3. Didache

With the Didache, we enter a world that is different, at least partly. The term τέλειος occurs twice in this document (1:4; 6:2); furthermore, the use of the verb τελειόω in 10:5 and 16:2 is important.

In 1:4, τέλειος occurs in a passage that partly consists of logia from the Jesus tradition and therefore is usually called the evangelical section (1:3b–2:1). On the basis of text-critical and literary-historical arguments, Van de Sandt comes to the conclusion "that the section was inserted into Did. 1–6 at the time when the earlier Two Ways form was incorporated in the Didache as a whole."[44] In the final redactional form of the Didache, this section has the nature of an explanation of 1:2 where we find a summary of the Torah on the basis of the double love commandment (Deut 6:5; Lev 19:18) and the Golden Rule, which itself belongs to the doctrine of the Two Ways. The evangelical section contains a series of radical requirements. Although the statement on perfection is not the conclusion of that series (as in Matt 5:48) but is linked to one particular exhortation ("if someone strikes you on your right cheek, turn your other one to him too"), it may safely be assumed that the qualification τέλειος refers to the whole series and that someone is considered to be perfect if he or she makes radical choices that exceed what is ethically customary.

Τέλειος occurs again in 6:2–3. In translation, the text of this passage is as follows: "If you can bear the entire yoke of the Lord, you will be perfect, but if you cannot, do what you can. As for food, bear what you can, but be very much on your guard against food offered to idols, for it is [related to] worship of dead gods." In this case, too, Van de Sandt is of the opinion that these sentences are a redactional addition and originally did not form part of the tradition of the Two Ways which we find in chapters 1–5.[45] In his view, Did. 6:2–3 is from the same hand as 1:3b–2:1.

The fact alone that the redactor incorporates the doctrine of the Two Ways in his text indicates that he considers this doctrine important for the Christian community or communities at which his booklet is aimed. He applies the contents of this doctrine fully to his readers. This is shown by the fact that he considers the person who is able to bear "the entire yoke of the Lord" as perfect. What exactly is meant by "the yoke of the Lord" (6:2) is disputed. To this question, two answers are possible:

I refer, for example, to Zmijewski, "Christliche 'Volkommenheit,'" 74, who argues that the "perfect law" refers exclusively to the love commandment "und *nicht auf das alttestamentliche Gesetz*" (italics his).

44. Huub van de Sandt and David Flusser, *The Didache: Its Jewish Sources and Its Place in Early Judaism and Christianity* (CRINT 3/5; Assen: Van Gorcum, 2002), 40.

45. Van de Sandt and Flusser, *The Didache: Its Jewish Sources*, 238–39.

- This expression refers to the exhortations bound up in the doctrine of the Two Ways and probably even the entire Torah, of which this doctrine is a particular elaboration. In this option, "the Lord" refers to God, who was mentioned shortly before, in 6:1.
- Another possibility is that "the Lord" refers to Jesus. An argument in favor of this option is that 6:2a calls forth associations with Matt 11:29, where Jesus exhorts his disciples to take up his yoke. Still, there is a remarkable difference: in the Didache, the yoke is heavy whereas in Matthew the yoke is called light. Within this second option, the yoke also refers to the Torah, but then the Torah as interpreted and lived by Jesus.

In 4:16, it says: "You shall not abandon the commandments of the Lord but shall keep what you have received, without adding or subtracting anything." The Torah must thus be seen as an organic whole and must be observed fully. It is remarkable that the didachist in 6:2b keeps open the possibility that not everyone observes all the provisions of the Torah. It is sufficient that they do what they can. The following verse shows that he wants to relieve certain community members from the obligation to keep the dietary laws, but immediately adds that everyone must refrain from eating food offered to idols. To keep the whole Torah should be the norm (whoever accomplishes this is perfect), but certain groups may have to settle for less. This is a Zweistufenethik, in other words, within the community there are two distinct classes, which nevertheless can live together on the condition that nobody practices idolatry.

It is an obvious guess that the group that keeps the whole Torah and is qualified as perfect may have consisted of Christians with a Jewish background and that the group that did not have to observe the dietary laws strictly consisted of community members with a Gentile past. In a recent monograph, Slee has argued, following Draper among others, that the doctrine of the Two Ways already functioned within Judaism in the framework of teaching proselytes who, on the basis of this doctrine, were encouraged to break with their Gentile past, especially by turning away from idolatry.[46] This doctrine fulfills a similar function in the Didache, but here the issue is the admission of Gentiles to a community that consists largely of Jewish Christians. Of this category of newcomers, no full observance of the Torah is required. However, they must try to keep as many of the dietary laws and, as a minimum requirement, abstain from food offered to idols, otherwise no joint meals would be possible; especially the celebration of the Eucharist would suffer. According to Slee, the newcomers from the world of the Gentiles must not resign themselves to their imperfect state, but try to grow into people who do meet the ideal of full observance of the Torah. Slee bases her argument on 16:2 where τελειόω, a word related to τέλειος is used ("the whole

---

46. Michelle Slee, *The Church in Antioch in the First Century CE: Communion and Conflict* (JSNTSup 244; London: Sheffield Academic Press, 2003).

time of your belief will be of no profit to you unless you are perfected at the final hour"; see also 10:5).

3.4. Conclusion

In Matthew and James, the concept of perfection is elaborated along the same lines, although there are differences in emphasis. The didachist takes up a position of its own, not because the ideal of perfection is interpreted differently here, but because he does not (yet) fully apply this ideal to all community members and, for the time being and by way of compromise, considers a less stringent regime acceptable for Christians from the world of the Gentiles.

4. Final observations

In this contribution, I have tried to establish, on the basis of three topics, what perception of the ideal community emerges from Matthew, James, and the Didache. The results can be summarized as follows:

- The community is referred to as ἐκκλησία. This term does not only refer to the local house-church but also the totality of such communities, the universal church.
- The three documents suggest that the community has special knowledge that it has received from God and that co-determines the selection of norms and values that are recommended in these documents and of negative values that are challenged in them. As a result of this special knowledge, the community has a profile of its own that distinguishes it from other groups.
- That this special knowledge is conveyed by Jesus is made explicit in Matthew, who presents Jesus in his role of teacher as the only one who interprets the Torah in a legitimate way. In some instances, the didachist indicates that a statement was made by Jesus or can be found in "his gospel." James expresses the statements in his letter as his own and does not explicitly refer to Jesus as their source or inspiration.
- In all three documents, being perfect is a prerequisite for all community members. The three documents also have in common that being perfect is perceived as a growing process, which will not culminate until the eschatological age.
- Being perfect means that the whole Torah is fulfilled, in all respects. In none of the three documents is the Torah reduced to the commandment to love one's neighbor or to the ethical provisions in the second table of the Decalogue. In James, such a reduction is even one of the misconceptions against which the author speaks out strongly. In Matthew and James, the requirement of full observance of the Torah applies as a prerequisite for admission to the Christian community. Matthew indicates that ritual prescriptions must also be observed (15:1–20). James is not explicit on this, but it may

not be concluded that he would want to make an exception for such rules. The didachist, however, suspends the requirement to keep the dietary laws for non-Jewish applicant Christian community members to the time of the eschatological age and, in the meantime, settles for the minimum requirement that they abstain from food offered to idols. Because he does not apply the same ethical norm to all community members, he in fact uses a Zwei-stufenethik.

- In none of the three documents is circumcision mentioned as a prerequisite for admission to the Christian community. Given the absence of evidence on this point, it may not be assumed that there is evidence of absence: the fact that circumcision is not mentioned does not mean that this ritual was not advocated. In neither Matthew nor the Didache, where baptism in the name of the Father and the Son and the Holy Spirit is mentioned, nor James, where baptism is not explicitly mentioned (however, see 1:18), are there clear indications for the view that baptism has replaced circumcision.

- The Gospel of Matthew contains a fierce polemic against the Pharisaic movement; the reproach that, in their case, the necessary concord between preaching and doing is missing is also leveled against certain members of the community (the false prophets) in Matthew. James and the Didache are also polemically orientated, but the authors of these documents mainly oppose people with divergent views within the community.

- James and the didachist view the future restoration of the one Israel as an event that is also salutary for the Christian community, whereas Matthew is of the opinion that his community is the authentic guardian of Israel's heritage and that Jewish groups that also claim this prerogative will not share in the eschatological kingdom. However, the latter view does not imply that he perceives the church as replacing Israel or that Israel has lost its special position as God's people.

The above results show that, as regards contents, the three documents are closely related where the construction of ideals that the Christian community must meet is concerned. In fact, they express three variants of the same basic idea, namely, that belonging to the Christian community provides the best situation to share in the eschatological salvation and that the way to life requires, in practice, fulfilling God's will, which can be found in the Torah given by him (and authoritatively interpreted by Jesus).

The differences are likewise striking. Most differences originate from the fact that one document raises issues that are missing in the other documents or are less prominent. These differences can be explained by the fact that the three documents do not belong to the same literary genre. Matthew is the author of a gospel, which, as a genre, is related to the Greco-Roman biographies, in which the person portrayed is the central figure; James's letter belongs to the genre of the Diaspora letter and does not focus so much on that which binds the members of the community but rather on matters that divide the minds at a particular moment; the Didache is a text with instructions for the initiation into the Christian community and, as such, focuses on the minimum requirement that applicant Christian community members with a non-Jewish background must meet, and also takes a stand against preachers and leaders with different views than those of the author.

In one instance, a difference of opinion was encountered as regards the question of whether the Gentiles can be admitted to the Christian community. It is tempting to seize upon this difference for a reconstruction of the historical, social, and religious setting of the three documents. Do they originate from the same environment or even from the same area and do they go back to the same period? If so, how can it be explained that they differ so much on this one matter? Or does the difference reflect gradual development in which the original orientation on the whole Jewish Torah is put in perspective to open up the community to people from the world of the Gentiles? Do Matthew and James represent an older phase in this process and the didachist a later period? The answers to these questions go beyond the scope of my contribution, which is based on a semantic and intertextual analysis, and requires the application of methods from historical criticism and the social sciences. My observations are therefore open for supplementation and any corrections from different research perspectives. Conversely, these different research perspectives may profit from the picture, sketched here on the basis of semantic research, of the ideal community in Matthew, James, and the Didache.

POVERTY AND PIETY IN MATTHEW, JAMES, AND THE DIDACHE

John S. Kloppenborg

εἰρήνη δὲ πᾶσι καὶ πράγματα ἐς τὸ ἔμπαλιν ἀνεστραμμένα·
ἡμεῖς μὲν οἱ πένητες γελῶμεν, ἀνιῶνται δὲ καὶ οἰμώζουσιν οἱ πλούσιοι.
Lucian, *Cataplus* 15

Armenfrömmigkeit—the notion that the poor and the pious were equated in biblical tradition prior to the first century c.e.—provides a common exegetical resort when discussing such texts as James, Matthew, and the Didache. In regard to the Didache, Jean-Paul Audet opined that in Did. 3:7–4:4, which Audet called an "instruction aux pauvres," the author encourages the addressees to identify with the δίκαιοι and ἅγιοι (4:2), who "ne sont pas autres, évidemment, que les πτωχοί, pauvres"—the pious poor of the Psalms.[1]

A propos of the conceptual background of James, Martin Dibelius argued that in post-exilic Israel the term *'ănāwîm* connoted not merely the socially disadvantaged but had come to refer, on the one hand, to the nation itself insofar as Israel was weak in relation to its strong neighbors and, on the other hand, to a special group within the people of Israel who enjoyed divine favor by virtue of their humble status. Both in prophetic literature and in the Psalms the castigation of the rich and powerful for their ill-treatment of the poor was taken to imply conversely that the poor were advantaged:

> The more piety was understood as humbling oneself before God's will, the more poverty could function as intrinsically fertile soil for piety. As a result, "poor" and "pious" appear as parallel concepts (Ps 86:1–2; 132:15–16), and the typical enemy of the poor is also the enemy of God (Ps 109:31).[2]

---

1. Jean-Paul Audet, *La Didachè: Instructions des apôtres* (EBib; Paris: Gabalda, 1958), 317.

2. Martin Dibelius, *James: A Commentary on the Epistle of James* (revised H. Greeven; Hermeneia; Philadelphia: Fortress, 1976), 39.

Following Isidore Loeb's famous 1890 article on the "literature of the poor," Dibelius concluded that those who called themselves poor might have been economically disadvantaged. But that was not the main point: "the pious thought of themselves as the poor because *poverty had become a religious concept.*"[3] James's desire was to be poor, i.e., pious, and thus not to participate in the contaminating elements of the world. "He wanted all Christian to continue to belong to the "poor". . . . He wanted to barricade every door through which the spirit of the world might enter."[4] The salient feature of "poverty" in this view is not so much its economic or social aspect as its religious and moral ones. Theoretically a wealthy person could be numbered among the "poor" if she or he put trust in God.[5]

The identification of poverty with piety continues to be invoked in order to account for James. Ralph Martin described "piety of the poor" as a "handy phrase" and argued that

> in some way not quite clearly defined these groups ['the poor'] represented people who trusted in God for help, and so their poverty was equally a "poverty in spirit" in the sense of Matt 5:3; 11:5 (cf. Luke 4:18), and their religious outlook was similar to that of the pious ones in the Lukan nativity stories (Luke 1–2).[6]

---

3. Dibelius *James: A Commentary on the Epistle of James*, 40 (emphasis his); Isidore Loeb, "La littérature des pauvres dans la Bible," *REJ* 20 (1890): 179–80: "du moins le dénûment du Pauvre n'est pas l'essence même de sa pauvreté." Ernst Bammel, "πτωχός, πτωχεία, πτωχεύω," *TDNT* 6: 896, on the use of πτωχός in the *Psalms of Solomon*: "Where used, πτωχός is always the chief term and it thus represents an essential aspect in the selfunderstanding of the community which expresses itself in the Ps. Since this is undergoing various forms of affliction, πτωχός can include material poverty, though this is not the essential characteristic of the community nor does the climax of the statement lie here. πτωχός is in this sense the relic that brings to light a piety which is seeking release from a powerful ideology of poverty"; on James: Peter H. Davids, *The Epistle of James: A Commentary on the Greek Text* (NIGTC: Grand Rapids: Eerdmans, 1982), 111: "This election [of favoured groups] is based on the OT passages in which God is said to care for the poor . . . and the resulting fact that 'poor' became a term for the pious. . . ."

4. Dibelius, *James: A Commentary on the Epistle of James*, 48.

5. James B. Adamson, *The Epistle of James* (NICNT; Grand Rapids: Eerdmans, 1976), 108–9: "Not every rich man is doomed to be damned (e.g., Joseph of Arimathea, Mark 15:43–47), and not every poor man is sure to be saved, but for the purposes of this chapter [James 2] there is a deep difference between the rich, in general, and the poor, in general, and there is, in general, an equation of the poor and the world's despised." Recently Johannes Un-Sok Ro (*Die Sogennante "Armenfrömmigkeit" im Nachexilischen Israel* [BZAW 322; Berlin: de Gruyter, 2002]) has argued that "poverty" has no socio-economic connotations at all, but refers in postexilic literature to "spiritual poverty (humility, openness to the divine, etc.)."

6. Ralph P. Martin, *James* (WBC 48; Waco, Tex.: Word Books, 1988), lxxxv.

By the time of James, πτωχός was a technical term for the class of pious and humble people who put their trust in God for redemption and not in material wealth.[7]

The conflation of piety and poverty has been both embraced and strenuously resisted by theologies of liberation, although on ideological rather than historical or exegetical grounds. Some claim that the "poor" enjoy an epistemic privilege such that only the poor are able to understand fully the moral message of the Jesus movement and to appropriate it. This of course is not a historical or exegetical assertion. Rather, it claims either that the poor are somehow able to escape from the ideological framework of bourgeois or privileged discourse, or that the epistemic perspective of the poor is ideological only in the benign sense of that term. Hence, they enjoy unencumbered access to truth.[8] Both views are in fact quite problematic philosophically. But the notion of an epistemic privilege of *the poor* is also problematic insofar it conflates the world's "poor," both historically and translocally, into a single group, irrespective of the specifics of cultures, ideologies, economies, and social practices that serve to differentiate these "poors" one from another.

On the other hand, Elsa Tamez stresses the negative ideological consequences of the identification of poverty and piety:

> if we make the poor and the pious synonymous then real economic oppression and God's concern for this very class of people are lost. The rich become the piously poor and the poor rich in piety, and the economic order and the unjust power stay as they are. Thus the rich always come out ahead: they are rich in real life and piously poor before God and thus heirs of God's reign.[9]

While Tamez's comments are also not exegetical, they underscore the potential ideological entailments in *Armenfrömmigkeit* as an exegetical construct. It might be that this construct is *historically* justified, irrespective of how it might also mask the bitter reality of poverty. On the other hand, Tamez's observations should alert us to the possibility that *Armenfrömmigkeit* commended itself to modern North Atlantic interpreters precisely because it stressed values (morality and piety) as a key to the construction of Christian identity and suppressed other features (material poverty) that by the early-twentieth century had come to belong to other realms of cultural discourse and hence were supposed to be irrelevant or peripheral to genuinely "religious" claims.

---

7. Ibid., 65.

8. Delwin Brown, "Thinking About the God of the Poor: Questions for Liberation Theology from Process Thought," *JAAR* 57 (1989): 267–81.

9. Elsa Tamez, *The Scandalous Message of James: Faith Without Works is Dead* (rev. ed.; New York: Crossroad, 2002), 36.

Richard Bauckham endeavors to avoid the masking of genuinely economic concerns in the discourse of the early Jesus movement and at the same time is aware of the rhetorical function of discourse on poverty. According to Bauckham, James stresses the exemplary status of the πτωχοί—not merely the "working poor" (πένηται) but the destitute and indigent. James's addressees are neither the rich nor the poor, but rather those living between these extremes, those who might be tempted to identify with the élite *via* mechanisms of patronage.[10] Against this, James insists that

> [the poor] are not only members, for the kingdom they will inherit God has promised, like the crown of life (1:12), to 'those who love him'. . . . But they are the paradigmatic members, in some sense the model to which all other members must conform. Thus, just as Old Testament Israel's election was not for herself alone, but for the sake of the nations, so God's choice of the poor is not for the sake of the poor themselves but also for others.[11]

Bauckham recognizes the rhetorical use of the figures of the "poor" and the "rich" and argues that while James has no expectation that his addressees will or should impoverish themselves by adopting a beggarly existence, they should embrace a "counter-cultural" view in which "all must adopt the humility of the poor towards God and the humility of the poor (i.e., their not claiming superiority) towards others."[12] Ultimately this amounts to a social praxis in which economic and social disparities are leveled by promoting generalized reciprocity and an acknowledgement of the equality of rich and poor—an acknowledgment that aims at ameliorating material disparities.[13]

In what follows I would like both to develop and qualify elements of Bauckham's approach. He has successfully avoided concealing the economic realities of poverty behind a notion of piety. And he is aware that the discourse on poverty—at least in James—is in the first place *rhetorical*, rather than a *description* of social reality. That is, use of the rhetorical *sygkrisis* of the beggar and the rich man should not naively be interpreted to mean that James directly addresses either beggars or the ultra-rich; nor does the seeming privileging of a beggarly existence serve to encourage the addressees' embracing of such an existence. On the contrary, the *sygkrisis* serves other functions. Whether Bauckham's proposal—that

---

10. Richard J. Bauckham, *James: Wisdom of James, Disciple of Jesus the Sage* (New Testament Readings; London: Routledge, 1999), 188: "Thus, when James addresses his readers/hearers in general, he speaks of both the poor and the rich as other people (2:2–7, 14–16; in 4:13–5:6 he employs rhetorically direct address to two different groups of the rich in turn). This certainly does not mean that he expected no poor people to belong to the communities he addresses (1:8; 2:15), but that he expected the majority not to be poor."

11. Ibid., 193.

12. Ibid., 195.

13. Ibid., 196.

James holds out the poor as moral exemplars—is an adequate reading must be examined more carefully. But before turning to the function of the *sygkrisis* of rich and poor in James, Matthew, and the Didache, it will be useful to discuss the construct of *Armenfrömmigkeit*.

1. Discourse on Poverty and Wealth

Discourse on poverty and riches is a frequent feature of biblical, indeed, all Near Eastern, literature. The discourse is highly variegated, appearing with differing nuances in legal, prophetic, sapiential, and hymnic texts.

In the Tanak the focus of legal texts is advocacy on behalf of the poor (*'ebyôn, dal, maḥsôr* and *'ānî*): that legal judgments concerning the poor not be subverted (Exod 23:3, 6; Lev 19:15); that the poor be allowed to use the produce that grows on fallow land (Exod 23:11) and to reap the corners of fields (Lev 19:9–10; 23:22); that loans be extended to the poor even if a sabbatical year is approaching (Deut 15:7–11); and that the wages of poor laborers not be withheld (Deut 24:14).

The treatment of the poor in Wisdom texts somewhat more varied. On the one hand, there are complaints against those who prey upon the poor (Prov 30:14; Job 20:19; 24:4, 9, 14) and contrasting definitions of piety that involve assisting and advocating for the poor. For example, when Job defends his character, acts of benefaction toward the poor are key elements in his auto-representation:

> When I went out to the gate of the city, when I took my seat in the square, the young men saw me and withdrew and the aged rose up and stood; the nobles refrained from talking and laid their hands on their mouths . . . because I delivered the poor (*'ānî*) who cried, and the fatherless who had none to help him. The blessing of the wretched came upon me and I caused the widow's heart to sing for joy; I put on righteousness and it clothed me; my justice was like a robe and a turban; I was eyes to the blind, and feet to the lame; I was a father to the poor (*'ebyônîm*), and I searched out the cause of him whom I did not know. (Job 29:7–9, 12–16)

Similar usages are found in Proverbs, where the benefaction of the poor is a mark of the true sage:

> He who oppresses a poor man insults his maker, but he who is kind to the needy honors him (14:31).
> He who is kind to the poor lends to the lord, and he will repay him for his deed (19:17).
> He who has a bountiful eye will be blessed, for he shares his bread with the poor (22:19).
> A righteous man knows the rights of the poor; the wicked have no such understanding (29:7).

Nevertheless, poverty is not treated as a virtue. On the contrary:

> A rich man's wealth is his strong city; the poverty of the poor is their ruin (10:15).
> The ransom of a man's life is his wealth, but a poor man has no means of redemption (13:8).
> The days of the poor are hard, but a cheerful heart has a continual feast (15:15)
> Wealth brings many new friends, but a poor man is deserted by his friend (19:4).
> All a poor man's brothers hate him; how much more do his friends go far from him! He pursues them with words, but does not have them (19:7).

There are, of course, constructions in which poverty is seemingly valued above wealth:

> It is better to be of a lowly spirit with the poor than to divide the spoil with the proud (16:19).
> Better is a poor man who walks in his integrity than a man who is perverse in speech, and is a fool (19:1).
> Better is a poor man who walks in his integrity than a rich man who is perverse in his ways (28:6).
> Better is a poor and wise youth than an old and foolish king, who will no longer take advice, even though he had gone from prison to the throne or in his own kingdom had been born poor (Qoh 4:13–14).

It would be wrong, however, to conclude that such contrasts constitute an exception to the generally negative view of poverty. These statements are directed to the rich, not the poor, and function to warn the rich against excessive or abusive behavior. Poverty is nowhere romanticized as virtuous; on the contrary, the extremity of poverty is used here rhetorically to underscore the even greater dangers of arrogance, hybris, foolishness, and other sapiential vices.

A different view of poverty is also encountered in wisdom literature, one that traces poverty to indolence. This should not be surprising, since the social location of wisdom discourse is in the upper scribal sectors, which idealized study and mental exertion. Thus, Proverbs warns that those who are lazy are punished with poverty (*reš*) (Prov 6:9–11; cf. 24:34) while hard work is idealized as something that brings profit (Prov 14:23; 21:5). Sirach lists as one of the three hateful kinds of persons the "beggar who is proud" (Sir 25:2; cf. Syriac Menander 354–8),14 and suggests that death is a welcome relief to the needy (42:2; cf. Syriac Menander 99–104). Syriac Menander opines that poverty in old age is "the dregs of all evil" (435–36; cf. 427–28).

---

14. Tjitze Baarda, "The Sentences of the Syriac Menander," in *The Old Testament Pseudepigrapha* (ed. James H. Charlesworth; Garden City, N.Y.: Doubleday, 1983–85), 2:602.

Nevertheless, generosity towards the poor remains a virtue and Proverbs expresses the view that, paradoxically, benefaction leads to an increase, not a decrease in wealth:

> One man gives freely, yet grows all the richer; another withholds what he should give, and only suffers want (Prov 11:24).
> He who oppresses the poor to increase his own wealth, or gives to the rich, will only come to want (Prov 22:16).

In the corpus of prophetic writings, the terms *'ebyôn*, *dal*, and *'ānî* occur in the context of complaints and threats concerning the rapacious activities of the rich, who abuse and devour the property of the poor (Isa 3:14–15; 10:2; 11:4; 32:7; Jer 2:34; 22:16–17; Ezek 16:49; 18:12; 22:29; Amos 2:6–7; 4:1; 5:11–12), forecasts of an idyllic state in which the poor are treated equitably (Isa 11:4; 14:30; 26:5–6; 29:19) and expressions of God's advocacy on behalf of the poor (Isa 25:4; 41:17; 58:7; Zeph 3:12).

An important source of statements on poverty is found in the Psalms of Lament, which not only depict the poor as the victims of the evil and the rich (10:2, 9; 37:14; 109:16), but also represent God as the defender of the poor:

> "Because the poor (*'ānî*) are despoiled, because the needy (*'ebyôn*) groan, I will now arise," says the LORD; "I will place him in the safety for which he longs." (Ps 12:5)
> This poor man (*'ānî*) cried, and the LORD heard him, and saved him out of all his troubles (Ps 34:6).
> As for me, I am poor (*'ānî*) and needy (*'ebyôn*); but the LORD takes thought for me. You are my help and my deliverer; do not tarry, O my God! (Ps 40:17)
> For the LORD hears the needy (*'ebyôn*), and does not despise his own that are in bonds. (Ps 69:33)
> But I am poor (*'ānî*) and needy (*'ebyôn*); hasten to me, O God! You are my help and my deliverer; O LORD, do not tarry! (Ps 70:5)
> He raises the poor (*'ānî*) from the dust, and lifts the needy (*'ebyôn*) from the ash heap. (Ps 113:7).

It will be noticed that *'ānî* is frequently paired with *'ebyôn*, and that both appear to refer to straitened social and economic circumstances. The *'ebyônîm* are said to be despoiled by the strong (Ps 35:10); they are "brought down" by the wicked (Ps 37:14); and Ps 132:15 promised that God will "satisfy her poor (*'ebyôn*) with bread," which suggests that "poor" refers in fact to those who lack basic essentials. There is nothing here to suggest that the "poor" are idealized as those who patiently and piously endure misery. Pleins is right to conclude that

> the term [*'ebyôn*] simply points out severe economic deprivation. This condition may evoke the concern of God and the community, but the poverty of the

'ebyôn in and of itself is not considered a virtue or a way of life to be pursued for religious reasons.[15]

1.1. 'Anāwîm Piety[16]

The term 'ănāw (mostly in the plural 'ănāwîm), which appears predominantly in the Psalms (9:13, 19; 10:12, 17; 22:27; 25:9; 34:3; 37:11; 69:33; 76:10; 146:6; 149:4) and Isaiah (11:4; 29:19; 32:7; 61:1) became the special focus of attention in the late-nineteenth century. Heinrich Graetz's commentary on the Psalms conjectured that the Psalms of complaint reflected the discourse of a social "class" of impoverished Levites, disadvantaged by the Aaronite priesthood.[17] A similar view was soon promoted by Isidore Loeb, even though he did not endorse the identification of the "poor" with the Levites. According to Loeb,

> during the Babylonian exile there arose among the Jews a class of persons claimed to the *servants of God* in a special way, and believed themselves to be more faithful to Judaism than any other Jews. We know them from deutero-Isaiah or Pseudo-Isaiah, who described their situation vis à vis their coreligionists, expressed their sentiments, thinking, and hopes. They had taken a vow of poverty and humility, believed that they would atone for the sins of the Jewish people, and would suffer for them in order to earn their deliverance. They regarded themselves as the heart and core of the nation, as it were a living symbol of the Jewish people.... [After the exile] these courageous souls probably formed associations or confraternities, called "the pious," "the righteous," "the holy ones," "the poor," "the humble." They seem to have been especially numerous and influential during the Syrian dominion, but they were not dissolved under the Hasmoneans and occupied an even more important place in primitive Christianity.[18]

Independently of Loeb, Alfred Rahlfs also rejected Graetz's theory that the "poor" represented a party of Levites, but concluded that the 'ănāwîm were a "party" that arose during the Exile, convinced that Israel itself had become "the poor." The Servant of the Lord of Deutero-Isaiah served as a personification of this party:

> Die Anawim = Knechte Jahwes sind eine Partei innerhalb des Volkes, aber nichts führt darauf, sie als Leviten oder überhaupt als Angehörige eines bes-

---

15. J. David Pleins, "Poor, Poverty," *ABD* 5 (1992): 404.

16. On what follows, see the survey by Gerhard Lohfink, "Von der 'Anawim-Partei' zur 'Kirche der Armen': Die bibelwissenschaftliche Ahnentafel eines Hauptbegriffs der 'Theologie der Befreiung'," *Bib* 67 (1986): 153–76.

17. Heinrich Graetz, *Kritischer Commentar zu den Psalmen: Nebst Text und Uebersetzung* (Breslau: S. Schottlaender, 1882–83), 20–37.

18. Isidore Loeb, "Les dix-huit bénédictions," *REJ* 19 (1889): 23.

timmten Standes zu fassen. Die Anawim sind vielmehr die Frommen, die entschlossenen Anhänger Jahwes im Exil überhaupt. Ob diese Partei sich selbst den Namen Anawim als Parteinamen beigelegt hat, ist nicht sicher auszumachen. Möglich wäre es.[19]

By the early-twentieth century doubts were expressed about whether the 'ănāwîm represented a "party" rather than simply a "direction" (Richtung) or tendency in Israelite piety. Wolf Wilhelm Graf Baudissin contended that one could speak of a "party" of the poor in the Maccabean period at the earliest.[20] But the tendency in Israelite piety to identify the poor with the virtue of humility came with Deutero-Isaiah's characterization of Judah as God's 'ănāwîm (Isa 61:1). The exile was interpreted as a humbling act of God that constituted Israel's identity. Thereby poverty, once a negative term, received a positive valuation. For Baudissin, as Pleins puts it, "poverty and humility eventually dovetail as theological concepts: they are the precondition for experiencing the compassion of God."[21]

Max Weber's Das antike Judentum, published in 1921, also saw the Exile and Deutero-Isaiah as pivotal in the transvaluation of older views of poverty into something positive, equated with "the plebian virtue of humility."[22] Weber, however, emphasized the Maccabean period as the period of ascendancy of the 'ănāwîm:

> The "pious," the Hasidim as they were called especially in early Maccabean times, the 'ănāwîm as they were also named in the Psalms now became the main champions of a newly developing Jewish religiosity. They represent primarily an urban demos of town-farmers, artisans, traders, and as typical of antiquity, often stand sharply opposed to the wealthy urban and landed sibs both secular and priestly. . . . New was only the form and intensity of the struggle. This was essentially due to the urban character of the demos. Whereas the pious in pre-Exilic prophecy still represented a mere object of charity as preaching by the prophetic and Levitical and especially Deuteronomistic circles, they now became vocal and came to feel themselves to be the chosen people of Yahwe in contrast to their opponents. In our sources their religious mood is brought to clearest expression by the Psalms.[23]

It is obvious that Weber's equation of the 'ănāwîm/pious with the urban proletariat is precisely the kind of identification against which Tamez protests, since

---

19. Alfred Rahlfs, 'ānî und 'ānāw in den Psalmen (Göttingen: Dieterich, 1892), 83.

20. Wolf Wilhelm Graf Baudissin, "Die alttestamentliche Religion und die Armen," Preussische Jahrbücher 149 (1912): 219.

21. Pleins, "Poor, Poverty," 411.

22. Max Weber, Ancient Judaism (trans. H. H. Gerth and D. Martindale; New York: The Free Press, 1952), 370.

23. Ibid., 382.

it obscures from view those much further down the economic ladder than the urban working poor—smallholders who typically farmed plots too small to support a family and day laborers who suffered from chronic and structural underemployment,[24] not to mention various expendables. Weber's view also makes possible the claim that Tamez finds so problematic—that moderately wealthy urban dwellers could claim to be among the "poor" by virtue of the fact that they did not belong to the hated civic élite.

For his part, Antonin Causse located the "poor" further down the social ladder than Weber. He argued that the Psalter was not a book written by or for the priests; on the contrary, "[il] est l'oeuvre du peuple, il a été écrit par «les pauvres» et pour «les pauvres»" as a book of consolation and edification.[25] These poor

> truly dwelt in the countryside of ancient Palestine, in the unknown village, in the village on the hillside, in the village in the valley. It is there that they suffered, prayed, hoped. They were the peasants, labourers, and shepherds like their fathers. Every day they toiled, cultivated the rocky soil under the scorching sun; every night they came back to their homes and, under the oriental night, breathed out complaints of their souls; they called on God for help.[26]

Key to the piety of the 'ănāwîm, however, was how it surpassed "infinitely" that of the sacerdotal institutions of Judaism:

> Forgiveness and deliverance we not obtained through exterior acts, by ritual expiation, by sacrifices for sins as in the levitical Torah. The Ebionites had understood the great emptiness of the religion of external signs and magical forms. What God demanded of the faithful is to love justice and kindness and to walk humbly before him.[27]

---

24. John S. Kloppenborg, "The Growth and Impact of Agricultural Tenancy in Jewish Palestine (III BCE—I CE)," *JESHO* 51 (2008): 33–66.

25. Antonin Causse, *Les «Pauvres» d'Israël* (Prophètes, Psalmistes, Messianistes) (Strasbourg: Librairie Istra, 1922), 80.

26. Ibid., 81: "[i]ls ont vraiment habité là dans les campagnes de l'ancienne Palestine, dans le village innommé, le village au flanc de la colline, au creux du vallon. C'est là qu'ils ont souffert, qu'ils ont prié, qu'ils on espéré. C'étaient des paysans, laboureurs et bergers comme leurs pères. Le jour ils ont travaillé, cultivé le sol rocailleux sous le soleil brûlant; le soir ils sont rentrés dan leur maison, et sous la nuit d'Orient, ils ont exhalé le plainte de leur âme; ils ont appelé Dieu à leur secours."

27. Ibid., 129–30: "Ici l'expérience religieuse dépasse infiniment le cadre des institutions cultuelle du judaïsme. Le pardon et la délivrance ne sont pas obtenus par des actes extérieurs, des expiations rituelles, des sacrifices pour le péché comme dans la tora lévitique. Les ébionim ont compris la grande vanité de la religion des gestes et des formules magiques. Ce que Yahwe demande au fidèle c'est d'aimer la justice et la bonté et de marcher humblement devant lui," referring to Ps 32:1, 2, 5; Mic 6:8.

This was a completely interiorized piety, replacing the formalism of cultic practices, assured of God's bounty and justice, dependent upon God, and faithful to the Torah.[28]

Striking in these descriptions of the piety of the poor is the almost complete neglect of attention to economic factors; indeed, the characteristics of the "poor" have more to do with sturdy, individualistic north-European (and probably Protestant) values than they do with the situation of the economically dispossessed of the Levant.[29]

The stress on "poverty" as an interiorized piety reached its apogee in the work of the Catholic Albert Gelin who saw the beginnings of *Armenfrömmigkeit* in the eighth century, in Zephaniah, who transvalued the terms *'ānî* and *'ānāw*, once terms denoting failure, into positive terms indicating God's protection.

> Man must be poor before God, just as he was already poor in the presence of Asshur. Specifically, this meant the rooting out of all pride. . . .
> Spiritual poverty has rarely been so beautifully described: total openness to God, absolute humility, respect, obedience, consciousness of guilt, or better, still, compunction. All this points to perfect faith.[30]

Because of this highly theologized view of poverty, when Gelin came to the literature of the Jesus movement he could argue that Jesus did not intend to "beatify a social class" or "canonize" poverty. On the contrary, what he advocated was "spiritual poverty"—openness to God.[31] This for Gelin made sense of the fact that the Twelve were "small landowners." Jesus did not condemn wealth, had well-off friends, and "was accustomed to social amenities" such as banquets.[32] Indeed, Gelin declares that "in those days no segment of the population corresponded to our suffering proletariat."[33]

Like Gelin, Augustin George saw the full flowering of *Armenfrömmigkeit* to exist only with Jesus himself. "If we understand the expression to mean that the poor of the Old Testament arrived at a mystique of renouncing temporal goods, we must admit that this kind of detachment simply does not exist in the Old Testament. This is the new contribution of Jesus. Until he came, poverty in any

---

28. Ibid., 127–35.

29. S. T. Kimbrough, "A Non-Weberian Sociological Approach to Israelite Religion," *JNES* 31 (1972): 201–2 traces Causse's stress on individualism not to his Protestantism but to the influence of Lévy-Bruhl's theory of anthropological development from prelogical (and collectivist) thinking from the Stone Age to the emergence of the individual and ethical teaching based on personal responsibility in the VI/V B.C.E.

30. Albert Gelin, *The Poor of Yahweh* (Collegeville, Minn.: Liturgical, 1963), 30, 34.

31. Ibid., 107–8.

32. Ibid., 102.

33. Ibid., 105.

meaning of the term, was considered an evil. . . ."[34] The experience of poverty in
the Old Testament indeed led the poor not only to accept their condition, since
God "loved" the poor, but also to put their trust in a God who would deliver
them. Although poverty was an evil, it was also valorized, according to George,
and turned into "spiritual poverty which is a submission in faith, an accepted
smallness, a religious humility."[35] George insists that this is not an idealization
of poverty, but that in fact is what his description amounts to: "Poverty *did* have
an indisputable religious richness for [the people of the Old Testament]: it called
them to open themselves to God and prepared them to receive both the demands
and the gifts of Jesus."[36] It was Jesus and the Jesus movement that took the final
step of calling for the renunciation of worldly goods in the service of God.

The descriptions of Gelin and George are rather blatant instances of the
interpretations against which Tamez inveighs: the transfiguration of material
poverty into a virtue by placing it in a theological teleology that runs from the
rationalization of material deprivation as a catechetical state that fosters the
"higher" value of dependence on the divine to a voluntary embracing of renunciation as something inherently virtuous.

Despite the strong legacy of scholarship that wishes to find an equation of
poverty and piety, and notwithstanding Tamez's reservations concerning the
conflation of poverty with piety, strong exegetical objections have been registered against the notion of *Armenfrömmigkeit*. Kuschke's 1939 study of rich and
poor in post-exilic literature concluded that *'ănî* simply referred to the powerless,
oppressed poor and that it was impossible to conclude to what extent the pious
(*'ănāwîm*) were poor (*'ănî*) in a social sense. "Auf jedem Fall haben wir es nicht
mit einer 'Partei der gottlosen Reichen' und einer 'Partei der frommen Armen'
zu tun, die sich gegenseitig Klassenkämpfe geliefert hätten."[37]

Even the word *'ănāwîm* seems to have the same semantic range as *'ănî*. In
the Psalms the *'ănāwîm* are without food (22:27), landless (37:11), and in bonds
(69:33). God will not forget the poor (9:13, 19; 10:12, 17; 69:33). And Ps 147:6
contrasts them with the wicked (*rĕšā'îm*). The situation is not significantly different in the prophetic corpus, where the *'ănāwîm* appear in parallel with *dalîm*
(Isa 11:4; Amos 2:7) or *'ebyônîm* (Isa 29:19; 32:7; Amos 8:4). In Isa 61:1 they
are exiles to whom liberty and release is offered. As Pleins notes, the social and

---

34. Augustin George, "Poverty in the Old Testament," in *Gospel Poverty: Essays in Biblical
Theology* (ed. A. George, *et al.*; Chicago, Ill.: Franciscan Herald, 1977), 15.

35. Ibid,. 17.

36. Ibid., 19.

37. Anton Kuschke, "Arm und Reich im Alten Testament mit besonderer Berücksichtigung der nachexilischen Zeit," *ZAW* 57 (1939): 57. Cf. Pleins' comment on Deutero-Isaiah: "the
general and terribly concrete situation of political and economic oppression indelibly stamps
Second Isaiah's concept of poverty. This is not a theology of humility in the more detached or
spiritualized sense" (Pleins, "Poor, Poverty," 409).

economic connotations of *'ǎnāwîm* are less clear in Zeph 2:3 ("Seek the Lord, all you humble [*'ǎnāwîm*] of the land, who do his commands; seek righteousness, seek humility [*'ǎnāwa*]"). But "this is the only passage in the entire Hebrew Bible where the term *'ǎnāwîm* seems to have the less concrete meaning of "humble," although even here this is not altogether certain."[38] It is in fact possible that *'ǎnāwîm* is simply a variant of the plural of *'ānî*, despite the fact that the LXX does not render these two substantives in the same way.[39] Pleins concludes:

> If *'ǎnāwîm*, then, is nothing more than a plural form of *'ānî*, the meaning of *'ǎnāwîm* must be sought in conjunction with all the *'ānî* texts. Three things will follow from this. (1) The term *'ǎnāwîm* will be understood to denote concrete socioeconomic forms of poverty: it cannot be viewed as a condition that occurs by chance or by not being upright; rather, it is the product of oppression. . . . (2) The religious connotation of "humbleness" will be rejected, although it will not be necessary to lay aside the biblical idea that God is concerned for the oppressed, and we can still see that the poor are depicted as those who do call on God in their oppression . . .; in other words, the relation between God and the poor is a matter of justice, not based on piety. . . . (3) The statistics for word distribution will be combined, making *'ānî/'ǎnāwîm* the predominant word for poverty in the Hebrew Bible.[40]

In later Judaean literature it is no clearer that poverty and piety are equated. In the *Psalms of Solomon*, God is depicted as the hope and refuge of the poor (5:2, 11; 10:6; 15:1; 18:2); in the *Testaments of the 12 Patriarchs* poverty is an evil to be relieved by the benefaction of the well-to-do.[41] There are forecasts of the escha-

---

38. Pleins, "Poor, Poverty," 411, emphasis added. Similarly, Bammel, "πτωχός, πτωχεία, πτωχεύω," 890: "Only in Zeph. 3:12 is there as yet a true religious estimation of the poor; here God will leave only a *'am 'ānî wadal* (λαὸς πραΰς καὶ ταπεινός), and this will trust in Him."

39. The LXX translates *'ǎnāwîm* as πραΰς ("mild", "gentle") at Num 12:3; Ps 25:9 (twice); 34:4 [33:3]; 37:11 [36:11]; 76:9 [75:10]; 147:6 [146:6]; 149:4; as ταπεινός ("humble") at Isa 11:4; 32:7; Amos 2:7; Zeph 2:3; Prov 3:34; as πτωχός ("poor") at Isa 29:19; 61:1; Amos 8:4; Ps 69:33 [68:33]; Prov 14:21; and as πένης ("poor") at Ps 9:13, 19; 10:12 [9:33], 17 [9:38]; 22:27 [21:27].

In contrast, *'ānî* is rendered overwhelmingly as πτωχός in Lev 19:10; 23:22; 2 Kgs 22:28; Job 29:12; 34:28; 36:6; Ps 9:23, 30, 35; 12:5 [11:5]; 14:6 [13:6]; 22:24 [21:24]; 25:16 [24:16]; 34:6 [33:6]; 35:10 [34:10]; 37:14 [36:14]; 40:17 [39:17]; 68:10 [67:10]; 69:29 [68:29]; 70:5 [69:5]; 72:2 [71:2]; 72:4 [71:4]; 74:21 [73:21]; 86:1 [85:1]; 88:15 [87:15]; 102:1 [101:1];109:22 [108:22]; 140:12 [139:12] or ταπεινός at (Ps 18:27 [17:27]; 82:2 [81:3]; Prov 3:34; Qoh 10:6; Isa 14:32; 32:7; 49:19; 54:11; 58:4; 66:2; Jer 22:16) or πένης (Deut 15:11; 24:14, 15; Ps 9:12, 18; 72:4 [71:4]; 74:19 [73:19]; 109:16 [108:16]; Prov 31:9 [24:77]; 31:20; Zech 7:10; Isa 10:2); Prov 14:21) and less frequently as πραΰς (Job 24:4; Zeph 3:12; Zech 9:9; 26:6).

40. Pleins, "Poor, Poverty," 413.

41. *T. Iss.* 3.8; 5.2; 7.5; *T. Ash.* 2.5, 6; *T. Jos.* 3.5; *T. Benj.* 4.4; 4Q424 III, 9–10. The statement of *T. Gad* 7.6, that a poor man who is not envious is richer than all does not amount to a valorization of poverty.

tological elevation of the poor in *T. Jud.* 25.4 and *Sib. Or.* 8.208. *1 Enoch* 92–105 conducts a strenuous campaign against the wealthy and the powerful claiming that these oppress the righteous (96.8).[42] Yet it is noteworthy that neither πένης nor πτωχός appears in the Epistle. Although it is obvious that the authors of the Epistle do not classify themselves among the rich, and do consider themselves to be δίκαιοι, there is no claim that poverty and piety or righteousness are necessarily connected.

The writer of 4QInstruction positions both himself and his addressees among the poor with the repeated address, "you are poor" אביון אתהע, 4Q415 6 2; 4Q416, 2 III, 12; ראש אתה, 4Q416 2 III, 2; רש אתה, 4Q418 177 5).[43] The content of the instruction, as Benjamin Wright has observed, indicates that the "poor" are actually poor. "The sage of *4QInstruction* . . . intends his advice to rescue the mevin from the oppressive results of poverty, such as falling into the hands of creditors, lenders, and others who would take advantage of him."[44] For 4QInstruction, poverty is not a virtue or an ideal, nor do the poor have an advantage over the rich simply by virtue of their economic state:

> 4QInstruction teaches that the poor are indeed considered insignificant in the eyes of others, and they are not justified before God by the fact of their poverty. . . . The poor who sin require God's forgiveness (4Q417 2 I). God will, however, raise up the poor who have been wronged (4Q418 126 —interestingly enough, not explicitly by the rich). One fragmentary line might indicate that the sage of 4QInstruction prefers a way of life characterized by poverty: 4Q416 2 II, 20–21 reads, "Do not esteem yourself for your poverty (במחסורכה) when you are (anyway?) a pauper (רוש), lest vacat you bring into contempt your (own way) of life."[45]

Even this last quoted text seems to suggest, on the contrary, that poverty in itself should not be a badge of pride.

While 4QInstruction may be pre-Qumranic in origin and hence not necessarily represent precisely the diction of the *Yaḥad*, other texts with a strong claim to represent the self-understanding of the *Yaḥad* indeed use terms for poverty. 4QpIsaᵃ (4Q161 8–10 III, 3–4), commenting on Isa 10:33–34, interprets the

---

42. George W. E. Nickelsburg, "Riches, the Rich, and God's Judgment in 1 Enoch 92–105 and the Gospel According to Luke," in *George W. E. Nickelsburg in Perspective: An Ongoing Dialogue of Learning* (ed. J. Neusner and A. J. Avery-Peck; JSJSup 80; Leiden: Brill, 2003), 521–46.

43. Text: John Strugnell, *et al.*, *Qumran Cave 4. XXIV: Sapiential Texts, Part 2* (DJD 34; Oxford: Clarendon, 1999).

44. Benjamin G. Wright, "The Categories of Rich and Poor in the Qumran Sapiential Literature," in *Sapiential Perspectives: Wisdom Literature in Light of the Dead Sea Scrolls* (ed. J. J. Collins *et al.*; STDJ 51; Leiden: Brill, 2004), 113.

45. Wright, "Categories of Rich and Poor," 122.

destruction of the tall trees as the defeat of the Kittim at the hands of Israel, the "gentle of the [earth] (ענוי ארץ)." (similarly, 1QM XI, 13: enemies will be delivered up into the hand of the poor [ביד אביונים]). Yet the current state of Israel is due, according to the *pesher*, to the depredations of the evil. Catherine Murphy comments,

> They are reduced to that state because of the rogues who hatch plots to destroy the hungry and thirsty (Isa 32:5–7; 4QpIsa^c 26 1–3 [4Q163]; see 4QpIsa^e 6 2–7 [4Q165]). In their current deprivation they long for the day when God will reverse their fortunes and provide them with the bread they need and the water for which they thirst (4QpIsa^c 23 13–19), when God will free them and provide justice (4QpIsa^c 8–10 11–14; 18–19 1–6).[46]

A similar use of poverty is attested in 4QpPs^a (4Q171 II, 9–12):

> And the poor (ענוים) shall possess the land and enjoy peace in plenty [Ps 37:11]. Its interpretation concerns the congregation of the poor (עדה האביונים) who will tough out the period of distress and will be rescued from all the snares of Belial. Afterwards, all who shall possess the land will enjoy and grow fat with everything enjoyable to the flesh.[47]

Like 4QpIsa^a this pesher indicates that "poor" became a self-designation of the Qumran group. Yet there is no indication that the group's poverty (= piety) is the ground for its hope of eventual triumph. Similarly, the speaker of the Hodayot—perhaps the Righteous Teacher—frequently refers to himself as נפש עני (XIII, 13, 14) or נפש אביון (XI, 25; XIII, 18). This designation, however, points to actual poverty as is made clear by XI, 24–25:

> For I find myself at the boundary of wickedness and share the lot of the scoundrels. The soul of the poor person lives among great turmoil, and the calamities of hardship are with my footsteps.

Mansoor concludes appropriately that while *'ebyôn* seems to have become a favorite self-designation of the sect, the term also points to "the permanent social, economic and political state of the person or the group in question."[48]

---

46. Catherine M. Murphy, *Wealth in the Dead Sea Scrolls and the Qumran Community* (STDJ 40; Leiden: Brill, 2002), 238.

47. Florentino García Martínez and Eibert J. C. Tigchelaar, *The Dead Sea Scrolls: Study Edition* (Leiden: Brill, 1997–1998), 1:343.

48. Menahem Mansoor, *The Thanksgiving Hymns: Translated and Annotated with an Introduction* (STDJ 3; Grand Rapids: Eerdmans, 1961), 49. "These words [עני and רש] have in themselves no special religious meaning, even if the nuance of 'humble (meek)' may sometimes be included. They denote a man (or a people) as actually 'afflicted' and 'destitute' because of his suffering, his being oppressed, helpless, etc." (ibid., 134).

By the first century B.C.E., then, there is ample evidence of discourse about the impoverished. Poverty is nowhere treated as a state to be sought and those in the state of poverty were not thought to be privileged by virtue of their poverty. Of course, as in other instances of Near Eastern literature, God or the king were routinely represented as concerned with the plight of the poor and able to intervene to mitigate their dire situation.[49]

It is true that documents such as the Epistle of Enoch tend to treat the rich as inherently wicked, but these documents do not conversely consider the poor to be naturally advantaged. And it is true that "the Poor" became a self-designation at Qumran; but this term should not be robbed of its social and economic aspects and turned into a cipher for "the pious"; on the contrary, it points to the actual disadvantagement of the Righteous Teacher and the *Yaḥad* relative to their enemies.

2. The Poor in the Two Ways, Matthew, and James

Of the various terms that might be used to describe poverty (ἄπλουτος, ἄπορος, ἐνδεής, πενιχρός, πένης, πτωχός), Matthew and James prefer πτωχός and never use any of the other lexemes. The Didache uses πένης once (5:2), ἐνδεῖν once (5:2), and πτωχός twice (5:2; 13:4). It has been common to argue for a significant distinction between πένης and πτωχός, the former referring to the working poor and the latter to the destitute. The text most commonly cited to support this distinction is Aristophanes' *Plutus* 549–550:

Χρεμύλος· Οὔκουν δήπου τῆς πτωχείας πενίαν φαμὲν εἶναι ἀδελφήν;

Πένης· Ὑμεῖς γ' οἵπερ καὶ Θρασυβούλῳ Διονύσιον εἶναι ὅμοιον. Ἀλλ' οὐχ οὑμὸς τοῦτο πέπονθεν βίος οὐ μὰ Δι'-, οὐδέ γε μέλλει. Πτωχοῦ μὲν γὰρ βίος, ὃν σὺ λέγεις, ζῆν ἐστιν μηδὲν ἔχοντα· τοῦ δὲ πένητος ζῆν φειδόμενον καὶ τοῖς ἔργοις προσέχοντα, περιγίγνεσθαι δ' αὐτῷ μηδέν, μὴ μέντοι μηδ' ἐπιλείπειν.

Chremyulus: Well, don't we say that poverty (*penia*) is a sister of beggary (*ptōcheia*)?

Poverty: Ah, according to you Thrasybulus and Dionysius are one and the same. No, my life is not like that, nor by Zeus will ever be. For the life of the beggar, whom you describe, is to live never possessing anything. But the

---

49. Chester Charlton McCown, "The Beatitudes in the Light of Ancient Ideals," *JBL* 46 (1927): 50–61.

50. See Arthur Robinson Hands, *Charities and Social Aid in Greece and Rome* (London: Thames & Hudson, 1968), 64–65, who also notes the "Greek tendency to hyperbole and variation of language for its own sake" and conjectures that the higher frequency of πτωχός in "Greek-Oriental literature as compared with classical has been taken to reflect a higher incidence of dire poverty in this period" (ibid., 65).

life of a poor man is to live by scrimping and being attentive to his work:
he has no surplus, but there is no shortfall either.

Relying on Aristophanes it is usual to suppose that the early Jesus movement,
by preferring πτωχός in its discourse, had in view not the working poor but the
utterly destitute.[51] The validity of this distinction is, however, undermined by the
observation that the Septuagint constantly uses πτωχός generically to refer to the
poor. For example, 4 Kgdms 25:12, referring to the deportation of the population from Judah, states that "the captain of the guard left some of the πτωχοί of
the land as vinedressers and plowmen," where πτωχοί cannot mean "beggars."[52]
Moreover, Ps 39:18, 69:6, 85:1 and 108:22 use the phrase ἐγὼ δὲ πτωχός εἰμι καὶ
πένης, where the two nouns must be synonymous; if the πτωχός signified a status
much lower than that of πένης, one should expect ἐγὼ δὲ πένης εἰμι, καὶ πτωχός,
"I am poor, nay, a beggar."[53] Additionally, Prov 22:22 reads μὴ ἀποβιάζου
πένητα, πτωχὸς γάρ ἐστιν, "do not rob the *penēs*, for he is a *ptōchos*." It makes
little sense to render this, "do not rob the poor for he is a beggar."[54]

If the Septuagint tended to assimilate πτωχός to πένης, ordinary Greek usage
could include the destitute among the poor. In the *Symposium*, Plato describes
Penia (poverty) as coming to the door to beg (203A) and Erōs, Penia's child, as
"rough and squalid, and has no shoes, nor a house to dwell in [and] always in
distress," that is, as a beggar (203CD). Πενία is a much more comprehensive category than is suggested by Aristophanes' distinction. Rosivach in fact notes,

---

51. Thus John Dominic Crossan, *The Historical Jesus: The Life of a Mediterranean Jewish
Peasant* (San Francisco: Harper & Row, 1991), 270–73: "The beatitude of Jesus declared blessed,
then, not the poor but the destitute, not poverty but beggary" (ibid., 273), referring to Gildas H.
Hamel, *Poverty and Charity in Roman Palestine: First Three Centuries C.E.* (University of California Publications: Near Eastern Studies 23; Berkeley and Los Angeles: University of California
Press, 1990), 170: "A πένης remained on a somewhat equal footing with the rich, at least in religious and political matters. He had a voice in the community and was conscious of supporting
the whole edifice of society. If the πένης was the opponent of the πλούσιος he was also on the
same side of the fence. Both πένης and πλούσιος determined each other's identity, whereas a
πτωχός was on the margins and recognized by everyone as such. Poor and rich belonged to the
same world and placed themselves on a common, ever-sliding scale, but beggars could not. The
πτωχός was someone who had lost many of all of his family and social ties."

52. The MT has וּמִדַּלַּת הָאָרֶץ.

53. L. Gregory Bloomquist, "The Rhetoric of the Historical Jesus," in *Whose Historical
Jesus?* (ed. W. E. Arnal and M. Desjardins; ESCJ 7; Waterloo, Ont.: Wilfred Laurier University
Press, 1997), 107. The two nouns appear in synonymous parallelism elsewhere: 1 Sam 2:8; Job
34:28; Ps 11:6; 34:10; 36:14; 40:2; 69:6; 71:4; 71:12, 13; 73:21; 81:3, 4; 85:1; 108:16, 22; 112:7;
139:13; Prov 31:20; Isa 10:2; Ezek 16:49; 18:12; 22:29; Amos 4:1; 8:4; Ps Sol 5:11.

54. Benjamin G. Wright and Claudia V. Camp, "'Who Has Been Tested by Gold and
Found Perfect?' Ben Sira's Discourse of Riches and Poverty," *Henoch* 23 (2001): 154 note that
the LXX translator of Sirach "often seems to regard the two roots [πτωχ- and ταπειν-] as synonymous," citing Sir 13:20–23 where עֲנָוָה/ταπεινότης appears in parallel with אֶבְיוֹן/πτωχός.

The passage from *Wealth* quoted above is taken . . . to show that beggars (*ptōkhoi*) were a distinct underclass, as it were, beneath the *penētes*, but this is not quite correct, since, properly speaking, all non-wealthy, including beggars, were *penētes*. The word *ptōkhos* is rarely used to describe actual real beggars. Rather it is used most often in two contexts, first to elicit sympathy in describing people who have lost everything . . . and second as an exaggerated synonym for *penēs*, particularly as a term of abuse.[55]

If the distinction between πτωχός and πένης is not overdrawn, then the language of the early Jesus movement appears for the most part conventional when viewed against the background of other Judaean literature.

2.1. The Didache and the "Poor"

I will begin with the Two Ways document of the Didache for two reasons. First, whether or not Did. 1:1–2; 2:2–6:1 is thought already to belong to the Jesus movement, it reflects virtually nothing of the tradition of Jesus's sayings that was eventually enshrined in Q and Matthew and which, as I have argued elsewhere, was known to James.[56] The catena of Jesus-sayings in 1:3–2:1, which betrays knowledge of Luke and either Matthew or Q,[57] is almost universally acknowledged to be a later addition to the Two Ways. As will become clear, the references to the poor in Matthew and James are due in large measure to Q sayings concerning poverty.

Second, the Didache is very lean when it comes to references to the poor. Did. 13:4 recommends that if a prophet is not available in the community to be the recipient of first fruits, these should be given to τοῖς πτωχοῖς.[58] This provi-

---

55. Vincent J. Rosivach, "Some Athenian Presuppositions About 'The Poor'," *GR* 38 (1991): 196, n. 5.

56. On the slight evidence of "christianizing" of the Two Ways document prior to the addition of 1:3–2:1, see John S. Kloppenborg, "The Transformation of Moral Exhortation in Didache 1–5," in *The Didache in Context: Essays on Its Text, History and Transmission* (ed. C. N. Jefford; NovTSup 77; Leiden: Brill, 1995), 97–98. On James and the Jesus tradition, see John S. Kloppenborg, "The Reception of the Jesus Tradition in James," in *The Catholic Epistles and the Tradition* (ed. J. Schlosser; BETL 176; Leuven: Peeters, 2004), 93–139; "Emulation of the Jesus Tradition in James," in *Reading James with New Eyes* (ed. R. L. Webb and J. S. Kloppenborg; Library of New Testament Studies 342; London: T&T Clark, 2007), 121–50.

57. See John S. Kloppenborg, "The Use of the Synoptics or Q in Did 1:3b–2:1," in *The Didache and Matthew: Two Documents from the Same Jewish-Christian Milieu?* (ed. H. van de Sandt; Assen: Van Gorcum, 2005), 105–29.

58. Did. 13:4, which uses the second person plural instead of the second person singular of 13:3, 5–6, has been regarded as a later, though still old, gloss: Audet, *La Didachè: Instructions des apôtres*, 458; Kurt Niederwimmer, *The Didache: A Commentary* (Hermeneia; Minneapolis: Fortress, 1998), 192.

sion is evidently an imitation of Num 18:8–32, which mandated a tithe to be paid to the priests and Levites, and Deut 14:28–29, which adds καὶ ὁ προσήλυτος καὶ ὁ ὀρφανὸς καὶ ἡ χήρα ἡ ἐν ταῖς πόλεσίν σου as additional recipients of the tithe.

The only other explicit references to the poor comes in the Two Ways section in 5:2, in a lengthy list of the partisans of the "way of death," which includes those who "show no mercy to a poor person" (οὐκ ἐλεοῦντες πτωχόν), who "do not make an effort for the oppressed" (οὐ πονοῦντες ἐπὶ καταπονουμένῳ), who "turn their backs on the needy person" (ἀποστρεφόμενοι τὸν ἐνδεόμενον), who oppress the afflicted (καταπονοῦντες τὸν θλιβόμενον), "advocates for the rich" (πλουσίων παράκλητοι) and the lawless judges of the poor (πενήτων ἄνομοι κριταί). The explicit condemnation of friends of the rich coupled with the condemnation of their neglect of the poor and oppressed recalls much of the polemic of the Epistle of Enoch, which in turn developed the language of the Psalms and prophetic complaints against the wealthy. Neither the call to support the poor nor complaints against the abuses of the wealthy, however, is terribly novel when viewed in the context of the discourse of the Tanak on wealth and poverty. None of these suggests that piety is a special mark of the poor.

The point in the Two Ways document that has been thought to reflect ʿănāwîm piety is Did. 3:7–4:4. Jean-Paul Audet called this section an "instruction aux pauvres."[59] Citing Causse,[60] Audet saw the typical features of ʿănāwîm piety: the appeals to patience, mercy, and fidelity to the Torah; warnings against anger and hybris; and the encouragement to seek the company not of the arrogant but of the δίκαιοι-ἅγιοι (4:2). Even though none of the terms for "poor" appears in 3:7–4:4, Audet concluded that the addressees "ne sont pas autres, évidemment, que les πτωχοί, pauvres, plus directement reconnaissables sous ce nom dans l'exhortation sur l'aumône" (4:5–8).[61] Niederwimmer for his part calls the section "the ʿănāwîm sayings," evidently because this section employs language typically associated with ʿănāwîm piety.[62]

It should be said, initially, that it seems very unlikely that 3:7–4:4 or the Two Ways in general intends to address the "poor." The immediately preceding section, Did. 3:1–6, is concerned to articulate an aetiology and genealogy of vices, arguing that there is a direct and necessary connection between lesser vices such as anger not expressly proscribed by the Torah, and murder, part of the Decalogue. This kind of discourse, which seeks to establish family resemblances among certain behaviors, and which operates from and seeks to illustrate the theoretical claim of the unity of the Torah, belongs to a fairly sophisticated moral speculation, hardly consonant with addressees far down the social ladder. The

59. Audet, La Didachè: Instructions des apôtres, 311.
60. Causse, Les «Pauvres» d'Israël.
61. Audet, La Didachè: Instructions des apôtres, 317.
62. Niederwimmer, The Didache: A Commentary, 100–102.

advice not to associate with the ὑψηλοί (3:9; cf 5:2, ὕψος, ἀλαζονεία) but instead with the δίκαιοι also implies addressees who, on the one hand, like the Epistle of Enoch identify the wealthy and arrogant with the wicked,[63] and on the other, have some degree of *choice* in their associations, and could avoid contact, e.g., with wealthy benefactors and the elite of Roman society. The counsel not to show partiality in correction (οὐ λήψῃ πρόσωπον ἐλέγξαι ἐπὶ παραπτώμασιν; 4:3) likewise points to persons who might from time to time enjoy authority over others.

Comparison of the Didache's Two Ways with that of Barnabas suggest, first, that the τέκνον section (Did. 3:1–6) was inserted in the source common to the Didache's Two Ways, the *Doctrina Apostolorum* and the *Canons of the Holy Apostles*.[64] Second, comparison of Did. 3:7–4:4 with *Barn.* 19.2–7 indicates that either the didachist or his source rearranged extensively, extracting some of the material to create Did. 2:2–7 and rearranging the remaining sayings of Barnabas to form two small clusters of imperatives, 3:7–10 and 4:1–4.

While the sayings in Barnabas are rather chaotic, the Didache is much better organized, with the first cluster (3:7–10) stressing humility, quiet, and acceptance of fate, and the second recommending reverence for teachers and the fostering of strong inner-group solidarity. In fact submission to teaching is common to both clusters, since 3:8 valorizes an awe-filled posture towards οἱ λόγοι οὓς ἤκουσας. The allusion is to Isa 66:2b, καὶ ἐπὶ τίνα ἐπιβλέψω ἀλλ᾽ ἢ ἐπὶ τὸν ταπεινὸν καὶ ἡσύχιον καὶ τρέμοντα τοὺς λόγους μου,[65] "but this is the man to whom I will look, he that is humble and quiet and trembles at my word," which suggests that οἱ λόγοι are meant to be divine words, conveyed through the voice of a teacher. That is, both units are concerned with the student's posture vis à vis teaching.

Comparison of Did. 3:7–10 with Barnabas indicates considerable expansion, as well as rearrangement. For Barnabas' lapidary imperative, ἔσῃ πραΰς, the

---

63. On arrogance as a stereotypical vice of the rich, see Vincent J. Rosivach, "Class Matters in the «Dyskolos» of Menander," *CQ* 51 (2001): 129 and Aristotle, Rhet. 1378b26: αἴτιον δὲ τῆς ἡδονῆς τοῖς ὑβρίζουσιν, ὅτι οἴονται κακῶς δρῶντες αὐτοὶ ὑπερέχειν μᾶλλον. διὸ οἱ νέοι καὶ οἱ πλούσιοι ὑβρισταί· ὑπερέχειν γὰρ οἴονται ὑβρίζοντες, "the cause of pleasure for those who act in an insulting way is the idea that, by ill-treating others, they are able more fully to demonstrate superiority. For this reason the young and the rich are given to insults: for they suppose by acting in an insulting fashion they are showing their superiority."

64. Thus Niederwimmer, *The Didache: A Commentary*, 124 n. 1. Interestingly, P.Oxy. 1782 has a series of wedge-shapes signs at the ends of fol. 2r.20 followed by horizontal dashes (fol. 2r.21), thus separating 2.7 from 3.1; see Richard Hugh Connolly, "New Fragments of the Didache," *JTS* 25 (1924): 152. Niederwimmer (*The Didache: A Commentary*, 37) thinks that the copyist wished to signal that nothing was missing from l. 20 and that a new section began after l. 21 (i.e., 3:1–6). Audet (*La Didachè: Instructions des apôtres*, 55): "Il est beaucoup plus naturel de supposer une addition projectée, puis omise après coup pour une raison ou pour une autre."

65. 1 Clem. 13.4 cites Isa 66:2b but uses πραΰς instead of ταπεινός: ἐπὶ τίνα ἐπιβλέψω ἀλλ᾽ ἢ ἐπὶ τὸν πραὺς καὶ ἡσύχιον καὶ τρέμοντα τοὺς λόγους μου.

Didache provides a full motive clause: ἐπεὶ οἱ πραεῖς κληρονομήσουσι τὴν γῆν, citing Ps 36:11 LXX, οἱ δὲ πραεῖς κληρονομήσουσιν γῆν (MT: וַעֲנָוִים יִירְשׁוּ־אָרֶץ). Van de Sandt draws attention both to the wording of the *Doctrina*, *esto autem mansueti quia mansueti possidebunt sanctam terram*, and to the pesher on Ps 37:11 in 4QpPsᵃ II, 9–11, and the pesher on Ps 37:21–22:

> And the poor (ענוים) shall possess the land and enjoy peace in plenty [Ps 37:11]. Its interpretation concerns the congregation of the poor (עדה האביונים) who will tough out the period of distress and will be rescued from all the snares of Belial. Afterwards, all who shall possess the land will enjoy and grow fat with everything enjoyable to the flesh. . . . (4QpPsᵃ II, 9–11)

> The wicked borrows but does not pay back, while the just man is sympathetic and gives. For those who are blessed [by him shall pos]sses the land, but those who are cursed by him [shall be cu]t off. Its interpretation concerns the congregation of the poor [to whom is] the inheritance of the whole . . .[. . .] They will inherit the high mountain of Isra[el and] delight [in his] holy mountain. (4QpPsᵃ III, 8–11).[66]

Both *pesharim* refer to Ps 37:11 and as the second pesher makes clear, the *Yaḥad* expected to inherit the temple (=the high mountain of Israel).[67] Van de Sandt sees this "patriotic" or "national-political" interpretation also in the *Doctrina*. Yet it is crucial to note that neither Did. 3:7 nor Matt 5:5 follows this interpretation, as van de Sandt himself notes.[68] Ps 37:11 is not given the political interpretation it has in 4QpPsᵃ.

Niederwimmer proposes that the didachist expresses the belief typical of *'ănāwîm* piety that "those who are oppressed and without possessions . . . will eventually (an eschatological hope, but not for the near future) be the possessors of the (holy) land" and that "the humble and pious person [who] . . . accepts everything that befalls him or her without grumbling" (3.10) will be compensated.[69] But nothing in particular in 3:7–10 indicates poverty; on the contrary,

---

66. Trans. García Martínez, *Dead Sea Scrolls*, 1:343–45.

67. Huub van de Sandt and David Flusser, *The Didache: Its Jewish Sources and Its Place in Early Judaism and Christianity* (CRINT 3/5; Assen: Van Gorcum, 2002), 134.

68. On Matt 5:5, William D. Davies and Dale C. Allison, Jr. (*A Critical and Exegetical Commentary on the Gospel according to Saint Matthew* (ICC; Edinburgh: T&T Clark, 1988–97], 1:450) consider the possibility that τὴν γῆν refers to the Land of Israel but reject this on the grounds that elsewhere Matthew uses ἡ γῆ to mean "the earth." "It would seem to follow, then, that in Mt 5.5 'to inherit the land' has been spiritualized, and 5.5b is no more concrete than any of the other promises made in the beatitudes. It is just another way of saying, 'The one who humbles himself will be exalted (in the Kingdom of God)'" (Davies and Allison, *A Critical and Exegetical Commentary on . . . Matthew*, 450–51).

69. Niederwimmer, *The Didache: A Commentary*, 100, 102.

when πραΰς is paired with ἡσύχιος (and μακροθυμία), as it also is in Hermas, *Mand.* 5.2.3; 6.2.3 and *1 Clem.* 13.4, its primary referent is not to economic states but to mildness or gentleness. The economic associations of *'ănāwîm* are not carried over into Greek.

Rather than expressing beliefs about the redemption of the poor, Did. 3:7–8 strings together virtues associated with moral instruction. A similar set of adjectives is found in *T. Dan* 6.9 (in what may be a Christian insertion): ἔστι [ὁ πατὴρ τῶν ἐθνῶν] γὰρ ἀληθὴς καὶ μακρόθυμος, πρᾶος καὶ ταπεινός, καὶ ἐκδιδάσκων διὰ τῶν ἔργων νόμον Θεοῦ, "for [the father of the nations] is true and patient and mild and lowly and teaches through his works the Law of God." Didache 3:7–10, like 4:1–4, aims to inculcate the virtues of a student. *'Anāwîm* piety has nothing to do with this unit.

2.2. MATTHEW AND THE POOR

Most of Matthew's uses of "poor" are also quite conventional. Matt 19:21 (editing Mark 10:21) advises almsgiving to the πτωχοῖς as a means of obtaining "treasure in heaven" in a manner not significantly different from the advice proffered by Sirach or Tobit:

> Σύγκλεισον ἐλεημοσύνην ἐν τοῖς ταμείοις σου, καὶ αὕτη ἐξελεῖταί σε ἐκ πάσης κακώσεως.
> Store up almsgiving in your treasury, and it will rescue you from all affliction.
> (Sir 29:12)

> Ἐλεημοσύνη γὰρ ἐκ θανάτου ῥύεται, καὶ αὐτὴ ἀποκαθαριεῖ πᾶσαν ἁμαρτίαν· οἱ ποιοῦντες ἐλεημοσύνας καὶ δικαιοσύνας πλησθήσονται ζωῆς.
> For almsgiving delivers from death, and it will purge away every sin. Those who perform deeds of charity and of righteousness will have fullness of life. (Tob 12:9).[70]

Almsgiving as a means of relieving poverty is also presupposed in the exchange in Matt 26:9–11. Also conventional is the sentiment expressed in Matt 11:5 (from

---

70. Sir 3:30 πῦρ φλογιζόμενον ἀποσβέσει ὕδωρ, καὶ ἐλεημοσύνη ἐξιλάσεται ἁμαρτίας, "Water extinguishes a blazing fire: so almsgiving atones for sin"; 17:22 ἐλεημοσύνη ἀνδρὸς ὡς σφραγὶς μετ- αὐτοῦ, καὶ χάριν ἀνθρώπου ὡς κόρην συντηρήσει, "A man's almsgiving is like a signet with the Lord and he will keep a person's kindness like the apple of his eye"; 29:12 σύγκλεισον ἐλεημοσύνην ἐν τοῖς ταμείοις σου, καὶ αὕτη ἐξελεῖταί σε ἐκ πάσης κακώσεως, "Store up almsgiving in your treasury, and it will rescue you from all affliction"; 40:17 χάρις ὡς παράδεισος ἐν εὐλογίαις, καὶ ἐλεημοσύνη εἰς τὸν αἰῶνα διαμενεῖ, "Kindness is like a garden of blessings, and almsgiving endures for ever"; 40:24 ἀδελφοὶ καὶ βοήθεια εἰς καιρὸν θλίψεως, καὶ ὑπὲρ ἀμφότερα ἐλεημοσύνη ῥύσεται, "Brothers and help are for a time of trouble, but almsgiving rescues better than both."

Q 7:22) that the πτωχοί will be favored by God's saving actions. There is an obvious allusion to Isa 61:1, מָשַׁח יְהוָה אֹתִי לְבַשֵּׂר עֲנָוִים / ἔχρισέν με εὐαγγελίσασθαι πτωχοῖς, and now a remarkable parallel in 4Q521 2 II, 12, "the Lord will heal the wounded and will enliven the dead and give good news to the poor (יבשׂר ענוים). Less conventional is what is expressed in Matt 5:3, adapted from Q 6:20.

Q 6:20b: μακάριοι οἵ πτωχοί, ὅτι [[ὑμετέρα]] ἐστὶν ἡ βασιλεία τοῦ θεοῦ.[71]
Matt 5:3: μακάριοι οἱ πτωχοὶ τῷ πνεύματι, ὅτι αὐτῶν ἐστιν ἡ βασιλεία τῶν οὐρανῶν.

As is well known, it is usual to argue that Matthew has redactionally ethicized what in Q is referred to as the social or economic state of poverty. This conclusion is obvious from the attributes that Matthew added to Q's beatitudes and from the extra beatitudes added. Davies and Allison resist this conclusion, pointing out that "there are no explicit imperatives" except in 5:11–12, and that the qualities enunciated by the makarisms are not frequent in New Testament catalogues of virtues.[72] But Davies and Allison themselves concede that πτωχοὶ τῷ πνεύματι, like עני רוח of 1QM XIV, 7, means "humble."[73] Likewise, οἱ πραεῖς (5:5), οἱ πεινῶντες καὶ διψῶντες τὴν δικαιοσύνην (5:6), οἱ ἐλεήμονες (5:7), οἱ καθαροὶ τῇ καρδίᾳ (5:8), and οἱ εἰρηνοποιοί (5:9) all point to ethical, not to social or economic states. That these statement are not framed as imperatives is quite irrelevant to their illocutionary function: it should be obvious that makarisms such as Ps 1:1 (μακάριος ἀνήρ, ὃς οὐκ ἐπορεύθη ἐν βουλῇ ἀσεβῶν καὶ ἐν ὁδῷ ἁμαρτωλῶν οὐκ ἔστη καὶ ἐπὶ καθέδραν λοιμῶν οὐκ ἐκάθισεν) or 40:2 (μακάριος ὁ συνίων ἐπὶ πτωχὸν καὶ πένητα· ἐν ἡμέρᾳ πονηρᾷ ῥύσεται αὐτὸν ὁ κύριος) have an implied imperative, as Davies and Allison themselves admit.[74]

The issue for Davies and Allison is whether Matthew's makarisms are "entrance requirements"[75] or "eschatological blessings,"[76] that is, whether their "primary function . . . is moral" or "whether a moral dimension excludes a promissory or conciliatory dimension."[77] Put this way, the answer seems clear: surely the beatitudes both recommend certain behaviors and promise rewards to the

71. Reconstruction: James M. Robinson, Paul Hoffmann, and John S. Kloppenborg, eds., *The Critical Edition of Q: A Synopsis, Including the Gospels of Matthew and Luke, Mark and Thomas, with English, German and French Translations of Q and Thomas* (Hermeneia; Minneapolis: Fortress, 2000), 46.

72. Davies and Allison, *A Critical and Exegetical Commentary on . . . Matthew*, 1:439.

73. Ibid., 1:444.

74. Ibid., 1:439.

75. E.g., Georg Strecker, *Die Bergpredigt: Ein exegetischer Kommentar* (Göttingen: Vandenhoeck & Ruprecht, 1984), 34.

76. Robert Guelich, "The Matthean Beatitudes: 'Entrance-Requirements' or Eschatological Blessings," *JBL* 95 (1976): 415–34.

77. Davies and Allison, *A Critical and Exegetical Commentary on . . . Matthew*, 1:440.

faithful. The tension that exists within the string of Matthaean makarisms—between "blessed are those who mourn" (5:4), which has no obvious imperatival function, and "blessed are the gentle," which does—can be resolved by noting that the markarisms that are "purely ethical" (5:5, 7–9) are those that Matthew has added to Q; two of the makarisms taken from Q have been edited to enhance their ethical dimension (5:3, 6); the remaining two (5:4, 11–12) already included the nuance of patient endurance of adversity and so were left more or less unchanged. The key point is that Matthew's editing has shifted Q's makarisms, which concerned social conditions, into ethical discourse.

Some commentators seem desperate to retain a strong economic perspective for Matthew's beatitudes.[78] Yet Matthew has relatively little to say about the poor or poverty generally.[79] When speaking of money, he uses high denominations (τὰ δίδραχμα, 17:24; τάλαντον/τα, 18:24; 25:15, 16, 20, 22, 24, 25, 28; στατήρ, 17:27). And where he speaks of alimentary and other means of support, for example in the mission instructions, in 10:10, he changes Q 10:7's ἄξιος γὰρ ὁ ἐργάτης τοῦ μισθοῦ αὐτοῦ to τῆς τροφῆς αὐτοῦ, signaling a shift from the payment of day laborers (ἐργάται)—that is, payment to persons outside to household—to the maintenance of workers within the household.[80]

Matthew's relocation of Q 12:51–53 and 14:26–27; 17:33 to the end of the mission discourse also shows his interest in the household: Q 12:51–53 predicts division within the household, now apparently the direct result of the admonition to fearless confession (Matt 10:26–33 = Q 12:2–9, also relocated), while Q 14:26, which speaks of "hating parents"[81] is moderated to "loving parents *more*

---

78. E.g., Michael Crosby, *House of Disciples: Church, Economics, and Justice in Matthew* (Maryknoll, N.Y.: Orbis, 1988), 152–55, who rejects the view that Matthew "waters down" the original by "spiritualizing" the beatitudes, and dismisses this with the dubious characterization that "the Hebrew mentalitiy did not 'spiritualize' or 'materialize'; it united the two" (ibid., 154).

79. W. D. Davies, *The Setting of the Sermon on the Mount* (Cambridge: Cambridge University Press, 1966), 213: "nowhere does Matthew reveal an emphasis on poverty and ascetic rejection of wealth."

80. I am indebted to Giovanni Battista Bazzana, "Early Christian Missionaries as Phyisicians: Christian Sources in the Context of Greco-Roman Medical Practice," paper presented at the annual meeting of the Context Group, Ashton Pa., March 15–18 (2007) for this observation: "What is implied in Matthew's change of the Q wording? At first sight it is clear that the saying 'the laborer deserves his nourishment' has lost a good deal of its significance: which laborer would have worked without salary and only on the promise to receive some food? He would have been immediately equated to a slave. It is worth remarking that probably this is the exact meaning implied by the Matthean redaction of our passage: the redactor intended to depict Jesus' missionaries not as paid laborers but as members of God's household who perform their duty without expecting any wage." See also A. E. Harvey, "The Workman is Worthy of His Hire: Fortunes of a Proverb in the Early Church," *NovT* 24 (1982): 209–21.

81. Reconstruction: Robinson, Hoffmann, and Kloppenborg, *Critical Edition of Q*, 450.

than me." Matthew's redaction of chapter 18 likewise stresses the household as a locus: Matt 18:6 adds τῶν πιστευόντων εἰς ἐμέ to Q 17:2's τῶν μικρῶν τούτων, thus making clear that Matthew is speaking to members of the households of the Jesus movement. The use of Q 17:3–4 on forgiveness in this context likewise indicates Matthew's strong interest in establishing rules for interaction among "brothers" (18:15, 21). The concluding parable, Matt 18:23–35, takes the metaphor of relationships of domestic slaves within a (large!) household to illustrate relationships within the Jesus movement. And the quartet of parables in 24:45–51; 25:1–13, 14–30, 31–46, two of them taken from Q and relocated here, stress faithful household management and the distribution of τροφὴ ἐν καιρῷ (24:45) to fellow domestics, attentiveness to the moral demands of the householder (25:1–13),[82] and faithful service of domestic slaves to an absentee owner (25:14–30). It is only in the final parable, 25:31–46, that there is any hint of interest in the benefaction of the poor, here characterized as the hungry, thirsty, strangers, naked, ill, and imprisoned. However, these are further qualified as ἑνὶ τούτων τῶν ἀδελφῶν μου τῶν ἐλαχίστων (25:40), which can only refer to members of the Jesus movement.[83] Hence, Matthew's concern is not primarily with the poor or dispossessed outside the Jesus movement, but with negotiating relationships *within* the Jesus groups.

In view of Matthew's concentration of the moral economy of the household of the Jesus movement, his ethicizing of the makarisms is perfectly intelligible. In fact, given his general neglect of the "poor" as a social category, it would be odd for him simply to have taken over Q's makarisms unchanged. The makarisms thus become a catalogue of virtues that draw upon and transform the older list of makarisms from Q, adapting Q's discourse about the inversion of the social states to discourse concerning maintenance of the households of the Jesus movement.

2.3. James and the Discourse on the Poor

As is well known, James offers a dense configuration of discourse on wealth and poverty, contrasting ὁ ταπεινός and ὁ πλούσιος in 1:9–11; the πλούσιος and the πτωχός in 2:1–7, and attacking οἱ πλούσιοι and wealth in 5:1–4. James also employs the πραΰ- root twice, in 1:21 and 3:13. In neither case, however, does the term connote either material poverty or oppression as it does in Ps 34:3 [33:3]

---

82. See here Karl Paul Donfried, "The Allegory of the Ten Virgins (Mt 25:1–13) as a Summary of Matthean Theology," *JBL* 94 (1974): 415–28, who notes the stress on the virtues of prudence (25:4, 9), preparedness, and especially the acquisition of good works.

83. Ulrich Luz, *Matthew 21–28* (Hermeneia; Minneapolis: Fortress, 2005), 271–73, 279–82 argues that the "least of these my brothers" are the itinerant radicals of the Jesus movement who, according to 10:40 are to be "received" as the Lord.

and 147:6 [146:6], translating *'ānāwîm*. On the contrary, as the context makes clear, πραΰτης connotes a favorable disposition to receive teaching:

> 1:21 διὸ ἀποθέμενοι πᾶσαν ῥυπαρίαν καὶ περισσείαν κακίας ἐν πραΰτητι, δέξασθε τὸν ἔμφυτον λόγον τὸν δυνάμενον σῶσαι τὰς ψυχὰς ὑμῶν.
> Therefore put away all filthiness and abundance of evil and accept with gentleness the implanted *logos* which is able to save your souls.

> 3:13: Τίς σοφὸς καὶ ἐπιστήμων ἐν ὑμῖν; δειξάτω ἐκ τῆς καλῆς ἀναστροφῆς τὰ ἔργα αὐτοῦ ἐν πραΰτητι σοφίας.
> Who is wise and understanding among you? Let him show by his good conduct his works through the gentleness of wisdom.

This usage of πραΰτης is fully in accord with ordinary Greek usage, especially in connection with virtues of the wise,[84] and with its use in Psalms such as 25:9 [24:9] and Prov 16:19, where the term appears in the context of the reception of teaching, or in the Sentences of Sextus, where it is a mark of a sage, or in Hermas, *Mand.* 11.8, where gentleness is the mark of a true believer rather than a false prophet:

> Ps 24:9: ὁδηγήσει πραεῖς ἐν κρίσει, διδάξει πραεῖς ὁδοὺς αὐτοῦ.
> He leads the humble in what is right, and teaches the humble his way.

> Prov 16:19: κρείσσων πραΰθυμος μετὰ ταπεινώσεως ἢ ὃς διαιρεῖται σκῦλα μετὰ ὑβριστῶν.
> It is better to be of a lowly spirit with the poor than to divide the spoil with the proud.

> *Sent. Sextus* 453: ἄρχων μὲν ἐπιτήδευε πραΰς εἶναι, ἀρχόμενος δὲ μεγαλόφρων.
> Begin by making a practice of being gentle, beginning with (being) generous.

> Hermas, *Mand.* 11 [43].8: πρῶτον μὲν ὁ ἔχων τὸ πνεῦμα τὸ ἄνωθεν πραΰς ἐστι καὶ ἡσύχιος καὶ ταπεινόφρων καὶ ἀπεχόμενος ἀπὸ πάσης πονηρίας καὶ ἐπιθυμίας ματαίας τοῦ αἰῶνος τούτου.

---

84. Friedrich Hauck and Siegfried Schulz, "πραΰς, πραΰτης," *TDNT* 6: 646: "It is a mark of the high-minded (μεγαλόθυμος, Epictetus Fr., 12) and noble (Plato, *Phaedr.* 243C; *Leg.* 5.731D), of the cultured (παιδευτικὸς ἄνθρωπος θέλων εἶναι ἄσκει πραότητα), and therefore of the wise (with κόσμιος and ἡσύχιος in Stobaeus 2.115.10), who remains calm even in face of abuse (Epictetus, *Ench.* 42); Socrates is a model here (Plato, *Phaedr.* 116C). Hence the gentleness of leading citizens is constantly extolled in encomiums, and it has a prominent place in depictions of rulers. Rhetoric counts it among the *commoda animi*. For Lucian it is an adornment of the soul like δικαιοσύνη, εὐσέβεια, ἐπιείκεια etc., *Somnium*, 10."

In the first place whoever has the spirit that comes from above is gentle and quiet and humble, and abstains from all evil and the empty desires of this age.

Turning to the discourse on rich and poor, one of the central debates in the interpretation of James is his posture towards rich and poor. On the face of it, it would appear that James identifies solidly with the poor against the rich, declaring that the rich will perish (1:10–11; 5:1) and that the poor and humble will be elevated (1:9–11). Peter Davids, invoking the notion of the piety of the poor, argued:

> It is clear first of all that James has great sympathy for the poor and that the term is virtually identical in his mind with "Christian," probably due to the community's circumstances and the traditional piety-poverty link. . . . Each place [Jas 1:9, 12; 2:5; 5:7] identifies the community with the poor and oppressed group.[85]

Earlier Dibelius had concluded similarly:

> Ja[me]s can express his sympathy with the poor with so little reserve because for him being poor and being Christian were coincidental concepts, not only by virtue of his archaizing dependence on the literature [of the poor], but also by virtue of is own personal conviction.This can be stated with all confidence because the entire document bears witness to a pietistic-patriarchal thought-world which was especially propitious for the revitalization of the attitude of the Poor; antipathy toward the world, mistrust of "secular" affairs, warning against arrogance, humble submission before God.[86]

Windisch took this even further, declaring that James was a representative of Ebionite Christianity.[87] Conversely, for Dibelius the rich mentioned in the letter are either non-Christians or "people whom he considers no longer to be included in a proper sense within Christendom."[88]

There are several problems with the notion of James's identification with the poor via the construct of *Armenfrömmigkeit*, however. In the first place, the scene in 2:1–5 involving the rich man and the πτωχός in rags is not constructed to lead to the conclusion that the πτωχός belongs to the Jesus-group in virtue of his piety. On the contrary, the focus of this unit is to argue that the προσωπολημψία displayed (or imagined to be displayed) by his addressees amounts to a violation

---

85. Davids, *Epistle of James*, 45.

86. Dibelius, *James: A Commentary on the Epistle of James*, 44.

87. Hans Windisch, *Die katholischen Briefe* (3rd ed.; rev. by H. Preisker; HNT 15; Tübingen: Mohr Siebeck, 1951), 36.

88. Dibelius, *James: A Commentary on the Epistle of James*, 87–88. Compare Tamez, *Scandalous Message of James*, 25: "The rich (plousios) in the letter do not belong to the Christian community, or at least the author does not think that they should belong to it."

of the Torah. Moreover, as Kelly points out, the use of Abraham, proverbially a wealthy man, as an exemplar of piety in 2:21 is odd if James were really committed to the proposition that the rich are inherently evil.[89] Likewise the complaint against merchants in 4:13–17 does not concern their wealth but their arrogance.

Rather than treating the πτωχός in James as a *description* of either the intended addressees, or the ideal condition of those addressees, or even claiming with Bauckham that James's discourse on the "poor" aimed at encouraging emulation of certain characteristics of the poor—openness, humility, dependence—it is worth considering the fact that the contrast of rich and poor was a standard rhetorical trope in Graeco-Roman moralizing literature. Philostratus names as ἀρχαία σοφιστική the contrast of rich and poor and the figure of the rich man or tyrant,[90] and one of Stobaeus's topic in his anthology is σύγκρισις πενίας καὶ πλούτου. When Petronius, speaking through Trimalchio, wishes to lampoon rhetoric, he has Trimalchio ask Agamemnon to deliver the speech (*controversia*) that he practiced in school that day. Agamemmnon begins, *pauper et dives inimici erant*, at which point Trimalchio interrupts and proceeds with an attack on rhetoric.

Example of this sort could be multiplied almost indefinitely; the point is clear, however, that the contrast of rich and poor was a standard rhetorical figure. The question to be raised, now, is the function of this contrast.

Lucian of Samosata's *Cataplus* offers a telling example of the use of this trope. The story features three of the day's dead, whom Hermes has brought down to Clotho and Charon. They are Megapenthes, a tyrant, Micyllus a penniless cobbler, and Cyniscus, a Cynic philosopher. After Megapenthes makes a run for the mouth of the cave and is run down by Hermes, assisted by Cyniscus, and after Megapenthes unsuccessfully tries to bribe his way back to life, Clotho reveals to him how it will turn out after his death. The picture is not a pretty one: he was slain by the new ruler, who took his daughter as a concubine; his slave

---

89. Francis Xavier Kelly, "Poor and Rich in the Epistle of James" (Ph.D. diss., Temple University, 1973), 208.

90. Philostratus, *Vita sophistarum* 481: Ἡ μὲν δὴ ἀρχαία σοφιστικὴ καὶ τὰ φιλοσοφούμενα ὑποτιθεμένη διῄει αὐτὰ ἀποτάδην καὶ ἐς μῆκος, διελέγετο μὲν γὰρ περὶ ἀνδρείας, διελέγετο δὲ περὶ δικαιότητος, ἡρώων τε πέρι καὶ θεῶν καὶ ὅπη ἀπεσχημάτισται ἡ ἰδέα τοῦ κόσμου. ἡ δὲ μετ᾽ ἐκείνην, ἣν οὐχὶ νέαν, ἀρχαία γάρ, δευτέραν δὲ μᾶλλον προσρητέον, τοὺς πένητας ὑπετυπώσατο καὶ τοὺς πλουσίους καὶ τοὺς ἀριστέας καὶ τοὺς τυράννους καὶ τὰς ἐς ὄνομα ὑποθέσεις, ἐφ᾽ ἃς ἡ ἱστορία ἄγει. "Now ancient sophistic, even when it propounded philosophical themes, used to discuss them diffusely and at length; for it discoursed on courage, it discoursed on justice, on the heroes and gods, and how the universe had been fashioned into its present shape. But the sophistic that followed it, which we must not call 'new,' for it is old, but rather 'second,' sketched the types of the poor man and the rich, of princes and tyrants, and handled arguments that are concerned with definite and special themes for which history shows the way."

is sleeping with Megapenthes' wife; his retainers had no real loyalty and one of them poisoned him. In short, Lucian paints Megapenthes as a pathetic figure, petty and grasping, cowardly before death, and shackled by his attachments.

Micyllus, by contrast, is happy to die:

> By Zeus I see that everything is quite spendid here. For that all should be equal in rank and that none should be different from his neighbour seems indeed very pleasant to me. And I infer that here those who are in debt do not have their goods seized, that there is no paying of taxes, that above all there is no freezing in winter nor sickness nor getting beaten up by those who are more powerful. All are at peace and the tables are turned, since we who are poor are laughing, but the rich are in distress and lamenting. (Lucian, *Cataplus* 15)[91]

Micyllus does admit that he once considered Megapenthes to be ἰσόθεός τις, somone who was like a god, impressed by his finery. Now he sees Megapenthes for what he is. Throughout *Cataplus* and *Dialogues of the Dead*, Lucian holds forth the ideal of ἰσοτιμία, a society without stratification.[92] But this state, for Lucian, only exists in Hades.

This is not the end of the story, since in *Cataplus*, the rich tyrant is punished by Rhadamanthos by *not* being permitted to drink the waters of *Lethē* and thus forced forever to remember "what he was and how much power he had in the upper world" (28). In *Menippus*, Lucian has the οἱ πλούσιοι καὶ τοκογλύφοι, lined up in Hades, each with neck irons, and the town council of Hades passing a special decree against the rich:

> Whereas the rich have committed many lawless deeds in like, plundering and doing violence and in every manner humiliate the poor, be it resolved by the senate and the people that when they die their bodies be punished like those of the other malefactors, but their souls be sent back up into life and enter into donkeys until they shall have passed 250,000 years in the said condition, transmigrating from donkey to donkey, bearing burdens, and being driven by the poor; and that thereafter it be permitted for them do die.[93]

---

91. καὶ νὴ Δι'- ἤδη καλὰ τὰ παρ' ὑμῖν πάντα ὁρῶ· τό τε γὰρ ἰσοτιμίαν ἅπασιν εἶναι καὶ μηδένα τοῦ πλησίον διαφέρειν, ὑπερήδιστον ἐμοὶ γοῦν δοκεῖ. τεκμαίρομαι δὲ μηδ' ἀπαιτεῖσθαι τὰ χρέα τοὺς ὀφείλοντας ἐνταῦθα μηδὲ φόρους ὑποτελεῖν, τὸ δὲ μέγιστον, μηδὲ ῥιγοῦν τοῦ χειμῶνος μηδὲ νοσεῖν μηδ' ὑπὸ τῶν δυνατωτέρων ῥαπίζεσθαι. εἰρήνη δὲ πᾶσι καὶ πράγματα ἐς τὸ ἔμπαλιν ἀνεστραμμένα· ἡμεῖς μὲν οἱ πένητες γελῶμεν, ἀνιῶνται δὲ καὶ οἰμώζουσιν οἱ πλούσιοι.

92. The notion of ἰσοτιμία is frequent in Lucian, *Phaleris* 1.3.7; *Cataplus* 15.11; *Contemplantes* 18.10; *Piscator* 34.9; *De Mercede Conductis* 16.9; *Imagines* 9.24; *Saturnalia* 7.29; 13.5; 31.5; 32.20; *Apologia* 11.35; *Dialogi Mortuorum* 1.4.4; 8.2.1; 30.2.12.

93. Lucian, Menippus 20: Ἐπειδὴ πολλὰ καὶ παράνομα οἱ πλούσιοι δρῶσι παρὰ τὸν βίον ἁρπάζοντες καὶ βιαζόμενοι καὶ πάντα τρόπον τῶν πενήτων καταφρονοῦντες, δεδόχθω τῇ βουλῇ καὶ τῷ δήμῳ, ἐπειδὰν ἀποθάνωσι, τὰ μὲν σώματα αὐτῶν κολάζεσθαι καθάπερ καὶ τὰ τῶν

Addressing the question of what Lucian was out to accomplish in these satires, Baldwin argues that

> the extent to which Menippus and Diogenes monopolize these dialogues [viz. *Dialogi Mortuorum*] and the consistent attitude they adopt against the rich is deliberately created by Lucian for a purpose and this purpose is to establish a programme of social criticism unmistakably associated with the Cynics.[94]

Yet in the *Saturnalia*, when Cronosolon, a priest of Cronos, points to social inequities and asks Cronos to make a more equitable distribution of property (11) and to "abolish this inequality" (19), Cronos rejects a redistribution but writes to the rich to ask them to share a bit more in order to forestall an outcry for redistribution (31). The context for this, of course, is the Roman *Saturnalia* when slaves and the poor were feted by the rich which, as Baldwin points out, "served only to emphasize the injustice and inequality of 'normal' conditions."[95]

Although Lucian was quick to lampoon the rich and to paint vivid pictures of the pathetic nature of their existence and even the punishments that might await them, it seems unlikely that Lucian proposed *isotimia* as anything more than a theoretical ideal. That is, there is little to suggest that Lucian actually identified with the plight of the poor or that he addressed the poor, still less that he imagined *isotimia* as a real social possibility. Although Lucian came from a poor family (*Somnium*), he addressed his peers—educated urbanites. The best he could do was to undermine the self-evident value that these peers attached to the pursuit of wealth and the honor that could come with this. The most his Cronosolon was able to extract from Cronos is a *temporary* inversion of status hierarchies at the *Saturnalia*. But as Victor Turner has shown, role inversions of this sort, because they are limited to festivals, in fact reinforce status hierarchies, rather than subverting them.[96]

Mary Douglas has drawn attention to the relationship between joking—and Lucian's satire belongs generally to joking—and social structure:

> My hypothesis is that a joke is seen and allowed when it offers a symbolic pattern of a social pattern occurring at the same time. As I see it, all jokes are expressive of the social situations in which they occur. The one social condition necessary for a joke to be enjoyed is that the social group in which it is received

---

ἄλλων πονηρῶν, τὰς δὲ ψυχὰς ἀναπεμφθείσας ἄνω εἰς τὸν βίον καταδύεσθαι εἰς τοὺς ὄνους, ἄχρις ἂν ἐν τῷ τοιούτῳ διαγάγωσι μυριάδας ἐτῶν πέντε καὶ εἴκοσιν, ὄνοι ἐξ ὄνων γιγνόμενοι καὶ ἀχθοφοροῦντες καὶ ὑπὸ τῶν πενήτων ἐλαυνόμενοι, τοὐντεῦθεν δὲ λοιπὸν ἐξεῖναι αὐτοῖς ἀποθανεῖν.

94. Barry H. Baldwin, "Lucian as Social Satirist," *ClQ* NS 11 (1961): 201.

95. Ibid., 203.

96. Victor Turner, *The Ritual Process: Structure and Anti-Structure* (Chicago: Aldine, 1969).

should develop the formal characteristics of a 'told' joke: that is, a dominant
pattern of relations is challenged by another. If there is no joke in the social
structure, no other joking can appear.[97]

The joke, then, renders explicit the social situation in question and exposes its
frailty and contingency. For this reason the joke is hardly a strong instrument
of social deconstruction and reconstruction, since it in fact only assumes what
is already perceived at some level as problematic in social structures and puts a
spotlight on these. Joking serves as a kind of social safety valve that relieves pressures and ambivalences, without actually undoing the structures that cause those
pressures. Had Lucian's satire been able really to deconstruct the social hierarchies of antiquity, it is doubtful that his works would have survived, since they
would likely have been suppressed.

Returning to James, I suggest that the *sygkrisis* of rich and poor that is bela-
bored there is not designed to address the poor, whether the working poor or the
destitute, but rather James's peers. To judge from the level of his Greek and from
the scenario of a patron appearing in a *synagogē* advertising for clients in chapter
2,[98] these addressees likely belong to urban, reasonably well educated groups of
diaspora Judaeans. Although the *sygkriseis* in James 1 and 2 are not "jokes," they
have a "joke structure," as Douglas has also termed the parables of Jesus[99]: the
comparison exaggerates difference—thus selecting not a πένης but a πτωχός, and
describing in elaborate detail the clothing and rings of the rich man and the rags
of the poor man in chapter 2. James concludes with an equally graphic and exaggerated depiction of the fate of the rich, "weeping and howling" at their losses.
The picture is not at all unlike Lucian's depiction of the fate of the rich in Hades,
who both cling in vain to their wealth but also appear as objects of derision and
laughter by the poor.

James, of course, does not wish to defer a notion of *isotimia* to the afterlife.
In the dark of Hades and when all are reduced to skulls, it is hard to distinguish
Helen of Troy from anyone else, as Menippus finds out in *Dialogi Mortuorum*.
James, however, seemingly proposes that something like *isotimia* should begin
in the assembly, and in fact argues in 2:1–13 that anything less amounts to
προσωπολημψία, which in turn puts the lie to his addressees' claim to be Torah
observant. Thus he not only uses the rhetorical topos of rich and poor in order to
expose the inequality that was already generally lamented in Graeco-Roman society, at least among Hellenistic moralists, but brings to bear an argument from the

---

97. Mary T. Douglas, "Jokes," in *Implicit Meanings: Essays in Anthropology* (London and
Boston: Routledge & Kegan Paul, 1975), 98.

98. See Nancy J. Vyhmeister, "The Rich Man in James 2: Does Ancient Patronage Illumine
the Text?" *AUSS* 33 (1995): 265–83; John S. Kloppenborg, "Patronage Avoidance in the Epistle
of James," *HvTSt* 55 (1999): 755–94.

99. Douglas, "Jokes," 99–100.

Torah, especially the Holiness Code, to buttress his attack on differential treatment of persons.

I think it doubtful, however, that James's use of the comparison of rich and poor in fact "undermined the system." Status hierarchies were simply too deeply ingrained in Greek and Roman society, and supported by a nexus of legal, economic, familial, and political provisions. What he could accomplish, however, was to produce a kind of "joke," which exposed again the fragility and contingency of status hierarchies, and to undermine the self-evident nature of the categories and distinctions required to maintain such hierarchies. This is not "revolutionary" discourse; as with Lucian it probably amounted to a plea for increased benefaction of the poor by the rich, as indeed James himself recommends in 2:14–26.

3. Conclusion

This paper has been critical of the construct of *Armenfrömmigkeit* on ideological grounds—that is masks real poverty—but especially on exegetical grounds, that there is very slender evidence of an equation of poverty and piety in Israelite discourse. If this is so, it is even more problematic to invoke *Armenfrömmigkeit* in order to account for the discourse of the Didache, Matthew, and James on poverty.

The Didache's use of πραΰτης and the citation of Ps 37:11, far from belonging to discourse about the poor, concerns the correct posture of the learner. Discourse on poverty in both Matthew and James begins with Q 6:20b, which used the rhetorical figure of the πτωχός to deconstruct the more dominant cultural discourse on the relationship between wealth and the blessings of the deity, and hence to valorize the status of town and village dwellers in Jewish Palestine. Matthew absorbed Q 6:20b into discourse on the management of the Christian household and the virtues appropriate to that household. This involved ethicizing Q. James also employs Q 6:20b, and *is* in fact speaking of the poor. But he uses the trope of the πτωχός not because he addresses the indigent among them, or identifies with them, still less that he "equates the poor with the believers" or even holds them out as a model for emulation, but because, like Lucian, he wishes to problematize for educated Judaean urbanites one of the dominant ideological structures of Graeco-Roman society and the mechanisms of social exchange (patronage) that flow from those structures.

Jesus Tradition in Matthew, James, and the Didache: Searching for Characteristic Emphases

Jens Schröter

1. Matthew, James, and the Didache as Early Christian Writings

In contemporary discussion about the beginnings of Christianity there is growing awareness of the complex developments that eventually lead to a "parting of the ways" between "Judaism" and "Christianity." It is widely acknowledged that Judaism was by itself a multi-faceted phenomenon, and that the early Christian writings are deeply ingrained with Jewish traditions. The distinction between "Judaism" and "Christianity" may, therefore, be productive from a heuristic viewpoint, but by the same time misleading with regard to the actual situation of the communities of Jesus's followers in the first decades and also as description of the perspective of at least some early Christian texts, including Matthew, James, and the Didache.

Against this background, the symposium in Tilburg, 7–8 April 2003, has brought the relationships between two of these writings, namely, Matthew and the Didache, into sharper focus. Although the papers read at this symposium[1] differ in some aspects, e.g., whether the relationship can be specified as literary dependence,[2] there is general agreement that both writings have to be interpreted as originating from a common milieu of early Christianity with close connections

---

1. See Huub van de Sandt, ed., *Matthew and the Didache: Two Documents from the Same Jewish-Christian Milieu?* (Assen: Van Gorcum, 2005).

2. Whereas Joseph Verheyden argues that the Didache reveals knowledge of Matthew's Gospel, Jonathan A. Draper denies such a relationship. See Joseph Verheyden, "Eschatology in the Didache and the Gospel of Matthew," in van de Sandt, ed., *Matthew and the Didache*, 193–215; Jonathan A. Draper, "Do the Didache and Matthew Reflect an 'Irrevocable Parting of the Ways' with Judaism?," ibid., 217–41. The discussion becomes even more complex if one includes the study of Alan J. P. Garrow, *The Gospel of Matthew's Dependence on the Didache* (JSNT 254; London: T&T Clark, 2004), who develops a complicated model of relationships between Matthew and the Didache in several stages.

to Jewish traditions.[3] If now the letter of James is included as well, the matter becomes more complex.[4] The three writings that are now compared with each other belong to different genres: a biography of Jesus, a (probably) pseudonymous letter,[5] and a church manual. The difference in genre also has consequences for the respective treatment of the so-called "Jesus traditions." In Matthew's story of Jesus these traditions are regularly ascribed to Jesus, whereas in the two other writings the case is different. It can, therefore, already at this point tentatively be assumed that there is a relationship between genre and dealing with "Jesus traditions" in early Christian writings. I will return to this issue later.

Despite the difference in genre, the three writings share a remarkable characteristic: There is sound evidence that they are not, or at least not exclusively, addressed to a specific community, but to "all Christians."[6] This is not to deny that they show features that allow placing them within a certain cultural and religious context. But still, they belong to those early Christian writings that are addressed to a wider audience. Within this concept each of them presents a distinct concept of continuity with, and divergence from, Judaism.[7]

To interpret Matthew's Gospel, it is of crucial importance to define the relationship of the community of Jesus's followers to the synagogue, and especially their perspective on the torah. As is well known, Matthew contains the unambiguous statement that Jesus did not come to abolish the law but to fulfill it, but at the same time the author points out that Jesus interprets the law according to

---

3. See, e.g., the articles of Bas ter Haar Romeny and Jonathan A. Draper in H. van de Sandt, ed., *Matthew and the Didache*.

4. For an attempt to bring the three writings in a closer relationship see Gunnar Garleff, *Urchristliche Identität in Matthäusevangelium, Didache und Jakobusbrief* (BVB 9; Münster: Lit, 2004). Garleff works with a concept of "kollektive Identität" and with a definition of "Judenchristentum" as "eine Sonderform des Judentums" (ibid., 208) in contrast to "Heidenchristentum" (see ibid., 207–14). From my perspective it is questionable whether this distinction—which goes back to Ferdinand Christian Baur—is a fruitful approach to the history of early Christianity. The relationships between Jews and Gentiles within early Christianity were much more complex than such an approach suggests. Moreover, it is doubtful whether Matthew, James, and the Didache should be compared with each other along the lines of the rather vague category "Identität."

5. The pseudonymity of James is still contested. For a concise summary of the arguments pro and con see Christoph Burchard, *Der Jakobusbrief* (HNT 15/1; Tübingen: Mohr Siebeck, 2000), 3–5; Wiard Popkes, *Der Brief des Jakobus* (THKNT 14; Leipzig: Evangelische Verlagsanstalt, 2001), 64–68. Burchard and Popkes themselves plead for pseudonymous origin.

6. With regard to the gospels Richard Bauckham has argued in that direction. See his "For Whom Were Gospels Written," in *The Gospels for all Christians. Rethinking the Gospel Audiences* (ed. R. Bauckham; Edinburgh: T&T Clark, 1998), 9–48.

7. It might therefore be dangerous to work with a concept of "Jewish Christianity" to compare the three writings. It is not quite clear how this category can be related to early Christian writings and communities and whether the distinct features of the three writings are rather concealed than revealed by this concept.

his own authority and criticizes the Pharisees for their defective righteousness.[8] Matthew's perspective on the law is therefore a controversial and much-debated issue in scholarship still today. While, on the one hand, a consensus has developed that Matthew depicts Jesus's activity as directed towards the renewal of Israel, this consensus was called into question by two more recent publications that emphasize the radical interpretation of the law and the prophets by the Matthean Jesus and regard the Gentile mission as an integral part of Matthew's story of Jesus.[9] This position may be regarded as a legitimate corrective over against approaches that neglect all those features in Matthew that point to a separation from the synagogue.[10] In any case, there can be no doubt that the law and the prophets still function as the basis for the Jesus community, although now as interpreted by Jesus. This means that the Jesus traditions in Matthew gain their importance within a concept that emphasizes the meaning of Jewish identity for a community that no longer belongs to the synagogue and consists of Jews and Gentiles alike.[11]

As far as the Didache is concerned, I refer to the volume co-authored by Huub van de Sandt and David Flusser, published in 2002, to the collections of articles edited by Clayton N. Jefford and Jonathan A. Draper, and to the investigation ("Didache and Judaism") by Marcello Del Verme from 2004.[12] These and other publications of the last fifteen years demonstrate a remarkable interest in the Didache in recent research, leading to the conclusion that this writing belongs to a historical situation where Christianity was on its way to form its own identity over against Judaism, and at the same time separates itself from the Gentiles. What makes it more difficult to define the place of the Didache within this process more precisely is the fact that it is a composite document with a complex literary history. Some of the traditions in the Didache reveal traces of

---

8. Matt 5:17–20.

9. See Roland Deines, *Die Gerechtigkeit der Tora im Reich des Messias: Mt 5,13–20 als Schlüsseltext der matthäischen Theologie* (WUNT 177; Tübingen: Mohr Siebeck, 2004); Paul Foster, Community, *Law and Mission in Matthew's Gospel* (WUNT 2/177; Tübingen: Mohr Siebeck, 2004).

10. See the evaluation of the studies by Deines and Foster by Wolfgang Reinbold, "Matthäus und das Gesetz. Zwei neue Studien," *BZ* 50 (2006): 244–50.

11. See Matthias Konradt, "Die vollkommene Erfüllung der Tora und der Konflikt mit den Pharisäern im Matthäusevangelium," in *Das Gesetz im frühen Judentum und im Neuen Testament* (ed. D. Sänger und M. Konradt; NTOA 57; Göttingen: Vandenhoeck & Ruprecht, 2006), 129–52.

12. Huub van de Sandt and David Flusser, *The Didache: Its Jewish Sources and its Place in Early Judaism and Christianity* (CRINT 3/5; Assen: Van Gorcum, 2002); Clayton N. Jefford, ed., *The Didache in Context: Essays on Its Text, History and Transmission* (NovTSup 77; Leiden: Brill, 1995); Jonathan A. Draper, ed., *The Didache in Modern Research* (AGJU 37; Leiden: Brill, 1996); Marcello Del Verme, *Didache and Judaism: Jewish Roots of an Ancient Christian-Jewish Work* (New York: T&T Clark, 2004).

earlier stages of the separation process between "Judaism" and "Christianity" more distinctly than others. Moreover, it has to be kept in mind as well that the relationship to other early Christian writings, especially to the Gospel of Matthew, can only be defined with caution. One has to allow for the possibility that at least some of the traditions in the Didache might be older than, and independent from, the Synoptic Gospels.

The letter of James poses even more complex problems. James's familiarity with Hellenistic-Jewish wisdom traditions has frequently been pointed out in recent research, for example, in the commentaries of Hubert Frankemölle, Christoph Burchard, and Wiard Popkes as well as in the monograph of Matthias Konradt.[13] Many scholars have also pointed out that James is not just a random collection of parenetic material but instead develops a distinct perspective within early Christian theology focused on a way of life corresponding to the "perfect gift from above" (Jas 1:17). The detection of James's particular theological viewpoint became possible when the letter was no longer regarded as an inferior counterpart to Paul but evaluated in its own right as an early Christian writing in the tradition of Jewish Wisdom literature.[14] Frankemölle is even more specific. According to him James not only took up oral and written sapiential traditions but presents itself as a deliberate relecture of Sirach.[15] Whether one follows that assumption or not, strong connections between James and Jewish wisdom traditions are obvious.

At the same time, James demonstrates a rather general approach to Christian ethics that is not exclusively confined to a "Jewish identity." Rather, the author uses Jewish "identity markers," like, for example the designation "the twelve tribes in the dispersion," in an unspecified manner for the Christian communities. Comparable to 1 Peter, then, the author can apply Jewish terminology to Christians regardless of their origin from Judaism or Paganism.[16] Biblical and other Jewish traditions in James are, therefore, part of a wider context of ancient Wisdom literature. In contrast to Matthew and the Didache, James uses terms, for example, like συναγωγή, καθαρίζειν, or even νόμος[17] in a general sense and

---

13. Hubert Frankemölle, *Der Brief des Jakobus* (2 vols.; ÖTK 17/1.2; Gütersloh: Gütersloher Verlagshaus, 1994); Burchard, *Jakobusbrief*; Popkes, *Brief des Jakobus*; Matthias Konradt, *Christliche Existenz nach dem Jakobusbrief: Eine Studie zu seiner soteriologischen und ethischen Konzeption* (SUNT 122; Göttingen: Vandenhoeck & Ruprecht, 1998).

14. The relationship of James to Paul is still a controversial issue. Frankemölle, Konradt, and Burchard have presented important arguments for an independent perspective on faith and works in James. The opposite view is supported by Popkes; Martin Hengel; Peter Stuhlmacher and more recently by Friedrich Avemarie.

15. Frankemölle, *Brief des Jakobus*, 1:85.

16. See, e.g., 1 Pet 2:9.

17. In Jas 2:1, the Christian assembly is called συναγωγή, whereas in 5:14, James uses the term ἐκκλησία. Hence, he uses two terms side by side that in Matthew are strongly opposed to

not exclusively with Jewish connotations. Hence it must remain an open question whether James can be put into the same framework as Matthew and the Didache.

The three writings, therefore, in one way or another, represent a form of early Christianity for which Jewish traditions remained an important heritage with regard to the formation of Christian identity. But within this broad spectrum—to which other early Christian writings belong as well—each one's place needs to be defined separately. In what follows, it will be shown that Matthew and the Didache belong more closely together than either one of them of them does with James.

It is against this background that I set out in the following paragraphs to examine the use of the so-called "Jesus traditions" in these writings. Because it is not self-evident what "Jesus traditions" exactly means, the clarity of my argument requires starting with a few remarks on how I understand the term "Jesus traditions."

2. "Jesus tradition," "Synoptic tradition," and "Words of the Lord" in early Jewish-Christian writings

The phrase "Jesus tradition" can be defined in different ways. If it is understood as referring to traditions that with a certain degree of probability can be ascribed to Jesus himself, or were at least attributed to him in the early church, the letter of James and most of the traditions in the Didache would automatically fall outside of this category. It is only the Gospel of Matthew in which the traditions are entirely ascribed to Jesus, although there is agreement that a substantial part of them does not go back to Jesus himself. What we call "Jesus tradition," then, consists of traditions of different origin that can only partly be traced back to Jesus himself and that only in some writings were ascribed to him, while other texts transmitted them anonymously or under the authority of other representatives of early Christianity.

This observation is corroborated by Paul's letters.[18] Paul only occasionally refers to "the Lord" as authority behind certain commandments, whereas he more frequently quotes traditions with parallels in the Synoptic Gospels without mentioning "the Lord" or "Jesus." Therefore, the question arises whether in these instances Paul is referring to "Jesus tradition" as well. Does he, as, for example,

---

each other. In 4:8, καθαρίζειν and ἁγνίζειν are used metaphorically. The νόμος τέλειος in 1:25 does not necessarily refer exclusively to the Jewish law but can also be understood in a wider sense.

18. See Jens Schröter, *Von Jesus zum Neuen Testament: Studien zur urchristlichen Theologiegeschichte und zur Entstehung des neutestamentlichen Kanons* (WUNT 204; Tübingen: Mohr Siebeck, 2007), 81–104.

James Dunn has argued,[19] in these cases also quote sayings from Jesus without explicitly mentioning where they come from, or does he refer to traditions that had not been attributed to Jesus when Paul became aware of them? In James, 1 Peter, and the Didache we are confronted with a similar phenomenon. Traditions that the Synoptic Gospels refer to as coming from Jesus are quoted here without such an attribution.

The author of James mentions Jesus's name only once[20] and puts the whole teaching under the authority of his brother James. It is therefore not certain whether the traditions he shares with the Synoptic Gospels, especially with Matthew or Q, had already been associated with Jesus at all when James incorporated them in his letter.[21] The alternative would be either that James made originally named sayings of Jesus pseudonymous or anonymous, or that this tradition had not been connected with Jesus at all when he took it over. If the latter were the case, it would have been Matthew in most instances who attributed the traditions to the authority of Jesus.[22]

In a recent article, John Kloppenborg has listed six options to come to grips with this problem, reaching from the extreme position that there is no Jesus tradition in James at all on the one end to the explanation that these traditions go back to the historical James's own memories on the other.[23] Kloppenborg himself, following Richard Bauckham, favors a controlled oral-tradition-model without taking over Bauckham's assumption of authentic Jacobean authorship. As this discussion shows, the term "Jesus tradition" in James is in need of qualification because it is by no means self-evident that James had access to traditions that originated with Jesus himself.

At several places, the Didache refers to "the Lord" or "the Gospel" as authority behind its traditions.[24] In Did. 6:2 "the whole yoke of the Lord" is mentioned, probably referring, as I will argue later, to the evangelical section inserted into the Two Ways teaching. In Did. 8:2 the Lord's Prayer is introduced by the admo-

19. James D. G. Dunn, "Jesus Tradition in Paul," in *Studying the Historical Jesus: Evaluations of the State of Current Research* (ed. B. Chilton and C. A. Evans; NTTS 19; Leiden: Brill, 1994), 155–78.

20. Jas 2:1: ἔχετε τὴν πίστιν τοῦ κυρίου ἡμῶν Ἰησοῦ Χριστοῦ τῆς δόξης. In 5:7–8, 11 the κύριος is mentioned four times, in 5:11 probably referring to God.

21. See Burchard, *Jakobusbrief*, 17.

22. Attributing this step to Q is not helpful because it is not certain whether the isolated sayings or sayings collections of Q were transmitted in general under the authority of Jesus.

23. John S. Kloppenborg, "The Reception of the Jesus Traditions in James," in *The Catholic Epistles and the Tradition* (ed. J. Schlosser; BETL 176; Leuven: Peeters, 2004), 93–141.

24. In the Didache, κύριος refers to the authority of Jesus (see 9:5; 11:2, 4, 8; 12:1; 14:1: κυριακὴ κυρίου; 15:1), his coming at the end of time (10:6: μαρὰν ἀθά; 16:1, 7–8) and traditions that are ascribed to him (6:2: ζυγὸν τοῦ κυρίου; 8:2; 9:5; 15:4). In 4:1, 12–13; 10:5; 14:3 also God can be called κύριος.

nition not to pray like the hypocrites, but instead as the Lord has directed in his Gospel.[25] This rule belongs to a section on fasting and praying (Did. 8) that stands somewhat awkwardly between the passages on baptism (Did. 7) and on thanksgiving (Did. 9–10).[26] The rule on fasting was probably inserted here on the basis of the catchword "fasting" (νηστεῦσαι) in 7:4, which is taken up in 8:1 by νηστεῖαι and leads to an instruction about fasting and praying, two rites that are traditionally connected in Jewish writings. As has already been argued several times, chapter 8 is a later insertion introducing more traditional material— instructions on fasting on the fourth and sixth day of the week and the Lord's Prayer—into the liturgical section in Did. 7–10.[27] The reference to the Lord's teaching in his Gospel was thereby probably added by the redactor himself and therefore belongs to the redactional layer of the Didache.

The other cases are similar. In 9:5 the saying of the Lord "Do not give what is holy to the dogs" is introduced as justification for the restriction of the Eucharist to the baptized. In 11:3 the tradition about wandering apostles and prophets is introduced with the phrase περὶ δὲ τῶν ἀποστόλων καὶ προφητῶν, κατὰ τὸ δόγμα τοῦ εὐαγγελίου οὕτω ποιήσατε, and in 15:3 and 4 the admonitions to correct one another in peace as well as to prayer and almsgiving are motivated by a reference to "the Gospel" or "the Gospel of the Lord." With regard to all these instances it has been argued persuasively that the references to the "Lord" and the "Gospel" belong to a late redactional stage in the composition history of the Didache. With these references the redactor does in all probability not refer to a written Gospel.[28] Instead, the term εὐαγγέλιον is used as designation for the teaching of the Lord and not for a written text. This does of course not answer the question whether the redactor had knowledge of a written Gospel. But, as will be shown later, the Didache's versions of these traditions are more appropriately explained as analogies to those in the Synoptic Gospels than as literarily dependent upon one or several of them.

The redactor of the Didache, then, ascribes some traditions to the authority of "the Lord and his Gospel," but not to "Jesus." This can be compared to Paul and 1 Clement, where traditions are ascribed to "the Lord" or "the Lord Jesus" in a similar way,[29] showing that the exalted Lord is the authority behind these

---

25. Μηδὲ προσεύχεσθε ὡς οἱ ὑποκριταί, ἀλλ' ὡς ἐκέλευσεν ὁ κύριος ἐν τῷ εὐαγγελίῳ αὐτοῦ.

26. See van de Sandt and Flusser, The Didache: Its Jewish Sources, 291.

27. See, e.g., Kurt Niederwimmer, Die Didache (Kommentar zu den Apostolischen Vätern 1; Vandenhoeck & Ruprecht, 1989), 165; Jonathan A. Draper, "Christian Self-Definition against the 'Hypocrites' in Didache VIII," in J. A. Draper, ed., Didache in Modern Research, 223–43. Draper draws attention to the fact that in the Ethiopic version Did. 8:1–2 only follows after 11:3–13, which points to an instability of that material in the textual tradition (ibid., 227).

28. If that were the case, one would naturally have to think of Matthew's Gospel.

29. 1 Cor 7:10 (see also 7:12 and 25); 9:14; 11:23; 1 Thess 4:15; 1 Clem. 13.1; 46.7.

traditions. The Didache introduces these references to highlight the importance of the exhortations. At the same time, it is obvious that the redactor regards not only these traditions as coming from the earthly Jesus. Instead, the reference to the Lord and his Gospel is part of the redactional activity of collecting different traditions into a composite manual and interpreting them from a common viewpoint.[30]

This is corroborated by a further observation. The name "Jesus" appears in the eucharistic prayers in chapter 9 and 10 in phrases that mention God's activity through Jesus (διὰ Ἰησοῦ), but not the teaching of Jesus himself. In a characteristic deviation from the references to "the Lord" and "his Gospel," Jesus is designated here as God's servant (παῖς). The title "Lord" instead presupposes that Jesus in his divine authority stands behind the teaching in his Gospel. Consequently, also with regard to the Didache, one should only speak with caution of "Jesus tradition."

Without the Synoptic Gospels it would therefore be almost impossible to recognize traditions in James or the Didache as Jesus traditions. They rather appear as catechetical instructions with close affinities to Jewish traditions, sometimes combined with quotations from Scripture and occasionally ascribed to the authority of the Lord. If we take into account the tendency of the Synoptic Gospels to collect diverse traditions and ascribe them to the authority of Jesus, it cannot be decided from the outset whether a tradition originally comes from Jesus and was made anonymous or put under a different authority only later, or whether it was first transmitted as anonymous Christian catechesis—what Luke calls "teaching of the apostles" (διδαχὴ τῶν ἀποστόλων, Acts 2:42)—and only secondarily ascribed to Jesus.

It would therefore not be practical to start our inquiry with a distinction between "Jesus tradition" and other catechetical or parenetical traditions in early Christianity. Instead, one has to compare the use of common traditions and their function within the concept of the respective writings. It is perhaps more appropriate to speak of "synoptic traditions" and bear in mind that they can appear in and outside the Synoptic Gospels. Whether they originated from Jesus himself or were attributed to him in early Christianity can remain open. But it can already be formulated at this point as a first "result" that, irrespective of the historical question, it seems important for Matthew to refer to Jesus as the authority behind the traditions, whereas James does not appear to feel the necessity to do so. And in the Didache only slight traces of ascribing some traditions not to Jesus but to the Lord and his Gospel are discernible, and the bulk of Didache's tradi-

---

30. For a discussion of the composition of the Didache see Niederwimmer, *Die Didache*, 64–80; van de Sandt and Flusser, *The Didache: Its Jewish Sources*, 28–48. See also Kurt Niederwimmer, "Der Didachist und seine Quellen," in C. N. Jefford, ed., *Didache in Context*, 15–36. In my view it is not necessary to postulate multiple stages of redaction. Instead, the redactional activity shows a coherent perspective on the material.

tions remains unaffected by this redactional tendency. Against this background I will take a closer look at some of these traditions in the following.

3. Perfection as the interpretative key for "Jesus traditions" in Matthew, James, and the Didache

Because each of the three writings uses "synoptic traditions" or "Jesus traditions" in its own way and because it cannot be decided from the outset how they are related to each other, it is useful to begin with a concept that occurs in all three writings and functions as an interpretative key for these traditions, namely, "perfection" (τελειότης, τέλειος εἶναι). Perfection is a central element in James's concept of ethics and soteriology that occurs immediately at the beginning of the letter.[31] It appears also at a prominent place in Matthew, namely, in Matt 5:48 as a summary of Jesus's interpretation of the Torah as well as in Matt 19:21 in the debate between Jesus and the rich young man. Finally, the Didache refers to perfection in the *sectio evangelica* (1:4) as well as in the summary of the Two Ways section in 6:2. Moreover, it is no incident that this concept interprets traditions that appear in James at different places, which Matthew has collected in the Sermon on the Mount and that occur in the Didache in the *sectio evangelica*. At the outset it can be stated, therefore, that perfection is a prominent concept in all three writings and a characteristic element of their interpretation of "Jesus traditions." But, as we will see, each of the three writings develops the topic in a distinct way.

Apart from the concept of perfection, the three writings share other topics in their ethical instructions. All three texts exhort the addressees to be merciful[32] and not to be hypocritical,[33] and they contrast the doers of the word to those who only hear it.[34] Moreover, all three writings interpret wealth as danger and warn against oppressing the poor. In their eyes, such behavior is typical of people who do not follow God's will.[35] They are therefore related to each other by a parenetical perspective that also characterizes their respective use of Jesus traditions. To put this into sharper focus, I begin with James.

---

31. Jas 1:2–4 (see next section).

32. Matt 5:7; Jas 2:13; 3:17; Did. 3:8; 5:2.

33. Matt 6:2, 5, 16 (see also the accusations in 7:5; 15:7; 22:18; 23:13–29); Jas 3:17; Did. 2:6; 4:12.

34. Matt 7:24–27; Jas 1:22–25; Did. 2:5.

35. Matt 6:19–21; 19:16–22; Jas 1:9–11; 2:1–13; 5:1–5; Did. 5:2.

3.1. James: Wisdom as the way to perfection

In James the topic of perfection occurs immediately at the beginning of the letter in 1:4. The τέλειος-terminology is used twice here: first in connection with ἔργον in the phrase ἔργον τέλειον, and second as description of the status of those who perform "perfect works" and will therefore be themselves "perfect": τέλειος εἶναι. As the ἵνα-construction shows, there exists a close connection between performing perfect works and being perfect. This is corroborated by the phrases δώρημα τέλειον in 1:17 and νόμος τέλειος in 1:25, as well as by the statement in 2:22: faith is brought to completion by the works (ἐκ τῶν ἔργων ἡ πίστις ἐτελειώθη). The concept of perfection is therefore of crucial importance for James's theology as a whole.[36] As the combination of τέλειος εἶναι with ὁλόκληροι and ἐν μηδενὶ λειπόμενοι in 1:4 shows, "perfection" depicts the status of those who lack nothing and live in complete agreement with God's will.

To describe how this can be achieved, James confronts his addressees with a reminder of what they already know (1:3 γινώσκοντες). The content of this knowledge is that "trials of any kind" (πειρασμοὶ ποικίλοι) that the addressees face are a reason for joy because they are to be regarded as a test of faith, which produces endurance. Endurance itself shall bring forth "perfect work" and thus will lead to perfection. James, then, opens his letter with a call to perfection that demonstrates that the addressees are able to endure diverse trials.

Included in this admonition is an allusion to an early Christian tradition that has analogies in 1 Pet 1:6–7 and Rom 5:3–4. The common theme of these three texts is that all of them contrast afflictions with the status of perfection, including close literal agreement between Jas 1 and Rom 5 in the phrase ὑπομονὴν κατεργάζεται. A further verbal link exists between δοκίμιον in Jas 1:3 and δοκιμή in Rom 5:4, whereas the terms for describing afflictions and the corresponding positive state as well as the sequence of the terms differ.[37] Closer agreements exist between James and 1 Peter. In both texts the present afflictions are called πειρασμοὶ ποικίλοι and the addressees are encouraged to rejoice (Jas 1:2: χαρὰν ἡγήσασθε; 1 Pet 1:6: ἀγαλλιᾶσθε). Moreover, both writings use the phrase τὸ δοκίμιον ὑμῶν τῆς πίστεως. Because this is a unique formulation, this agreement cannot be incidental but points to a common tradition.

The main difference between James and the other two texts is that in Rom 5 and 1 Pet 1 the afflictions appear as concrete sufferings the addressees have to endure. Paul uses the term θλίψεις, while 1 Peter specifies the πειρασμοί with the verb λυπεῖσθαι. The opening of James, however, does not explain what the

---

36. See Konradt, *Christliche Existenz nach dem Jakobusbrief*, 267–85.

37. Jas: πειρασμοί, δοκίμιον τῆς πίστεως, ὑπομονή, ἔργον τέλειον, τέλειος εἶναι; Rom: θλίψεις, ὑπομονή, δοκιμή, ἐλπίς.

"diverse afflictions" are. But at the beginning of the corpus of the letter in 1:12,[38] it becomes clear that temptation does not come from God and that the addressees do not suffer from persecution or imprisonment. Instead they are endangered by their own desires, which eventually lead to sin and death.[39] Later this is specified by the references to the lack of works that could prove their faith (2:14–25), or to their bitter envy and selfish ambition that demonstrates their lack of wisdom from above (3:13–18). The πειρασμοί are, therefore, ethical challenges that lead the addressees astray.

This corresponds to the other main difference between James on the one hand and Romans and 1 Peter on the other: In 1:4 James changes the verbal aspect from the indicative (κατεργάζεται) to the imperative (ἐχέτω). According to James, the status of perfection therefore needs to be achieved by the addressees alone who are required to perform the ἔργον τέλειον, whereas in Rom 5 and 1 Pet 1 it will be provided by God, who has already given the Holy Spirit (Rom) or will give the addressees a reward for their endurance when Jesus Christ is revealed (1 Pet).

Consequently, James interprets an early Christian tradition about the correspondence of afflictions and eternal reward in the light of his specific understanding of perfection. The reason for bringing together the topic of perfection with the tradition about afflictions, testing, and endurance is probably that Jewish Wisdom literature frequently uses the motif that trials are tests for genuine faith.[40] It is a widespread conviction that God educates his people with punishments, and that sufferings and hardships can therefore originate with God himself. But James interprets that concept differently: Tribulations are explicitly not attributed to God who educates by trial or punishment. Instead, they are presented as ethical challenges for the faith of the addressees and can therefore demonstrate that a believer is matured and possesses "wisdom from above" (3:17). James, then, uses early Christian traditions that have parallels in other early Christian writings—in some elucidating cases in 1 Peter[41]—to develop the theme of perfection, which occurs in Matthew and the Didache as well.

---

38. With Burchard, *Jakobusbrief*, 12, 67–68, I regard 1:12 as the beginning of the corpus of James's letter.

39. Jas 1:12–15.

40. See, e.g., Sir 2:5a ἐν πυρὶ δοκιμάζεται χρυσός; 4:17: πειράσει αὐτὸν ἐν τοῖς δικαιώμασιν αὐτῆς; Prov 27:21 δοκίμιον ἀργύρῳ καὶ χρυσῷ πύρωσις, ἀνὴρ δὲ δοκιμάζεται διὰ στόματος ἐγκωμιαζόντων αὐτόν.

41. See Matthias Konradt, "Der Jakobusbrief als Brief des Jakobus: Erwägungen zum historischen Kontext des Jakobusbriefes im Lichte der traditionsgeschichtlichen Beziehungen zum 1. Petrusbrief und zum Hintergrund der Autorfiktion," in *Der Jakobusbrief: Beiträge zur Rehabilitierung der "strohernen Epistel"* (ed. P. von Gemünden, M. Konradt and G. Theißen; Beiträge zum Verstehen der Bibel 3; Münster: Lit, 2003), 19–30.

A specific link with a synoptic tradition becomes evident immediately after the tradition that James shares with Romans and 1 Peter. In 1:5 James, taking up the term λείπειν from 1:4, turns to the topic of wisdom. It now becomes clear that what must not be lacking if somebody wants to attain perfection is wisdom. Otherwise, one should ask God and it will be given. At this point James picks up a "synoptic tradition" or "Jesus tradition." The correspondence between asking and receiving has an analogy in a Q tradition (Matt 7:7–8/Luke 11:9–10) and in Mark 11:23–24.[42] In James and Q there is a direct correspondence between the imperative of αἰτεῖν (αἰτεῖτε, αἰτείτω) and the passivum divinum of διδόναι (δοθήσεται). The construction in Mark is somewhat different: πάντα ὅσα προσεύχεσθε καὶ αἰτεῖσθε, πιστεύετε ὅτι ἐλάβετε, καὶ ἔσται ὑμῖν. But there is also a close link between James and Mark: In both texts we find the admonition to believe without any doubt, although the content of the requests varies.[43] Furthermore, James and Mark provide a semantic opposition between the verbs πιστεύειν and διακρίνειν.

In 1:5, then, James relies on an early tradition that the Synoptic Gospels transmit as a saying of Jesus in different variants. In James this tradition is connected with the Jewish conviction that God gives without reservation and degradation (ἁπλῶς καὶ μὴ ὀνειδίζοντος). Hence, perfection is the result of the ἔργον τέλειον, which, according to James, is only possible if one possesses the wisdom from God. To establish this conviction James uses Jewish traditions referring to temptations for those who want to serve the Lord, to God's eternal reward and his generosity in giving. He connects these traditions with early Christian traditions about suffering and reward and the correspondence of giving and receiving. Only one of these traditions is a synoptic or a "Jesus" tradition. For James it is characteristic, then, that he integrates the different traditions in his own concept of testing, perfection, and wisdom.

A similar overlap between James, the synoptic tradition, and 1 Peter appears in the topic of humiliation and exaltation in Jas 4:10.[44] The saying has a parallel in Matt 23:12/Luke 14:11, which perhaps goes back to a Q tradition. A further analogy occurs in Luke 18:14, at the conclusion of the parable of the Pharisee and the tax collector. Finally, there is a parallel in 1 Pet 5:6. To evaluate the tradition history of the saying in early Christianity, all of these instances have to be considered.[45]

---

42. The tradition is referred to again in Jas 4:3: αἰτεῖτε καὶ οὐ λαμβάνετε διότι κακῶς αἰτεῖσθε.

43. In Mark it is the request for the power to perform miracles, James urges his readers to ask God for wisdom.

44. Ταπεινώθητε ἐνώπιον κυρίου καὶ ὑψώσει ὑμᾶς.

45. See Matthias Konradt, "Der Jakobusbrief im frühchristlichen Kontext: Überlegungen zum traditionsgeschichtlichen Verhältnis des Jakobusbriefes zur Jesusüberlieferung, zur pau-

All sayings are characterized by the opposition of ταπεινοῦν and ὑψοῦν. Thereby, the closest parallel to James within early Christian tradition occurs again in 1 Peter. Both writings use the imperative of ταπεινοῦν (ταπεινώθητε) as well as an active form of ὑψοῦν with God as subject (Jas: ὑψώσει; 1 Pet: ὑψώσῃ) Moreover, in both writings the admonition to humble oneself is connected with Prov 3:34, which is quoted in Jas 4:6 and 1 Pet 5:5, and in both writings the devil (διάβολος) is mentioned in the immediate context as the representative of the endangering and hostile world. Furthermore, it is remarkable that neither 1 Peter nor James connect the saying with Jesus but instead relate it to a quotation from Scripture. Hence, one can detect two ways of how the early Christian tradition about humiliation and exaltation was adopted, one in the Synoptic Gospels and the other in James and 1 Peter.

The interpretation of the saying in James and 1 Peter varies, comparable to the reception of the tradition on trials and endurance mentioned above. In 1 Peter it is interpreted in light of the situation of the community in the context of a hostile pagan world, symbolized by the devil who prowls around like a roaring lion, whereas in James the addressees are endangered by their friendship with the world, which equals enmity to God (Jas 4:4). Being "humble before the Lord" in 1 Peter means to bear the sufferings in the present world by casting all anxieties on God (1 Pet 5:7), whereas in James the phrase describes an attitude of detraction from the pleasures of the world. This is confirmed by Jas 1:9–11, where humiliation and exaltation occur as well. Taking up the motif of the withering grass and the falling flower from Isa 40:7, James explains why the humble brother shall boast in being raised up, while the rich shall boast in being brought low, because he will fade away with his wealth like a flower in the field.

As in the former case, "Jesus traditions" in James appear in the context of parenese and have analogies in various other writings: in the Synoptic Gospels, 1 Peter, and in the Septuagint.[46] Thus, in James, "Jesus traditions" or "synoptic traditions" do not appear as a specific kind of tradition. Instead, they are used side by side with quotations from Scripture or other Jewish and early Christian traditions in order to develop the idea of wisdom as the way to perfection. The combination with other traditions may indicate that James has independent access to "Jesus traditions" and uses them in a distinct way.

linischen Tradition und zum 1. Petrusbrief," in J. Schlosser, ed., *The Catholic Epistles and the Tradition*, 171–212, 193–94.

46. An interesting overlap between James and Paul is the topic of election of the poor or weak in Jas 2:5 and 1 Cor 1:26–28.

3.2. MATTHEW: JESUS'S INTERPRETATION OF THE LAW AND THE PERFECTION OF
THE HEAVENLY FATHER

We begin again with a look at the concept of perfection. In Matt 5:48, Jesus's interpretation of the law in the so-called antitheses is summarized with an appeal to perfection: ἔσεσθε οὖν ὑμεῖς τέλειοι ὡς ὁ πατὴρ ὑμῶν ὁ οὐράνιος τέλειός ἐστιν. This corresponds with the sayings about fulfilment of the law in 5:17–20, because righteousness can only be achieved by fulfilment of the law as it is interpreted by Jesus. At the same time, this leads to the perfection of the heavenly father himself. The exhortation ἔσεσθε οὖν ὑμεῖς τέλειοι in 5:48 therefore forms an inclusio with the saying about the fulfilment of the law in 5:17 and interprets the antitheses as fulfilment of the law.[47] This is corroborated by the observation that Matthew has used a Q-tradition parallel to Luke 6:36. Differing from Luke who exhorts his readers to be "merciful," Matthew urges them to be "perfect." In this way Matthew stresses the importance of obedience to the law as God's own will according to what was explained in the antitheses. Although one can probably assume a special relationship between the commandment to love one's enemies and the exhortation to perfection, the latter certainly refers back to the antitheses as a whole. Therefore, Matt 5:48 summarizes Matthew's understanding of the Torah: Jesus's interpretation does in no way abolish the Law, but instead reveals its true meaning as the way to perfection.[48]

The second instance in Matthew is the dialog between Jesus and the rich young man in chapter 19. In verse 21 the phrase τέλειος εἶναι is used as description of those who are able not only to keep the law but to gain a treasure in heaven by doing more than the law requires, namely, selling their possessions, giving their money to the poor, and following Jesus. A similar distinction between fulfillment of the law and going beyond what it requires by following Jesus's commandments and becoming perfect occurs in Did. 6.[49] Both texts show that God's commandments, as they appear in Scripture, do not lead to perfection per se, but only if they are supplemented by Jesus's (or the Lord's) interpretation. I will return to how the Didache deals with this topic in the next paragraph.

A distinctive feature of Matthew, then, is the close relationship between righteousness, fulfilment of the law, and perfection. As for James, also for Matthew, perfection can only be achieved by unrestricted obedience to God's will. Unlike James, however, Matthew does not link perfection with σοφία, but instead with Jesus's interpretation of the Law and with "following Jesus." Whereas Jas 1:5 emphasizes that God will give wisdom if one asks in faith without doubt and that

---

47. See the discussion in van de Sandt and Flusser, *The Didache: Its Jewish Sources*, 204–37.

48. See Konradt, "Die vollkommene Erfüllung der Tora," 139–41.

49. See next paragraph.

wisdom enables one to endure tribulations, Matthew claims that it is the encounter with Jesus and the association with him that will lead to perfection.

This can be demonstrated by a comparison of the prohibition of oath in Jas 5:12 and Matt 5:33–37. As is well known, James and Matthew share a general prohibition of oath (ὀμνύειν), while in Jewish literature it is only forbidden to swear falsely (ἐπιορκεῖν). This latter tradition also appears in Did. 2:3 within the Two Ways section, but outside the *sectio evangelica*. The Two Ways section of the Didache therefore reflects traditional Jewish ethics, whereas James and Matthew propose a radicalized interpretation that exceeds the "ordinary" way. With regard to the Didache it may be mentioned in passing that this could indicate that the Two Ways section was only slightly reworked by a Christian redactor and only later radicalized by the inclusion of the *sectio evangelica*.

Turning back to James and Matthew, one wonders how the agreement of the absolute prohibition of oaths might be explained. James and Matthew have three elements in common: first the prohibition to swear itself (Jas: μὴ ὀμνύετε; Matt: μὴ ὀμόσαι ὅλως), second the reference to heaven and earth by which one must not swear, and third the admonition that a "yes" must be a "yes" and a "no" a "no." The main differences are that Matthew is more detailed in his explanation of heaven and earth as the throne of God and his footstool, as well as by mentioning other objects by which one is not allowed to swear (Jerusalem, one's head), whereas James has the general exhortation not to swear any other oath at all. Moreover, the Matthean wording forms the "antithesis" to the preceding "thesis" οὐκ ἐπιορκήσεις, ἀποδώσεις δὲ τῷ κυρίῳ τοὺς ὅρκους σου. James's version, therefore, is usually, and probably rightly, regarded as closer to the original tradition.[50] But this of course does not explain where the tradition comes from and how it functions in both writings.

The prohibition to swear is often regarded as an authentic Jesus saying.[51] But in this case the difficulty results from the fact that the older version in James does not indicate that it is a Jesus tradition at all. Only a secondary, revised version in Matthew's antitheses is ascribed to Jesus's authority. Therefore, the possibility cannot be excluded that an anonymous early Christian parenetical tradition was secondarily attributed to Jesus.[52] The assumption that such a harsh saying was in fact created in the early Christian community is just as difficult as to explain why James could dare to put such a saying under his own authority although it originally circulated as a Jesus saying.

---

50. See, e.g., Ulrich Luz, *Das Evangelium nach Matthäus (Mt 1–7)* (5th ed.; EKKNT 1/1; Düsseldorf and Zürich: Benziger and Neukirchener, 2002), 371; Burchard, *Jakobusbrief*, 207; Popkes, *Brief des Jakobus*, 334.

51. See, e.g., Luz, *Das Evangelium nach Matthäus (Mt 1–7)*, 372.

52. See Konradt, "Jakobusbrief im frühchristlichen Kontext," 198–200; Burchard, *Jakobusbrief*, 207; Frankemölle, *Brief des Jakobus*, 2:700–702.

Whether the saying comes from Jesus or not, both writings present it as a very special commandment. James highlights it by the emphatical introduction πρὸ πάντων δέ, ἀδελφοί μου, which refers either to verse 12 itself or to the following admonitions.[53] Obviously, the phrase introduces exhortations that James wants to emphasize in the final part of his letter. With this commandment James criticises the practice of swearing and stresses the necessity of reliable speech. The importance of the prohibition of oaths is underlined even more by the threat of being condemned to eternal judgement at the end of verse 12.

For Matthew, the prohibition to swear instead belongs to Jesus's interpretation of the Torah in the antitheses. It is introduced as an aggravation of the traditional commandment not to swear falsely that occurs in several Jewish texts.[54] The broader context of both versions is the critique of oaths in Jewish and Hellenistic tradition. As in James, the pointed interpretation of that tradition as a general prohibition of oaths shows that authentic, reliable speech was an important part of early Christian ethics. But whereas in James the phrase is part of admonitions at the end of the letter, in Matthew it belongs to those commandments that separate the followers of Jesus from the Pharisees and scribes because it is a "perfect" fulfillment of Jewish tradition that by itself cannot lead to perfection.

For Matthew it is characteristic, then, that "Jesus traditions" are presented in the form of Jesus's ethical teaching, which brings traditional Jewish commandments to its completion. The central passage in Matthew's Jesus story relevant to this issue is certainly the Sermon on the Mount, especially the so-called antitheses. It is therefore not by accident that in the antitheses many Jewish traditions are taken up and integrated into the teaching of Jesus.[55] Because these traditions and even the law itself are only effective as far as they are interpreted by Jesus, Jesus's teaching implies a separation from the synagogue and the deficient righteousness of the Pharisees and scribes. Hence, although Matthew and James share many Jewish and early Christian traditions, in Matthew they are interpreted in a polemical way by emphasizing that they are only valid if interpreted from Jesus's radical perspective.

---

53. The closest parallel to πρὸ πάντων in the New Testament is 1 Pet 4:8, followed by an admonition to love one another.

54. See, e.g., Zech 5:3; Ps.-Phoc. 16; Wis 14:25; Philo, Decal. 88.

55. See, e.g., Sir 34:22 φονεύων τὸν πλησίον ὁ ἀφαιρούμενος ἐμβίωσιν, καὶ ἐκχέων αἷμα ὁ ἀποστερῶν μισθὸν μισθίου; T. Benj. 8.2 ὁ ἔχων διάνοιαν καθαρὰν ἐν ἀγάπῃ οὐχ ὁρᾷ γυναῖκα εἰς πορνείαν; Ps.-Phoc. 3 μήτε γαμοκλοπέειν μήτ' ἄρσενα Κύπριν ὀρίνειν. See also n. 54.

3.3. The Didache: "Perfect" and "Ordinary" Christians

In the Didache, as in Matthew, the topic of perfection occurs at three places.[56] First, in 1:4 the exhortation to turn the other cheek is interpreted with the phrase καὶ ἔσῃ τέλειος. It is not quite clear why the Didache regards especially this commandment as leading to perfection. In any case, it belongs to the redactional material the *sectio evangelica* adds to the Two Ways passage, which provides the reader with commandments that surpass the Two Ways teaching itself. The phrase καὶ ἔσῃ τέλειος probably does not reflect Matthean influence, but goes back to the redactor himself who inserted the *sectio* into the Didache and emphasized its specific character by depicting it as the way to perfection.

The second instance is 6:2, a summary of the whole section of chapter 1–5. Here the phrase καὶ ἔσῃ τέλειος follows the conclusion of the Two Ways section in 6:1 and refers back to the *sectio evangelica*.[57] The difference between those who are able to bear the "entire yoke of the Lord" and those who are not, then, represents the same redactional perspective that also appears in the intrusion of the *sectio evangelica* into the Two Ways section itself. This is confirmed by the repetition of the phrase καὶ ἔσῃ τέλειος and by the interpretation of the Two Ways section as a whole. The distinction between the two ways leading to life or death is necessary for everyone, whereas the way to perfection goes beyond that distinction. The "entire yoke of the Lord," therefore, entails all radical commandments of the *sectio* necessary to keep for attaining perfection. The *sectio* thereby functions as a specific interpretation of the double commandment to love God and the neighbor as well as of the Golden Rule (Did. 1:2) by using Synoptic traditions. Unlike the commandments in the *sectio*, 6:3 requires from all Christians to abstain from food offered to idols.[58] This is a clear indication that the Didache expects Gentiles to become part of the Christian community. The Two Ways doctrine constitutes the pre-baptismal instruction for them, including the "way to perfection" in the evangelical section.

With this interpretation, the redactor of the Didache not only transcends the traditional Two Ways teaching, but also allows for the possibility that not all Christians might be able to keep these more demanding commandments. For these "ordinary Christians" there is still the possibility to follow the Two Ways teaching without keeping the commandments for perfection. It is possible, therefore, to belong to the "Christian" community and to stay with the "ordinary"

---

56. In 10:5, in the eucharistic prayer, God is asked to lead the church to perfection in his love (τελειῶσαι αὐτὴν ἐν τῇ ἀγάπῃ σου). For discussion of the topic see also Draper, "Didache and Matthew," 225–57.

57. See Niederwimmer, *Die Didache*, 152–56.

58. An interpretation of 6:2 in the light of 6:3 is developed by van de Sandt and Flusser, *The Didache: Its Jewish Sources*, 238–70.

way of observing the traditional Jewish commandments as presented in the Two Ways teaching. The ethical distinction between those who are able to bear "the whole yoke of the Lord" and those who are not, then, does not divide the community, but only demonstrates how perfection can be achieved. This solution is less radical than in Matthew. It shows that the separation from Judaism in the Didache is not a consequence of ethical radicalism but of liturgical practice: The community is advised to celebrate baptism and Eucharist, to pray as the Lord has commanded and to fast on other days than the "hypocrites."

As is well known, several overlaps exist between the evangelical section and the Synoptic Gospels, especially with Matthew. This does of course not answer the question of how the *sectio* is related to the Synoptic Gospels. Scholarly opinion is divided here between those who argue for literary dependence and those who plead for independence. If one favors the first option, it is necessary not only to explain the relationship of the *sectio* to Matthew, but also to Luke, Justin Martyr, and the Shepherd of Hermas, because all these writings consist of traditions parallel with the *sectio*.[59] The closest agreements between the Didache and Matthew are the exhortation to turn the other cheek and the admonition immediately afterwards to go along for two miles.[60] Showing close contacts with Luke are the formulation εὐλογεῖτε τοὺς καταρωμένους ὑμῖν καὶ προσεύχεσθε . . .;[61] the order ἱμάτιον – χιτών, which Matthew has in the reversed sequence; and the phrase παντὶ τῷ αἰτοῦντί σε δίδου καὶ μὴ ἀπαίτει in Did. 1:5a, which is in close affinity to Luke 6:30: παντὶ αἰτοῦντί σε δίδου, καὶ ἀπὸ τοῦ αἴροντος τὰ σὰ μὴ ἀπαίτει. There is also strong agreement between Did. 1:5 and Herm. *Mand.* 2, 4–6. If one opts for dependence of the *sectio* on other early Christian writings, one should acknowledge, therefore, that it is influenced by several texts, not only by Matthew.

The other possibility is that the *sectio* belongs to a spectrum of thematically related texts in which essential themes of early Christian teaching are brought into the form of an epitome.[62] The latter possibility clarifies why the *sectio* appears as a text that has analogies to Matthew's and Luke's sermons in Hermas and also in Rom 12:14–21, where the commandments to bless the persecutors and to be peaceful to one's enemy occur as well. This would also explain why the *sectio* appears as a teaching of the Lord that leads to perfection and thereby

---

59. See Niederwimmer, *Die Didache*, 93–100, with helpful tables.

60. Did. 1:4b–5a: ἐάν τίς σοι δῷ ῥάπισμα εἰς τὴν δεξιὰν σιαγόνα, στρέψον αὐτῷ καὶ τὴν ἄλλην καὶ ἔσῃ τέλειος· ἐὰν ἀγγαρεύσῃ σέ τις μίλιον ἕν, ὕπαγε μετ' αὐτοῦ δύο.

Matt 5:39b: ὅστις σε ῥαπίζει εἰς τὴν δεξιὰν σιαγόνα [σου], στρέψον αὐτῷ καὶ τὴν ἄλλην; 5:41: καὶ ὅστις σε ἀγγαρεύσει μίλιον ἕν, ὕπαγε μετ' αὐτοῦ δύο.

61. Did. 1:3b; Luke 6:28.

62. See Jonathan A. Draper, "Jesus Tradition in the Didache," in Draper, *Didache in Modern Research*, 72–91, 79–85; van de Sandt and Flusser, *The Didache: Its Jewish Sources*, 40–48.

surpasses the Two Ways section. Finally, because the evangelical section shares several aspects with other early Christian writings and at the same time has its own characteristics[63] it seems more appropriate to assume that the Didache is not literarily dependent here on the Synoptic Gospels but rather had its own access to early Christian traditions.

The two other sections in the Didache in which analogies to the Synoptic Gospels appear in concentrated form are the Lord's Prayer in chapter 8 and the eschatological discourse in chapter 16. I have already argued above that the Lord's Prayer, together with the admonitions not to fast and to pray with the hypocrites, was probably later inserted between the sections on baptism and Eucharist. The characteristic feature of this insertion is the separation of the fasting and praying of the "hypocrites" from that of the addressees of the Didache. There are several observations highlighting a distinct perspective of the Didache that is not dependent on Matthew.

First, the liturgical section in chapters 7–10 as a whole shows that the Didache develops rules for ritual life in its own way. There is no comparable description of baptism in Matthew; the Eucharist in Matthew is depicted as Jesus's Last Supper whereas the Didache calls it "thanksgiving" (εὐχαριστία) and it is characterized by two prayers over the cup and the fragment and a third one after the fill.[64] The Lord's Prayer itself has some minor but characteristic divergences from Matthew's version. These are the formulation ἐν τῷ οὐρανῷ instead of Matthew's ὁ ἐν τοῖς οὐρανοῖς, the singular τὴν ὀφειλήν in Did. where Matthew has the plural τὰ ὀφειλήματα, and the present tense ἀφίεμεν where Matthew has the aorist ἀφήκαμεν. In all these instances Luke has a third version: He does not qualify the father as *heavenly* father at all; instead of ὀφειλήματα he has ἁμαρτίας, and instead of ἀφήκαμεν he uses ἀφίομεν. This strengthens the assumption that these are cases of Matthew's redactional activity. The formulation ὁ ἐν τοῖς οὐρανοῖς is characteristic for Matthew, and the aorist ἀφήκαμεν reflects the Matthean understanding of forgiveness among community members as a prerequisite for God's forgiveness. That this a central aspect in Matthew's interpretation of the prayer becomes also evident from the verses which immediately follow the prayer itself (6:14–15). Here, a plural occurs for the designation

---

63. See, e.g., the phrase καὶ οὐχ ἕξετε ἐχθρόν in Did. 1:3, which does not occur in the Synoptic Gospels but is thematically related to the commandment to overcome evil with good in Rom 12:21 and not to resist the evil in Matt 5:39. Also the interpretations of the commandment not to demand back with the formulation οὐδὲ γὰρ δύνασαι in Did. 1:4 and εἰ μὲν γὰρ χρείαν ἔχων λαμβάνει τις, ἀθῷος ἔσται· ὁ δὲ μὴ χρείαν ἔχων δώσει δίκην in 1:5 are characteristic for their understanding in the Didache.

64. For my interpretation of the Eucharist in the Didache see Jens Schröter, *Das Abendmahl. Frühchristliche Deutungen und Impulse für die Gegenwart* (SBS 210; Stuttgart: Katholisches Bibelwerk, 2006), 60–72.

of human trespasses, παραπτώματα, which may explain why Matthew uses a plural, ὀφειλήματα, also in the prayer itself.

The version of the Didache is not affected by these redactions. Instead, the interpretation of the prayer becomes evident in a different way, namely, in the doxology at the end of the prayer, which has analogies in the eucharistic prayers in chapters 9 and 10,[65] as well as in the following command to pray three times a day. Moreover, it is remarkable that although the section on fasting and prayer begins with a polemical remark against the "hypocrites," directed toward fellow Jews from whom the addressees shall keep away, the passage ends with a commandment to follow Jewish practice of praying three times every day. The Didache, then, develops ritual life in close affinity to Jewish customs, a feature that appears somewhat differently also in the section on the Eucharist. Here, the order cup – bread is probably adapted from Jewish practice, and the eucharistic prayers in chapter 9 and 10 are loaded with Jewish terms and ideas.[66]

The separation from the "hypocrites" is described in a different way than in Matthew.[67] Matthew promotes a sharp ethical distinction between the synagogue and the community. The hypocrites are thereby identified as scribes and Pharisees as representatives of the Jewish community whose righteousness is defective. In the Didache, however, it is rituals that separate "Jews" from "Christians." The label "hypocrites" thereby functions as polemical justification for the separation of the community of the Didache from other Jewish groups.[68]

The third instance of "perfection" occurs in 16:2. The admonition to be "perfect" at the final hour is somewhat different from 6:2. Whereas according to 6:2 it is sufficient to "do what you can," in 16:2 perfection is necessary for salvation in the final judgement.

With regard to the synoptic tradition a similar picture as in the preceding passages emerges.[69] The specific combination of the commandment to keep vigil, let the lamps not go out, leave the waists not ungirded and to be ready, as well as the unknown hour of the Lord's coming and the warning against false prophets has several analogies in the Synoptic Gospels.[70] But it is improbable that this chapter is literarily dependent on Matthew's version of the apocalyp-

---

65. In Did. 9:3 and 10:2 the formulation σοὶ ἡ δόξα εἰς τοὺς αἰῶνας is used.

66. See Niederwimmer, *Die Didache*, 173–209; van de Sandt and Flusser, *The Didache: Its Jewish Sources*, 296–329.

67. See Draper, "Didache and Matthew," 230–35.

68. See the intensive discussion of the identity of the "hypocrites" in the Didache by Del Verme, *Didache and Judaism*, 143–88.

69. See the discussion in Niederwimmer, *Die Didache*, 247–69. See also John S. Kloppenborg, "Didache 16,6–8 and Special Matthean Tradition," *ZNW* 70 (1979): 54–67. Verheyden, "Eschatology in the Didache," takes a different view.

70. The parallels occur in Matt 24:42–25:13; Luke 12:35–40 and Mark 13:33–37 and Matt 7:15.

tic discourse. Instead the eschatological discourse of the Didache appears as an independent reception of an early Christian apocalyptic tradition that Matthew has used as well. This becomes especially evident in Did. 16:4 where several differences between the Didache and the synoptic versions in Mark 13:19–22 and Matt 24:21–24 occur but also by comparing Did. 16:7–8 with Mark 13:26; Matt 24:30 and Luke 21:27. Moreover, Did. 16:2b has a parallel in Barn. 4:9, and the scenario described in Did. 16:6, based on synoptic traditions but also in 1 Thess 4:16; 1 Cor 15:52, is developed with its own characteristics.[71] A special feature of the Didache is the commandment to assemble frequently.[72] Hence, the traditions in Did. 16 have analogies in several early Christian writings and were independently collected in the Didache into an apocalyptic discourse that at the same time concludes the whole instruction.

The so-called "Jesus traditions" in the Didache, then, are taken from a multitude of early Christian catechetical traditions which James and Matthew had access to as well. In the Didache these traditions appear as ethical teachings partly ascribed to the authority of "the Lord" and his Gospel. In two cases—the *sectio evangelica* and the teaching on fasting and prayer—they surpass traditional Jewish ethics and function to explain the separation from fellow Jews. In this respect, the process of separation is motivated in a different way than in Matthew.

4. Conclusions

In Matthew, James, and the Didache, the concept of "perfection" functions as an important clue for the interpretation of the so-called "Jesus traditions." This concept has its roots in Jewish writings that emphasize the necessity to live according to God's will. Despite this agreement, there is no evidence for a literary dependency between any of the three writings. Instead, each of them had access to early Christian ethical and parenetical traditions, interspersed with Jewish traditions and quotations from Scripture. Each of the three writings adopted these traditions independently and used them to develop its own, specific version of early Christian theology.

James proposes a close connection between perfection and wisdom. Wisdom is a gift from God that enables the addressees to live their faith in a perfect way. To explain this in detail, James picks up different traditions that in several instances have analogies in the Synoptic Gospels. But there is no hint at all that James knew that these traditions were related to Jesus, nor does the author ascribe them to the authority of "the Lord." Instead they appear side by side with other early Christian and Jewish traditions that for James are equally important as ethical instructions.

---

71. See, e.g., Did. 16:4: τότε φανήσεται ὁ κοσμοπλανὴς ὡς υἱὸς θεοῦ; 16:5: τότε ἥξει ἡ κτίσις τῶν ἀνθρώπων εἰς τὴν πύρωσιν τῆς δοκιμασίας; 16:6: τὰ σημεῖα τῆς ἀληθείας.

72. See also Ignatius, *Eph.* 13.1.

There is also no need for James to emphasize a difference between Jewish traditions and Christian ethics. Instead, he mixes Jewish parenetical traditions and quotations from Scripture with early Christian traditions in order to face ethical deficiencies of his addressees with his concept of ethical perfection.

With regard to Matthew a close affinity of perfection and interpretation of Jewish law can be observed. Early Christian traditions are used here to emphasize that the Jewish law leads to righteousness and perfection only in its "Christian" version, namely, as interpreted by Jesus. The polemical gesture shows in this context that Matthew already looks back at a process of separation between the Jesus followers and the synagogue and legitimizes this parting of the ways by depicting the Jesus community as obliged to exceed the defective righteousness of the scribes and Pharisees.

Finally, the Didache interprets the common traditions in a way that separates Christians from Jews not by ethical radicalism but by ritual life. Diverse traditions from different origins—the Two Ways section, the *sectio evangelica*, the liturgical section on baptism and Eucharist, instructions on fasting and the Lord's Prayer, instructions about wandering apostles and prophets, and eschatological traditions—are all brought together to instruct the community about ethical, liturgical, and eschatological matters. For this purpose the redactor uses synoptic traditions, especially in the evangelical section, in the Lord's Prayer and in the eschatological discourse. But these traditions are neither dependent on a written Gospel nor are they identified as "Jesus traditions." Instead, they appear as general "apostolic" instructions, whereas references to "the Lord" and "the Gospel" are used to surpass the Two Ways teaching with the "whole yoke of the Lord," as well as to emphasize the importance of prayer, the restriction of the Eucharist to the baptized, how to deal with wandering apostles and prophets and how to preserve peace within the community.

From the insertion of the evangelical section in the Two Ways teaching, the polemic against the "hypocrites" and the restriction of the Eucharist one can conclude that the redactor of the Didache uses these traditions to develop a "Christian" over against a "Jewish" identity. The Didache accomplishes this goal by taking over Jewish ethical instructions, surpassing them with a "way to perfection" and presenting them as part of a manual that also consists of specific liturgical instructions for a "Christian" community. Here, separation from fellow Jews is not based on ethical rigor like in Matthew. Rather, the Didache reflects a traditional Jewish ethos and separates the "Christian" community by introducing specific rituals like baptism and Eucharist, and by polemic against fasting and prayers of the "hypocrites."

In sum, James, Matthew, and the Didache share the conviction that "Christianity,"—a term that has to be used with caution in regard to all three writings—should be understood as a way to perfection. In James this is developed by emphasizing the importance of wisdom as the gift from God that enables Christians to live according to their calling as those who were (re)born by the word of truth, whereas in Matthew and the Didache perfection is connected to ethical or liturgical separation. The "Jesus traditions"—more aptly described as general, early Christian parenetical or ethical traditions—function to develop these perspectives in three different ways.

PART 4
INTERPRETING TORAH

Problems with Pluralism in Second Temple Judaism: Matthew, James, and the Didache in Their Jewish-Roman Milieu

J. Andrew Overman

One of the most important insights from the last generation of scholarship on early Christianity and Judaism has been the recognition that both of these terms are anachronistic when applied to the early Roman period. Neat distinctions between these two related traditions cannot be maintained in the dynamic and ultimately messy years between the reign of Tiberius and, let us say for convenience, Constantine. The distinction between these two monotheistic traditions evolved variously over time depending upon locale and context.

Up to the fourth century it is difficult to speak reliably about so-called Christianity and Judaism. The distinction between these two groups across the Roman Empire simply does not obtain in a consistent and thorough enough manner. Distinguishing between Judaism and Christianity is difficult enough. But, in addition to this, we now recognize that there were multiple forms of both within this fluid period. Christianity and Judaism did not simply compete with one another and ultimately go in separate directions. Such a sentence now, in light of the last few decades of research, seems crude and oversimplified in the extreme.[1]

The welcome recognition of the impressive plurality that existed within Second Temple or Early Roman Judaism—both at home and abroad—makes defining or naming groups very difficult. The diversity that existed within these two broad traditions during the Roman period makes defining a member of either group extremely challenging at the least and wrongheaded at worst. There are certainly so-called Jewish groups that would have had nothing to do with one another when one looks across the range of both Palestinian and Diaspora

---

1. A much fuller discussion of the plurality within and among Judaisms of this period can be found in J. Andrew Overman and William S. Green, "Judaism in the Greco-Roman Period," *ABD* 3:1137–54. I would like to express my gratitude to the organizers of the conference at Tilburg University where these papers were presented. Their hospitality and the setting of Tilburg produced a most stimulating and successful discussion and conference.

groups. And the same can and has been said of so-called early Christian groups of the same period. An instructive case in point is the catalog of those who will inherit the world to come and those who will not, as found in the *Mishna*:

> All Israelites have a share in the world to come, as it is said, "Your people also shall be all righteous, they shall inherit the land forever; the branch of my planting, the work of my hands, that I may be glorified" (Isa 60:21).
> And these are the ones who have no portion in the world to come:
> He who says the resurrection of the dead is a teaching which does not derive from Torah, and (he who says) the Torah does not come from Heaven, and an Epicurean. And R. Akiba says, "Also he who reads heretical books . . . Abba Saul says "Also he who pronounces the divine Name as it is spelled out. (*m. Sanh.* 10:1)

Similarly in Matthew we find a denunciation of a group closely related to the Matthean community both in terms of proximity and ideology, yet famously vilified because of their interpretation of Law/Torah, which the author finds destructive.

> But woe to you scribes and Pharisees, hypocrites, because you shut off the king-dom of heaven from people; for you do not enter in yourselves, nor do you allow those who are entering to go in. (Woe to you Scribes and Pharisees, hypo-crites, because you devour widows' houses, even while for a pretense you make long prayers; therefore you shall receive greater condemnation.) Woe to you scribes and Pharisees, hypocrites, because you travel about on sea and land to make one proselyte and when they become one you make them twice as much a son of hell as yourself. (Matt 23:13–15).

In the cases of Mishna and Matthew cited here, from the point of view of an outsider, let us say a Roman official or judge in the province of Judaea or Syria, these look like quite similar groups, perhaps virtually indistinguishable. They are monotheistic, basically Jewish groups arguing about the law / *nomos* / Torah they hold in common. Romans would have appreciated at least the importance of the law in this debate. It is striking to note how often it is the law and legal interpre-tation that emerges as the cause of the tension between competing closely related groups.[2] The two passages above highlight how closely related various Jewish groups may seem on the one hand and the intense, deeply felt enmity between such closely aligned groups on the other. In both passages we can apprehend closely related Jewish groups who apparently, at least on paper, will have nothing to do with one another.

---

2. Discussed in J. Andrew Overman, *Matthew's Gospel and Formative Judaism: The Social World of the Matthean Community* (Minneapolis: Fortress, 1990), 23–29.

To those on the inside the difference and tension over the law and legal interpretation is great, if not grave, but to even a relatively well-informed Roman these appear to be members of the same group arguing about their shared laws and traditions. Roman distinctions between Jews and Christians are of course a development from a far later period than our texts here. And in our earlier period Roman elites understandably do not make nuanced distinctions between various kinds of Jews as if they had read Josephus.[3] Recognizing Jews, Christians, or so-called Jewish-Christians in this period is complicated yet further by the shared influences most groups encountered simply by virtue of being modestly engaged in the commerce and culture of the omnivorous Roman imperial world. Roman philosophy, political realities, and religious influences, forms of which existed from Gibraltor to the Euphrates, are recognizable in the literature coming from the very groups we are trying to define and distinguish between. Were some of the texts and voices we analyze Jewish? Christian? Stoic? Judeo-Christian? Judeo-Christian-Stoic? The short answer to all of this is *yes*. That is to say, many monotheistic texts from this period were indeed a combination of all these influences and more. How do we measure or weigh these influences? As many have recognized, there is a continuum here in sorting out influences and placing groups and their texts on a map of early Christianities and Judaisms of the Roman period. Sometimes the categories we utilize or rely upon can be more misleading than helpful and the names too anachronistic to shed light or constructively distinguish.[4] The documents of James, Matthew, and the Didache put the problems associated with identifying or defining groups in the Second Temple period in bold relief. In this paper I wish to offer a brief summary of where these three texts might fall on the fluid maps of Judaism and Christianity in the early Roman period.

1. MATTHEW

Concerning Matthew I have argued with many others that the defining feature of this text is the conflict between the community behind the Gospel and a rival group in the author's setting. Matthew believes that Matthean Jews centered on the teachings of Jesus is the group that should assume leadership in their milieu. For the author, leadership means Torah interpretation, defining appropri-

---

3. While a great deal has been written on this subject, a most helpful discussion of Roman views of Jews can be found in Erich S. Gruen, "Roman Perspectives on the Jews in the Age of the Great Revolt," in *The First Jewish Revolt: Archaeology, History, and Ideology* (ed. A. Berlin and J. A. Overman; London: Routledge, 2002), 27–42.

4. With regard to this complicated historical process and development, two works of Ramsay MacMullen remain illuminating: *Christianizing the Roman Empire (A.D. 100–400)* (New Haven, Conn.: Yale University Press, 1984) and *Christianity and Paganism in the Fourth to Eighth Centuries* (New Haven, Conn.: Yale University Press, 1997).

ate piety in their time and place, and claiming ownership of (certain) traditions and expectations in Israel. The other group is characterized as poor leaders and teachers, treacherous for Israel, and as having brought nothing but woe for the people of Matthew's setting. For Matthew, Jesus has framed and explicated traditions important to the group in a definitive manner. Traditions and teachings associated with Jesus common to the community are the authoritative version of how to understand laws, prioritize ethics, and approach the future. Like Qumran, for example, Matthew seems to care little about the one thing most Judaisms have in common, namely, Roman imperial realities. He focuses instead on the competition with this other closely related group of Jewish leaders captured somewhat artificially in the conflation, "scribes and Pharisees."

While Matthew does not mention Roman and Roman realities explicitly, as do some other writers from his epoch and setting, he does address issues that we can recognize as related to Roman imperial realities. The so-called parable of the landowner in 21:33–44 is one place where Matthew addresses client lordship in his setting in the Roman east. The failure of the local leadership to "pay their proceeds on time" led to the loss of the land. He concludes the parable by stating clearly that the story was aimed at the scribes and Pharisees. They and people like them brought this suffering upon the people. A similar though arguably more theologized parable follows after this one in 22:1–7. The disregard of some of the local leaders led in this case to the destruction of their city. These two parables back-to-back in Matthew precipitate the plot on the part of the scribes and Pharisees— or we would say local leadership (22:15)—to put Jesus to death. They constitute the beginning of the end for the Matthean Jesus.[5]

Also in terms of Roman provincial realities, Matthew alone stresses the appropriateness, if not absolute need, to pay one's taxes. Matthew's addition to this broader colonial reality takes place in Capernaum and is found in 17:24–27. Matthew concludes unequivocally that taxes should be paid. Technically, according to 17:26, his group should not have to pay being "sons" but, "in order not to give offense," taxes will be paid. Here we see another critique by Matthew of what was obviously an approach to taxes in his setting that he associates with poor leaders and poor interpretation. An interpretation of "freedom" (17:26) as meaning that one does not have to pay the tax is woefully misguided and has led to tremendous pain and destruction. These three passages from Matthew most clearly bear the signs of an immediate post-70 situation where poor leaders and misguided Jewish groups have led the land to ruin. Matthew asserts that his community and their application of Torah through Jesus is the remedy for these problems.

---

5. The theme of Roman influences in Matthew is developed further in J. Andrew Overman, *Igreja e Comunidade em Crise: O Evangelho Segundo Mateus* (São Paulo: Paulinas, 1996), 303–32.

Finally, in this regard Matthew's ethic articulated in the Sermon on the Mount can justifiably be read as counsel toward a *modus vivendi* with those in power. It is true this counsel can at the same time be viewed as a form of resistance, as has been so often noted. But this would be a kind of resistance that up to this point has not been heard of in Palestine or elsewhere. The second half of Matt 5 articulates both his ideas about fulfilling the law, but also how his community can live in a world controlled by alien forces. The double-love command is the hermeneutical and ethical guide for the community and the way in which one truly fulfills the law. But it is also sagacious and utilitarian counsel for surviving in his Roman provincial setting in the post-70 era. The author is explicit about this in at least 5:22, 25, 29–30, 38–41, and 44–45. What is an articulate expression of Torah interpretation and fulfillment is also at the very same time savvy counsel for a post-revolutionary colonial setting in Syro-Palestine.

What is important here is recognizing that Matthew has taken issue with local Jewish leaders or retainers.[6] This is evident throughout most of his Gospel. The nub of this contention is legal interpretation and piety or praxis. He believes the competing group distorts the law for their agenda and ends. His community, as a result of the interpretation provided for them through Jesus, is the group that should guide God's people in this place and time. But, just as important as, and even related to this argument by Matthew, he places his community in a middle ground with respect to Roman provincial authorities. At the very least, Matthew urges a way of living with the powers that be and charts a course of slightest offense. This sets him apart from some of his contemporaries. He seems to believe his community would be much better suited to guide the local population and handle legal interpretation. Those currently in charge locally are nothing but evil in his view.

With regard to Matthew we are not talking here about early Rabbinic groups. Matthew seems a bit too early for that in my opinion. We are as yet in the midst of this very fluid post-70 period where apocalyptic options are still on the table in a Syro-Palestinian setting. The Jewish groups that do not require a literal temple in their theology and praxis still appear viable; this would be some version of Pharisaism and Matthean Judaism. The objective of obtaining leadership and authority in their setting is not a complete fantasy for Matthew, though he admits the others hold the upper hand in this struggle. Books like *2 Baruch*, *4 Baruch*, *4 Ezra*, extra- or proto-rabbinic texts like the early sections of *Pirqe 'Abot* or *'Abot de Rabbi Nathan*, maybe the *Odes of Solomon*, aspects of Josephus like his atten-

---

6. The concept of "retainer" is taken from Lenski but developed by Anthony J. Saldarini in *Pharisees, Scribes and Sadducees in Palestinian Society: A Sociological Approach* (Wilmington, Del.: Michael Glazier, 1988).

tion to popular rebel groups, and some others are examples of texts that share both points of view as well as this interim, ill-defined period with Matthew.[7]

2. Didache

When we turn out attention to the Didache, several differences strike us immediately. We are now reading about a group that takes its lead and instruction from *HO KURIOS*. Jesus is rarely mentioned. His name comes up in a curious formulation in the eucharist, "Jesus your child (Ἰησοῦ τοῦ παιδός σου)," which reads like a very early liturgical formulation inherited by the group.

The notion of the *ekklesia* has a Matthean ring but seems to have assumed a broader geographic and philosophical sense. The *ekklesia* is scattered and recognized as an association beyond the local realm. Related to this church, roles and offices have clearly gained recognition and currency ("Apostle," "Prophet," "Deacon," "Teacher," and "Bishop"). Structure and order with respect to ecclesial rites seems to be a matter of substantial importance for the Didache. The followers are known—at least to one another—as *Christianoi* and the term Gospel carries a freight that suggests a taken-for-granted knowledge of its message and content. All these substantial sociological developments do not sound much like Matthew and a lot more like a set and stage of developments we might find in, say, the Pastoral Epistles.

The Didache is rightly designated a manual for a community that is well on the way to being organized. It sees itself as part of a regional network. The document focuses, as manuals would, on proper liturgical life but stresses above all ethics, right behavior, treatment of others, and piety, emphasizing right attitudes and actions for the members *within the context of the group.*

Based on the information the document provides, the Didache shows little interest in issues beyond the association. There is no obvious quarrel with those in its milieu outside the group. Take for example the logion concerning the courts in 1:5. In Matthew this saying (5:26) is intended to highlight the hostility of the courts toward the Matthean community and is part of offering a broader strategy for getting along in the city where legal authorities are out to get members. In the Didache the saying is clearly and awkwardly dislodged from this earlier setting and now is about sharing possessions and appropriate use of alms within the community. The saying is about internal piety, not political realities. Similarly, "Hypocrites" (Did. 8:1, 2) is not a term for errant authorities in the city or the setting of the group, as is the case in Matthew. It is a term that denotes

---

7. I still find Graham Stanton's ("5 Ezra and Matthean Christianity in the Second Century," *JTS* 28 [1977]: 67–83) notion of a "Matthean Circle" quite helpful in thinking about the other forms of Judaism or Jewish-Christianity that would have found affinity with Matthew's interpretations.

aberrant behavior or attitudes in the Didache. It is not a term associated with an identifiable group. Being a hypocrite is like being lustful, or proud, "consorting with the lofty," or a host of other negative behaviors and attitudes. It is a trait to be avoided, an ethical injunction. This is a far cry from Matthew's application of the term.

The focus in the Didache is on life within the community and does not portray a position of alienation vis-à-vis the world. The setting of the Didache, so far as we can tell, does not suggest a reality where the followers of the Lord are at odds with their broader setting. Schism or Schismata within the community is a far greater concern (2:6–7; 4:3; 15:3). Schism is revealed in the tension concerning treatment of slaves (4:10, 11, itself an astonishing inclusion). And one is struck with the oft-noted tension over "rich" and "poor," which do not read like spiritualized terms but honest reflections of the economic diversity of the group. Some followers or members are now Roman *Optimates* of grander social standing.

There is something that strikes the reader as a *Matthean veneer* or *kinship* to parts of the Didache. What appealed to the author or compiler of the Didache was the more-obviously ethical portions of early Jesus traditions with which Matthew also found resonance. He is not alone of course. The ethical traditions given fuller expression in Matthew have resonated with many over the centuries. There is nothing in the Didache, as far as I can see, that would require us to relate the document to Matthew beyond this significant ethical *Vorlage*. And, significantly, there is little here that would compel us to conclude that this is a document somehow associated with Second Temple Judaism, however broadly we define that category. The Christology of the Didache is somewhere between low and non-existent, so there is little here to help us place the text on maps of early Christianities or Judeo-Christianities. It may be wisest to declare the document *non-aligned* at this point. The Didache is trying to supply order and structure to a growing community that has an obvious measure of sociological sophistication when compared to a host of other early Christian and Jewish communities from roughly the same period. They are connected to Jesus in some way, more to *the Lord*. The two titles are related but not coterminus. As Matthew reflects a kind of Judaism in Palestine that did not ultimately survive, so the Didache strikes us as a stage of quasi-*Christian* sociological and theological development that likewise did not survive long past the Roman period.

Thus, we do admit the presence of Matthean language or echoes of Matthew in the Didache seemingly suggesting a Matthean veneer or relationship to Matthew. Beyond this there is little to connect the two documents. But this is not where the matter ends for here is where recent work on the Didache helps us better to understand what these two quite different texts also have in common. Huub van de Sandt and others have demonstrated convincingly that these two different genres and texts do in fact share an affinity for an earlier tradition bound to ethics and legal interpretation.[8] Very early Rabbinic traditions along with the tradition as it finds expression in formative Jewish groups lies behind the ethical instructions found in both Matthew and the Didache manual. Here the recent continental and especially Dutch scholarship has pointed a way forward in uncovering a connection between Matthew and the Didache. These are two very different texts reflecting groups that faced quite different fundamental issues. The Didache is focused on internal issues and behavior and reflects a stage of sociological development we do not find in Matthew. Matthew, on the other hand, faces a struggle with a real rival in his setting that threatens the very survival of the group. The aim and purpose of these two texts are quite disparate. Yet we can hear and sense in these two texts a connection. The connection is that kinship rooted in the earlier Jewish ethical tradition of the Two Ways.[9]

What is important to note here is the different ways in which the two documents employ the Two Ways stratum. The Didache presents the Two Ways as instruction for living an ethical, Torah-guided life within the community. Matthew, especially when placed within the larger context of the antithesis in chapter 5, transforms the Two Ways into ethics that serve the community well when exercised internally. But just as importantly, it serves the adherent well when lived out externally in Matthew's broader social and political context. Clearly and significantly both authors view this tradition as the way in which the law is fulfilled. Here we can see obvious agreement. The manner in which the Two Ways informs the life, behavior, even strategy of the members is different in the two documents. Both Matthew and the Didache transform or utilize this shared ethical tradition in a manner that reveals the station of each community in their respective settings.

3. JAMES

When we turn to James we see another stage in the messy early-Roman history of formative Judaism and Christianity. The substantial work done on this document recently appears to have concluded—if such a word is possible—that we have in James the emergence of a rather sophisticated measure of Hellenistic philosophy merging with a Diaspora group that honors Jesus. The honoring of Jesus, so far as the document discloses, does not include any significant theological freight. For example there is no obvious soteriological discussion apart from the notion or act of "doing," no mention of the resurrection, and the document

---

8. Noted in many works but put forth most persuasively in the article in this volume on the "Two Ways" tradition.

9. Van de Sandt, ibid., with respect to Matthew, James, and the Didache, "the correspondence in perspective . . . results from their common orientation on a section of the Jewish Two Ways that is best preserved in Didache 3:1–6."

is lacking the liturgical life and counsel prominent in the Didache. James is fundamentally a theocratic tractate on faith and ethics. This tractate or instructional exhortation is substantially influenced by Hellenistic ethics and principles. One is stuck with the level of philosophical sophistication in this short work. Perhaps we have in James, as Sophie Laws suggested some time ago, the presentation of Jesus as a Hellenistic teacher and ethicist by a "God-Fearer."[10]

The notions and terms from James that would punctuate this level of philosophical sophistication is a long list. In short there is much this dense text has in common with Stoic traits of the Roman period. An emphasis on ethics is a feature of Stoicism put in bold relief when we come to the Roman period, as Gretchen Reydams-Schils has shown again quite recently with considerable force.[11] The God of James's Letter is construed in Stoic terms and notions common to the Second Sophistic.[12] The religious language of James in, for example, 1:26–27 and elsewhere is at home in the Roman religious milieu of the cities of Greece or Anatolia. Eschatological notions here are less apocalyptic and imagery much more like the Stoic notion of life in the next realm and epoch (1:17–18). The perfect law (of liberty) is the language of the Stoicism that had gained substantial popularity and accessibility in the Roman period (1:25; 2:12). Liberty, love, and ethics had coalesced in Stoic thought by our period, but was a notion firmly grounded in Stoic thought from the outset. The city is held together by a common commitment of its citizens to one another, and the order of the polis by an ethic that conflated love and liberty.[13]

In concrete terms we see again possible tension over pretention and economic diversity in the letter. This James shares with the Didache. Those who are rich have provoked dissention. The theme is prominent enough that one wonders if this tension in fact constitutes the occasion of the Epistle? Humility is a trait of members that comes close to being a *sine qua non* for the group: "Distinctions are not made among yourselves" (2:4, 9). Quarrels and divisions are referred to explicitly in the letter (e.g., in 4:1). Trials or tests are part of their thought-world. These are welcome insofar as they cultivate the pivotal trait of ὑπομονή and finally τέλειος. Monotheism alone seems to mean little (2:19). Proper ethics and actions along with trust/belief is what make a difference. I should think to a moderately educated or engaged Roman thinker or speaker this would make

---

10. Sophie Laws, *A Commentary on the Epistle of James* (San Francisco: Harper & Row, 1980), 37.

11. *The Roman Stoics: Self, Responsibility, and Affection* (Chicago: University of Chicago Press, 2005).

12. Demonstrated fully by Matt A. Jackson-McCabe, *Logos and Law in the Letter of James: The Law of Nature, the Law of Moses, the Law of Freedom* (NovTSup 100; Leiden: Brill, 2001).

13. Developed by Malcolm Schofield in *The Stoic Idea of the City* (Cambridge: Cambridge University Press, 1991), 22–55. Zeno himself stressed this connection according to later sources.

perfect sense. True or right *reason* leads to perfection (Seneca, *Ep.* 124.14–15). Here πίστις, appropriately enough, plays the role of reason in the development or evolution of the believer. Concern for the common good and to live without distinction were prominent Roman Stoic beliefs that James would celebrate with the likes of Cicero, Epictetus, or Seneca. "We were all born under the law and derive the principles from nature that all ought to obey and follow, that one's advantage should be the common advantage which is in turn yours as well" (Cicero, *Off.* 3.52). James stresses the health and commonwealth of the community based on πίστις. James is its own Jewish-Stoic *community of reason* (Cicero, *Fin.* 3.64).

I take James's address to the Diaspora seriously. I cannot see how συναγωγή in 2:2 refers to anything but a Diaspora community. The analogies drawn from Abraham and Rahab in chapter 2 signal for us that this is a Jewish Diaspora community from the early Roman period. Notions of *pronoia*, the Decalogue, and the by-now well-entrenched notion of the Diaspora community as a *synagogue* all point to a Greco-Roman Jewish Diaspora group. His is a Jewish community that has little to do with the issues characterizing Palestinian communities in the post-70 period, and still less to do with the Judaism that takes shape slowly after Bar Kokhba. James's own community represents a type of Judaism which found certain Greek philosophical notions quite compatible with their understanding of Jewish history and whatever Jesus came to accomplish. They would have lived around and among other Jewish groups with little distinction and disturbance.[14]

But notions like "the implanted word," "the law liberty," the "shadow of turning," and even the notion of πίστις in James all place the text squarely in the Roman Stoic cultural and philosophical milieu. And this means that he has a lot to talk about when we consider someone like Philo of Alexandria or what we know of the Jews from Sardis for example.[15] These Greco-Roman Diaspora communities remain a fascinating but far too under-explored a part of the history of Judaism in this period. James would be a voice that fits quite well on the map of these Greco-Roman diaspora communities. We could call him Christian too by virtue of the opening line of the first two chapters, but little else.

As we look at the history of the development of texts and communities such as Matthew, the Didache, and James I think we are wisest to place our bets on James in terms of survival and longevity. Matthew was extinguished or re-absorbed back into a proto-Rabbinic community that for a time tolerated the emphasis on Jesus. Except for the preservation of the liturgies, the Didache leads to a cul-de-sac in the history of Christian development. It seems to me James had

---

14. Matt Jackson-McCabe, "The Messiah Jesus in the Mythic World of James," *JBL* 122 (2003): 725.

15. J. A. Overman and R. S. MacLennan, eds., *Diaspora Jews and Judaism: Essays in Honor of and in Dialogue with A. Thomas Kraabel* (South Florida Studies in the History of Judaism 41; Atlanta: Scholars Press, 1992).

the best run. These Greco-Roman Diaspora communities lasted a very long time. But in the end what preserved James was what preserved Christianity as well. The merging of fundamental Greco-Roman philosophical and political notions with a "community of reason" provided for the survival of a number of faith communities and ultimately led to the indistinguishable coalescing of Athens and Jerusalem.

While strikingly different in tone, language, philosophical orientation, and certainly setting and purpose, we do find James employing the same ancient Two Ways tradition utilized by Matthew and Didache—two texts with which he otherwise has very little in common. Yet again we see this influential, early tradition being applied and transformed in a manner that makes perfect sense for James's setting. The extension of ethical mandates to attitudes and dispositions not surprisingly also is at home in the emerging Stoic ethic of the early Roman period and Second Sophistic.

In 1:14–20 and 4:1–4, but especially 2:8–11, we find allusion to this earlier Jewish tradition. Of course in the hands of the author of James one need not think of this as a "Jewish" tradition any longer. On the contrary, it is a tradition that Roman readers would identify as in consonance with the dominant ethical formulations of the day. The connection between love, freedom, and the life of the polis was explicit in Stoic thinking from the time of Zeno and that never changed. Roman Stoicism focused on ethics. From Zeno's formulation of the ideal city where love ruled, Roman Stoics developed a code of ethics that would have found much in common in the two traditions.[16] Or as Cicero said, "those who have law in common have justice in common. And those who have these things in common must be held to belong to the same commonwealth (*civitas*)" (*Leg.* 1.23). Clement of Alexandria (*Strom.* 4 26) reinforces this common acceptance of Stoicism as a fundamentally ethical framework for the life and prospering of a city. "The Stoics say the Universe is in the proper sense a city, but that those here on earth are not—they are called cities, but are not really. For a city or a people is something morally good, an organization or group administered by law which exhibits refinement (ἀστεῖον)."[17]

4. Conclusion

When we view the three texts under review here, we do indeed find a shared interest, commitment, and outlook on law and ethics. That ethical framework can justifiably, in notable instances, be traced to an early independent tradition that we have referred to as "the Two Ways." Was this early Jewish tradition the foundation of Jesus's own ethic and therefore embedded in an amalgam of early

---

16. Moses Hadas, *The Stoic Philosophy of Seneca* (New York: Norton, 1958), 22, 26.

17. Clement cited in Schofield, *The Stoic Idea of the City*, 24.

Jewish, Christian, Jewish-Christian and finally Jewish-Christian-Stoic texts and communities? Such an assertion seems plausible, though equally unverifiable. What we do see in this early tradition is an impressive, widespread embrace of the basic tenants of this ethic. And at the same time we see an adaptability and applicability for this approach to law and ethics that found a home across the early Roman world in an extraordinary range of communities.

The popular and oft-relied-upon ethical tradition of the Two Ways found resonance in early Christian, Jewish, and Roman communities across the Greek East. This tradition could be claimed and owned by a broad range of religious and cultural contexts. This speaks to the strength and reason underlying this tradition. Its adoption across a wide range of communities of the early Roman world, however, contributes yet further to our perception of a quite fluid and finally wonderfully messy picture of Jews, Christians and Romans mixing together. While they may have been able to determine the difference between the three, in this instance, we cannot.

THE LOVE COMMAND IN MATTHEW, JAMES,
AND THE DIDACHE

Matthias Konradt

As is well-known, the fundamental importance of the love command is
not an exclusive feature of Jewish Christianity, as, for example, represented by
the Gospel of Matthew, but is a *common* trait in Early Christianity.[1] In dealing with the question whether the Gospel of Matthew, the Epistle of James, and
the Didache represent one and the same religious milieu, it therefore does not
seem possible to identify a common milieu of Matthew, James, and the Didache
through, metaphorically speaking, "surface mining" by considering the topic
of neighborly love. Moreover, a thorough analysis of the relationship between
Matthew, James, and the Didache[2] would have to take the *entire* writings into
account. Thus, I have to confine myself to giving an overview of the relevance,
meaning, and thematic contexts of applications of the love command in the three

---

1. See in the synoptic tradition Mark 12:31; Luke 10:27; in Johannine literature John
13:34–35; 15:12–13, 17; 1 John *passim*; in Pauline and Deuteropauline letters Rom 12:9; 13:9–
10; 1 Cor 8:1–3; 13; Gal 5:14; 1 Thess 4:9; Col 3:14; see moreover Jas 2:8; 1 Pet 1:22; 2:17; 4:8; *1
Clem.* 49.1–50.7; *Sib. Or.* 8.481. I thank Greta Konradt, Delia Richner and Esther Schläpfer for
their assistance.

2. With regard to the relationship between Matthew and the Didache, most, although not
all, scholars now tend to postulate independence. See, e.g., the discussion in Aaron Milavec,
"Synoptic Tradition in the *Didache* Revisited," *JECS* 11 (2003): 443–80 (with references to
literature in nn. 1–13). For the dependence of the Didache on Matthew's Gospel, see, e.g.,
Klaus Wengst, *Didache (Apostellehre), Barnabasbrief, Zweiter Klemensbrief, Schrift an Diognet*
(Schriften des Urchristentums 2; Darmstadt: Wissenschaftliche Buchgesellschaft, 1984), 24–30.
Recently Alan J. P. Garrow, *The Gospel of Matthew's Dependence on the* Didache (JSNTSup
254; London: T&T Clark, 2004) argued that Matthew is dependent on (a previous form of)
the Didache, not the Didache on Matthew. For a critical evaluation of Garrow's approach, see
the review of Garrow's monograph by Jens Schröter in *TLZ* 131 (2006): 997–99. For the relationship of Matthew and James see the discussion in Matthias Konradt, "Der Jakobusbrief im
frühchristlichen Kontext: Überlegungen zum traditionsgeschichtlichen Verhältnis des Jakobusbriefes zur Jesusüberlieferung, zur paulinischen Tradition und zum 1Petr," in *The Catholic
Epistles and the Tradition* (ed. J. Schlosser; BETL 176; Leuven: Peeters, 2004), 190–207.

writings. For that purpose, I will try to point out some convergences and congruencies in the reception of the topic of neighborly love. I will close with some preliminary remarks on the question whether Matthew, James, and the Didache can be grouped together as representatives of the same milieu.

1. LOVE OF ONE'S NEIGHBOR IN THE GOSPEL OF MATTHEW

Matthew explicitly refers to the love command no fewer than three times in his Gospel (5:43; 19:19; 22:39). In the first occurrence in 5:43 (the last antithesis), the quotation of Lev 19:18 is incomplete—"like yourself" is missing—and there is the addition of "you shall hate your enemy." As I have argued elsewhere,[3] the so-called antitheses are not directed against the Torah itself,[4] but against its interpretation by the scribes and Pharisees.[5] In other words, in the theses, Matthew quotes the Torah as it is insufficiently interpreted by the scribes and Pharisees. Due to this "distorted" understanding, the "righteousness" of the scribes and Pharisees does not suffice for entering the kingdom of Heaven (5:20), whereas the better righteousness expected from the disciples is based on Jesus's interpretation of the Torah, which develops its full and deepest meaning. The last antithesis clearly demonstrates this approach. In his other two citations of the love command (Matt 19:19; 22:39), Matthew refers to it as a major commandment of the Torah without feeling bound to give any further explanation. Therefore, it is obvious that for Matthew himself, the opposition of neighbor and enemy that is

---

3. See Matthias Konradt, "Die vollkommene Erfüllung der Tora und der Konflikt mit den Pharisäern im Matthäusevangelium," in *Das Gesetz im frühen Judentum und im Neuen Testament* (ed. D. Sänger and M. Konradt; NTOA/SUNT 57; Göttingen: Vandenhoeck & Ruprecht, 2006), 134–41.

4. For the opposite thesis, see, e.g., Ingo Broer, *Freiheit vom Gesetz und Radikalisierung des Gesetzes: Ein Beitrag zur Theologie des Evangelisten Matthäus* (SBS 98; Stuttgart: Verlag Katholisches Bibelwerk, 1980), 75–81; Ulrich Luz, *Das Evangelium nach Matthäus (Mt 1–7)* (5th ed.; EKKNT 1/1; Düsseldorf: Benziger, 2002), 330; Hans-Joachim Eckstein, "Die Weisung Jesu Christi und die Tora des Mose nach dem Matthäusevangelium," in *Jesus Christus als die Mitte der Schrift: Studien zur Hermeneutik des Evangeliums* (ed. C. Landmesser *et al.*; BZNW 86; Berlin: de Gruyter, 1997), 396–403; Karl-Wilhelm Niebuhr, "Die Antithesen des Matthäus: Jesus als Toralehrer und die frühjüdische weisheitlich geprägte Torarezeption," in *Gedenkt an das Wort* (ed. C. Kähler *et al.*; Leipzig: Evangelische Verlagsanstalt, 1999), 176–77.

5. For this approach, see Christoph Burchard, "Versuch, das Thema der Bergpredigt zu finden," in *Studien zur Theologie, Sprache und Umwelt des Neuen Testaments* (ed. D. Sänger; WUNT 107; Tübingen: Mohr Siebeck, 1998), 40–44; Christian Dietzfelbinger, "Die Antithesen der Bergpredigt im Verständnis des Matthäus," *ZNW* 70 (1979): 3; Heinz-Wolfgang Kuhn, "Das Liebesgebot Jesu als Tora und als Evangelium: Zur Feindesliebe und zur christlichen und jüdischen Auslegung der Bergpredigt," in *Vom Urchristentum zu Jesus* (ed. H. Frankemölle *et al.*; Freiburg: Herder, 1989), 213–18; J. Daryl Charles, "Garnishing with the 'Greater Righteousness': The Disciple's Relationship to the Law (Matthew 5:17–20)," *BBR* 12 (2002): 8.

evident in 5:43 is not part of the commandment itself, but is only introduced to it by false interpretation. The Matthean Jesus liberates the commandment from its restrictive interpretation, which is polemically assigned to the Pharisees, and thereby points out its true significance.

There is no indication that this criticized restriction is to be seen along the lines of national or ethnic boundaries. As 5:46 suggests, it is a rather ordinary-ethical common sense that has to be overcome, a restriction of love to friends according to the principle of mutuality.[6] In other words, Matt 5:43 is a variation of the vulgar-ethical maxim "to benefit his friends and harm his enemies" (Plato, *Menon* 71e)[7] in biblical language.[8] Against this background, the Matthean Jesus demands that the love command should be followed without any limitation; it is valid even with regard to the enemy. Thus, the Matthean Jesus radicalizes the love command by claiming that loving care for the well-being of others is entirely independent of how the other acts towards oneself.

Matthew substantiates this claim with the argument of conformity: Acting indiscriminately to all people conforms to the loving kindness of the creator who "makes his sun rise on the evil and on the good" (5:45). In the overall context of Matt 5, loving one's enemy takes up the blessing of the peacemakers in 5:9, as is indicated by the promise that the peacemakers as well as those who love their enemies will be sons of God.[9] Thus, love of one's enemy is understood as an act of peacemaking,[10] and due to the fundamental nature of the requirement in Matt 5:44, this appears as a principal demand to reshape social relations by countercultural behavior, which overcomes the principle of retribution according to

---

6. See the discussion in Matthias Konradt: ". . . 'damit ihr Söhne eures Vaters im Himmel werdet': Erwägungen zur 'Logik' von Gewaltverzicht und Feindesliebe in Mt 5,38–48," in *Gewalt wahrnehmen – von Gewalt heilen: Theologische und religionswissenschaftliche Perspektiven* (ed. W. Dietrich and W. Lienemann; Stuttgart: Kohlhammer, 2004), 84–85.

7. See also Plato, *Resp.* 332e; 336a ("'Do you know whose view I think it is,' I said, 'that it's right to help one's friend and harm one's enemies?'"); Epictetus, *Diatr.* II 14.18 (οἶδας τὸν εὖ ποιοῦντα ἀντευποιῆσαι καὶ τὸν κακῶς ποιοῦντα κακῶς ποιῆσαι); Isocrates, *Demon.* 29 ("Bestow your favors on the good. . . . If you benefit bad men, you will have the same reward as those who feed stray dogs; for these snarl alike at those who give them food and at the passing stranger."), as well as Ps.-Phoc. 80 on the one hand ("It is proper to surpass [your] benefactors with still more [benefactions]."), and 152 on the other ("Do no good to a bad man; it is like sowing into the sea."). For other early Jewish writings see, e.g., Tob 4:17.

8. See William Klassen, *Love of Enemies: The Way to Peace* (Philadelphia: Fortress, 1984), 84; Gordon M. Zerbe, *Non-Retaliation in Early Jewish and New Testament Texts: Ethical Themes in Social Contexts* (JSPSup 13; Sheffield: JSOT Press, 1993), 206.

9. For this connection see Dieter Lührmann, "Liebet eure Feinde (Lk 6,27–36; Mt 5,39–48)," *ZTK* 69 (1972): 414–15 and Rudolf Schnackenburg, "Die Seligpreisung der Friedensstifter (Mt 5,9) im matthäischen Kontext," *BZ* NF 26 (1982): 167–70.

10. See Konradt, "Erwägungen zur 'Logik' von Gewaltverzicht und Feindesliebe," 89.

which love is answered by love and hate by hate. Instead, hate shall be overcome by love.

It is important to take into consideration that, to some extent, the command to love one's enemy in Matt 5 takes up the love command from its original context in Lev 19, where the phrase primarily addresses the question of how one shall deal with a "personal enemy."[11] One shall not hate, but reprove the neighbor. One shall not take vengeance, but shall love one's neighbor as oneself. This original application is further elaborated in the *Testaments of the Twelve Patriarchs*, where the story of Joseph, who does not take vengeance on his brothers but rather cares for them in Egypt, and the love command mutually interpret each other.[12] If one compares this to Matt 5, one can of course call attention to the fact that in Lev 19 and the *Testaments* the application of love of one's personal enemy does not actually exceed the Jewish community, whereas the interpretation in Matt 5 is of a more principal nature. Love of one's enemy is not confined to persons within the community who have acted improperly towards oneself, but it also refers to outsiders. On the other hand, no principal confinement of the love command to the Jewish community appears in Lev 19 or in the *Testaments*, but rather a focus on the concrete ethical need of the community.[13] Of greater importance is the fact that Matt 5 can be read as a development of an original aspect of the love command in the Torah and in early Jewish tradition.[14]

The second occurrence of the love command in Matthew's Gospel goes back to the redactional hand of the evangelist. In his reply to the rich young man's question on which commandments he has to obey in order to enter the kingdom in Matt 19:18–19, the Matthean Jesus not only quotes the socio-ethical commandments of the decalogue, but the love command as well. In the light of Matt 22:37–40, it is certainly not incorrect to postulate that the love command functions as a summary of the social will of God and thus as a summary of the commandments from the Decalogue, which themselves represent main sentences of the Torah.[15]

---

11. See Hans-Peter Mathys, *Liebe deinen Nächsten wie dich selbst: Untersuchungen zum alttestamentlichen Gebot der Nächstenliebe (Lev 19,18)* (OBO 71; Göttingen: Vandenhoeck & Ruprecht, 1986), 81 and also John Piper, *'Love Your Enemies': Jesus' Love Command in the Synoptic Gospels and in the Early Christian Paraenesis: A History of the Tradition and Interpretation of Its Uses* (SNTSMS 38; Cambridge: Cambridge University Press, 1974), 32.

12. See Matthias Konradt, "Menschen- oder Bruderliebe? Beobachtungen zum Liebesgebot in den Testamenten der Zwölf Patriarchen," *ZNW* 88 (1997): 301–3.

13. See Thomas Söding, *Das Liebesgebot bei Paulus: Die Mahnung zur Agape im Rahmen der paulinischen Ethik* (NTAbh NF 26; Münster: Aschendorff, 1995), 48: "Das Liebesgebot will nicht exklusiv, sondern positiv die Pflichten gegenüber den Mit-Israeliten einschärfen."

14. See Konradt, "Erwägungen zur 'Logik' von Gewaltverzicht und Feindesliebe," 71–77.

15. For the reception of the decalogue in Early Judaism and Early Christianity see Günter Stemberger, "Der Dekalog im frühen Judentum," *Jahrbuch für biblische Theologie* 4 (1989):

In our context, the question whether the insertion of the love command is correlated to the discourse between Jesus and the rich man in verses 20–21 is of crucial importance. The rich man maintains that he has kept all the command-ments quoted by Jesus and asks what he still lacks. Jesus now answers that if he wants to be perfect, he has to sell all his possessions, give them to the poor and follow Jesus. The decisive alternative is whether selling his possessions for the benefit of the poor is an additional requirement,[16] or whether this demand is to be read as an interpretation of the love command with reference to the con-crete life situation of the rich man.[17] In the first case, Jesus would accept the rich man's statement about fulfilling the commandment; in the second case, he would implicitly call it into question: If the rich man will not use his possessions for the benefit of the poor, he would, at least in this special instance, have fallen short of the requirement set out by the love command.

What emphatically speaks for this second option is the fact that Jesus coun-ters the rich man's departure with the statement that it is hard for a rich person to enter the kingdom of heaven (v. 23). This refers back to the opening question about the requirements for receiving eternal life. In Matthew's version, differently from Mark, this initial question is answered by Jesus with an explicit reference to "keeping the commandments" as the entrance requirement. When, at the end of the story, no *prominent* place in heaven, but exactly what he asked for, that is, mere entrance into the kingdom, is denied to the rich man, this implies logi-cally that he has not fulfilled the commandments,[18] at least not in his encounter

---

91–103; Dieter Sänger, "Tora für die Völker: Weisungen der Liebe: Zur Rezeption des Deka-logs im frühen Judentum und Neuen Testament," in *Weisheit, Ethos und Gebot: Weisheits- und Dekalogtraditionen in der Bibel und im frühen Judentum* (ed. H. Graf Reventlow; Biblisch-theologische Studien 43; Neukirchen-Vluyn: Neukirchener Verlag, 2001), 97–146 and Ulrich Kellermann, "Der Dekalog in den Schriften des Frühjudentums: Ein Überblick," in Graf Reven-tlow, ed., *Weisheit, Ethos und Gebot*, 147–226.

16. See Alexander Sand, *Das Evangelium nach Matthäus* (RNT; Regensburg: Pustet, 1986), 396 and also Ulrich Luck, *Das Evangelium nach Matthäus* (ZBK NT 1; Zürich: Theologischer Verlag, 1993), 215–17.

17. See Hubert Meisinger, *Liebesgebot und Altruismusforschung: Ein exegetischer Beitrag zum Dialog zwischen Theologie und Naturwissenschaft* (NTOA 33; Göttingen: Vandenhoeck & Ruprecht, 1996), 40–41; Martin Meiser, "Vollkommenheit in Qumran und im Matthäusevan-gelium," in *Kirche und Volk Gottes* (ed. Martin Karrer *et al.*; Neukirchen-Vluyn: Neukirchener Verlag, 2000), 198; Roland Deines, *Die Gerechtigkeit der Tora im Reich des Messias: Mt 5,13–20 als Schlüsseltext der matthäischen Theologie* (WUNT 177; Tübingen: Mohr Siebeck, 2005), 391: "Indem er [sc. der reiche Jüngling, M.K.] seinen Besitz nicht zu verkaufen und zu verteilen vermag, gesteht er ein, dass er eben seinen Nächsten nicht so liebt wie sich selbst."

18. See E. Yarnold, "Τέλειος in St. Matthew's Gospel," in *Studia Evangelica* (ed. F. L. Cross; vol. 4; TU 102; Berlin: Akademie-Verlag, 1968), 271. See also the contribution by Wim Weren to this volume.

with Jesus. And this means that, contrary to Mark's version,[19] Jesus's demand that he should sell his possessions for the benefit of the poor has to be understood as Jesus's unfolding of the meaning of the love command for the young man in his specific life situation. Furthermore, following Jesus and fulfilling the commandments are not to be viewed as separate items, but fulfilling the commandments according to Jesus's interpretation is an integral part of following him.[20]

This interpretation can be substantiated by including the motif of perfection in Matt 19:21. There are only two occurrences of the adjective "perfect" in Matthew's Gospel; the other is in 5:48. Both are redactional, and both occur in the context of the love command. This is certainly not accidental. In both sections, Matthew links perfection to the fulfillment of the love command in its true and deepest sense. Perfect love does not permit any limitation of the objects of love, and it embraces the generous (or even total) use of one's possessions for the benefit of the poor. The insertion of the love command in 19:19 certainly does not only pursue the purpose of pointing to the supreme position of the love command as a summary even of the commandments from the decalogue; predominantly, this insertion is necessary for Matthew because he wants to present the demand to charitably use one's possessions, which he found in Mark, as an application of the Old Testament love command. To put it another way, in the Matthean version, Jesus's request appears as an authentic interpretation of what it means to live in accordance with the Torah.

Although the concrete application of the love command in Matt 19:16–22 cannot be regarded as a general requirement irrespective of one's life situation, it also cannot be declared meaningless for the community by referring to the specific situation of the rich young man in his encounter with the earthly Jesus. Rather, it points to a community that is characterized by an intensive care for the poor. The context of such behavior is the expectation of the near kingdom, which results in a reversal of values. Because one cannot serve two masters at the same time, God *and* Mammon (see 6:24), every disciple must primarily strive for the kingdom of God and his righteousness (6:33).

While Matt 5:43–48 is in line with the original context of the love command in Lev 19:17–18 as it is developed in the *T. 12 Patr.* with regard to the figure of Joseph, Matt 19:16–22 follows a second option of application, namely, charitable love, as it appears in the *T. 12 Patr.*, namely, in the *Testament(s) of Issachar* (and

---

19. See Hermut Löhr, "Jesus und der Nomos aus der Sicht des entstehenden Christentums: Zum Jesus-Bild im ersten Jahrhundert n. Chr. und zu unserem Jesus-Bild," in *Der historische Jesus: Tendenzen und Perspektiven der gegenwärtigen Forschung* (ed. Jens Schröter and Ralph Brucker; BZNW 114; Berlin: de Gruyter, 2002), 346.

20. For a different interpretation see Rudolf Hoppe, "Vollkommenheit bei Matthäus als theologische Aussage," in *Salz der Erde – Licht der Welt: Exegetische Studien zum Matthäusevangelium* (ed. L. Oberlinner and P. Fiedler; Stuttgart: Katholisches Bibelwerk, 1991), 159–64.

Zebulon).[21] This analogy presents exemplary evidence that Matthew is firmly rooted in early Jewish Torah paraenesis. At the same time, the aspect of radicalization, which has often been mentioned, cannot be overlooked, with regard either to Matt 5 or to Matt 19.

The fact that "perfection" is linked with the fulfillment of the love command in Matthew's Gospel points to its central position in Matthew's understanding of the law as it is explicitly stated in 22:34–40. With regard to the position attributed to love of one's neighbor, one important feature of the Matthean version is that in Jesus's answer to the question of the Pharisaic lawyer, loving one's neighbor is explicitly assessed as equivalent to love of God.[22] This directly corresponds to Matthew's emphasis on mercy over against sacrifices, which he states twice by citing Hos 6:6 (Matt 9:13; 12:7). On the whole, Matthew's focus on the social will of God (see Jas 1:26–27) is of utmost importance in his story of Jesus.

This focus is embedded in the sharp conflict between Jesus and the Pharisees with their allegedly one-sided emphasis on ritual norms, at least as Matthew presents it. In this light, it becomes understandable why Matthew changed the friendly atmosphere of the Marcan pericope to a conflict scene in which a *Pharisaic* lawyer approaches Jesus to *test* him in the negative sense of Matt 22:15 "to entrap him in his words." The Pharisaic lawyer tries to elicit an explicit statement from Jesus, which proves that—by emphasizing mercy to men—he does not give adequate (that is, highest) priority to honoring God.[23] Although Jesus joins the Jewish consensus[24] in his answer by quoting Deut 6:5 as the greatest commandment, he then elevates the love command to an equal level. He thereby interprets the Jewish consensus with regard to his emphasis on the merciful care for one's neighbor and, at the same time, indicates that love to God cannot be realized sufficiently by a rigorous observance of purity or Sabbath regulations or by extensifying tithing, but only by doing God's social will. Surely, love of God and love of one's neighbor cannot be equated with one another,[25] but neither can they be played off against one another: Love of one's neighbor is a central and indispensable element of love of God.

In v. 40, Matthew adds: "On these two commandments hang all the law and the prophets." In the Matthean context, this does not mean an actual reduction

21. See especially *T. Iss.* 5.2 and *T. Zeb.* 5.1–8.3.

22. Christoph Burchard, "Das doppelte Liebesgebot in der frühen christlichen Überlieferung," in *Studien zur Theologie, Sprache und Umwelt des Neuen Testaments* (ed. D. Sänger; WUNT 107; Tübingen: Mohr Siebeck, 1998), 25 aptly calls this a "Gleichordnung trotz Differenz."

23. For this interpretation see Konradt, "Die vollkommene Erfüllung der Tora," 146–49.

24. See *Let. Aris.* 132; Ps.-Phoc. 8; Philo, *Decal.* 65; Josephus, *Ag. Ap.* 2.190.

25. See Ulrich Luz, "Überlegungen zum Verhältnis zwischen Liebe zu Gott und Liebe zum Nächsten (Mt 22,34–40)," in *Der lebendige Gott: Studien zur Theologie des Neuen Testaments* (ed. T. Söding; Münster: Aschendorff, 1996), 147.

of the law to the double love commandment,[26] as the coordination of commandments from the decalogue and the love command in Matt 19:18–19 confirms
with regard to loving one's neighbor: the social commandments from the decalogue unfold the love command.

To summarize, two important fields of application of the love command
emerge, namely, the relationship to an enemy, or more specifically, any enemy,
and charitable love for the benefit of the poor. In both cases, Matthew radicalized
the demand and linked the love command with the motif of perfection. Perfect
love in its Matthean understanding is not just an intensification of normal cultural behavior but overcomes the principle of mutuality, and it is embedded in a
redefinition of social values with regard to one's possessions.

2. Love of One's Neighbor in the Epistle of James

The love command is formally quoted in Jas 2:8: "If you really fulfill the royal
law according to the Scripture, 'You shall love your neighbor as yourself,' you
do well." The function of the love command in James is disputed. Is it, contrary
for example to Paul, just one commandment among the others, even if it might
be of more importance than others?[27] Or does it function as a summary of the
law or at least of its social part?[28] Or does it even function as its hermeneutical
center?[29] The decisive argument for a summarizing function (as in Matthew) is
that elsewhere in James νόμος always means the law as a whole, but never only
a single commandment (Jas 1:25; 2:9–12; 4:11). This should then also be valid
for Jas 2:8. In other words, the love command is not just a single commandment
among others, even if it might have a more prominent rank. Rather, the entire
law is called "royal" in Jas 2:8, and through love the entire law is fulfilled. Again
as in Matthew, this is not to be understood as a reduction of the law to the love

---

26. Against Deines, *Die Gerechtigkeit der Tora*, 400.

27. See, e.g., Martin Dibelius, *Der Brief des Jakobus* (ed. F. Hahn; 12th ed.; KEK 15;
Göttingen: Vandenhoeck & Ruprecht, 1984), 177; Martina Ludwig, *Wort als Gesetz: Eine
Untersuchung zum Verständnis von "Wort" und "Gesetz" in israelitisch-frühjüdischen und neu-
testamentlichen Schriften: Gleichzeitig ein Beitrag zur Theologie des Jakobusbriefes* (Europäische
Hochschulschriften, Reihe 23, Theologie 502; Frankfurt a.M.: Peter Lang, 1994), 174–75.

28. See Rudolf Hoppe, *Der theologische Hintergrund des Jakobusbriefes* (2nd ed.; FB 28;
Würzburg: Echter, 1985), 88–89; Ulrich Luck, "Die Theologie des Jakobusbriefes," *ZTK* 81
(1984): 17; Matthias Konradt, *Christliche Existenz nach dem Jakobusbrief: Eine Studie zu seiner
soteriologischen und ethischen Konzeption* (SUNT 22; Göttingen: Vandenhoeck & Ruprecht,
1998), 184–87.

29. See Martin Klein, *"Ein vollkommenes Werk": Vollkommenheit, Gesetz und Gericht als
theologische Themen des Jakobusbriefes* (BWANT 139; Stuttgart: Kohlhammer, 1995), 148 and
Wiard Popkes, *Der Brief des Jakobus* (THKNT 14; Leipzig: Evangelische Verlagsanstalt, 2001),
174: "Wie auch anderswo im Frühchristentum gilt das Liebesgebot als *norma normans*, als
Kanon des Gesetzes."

command, as the allusion to Lev 19:15 in Jas 2:9 and the quotation of two commandments of the decalogue in Jas 2:11 show. But the love command formulates the basic intention or nature of the law, which is then explicated by other regulations.

With regard to the relationship of 2:8 and 2:9, the summarizing function of the love command implies that the claim that one has fulfilled the love command and, thereby, the law as a whole (2:8) is disproved by showing partiality in one's social interaction with rich and poor people (2:9). In 2:1, James points out the incompatibility of faith in the glory of our Lord Jesus Christ[30] and partiality. The explicit mention of the glory of the exalted Lord relates antithetically to the orientation to worldly glory, so to say, which comes to the fore by showing favoritism towards the rich. In other words, Jas 2:1 calls for a radical invalidation of wealth as a criterion for social status due to faith in the one and only glory of the exalted Lord, in which Christians hope to participate when they receive the "crown of life that God has promised to those who love him" (Jas 1:12). Such a demand implies a total abrogation of the established social order, an inversion of social values that is then spelled out in 2:5–7, where James contrasts negative experiences that Christians had to make with rich people on the one hand with God's election of the poor on the other: "Has not God chosen those who are poor in the eyes of the world to be rich through faith and to inherit the kingdom he promised to those who love him?" (2:5).

In 2:13 James moves from love to mercy. Thus, the love command in James is closely connected with a merciful attitude towards the poor. The importance of merciful, charitable love in James is underlined by Jas 1:27 and 2:15–16. In 1:27, James refers to caring for orphans and widows in their distress when defining true religion. And in 2:15–16, James illustrates worthless practice of religion by referring to a Christian who provides a needy brother or sister with good wishes, but does not take care of their bodily needs. Moreover, for James, mercy does not only mean almsgiving; mercy begins with the respectful attitude towards the poor, as James's example in 2:2–4 illustrates. In other words, alms given condescendingly are not what James has in mind.

The respectful attitude towards the poor called for by James is an expression of his countercultural model of social order with its anti-hierarchical leveling of social positions as a crucial element of the Christian belief system. In this context, love of one's neighbor is neither to be confused with an ethos of friendship between people of equal social rank, nor to be envisioned as a move of the afflu-

---

30. On the difficult construction in Jas 2:1, see Christoph Burchard, "Zu einigen christologischen Stellen des Jakobusbriefes," in *Anfänge der Christologie* (ed. C. Breytenbach and H. Paulsen; Göttingen: Vandenhoeck & Ruprecht, 1991), 354–57.

ent down to the poor, but as behavior among people who—in contradiction with "worldly" standards—*are* of equal rank.[31]

If compared to the Gospel of Matthew, the application of the love command in Jas 2:1–13 shows affinity with Matthew's addition of it in Matt 19:16–22. In both instances the relevance of the love command is spelled out in terms of the attitude towards the poor, and in both instances the claim to (have) fulfill(ed) the commandment (Matt 19:20; Jas 2:8)[32] serves as a foil for unfolding its inmost meaning. Furthermore, this interpretation is embedded in a countercultural model of social life, in which striving for the kingdom of God is regarded as the highest priority. In Jas 2:8, the law is called νόμος βασιλικός. In the immediate context, the phrase refers back to 2:5, where James spoke about the heirs of the kingdom that God promised to those who love him. In this context, the designation of the law as "royal" probably implies that it defines the life order of the kingdom given by God as the king, which is already binding in this world with its different social order for those who wish to inherit the kingdom.[33] In 4:4, James directly contrasts friendship with God and friendship with the world. Traditio-historically, Jas 4:4 seems to be influenced by the Q-logion that Matthew integrated into his Sermon on the Mount in Matt 6:24.[34] Furthermore, the anti-hierarchical impetus of Jas 2 finds a counterpart in Matt 23:8–12. In short, in Matthew and in James, the emphasis on the love command gains its contours in the context of an overall social ethos in which the normal status positions are leveled off[35] and possessions do not qualify as a desirable goal of one's personal aspirations, but are consequently regarded as a means for helping the needy.

After the direct quotation of the love command in Jas 2:8, there is a second passage that is of importance here, namely, 4:11–12. The conspicuous change from "brother" to "neighbor" in 4:12 (2:8 and 4:12 contain the only occurrences of πλησίον in James) suggests that 4:12 intentionally refers back to 2:8 and thus to the love command.[36] This approach can be confirmed by the thematic aspect

---

31. For the combination of love and equality or status indifference see Gerd Theißen, "Nächstenliebe und Egalität: Jak 2,1–13 als Höhepunkt urchristlicher Ethik," in *Der Jakobusbrief: Beiträge zur Rehabilitierung der "strohernen Epistel"* (ed. Petra von Gemünden et al.; Beiträge zum Verstehen der Bibel 3; Münster: Lit, 2003), 124–35.

32. For the interpretation of the conditional clause in Jas 2:8 see Konradt, *Christliche Existenz nach dem Jakobusbrief*, 185–86. See also Theißen, "Nächstenliebe und Egalität," 128.

33. For interpretational options for the phrase νόμος βασιλικός, see Meisinger, *Liebesgebot*, 136–38 and Theißen, "Nächstenliebe und Egalität," 132–34.

34. See Konradt, "Der Jakobusbrief im frühchristlichen Kontext," 194–95.

35. See Meisinger, *Liebesgebot*, 147: "Das Nächstenliebegebot bedeutet für ihn (sc. für Jakobus, M.K.) die Verpflichtung zu egalitärem Verhalten. . . . Reiche und Arme sollen sich nicht als solche, sondern als Nächste, die ihren Nächsten lieben, begegnen. Statusunterschiede soll es innerhalb der Gemeinde nicht geben."

36. See, e.g., Dibelius, *Der Brief des Jakobus*, 273; Ralph P. Martin, *James* (WBC 48; Waco, Tex.: Word Books, 1988), 163.

treated in 4:11–12. καταλαλεῖν and κρίνειν are not synonymous, but their juxtaposition indicates that they refer to related aspects. The phrase κρίνειν τὸν ἀδελφόν, which is probably influenced by the Jesus saying in Matt 7:1; Luke 6:37, refers to an incorrect way of dealing with sins of others. In this context, καταλαλεῖν does not mean slander, but more generally "to tell bad things about another person" (see, e.g., Num 12:8; 21:5; Ps 77:19 [LXX]).[37] Instead of fraternal correction in a private conversation, as outlined in Matt 18:15, the sin committed by the other is made public. This does not only take up the original context of the love command in Lev 19:17–18, but can also be contextualized by its reception in early Judaism, especially again in the *T. 12 Patr.* According to the *Testament of Gad* 4.2–3, hatred (τὸ μῖσος) "does not want to hear the words of his [sc. God's] commandments concerning the love of one's neighbor, and it sins against God. For if a brother stumbles, it wants to proclaim it immediately to all men and it urges that he should be judged for it. . . ."[38] James 4:11–12 picks up this application of the love command. Those who judge others because of their sins and try to put someone in an unfavorable light by talking about his transgressions in public, transgress the law themselves because they do not act according to the love command. Interpreted in this way, the compositional placement of the admonition in 4:11–12 makes good sense: In 4:7–10 James called upon the *sinners* to repent; in 4:11–12, he added an admonition to the *brothers* on how to treat the sinners.

To summarize: When James's reception of the love command is compared to Matthew's, a significant overlap can be detected. First of all, differently from Paul and John, Matthew and James lack an explicit christological argument for love, e.g., with reference to Jesus's death. When Matthew and James speak of love, the natural point of reference for them is the Old Testament love command, to which prominent status is given in both writings. What is implied in the references to the love command in Jas 2:8 and in Matt 19:19 is explicitly stated in Matt 22:34–40: The love command functions as a summarizing statement of God's social will. In both writings, this does not mean a reduction of the law to the love command, but the love command is unfolded by other regulations, whereby the second table of the decalogue is of major importance in both writings. Again, this is a phenomenon that can also be found in early Jewish writings.[39] Furthermore, the assignment of highest status to the love command is linked with similar thematic fields of its concrete application in James and Matthew: Matt 19:16–22 and Jas 2:1–13 similarly unfold the requirement of the love command in the face of its claimed fulfillment. In both cases, the problem of wealth plays an important

---

37. See also the juxtaposition of καταλαλεῖν and ψέγειν βίον ἀνθρώπου in *T. Iss.* 3.4.

38. See also the reception of Lev 19:17–18 in 1QS V, 24–VI, 1 and the shorter version in 4Q258 1 II, 4.

39. See the literature in n. 15.

role, and there is a close connection of love and mercy in Matthew and James. Moreover, Jas 4:11–12 can at least remotely be compared to the love of enemy in Matt 5: What Matt 5 states in a programmatic way is applied to a congregational setting in Jas 4. The topic of forgiveness is of great importance in Matthew's Gospel.[40] It is not directly connected with the love command anywhere. But if the explicit prominent status of the love command in Matthew's Gospel is taken into account, one can ask whether Matthew's emphasis on forgiveness might be regarded as an expression of the love command's central position. Moreover, to love one's enemy certainly includes the willingness to forgive. At any rate, the two main applications of the love command found in the *T. 12 Patr.*, which can be regarded as exemplary evidence for the developments in Early Jewish Torah paraenesis, reappear in James: forgiving love and charitable love. And this demonstrates how firmly James is embedded in Early Jewish Torah interpretation, which is also a characteristic of Matthew's Gospel.

3. The Love Command in the Didache

As is well-known, in the Didache's version of the Two Ways-instruction, the description of the "way of life," is introduced by the double love command plus the Golden Rule in its negative formulation as a summary statement of God' will (1:2). This feature distinguishes Didache from the related passage in the Epistle of Barnabas, but, as the *Doctrina apostolorum*,[41] the *Canons of the Holy Apostles*[42] and the *Epitome of the Canons*[43] suggest, it was already a feature of the recension of the Two Ways-instruction used by the didachist,[44] which—with Niederwimmer's designation—I will call recension C.[45] The combination of the admonitions to love God and one's brother or neighbor and their function as a summary of God's will are features that appear in Jewish sources prior to the emergence of Christianity.[46] However, the direct citation of the two love commands combined with their designation as πρῶτον and δεύτερον is evidenced only in Christian sources, namely, in Mark 12:29, 31 and Matt 22:38–39. This might be taken as—at

---

40. See esp. Matt 1:21; 6:14–15; 9:2–13; 18:21–35; 26:28.

41. See Joseph Schlecht, *Doctrina XII apostolorum, Die Apostellehre in der Liturgie der katholischen Kirche* (Freiburg i.Br.: Herder, 1901), 101, 105–6.

42. See Theodor Schermann, *Die allgemeine Kirchenordnung, frühchristliche Liturgien und kirchliche Überlieferung 1: Die allgemeine Kirchenordnung des zweiten Jahrhunderts* (Studien zur Geschichte und Kultur des Altertums, Supplement 3; Paderborn: Schöningh, 1914), 15.

43. See Theodor Schermann, *Eine Elfapostelmoral oder die X-Rezension der „beiden Wege"* (Veröffentlichungen aus dem Kirchenhistorischen Seminar München 2/2; München: Lentner'schen Buchhandlung, 1903), 16.

44. See Kurt Niederwimmer, *Die Didache* (Kommentar zu den Apostolischen Vätern 1; Vandenhoeck & Ruprecht, 1989), 91.

45. Niederwimmer, *Die Didache*, 61–63.

46. See esp. *T. Iss.* 5.2; 7.6; *T. Dan* 5.3; *T. Jos.* 11.1; *T. Benj.* 3.3 and Philo, *Spec. Laws* 2.63.

least—tentative evidence that this recension stems from a Jewish *Christian* or *Christian* Jewish circle.[47]

The juxtaposition of the double-love command with the Golden Rule in Did. 1:2 is of special interest if compared to Matthew, because *both* function as summary statements of the law also in Matthew. Whereas Matt 22:40 defines that the entire law and the prophets hang on the two love commands, the reference to the Golden Rule in 7:12 is commented upon by the statement, "for this is the law and the prophets." At this point, there is no evidence in favor of direct dependence of one source on the other.[48] Like Luke, Matthew cites the Golden Rule in its positive formulation, which goes back to the Saying Source, whereas in Did. 1:2 the negative formulation appears.[49] But one might ask whether Matthew's assignment of a summarizing function to the Golden Rule in 7:12 as well as to the double love command in 22:40 might be inspired by a combination of both as it is evidenced by recension C.[50] In other words, Did. 1:2 might be a witness of a tradition that also influenced Matthew. At any rate, Matthew's remark about the *equal* rank of the command to love one's neighbor in 22:39 remains his own individual contribution, which has no counterpart in Did. 1:2.

The plausibility of a common tradition is underlined by the fact that in the pre-Didache recension of the Two Ways-instruction, the explication of the programmatic opening references to the double love command and the Golden Rule

---

47. See Jonathan Draper, "The Jesus Tradition in the Didache," in *The Jesus Tradition Outside the Gospels* (ed. David Wenham; Gospel Perspectives 5; Sheffield: JSOT Press, 1985), 272; John S. Kloppenborg, "The Transformation of the Moral Exhortation in *Didache* 1–5," in *The* Didache *in Context: Essays on Its Text, History and Transmission* (ed. C. N. Jefford; NovTSup 78; Leiden: Brill, 1995), 98; Niederwimmer, *Die Didache*, 91. For a different position see Huub van de Sandt and David Flusser, *The Didache: Its Jewish Sources and its Place in Early Judaism and Christianity* (CRINT 3/5; Assen: Van Gorcum, 2002), 158, n. 58.

48. Against this, Christopher M. Tuckett, "Synoptic Tradition in the Didache," in *The* Didache *in Modern Research* (ed. J. Draper; AGJU 37; Leiden: Brill, 1996), 106–7 favors the dependence of πρῶτον – δεύτερον (Did. 1:2) on Matt 22:38–39. Against Tuckett see Milavec, "Synoptic Tradition in the *Didache* Revisited," 460.

49. Moreover, the command to love God in Did. 1:2 does not follow Deut 6:5, but parallels *Barn.* 19:2 (ἀγαπήσεις τὸν ποιήσαντά σε) and has an analogy in Sir 7:30 (ἐν ὅλῃ δυνάμει ἀγάπησον τὸν ποιήσαντά σε).

50. See Clayton N. Jefford, *The Sayings of Jesus in the Teaching of the Twelve Apostles* (VCSup 11; Leiden: Brill, 1989), 37: The "notation concerning the 'double love commandment' and the Golden Rule as the summation of 'the law and the prophets' appears only here [sc. in Matt 7:12; 22:40, M.K.] in the Gospels, and thus may imply that the Matthean redactor was familiar with a tradition in which the 'double love commandment' and the Golden Rule were recognized as two elements of a single *inclusio* concerning the parameters of the OT law." Jefford concludes: "This lends some support for the position that the Didachist and the Matthean redactor are dependent upon a common tradition of scriptural interpretation" (ibid.).

is obviously structured by the influence of the decalogue in Did. 2:2–6.[51] There seems to be a similar relation of the love command and the decalogue in all three writings under discussion here: Matthew, James, and the Didache, or respectively, the pre-Didache-recension. Furthermore, this is complemented by a wide understanding of the Decalogue commandments, which is evidenced for Matthew in Matt 5:21–30 and for the Didache in the τέκνον-sayings in 3:1–6 and can be assumed for James on the basis of the usage of φονεύειν in 4:2.[52]

The love command is taken up in the form of an allusion in Did. 2:7, which shows some reverberations of its original context in Lev 19:17–18. No close relationship to Jas 4:11–12 can be detected here, but at least both documents point to an ongoing reflection of the love command in its original context. This is underlined by several links between the Didache material and the passage in Lev 19:11–18,[53] among them the demand not to show favoritism in Did. 4:3 (see Lev 19:15). This passage from Lev 19 also seems to make up the background of Jas 2:8–9.[54]

An aspect that must be treated separately from the question of possible influences of the sources of the Didache on the Gospel of Matthew is the redactional level of the Didache itself. All Didache texts to which I have referred until now were already extant in recension C. This is not the case with regard to the *sectio evangelica* in 1:3b–2:1,[55] in which the love of one's enemy appears. I think that this section is not a post-didachist interpolation, but an insertion by the didachist himself.[56] The section shows convergences with Matthew in some points and with Luke in others, and this includes that these convergences are accompanied by differences with Matthew *and* Luke. As is well-known, the question of exact relationships is a notorious crux. Is the didachist dependent on Matthew (and also

---

51. See on this Jefford, *The Sayings of Jesus*, 53–58; Kloppenborg, "Transformation of the Moral Exhortation," 99–100.

52. See on this Konradt, *Christliche Existenz nach dem Jakobusbrief*, 129–30.

53. See Did. 2:3 with Lev 19:12 and 19:16, Did. 2:5 with Lev 19:11 and Did. 4:3 with Lev 19:15. See Kloppenborg, "Transformation of the Moral Exhortation," 103.

54. See Luke T. Johnson, "The Use of Leviticus 19 in the Letter of James," *JBL* 101 (1982): 391–401.

55. For an analysis of this section see, e.g., Niederwimmer, *Die Didache*, 93–116.

56. See for this position, e.g., Niederwimmer, *Die Didache*, 93–98. For a post-didachist interpolation, see, e.g., Wengst, *Didache (Apostellehre)*, 18–20.

on Luke?) here[57] or did he use an independent tradition?[58] Since I cannot go into a detailed analysis of this section here, I have to confine myself to pointing out an intriguing convergence on the conceptual level: In the overall architecture of the Two Ways instruction, the love of one's enemy in the *sectio evangelica* appears as an explication of the love command cited in 1:2. Thus, Jesus's instructions are positively incorporated into the conception of the Torah, which is close to Matthew's approach in Matt 5:17–48.

Another feature that should be considered in this context is the motif of perfection in the Didache. Since the appendix in 6:2–3 seems to be a redactional element,[59] one can ask if the second reference to the motif of perfection in 1:4 also goes back to the hand of the redactor.[60] In the Synoptics, perfection only occurs in Matthew's Gospel, namely, as we have seen, in the context of the interpretation of the love command. In the Didache, the motif of perfection appears in a similar, but not in exactly the same context. It is not directly linked to love of enemy, but to turning the other cheek as well. The point of reference in Did. 6:2 is difficult to define. Does "the entire yoke" refer to the whole Torah, inclusive of all food regulations and so on, so that the didachist would allow for some

---

57. See Tuckett, "Synoptic Tradition," 128, who postulates that the Didache "presupposes the finished gospels of Matthew and Luke." Jefford, *The Sayings of Jesus*, 52 does not only maintain that the interpolator "shows an awareness" of the text of Matthew's Gospel and "seems to know the Lucan Gospel as well," but he also postulates that "the interpolator writes from within the same tradition as that of the Matthean Gospel." One of his arguments is that the association of εὐλογέω, προσεύχομαι, and νηστεύω in Did. 1:3 would give witness to a tradition that Matthew took up in 6:1–18 (44–46, 52). On the other hand, John S. Kloppenborg, "The Use of the Synoptics or Q in Did. 1:3b–2:1," in *Matthew and the Didache: Two Documents from the Same Jewish-Christian Milieu?* (ed. H. van de Sandt; Assen: Van Gorcum, 2005), 129 concludes that "the compiler of Did. 1:3b–2:1 knew Luke," but he sees no clear indication whether in addition to Luke, the compiler was also familiar with Matthew, or only with Q.

58. For this option, see, e.g., Draper, "Jesus Tradition," 273–79, and van de Sandt and Flusser, *The Didache: Its Jewish Sources*, 40–48. See also the discussion in Willy Rordorf, "Does the Didache Contain Jesus Tradition Independently of the Synoptic Gospels?," in *Jesus and the Oral Gospel Tradition* (ed. Henry Wansbrough; JSNTSup 64; Sheffield: JSOT Press, 1991), 399–412 with references to the works of Christopher M. Tuckett (s. above n. 48 and n. 57) and Clayton N. Jefford (s. above n. 50). Rordorf concludes, "that in this passage of the doctrine of the Two Ways the Didache has preserved a Jesus tradition independently of the Synoptic Gospels" (ibid., 411). See also the critical discussion of Tuckett's approach in Milavec, "Synoptic Tradition in the Didache Revisited," 461–71.

59. Van de Sandt and Flusser, *The Didache: Its Jewish Sources*, 241, however, see a tension between the position in 6:2–3 and the anti-Jewish standpoint in 8:1–2 and thus postulate "that the appendix [sc. 6:2–3, M.K.] can hardly be explained as an original contribution by the final author-editor of the Didache."

60. See Niederwimmer, *Die Didache*, 94, 107.

alleviation in this regard?[61] Or does the didachist here refer back to the love of enemy and the renunciation of retaliation in the *sectio evangelica*[62] or to the preceding chapters on the whole[63] (which appears to me to be the most probable solution)? At any rate, a significant difference between Matthew and the Didache emerges here: For Matthew, the perfect fulfillment of the Torah is not arbitrary, but a binding requirement for the disciples and should be a characteristic of the *ecclesia*, which through that feature positively stands out from the Pharisaic synagogue. The didachist seems to be aware of the high ethical demand formulated in the instruction; on these grounds, he presents perfection as the goal for which one should strive,[64] but it is obviously not a prerequisite of salvation. Perfection is also an important topic in the Epistle of James,[65] where it appears as an ideal that ought to be aimed at, as in the Didache. James, however, knows that no one can really attain this goal, and here, the sins of the tongue are the major problem (see 3:2).

4. Matthew, James, and the Didache as Representatives of One and the Same Branch of Early Christianity?

If one compares the reception of the love command in Matthew, James, and the Didache with one another, some convergences emerge. As in Matthew and James, there is no evidence in the pre-Didache recension or in the Didache itself for a christological coloring of the love command through an interpretation of Jesus's death as an act of love (see Gal 2:20), but, again, we find a natural recourse to the Old Testament love command.[66] In comparison with Pauline and Johannine literature, this is remarkable to some extent. All three writings show a similar understanding of the love command as a summary statement of God's will, which is foreshadowed in Early Jewish writings. There is no sign of a reduction of the law to the love command, but the natural recourse to it in establishing love as the main ethical guideline is exemplary evidence for the continuity

---

61. See Wengst, *Didache (Apostellehre)*, 96; Van de Sandt and Flusser, *The Didache: Its Jewish Sources*, 269; Jonathan A. Draper, "Do the Didache and Matthew Reflect an 'Irrevocable Parting of the Ways' with Judaism?" in H. van de Sandt, ed., *Matthew and the Didache*, 227–30.

62. So Niederwimmer, *Die Didache*, 155–56.

63. See Gunnar Garleff, *Urchristliche Identität in Matthäusevangelium: Didache und Jakobusbrief* (Beiträge zum Verstehen der Bibel 9; Münster: Lit, 2004), 135–44.

64. See the conclusion of Garleff, *Urchristliche Identität in Matthäusevangelium*, 144 that the didachist "in 6,2 die Radikalität seines Lebensweges wahrnimmt und diesen gerade durch 2b begehbar macht."

65. On the topic of perfection in James see Konradt, *Christliche Existenz nach dem Jakobusbrief*, 267–85.

66. See Kloppenborg, "Transformation of the Moral Exhortation," 104.

with the Torah on the whole. All three writings also demonstrate continuity with the main thematic fields of applying the love command in Early Judaism, as it is especially documented in the *Testaments of the Twelve Patriarchs*. Moreover, in all three writings, the central importance of the love command is connected to the prominent role of the decalogue (but see also Rom 13:8–10). The congruence in the reception of the Torah in Matthew, James, and the Didache is linked with a common recourse to the motif of perfection, which however is developed in different ways. Other differences also exist[67] on which I cannot elaborate here.[68]

Do these findings support the idea that "in addition to the Pauline and Johannine "schools," Matthew, James and the Didache represent a third, important religious milieu within earliest Christianity, which is characterized by its distinct connections to a particular ethical stream of contemporary Jewish tradition"?[69] The question is complex and, as mentioned in the introduction, it cannot be dealt with in an adequate manner in the (thematic) framework of this essay. I can only indicate my preliminary position here. In my opinion, a close relation must be assumed between Matthew's Gospel and the Didache, but one has to distinguish between different steps of the formation of the documents. As has been shown above, there seems to be an interrelationship between the ethical traditions that were taken up in the pre-Didache recension C on the one hand, and those that influenced the evangelist on the other. On the level of the didachist himself, I still consider it to be a reasonable assumption that the didachist was familiar with Matthew's Gospel itself and, given the relationship between Matthew's Gospel and traditions that were taken up in recension C, that he lived in the near surroundings of the origin of the Gospel.[70] In other words, it is worth

---

67. I briefly point only to two other differences between Matthew and James. Whereas Matthew operates with a contrast of ἐκκλησία (16:18; 18:17) and "their synagogues" (see esp. Matt 10:17; 12:9 and 23:34), in James both terms are used with regard to the Christian congregation (see Jas 2:2 and 5:14). And while James identifies the believers in Christ with the "twelve tribes" (1:1) and thus with Israel, Matthew never postulates such an identity for the church. On the latter question see Matthias Konradt, *Israel, Kirche und die Völker im Matthäusevangelium* (WUNT 215; Tübingen: Mohr Siebeck, 2007), 349–77.

68. I mention only that on the whole, James displays a much stronger Hellenistic character than Matthew. Christoph Burchard (*Der Jakobusbrief* [HNT 15/1; Tübingen: Mohr Siebeck, 2000], 5) rightly calls the author of James a theologian "mit guter (jüdisch-) hellenistischer Bildung" and points to the "hellenistischen, wenn auch oft jüdisch vermittelten Züge seiner Theologie und Ethik" (ibid., 4; see also Konradt, *Christliche Existenz nach dem Jakobusbrief*, 317).

69. So Huub van de Sandt and Jürgen Zangenberg on pp. 1–2 in the introduction to this volume.

70. See the convincing argument for an intertextual reference of the Didache to Matthew's Gospel in Garleff, *Urchristliche Identität in Matthäusevangelium*, 199–206. Differences can be interpreted as "Modifikationen der Lehren des Evangeliums hinsichtlich der veränderten Situation" (ibid., 204).

considering that the Didache in its final form represents a later stage of Matthean "Christianity" and thus gives insight into its further development.

Some affinity between Matthew and James does also exist, which, however, cannot be equated with the close relationship of Matthew and the Didache.[71] As far as localizing is concerned, I agree with many exegetes that Syria is the most probable place for James[72] as it is for Matthew and the Didache. But Syria is large, and due to the divergences between James and Matthew, which might include different social compositions of the communities,[73] I prefer the possibility that James and Matthew/Didache represent "only" two (closely) related branches of Early Syriac Christianity, instead of assigning James to exactly the same "milieu" as Matthew and the Didache.

---

71. See the exemplary points of difference mentioned above in n. 67 and also n. 68.

72. See Matthias Konradt, "Der Jakobusbrief als Brief des Jakobus: Erwägungen zum historischen Kontext des Jakobusbriefes im Lichte der traditionsgeschichtlichen Beziehungen zum 1 Petr und zum Hintergrund der Autorfiktion," in Gemünden, *et al.*, eds., *Der Jakobusbrief: Beiträge zur Rehabilitierung,* 16–53: 42 with n. 132.

73. According to Did. 7:1, the Two Ways-tractate in Did. 1–6 served as a pre-baptismal instruction for Gentile converts (see, e.g., Willy Rordorf, "An Aspect of the Judeo-Christian Ethic: The Two Ways," in Draper, ed., *The Didache in Modern Research,* 153–59); this, however, does not speak against a predominantly Jewish-Christian community, which is open for Gentiles as its context. With regard to Matthew, most scholars today agree that the members of the community were at least predominantly of Jewish origin (see on this Konradt, *Israel, Kirche und die Völker,* 386–93). I do not see, however, that this can be taken for granted in the case of the Epistle of James (see on this Konradt, "Der Jakobusbrief als Brief des Jakobus," 44, 45, 53). At the same time, the principal theological convergence of the three writings must be stressed in this context: All three writings display a kind of Christianity that is characterized by a strong Jewish fundament and a rather smooth theological transformation of Jewish traditions in the process of opening the communities for Gentiles—without any severe break with Torah in principle.

Ethics in the Letter of James, the Gospel of Matthew, and the Didache: Their Place in Early Christian Literature

Patrick J. Hartin

1. Preliminary remarks

In considering the ethical dimensions of the three texts, the Letter of James, the Didache, and the Gospel of Matthew, this paper will examine their relationship to the ethical worlds of the people of Israel and of nascent Christianity. Each investigation will begin with the Letter of James for two reasons. In the first place, my field of scholarship has largely been devoted to an investigation of the Letter of James. In the second place, I am convinced that the Letter of James is an early writing, preceding that of the Gospel of Matthew and the Didache. Scholarship has long been divided over the question of the date of the Letter of James. However, based on a careful examination of the evidence, the Letter of James emerges as an early writing from the hand of a follower of James of Jerusalem, written shortly after his death (in 62 C.E.) from Jerusalem to followers of Jesus the Messiah living outside of Palestine (Jas 1:1). The letter aims at reminding its hearers/readers of James's teaching and to encourage them to live in "friendship with God" (4:4).[1]

---

1. For a discussion of the date and authorship of the Letter of James see Patrick J. Hartin, *James* (SP 14; Collegeville, Minn.: Liturgical Press, 2003), 16–25. "An early date for this writing is required from the evidence noted above, namely, (1) the way the author refers to himself, expecting his hearers/readers to know his identity; (2) the closeness of the author to the heritage of Israel (he still sees himself as belonging to that world); (3) the use made of the Jesus traditions (prior to the appearance of the canonical gospels); (4) the closeness to the spirit and vision of Jesus; (5) the total lack of reference to the Gentiles in any form; and (6) the omission of any reference to the destruction of the Temple of Jerusalem" (ibid., 24).

2. Ethics in the Letter of James, the Gospel of Matthew, and the Didache

2.1. Ethos and Identity

The ethical vision of an author or a community is referred to as its *ethos*. Webster's Dictionary defines *ethos* in the following way:

> ethos 1. the fundamental character or spirit of a culture; the underlying senti-
> ment that informs the beliefs, customs, or practices of a group or society. 2. the
> distinguishing character or disposition of a community, group, person, etc.[2]

Ethos points to the very identity of a people or a community: this is who we are and this is what distinguishes us from other groups or communities. The *ethos* directs the way members of a group or community lead their lives. Consequently, this *ethos* gives rise to the *ethics* of that group or community, namely, those rules, values, and guidelines to which members adhere and by which they express their identity. Webster's defines "ethics" as "1. a system or set of moral principles. 2. the rules of conduct governing a particular class of human actions or a particular group, culture, etc."[3] In examining James, Matthew, and the Didache, attention will be given to the *ethos* that points to the vision and identity of the group or community behind each text. Then, an examination will be made of the ethics that emerges from that vision and that is expressed through the various ethical admonitions in the texts.

2.1.1. The Letter of James

James writes to those who see themselves within the context of Israel's heritage and traditions. Two points demonstrate this most specifically:

The Eschatological Hope of the Twelve-Tribe Kingdom.[4] In the opening verse of the letter, James[5] identifies those to whom he writes as "the twelve tribes in the

---

2. *Random House Webster's Collegiate Dictionary* (New York: Random House, 1995), 459.

3. Ibid.

4. I have examined this phrase in detail elsewhere, for example, Patrick J. Hartin, "'Who Is Wise and Understanding among You?' (James 3:13): An Analysis of Wisdom, Eschatology, and Apocalypticism in the Letter of James," in *Conflicted Boundaries in Wisdom and Apocalypticism* (ed. B. G. Wright, III and L. M. Wills; SBLSymS 35, Atlanta: Society of Biblical Literature, 2005), 149–68; and idem, *James*, 53–55.

5. When referring to James (and in like manner to Matthew) as the author of the text, I do not intend to take a position on the actual identity of the writer. The use of the name James (and analogously Matthew) is merely a handy tool since the writers and tradition identify themselves in this way.

Dispersion"[6] (ταῖς δώδεκα φυλαῖς ταῖς ἐν τῇ διασπορᾷ χαίρειν) [1:1]). In using the article in conjunction with "the Dispersion" (ἐν τῇ διασπορᾷ), James indicates a literal understanding of the Diaspora, as those areas outside Palestine where people of the house of Israel live.[7] James is not speaking metaphorically as some commentators wish to assert.[8] This would be possible only if the writer were addressing Christians from the pagan world. Indeed, the whole letter bears the stamp that its hearers/readers are from the people of Israel.

The reference to the "twelve tribes" originally refers to the people of Israel who trace their origins back to the twelve sons of Jacob (see Exod 24:4; 28:21; 39:14). The reign of King David gave impetus to the hope that his kingdom would last indefinitely. As the prophet Nathan said to King David, "Your house and your kingdom shall be made sure forever before me; your throne shall be established forever" (2 Sam 7:16). With the division of the twelve tribe kingdom after Solomon and the subsequent destruction of both the northern and southern kingdoms, the hope emerged for a restored twelve-tribe kingdom: "Thus says the Lord God: I will take the people of Israel from the nations among which they have gone, and will gather them from every quarter, and bring them to their own land. I will make them one nation in the land . . ." (Ezek 37:21–22). This hope in the reconstituted twelve-tribe kingdom continues on into the period of the first century C.E., as is evident from writings from this period: "He will gather a holy people whom he will lead in righteousness; and he will judge the tribes of the people that have been made holy by the Lord their God" (*Pss. Sol.* 17:26;[9] see also 1QS VIII,1).

James, then, reflects the hope in the fulfillment of this twelve-tribe kingdom. He further strengthens this identity by referring to them as "the first fruits of (God's) creatures" (1:18). In this context, those to whom James writes are identified as believers from the people of Israel who have accepted Jesus's message. They are heirs to the promises and hopes of the past in that God's eschatological kingdom is being brought to fulfillment in their presence. Through this self identification, James situates his hearers/readers, living outside of Palestine, firmly within the people of Israel, laying claim to the fulfillment of its most foundational

---

6. Unless otherwise noted, the translation of the Bible that is used throughout this paper is that of the NRSV.

7. See Hartin, *James*, 50–51.

8. See Martin Dibelius, *James: A Commentary on the Epistle of James* (trans. M. A. Williams; ed. H. Koester; Hermeneia; Philadelphia: Fortress, 1976), 66–67.

9. Translation of the *Psalms of Solomon* is by R. B.Wright, "The Psalms of Solomon," in *The Old Testament Pseudepigrapha* (ed. J. H. Charlesworth; Garden City, N.Y.: Doubleday, 1983–85), 2:667.

hopes. For James, a believer can be both a member of the people of Israel and a follower of Jesus.[10]

The Torah. James discusses the law on three occasions in his letter (1:25; 2:8–12; and 4:11–12) identifying the law as "the law of freedom," "the perfect law," and "the royal law." I have examined James's concept of law elsewhere.[11] I see this term referring to the biblical Torah[12] as the expression of God's will for God's covenant people. Here, attention will be given as to how the concept of law/Torah functions in the Letter of James. To understand this, it must be viewed against the background of the purity rules that were essential for the proper functioning of every first-century C.E. Mediterranean society. James's very definition of religion presupposes the importance of this concept: "Religion that is pure and undefiled before God, the Father, is this: to care for orphans and widows in their distress, and to keep oneself unstained by the world" (1:27). The purpose of the Torah is to make known for the members of the community what those purity rules are: what rules are needed to maintain their access to God and what will keep them "unstained by the world" (ἄσπιλον ἑαυτὸν τηρεῖν ἀπὸ τοῦ κόσμου [1:27]). This is what James has in mind in 4:4 in his contrast between "friendship with God" and "friendship with the world." Again, rich in the language of purity, James calls on his hearers/readers: "Draw near to God, and he will draw near to you. Cleanse your hands, you sinners, and purify your hearts, you double-minded . . . Humble yourselves before the Lord, and he will exalt you" (Jas 4:8–10).

The Torah expresses how they are to maintain their relationship as God's covenant people. The Torah exercises a socializing function in the way in which Berger and Luckmann have defined the concept of socialization as "the comprehensive and consistent induction of an individual into the objective world of a society or sector of it."[13] The rhetorical function of the Letter of James is to socialize the hearers/readers of this letter so that they understand their identity as members of the twelve-tribe kingdom while the law/Torah makes known to them what they must do to preserve that identity. The Torah preserves the boundary that separates them from the wider society. Nowhere does James refer to cere-

---

10. See Scot McKnight, "A Parting within the Way: Jesus and James on Israel and Purity," in *James the Just and Christian Origins* (ed. B. Chilton and C. A. Evans; Leiden: Brill, 1999), 129.

11. See Hartin, *James,* 111–15; see also "The Religious Context of the Letter of James," chapter 8 in *Jewish Christianity Reconsidered* (ed. M. Jackson-McCabe; Minneapolis: Fortress Press. 2007), 203–31.

12. I acknowledge my debt in this regard to Robert W. Wall, *Community of the Wise: The Letter of James* (New Testament in Context; Valley Forge, Pa.: Trinity Press International, 1997), 83–98.

13. Peter L. Berger and Thomas Luckmann, *The Social Construction of Reality: A Treatise in the Sociology of Knowledge* (Garden City, N.Y.: Doubleday, 1966), 120.

monial, cultic, or ritual laws. Instead, the aspect of the Torah to which he gives attention is the moral or social law that God's people needed. Specifically, it is the law of love as expressed in the *Shema Israel* (Deut 6:4–5) and in the command to love one's neighbor (Lev 19:18). As I have expressed elsewhere, the function of the law/Torah in the lives of the members of James's community[14] is fourfold:

- It creates a collective identity for the twelve-tribe kingdom that distinguishes it from the world.
- It encourages internal solidarity and cohesion among the members of the community.
- It promotes a steadfast commitment to God by showing "friendship with God" as the prime identification marker for the community.
- It requires a choice for God as opposed to the world.[15]

2.1.2. The Gospel of Matthew

This Gospel is also firmly set within the contours of the people of Israel and its heritage. Jesus is a member of the people of Israel (2:6, 20, 21; 8:10; 9:33; 10:23; 15:31; 19:28; 27:9, 42). "The house of Israel" is a term used to identify those among whom Jesus is actively preaching and teaching (10:6; 15:24). By implication, Matthew's community sees itself as part of the people or house of Israel.

Matthew's Gospel is also conscious of those traditions relating to the establishment of the twelve-tribe kingdom to which the Letter of James drew attention. Matthew's Jesus conducts a ministry that aims at reconstituting this twelve-tribe kingdom. When Matthew's Jesus sends out the twelve, he instructs them: "Go nowhere among the Gentiles, and enter no town of the Samaritans, but go rather to the lost sheep of the house of Israel" (10:5–6). While Matthew's Gospel does envisage an outreach to the Gentiles at the end (28:19–20), Jesus restricts his ministry and that of his disciples to the people of Israel. When speaking to the Canaanite woman, Jesus specifically identifies his mission in these words: "I was sent only to the lost sheep of the house of Israel" (15:24). Matthew presents Jesus gathering together the lost tribes of Israel and reconstituting God's twelve-tribe kingdom.

The disciples share in this task (10:5–6). They continue to build up God's kingdom. At the conclusion to the Gospel, Jesus sends out his disciples to continue his mission: "Go therefore and make disciples of all nations . . ." (Matt

---

14. When speaking about "James's community," I intend *those who receive* his letter, namely, the hearers/readers of the letter. I do not intend by this term the community *from which* James is writing. Also, given the more general address of the Letter of James, "to the twelve tribes in the Dispersion," I do not intend one single community, but rather all those to whom James writes, which would include many "communities" scattered outside Palestine that together comprise "the twelve tribes."

15. Hartin, *James*, 115.

28:19–20). Only at the end time will this ingathering of the people of Israel, which Jesus began in his ministry, be completed: "Jesus said to them: 'Truly I tell you, at the renewal of all things, when the Son of Man is seated on the throne of his glory, you who have followed me will also sit on twelve thrones, judging the twelve tribes of Israel" (Matt 19:28).

The Torah in Matthew. As with the Letter of James, the Gospel of Matthew envisages the fulfillment of the whole law. "(Jesus said:) 'Do not think that I have come to abolish the law or the prophets; I have come not to abolish but to fulfill. For truly I tell you, until heaven and earth pass away, not one letter, not one stroke of a letter, will pass from the law until all is accomplished'" (Matt 5:17–18).

Matthew's Jesus does not take issue with the Torah as such, for the Torah is God's expressed will. Instead, Matthew's Jesus claims the role as official interpreter of God's will, of God's Torah. Matthew's Jesus takes issue with the way the rabbis of the synagogue interpret the Torah through their oral law.[16] After stating unambiguously that he has come not to abolish the law but to fulfill it, Jesus shows by means of six antitheses that his fulfillment entails more than the legalistic carrying out of the law. It embraces one's interior dispositions, which precede and ultimately result in the breaking of the law. Matthew's Jesus undermines the whole Pharisaic way of interpreting the law. In effect, Jesus shows in 5:21–47 that no one can claim to be not guilty of breaking this or that law—everyone is guilty![17] Instead, one has to rely upon God's righteousness.

Matthew uses another expression to show Jesus's relationship to the Torah: "*Take my yoke upon you,* and learn from me; for I am gentle and humble in heart, and you will find rest for your souls. For *my yoke* is easy, and my burden is light" (11:29–30). When Jesus says here, "Take my yoke upon you" (ἄρατε τὸν ζυγόν μου ἐφ' ὑμᾶς), he is contrasting himself to "the yoke of the Torah." The passage in *2 Bar.* 41:3 shows that the phrase "the yoke of the Torah" was a common expression of the time: "For behold, I see many of your people who separated themselves from your statutes and who have cast away from them *the yoke of your Law.*"[18] Jesus is in effect stating that his interpretation of the Torah is easy and light in contrast to the other rabbis who place a heavy burden on their followers through their interpretations.

---

16. See Leander E. Keck, "Ethics in the Gospel according to Matthew," *The Illiff Review* 41 (1984): 49.

17. Ibid., 50.

18. This translation of *2 Baruch* is by A. F. J. Klijn, "2 (Syriac Apocalypse of) Baruch," in *The Old Testament Pseudepigrapha* (ed. J. H. Charlesworth; 2 vols.; Garden City, N.Y.: Doubleday, 1983–85), 1:633.

2.1.3. The Didache

The Didache is also firmly set within the context of the heritage of Israel and its traditions. However, a decided difference is evident in comparison with the Letter of James. While the Letter of James nowhere envisages an outreach to the Gentiles (its focus is exclusively within the framework of the people of Israel), the Didache aims at instruction directed to those Gentiles wishing to become members of the community.[19] In doing so, the requirements laid upon them are those that the people of Israel would require of all Gentiles. The Two Ways instruction that forms the opening section of the Didache (1:1–6:3) applies those ethical instructions of the Torah to Gentiles, while omitting all the cultic and ritual instructions of the Torah.[20]

The Didache does not use James's reference to the community as the "twelve tribes." In fact, the Didache does not identify the community it addresses through the use of terms or labels. The only identifying terms are the references to David: "the holy vine of David, your child" (9:2)[21] and "Hosanna to the God of David" (10:6). While the two titles associated with the Didache make reference to the "twelve apostles," the Didache is certainly not the product of these twelve apostles. Nevertheless, the title intends to connect the instructions contained in this Two Ways document with the teaching the twelve handed on, a teaching that ultimately came from Jesus.

The Torah in the Didache. The Didache envisaged a situation as noted above where the community had accepted Gentiles into their midst. What were the new members required to do in order to be part of this community of followers of Jesus, the Messiah? The document of the Didache speaks to this. Once more the Torah lies at its heart. The first part of the text, the Two Ways (Did. 1:1–6:3), begins by laying out the essence of the path to life, namely, love of God and love of neighbor (1:2). The instructions focus largely on applications of the second part of the Decalogue and on practices that occurred among the Gentiles, but were considered evil among the teachers of the house of Israel, such as pederasty, the practice of magic, abortion, the killing of a newly born child (2:1–2). This attention to actions

---

19. The Didache has a twofold title: "The Teaching of the Twelve Apostles," and "The Teaching of the Lord through the Twelve Apostles to the Gentiles (Or: *nations*)." This title has been the subject of much debate especially regarding its authenticity and originality (see Jean-Paul Audet, *La Didachè: Instructions des Apôtres* (Paris: Gabalda, 1958), 91–103.

20. See Jonathan A. Draper, "Do the Didache and Matthew Reflect an 'Irrevocable Parting of the Ways' with Judaism?" in *Matthew and the Didache: Two Documents from the Same Jewish-Christian Milieu?* (ed. H. van de Sandt; Assen: Van Gorcum, 2005), 240.

21. Unless otherwise noted, the translation of the Didache that is used throughout this paper is that of Bart D. Ehrman, "The Didache," in *The Apostolic Fathers* (2 vols.; LCL 24–25; Cambridge, Mass.: Harvard University Press, 2003), 1:405–43.

in which Gentiles might be involved functions as a way of socializing the Gentiles into this community by laying out the boundary markers for the members of this community. Once again, the Torah gives inspiration to all these instructions.

At the conclusion to the Two Ways section, the writer gives attention to the issue of whether Gentiles joining the community are required to observe the food laws that were central to every member of the house of Israel. This is the same issue that caused such consternation in the early communities of the followers of Jesus, as Acts 15:1–29 indicates.

> For if you can bear the entire yoke of the Lord, you will be perfect; but if you cannot, do as much as you can. And concerning food, bear what you can. But especially abstain from food sacrificed to idols; for this is a ministry to dead gods. (Did. 6:2–3)

Gentile members of the community of the Didache are accepted where they are and burdens are not laid upon them that would be impossible for them to carry out. They are not required to take upon themselves "the entire yoke of the Lord" (ὅλον τὸν ζυγὸν τοῦ κυρίου). As in the Gospel of Matthew, the expression "yoke of the Lord" is contrasted to the "yoke of the Torah." The term is used in a positive sense as it always is in the context of the house of Israel. Paul, on the other hand, uses the term in a negative sense and sees Christ as having liberated his followers from a "yoke of slavery" (ζυγῷ δουλείας): "For freedom Christ has set us free. Stand firm, therefore, and do not submit again to a yoke of slavery" (ζυγῷ δουλείας; Gal 5:1).

In particular, the Gentile members of the community are not required to adhere to the dietary or food laws that are prescribed by the Torah. They are, however, required to abstain from food offered to idols for this is judged to run counter to the basic law of the Decalogue that prescribes the worship of the one true God. The Gentile convert is called to strive toward carrying out *the whole Law,* but it is not something he is expected to fulfill. Members of the house of Israel, however, are obligated to carry out the dietary or food laws since this is part of the "yoke of the Lord" that they have always accepted. Gentile members of the community, on the other hand, do have a choice of following them or not. The ideal would be for the Gentile member to observe the whole Torah, including food laws, but this remains an ideal and a tolerant approach is accepted for those who are not able to "bear the entire yoke of the Lord": "εἰ μὲν γὰρ δύνασαι βαστάσαι ὅλον τὸν ζυγὸν τοῦ κυρίου, τέλειος ἔσῃ."[22]

---

22. As van de Sandt and Flusser state: "The composer of *Did.* 6:2–3 was an exponent of a group of Jewish-Christians who remained within the ambit of Tora-observance. Compliance with the entire Tora is the ideal but the text shows a tolerant attitude to those who are not capable of bearing 'the whole yoke of the Lord'" (Huub van de Sandt and David Flusser,

2.1.4. Summary

These three texts speak to groups with a common *ethos* and a common vision, but at different moments in time. *The communities to whom James writes* still lie at the heart of Israel. There is no evidence or at least no concern relating to the admission of Gentiles into their communities who are judged to reconstitute "the twelve tribes in the Dispersion" (1:1). With the Torah at its heart, they aim at maintaining friendship with God (4:4) through carrying out the stipulations of the Torah. *Matthew's community,* on the other hand, indicates that it has moved beyond the initial stages of James's communities where *all the members* were seen to belong to the house of Israel. Matthew's Gospel has embarked upon an outreach to the Gentile world showing this was clearly Jesus's intent. *The Didache* reflects a community at a more developed stage than that of the Gospel of Matthew. Gentiles have been accepted into their midst and the need arises for a framework for socializing them into the community by showing what is required of them as part of the community. This need is answered by the directions that the Didache sets forth. All three texts reflect different stages in the development of communities emerging from a common milieu whereby the members continue to view themselves as firmly rooted within the house of Israel, yet at the same time following Jesus, the Messiah.

2.2. ETHICAL ADMONITIONS

The ethical admonitions occur as boundary markers expressing the identity (*ethos*) of the members of the respective communities. Beginning with the Letter of James, I identify a number of these boundary markers, which I seek to find reflected in the other two texts, the Gospel of Matthew and the Didache.

2.2.1. "Being perfect" (τέλειος)

The Letter of James. A noteworthy feature of the Letter of James is the frequency that the adjective τέλειος ("perfect") occurs within this brief letter. The word τέλειος appears four times in the opening chapter (1:4 [twice]; 1:17 and 1:25). It also occurs at 3:2. While the verb τελειόω ("to make perfect, to complete") is found at 2:22, the verb τελέω ("to fulfill, to accomplish") is used at 2:8.

The Didache: Its Jewish Sources and its Place in Early Judaism and Christianity [Assen: Van Gorcum, 2002], 269). Van de Sandt and Flusser argue that Didache 6:2–3 is a later insertion into the Two Ways text of 1:1–6:1. This is an issue that is beyond the scope of this paper, but their basic insight is significant, namely, that these verses 6:2–3 offer a tolerant attitude to the converting Gentile especially in relation to the observance of dietary laws.

An overview of the use of the word τέλειος in the Septuagint gives an insight into its intended meaning.[23] Together with the word ἄμωμος, it translates the Hebrew word תמים, which bears the meaning of "unblemished, blameless." For example, "Your lamb shall be without blemish (τέλειος), a year-old male" (Exod 12:5). Its origin arises from the sacrificial worship within Israel that required that the sacrificial animal should be without defect, namely, "unblemished."

While the concept τέλειος went through a development by applying the cultic reference to human behavior,[24] the idea of wholeness or completeness remained its basic meaning. James refers to his hearers/readers as "the first fruits of God's creatures" (1:18). As the first fruits of every harvest offered to God were without blemish (whole), James's hearers/readers in a similar way are perceived to be whole, complete, without blemish. As "the twelve tribes in the Dispersion," they epitomize the wholeness of God's chosen people—they conform to the original idea God had of them as God's holy people. Taken together, these two images convey the insight that James's communities reflect the start of the reconstituted people of God—they are the first to be part of this people that conforms to the image God had of them at the very beginning.[25] In connecting with the roots of this idea of τέλειος in the Septuagint, James also holds to the cultic origins of this concept by presenting instructions or laws that express the notions of purity and holiness within his society. All purity rules aimed at structuring life so that right relationships between God, community, and believer would be maintained. [26]

Since God recreated them as the "first fruits of (God's) creatures (1:18), their response is to remain in *wholehearted dedication to the Lord* (4:7–10). James draws a sharp contrast between two ways of life, one life led in "friendship with God," the other led in "friendship with the world" (4:4). These two "friendships" are diametrically opposed to each other. This explains James's definition of religion as "keeping oneself unstained by the world" (1:27).

This wholehearted dedication to the Lord is demonstrated by remaining steadfast in fulfilling the Law/Torah, as the expression of God's will. Consequently, James calls on his hearers/readers *to fulfill the whole law* (2:10–11). The

---

23. See Patrick J. Hartin, *A Spirituality of Perfection: Faith in Action in the Letter of James* (Collegeville, Minn.: Liturgical Press, 1999), 17–39.

24. For example, "You must remain completely loyal (τέλειος) to the LORD your God" (Deut 18:13). This called one to give oneself wholeheartedly to the Lord, worshipping the Lord God alone. As Rudolf Schnackenburg ("Christian Perfection according to Matthew," in *Christian Existence in the New Testament* (ed. Rudolf Schnackenburg; Notre Dame, Ind.: University of Notre Dame Press, 1968], 162) explains: "To be 'blameless' before the Lord (Deut 18:13) means to belong to him wholeheartedly, without practicing idolatry, sorcery and other abominations (cf. 18:9–12)."

25. Hartin, *A Spirituality of Perfection*, 89.

26. See Bruce J. Malina, *The New Testament World: Insights from Cultural Anthropology* (3rd edition, rev. and enl.; Louisville, Ky.: Westminster John Knox, 2001), 189.

focus in the Letter of James on "being perfect" is one that gives expression to their very being as "the twelve tribes in the Dispersion." Called to wholeness, they live out their lives together as members of this twelve-tribe kingdom in fidelity to their relationship with God and to the law that gives their lives direction.

The Gospel of Matthew. The concept of "being perfect" occurs on two occasions in the Gospel of Matthew (5:48 and 19:21). In both instances, it conforms to the usage found in the Letter of James.[27] Matthew 5:48 brings the first part of his Sermon on the Mount to a culmination with the call: "Be perfect, therefore, as your heavenly Father is perfect" (Ἔσεσθε οὖν ὑμεῖς τέλειοι ὡς ὁ πατὴρ ὑμῶν ὁ οὐράνιος τέλειός ἐστιν).[28] Since the only occurrence of the word τέλειος in the Synoptic Gospels is found in the Gospel of Matthew, and since it is redactional in 19:21, it is logical to presuppose that it is also redactional here in 5:48.[29]

In the context of Matt 5:48, God's actions are presented for imitation. For example, "For (God) makes his sun rise on the evil and on the good, and sends rain on the righteous and on the unrighteous" (5:45). Since God shows concern for the good and the bad without distinction, the believer must do likewise. The phrase Ἔσεσθε οὖν ὑμεῖς τέλειοι ὡς ὁ πατὴρ ὑμῶν ὁ οὐράνιος τέλειός ἐστιν (5:48) refers specifically to the imitation of God's actions, not his essence or being. Once again it is the concept of completeness or wholeness that Matthew envisages. If you wish to be whole, you must imitate the actions of God by showing love and care for all.

In Matt 19:21, Jesus responds to the rich young man's question, "I have kept all these, what do I still lack?" by saying, "If you wish to be perfect, go sell your possessions, and give the money to the poor and you will have treasure in heaven; then come, follow me." A comparison of this text with that found in the Gospel of Mark (10:21)[30] shows that Matthew has replaced Mark's phrase, "You lack one thing" (Ἕν σε ὑστερεῖ [Mark 10:21]) with the phrase, "If you wish to be perfect" (Εἰ θέλεις τέλειος εἶναι). Since the word τέλειος occurring in both Matt 5:48 and 19:21 is Matthew's, the redactor's, addition to the text, it must bear a common meaning in both instances. Matthew 5:48 refers to the call to wholeness or completeness in the context of God's love and care for all. In Matt 19:21,

---

27. I have examined this in detail in Hartin, *A Spirituality of Perfection,* 129–47.

28. The Gospel of Luke has a variation of this saying in his Sermon on the Plain: "Be merciful, just as your Father is merciful" (Γίνεσθε οἰκτίρμονες καθὼς [καί] ὁ πατὴρ ὑμῶν οἰκτίρμων ἐστίν [Luke 6:36]).

29. This view is supported by William D. Davies and Dale C. Allison, Jr., *A Critical and Exegetical Commentary on the Gospel according to Saint Matthew* (3 vols.; ICC; Edinburgh: T&T Clark, 1988), 1:560–61.

30. Matthew draws this pericope from Mark who has simply, "Jesus, looking at him, loved him, and said, 'You lack one thing; go, sell what you own, and give the money to the poor, and you will have treasure in heaven; then come, follow me'" (Mark 10:21).

a similar idea is stressed: this young man is called to wholeness or completeness in his obedience to God's will. This rich young man is called to follow Jesus in a particular situation that applies to him alone. It is not intended to be taken as a generalized teaching that Jesus is asking all followers to eschew wealth. For this young man, wealth is an obstacle to maintaining completeness/wholeness in his relationship with God and his fellow believers. Where this story acts as a paradigm for every believer is that everyone is called to wholeness or completeness in relationship with God and one another. Everyone has to respond with a generosity of spirit and a wholeness of obedience.[31]

The above examination has focused upon how the concept of completeness or wholeness features in Matthew's usage of τέλειος in both 5:48 and 19:21. At the same time, it is a call to a right relationship with God. This relationship is demonstrated through one's way of life: a life of wholehearted love (5:48), or wholehearted obedience to God's will (19:21).

The Didache . The concept of "being perfect" is also characteristic of the Didache. The first occurrence of the word τέλειος appears in the opening section containing teaching clearly derived from the tradition of the Sayings of Jesus: "If anyone slaps your right cheek, turn the other to him as well, and you will be perfect" (ἐάν τὶς σοι δῷ ῥάπισμα εἰς τὴν δεξιὰν σιαγόνα στρέψον αὐτῷ καὶ τὴν ἄλλην καὶ ἔσῃ τέλειος [1:4]). This closely resembles the sayings in Matthew's Gospel (Matt 5:39; and 5:48) although the statement about "being perfect" in Matthew comes at the end of the series of sayings on loving one's enemies and acts as the culmination of the preceding teaching in chapter 5. In the Didache, the call to "be perfect" is inserted between two sayings on turning the other cheek and going the extra mile.

The second occurrence of the term τέλειος is found at the end of the section on the Two Ways (6:2). The new Gentile members of the community are told to do what they can, but if they carry out the whole Law, they will be perfect: "For if you can bear the entire yoke of the Lord, you will be perfect" (εἰ μὲν γὰρ δύνασαι βαστάσαι ὅλον τὸν ζυγὸν τοῦ κυρίου, τέλειος ἔσῃ). These two references to "being perfect" (τέλειος) act like bookends to the first section containing the two ways: they frame all the teachings contained within it. The concept of τέλειος is used in a way analogous to its usage in James, and remains true to the roots of its appearance in the Septuagint. The members of the community are called to wholeness by carrying out the teachings that are laid before them. In particular, this wholeness comprises their identity as God's people who strive to keep the whole Law. This is who God has called you to be—this is the way of life God intended the people to lead. Wholeness comes from walking according to the fullness of the law.

---

31. See Davies and Allison, Jr., *A Critical and Exegetical Commentary on . . . Matthew*, 48.

The ethical instructions act as guides or boundary markers identifying the members of this community. As with the Letter of James, the ethical admonitions (1:1–6:3) operate as purity rules. They identify the path to follow (the way of life) in which one lives in relationship with God and one another. Through obeying these laws, their identity emerges in their relationship with God and one another.

Jonathan Draper has interpreted the use of this term τέλειος as an indication that the members of the community of the Didache (and Matthew's Gospel) who come from the house of Israel are called to do more than their fellow Israelites who are not members of their community are called to do. [32]

While it is true that the context does include doing more than is required, the use of the word τέλειος rather gives expression to their identity: they will attain wholeness and integrity in their relationship with God, one another and themselves. This understanding of the concept of "being perfect" is supported at the conclusion to the Didache where the verb τελειόω is used (as in James 2:22): "Gather together frequently, seeking what is appropriate for your souls. For the entire time of your faith will be of no use to you if you are not found perfect (τελειωθῆτε) at the final moment" (Did. 16:2). Their life of faith and the carrying out of the instructions that have been laid before them will result at the end of time in their identity being known: they are people who have attained wholeness in their relationship with God and one another. This is who God intended them to be from the very beginning—God's "holy ones" (οἱ ἅγιοι) (Did. 16:7).

This detailed examination of the use of the term τέλειος in the three texts of the Letter of James, the Gospel of Matthew, and the Didache reveals an identical understanding. The members of their communities are all called to wholeness, to live out their lives together in fidelity to their relationship with God and to the law that gives their lives direction.

2.2.2. The Imitation of God

The Gospel of Matthew connects the theme of "being perfect" with the call to imitate God in God's actions. Much scholarly discussion has been given to the question of whether the concept of the imitation of God actually occurs in the Hebrew Scriptures. [33] While there are passages that appear to call on the people of Israel to imitate God's actions, a careful examination reveals that something

---

32. Jonathan Draper, "Do the Didache and Matthew indicate an 'Irrevocable Parting of the Ways' with Judaism?" in van de Sandt, ed., *Matthew and the Didache*, 227.

33. See Sophie Laws, "The Doctrinal Basis for the Ethics of James," *SE* 7 (Papers Presented to the Fifth International Congress on Biblical Studies Held at Oxford, 1973; Berlin: Akademie-Verlag, 1982), 302. See, as well, my discussion on this aspect of the imitation of God, in *Spirituality of Perfection*, 140–44.

else is actually the focus. For example, in the instruction, "You shall be holy, for I the LORD your God am holy" (Lev 19:2), the Israelites are called to holiness, not in imitation of God, but as a consequence of their relationship with God. The Hebrew conjunction used here (כִּי) expresses a result, not a comparison. God is holy by nature. In leading the Israelites out of Egypt, God formed them into God's own nation at Sinai (Exod 19:5–6). As a "holy nation," they are separated from the nations of the world and belong to God. This has consequences for the Israelites. Their actions must reflect their nature. Because God has chosen them to be God's own people, they must lead their lives accordingly. Basically, the understanding in Lev 19:2 is that one is to live in obedience to the Torah, to the will of God."[34]

In the Greek world, there are indications that point to an insight into the imitation of God. Plato, for example, speaks of "imitating God" in reference to his thought concerning the shadow and the ideal.[35] Philo, probably through the influence of the Hellenistic world, also speaks about the imitation of God by parents who imitate God in the procreation of their children.[36] This overview points to the conclusion that for the house of Israel the idea of the imitation of God did not play any important role, while in the wider Hellenistic world it did.

The Letter of James. The Letter of James is a theological text rather that a Christological one. The focus in this writing is on God rather than on Jesus. On only two occasions is the name of Jesus Christ mentioned directly (1:1; 2:1).[37] This is very different from the writings of Paul. At the same time there is no reference to the death and resurrection of Jesus. While James does not specifically address the aspect of the imitation of God, some of his sayings point the hearer/reader in this direction. For example, when the text speaks of humans being created in "the likeness of God" (3:9), it points backwards to the account of the biblical creation story. However, it also says that the believer is even now in God's likeness. This implies that believers must therefore act in the way in which God acts. When religion is defined as "to take care of orphans and widows" (1:27), behind this definition lies the concept of the way God acts throughout the Septuagint. God is the champion of the poor and outcasts. Consequently, this concept of religion

---

34. Ibid., 140–41. See as well, Jacques Dupont, "L'Appel à imiter Dieu en Matthieu 5,48 et Luc 6,36," *Rivista Biblica* 14 (1966): 140.

35. See Henri Crouzel, "L'Imitation et la 'Suite' de Dieu et de Christ dans les Premières Siècles Chrétiens, ainsi que Leurs Sources Gréco-Romaines et Hébraïques," *Jahrbuch für Antike und Christentum* (Jahrgang 21; Münster: Aschendorffsche Verlagsbuchhandlung, 1978), 7–8.

36. Philo, *Decal.* 107, 120; *Spec.* 2.225.

37. The references to God are more frequent: (ὁ) θεός occurs sixteen times (1:1, 5, 13 (twice), 20, 27; 2:5; 19, 23 (twice); 3:9; 4:4 (twice), 6, 7, 8); πατήρ ("Father") occurs three times (1:17, 27; 3:9); κύριος ("Lord") occurs eleven times: it refers to God on six occasions (1:7; 4:10, 15; 5:4, 10, 11) and to Jesus on five occasions (1:1; 2:1; 5:7, 14, 15).

exhorts believers to imitate God's actions in concern for those who are marginalized within their community. In almost all the ethical admonitions that James puts before his hearers/readers, he draws attention to actions that would reflect God's actions, namely, concern for the poor, widows, and orphans (1:27), compassion and mercy (5:11), and care for the sick (5:13–18).

The Gospel of Matthew. As noted above in discussing Matthew's call to be perfect, Jesus instructs his hearers/readers to imitate God: "Be perfect, therefore, as you heavenly Father is perfect" (5:48). This forms a conclusion to the whole section on the antitheses, "You have heard that it was said. . . . But I say to you. . ." (5:21–48). Prior to this call to imitate God, Matthew's Jesus has issued a call to love all people, including one's enemies. As a reason for this call, Jesus gave God's actions of love and care for all people as an example of what they were to imitate: "So that you may be children of your Father in heaven; for he makes his sun rise on the evil and on the good, and sends rain on the righteous and on the unrighteous" (5:45). Because God's actions treat all people equally, Jesus instructs his followers to do likewise. They are to imitate God's actions (not his essence). The same concept is expressed in the following section of the Sermon on the Mount where Matthew presents Jesus's teaching on forgiveness contained in the Our Father: "For if you forgive others their trespasses, your heavenly Father will also forgive you; but if you do not forgive others, neither will your Father forgive your trespasses" (Matt 6:14–15). In all their actions, believers are called to strive to maintain a right relationship with God.

The Didache. No specific attention is given to the imitation of God. The ethical admonitions as well are generally presented in the form of direct prescriptions without any further elaboration. As with the Letter of James and the Sermon on the Mount, the ethical admonitions of the Didache occur in a theological rather than Christological context. The writer speaks of teaching them the "reverential fear of God" (4:9–10). He also instructs his hearers/readers to look on others as they would on God: for example, "My child, night and day remember the one who speaks the word of God to you; honor him as the Lord" (4:1). There is also a focus upon God's actions, rather than upon God's being: "Welcome whatever happens to you as good, knowing that nothing occurs apart from God" (3:10).

The above discussion shows that in the ethical teaching of all three texts God is the center of concern and that the ethical admonitions are founded upon God. In the Gospel of Matthew (and probably in the Letter of James), God's actions are held up for imitation. This is unique in New Testament texts because elsewhere the focus lies chiefly on the imitation of Jesus and of his actions.

2.2.3. Double-minded

Connections can also be noted among the three texts, The Letter of James, the Gospel of Matthew and the Didache, regarding specific ethical admonitions that are distinctive within these writings.

In the Letter of James, the Greek word δίψυχος ("double-minded") occurs twice (1:8 and 4:8). This word δίψυχος is not found in the Greek language prior to the Letter of James. After James, the word appears in a number of Christian writings: δίψυχος occurs in *1 Clem.* 11.2; *2 Clem.* 11.2; and Herm. *Mand.* 9.6 while the verb διψυχεῖν occurs in *1 Clem.* 23.2; *2 Clem.* 11.5; Did. 4:4 and Herm. *Vis.* 2.2.7. This tends to indicate that the Letter of James either coined this word[38] or introduced it into Christian literature.[39] While the word might not have occurred before James, the concept is certainly found in Platonic thought that discusses divisions within the soul. Literally, the word means "double-souled." In the Hebrew Bible there is a reference to being double-hearted (with "a double heart they speak;" Ps 12:2). A major theme running throughout the Letter of James is the division that faces a person between friendship with God and friendship with the world. For James, δίψυχος captures this theme of the letter and focuses at the very beginning on the need to have loyalty in one's life. One cannot be divided as though one's very soul is divided.

James 1:5–8 draws a contrast between God's generous giving and the picture of the double-minded person. God gives gifts unhesitatingly to believers. On the other hand, the double-minded person's lack of trust in God's actions emerges from doubting prayer. The double-minded are so fickle that they cannot make a decision to trust God. What James argues for is a single-minded relationship with God whether on the individual or the community level. This is the heart of his message: the community and the individual embrace the same vision, the same *ethos*. They strive to live out their identity as "God's twelve-tribe kingdom." This demands total allegiance to God—no compromise is possible between friendship with the world and friendship with God.

The word δίψυχος occurs again in 4:8, "Draw near to God, and he will draw near to you. Cleanse your hands, you sinners, and purify your hearts, you double-minded" (ἐγγίσατε τῷ θεῷ καὶ ἐγγιεῖ ὑμῖν. καθαρίσατε χεῖρας, ἁμαρτωλοί καὶ ἁγνίσατε καρδίας, δίψυχοι). While in 1:8 the context was that of trusting God unconditionally in prayer, here the vision is wider. They are called to single-minded dedication to God. The only way this can be achieved is by purifying their hearts for they are divided in loyalty between God and the world. The purity rules take on added significance in this context because they are the means of reestablishing a relationship with God and maintaining access to God.

---

38. Stanley Porter, "Is *dipsychos* (James 1:8; 4:8) a 'Christian' Word?" *Bib* 71 (1990): 469–98.

39. Joseph B. Mayor, *The Epistle of St. James. The Greek Text with Introduction, Notes and Comments* (3rd ed.; London: Macmillan, 1910; repr. Grand Rapids: Zondervan, 1954), 42.

In the Gospel of Matthew, the word δίψυχος does not occur. Nevertheless, the same fundamental idea of total allegiance to God is found. In the Sermon on the Mount, Jesus speaks to the need of having undivided loyalty in relationship to God: "No one can serve two masters; for a slave will either hate the one and love the other, or be devoted to the one and despise the other. You cannot serve God and wealth" (6:24).

In Didache 4:4, the verb διψυχεῖν appears: "Do not be of two minds, whether this should happen or not" (οὐ διψυχήσεις, πότερον ἔσται ἢ οὔ). Like the Letter of James, it is a call to place single-minded trust in God. While this passage is somewhat unclear, the *Canons* (13:2)[40] offer an interpretation: "Do not be double-minded in your prayer." This is similar to the context of James 1:8 that spoke of unconditional trust in God in one's prayer life. The Didache also speaks about being "double-minded "and "double-tongued": "Do not be of two minds or speak from both sides of your mouth, for speaking from both sides of your mouth is a deadly trap" (οὐκ ἔσῃ διγνώμων οὐδὲ δίγλωσσος. παγὶς γὰρ θανάτου ἡ διγλοσσία; 2:4). Central to the Didache is the choice to be made between two paths, the path of life or the path of death. The believer is called to choose uncon-ditionally the path of life (1:1–2).

In all three texts, the ethical admonition to be single-minded in trusting God occurs whether it is through prayer or through undivided loyalty to God. This term δίψυχος evokes a concept that is central to the thought of all three documents, namely, the exclusive choice of friendship with God as opposed to friendship with the world (James) or the inability to serve two masters (Matthew) or the choice between the two paths of life and of death (the Didache).

2.2.4. The Double Command of Love

Many other ethical admonitions could be examined in these three texts, such as the relationship of faith and works, or the relationship of rich and poor. How-ever, the final point of this examination will look at the twofold command of love, which gives direction to many of the specific ethical issues that do arise.

All three texts stress the importance of the twofold command of love. This is nothing surprising in the context of the New Testament, since almost every tradi-tion pays attention to the importance of this command which undoubtedly goes back to Jesus.[41] What is significant is the similarity in the way this love command functions in each of the writings.

---

40. *The Canons* referred to here are the so-called *Apostolic Church Order* or *Canons of the Holy Apostles* where chapters 4–13 offer parallels to the Didache 1:1–4:8 without the section *Did.* 1:3b–2:1. (For a discussion of these Canons see Kurt Niederwimmer, *The Didache* [Herme-neia; trans. L. M. Maloney; ed. H. W. Attridge; Minneapolis: Fortress Press, 1998], 13–14).

41. See, for example, Matt 19:19; 22:39; Mark 12:31; Luke 10:27; Rom 13:9; Gal 5:14; John 15:12; 1 John 3:11.

The Letter of James. The central aspects of James's faith and his admonitions come together in chapter 2. The writer shows how faith requires a response in action: love is the basic response. In Jas 2:19 a deliberate reference is made to the Israelite profession of faith: "You believe that God is one; you do well" (2:19). This statement reflects the *Shema Israel* of Deut 6:4–5. In this context, James shows the absurdity of separating faith and works. This profession of faith is not just an intellectual acceptance; but it also requires a response. Even demons respond by shuddering in fear. The response of love for God (Deut 6:5) called forth from the believer is the opposite of fear.

In Jesus's teaching, faith also calls for a response of love: in particular love for neighbor (Matt 22:36–40). James embraces this second response of love of neighbor in 2:8 and thereby shows that he is handing on the teaching not just of his Scriptures but also of Jesus. James 2:8 belongs to the context of 2:1–13, which argues that faith of Jesus Christ[42] was irreconcilable with any form of favoritism or discrimination. Again, the faith of Jesus requires a response of love for one's neighbor.

James 2:8 identifies the love of neighbor as "the royal law" or "the law of the kingdom" (νόμον . . . βασιλικὸν. . .). In referring to this law of love of neighbor, James is also clearly conscious of the context in which this admonition occurs in Lev 19,[43] which outlines the social demands that arise for the Israelites in carrying out the Torah. Many of these ethical admonitions are considered by James in the course of his letter. For example, "you shall not keep for yourself the wages of a laborer" (Lev 19:13 = Jas 5:4): "you shall not be partial to the poor or defer to the great" (Lev 19:15 = 2:1–7). This latter admonition is exactly what James refers to in this "parable," where he points to discrimination against the poor in favor of the rich within community assemblies. As the "royal law," the law of love is the basic requirement for those who belong to James's communities. Love of the poor is the concrete way the law of love is carried out in these communities and it identifies the communities as those that imitate God's actions. James's instructions parallel those of Lev 19 and function in a similar way. The instructions of Lev 19 are concrete social markers that identify the type of community Israel is and how the members of Israel's community are to lead their lives. In like manner, the Letter of James identifies how his communities are to live out this

---

42. In the much-discussed interpretation of Jas 2:1, the reference is to the "*faith of* our Lord Jesus Christ" rather than to the "*faith in* our Lord Jesus Christ." For the Letter of James, faith is always directed to God not to Jesus. The genitive used here is a subjective genitive ("*faith of* our Lord Jesus Christ"), not an objective genitive ("*faith in* our Lord Jesus Christ"). See Hartin, *James,* 116–17.

43. Luke T. Johnson ("The Use of Leviticus 19 in the Letter of James," *JBL* 101 [1982]: 391–401) has given a really insightful and important study of the connections between Jas 2:8 and Lev 19.

law of love of neighbor by providing those social markers necessary to lead their lives as communities of the poor in relationship with one another and with God.

The Gospel of Matthew. To love God and one's neighbor embraces the entirety of the Law and the prophets (Matt 22:34–40). The same basic stress identified in James occurs here. In the encounter with the rich young man, Jesus challenges him to go beyond simply carrying out the second half of the ten commandments: "If you wish to be perfect, go, sell your possessions, and give the money to the poor, and you will have treasure in heaven; then come follow me" (19:21). Beyond the carrying out of the basic commandments, Matthew's Jesus also draws attention to the need to show special concern for the poor.

The Didache. This text opens with the double profession of love: "This then is the path of life. First, love the God who made you, and second your neighbor as yourself" (Did. 1:2). By opening with an express reference to the twofold law of love, the writer defines the basic requirement for the path of life to be: love of God and love of neighbor. As with the Letter of James, these are the foundational laws of the community clearly defining their identity. The ethical admonitions that follow (1:1–6:3) are an expression of how this love of neighbor is to be carried out. The writer says this specifically: "This is the teaching relating to these matters" (Did. 1:3). As with the Letter of James, the writer of the Didache is also concerned with providing an authentic interpretation of how the members of the community are to behave and preserve their identity. In describing the path of death (Did. 5), the mistreatment of the poor and oppressed is singled out for special condemnation: "Showing no mercy to the poor nor toiling for the oppressed nor knowing the one who made them . . . who turn their backs on the needy, oppress the afflicted and are supporters of the wealthy (πλουσίων παράκλητοι)" (5:2). The phrase πλουσίων παράκλητοι is ironic since the word παράκλητος refers to someone who acts on behalf of another. They should in fact be supporting the poor in the spirit of the Hebrew Scriptures as well as of Jesus. Instead, they support the rich.[44]

What is noteworthy in all three texts is the way in which this double command of love functions. In all instances, the love of God and of neighbor functions as the foundational law for each community. Above all the love of neighbor is concretely demonstrated through a love and concern for the poor, for those who have no one to defend them since they have no power and are at the mercy of those who are more powerful in society.

---

44. As Niederwimmer (*The Didache,* 118) says: "Παράκλητος is someone who intervenes on behalf of another. Its use here is ironic: they ought to act as advocates for the poor and needy, but no; they turn out instead to be advocates for the rich! The whole thing recalls the style of prophetic cursing. . . ."

3. The Place of the Letter of James, the Gospel of Matthew, and the Didache in Developing Early Christian Literature

Having considered the ethical perspective of these three documents, I turn to examine very briefly the relationship of these documents to other traditions and other Christian literature emerging at a similar period of time. Again a brief focus on their ethical dimensions is intended.

3.1. The Jesus Sayings Traditions

3.1.1. The Letter of James[45]

The cultural text behind the Letter of James is clearly that of the Septuagint. For the religious world in which James functions, the Torah is above all the normative text that gives his communities direction.[46] While Jas 2:8 quotes from the Book of Leviticus in support of his understanding of the "royal law," the Letter of James seldom quotes directly from the normative cultural texts. Instead, the writer uses them in support of his exhortations or arguments. In other words, he uses the images and thoughts *in performing his own argument*. What James does here, is what Jan Assmann calls "*a will to form* that is a will of transmission, of transmitting a distinctive cultural identity to further generations."[47]

The Letter of James also has another normative entity that imbues itself upon his thought, and that is the teaching of Jesus of Nazareth. I have examined this connection between the Letter of James and the traditions of Jesus, especially the relationship to the Q Sayings of Jesus, in a number of publications.[48] Here I wish briefly to draw attention to the way in which James has used these sayings.

The writer of the Letter of James uses Jesus's teaching in a manner analogous to the way he used his Scriptures to bring across his teaching and message. For example, in Jas 2:1 the writer holds up "the faith of our Lord Jesus Christ" for imitation. The way in which Jesus has interpreted the teachings of the Hebrew Scriptures becomes normative for the author of the Letter of James. As indicated above, the message both of Jesus and of James is that God is in the process of reconstituting "the twelve-tribe kingdom." God's activity was at work in Jesus's

---

45. The substance of this section on the Letter of James formed part of a paper I read at the Annual Meeting of the Society of Biblical Literature held in Washington, D.C., November 18–21, 2006 in the Consultation on Jewish-Christianity.

46. See Jan Assmann, "Form as Mnemonic Device: Cultural Texts and Cultural Memory," in *Performing the Gospel: Orality, Memory and Mark. Essays dedicated to Werner Kelber* (ed. R. A. Horsley, J. A. Draper, J. M. Foley; Minneapolis: Fortress Press, 2006), 76.

47. Ibid., 69.

48. See Patrick J. Hartin, *James and the Q Sayings of Jesus* (JSNTSup 47; Sheffield: JSOT Press, 1991), 141–72; Hartin, *James*, 81–88.

teaching and ministry. In the opening verse of his letter, James shows his understanding that God's action is continuing and his letter is addressed to those who represent the beginnings of this new twelve tribe kingdom.

For James, there is a harmonious interplay between the two traditions of the Septuagint and the teachings/sayings of Jesus. Each is used to illuminate the other. A good example is found in Jas 2:1–13 where the readers are called upon not to show favoritism within the community.[49] As I have shown elsewhere, James uses the structure of a perfect argument as outlined in *Rhetorica ad Herennium* (2.18, 28). Behind James's argument lies the language of Jesus's saying in the beatitude: "Blessed are you who are poor, for yours is the kingdom of God" (Q 6:20//Matt 5:3).[50] In order to call his readers to avoid discrimination against others, he builds upon both Jesus's message as well as his Scriptures. His argument is based upon the royal law so central to the normative texts of the house of Israel and the traditions that handed on Jesus's message.[51] In effect, James is performing the memory of Jesus anew by weaving it together with the memory of his Scriptures. The memory of Jesus can be used in a sense to interpret the Septuagint, and the Septuagint in its turn illuminates the tradition of Jesus himself. There is an interplay that exists between the two sources for the argument that James constructs.

This rhetorical usage of the two major traditions that influence James's thought is a further convincing argument for seeing the relationship of the Letter of James within the cultural worlds and heritage of the house of Israel and the followers of Jesus in the way they were developing within the course of the first-century C.E.

3.1.2. The Gospel of Matthew

The existence of the Q Sayings Source of the Jesus Traditions is based upon the similarities in the sayings material found in the Gospels of Matthew and Luke. The way Matthew used this sayings material is very different from James's usage. He preserves the character of the saying and transforms it only slightly to accord with other traditional material at his disposal and his theological vision. There are many similarities between the sayings material that serves as the basis for James's performance and the material found especially in the Sermon on the Mount. I have examined these connections elsewhere.[52] James does not appear

---

49. For a fuller explanation of this passage, see ibid. 124–48.

50. Ibid., 119–20. For the Q form of this Beatitude see James M. Robinson, Paul Hoffmann and John S. Kloppenborg, *The Critical Edition of Q* (Hermeneia; Minneapolis: Fortress Press, 2000), 46–47.

51. Hartin, *James*, 134–37.

52. See Patrick J. Hartin. "James and the Sermon on the Mount/ Plain," in *SBLSP* 28 (ed. D. J. Lull; Atlanta: Scholars Press, 1989), 440–57; and *James and the Q Sayings of Jesus*, 140–98.

to show a knowledge of the Gospel of Matthew or of the Sermon on the Mount. James's usage of the sayings traditions appears to be prior to the way in which Matthew has developed some of these sayings within his Gospel.[53]

3.1.3. The Didache

Many studies have been done on the *sectio evangelica* (Did. 1:3b–2:1) introduced at the beginning of the Two Ways material (1:1–6:3). John S. Kloppenborg, for example, has presented a careful and painstakingly insightful examination of the *sectio evangelica* (Did. 1:3b–2:1) where he has shown that this section of the Didache is clearly using the Jesus sayings tradition,[54] but it is difficult to determine exactly which tradition is being used in a certain instance.

There is a decided difference in the way in which the Didache has used these sources of the Jesus tradition and the way in which James has done so. The Didache, as with the Gospel of Matthew, has remained closer to the form of the actual Jesus saying by reproducing it as the didachist received it. James, on the other hand, has performed the saying in his own particular manner, thus leading to a certain transformation of Jesus's saying in a way that speaks to the hearers of his text.

The above examination shows that the three texts in different ways and to different degrees all bear some knowledge and use of the Jesus sayings traditions, especially that of the Sayings Source Q. It must argue for a location where the Sayings Source Q was circulating and for a time period in which it was being used.

3.2. The Letter of Barnabas and the Two Ways

The second part of the Letter of Barnabas offers a form of the Two Ways teaching that appears at the beginning of the Didache (1:1–6:3 with the exclusion of the *sectio evangelica* [Did. 1:3b–2:1] referred to above). The similarities between the Letter of Barnabas and the Didache are not judged to derive from dependence on each other, but rather through dependence upon another Jewish source that was translated into Greek and circulated widely in the early Christian

---

53. A good example of this occurs in the one saying that is very close in both texts, namely, the condemnation of taking oaths (Jas 5:12; Matt 5:33–37). James is the shortest account, while Matthew's saying appears to have been developed further through the insertion of other biblical phrases (e.g., Isa 66:1).While this is not Q material, it is sayings material common to James and Matthew and I would argue that James is closer to the original saying.

54. John S. Kloppenborg, "The Use of the Synoptics or Q in *Did*. 1:3b–2:1," in van de Sandt, ed., *Matthew and the Didache*, 129.

world.[55] The concept of a duality of two ways of living is also found in the Letter of James (for example, the stress on "friendship with God and friendship with the world" as well as his discussion on the two kinds of wisdom: the wisdom from above and the wisdom that is earthly [Jas 3:13–18]). This does not necessarily point to contact with or to James's knowledge of the Two Ways document since it was a common religious ethical motif. The same is true of the Gospel of Matthew in the contrast between the parable of the wise man and foolish man who built their houses on rock and sand respectively. This parable contrasts two ways of life led either in conformity to the words of Jesus or in opposition to them (Matt 7:24–27).

3.3. The Letters of Paul

Much has been written about the relationship between James and Paul, and tragically James is most often approached only through Paul's eyes. In particular, Jas 2:14–26 has aroused much discussion regarding its relationship to Paul. James and Paul were contemporaries so it is natural to raise the question as to whether their writings were written in response to each other. While James and Paul share much common vocabulary,[56] their visions are very different. For Paul, the emphasis lies on God's action of justification that occurs through the death and resurrection of Jesus. This is contrasted with those who strive to work out their own salvation by carrying out the legalistic prescriptions of the Mosaic Law. James, on the other hand, is concerned that faith must demonstrate itself in works of love. True faith is demonstrated in action. Paul and James each have a different vision that concerns them. Paul is concerned with how someone attains justification: it is a work of God alone, not a human work. James is concerned with what happens when one believes: one has to demonstrate this faith through acts of love.

Both Paul and James stress the importance that faith plays in the path to salvation. While Paul was at pains to argue that justification does not come from one's own efforts, James contrasts a faith that was dead with a faith that was alive in God

A quick look at the Gospel of Matthew and the writings of Paul shows that central and characteristic ideas in Paul are significantly missing from Matthew's Gospel. Matthew contains no view of sin as holding a person or the human race in slavery as is the view of Paul. For Matthew as well, there is no reflection on why it is impossible for the believer to actually carry out the law. Paul struggled with

---

55. See Van de Sandt and Flusser, "The Influence of the Two Ways in Christian Literature," in *The Didache: Its Jewish Sources*, 81–111.

56. See, for example, words such as justification (δικαιοσύνη), to save (σῴζειν), faith (πίστις), law (νόμος), and works (ἔργα).

this issue and offered a solution that sees within each person a power preventing him/her from carrying out the law. In other words, for Matthew the important focus is on the actions that the believer performs. He does not go beyond the actions (as Paul does) to consider the one who performs the actions or to inquire about the nature of the person performing these deeds. Paul and Matthew show two very different ethical visions and concerns.

The same holds true in comparing Paul and the Didache. The latter text gives attention to the rules and way of life that the believer is to lead without considering the context in which all actions are to be performed, namely, the justifying action of God. The focus is solely on human actions.

Paul's writings and the writings of James, Matthew, and the Didache emerge from very different traditions within the early Christian world. These communities or traditions were not necessarily in opposition to each other. Instead, they point to the diversity of the early Christian world where each could walk to the pace of a different drummer.

3.4 THE GOSPEL OF JOHN

The other major tradition for which there is evidence in the New Testament is that of the writings of John. As with Paul, the ethical vision of John differs notably from that of James, Matthew, and the Didache. The most striking difference lies in the realm of ethical admonitions. For the Gospel of John, love is the only ethical directive: no further or specific ethical admonitions are given. The Gospel of John is a Gospel of relationships. It is concerned with portraying different levels of faith responses to the person of Jesus. The ideal to aim for is represented by the beloved disciple who shows that the essence of discipleship consists in faith expressed through love. Furthermore, the relationship with the house of Israel takes on a very different picture in the Gospel of John. John's community has been expelled from the synagogue. There has indeed been a "parting of the ways."[57] As argued throughout this paper, the texts of James, Matthew, and the Didache all maintain their roots within the traditions of the house of Israel. For the community of John these bonds have been irrevocably broken. Consequently, the community of the Gospel of John and the communities of James, Matthew, and the Didache are very diverse communities with no interaction among them, each striving to uphold a very different vision and identity.

---

57. To adopt the phrase that James D. G. Dunn (*The Partings of the Ways between Christianity and Judaism and their Significance for the Character of Christianity* [Philadelphia: Trinity Press International, 1991]) has used to characterize the separation between the world of the house of Israel and the world of the followers of Jesus the Messiah.

4. Conclusion

Besides the Christian writings and traditions examined above, other early Christian writings also existed within the nascent Christian movement, such as those that focused around the figure of Thomas. *The Gospel of Thomas,* for example, had a very different ethos than that found in the above texts. Its focus was primarily on providing secret wisdom needed for leading life and acquiring salvation. The community from which the Gospel of Thomas and its associated writings drew their inspiration was Gnostic in heart and vision, which was very different from what lay behind the Letter of James, the Gospel of Matthew, and the Didache.

The instructions in these three texts, the Letter of James, the Gospel of Matthew, and the Didache, are at heart a call to fulfill God's will in order to maintain access to God, and to develop a right relationship with God and with one another. All three texts in their own way give expression to their understanding that faith has to be expressed through action. As James says, "But someone will say, 'You have faith and I have works.' Show me your faith apart from your works, and I by my works will show you my faith" (Jas 2:18). Matthew expresses this in a similar way: "Not everyone who says to me, 'Lord, Lord,' will enter the kingdom of heaven, but only the one who does the will of my Father in heaven" (Matt 7:21).

This examination of the ethos and ethical admonitions of these three texts has demonstrated that their identity and vision clearly point to a common, developing milieu that was still at home within the heritage and traditions of Israel, a heritage now influenced by the direction and interpretation that Jesus gave these traditions. The Letter of James (written toward the middle 60s C.E.) is the first witness to the vision and ethical directives of this milieu. This letter presents a vision for communities of the Diaspora to live faithfully according to Israel's traditions as interpreted by the teachings of Jesus in order to preserve their identity as God's twelve-tribe kingdom. The ethical admonitions reflect this identity. Matthew's Gospel (written in the early 80s C.E.) takes the story of Jesus and uses it to speak to his community concerned with remaining true to the traditions of the past while at the same time moving forward to grapple with new issues and concerns. In painting a narrative where the outreach to the Gentiles occurs after the ministry of Jesus, Matthew shows that this development was planned and envisioned by Jesus. With *the Didache* (written at the end of the first century and beginning of the second century C.E.), one notices that a shift has occurred within the community whereby many Gentiles have been admitted. The concern with which the Didache grapples is, "What are the requirements for these new members within their community?"

Based on the above investigation, I would suggest that the relationship between these three documents should be conceived in this manner: The Letter of James was the first writing to appear. It is addressed to communities in the Diaspora that were still clearly within the orbit of the house of Israel, but as a result of the teaching of Jesus saw themselves as the beginning of a reconstitution of the "twelve tribes of Israel." The Gospel of Matthew was written from one of these communities in the Diaspora within two decades of the writing of the Letter of James. The traditional location of Antioch as the home of Matthew's Gospel would also correspond well for the home of the Sayings Source Q. Distinctive to the Gospel of Matthew was the openness that it urged for the acceptance of Gentiles into their community. Finally, the Didache would be seen to emerge from this same community (Antioch) a few decades later than the Gospel of Matthew in which it aimed at giving form and direction to a community where many Gentiles were accepting faith in the message of Jesus.

It is interesting to observe what happened to our three texts. The Didache was not incorporated into the Canon (not for any heretical teaching that it contained, but probably simply because it had stayed too closely bound to its roots within Israel). The Letter of James was relegated to the margins of Christianity. It struggled to gain admission into the Canon and was clearly not seen to be on the same level as the Gospels and the writings of Paul. Only the Gospel of Matthew, and in particular the Sermon on the Mount, emerged from early Christianity as an embodiment of what was considered to be the Magna Carta of Christianity. So familiar is the Sermon to Christians that it is considered to be characteristic of Jesus's message. Ironically, the Gospel of Matthew would claim central place within the worship life of the Christian community for many centuries.

Law and Ethics in Matthew's Antitheses and James's Letter: A Reorientation of Halakah in Line with the Jewish Two Ways 3:1-6

Huub van de Sandt

Many scholars agree that Matthew's Sermon on the Mount, especially the Antitheses (5:17–48) section, is in many respects comparable to the Letter of James.[1] Matthew and James share the view that the followers of Jesus belong to law-abiding Israel. Neither argues for Jewish law, but simply takes it for granted. Second, both the Antitheses and James are more interested in moral imperatives than the ceremonial aspects of the law. They make no reference to the issues of circumcision, dietary laws, or other aspects of Mosaic law. On the contrary—and this is the third similarity—they share a focused interpretation of the law that is epitomized in the commandment to love thy neighbor (Matt 5:43–48; Jas 2:8). Fourth, the Antitheses and James speak of perfection as the goal of the Christian life (Matt 5:48; Jas 1:4). Fifth, the content assigned to the concept of righteousness in the two texts is strikingly similar as well. Both the Antitheses and James consider righteousness within the context of human actions. In Jas 1:20 the term refers to the standard God sets for humanity and this is in line with the use of the concept of righteousness in the Antitheses where righteousness exceeds that of the scribes and Pharisees (Matt 5:20). Finally, both the Antitheses and James urge the necessity of carrying out the full stipulations of the law (see Matt 5:18 and Jas

---

1. Patrick J. Hartin, *James and the Q Sayings of Jesus* (JSNTSS 47; Sheffield: JSOT Press, 1991), 208 and 168; see also Wiard Popkes, *Adressaten, Situation und Form des Jakobusbriefes* (Stuttgarter Bibelstudien 125/126; Stuttgart: Katholisches Bibelwerk, 1986), 174–75; Peter H. Davids, *The Epistle of James: A Commentary on the Greek Text* (NIGTC; Grand Rapids: Eerdmans, 1982), 47–49; Dean B. Deppe, *The Sayings of Jesus in the Epistle of James* (Chelsea, Mich.: Bookcrafters, 1989), 161; Gerhard Kittel, "Der geschichtliche Ort des Jakobusbriefes," *ZNW* 41 (1942): 71–105: 87; Virgil V. Porter, "The Sermon on the Mount in the Book of James: Part 1," *BSac* 162 (2005): 344–60; see also Wiard Popkes, *Der Brief des Jakobus* (THKNT 14; Leipzig: Evangelische Verlagsanstalt, 2001), 32–35. See also the contribution of Patrick J. Hartin in this volume.

2:10) and each does so by quoting examples of adultery and murder, albeit in reverse order (Matt 5:21–22, 27–28 and Jas 2:11).

Heading the list of themes in which James and Matthew stand in the same theological camp is the concept of the law. Matthew and James agree that fulfillment of the law—with a special emphasis upon moral consequences and high ethical standards—is the appropriate interpretation of the teachings of Jesus. How shall we account for this similarity of outlook in Matthew and James? Of course, one text may be dependent upon the other. James might have used material written by Matthew or Matthew by James. This is, however, most improbable.[2]

This paper argues that the correspondence in perspective between Matthew and James with regard to the law results from their common orientation on a section of the Jewish Two Ways that is best preserved in Did. 3:1–6. We will see first that both the theme and terminology of the *teknon* section in Did. 3:1–6 betray close affinities with material collected and preserved in the pious milieu of early Hasidic Sages. This specific ethical stream within early Rabbinic Judaism is probably the concrete life situation of the *teknon* passage. I then examine the Matthean Antitheses and James's Letter. Both Matthew's formulation of the Antitheses part (5:17–48) of the Sermon on the Mount and James's creation of specific segments of his letter (1:13–21; 2:8–11 and 4:1–4) used traditional materials identical or similar to those transmitted in Two Ways 3:1–6. The ethical code in the Antitheses and James—higher standards for the halakic way of life—finds its best explanation in light of Did. 3:1–6 and current traditions in Jewish Hasidic circles (*section 2*). This traditional type of instruction does not provide us with a full understanding of Matthew's Antitheses and the Letter of James, however. The argument in the latter writings is more rigorous than that in the Two Ways or the Hasidic literature. Matthew and James independently represent a further development and radicalization of the warnings in Did. 3:1–6, as will be shown in the final part of this paper.

---

2. For James's dependence upon the Gospel of Matthew, see, among others, Deppe, *The Sayings of Jesus in the Epistle of James*, 28; Massey H. Shepherd Jr., "The Epistle of James and the Gospel of Matthew," *JBL* 75 (1956): 40–51; Feliks Gryglewicz, "L'Épitre de St. Jacques et l'Évangile de St. Matthieu," *Roczniki Teologicano-kanoniczne* 8 (1961): 33–55, R. M. Cooper, "Prayer: A Study in Matthew and James," *Enc* 29 (1968): 268–77. The possibility of dependence is often postulated if a second-century dating for James is accepted. Nevertheless, "most scholars," according to Luke T. Johnson, "correctly agree that neither James nor Matthew knows the other"; see Luke T. Johnson and Wesley H. Wachob, "The Sayings of Jesus in the Letter of James," in *Authenticating the Words of Jesus* (ed. B. Chilton and C. A. Evans; NTTS 28/1; Leiden: Brill, 1999), 431–50; repr. in Luke T. Johnson, *Brother of Jesus, Friend of God: Studies in the Letter of James* (Grand Rapids: Eerdmans, 2004), 142.

1. The Two Ways 3:1–6

The Two Ways opens with two contrasting moral instructions that serve as a framework for the subsequent exposition of two sets of opposing ethical characteristics or antagonistic groups of people associated with the way of life and the way of death. This basic tradition circulated in Christian communities apart from its eventual incorporation and modification in the Didache.

1.1. The Two Ways in the Didache

Early versions of the Two Ways are found in Did. 1–6, the *Letter of Barnabas* 18–20, and the *Doctrina Apostolorum*, but there are also later recensions of the Two Ways tradition that include church orders, letters, and monastic writings.[3] They all prove that the doctrine was widely known in the first Christian centuries and attest to its popularity. Additional evidence supporting this assumption is that the doctrine of the Two Ways was employed within Christian circles in pre-baptismal instruction. This is explicitly stated in Did. 7:1, in a verse that follows right after the rendering of the Two Ways section. "Concerning baptism, baptize as follows: after having previously said these things (ταῦτα πάντα προειπόντες), baptize" (7:1).[4]

Early and later Christian writings thus attest to a separate circulation of a form of the Two Ways closely related to Did. 1–6. Recently, David Flusser and I have attempted to produce a reconstruction of the original teaching. Because the text of this pre-Didache source was in Greek, the document may be called the Greek Two Ways.[5] For our purpose, it is important to establish that this (hypothetical) version is generally reproduced in the precise wording of the Two Ways in the Didache, excepting only the Christianized sections 1:3b–2:1 and 6:2–3.[6] In

---

3. The Two Ways tradition in the later recensions as represented by the Apostolic Church Order, the Epitome of the Canons of the Holy Apostles, the Life of Shenoute, the Ps. Athanasian Syntagma Doctrinae, and the Fides CCCXVIII Patrum, demonstrate numerous links with the content and structure of the Doctrina and the Didache; see Huub van de Sandt and David Flusser, *The Didache: Its Jewish Sources and its Place in Early Judaism and Christianity* (CRINT 3/5; Assen: Van Gorcum, 2002), 63–70.

4. In Egypt as late as fourth century, the Two Ways manual was used as a pre-baptismal didactic tool and provided basic instruction about Christian life to neophytes. See Van de Sandt and Flusser, *The Didache: Its Jewish Sources*, 86–89. See also the contribution of Alistair Stewart-Sykes in this volume.

5. For the above information and a reconstruction of the Greek Two Ways, see Van de Sandt and Flusser, *The Didache: Its Jewish Sources*, 112–39.

6. Van de Sandt and Flusser, *The Didache: Its Jewish Sources*, 55–72. Also the Didache text itself shows the awkwardness of these verses. After the warning in 6:1 to sustain and observe the aforesaid prescriptions in the comprehensive ethical treatise, the subsequent verses (6:2–3) suddenly present a reduction of the previous standards for those unable to "bear the entire

this paper, therefore, I follow the Christian Didache excluding those parts and details that differ from the hypothesized Greek Two Ways.

Once one accepts that Did. 1–6 reflects the pre-didachist Two Ways teaching, the section could be taken to independently reproduce the early Jewish manual that might have been reworked by Matthew and James. Thus, as utilized in the Didache, the Two Ways conceivably provides us with a direct view of the unique material used by Matthew in writing Matt 5:17–48 and one of the sources employed by James. Admittedly, one could refer to other sources as well which show the Antitheses and James to be in line with the agenda of first-century Judaism.[7] None of these materials, however, has so far provided any external evidence of a similar line of reasoning, a corresponding topical organization or an analogous elaboration of the law. In this respect the comparison of the similarities between the Antitheses and James on the one hand and Did. 3:1–6 on the other turns out to be more relevant.

1.2. DID. 3:1–6 WITHIN ITS JEWISH SETTING

Did. 3:1–6 contains a general introduction followed by five small textual units. Apart from some slight changes, they are constructed in the same framework and employ the same terminology. The verses 2–6 display a particular

---

yoke of the Lord." Didache 6:2 unexpectedly indicates that partial compliance with all previous admonitions is sufficient. Furthermore, with respect to food, everyone is allowed to determine what is to be eaten and only a minimum requirement is stipulated (6:3). A second remarkable feature occurs in Did. 1:3b–2:1. The passage clearly interrupts the connection between Did. 1:3a and 2:2 and it stands out from the immediate context in chapters 1–6 with respect to its large number of close parallels to the Gospels of Matthew and Luke. This is all the more striking because a similar accumulation of traditional Gospel motifs is absent from the remainder of the Two Ways manual of Did. 1–6.

7. As for Matthew, see Ingo Broer, "Anmerkungen zum Gesetzesverständnis des Matthäus," in *Das Gesetz im Neuen Testament* (ed. K. Kertelge; QD 108; Freiburg: Herder, 1986), 128–45: 131–33; Hans D. Betz, *The Sermon on the Mount: A Commentary on the Sermon on the Mount, including the Sermon on the Plain (Matthew 5:3–7:27 and Luke 6:20–49)* (Hermeneia; Minneapolis: Fortress, 1995), 277–85; Gerald Friedlander, *The Jewish Sources of the Sermon on the Mount* (Library of Biblical Studies; New York: Ktav 1969), 40–53; Str-B 1:276–82, 298–301; Claude G. Montefiore, *Rabbinic Literature and Gospel Teachings* (1st ed. 1930; repr. New York: Macmillan, 1970), 38–56; Ernst Percy, *Die Botschaft Jesu: Eine traditionskritische und exegetische Untersuchung* (LUÅ n.s. 49; Lund: Gleerup, 1953), 131–63.

As for James, see, among others, Louis Massebieau, "L'Épitre de Jacques est-elle l'oeuvre d'un Chrétien?" *RHR* 32 (1895): 249–83; Friedrich A. W. Spitta, "Der Buch des Jacobus," in *Der Brief des Jakobus: Studien zum Hirten des Hermas* (vol. 2 of *Zur Geschichte und Literatur des Urchristentums*; ed. F. A. W. Spitta; Göttingen: Vandenhoeck & Ruprecht, 1896); Hartwig Thyen, *Der Stil der jüdisch-hellenistischen Homilie* (FRLANT 65; Göttingen: Vandenhoeck & Ruprecht, 1955); Willi Marxsen, *Introduction to the New Testament* (trans. G. Buswell; Philadelphia: Fortress, 1968).

repetitive pattern in that each is divided into two parallel halves. The first half contains a warning against a specific minor transgression because such a sin, so it says, "leads to" a major transgression. Then, in the second half, an admonishment is offered against two or more minor sins, for these too are considered to "give birth to" a major transgression. With respect to the Matthean and Jacobean materials at issue, the first three verses are rendered here:

(3:1) My child (τέκνον μου), flee from all evil and from everything resembling it.

(3:2)

    a. Be not angry (μὴ γίνου ὀργίλος),

    b. for anger (ὀργή) leads to murder (φόνον),

    c. nor jealous (μηδὲ ζηλωτής) nor irascible (μηδὲ ἐριστικός) nor hot-tempered (μηδὲ θυμικός)

    d. for from these murders are born (φόνοι γεννῶνται).

(3:3)

    a. My child, be not desirous (μὴ γίνου ἐπιθυμητής),

    b. for desire (ἐπιθυμία) leads to fornication (πορνείαν),

    c. nor foul-mouthed nor indiscreetly peering

    d. for from all these adulteries are born (μοιχεῖαι γεννῶνται).

In two clauses (a and c) minor transgressions are mentioned that "lead to" or "bring about" major sins (b and d): murder (3:2), fornication and adultery (these two are classed together in 3:3),[8] idolatry (3:4), theft (3:5), and blasphemy (3:6). The concept that Did. 3:1–6 presupposes is the common Jewish distinction between minor and major commandments.[9] The passage not only requires strict

---

8. See below, n. 56.

9. See 4 Macc 5.19–21, dismissing the suggestion that less weighty sins are less serious: "Accordingly, you must not regard it as a minor sin for us to eat unclean food (μὴ μικρὰν οὖν εἶναι νομίσῃς ταύτην, εἰ μιαροφαγήσαιμεν, ἁμαρτίαν); minor sins are just as weighty as great sins (τὸ γὰρ ἐπὶ μικροῖς καὶ μεγάλοις παρανομεῖν ἰσοδύναμόν ἐστιν), for in each case the law is despised"; trans. H. Anderson, "4 Maccabees," in The Old Testament Pseudepigrapha (ed. J. H. Charlesworth; 2 vols.; Garden City, N.Y.: Doubleday, 1983–85), 550.

In Philo's view, the observance of the light commandments is as essential as having no basic part of a building removed or destroyed; see Legat. 117 and compare also Philo's Alleg. Interp. 3.241; further, Isaak Heinemann, Philo's griechische und jüdische Bildung: Kulturvergleichende Untersuchungen zu Philons Darstellung der jüdischen Gesetze (Breslau, 1929–32; repr. Hildesheim: Georg Olms, 1962), 478–80.

An equally strict or even more rigorous attitude is found in rabbinic sources:

> Ben Azzai said: Run to fulfill the lightest precept even as the weightiest and flee from transgression; for one precept draws another precept in its train, and one transgression draws

observance of the major precepts, but also adherence to the minor commandments as well.

The preoccupation of the *teknon* section as a whole, however, is expressed
in the introductory sentence: "My child (τέκνον μου), flee from all evil and from
everything resembling it" (3:1). A similar statement occurs in rabbinic literature[10]
and has played a formative role in a particular type of rabbinic Judaism, that is,
in a refined ethics represented by the rabbinic *Derek Eres* tractates. Oral tracts
with subjects concerning *Derek Eres* existed as early as the second century C.E.
and part of these writings reflect the teachings of pious circles on moral behavior.
The early layer reflects a lifestyle that is called "derek hasidut," the way of the
pious. It reveals the teachings of the early Hasidim who "placed extreme stress on
self-deprival and the performance of good deeds and acts of loving kindness in
lieu of pure academic 'ivory tower' scholarship."[11] The treatise *Yir'at Het* ("fear
of transgression") is a separate denotation of chapters I–IV and IX of the Derek

---

another transgression in its train; for the reward of a precept (done) is a precept (to be
done), and the reward of one transgression is (another) transgression (*m. 'Abot* 4:2).

See George F. Moore, *Judaism in the First Centuries of the Christian Era: The Age of the Tannaim* (3 vols.; Cambridge, Mass.: Harvard University Press, 1927–1930), 1:470–71. The focus
on the light commandments also occurs in other general instances of rabbinic literature: *m.
'Abot* 2:1; *b. Menaḥ* 44a, top; *b. Ned.* 39b; *y. Pe'ah* 1,15d; *Sipre Deut* 79 to Deut 12:28 (Louis Finkelstein, ed. *Siphre ad Deuteronomium* [CT 3/2; Berlin: Jüdischer Kulturbund, 1939; repr New
York: Jewish Theological Seminary, 1969], 145); *Sipre Deut* 82 to Deut 13:1 (ibid., 148), *Sipre
Deut* 96 to Deut 13:19 (ibid., 157). See also Wilhelm Bacher, *Die exegetische Terminologie der
jüdischen Traditionsliteratur* (2 vols.; Leipzig, 1899; repr. Hildesheim: Olms, 1965), 1:172–74.

An echo of the rabbinic usage of "light" and "weighty" precepts is also found in the wording of Jesus: "and you have neglected the weightier matters of the Law" (βαρύτερα τοῦ νόμου)
in Matt 23:23b.

10. "For R. Eliezer did teach: 'one should always flee from what is hideous and from whatever seems hideous'" and "But the Sages said: 'Keep distant from what is hideous and from
whatever seems hideous'"; see *t. Ḥul.* 2:24 (M. S. Zuckermandel, ed. *Tosephta* [Pasewalk 1881;
repr. Jerusalem: Wahrmann, 1970], 503) and *t. Yebam.* 4:7 (Zuckermandel, *Tosephta*, 245),
respectively. For detailed substantiation of the following, see Van de Sandt and Flusser, *The
Didache: Its Jewish Sources*, 140–90.

11. Myron B. Lerner, "The External Tractates," in *The Literature of the Sages* (ed. S. Safrai;
CRINT 2/3; Assen: Van Gorcum, 1987), 1:380. See also Shmuel Safrai, "Teaching of Pietists in
Mishnaic Literature," *JJS* 16 (1965): 15–33: 25–28; idem, "Hasidim we-Anshei Maase," *Zion* 50
(1984–85): 133–54; idem, "Jesus and the Hasidim," *Jerusalem Perspective* 42–44 (1994): 3–22;
idem, "Jesus and the Hasidic Movement," in *The Jews in the Hellenistic-Roman World: Studies
in Memory of Menahem Stern* (ed. I. M. Gafni, A. Oppenheimer, and D. R. Schwartz; Jerusalem:
Graphit Press, 1996), 413–36 (Hebrew). See also Van de Sandt and Flusser, *The Didache: Its
Jewish Sources*, 165–69 and 172–73.

Ereṣ Zuṭa tract. Chapters I–III of this tract represent an early segment, probably dating from Tannaitic times.[12] It states:

> Keep aloof from everything hideous and from whatever seems hideous (הרחק מן הכיעור ומן הדומה לו) lest others suspect you of transgression (I,13).[13]

The urge to abstain from anything hideous, which is synonymous with evil,[14] incited pietistic Sages to keep not only to the literal meaning of a command-ment but also to its broad intention, surpassing the scope of widely accepted precepts. It exceeds the halakah's legal corpus. The early layer of *Derek Eres* liter-ature embodied a refined human ethic highlighting acts of charity, modesty and humility. Prominent in this doctrine is a rigorous attitude towards the prevailing halakah and the propensity for good deeds in public life, such as the redemption of captives, the restoration of property, the consolation of mourners, the giving of alms. Because they believed that a literal interpretation of the commandments resulted from a lack of positive motivation, they did more than the law required.

The most pertinent parallel to the preamble in Did. 3:1 and the subsequent strophes in 3:2–6 is found in the treatise *Yir'at Het* II,16–17. It concerns the fol-

---

12. The early (Tannaitic) part of *Yir'at Het* is identical with Masseket Derek Ereṣ Zuṭa, chapters I–III (minus I,18–20) in M. van Loopik, ed., *The Ways of the Sages and the Way of the World* (TSAJ 26; Tübingen: Mohr Siebeck, 1991), 172–251 (with commentary) = Masseket Derek Ereṣ, chapters I–II, in *The Treatises Derek Erez: Masseket Derek Erez; Pirke Ben Azzai; Tosefta Derek Erez* (ed. M. Higger; New York, 1935; repr. Jerusalem: Makor, 1970), 1:55–96 (Hebrew) and 2:33–42 (English). See Van Loopik, *The Ways of the Sages*, 9 and 16–17. Lerner ("External Tractates," 383, n. 108) refers to Higger's Masseket Derek Ereṣ I–II,7 (= *Treatises*, 55–93) as representing the earlier segment, which portion corresponds with Masseket Derek Ereṣ Zuṭa I–III,15 in Van Loopik, *The Ways of the Sages*, 172–246.

13. According to Van Loopik, *The Ways of the Sages*, 194–7 (with commentary) = Masse-ket Derek Ereṣ I,12 according to Higger, *Treatises*, 1:63 (Hebrew) and 2:35 (English). Compare also the following saying: "Keep aloof from anything hideous and (even) from whatever seems hideous"; see Derek Ereṣ Zuṭa VIII,3 according to Van Loopik, *The Ways of the Sages*, 290 = Masseket Derek Ereṣ VII,2 according to Higger, *Treatises*, 1:126 (Hebrew) and 2:50 (English). See further Masseket Yir'at Het, version a, chapter 2 in *Minor Tractates* (Massekhtot Ẓeirot) (ed. M. Higger; New York, 1929; repr. Jerusalem: Makor, 1970), 76 (lines 3–5); and version b, Perek Yir'at Heta in Higger, *Minor Tractates*, 82 (line 22)–83 (line 1) and Masseket Derek Eres Zeira, chapter 4, in Higger, *Minor Tractates* 90 (lines 12–13).

14. For the term כיעור ("ugliness") as ethically offensive, see the warning in S. Eli. Rab., chapter 2: "for ugly things that aren't fitting" (דברים מכוערים ודברים שאינן ראויין) (*Seder Eliyahu Rabba and Seder Eliyahu Zuta* [ed. M. Friedmann, Jerusalem: Wahrmann, 1969], 13); see also S. Eli. Rab., chapter 25 (ibid., 139); chapter 7 (ibid., 32); chapter 14 (ibid., 67); chapter 18 (ibid., 104).

lowing ethical rule, which serves as a résumé of moral codes in the *Derek Eres*
tractates:[15]

> Keep aloof from that which leads to transgression, keep aloof from everything
> hideous and from what even seems hideous. Shudder from committing a minor
> transgression (מחטא הקל), lest it leads you to commit a major transgression
> (לחטא חמור). Hurry to (perform) a minor precept (למצוה קלה), for this will lead
> you to (perform) a major precept (למצוה [חמורה]).[16]

The saying shows that the popular apophthegm to be as careful of unimportant
precepts as of important ones,[17] was originally an alternative form of the advice
to "flee from all evil and from anything resembling it" in the *teknon* section.

These themes and terminology evidence sufficient parallels to suggest that
the early layer of *Derek Eres* tracts and the rabbinic traditions representing
similar spiritual and ethic thought provide the most appropriate framework for
understanding Did. 3:1–6. The agreement between the maxims in *Yir'at Het* I,13;
II,16–17 and Did. 3:1–6 is not surprising, since there is a close affinity between
the ideas and ethical principles in the early *Derek Eres* doctrine and the views
in the Greek Two Ways.[18] Both sets of instructions emphasize not a strict legal,
halakic approach to the law but a moral, personal and ethical attitude to life.
Within pious Jewish circles in the Tannaitic period the belief was prevalent that
fulfillment of explicit halakic duty did not exhaust moral responsibility. Rather
than scrupulously discussing the specificities of Torah, the Greek Two Ways and
the early parts of *Derek Eres* present high ethical rules that appeal to a universal
morality.

---

15. See Gottlieb Klein, *Der älteste christliche Katechismus und die jüdische Propaganda-
Literatur* (Berlin, 1909), 69: "Die kürzeste Formel für Derech Erez lautet: Halte dich fern von
der Sünde und von dem, was hässlich ist."

16. *Yir'at Het* (or Derek Eres Zuṭa) II,16–17 according to Van Loopik, *The Ways of the
Sages*, 229–31 (with commentary) = Masseket Derek Eres I,26 according to Higger, *Treatises*,
1:78–79 (Hebrew) and 2:38 (English). The phrase "keep aloof from everything hideous" in the
first sentence of this paragraph is not found in Higger's edition. Van Loopik acknowledges
that this clause is missing in some manuscripts (ibid., 229). He maintains the above translation
however with reference to the "nearly identical form" of this dictum in 'Abot R. Nat. A 2; see
Aboth de Rabbi Nathan (ed. S. Schechter; Vienna 1887; repr. New York, 1945; corr. repr. New
York: Feldheim, 1967), 5a. Further, see also Masseket Yir'at Het, version a, chapter 1, in Higger,
Minor Tractates, 75 (lines 20–23) and version b, Perek Yir'at Het a, in Higger, *Minor Tractates*,
83 (lines 23–25).

17. See Felix Böhl, *Gebotserschwerung und Rechtsverzicht als ethisch-religiöse Normen in
der rabbinischen Literatur* (FJS 1; Freiburg i. B.: Schwarz, 1971), 59–63 and 85–109. Further, see
above, n. 9.

18. See Van de Sandt and Flusser, *The Didache: Its Jewish Sources*, 172–79.

2. A Tradition like Did. 3:1–6 underlying the Matthean Antitheses and James's Letter

I will now demonstrate that the ethical code in Did. 3:1–6 or a comparable tradition underlies the high standards of the halakic way of life in both the Matthean section and James.

2.1. The Antitheses Section in Matthew

How are the *teknon* segment in Did. 3:1–6 and the Antitheses section in the Sermon on the Mount connected? Does the closely matching order and content of the Sermon on the Mount and the Sermon on the Plain (Luke 6:20–49) not preferably lead to the assumption that "Q" was the source of Matthew's sermon? Indeed, Luke's version is probably very close to the original version in Q.[19] Nevertheless, if one takes the traditions behind Luke 6:20–49 to reflect Jesus's sayings, it is not hard to observe that Matthew must have considerably changed and expanded the extent and profile of the traditional Q sermon.[20] As far as Matt 5:17–48 is concerned, he almost certainly had another source at his disposal with which he intertwined the materials from Q, especially the passage reflected in Luke 6:27–36.

2.1.1. The Antitheses Section (Matt 5:17–48) and the Law

In order to prove the relevance of Did. 3:1–6 to the Antitheses section, the initial concern must be to establish definitive connections.[21] Let us first consider

---

19. See Graham N. Stanton, *A Gospel for a New People: Studies in Matthew* (Edinburgh: T&T Clark, 1992), 288.

20. "The amount of material in Matt 5–7 added to the Q speech is so impressive that the question arises whether Matthew's redaction is understandable without previous catechetic collections besides the Q sermon"; see Kari Syreeni, "The Sermon on the Mount and the Two Ways Teaching of the Didache," in *Matthew and the Didache: Two Documents from the Same Jewish-Christian Milieu?* (ed. H. van de Sandt; Assen: Van Gorcum, 2005), 100.

21. A number of scholars have found important agreements between Matt 5:21–48 and Did. 3:1–6; see Franz X. Funk, *Doctrina duodecim Apostolorum. Canones Apostolorum ecclesiastici ac reliquae doctrinae de duabus viis expositiones veteres* (Tübingen: Laupp, 1887), 12; Leonhard Goppelt, *Christentum und Judentum im ersten und zweiten Jahrhundert* (BFCT 2/55; Gütersloh: Bertelsmann, 1954), 187; Hanns Lilje, *Die Lehre der zwölf Apostel. Eine Kirchenordnung des ersten christlichen Jahrhunderts* (Die urchristliche Botschaft 28; Hamburg: Furche, 1956), 51–52; Stanislas Giet, *L'Énigme de la Didachè* (PFLUS 149; Paris: Ophrys, 1970), 158–60; Clayton N. Jefford, *The Sayings of Jesus in the Teaching of the Twelve Apostles* (VCSup 11; Leiden: Brill, 1989), 65–67; Betz, *Sermon on the Mount*, 219; Günther Bornkamm, "Der Aufbau der Bergpredigt," *NTS* 24 (1978): 432; David Flusser, "A Rabbinic Parallel to the Sermon on the Mount," in *Judaism and the Origins of Christianity: Collected Articles* (ed. D. Flusser; Jerusalem:

Matthew's Sermon on the Mount (Matt 5:3–7:27). The central part of the Sermon opens and closes with references to "the Law and the Prophets" (5:17 and 7:12). This section is in turn bifurcated. While the second division (6:1–7:12) of the section touches only indirectly upon issues of the law, the first division in 5:17–48 is thoroughly linked to the law and its commandments. It begins with a unit containing a programmatic statement on the validity of the Torah in Matt 5:17–20. In the next segment (5:21–48) the Antitheses occur, each of which is made up of two parts including an initial quotation from the law and, so it seems at first glance, Jesus's refutation of it.

The six scenarios of the exposition in 5:21–48 report what Jesus, according to Matthew, taught about offences like murder, adultery, divorce, perjury, retaliation, and hatred of one's enemy. They include a thesis, an antithesis, and, with the exception of the third scenario, an illustration of the significance of the saying (see 5:23–26 elaborating on 5:21–22; 5:29–30 on 5:27–28; 5:34b–37 on 5:33–34a; 5:39b–42 on 5:38–39a and 5:45–48 on 5:43–44). The elaborations seem to be extraneous materials that once circulated as independent sayings. Because these additions are likely to have been attached to the simple antitheses in a later stage, they will not be discussed here.[22]

The six antitheses in 5:21–48 contain a premise or thesis, mostly citing from or referring to commandments in the Torah, and an antithetical response to these commandments, introduced by the formula, "But I say to you." Unfortunately, the term "antitheses" has become the traditional designation of this phraseology implying the conviction that Jesus contradicted the Law of Moses.[23] However, the remainder of the Gospel does not suggest that Jesus's demands be confused with abrogating or watering down Jewish law. On the contrary, in 5:17–19 Matthew offers the assurance that the Antitheses are not intended to abolish but to

---

Magnes, 1988), 497–99, 504–5; idem, "Die Tora in der Bergpredigt," in *Juden und Christen lesen dieselbe Bibel* (ed. H. Kremers; Duisburg: Braun, 1973), 106–9 and nn. 11–12. For a comprehensive corroboration of the following, see van de Sandt and Flusser, *The Didache: Its Jewish Sources*, 193–237.

22. See also John P. Meier, *Law and History in Matthew's Gospel: A Redactional Study of Mt. 5:17–48* (AnBib 71; Rome: Biblical Institute Press, 1976), 126.

23. The second member of the antithesis, "but I say to you," is introduced by δέ instead of ἀλλά. The conjunction δέ must not be taken as a strong adversative and translated as if ἀλλά were used. The translation "but" makes the contrast too strong and gives the impression that Jesus deliberately sets himself over against the law; see David Flusser, "'Den Alten ist gesagt': Zur Interpretation der sog. Antithesen der Bergpredigt," *Jud* 48 (1992): 38; Robert H. Gundry, *Matthew: A Commentary on His Literary and Theological Art* (Grand Rapids: Eerdmans, 1982), 83; John Levison, "A Better Righteousness: The Character and Purpose of Matthew 5:21–48," *Studia Biblica et Theologica* 12 (1982): 176; William D. Davies and Dale C. Allison, *A Critical and Exegetical Commentary on the Gospel according to Saint Matthew* (3 vols.; ICC; Edinburgh: T&T Clark, 1988), 1:507 who would translate the antitheses this way: "You have heard that it was said (to the ancients) . . . but I (in addition) say to you."

promote this law. He certainly ruled out the possibility of offering opposition to the law.

There is widespread agreement that the content of all the Antitheses is traditional. This does not extend to formal composition, however. Most commonly, the specific formulations of the first, second, and fourth Antitheses (Matt 5:21–22, 27–28, 33–34a) are considered pre-Matthean while the antithetical pattern in the remainder of the series is assumed to be a secondary arrangement based on the earlier three.[24] Thus, those antitheses that evidence a radicalization of the commandments rather than a direct opposite character are generally considered to have been received by Matthew in antithetical form. In these paragraphs the counterstatement radicalizes, intensifies, and transcends the premise rather than revoking or changing it. Not only must you not kill, you must not even get that angry (5:21–22). Not only must you not commit adultery, you must not even look desirously at another man's wife (5:27–28). Not only must you keep oaths sworn in God's name, you must not swear oaths at all (5:33–34a).[25] In these antitheses,

---

24. Most scholars subscribe to Bultmann's analysis that the first, second and fourth antitheses are traditional (pre-Matthean) while the the other three (with Lucan parallels) are assigned to Matthew's redaction; cf. Rudolph Bultmann, *Die Geschichte der synoptischen Tradition* (8th ed.; FRLANT 29; Göttingen: Vandenhoeck & Ruprecht, 1970), 143–44; Ulrich Luz, *Das Evangelium nach Matthäus: Mt 1–7* (EKKNT 1/1; Zürich: Benziger-Verlag, 1985), 246 (though he is inclined to believe that the fourth antithesis is redactional too); Maarten J. J. Menken, *Matthew's Bible: The Old Testament Text of the Evangelist* (BEThL 173; Leuven: Peeters, 2004), 265–66; Werner G. Kümmel, "Jesus und der jüdische Traditionsgedanke," *ZNW* 33 (1934): 125 and n. 75; Georg Eichholz, *Auslegung der Bergpredigt* (2nd ed.; Neukirchen-Vluyn: Neukirchener Verlag, 1970), 69–70; Reinhart Hummel, *Die Auseinandersetzung zwischen Kirche und Judentum im Matthäusevangelium* (2nd ed.; BEvT 33; München: Kaiser, 1966), 67; Leonhard Goppelt, "Das Problem der Bergpredigt," in idem, *Christologie und Ethik* (Göttingen: Vandenhoeck & Ruprecht, 1968), 28–29; Georg Strecker, *Die Bergpredigt. Ein exegetischer Kommentar* (Göttingen: Vandenhoeck & Ruprecht, 1984), 64–67; idem, "Die Antithesen der Bergpredigt (Mt 5,21–48 par)," *ZNW* 69 (1978): 39–47; Erich Klostermann, *Das Matthäusevangelium* (4th ed.; HNT; Tübingen: Mohr Siebeck, 1971), 42; Eduard Lohse, "'Ich aber sage euch,'" in *Der Ruf Jesu und die Antwort der Gemeinde* (ed. E. Lohse, Chr. Burchard und B. Schaller; Göttingen: Vandenhoeck & Ruprecht, 1970), 189–90; Jan Lambrecht, *The Sermon on the Mount. Proclamation and Exhortation* (Good News Studies 14; Wilmington, Del.: Glazier, 1985), 94–95; Davies and Allison, *Critical and Exegetical Commentary on . . . Matthew*, 1:504–5; Francis W. Beare, *The Gospel according to Matthew: A Commentary* (Oxford: Blackwell, 1981), 146.

25. Matt 5:33–37 has a parallel in Jas 5:12 but without the antithetic format. The first part of the premise in Matt 5:33–37 refers to swearing false oaths (5:33a), which is surpassed in the first part of the antithesis (5:34a) in the form of an apodictic command consisting of a negative infinitive (μὴ ὀμόσαι). Similar wording in a present imperative construction is found in Jas 5:12a (μὴ ὀμνύετε). While the premise 5:33a emphasizes that one should not swear a false oath, the first part of the antithesis in 34a warns not to swear at all. Matt 5:37a continues this negative prohibition with a positive demand: "Let your yes be yes and no no." The clauses in Matt 5:33a, 34a and 37a all deal with an oath by which one affirms or denies having done something. This call for honesty is found with even more clarity in Jas 5:12c. The same passage of Matt 5:33–37,

Jesus's demands transcend or surpass the requirements of the Law rather than opposing them.[26] These traditional or primary antitheses belong to Matthew's special materials, while the secondary antitheses (5:31–32, 38–39a, 43–44) have taken this form because they have been inserted into a context in which the antithetic framework was the primal one.[27]

---

however, also expresses an appeal to the faithfulness of one's word. The second part of the premise (5:33b) is related to keeping one's vows made before God, a command that appears to link up with the second element of the antithesis (5:34b–36). There is a shift in diction and connotation here because the thought of vows is loosely connected to the heart of the antithesis in 5:33a, 34a, 37a. Since these promissory oaths (5:33b, 34b–36) are clearly intrusive in the original context of the passage, they probably represent a later interpolation. Was this material inserted by Matthew? It is not likely since unambiguous traces of a similar secondary extension is found in a same context in Jas 5:12b where it says "either by heaven or by earth or by any other oath" (cf. Matt 5:34, 35: "neither by heaven . . . nor by earth . . . nor by Jerusalem"). James shows familiarity with both the prohibition of swearing a false oath and the promissory oaths, which implies that the process of combining the two must have taken place in the pre-Matthean tradition. See Robert A. Guelich, *The Sermon on the Mount: A Foundation for Understanding* (2nd ed.; Waco, Tex.: Word Publishing, 1983), 211–18; 248–50; 267–68. See also Peter H. Davids, "Palestinian Traditions in the Epistle of James," in *James the Just and Christian Origins* (ed. B. Chilton and C. A. Evans; NovTSup 98; Leiden: Brill 1999), 49.

26. See also Davies and Allison, *Critical and Exegetical Commentary on . . . Matthew*, 1:504–5; Eichholz, *Auslegung der Bergpredigt*, 70; Bultmann, *Geschichte der synoptischen Tradition*, 143–44; Werner G. Kümmel, "Jesus und der jüdische Traditionsgedanke," ZNW 33 (1934): 125, n. 75; William D. Davies, *The Setting of the Sermon on the Mount* (Cambridge: Cambridge University Press, 1964), 101; Helmut Merklein, *Die Gottesherrschaft als Handlungsprinzip: Untersuchung zur Ethik Jesu* (2nd ed.; FB 33; Würzburg: Echter Verlag, 1981), 260. The text referred to in the fourth thesis is not drawn verbatim from the written Hebrew text of the Bible, but made up of a number of citations and allusions from the Torah (e.g., Exod 20:7, 16; Lev 19:12; Num 30:2; Deut 5:20; 23:22), all intending to safeguard the sanctity of God's name. Since a prohibition of this sort is considered as belonging to the Torah in a wide range of mostly parenetic Jewish materials (1 Esd 1:46; Wis 14:25; *T. Ash.* 2.6; Ps.-Phoc. 16; *Sib. Or.* 2.68; see also Sir 23:9–11; *2 En.* 40.1–2), the decree may have been regarded in Matt 5:33 as a Torah prohibition (see Betz, *Sermon on the Mount*, 263–64).

27. The opinion arguing for the redactional character of the latter three antitheses does not rule out the possibility that their substance is traditional too. Because they present materials partially paralleled in Luke, their content is often assigned to the Q source. The third antithesis about divorce (Matt 5:32) parallels Luke 16:18; the fifth about retaliation (Matt 5:39b–43) corresponds with Luke 6:29–30, and the sixth about loving one's neighbor (Matt 5:44–48) parallels Luke 6:27–28, 33–36. Because the antithetical form of arguing in a pattern of juxtaposed contrasting formulas is missing from the Lucan parallels, however, the antagonistic statements in these Matthean instances are generally regarded as secondary. There is widespread agreement that Matthew patterned the materials he found in Q upon the formulations of the first, second, and fourth antitheses. Moreover, the parallels in Luke enable us to ascertain that fifth and sixth Matthean antitheses were combined at the earlier stage of the tradition in Q. It was Matthew who has separated them and who is responsible for the antithetical format of the two passages.

In view of the radicalizing tendency in the three primary antitheses, there can be little doubt that neither the tradition underlying Matt 5:17–20 nor its Matthean redaction considered Jesus as having "fulfilled" the Law by setting aside, abolishing, or breaking with the Law of Moses. Such explanations come too close to meaning the opposite of 5:17. Moreover, if this is what was meant by the fulfillment of the Law in verse 17, continuity with 5:18–19 would be awkward, leaving us with the question what the "jot" and "tittle" (verse 18) and "the least of these commandments" (verse 19) would signify. There is a wide consensus among scholars that the "fulfillment" of the Law "implies that Jesus modified in some ways contemporary understandings of the Law."[28] Fulfillment of the Law appears to be determined by one's interpretation of it. What is essential here is the distinction between violating the Law and fulfilling it through a different interpretation.

Emphasis in the introduction (5:17–20) is on the continuing obedience to the Torah down to the smallest details of its wording. Interestingly, these tiniest minutiae, underscoring the immutability of the Torah thus far, serve as a metaphorical designation for the least important commands in 5:19: "Whoever then relaxes one of the least of these commandments and teaches men so, shall be called least in the kingdom of heaven; but he who does them and teaches them shall be called great in the kingdom of heaven." The reference to "one of the least of these commandments" or, better, "one of these least commandments" (μίαν τῶν ἐντολῶν τούτων τῶν ἐλαχίστων) is to the "iota or a tittle" in 5:18.[29] The "iota and tittle" represent both the smallest graphic elements of the law in a literal (verse 18) and figurative (verse 19) sense.

The phrase "the least of these commandments" in Matt 5:19 can best be understood in the light of the discussion in Jewish sources about "light" and "heavy" // "minor" and "major" commandments. Indeed, such a differentiation can be variously documented in post-biblical Jewish thought,[30] not least

---

28. Matthias Konradt, "Die vollkommene Erfüllung der Tora und der Konflikt mit den Pharisäern im Matthäusevangelium," in *Das Gesetz im frühen Judentum und im Neuen Testament* (ed. D. Sänger and M. Konradt; NTOA/SUNT 57; Göttingen: Vandenhoeck & Ruprecht, 2006), 131–41. See also Graham N. Stanton, "The Origin and Purpose of Matthew's Gospel: Matthean Scholarship from 1945 to 1980," *ANRW* 25.3:1937. This does not solve all our problems however, since, as Stanton makes clear, some scholars have unconvincingly attempted to explain Jesus's attitude towards the Law in Matthew by appealing to the latter's christology or eschatology; see ibid., 1934–37.

29. See Heinz Schürmann, "'Wer daher eines dieser geringsten Gebote auflöst . . .' Wo fand Matthäus das Logion Mt 5,19?," *BZ* 4 (1960), 241; Luz, *Das Evangelium nach Matthäus: Mt 1–7*, 1:238; Davies and Allison, *Critical and Exegetical Commentary on . . . Matthew* 1:496; Guelich, *Sermon on the Mount*, 151–52; Meier, *Law and History*, 91–92.

30. See above, n. 9.

in rabbinic discussion.[31] The main point in Matt 5:19 is the importance of the light commandments. In contrast to what one would expect (in Matt 23:23 the weighty things in the law must be given precedence), it is not those who teach that the weighty commandments should be discarded who are least welcome in God's kingdom, but those who teach that the light commandments can be ignored. Although the introductory passage in Matt 5:17–20 does not pursue this topic, in 5:19 Jesus seems to reconfirm an understanding of the value of the light commandments.

Finally, Matt 5:20 serves as a pivot between 5:17–19, stating the principles for the correct interpretation of Scripture, and 5:21–48, a series of sayings expressing the intention behind biblical demands for those aspiring to enter the Kingdom: "For I tell you, unless your righteousness exceeds that of the scribes and Pharisees, you will never enter the kingdom of heaven." The Matthean features become particularly clear in Matt 5:20, which certainly exhibits Matthew's favorite diction.[32] Through redactional shaping Matthew seems to be countering contemporary issues of authority. The "scribes and Pharisees," his opponents, are negative counterparts to the disciples.[33] The expression about "righteousness" being "greater" (πλεῖον) than that of the scribes and Pharisees is echoed in 5:48: "You, therefore, must be perfect (τέλειοι), as your heavenly Father is perfect (τέλειος)." The idea of greater righteousness is found again in the idea of perfection in 5:48 and both verses 5:20 and 48 serve to frame the six antitheses in

---

31. See above, n. 9. About this concept, see already Johan Wettstein, *Novum Testamentum Graecum* 1 (Amsterdam 1752; repr. Graz: Akademische Druck- u. Verlagsanstalt, 1962), 295–96; see also *Str-B* 1:249, 901–2; Israel Abrahams, *Studies in Pharisaism and the Gospels* (2 vols.; Cambridge: Cambridge University Press, 1917 = New York: Ktav, 1967), 1.18–29; Efraim Urbach, *The Sages: Their Concepts and Beliefs* (2 vols.; repr. of 2nd ed.; trans. Israel Abrahams; Jerusalem: Magnes, 1987), 1:345–50.

32. See Ulrich Luz, "The Fulfilment of the Law in Matthew (Matt. 5:17–20)," in idem, *Studies in Matthew* (Grand Rapids: Eerdmans, 2005), 197; published previously as "Die Erfüllung des Gesetzes bei Matthäus (Mt 5,17–20)," *ZThK* 75 (1978): 398–435; Guelich, *Sermon on the Mount*, 135, 156; Luz, *Das Evangelium nach Matthäus: Mt 1–7*, 1:230; Albert Descamps, "Essai d'interprétation de Mt 5,17–48: Formgeschichte ou Redactionsgeschichte?," *SE* 1 (1959): 163; Jacques Dupont, *Les Béatitudes 3: Les évangélistes* (Études Bibliques; Paris: Gabalda, 1973), 251, n. 2; Meier, *Law and History*, 116–19; Davies and Allison, *Critical and Exegetical Commentary on . . . Matthew*, 1:501.

33. See also Matt 23, where Matthew levels the usual charge of hypocrisy (vv 4–7) against the "scribes and Pharisees" and attacks the Jewish community leadership (of his own post-70 C.E. situation ?) in seven woe oracles, in which Jesus condemns the "scribes and Pharisees" seven times; see David C. Sim, *The Gospel of Matthew and Christian Judaism: The History and Social Setting of the Matthean Community* (Studies of the New Testament and Its World; Edinburgh: T&T Clark, 1998), 130–31. See also Petri Luomanen, *Entering the Kingdom of Heaven: A Study on the Structure of Matthew's View of Salvation* (WUNT 2/101; Tübingen: Mohr Siebeck, 1998), 85, 120.

5:21–47. If Matt 5:20 has any historical value, we might deduce that rather than being commonly accepted, the light precepts were popular only in certain pious circles.

2.1.2. The Antitheses Section and Did. 3:1–6

The traditional material behind Matt 5:17–48 may have been derived from a source identical with, or similar to, the individual *teknon* passage. Because the instruction itself reflects the contemporary ethical sensitivity of pious Jewish circles, Jesus's demands in this part of the Sermon are likely to have a historical precedent in the Hasidic milieu. When one aligns the two texts, the parallels between Did. 3:1–6 and the early layer of Matt 5:17–48 (Matt 5:17–19, 21–22, 27–28, 33–34a) are clear. The similarities are extensive enough to establish an undeniable relationship between the two sections.

First, both sections presuppose a Decalogue background. They both treat the sixth and the seventh commandments of the Decalogue as the first two weighty commandments (murder and adultery). The Decalogue is even more likely to stand in the shadow of Matt 5:21–48 since the command to love one's neighbor found in the last unit (5:43–48) is often used in early Judaism to express in crystallized form the second table of the Decalogue.[34] Rather interestingly, the items "murder" and "adultery" (in this order) also head the rather long catalogue of prohibitions in Did. 2:1–7 and again the list of vices that serves as an explication of the Way of Death in Did. 5. Ultimately, it does not seem unreasonable to suppose that the first two on these lists, which are modeled after the second tablet of the Decalogue, are based more on tradition than the remainder, which rather seems a haphazard and free adaptation in the various lists.[35]

A second point of unique agreement between Did. 3:1–6 and the early layer of the Antitheses regards the arrangement of the preamble and the first two paragraphs (the sixth and seventh commandment). The passages Did. 3:1–3 and

---

34. See Rom 13:8–10; Gal 5:14; Matt 19:18–19, b. Šabb. 31a; 'Abot R. Nat. B 26; Sipra Qedoshim 2,12 and y. Ned. 9,41c; see also Van de Sandt and Flusser, *The Didache: Its Jewish Sources*, 162–65.

35. The traditional list of antitheses in Matt 5:21–48 offers the two offenses, murder and adultery (5:21–22, 27–28), and the other offense—despite the fact that the Decalogue is not cited here—refers to the third commandment: "for the Lord will not hold him guiltless who takes his name in vain" (Exod 20:7; cf. Lev 19:12; either instance forbids abuse of God's name for unworthy purposes); see Gerald Friedlander, *The Jewish Sources of the Sermon on the Mount* (The Library of Biblical Studies; New York: Ktav, 1969), 61–65; Betz, *Sermon on the Mount*, 262; Joachim Gnilka, *Das Matthäusevangelium I: Kommentar zu Kap. 1,1–13,58* (HTKNT 1/1; Freiburg: Herder, 1986), 174; Guelich, *Sermon on the Mount*, 212; see also Serge Ruzer, "The Technique of Composite Citation in the Sermon on the Mount (Matt 5:21–22, 33–37)," *RB* 103 (1996): 72–74.

Matt 5:17–19, 21–22, 27–28, have a corresponding topical organization. Their introduction is similar to the saying that a light commandment is as important as a weighty one. This is the fundamental essence of Jewish *Derek Ereṣ* teachings. Both Did. 3:1 and Matt 5:17–19 warn against committing even the slightest transgression. To prevent people from ignoring light commandments or committing light transgressions, the linkage of these minor items with the weighty ones is elucidated. Should one violate a light precept, one ends up committing a grave sin. Being bad tempered or angry leads to murder and a lustful person is likely to end up committing adultery (Did. 3:2–3; cf. Matt 5:21–22, 27–28).

Finally, both sections, Did. 3:1–6 and Matt 5:17–19, 21–22, 27–28, 33–34a, draw the same conclusions along the same line of reasoning. They share the method of applying the principle laid down in the preamble (Did. 3:1 and Matt 5:17–19). Did. 3:2–6 repeatedly asserts that minor sins lead to major ones. The kind of argumentation used here is a *minori ad maius* (קל וחומר), presupposing that what is known about something "light" can be known "all the more so" about something "heavy." One can hardly doubt that the first, second and fourth antitheses in Matthew presuppose the same logical method. Matthew has Jesus explain that the original intention of the prohibition of murder, adultery and oaths was to include all attitudes and actions that potentially lead to such acts. The disposition of such explanations is clearly from the light to the weighty demands, from the lesser to the greater commandments. In Matt 5:17–19, we face the transparent principles of hermeneutics that are applied to the traditional commandments of the Scripture in 5:21–48. When Matthew has Jesus demand that the disciples' righteousness must exceed that of the scribes and Pharisees (5:20), he not only validates the continuance of the Torah (verse 18) but also the keeping of the "least of these commandments" (verse 19). The saying provides the critical principle by which the Law is to be read, interpreted and evaluated within the early milieu of *Derek Ereṣ* and, as explained above, within the circles in which the Two Ways and Matt 5:17–48 were originally kept alive.

2.2. The Letter of James

James is mostly viewed as a redactional work, composed of traditional material that was applied with tremendous freedom to a new context and argument. This does not necessarily imply, however, that the casting of these materials lacks a coherent structure. For our purpose it is important to know that the various topics broached in the opening chapter are subsequently expanded in the letter body. Some scholars have even suggested that the opening chapter is the key to understanding the letter in its entirety.[36] To be more specific with respect to our

---

36. According to Luke T. Johnson, the chapter is "something of an epitome of the work as a whole"; see his *The Letter of James* (AB 37A; New York: Doubleday, 1995), 174–75. According

investigation, it is important to notice that the correlation drawn between desire, sin, and death in Jas 1:13–15 and 1:19–21 is further developed in 4:1–6 where the origin of strife is located in the human pursuit of their own pleasures.[37] In 1:14–15 James champions man's accountability for sin and returns to this theme later in 4:1–4 where he shows more fully how such distorted desire leads to the death of others.

2.2.1. The Letter of James and Did. 3:1–6

In order to evaluate the points of contact between the Didache unit and James properly, it is particularly instructive to study the brief passages in Jas 1:13–15 and 1:19–21. Considering Jas 1:13–15, three points may be noted. First, we find the vice ἐπιθυμία ("desire") in both James and the *teknon* section. Whereas the noun ἐπιθυμία and the adjective ἐπιθυμητής in Did. 3:3 specifically describe sexual passions, the context of the word ἐπιθυμία in James suggests a broader concept. It appears to highlight individual responsibility for sin. In accordance with the *teknon* passage, however, the term's sexual connotation is developed in Jas 1:14–15 with vivid metaphors. "Desire" is personified as a seductive female who, having actively enticed the person referenced in verse 14, conceives a bastard child by him.

Second, James describes the consequence of desire in terms of giving birth: personified Desire gives birth to (τίκτει) sin, and sin brings forth (ἀποκύει) death (1:15). The *teknon* section uses similar "birthing" language in connection with the major sins in the second part (the "d" clauses) of its symmetrical strophes.[38] Third, the concatenated form is found in both Jas 1:14–15 and in Did. 3:1–6. Like Jas 1:14–15, the *teknon* section encapsulates its teaching with a chain-like structure carrying the thought from step to step: "be not angry, for anger . . ." and "be not desirous, for desire . . .".

---

to Mark E. Taylor and George H. Guthrie, it "functions as a summary of the major concerns and themes expanded in the body of the letter"; see their "The Structure of James," *CBQ* 68 (2006): 688. Many other scholars "are convinced that ch. 1 holds the key to the letter's structure"; see Mark E. Taylor, "Recent Scholarship on the Structure of James," *Currents in Biblical Research* 3 (2004): 112.

37. See Matt A. Jackson-McCabe, *Logos and Law in the Letter of James: The Law of Nature, the Law of Moses, and the Law of Freedom* (NovTSup 100; Leiden: Brill, 2001), 206–8.

38. As seen above, however, James prefers the terms τίκτω and ἀποκύεω in this context rather than the usual verb γεννάω as employed in the *teknon* section. He keeps restating his source in his own words and thus developed it as his own teaching; John S. Kloppenborg, "The Reception of the Jesus Traditions in James," in *The Catholic Epistles and the Tradition* (ed. J. Schlosser; BETL 176; Leuven: Peeters, 2004), 116–21. The verb ἀποκύεω ("to bear young") is also used in 1:18, but with respect to the unusual female image for God as "the father of light" who gives birth.

In 1:19–20 the initial result of human ἐπιθυμία is specified as anger (ὀργή): "Let every man be quick to hear, slow to speak, slow to anger, for the anger of man does not work the righteousness of God." These verses not only give some first detailed information about the content of ἐπιθυμία mentioned in 1:14–15, but the formal characteristic of the figure also connects the two passages. The form of these two passages is best designated as concatenation because they repeat one word from the preceding phrase. In Jas 1:14–15 the catenated form of "desire" and "sin" leads to death while the chain-syllogism in Jas 1:19–20 draws attention to the result of anger: "(Let every man be) slow to anger (ὀργήν), for the anger (ὀργή) of man does not work the righteousness of God." The clauses might easily recall Did. 3:2ab: "Be not angry (μὴ γίνου ὀργίλος), for anger (ὀργή) leads to murder (φόνον)."

Jas 1:21 also reflects elements of the *teknon* section (esp. Did. 3:1) but space does not allow me to go into this matter here.[39] In any case, when all of these parallels are considered, the general case for a relationship between Jas 1:13–15, 19–21 and Did. 3:1–6 seems strong.

2.2.2. James 2:8-11 and the Law

The main section on the law in James's letter is 2:8–11.[40] The passage shows a similar ethical interest in the law as does the segment found in Did. 3:1–6 and the ancient kernel of *Derek Ereṣ* literature. The text runs as follows:

> 8. If you really fulfill the royal Law according to the Scripture, "You shall love your neighbor as yourself," you do well. 9. But if you show partiality (προσωπολημπτεῖτε), you commit a sin, and are convicted by the law as transgressors. 10. For whoever keeps the whole law but fails in one point (ἐν ἑνί) has become guilty of all of it. 11. For he who said, "Do not commit adultery," also said, "Do not kill." If you do not commit adultery but do kill, you have become a transgressor of the Law.

Jas 2:1–5 warns readers not to be partial in their assemblies. Proof comes in two main sections, verses 5–7 and verses 8–11, and we find a renewed admonition in 2:12–13. The first section endorsing the argument consists of three rhetorical

---

39. For more evidence, see Huub van de Sandt, "James 4,1–4 in the Light of the Jewish Two Ways Tradition 3,1–6," *Bib* 88 (2007): 38–63.

40. According to Wesley H. Wachob, Jas 2:1–13 "is the Jamesian argument that says more about the law than any other in the letter"; see *The Voice of Jesus in the Social Rhetoric of James* (SNTSMS 106; Cambridge: Cambridge University Press, 2000), 127. For the following, see also Van de Sandt, "James 4,1–4," 56–58.

questions (verses 5–6a, 6b, 7) each of which anticipates an affirmative response.[41] The second section (verses 8–11) seeks to prove that a sin such as is represented by "partiality" (προσωπολημψία) is a violation of the Torah. Apparently the readers of the letter did not experience it that way. This lack of consciousness regarding the equivalence of "major" and "minor" precepts might have encouraged James to act.

James makes the love commandment a significant criterion by which all action should be measured.[42] In verses 8–9[43] he emphasizes that those who claim to live within the kingdom defined by the "royal" law of love cannot practice partiality. In James's opinion, observance of the Torah without love is as inconceivable as the neglect of minor commandments. In verses 10–11 he argues that failure to obey "one point" (ἐν ἑνί) of the law is equivalent to failing all of it. To be sure, the command against partiality ("one point") is connected to the contemporary standard Jewish view of the unity of the law.[44] James suggests that favoritism be condemned as severely by the law as adultery or even murder. This argument concurs with the common Jewish distinction between minor and major commandments.[45] Seemingly negligible minor commandments, like the prohibition of partiality, are included within the scope of the commandment not to commit adultery and not to kill.[46] Interestingly—and this will be discussed below—in Jas 4 the writer declares that the readers do kill (4:2) and commit adultery (4:4).

---

41. Privileged treatment of the rich stands in stark contrast to God who has chosen the poor to be "rich in faith." Moreover, acts of partiality are against self interest (verses 6–7).

42. It is unlikely that 2:8 refers to the love commandment as one commandment among others. Rather, it is the commandment that summarizes the entirety of the law, "royal" because it summarizes the law as the law of the kingdom of God (see 2:5). See also Matthias Konradt in this volume.

43. These verses are clearly antithetical. The contrast between verse 8 and verse 9 is of "really" keeping the law of love (verse 8) while at the same time disobeying one of its stipulations (verse 9).

44. In fact, James agrees with a traditional Jewish view that "whoever violates one commandment, will end up by violating them all" as evidenced in verse 11. See for instance Martin Dibelius, *James: A Commentary on the Epistle of James* (trans. M. A. Williams; Hermeneia; Philadelphia: Fortress, 1975), 144–46 with reference to *b. Hor.* 8b and elsewhere. See also Yizhak Baer, "The Historical Foundations of the Halakha," *Zion* 27 (1962): 127–28 (Hebrew).

45. See Dibelius, *James: A Commentary*, 144–45 and n. 113; Douglas J. Moo, *The Epistle of James: An Introduction and Commentary* (TNTC; Grand Rapids: Eerdmans, 1985), 95.

46. This law's approach is also emphasized in Jas 4:11–12:

> Do not speak evil against one another, brethren. He that speaks evil against a brother or judges his brother, speaks evil against the law and judges the law. But if you judge the law, you are not a doer of the law but a judge. There is one lawgiver and judge, he who is able to save and destroy. But who are you that you judge your neighbor?

James 2:8–11 is thus most naturally in accordance with Did. 3:1–6, which begins with: "My child, flee from all evil and from everything resembling it." This basic rule is designed to prevent indulging in sin and is the central moral preventative reflected in *Yir'at Het*. The warning in Jas 2:8–11 was probably indispensable "because of the tendency to think that obedience to the 'heavier' commandments outweighed any failure to adhere to the 'lighter' requirements of the law."[47] Because James's readers might have lost the ability to assess the value of the minor commandments properly, he removes any grounds someone might have for a light-hearted attitude toward the prohibition against partiality. In his mind, "to show contempt for the poor is equivalent to committing adultery or even murder."[48]

In conclusion, both James and the Matthean Antitheses stand close to the ethos of the *teknon* section in stressing the unity of the law as an ethical code. The three passages, Did. 3:1–6; Matt 5:17–48 and Jas 2:8–11, are analogous in taking the sixth and seventh commandment of the Decalogue as the first two weighty commandments (murder and adultery). Matthew and James contain an interpretation of these commandments (Matt 5:21–22, 27–28; Jas 2:10–11) when urging the necessity of carrying out the full stipulations of the law (see Jas 2:10 and Matt 5:18–19). Matthew 5:19 considers the relaxation of the law in its least important commandments as nonobservance of the law in its totality, while Jas 2:10 equates breaking even one point of the law with breaking it entirely. To be sure, the "one point" in which James's readers were falling short—partiality—could be called a "light" requirement. Practicing partiality boils down to committing murder and adultery. The thinking in Did. 3:1–6; Matt 5:17–19, 21–22, 27–28 and Jas 2:8–11 amounts to exactly the same thing insofar as these passages specify moral norms based on properly interpreted law.[49]

One cannot pick and choose which commandments to keep. It is utterly wrong to disregard some prohibitions while obeying the others. Slandering is likely to have been taken as a minor transgression here. According to James, however, one sets oneself above the Law in deciding with which commands to comply and which not to observe. Since one excludes the weight of a minor sin like slander, one claims for oneself God's role as the ultimate lawgiver.

47. Moo, *Epistle of James*, 95.

48. Patrick J. Hartin, *James* (SP 14; Collegeville, Minn.: Liturgical Press 2003), 137. See the Venerable Bede (672/3–735) according to Johnson, *Letter of James*, 233.

49. The content of the law is understood from the perspective of the commandment to love one's neighbor as summarizing the law *in toto*. The halakah was to be expounded within the parameters of the love commandment. The strong emphasis on love (5:43) does not abolish concern for the observance of specific regulations and precepts, but it does imply a definite shift in focus and priorities. See also Did. 1:3–3:10 all of which is placed under the fundamental principle of the love command formulated in 1:2.

3. A Characteristic Development of the Tradition in both Matthew and James

The structure and themes of the teachings in Matt 5:17–48 can be accounted for in a meaningful way within the framework of pious Jewish thought. After mentioning that entering the kingdom of heaven requires someone to "add to righteousness," the logion of Matt 5:20 introduces the intensification of the commandments in 5:21–48. Jesus rejects a minimalistic understanding of the weighty commandments. The saying makes clear that doing the will of God or traveling the Way to Life implies strict observance not only of the major commandments, but of the minor ones as well. The Matthean Jesus based his interpretation of Scripture on the theological insight current within Hasidic circles into the basic intention of the Legislator.

In his treatment of the minor sins, however, Jesus's argument in Matthew seems rather more rigorous than is the line of reasoning in the Two Ways or in the early stratum of *Derek Ereṣ*. Although the loss of temper, a lustful look, or the taking of an oath do not replace acts of murder, adultery, and perjury, they are valued in the Antitheses as sins in their own right, incurring the same penalty as murder or adultery. The passage in Did. 3:1–3 and, for example, *Yir'at Het* II,16–17, however, object to anger and desire (or lust) because they lead to major sins. The latter teachings appear largely to represent preventive measures to protect someone from transgressing weighty commandments. A bad-tempered or lustful person runs the risk of ending up committing murder or adultery. Attention does not seem focused here on the minor sins of infuriation or desire, but on the perils of the grave sins of murder and adultery.

Thus the tenor of the Antitheses section is more rigorous than the ethical standards prevalent in the pious environment of the Hasidim. Matthew's Jesus does not explicitly highlight the active observance of minor commands with a view to avoiding the major ones. In 5:21–22, 27–28, 33–34a he attaches equal moral significance to being angry with one's brother *and* to killing him, to looking lustfully at a woman *and* to committing adultery with her, to taking oaths *and* perjury. Jesus made a strong enforcement and a high liability felt to his audience by equating the gravity of obviously more innocent and minor offences with the major legal transgressions. In this way he was able to set more store by the minor commandments than was common in early *Derek Ereṣ* circles. Jesus's spiritual reorientation of the halakah, although in line with the Hasidim, is clearly perceptible in the introductory passage in Matt 5:17–19 where he urges his disciples to carry out the Law down to the very jot and tittle.

In James a similar radicalization may be noticed; I refer to Jas 4:1–4. The passage points out that wars (πόλεμοι) and battles (μάχαι) were being fought among the readers of the letter. They are even accused of murder, an almost intolerably strong charge when written to a Christian community. Finally, the author charges those who are engaged in warfare and killing with being "adulteresses" in 4:4.[50]

It is of importance to remember here that the relevant background of Jas 4:1–6 is found in Jas 1:14–15 and 1:19–21, two passages that in their turn are closely related to the *teknon* section Did. 3:1–6. James champions human responsibility for sin in the first chapter of his letter and returns to this theme later in 4:1–4 where he shows more fully how such distorted desire leads to violence and murder. Moreover, he builds his accusations around the contrasts of two ways of life: one led in friendship with God, the other in friendship with the world (4:4). Let us focus on some details. In Jas 4:1 conflicting selfish desires (minor vice) are the source of wars and battles (major offence). James probably rearranged traditional material here by rephrasing it as rhetorical questions, a stylistic feature frequently found in this letter.[51] In consonance with the tendency exhibited in Did. 3:1–6, however, he asserts that hedonistic pleasures and internal passions lead to violence.[52]

This very same pattern probably underlies Jas 4:2 as well. In order to see this, the two phrases "you murder" and "you battle and wage war" should be regarded as resulting from the preceding observations in this verse, namely, "you desire" and "you are jealous." Thus, in the Greek text of Jas 4:2, one should place a full stop after "you murder":[53]

---

50. It is useful to assess these verses in their literary context. The passage in Jas 4:1–4 belongs to the division 4:1–6, which in turn is part of the coherent literary unit Jas 3:13–4:10. The latter section is composed of four subsections, an exposition presenting the distinction James makes between two types of wisdom, the one from above and the other from below (3:13–18), an accusation in which the author strongly criticizes what can be labeled a life led without wisdom (4:1–6), a call to repentance (4:7–10), and finally some concrete practical advice is given (4:11–12). Because a detailed treatment of Jas 4:1–6 is beyond the scope of this article, attention will be paid solely to some basic points.

51. Compare also 3:6 (2:4, 5, 6, 7, 14, 15, 16, etc). Note the wording ἐν τοῖς μέλεσιν as well. This might refer to Jas 3:5, where it says: "the tongue is a small member (μικρὸν μέλος), yet it boasts of great things."

52. Because the terms ἐπιθυμεῖν and ζηλοῦν were used interchangeably in his days (see Johnson, *Letter of James*, 271; Jackson-McCabe, *Logos and Law*, 204), James might have understood the term ζηλωτής in the *teknon* section as "jealous" or "desirous."

53. Modern editions of the Greek New Testament, however, do not seem to support this conclusion. Instead of a coherent literary pattern substantiating this line of thought, Jas 4:2 often is divided into three disconnected statements:

   a. You desire (ἐπιθυμεῖτε) and do not have;

   b. you murder and are jealous (ζηλοῦτε) and are unable to obtain;

   c. you battle and wage war.

The structure of the passage evidences a haphazard arrangement of a number of isolated vices and severe misdemeanors apparently applicable to the community. Moreover, the expression "you murder" does not fit well with the following "you are envious" (ζηλοῦτε). The difficulties resolve themselves when one assumes that the author picks up here ideas planted earlier in Jas

a. You desire (ἐπιθυμεῖτε) and do not have, so you murder.

b. And you are jealous (ζηλοῦτε) and are unable to obtain, so you battle and wage war.

The punctuation adopted here breaks the verse into two statements, each with a cause and effect.[54]

For our purposes, it is of great importance to note that Jas 4:2 closely corresponds with the form of moral exhortation in the *teknon* passage. The connection between envy, jealousy, and murder is also found in Did. 3:1–6. As seen above, the latter section is bent on highlighting that transgression of minor precepts leads to the transgression of major ones. In Jas 4:2 the same path is depicted: "desire eventuates in murder" and "jealousy results in war."[55]

Not just Jas 4:1–2 but also the entire arrangement of Jas 4:1–4 shows James's awareness of a tradition like the *teknon* section. The author reserves some of his harshest invectives for those who pursue their own desires, addressing them as "adulteresses" (μοιχαλίδες). In Did. 3:2–3, being angry, jealous, eager for battle, and hot-tempered are all connected to murder while a lascivious or lustful person (ἐπιθυμητής) is tied to adultery (μοιχεία);[56] these are the topics treated by James in 1:14–15, 19–20 and 4:1–4.

On the other hand, the style of Jas 4:1–4 is quite different from the more moderate approach of Jewish sages as reflected in *Derek Ereṣ* and the *teknon* section. James deviates from the conventional topic by suggesting that these battles are being fought just then by his readers. Thus his letter refers not to a potential, but to an actual, real and tangible situation. Severe violence is already in evidence among them. The situation among his readers seems to have gotten seriously out of hand. He accuses his addressees of being engaged in warfare and other conflicts (4:1–2). They are "killers" (4:2) and "adulteresses" (4:4).

1:13–15, 19–21. The two statements, "you murder" and "you battle and wage war" follow as a result of "you desire" and "you are jealous."

54. Similar punctuation can also be found in Joseph B. Mayor, *The Epistle of St. James: The Greek Text with Introduction, Notes and Comments* (1897; repr. Grand Rapids: Zondervan, 1954), 134–7; James H. Ropes, *The Epistle of St James* (ICC; Edinburgh: T&T Clark, 1916), 254; Johnson, *The Letter of James*, 267, 277.

55. In addition to these statements a psychological judgment is also found here which explains the transition from a minor to a weighty sin. The additions "(you) do not have" and "(you) are unable to obtain" in 4:2 indicate that untrammeled desires for pleasure and passions turn out to be unsatisfied and, thus, lead eventually to murder, social upheaval, battles and war.

56. Unlike the variety of light transgressions in the two halves of the separate strophes, the same weighty offense is repeatedly retained in each of the two halves, with the exception of 3:3 where the weighty sin is expressed in two different words ("fornication" and "adultery"). It is, however, hard to believe that the term "fornication" was used in the earlier layer of GTW 3:1–6 since "adultery" and not "fornication" is mentioned in the second part of the Decalogue. For further argumentation, see Van de Sandt, "James 4,1–4," 60, n. 65.

The pointed absurdity of the allegations in James 4:1–4 offers a clue to their ultimate intention. Since James argued in 2:8–11 that breaking any command amounts to violating the whole law, it follows that the "minor transgressions" are judged in terms of the most extreme consequences possible. James understands those actions in Did. 3:1–6 that might result in strife, war, murder, or adultery as being as equally grave as major transgressions. He assesses the minor transgressions of his addressees as major transgressions. When his readers allow themselves to be carried away by their passions, give in to desires and are jealous, it is just as if they had waged war or committed murder. James's discussion is based less on the supposed activities of his addressees than on his intensification of the argument in the *teknon* section. In James's moral approach to the law, armed conflict, murder, and adultery take place among his readers because they allow desire to entice them into minor offences.

4. CONCLUSION

The demands of Jesus in the Antitheses and accusations of James in his Letter are rooted in a Jewish Hasidic milieu. The stricter interpretation of the commandments implying a definite shift of moral focus, presents an attitude to life that is beneficial to one's neighbor and emphasizes a more generous, positive attitude towards people throughout (Matt 5:43–48; Jas 2:8). In stressing the minor commandments of the law as an ethical code, the core of which is the principle of neighborly love (Matt 5:43–48; Jas 2:8; cf. Did. 1:2), the teaching of the Matthean Antitheses and James's Letter stand close to the ethos of the wider stream of pietistic Judaism.

The matching outlook of James and Matthew on the subject of the law must be accounted for with a source similar to the Two Ways 3:1–6. The distinctiveness of James and Matthew, however, emerges in the radicalization of the teaching. The individual sayings in Matthew's Antitheses—almost substituting anger for murder, lust for adultery, etc.—are primarily presented as an interpretation of biblical commandments, whereas James—charging those who are partial, biased, envious, jealous, and desirous with being "killers" and "adulteresses"—offers simple and straightforward accusations. The fact that Matthew and James both independently transmuted and radicalized a similar Jewish *teknon* tradition is likely the result of their very close ties with a community or network of like-minded communities in which these highly refined ethical standards were prevalent. We are dealing here with an ethical intensification that at that time may have represented a new step to attaining moral perfection (Matt 5:48; Jas 1:4).

PART 5
OBSERVING RITUALS

Ἀποκύησις λόγῳ ἀληθείας: Paraenesis and Baptism in Matthew, James, and the Didache

Alistair Stewart-Sykes

Certain common themes between Matthew, James and the Didache are not difficult to discern[1] but direct comparison is complicated by the differing overarching genres of the three documents. Nonetheless, in spite of the distinct genres, there is a subgenre, or rather, as I will suggest, a subspecies of a genre, that appears in all three, that is to say that all three contain elements of paraenesis. The purpose of this paper is to explore the paraenetic content of the three documents in the light of another common trait, namely, the practice of baptism. Obviously the practice of baptism does not set the communities that produced these documents apart from other early Christian communities, but an identification in the Didache of pre-baptismal instruction, which may properly be described as paraenetic, allows us to note parallels within the other works that in turn shed light on the rhetorical strategies that they employ.

1. Defining Paraenesis

Paraenesis in modern scholarly discourse has been notably difficult to define. My allotted space might readily be filled with analysis of the various arguments, and so my treatment will be cursory to the point of being curt. The term is effectively defined by Ps-Isocrates in *Ad Demonicum*, when he states that, in a *protreptikos logos*, paraenesis is preferable to *paraklēsis*. What this means is expanded in what follows when he says that he is writing to advise Demonicus on the objects to which the young should aspire, on the actions from which they

---

1. Beyond the papers from the conference in this volume, see, e.g., Ralph P. Martin, *James* (WBC 48; Waco, Tex.: Word Books, 1988), lxxiv–lxxvi; Massey H. Shepherd jr., "The Epistle of James and the Gospel of Matthew," *JBL* 75 (1956): 40–51 (who also brings the Didache into his account); Gunnar Garleff, *Urchristliche Identität in Matthäusevangelium, Didache und Jakobusbrief* (Beiträge zum Verstehen der Bibel 9; Münster: Lit, 2004) who, while he discusses the documents separately, allows us to observe relationships between the three.

should abstain, with what sort of people they should associate and the manner in which they should regulate their lives.[2] In other words, Ps-Isocrates is sending a *logos protreptikos* in which paraenesis, that is to say ethical advice, rather than simple exhortation, predominates. It was on this basis that Burgess classified paraenesis alongside protreptic.[3] It is not, however, a genre as such. Possibly it is a subgenre, or perhaps even a subspecies of protreptic, for the *logos protreptikos* is itself a species of the *genos sumbouleutikon*.[4] Possibly we may read Ps-Isocrates as stating that the primary mark of paraenesis is stylistic rather than generic,[5] as this would account for the different contexts in which paraenesis comes to appear. But above all we should be aware that a (rhetorically constructed) hostility to rhetoric and an implicit claim of the superiority of philosophy lies behind this statement. Paraenesis amounts to protreptic given by a philosopher rather than a rhetorician.

But even as Burgess was writing, some understanding of paraenesis as a genre in itself was coming about, a view given classical expression by Dibelius.[6] However, as such, we may note that not only is it without ancient definition but that, beyond, perhaps, *Ad Demonicum* itself, there is no extant example of a paraenesis pure and simple.[7] We may, moreover, note Ps-Libanius's definition of a paraenetic letter as urging (προτρέποντες) somebody to embrace or to avoid a course of action,[8] again implying a proximity to protreptic.

Scholarship seems to have come full circle, therefore, when Popkes, on the basis of the semantic use of the term and its cognates in ancient literature and the contexts to which paraenesis is addressed defines the basic function of paraenesis as the promotion of "attitudes and actions which secure the future of the recipient, both short and long-range. The present time is a time of decision which

---

2. *Demon.* 1.1.

3. Theodore C. Burgess, "Epideictic Literature," *The University of Chicago Studies in Classical Philology* 3 (1902): 226–28.

4. On the three genera see Aristotle, *Rhet.* 3.1–3. Symbouleutic rhetoric is defined as either hortatory or dissuasive (προτροπή or ἀποτροπή) in much the same way that Ps-Libanius, centuries later, defines παραίνησις.

5. So, similarly Troels Engberg-Pedersen, "The Concept of Paraenesis," in *Early Christian Paraenesis in Context* (ed. J. Starr and T. Engberg-Pedersen; BZNW 125; Berlin: de Gruyter, 2004), 61.

6. Martin Dibelius, *Der Brief des Jakobus* (11th ed.; rev. H. Greeven; Göttingen: Vandenhoeck & Ruprecht, 1964), 16–23. There is, perhaps, some basis for this in Isocrates' admission that in *Nic.* the subjects did not flow as such, as each was under a distinct heading (*Antid.* 67–68), but this was nonetheless more than a random scattering of thoughts.

7. So Wiard Popkes, "Paraenesis in the New Testament: An Exercise in Conceptuality," in *Early Christian Paraenesis* (ed. J. Starr and T. Engberg-Pedersen), 15.

8. Ps-Libanius *Epistolary styles*, 5. See Abraham J. Malherbe, *Ancient Epistolary Theorists* (SBLSBS 19; Atlanta: Scholars Press, 1988), 66–81.

implies an element of transition. Someone has come into a state of reshaping his or her future and now needs competent advice."[9]

Nonetheless, the term may mean, in a general rather than a generic sense, "ethical encouragement and advice." Thus Malherbe identifies five aspects of paraenesis that he considers defining, namely, that paraenesis is conventional teaching rather than new or original material;[10] that it is general in application;[11] that it is frequently repetition of what is already known, intended to make the hearer act on prior knowledge;[12] that a significant figure in paraenesis is the *paradeigma*, the example held up for imitation or for avoidance;[13] and, closely related to this, that this is communication from a respected figure closely acquainted with a more-junior disciple.[14] Whereas all of these may be marks of persuasive literature, which may be called paraenetic, using the term as meaning "ethical encouragement and exhortation," and whereas as such it may be useful to observe such marks, they are not to be employed as defining generic terms since, as Malherbe himself is aware, they are part of a generalized ethical communicative *koiné*.[15]

Further comment on defining paraenesis is forthcoming from Perdue. He notes that in fictive settings at least the occasion for the imparting of paraenesis may be the death or departure of the teacher or a change in status of the person addressed. However, he also notes, in keeping with Malherbe's observation that the content of the paraenesis may be known already to the hearer, that the occasion for its delivery is an important step, and that it serves to remind the hearer of his original incorporation into a group.[16] Perdue's fundamental point, however, is that paraenesis comes to the fore in situations of liminality. Once again we are forced back to the close relationship of paraenesis and protreptic. Nonetheless, whereas protreptic is primarily addressed to an uncommitted audience, paraenesis is speech to the unconverted moreso than to the half-converted,[17]

---

9. Popkes, "Paraenesis in the New Testament," 17.

10. Abraham J. Malherbe, "Hellenistic Moralists and the New Testament," *ANRW* 26.1: 280 with reference to Nic. 40–41.

11. Ibid., 289, with reference to Seneca *Ep.* 94. 32–35.

12. Ibid., 280–281, with reference to Seneca *Ep.* 94. 25; 94. 21; Dio Chrysostom, *Ordin.* 17.2.

13. Ibid., 282–83, with reference to *Demon.* 8–11.

14. Ibid., 285–87, with particular reference to the relationship between Seneca and Lucilius.

15. Engberg-Pedersen, "Concept of Paraenesis," 60, also suggests that there is more (or less) to paraenesis than simply the general ethical *commune* of the ancient world.

16. Leo Perdue, "Paraenesis and the Epistle of James," *ZNW* 72 (1981): 247–48.

17. The distinction made by Stanley K. Stowers, *Letter-writing in Greco-Roman Antiquity* (LEC 5; Philadelphia: Westminster, 1986), 91–96. John G. Gammie, "Paraenetic Literature: Towards the Morphology of a Secondary Genre," in *Paraenesis: Act and Form* (ed. L. Perdue and J. G. Gammie; *Semeia* 50; Atlanta: Scholars Press, 1990), 43, 53–54, disputes this by sug-

and as such to persons setting out on a liminal stage of being.[18] In other words, whereas a liminal situation might not be definitory of paraenesis, it is a primary context in which such discourse might be found, and if discourse that would otherwise appear paraenetic is clearly addressed to a situation of liminality then we have greater assurance of the classification. One may note here that Ps-Libanius distinguishes paraenesis from what he calls sumbouleutic discourse (of which I have suggested, actually, that this is a subspecies) on the grounds that paraenesis does not admit of contradiction.[19] As such, this compares readily with Austin's distinction between illocutionary and perlocutionary acts.[20] Thus the heavy presence of conventional maxims that, according to Aristotle, are best used in speech addressed from a senior to a junior,[21] could well be an indication of paraenesis, in that the situation of the audience is that of learning as neophytes and the social setting is thus more likely to turn an illocution into a perlocution, and given that there are precepts that do not admit of contradiction.[22] However the presence of maxims should not of itself be definitory.[23]

We thus conclude, in agreement with Perdue, that "protrepsis and paraenesis refer . . . to two distinct, but connected, stages along the way to virtue: entrance to the path of life and continuance in the course undertaken."[24] Thus, in Isocratean terms, pure *paraklēsis* is unnecessary, but calmer advice and guidance is needed. This is a definition and distinction that not only does proper justice to the evidence but, perhaps more importantly, is of heuristic value. The heu-

---

gesting that some literary works that might be paraenetic are addressed to a mixed audience. This is less than relevant, however, as these are literary works rather than actual paraenetic speech.

18. It is the failure to observe these stages that mars the suggestion of James Starr)"Was Paraenesis for Beginners?" in Starr and Engberg-Pedersen, eds., *Early Christian Paraenesis*, 73–111), that paraenesis is aimed at those who are more advanced. Thus in observing what *Hebrews* says of initial learning (p. 108), he is actually observing initial protreptic rather than paraenesis proper. See also n. 25 below.

19. Ps-Libanius, *Epistolary styles* 5. The distinction is perhaps comparable to those types of letters described by Ps-Demetrius as νουθετητικός and συμβουλευτικός (Ps-Demetrius, *Eloc.*, 7 and 11; see Malherbe, *Ancient Epistolary Theorists*, 30–41).

20. John L. Austin, *How To Do Things with Words* (2nd ed.; Oxford: Oxford University Press, 1975), 102–8.

21. *Rhet.* 2.21.

22. So Seneca, *Ep.* 94. 43.

23. As Gammie, "Paraenetic Literature" makes it. In doing so he is heavily influenced, it seems, by Seneca *Ep.* 95.1, which refers to "haec pars philosophiae quam Graeci paraeneticen vocant, nos praeceptivam dicimus"; this letter, however, needs to be read carefully and critically as it is an engagement in the Stoic discussion of the validity of non-argued statements.

24. Leo G. Perdue, "The Social Character of Paraenesis and Paraenetic Literature," in Perdue and Gammie, eds., *Paraenesis: Act and Form*, 24. Similarly Stowers, *Letter-Writing in Greco-Roman Antiquity*, 91–96.

ristic value of the classification comes about when an identification of discourse as paraenetic allows us insights into the situation of the hearers, or attunes us to clues to the situation of the hearer(s) that otherwise might be missed, rather than when the situation of the hearer(s) is known and we are therefore able to identify paraenesis on that basis. If the possible presence of paraenesis alerts us to a liminal life-setting that can in turn be demonstrated from other literary clues, not only have we succeeded in a classification, but more importantly we are able to see how the discourse fits the hearers. Thus, in seeking paraenesis in Matthew, James, and the Didache, we specifically seek ethical exhortation that betrays an element of liminality as the context for the recipients, thus being aware in the first instance of the relationship obtaining between this and protreptic, and, having observed this, we may see if the situation of the hearers is consistent with that form of address. With regard to the other observed features that attach more to paraenesis as generalized moral discourse, we may seek to observe such features as are noticed by Malherbe without in any way making them determinative as to whether any given passage is technically paraenetic.

In general, we may readily recognize the Two Ways section of the Didache as paraenetic. We may recognize it, moreover, as specifically so, for beyond its ethical content, and beyond its generalizing tone and relative lack of specificity, it is, I need hardly argue, intended as a pre-baptismal address, setting out the conditions for behavior for one who is to be baptized in this community. As such it functions quasi-protreptrically and in a socially formative manner, in other words paraenetically, in instructing the addressee in preparation for his or her baptism. By having this assured understanding, moreover, of the social and religious function of this instruction, we are equipped to understand the appearance of similar material elsewhere in which the context of the hearers is less clear.[25]

Thus, turning to Matthew we may likewise recognize the content of Matt 5–7 as generally and unspecifically paraenetic. The question of whether it is specifically so is less certain, as in its fictive narrative setting there is nothing that readily indicates that it is intended as protreptic. However, there are two arguments that lead me to suggest that this is the original setting of the unit. The first derives from Hartman's suggestion that the instruction to teach all nations in the context of baptism refers back to the content of teaching that is to be found

---

25. This in turn is what enables us to see that Starr's denial in "Was Paraenesis for Beginners?" that paraenesis is intended principally for those at an early stage in their moral or religious journey is hopeless; he is unable to deny that this is the function of the Two Ways material in the Didache. At 109–10 he refers to Huub van de Sandt and David Flusser, *The Didache: Its Jewish Sources and Its Place in Early Judaism and Christianity* (CRINT 3/5; Assen: Van Gorcum, 2002), 31, to support his suggestion that the function of this material extended beyond that stated, but there is no support there, as discussion at this point concerns the document as a whole.

within the first Gospel.[26] Principal among these blocks of teaching is that found at Matt 5–7. In particular there is reference within this block to the Two Ways tradition: "Enter by the narrow gate, for one gate is wide and the way is spacious which leads to destruction,"[27] an exhortation that leads rapidly to an eschatological conclusion. As such, and on the assumption that Matthew and the Didache share at least a *Traditionskreis*, we may suggest that the Two Ways tradition, in its use as pre-baptismal instruction, has worked some influence here.

Secondly, quite apart from verbal parallels, there is a substantial degree of content in common between the Two Ways chapters of the Didache and Matt 5. Both redefine the extent of application of the commandments and both preach reliance upon God for all things; the substantial degree of confluence, moreover, between Did. 1:2–5 and Matt 5 hardly needs comment. I suggest that this material was circulating in the context of versions of the Two Ways employed in pre-baptismal catechesis.

Within this block of teaching there are nonetheless, it may be noted, a variety of forms. In particular a cultic didache may be found within the block of teaching, that itself has numerous points of contact, as well as difference, with the cultic instructions of the Didache following the direction to baptize, namely, directions on fasting and on prayer.[28] We may see this as circulating independently and being placed secondarily within what is effectively an epitome of Jesus's teaching.[29] All this may be the work of the redactor of the first Gospel, but the *Traditionskreis* lying behind it is bound up to the nexus of baptismal preparation.

To turn to James, there is no question that in the most general sense the epistle is paraenetic, indeed Dibelius classified James as a paraenetic text, "a stringing together of admonitions of general ethical conduct."[30] Insofar as Dibelius was speaking of a genre the very mark of which was an absence of order, we must, of course, deny such a characterization, but the content is nonetheless largely ethical and there are, moreover, a number of features identified by Malherbe as part of the *lingua franca* of Hellenistic ethical discourse. Thus, the fictive author is a person of agreed authority, the exhortation is general rather than particular, and *paradeigmata* are employed. What is less clear is the extent to which the epistle is paraenetic insofar as the term may be understood in indicating protrep-

---

26. Lars Hartman, *Into the Name of the Lord Jesus: Baptism in the Early Church* (Studies of the New Testament and its World; Edinburgh: T&T Clark, 1997), 149–50.

27. Matt 7:13.

28. So Hans D. Betz, "A Jewish-Christian Cultic *Didache* in Matt 6:1–18: Reflections and Questions on the Problem of the Historical Jesus," in H. D. Betz, *Essays on the Sermon on the Mount* (trans. L. Welborn; Philadelphia: Fortress, 1985), 55–69.

29. So Hans D. Betz, "The Sermon on the Mount (Matt 5:3–7:27): Its Literary Genre and Function," in Betz, *Essays on the Sermon on the Mount*, 1–16.

30. Dibelius, *Brief des Jakobus*, 19–20.

sis. There is no evidence that the audience is preparing for baptism, indeed there is evidence that the audience is already baptized, since reference is made to the name that has been invoked upon them (2:7), and to the new birth that they have already received (1:18). The question, therefore, is whether the paraenetic content of James is meant to recall instruction given before baptism as a means of restoring the hearers to their baptismal resolve through reminding them of their initial incorporation into James's group and therefore to reflect paraenesis proper.

This in turn can only be answered through an examination of what James says about baptism, to see whether this gives a clue to the nature of the pre-baptismal direction that had been given. If this direction may be seen to conform to patterns and contents of catechesis known elsewhere, then we may reasonably suggest that elements adduced from elsewhere, in the *Traditionskreis* may have formed part of that known within the James community. We might then recognize that the persuasive force of James's words comes about through the restatement of baptismal protrepsis.

2. Baptism in Matthew, James, and the Didache

Regarding the rite of baptism itself we are well-informed by the Didache of the practice of this community,[31] but rather than tread this ground again we begin with James, in an attempt to recover the understanding of baptism enunciated here, in order to see the extent to which it is shared by the other two documents under discussion.

As already noted, there are two passages that seem to reflect the baptized status of the hearers and that, in turn, may inform us regarding James's thoughts concerning baptism. In addition to these, Braumann argues that 2:5, 14; 4:10, 12; 5:15, and 5:20 are also baptismal references.[32] His arguments are, however, vague; for instance on 5:20 he simply notes that release from death might be a reference to baptism as the language is fitting. However, these are not obviously baptismal in the sense that the first two are. We will argue below that 5:20 at least bears the weight that Braumann puts upon it, albeit on different grounds from

---

31. Among treatments of baptism in the *Didache* see, beyond the standard commentaries, Nathan Mitchell, "Baptism in the *Didache*," in *The Didache in Context: Essays on Its Text, History, and Transmission* (ed. C. N. Jefford; NovTSup 77; Leiden: Brill, 1995), 226–55; Willy Rordorf, "Baptism According to the *Didache*," in *The Didache in Modern Research* (ed. J. A. Draper; AGJU 37; Leiden: Brill, 1996), 212–22; Jonathan A. Draper, "Ritual Process and Ritual Symbol in *Didache* 7–10," *VC* 54 (2000): 121–58.

32. Georg Braumann, "Der theologische Hintergrund des Jakobusbriefes," *TZ* 18 (1962): 406–8.

those that he adduces, once we have submitted the two clear references to closer examination.[33]

The first passage relates to the rebirth undergone in baptism, and is part of a statement of the beneficence of God: πᾶσα δόσις ἀγαθὴ καὶ πᾶν δώρημα τέλειον ἄνωθέν ἐστιν καταβαῖνον ἀπὸ τοῦ πατρὸς τῶν φώτων, παρ᾽ ᾧ οὐκ ἔνι παραλλαγὴ ἢ τροπῆς ἀποσκίασμα. βουληθεὶς ἀπεκύησεν ἡμᾶς λόγῳ ἀληθείας εἰς τὸ εἶναι ἡμᾶς ἀπαρχήν τινα τῶν αὐτοῦ κτισμάτων.[34] The baptismal reference is clear in the reference to the birthing of the Christian. The birthing is in order to make those so reborn an ἀπαρχή of his creation. The creation is, it would seem, not the old creation, as it is hard to see how those baptized should be first fruits of that, but rather a new creation being ushered in by God, an eschatological refashioning in which those who are baptized are already present, a creation that is God's own. The means of doing so is a λόγος ἀληθείας, here implying that the word is spoken in the baptismal context, as it is the means by which the birthing takes place.[35] It is, in other words, a perlocutionary act. Whereas it may be a reference to a baptismal formula, an utterance by which the new status of the baptized is brought about, even assuming that such a formula existed, the word that is the means of birth is the word of God whereas the performance of birth in baptism is the work as much of the water as any words that might be uttered, and therefore it is equally likely that it is a reference to the words spoken in paraenesis before the baptism itself, the instruction given, seen as the word of truth.[36] It is also conceivable that, just as in the practice of proselyte baptism within Judaism, voice was given to the greater and lesser commandments even while the candidate was in the water,[37] so directions and commandments were repeated during the baptism itself.[38] Leaving the question of the word for the moment,

33. Braumann's approach may be contrasted to that of Garleff, *Urchristliche Identität in Matthäusevangelium*, for whom ritual as an identity former is all but absent in James (note especially pp. 316 and 325.)

34. Jas 1:17–18.

35. See also the similar uses and context of the term at Col 1:5 and Eph 1:13. The context in Ephesians is clearly baptismal, that in Colossians is related closely to conversion. See, however, Martin, *James*, 40, for whom the word of God spoken in creation provides the sole background to the term.

36. So Franz Mussner, "Die Tauflehre des Jakobusbriefs," in *Zeichen des Glaubens: Studien zu Taufe und Firmung* (ed. H. Auf Der Maur and B. Kleinheyer; Freiburg: Herder, 1972), 63–64, who also notes the parallel with Eph 1:13. For other understandings of the term, such as reference to the Torah or to the word spoken in creation, with some discussion, see Wiard Popkes, "Tradition und Traditionsbrüche im Jakobsbrief," in *The Catholic Epistles and the Tradition* (ed. J. Schlosser; BETL 176; Leuven: Peeters, 2004), 153; Garleff, *Urchristliche Identität in Matthäusevangelium*, 276, n. 318 with refs.

37. *b. Yebam.* 47a–b.

38. We may note in this context the somewhat speculative but nonetheless attractive suggestion of Aaron Milavec, *The Didache: Faith Hope and Life of the Earliest Christian Com-*

however, we may state at this stage that baptism in James's understanding is a means by which the believer enters a new eschatological status, standing as the beginning of a new creation.

An eschatological element in Matthew's understanding of baptism is identified by Hartman within the first Gospel in that the Lord's instruction to baptize is set in the expectation of his coming again, and in the promise that the Lord will be with the believer to the end of the age.[39] Presence with the Lord is also understood by Nepper-Christensen as central to Matthew's understanding of baptism,[40] thus indicating an inaugurated eschatology by which the presence of the Lord is an earnest of the coming of the Son of Man. The Didache likewise sounds a note by which we may understand baptism as having a clear inaugurated eschatological orientation. In particular we may note that it is through baptism that persons are admitted to the eucharistic meal in which the eschatological presence of the Lord was enjoyed, even while his coming was besought.[41] The conclusion, moreover, exhorts the hearer in the light of the Lord's coming to continue in the state in which they were baptized. But for all that a similarity is arguable, there is not sufficient proximity in baptismal theologies here, nor is this similarity unique, for Pauline circles likewise see the Christian standing as part of a new creation.[42]

We may turn to the other clearly identified reference to baptism within James. In the context of a discussion concerning courts, reference is made to the name that has been called over the Christian. Of the rich who are dragging the hearers into the courts, James states: οὐκ αὐτοὶ βλασφημοῦσιν τὸ καλὸν ὄνομα τὸ ἐπικληθὲν ἐφ' ὑμᾶς.[43] We may note that the same phrase is found in Herm. Sim. 8.6.4 where the shepherd refers to apostates who have become ashamed of τὸ ὄνομα κυρίου τὸ ἐπικληθὲν ἐπ' αὐτούς.[44] In some sense the name is called out over a person, though Hartman doubts this, and suggests instead that the usage reflects the Hebrew Bible and that so "the expression hardly refers directly to baptism, but rather says that the Christians addressed are sanctified and dedicated to God and so belong to him, like the old Israel."[45] The aorist, however,

---

munities, 50–70 CE (New York: Newman, 2003), 266–68, that the Two Ways catechism was repeated during the baptism.

39. Hartman, Into the Name of the Lord Jesus, 153.

40. Poul Nepper-Christensen, "Die Taufe im Matthäusevangelium," NTS 31 (1985): 206–7.

41. For a general recognition of the Didache's understanding of baptism as eschatological see Mitchell, "Baptism in the Didache," 248, though the significance he attaches to the term "eschatology" is not altogether clear.

42. E.g., 2 Cor 5:17.

43. Jas 2:7.

44. See also Herm. Sim. 9.17.4.

45. Hartman, Into the Name of the Lord Jesus, 49, n. 52.

indicates a liturgical event[46] rather than a standing situation, which would more naturally be expressed by a perfect. The name is called out onto the Christian.

The name is either that of Jesus or, as implied in the baptismal rite of the Didache and in Matthew's directions for the baptism of the nations, that of the Trinity. My own suspicion is that the name is the name of Jesus.

Although it is possible that this is a reference to baptism ἐπὶ τῷ ὀνόματι Ἰησοῦ Χριστοῦ, and that it reflects a formula baptizing in the name of Jesus,[47] and that the same is true of the baptismal rites of Acts, there are grounds to doubt this. For whereas there are several references in Acts to baptism into the name of Jesus Christ[48] these do not allow us confidently to assert that this is the formula employed. Rather, as Hartman puts it, "in all probability the rite was accompanied with such interpreting prayers or allocutions or proclamations that it was clear to those who took part and those who assisted that it was naturally called a baptism into the name of the Lord Jesus."[49] Von Campenhausen similarly points out that everything in the church might be done "in the name of Jesus," and that therefore no special significance should be attached to baptism in this name.[50] Hartman and von Campenhausen thus give more than adequate explanations of the usage that therefore do not necessitate the assumption that the formula is employed in the ritual, and so it is all the more odd that Hartman, though not von Campenhausen, nonetheless assumes that the baptismal rite named Jesus in some way.

The model of proselyte baptism as of the other purification rites in water known in Judaism does not presume the use of a formula,[51] and in the earliest period, the early-third century, in which we are well informed concerning baptismal rituals, there is no formula spoken by the baptizer but rather a set of interrogations to which the candidate answers. These later interrogations are

---

46. So, also, Peter Davids, *The Epistle of James: A Commentary on the Greek Text* (NIGTC; Exeter: Paternoster, 1982), 113, who otherwise does not concentrate on the liturgical significance of this statement or on baptismal allusions in the letter, as witnessed by his comment (p. 90) that reference to catechesis in the λόγος ἀληθείας is "possible."

47. So Mussner, "Die Tauflehre des Jakobusbriefs," 62.

48. E.g., Acts 2:38; 8:16; 10:48; 19:5.

49. Hartman, *Into the Name of the Lord Jesus*, 140.

50. Hans F. von Campenhausen "Taufen in dem Namen Jesu?" *VC* 25 (1971): 3. Similar arguments were employed by Edward G. C. F. Atchley, *On the Epiclesis of the Baptismal Liturgy and in the Consecration of the Font* (London: Humphrey Milford, 1935), 7–8.

51. So, pertinently, Von Campenhausen, "Taufen in dem Namen," 7, though we should note *b. Yebam.* 47a–b as cited above, and, again as noted above, the suggestion of Milavec, who likewise rightly rejects the existence of any formula spoken by the baptizer. Von Campenhausen's argument at "Taufen in dem Namen," 6, that there is no formula found in the baptism of the Ethiopian eunuch at Acts 8 is on its own a weak argument from silence, but is strengthened by reference to silent rites elsewhere.

Trinitarian in form. We may thus note that just as the formula "baptism in the name of Jesus" need not reflect liturgical use, the same is true of the Trinitarian formula in Matthew and the Didache.[52] The point that bedevils this discussion is the unspoken assumption that there was a formula spoken by the baptizer, and yet there is no evidence for any such formula from the first four centuries but rather an interrogation which, in the third century at least, is threefold. The Didache does not state that the Trinity should be named in the baptismal process, and so we should anticipate that baptism, in accordance with the models of purification known in Judaism, should be silent. Hartman suggests that the Trinitarian formulation comes about having grown from an original naming of Jesus as there is reflection in debate with Jews on the fact that Jesus is the Father's Son and that the Spirit is active in his mission;[53] however, whereas this is a plausible process of theological reflection there is no necessity that this be ritually expressed, but rather implies an expansion of the idea of baptism into the name and power of God.

It is possible, however, to countenance some development of understanding even within the period during which the Didache was redacted, from talk of baptism into the Lord's name to talk of baptism into that of the Trinity. Yet that is not to say that there was a change in the baptismal formula, for there was no formula as such, but might rather be expressed in the number of immersions. So it is possible that the redactor of Did. 7:3, in stating that that infusion, when practiced, should take place three times in the name of the Trinity, is adding something new in that there may have been a change from a single immersion on the basis of an expression of faith in Jesus to a triple immersion on the basis of an expression of faith in the triad. Certainly as the baptism of Gentiles becomes more common an expression of faith in God the Father, which might be assumed to have been held by those of Israelite heritage, would be a reasonable addition.[54] This is slightly speculative, as it is based solely on one piece of evidence and on one (reasonable) assumption, but that is more evidence than can be brought for a baptismal formula beyond the possible repetition of elements of the catechism, before Nicaea.

On the assumption that the name to which reference is made is that of Jesus, James and Hermas provide the best evidence for the use of this name in a liturgical formula connected to baptism. Yet even though the name of Jesus is mentioned in the baptismal rite of James's community, there is no certainty that the formula was declaratory in the manner imagined; indeed the terms ἐπικληθὲν ἐφ' ὑμᾶς in James and ἐπικληθὲν ἐπ' αὐτούς in Hermas sound more

---

52. See Nepper-Christensen, "Die Taufe im Matthäusevangelium," 203, who assumes that this is a liturgical formula, whilst doubting its originality.

53. Hartman, *Into the Name of the Lord Jesus*, 151.

54. So also Rordorf, "Baptism According to the *Didache*," 217–28.

as though the formula to which reference is made might be epicletic. Once this is recognized there is other evidence that falls into place. Thus Cyprian refers to Marcionite belief that the efficacy of baptism comes about through the "maiestas nominis"[55] and the anonymous *De rebaptismate* from the same period likewise appears to indicate that baptism, particularly in Marcionite communities, might include an invocation of Jesus upon the candidate, and in such a way that this would appear to have been a pre- or post-baptismal ceremony.[56] The summit of the evidence, however, is in *Traditio apostolica* in which, immediately after baptism, the candidate is anointed by a presbyter with the words "I anoint you with holy oil in the name of Jesus Christ."[57] We may suggest that the oil has become the medium of the calling down of the name upon the candidate.[58] That all this evidence is Roman and/or Marcionite should not deter us, as these Roman rites reflect practice imported from the eastern Empire and Marcionite liturgical practice is not distinct from that of the *Großkirche*.[59]

This formula, therefore, should be understood separately from references in Acts to baptism "in the name of Jesus," or the direction of the Didache that those baptized "in the name of the Lord" are those with the exclusive rite to participate in the Lord's Supper. The name is the name of Jesus, but it is spoken not as a declaratory baptismal formula but as part of an epicletic pre- or post- baptismal ceremony.

If it is the case that baptism in the community of James included an epiclesis of the Lord onto the candidate as part of the complex of baptismal rites, then there is a distinct difference between this ritual and that of the Didache. With regard to Matthew we are less certain, as the Lord's promise to be with the disciples may reflect such an epiclesis. This is, of course, conjectural in the extreme, but we cannot, from the information available to us, totally exclude the possibility that there was such a rite.

---

55. *Ep.* 74.5.1.

56. Atchley, *On the Epiclesis*, 7 and 16, n. 44, suggests that this is simply a prayer, an *invocatio*. Whereas this is just feasible in *De rebaptismate* 10, which speaks vaguely of the *invocatio* of the name, in 12 the *invocatio* is specifically *super* the candidates. "Si sic perseuerunt," (i.e., should heretics who have been baptized but have not received the Holy Spirit through the imposition of a bishop's hands continue not to receive episcopal handlaying) "salui esse non possunt, quia non requisiuerunt Dominum post inuocationem nominis eius super eos."

57. This congruence of *Trad. ap.* with other Roman evidence tends to support my suggestion in *On the Apostolic Tradition* (Crestwood, N.Y.: St Vladimir's, 2001), 122, that this section is part of an underlying Roman rite. See Paul F. Bradshaw *et al.*, *The Apostolic Tradition: A Commentary* (Hermeneia; Minneapolis: Augsburg Fortress, 2002), 127.

58. Slightly more speculatively we may suggest that this practice in turn led to the epicletic prayers in Syrian rites over the oil for the *rušma*.

59. So my "Bread, Fish, Water and Wine: the Marcionite Menu and the Maintenance of Purity," in *Marcion und seine kirchengeschichtliche Wirkung* (ed. G. May and K. Greschat; TU 150; Berlin: de Gruyter, 2002), 207–20.

Beyond these two references within James we cannot safely go. We are also not in a position to argue from silence. That is to say, whereas Matthew's account of the baptizer's activity implies, on the basis of comparison with the other synoptic accounts, that forgiveness was not part of the complex of ideas surrounding baptism,[60] and whereas the Didache seems likewise not to promote such an idea,[61] its absence from James may simply be the result of an absence of opportunity rather than the absence of an idea.[62]

Thus on the basis of these two phrases we deduce that the rite described by James has the significant difference from that of the Didache in that there is an invocation of the name of Jesus; it is possible that Matthew's rite had this but we are far from sure of this. Secondly we note that although for all three baptism is the means by which the believer enters the eschatological realm this is not a mark of uniqueness.

3. James's Exhortation as Reflecting Baptismal Paraenesis

In spite of the fundamentally negative result, it is still worth exploring whether the sections in which James's baptismal allusions occur bear traces of pre-baptismal instruction, in particular insofar as the reference to rebirth makes explicit reference to such instruction. There are other grounds for attempting this undertaking, moreover, as, although we may concentrate on three particular documents that share a *Traditionskreis*, to a degree there are others that likewise in some way appear to reflect a common catechetical pattern. This pattern was identified by Carrington within the Pauline tradition,[63] and although the pattern itself is not found within the three documents under scrutiny, elements of its contents certainly appear that imply the circulation of material related to baptism quite independent of the differing rites by which baptism was administered.

Popkes had indeed argued that there was a debt within James to pre-baptismal direction. This conclusion was reached in part on the basis of a characterization of the letter as having an *Anredecharakter*, and on the ground of a thematic cohesion with 1 Peter, arguably also redacted from pre-baptismal instruction, in particular with regard to the theme of testing. He further observes that testing is also part of rabbinic instruction given to proselytes at baptism, that there is also allusion to testing in a baptismal context at 1 Cor 10, and that the baptism of Jesus is closely tied to his subsequent testing in the wilderness. This

---

60. Hartman, *Into the Name of the Lord Jesus*, 152; Nepper-Christensen, "Die Taufe im Matthäusevangelium," 201.

61. So Mitchell, "Baptism in the *Didache*," 234–35.

62. Though we should note that forgiveness is attributed to prayer with anointing at 5:15.

63. Philip Carrington, *The Primitive Christian Catechism: A Study in the Epistles* (Cambridge: Cambridge University Press, 1940).

thematic congruence and quasi-homiletic character are the bases on which the possibility is raised that James reflects catechetical paraenesis.[64] When I examined James to determine whether it might reflect a synagogue homily or other proclamation of the word within the Christian assembly I found these arguments unconvincing,[65] and still do. There is no particular reflection of a liminal character in James's hearers and although testing fits with the character of somebody approaching baptism and is linked in the tradition with baptism, this life-setting for testing is not unique as other situations might call forth such a trial of faith.

Nonetheless, Popkes's conclusion that James in some way reflects pre-baptismal instruction may well be correct, though it may be reached on different grounds, namely, a degree of cohesion between some of the content and material, which may be agreed on safer grounds to have been addressed to an audience approaching baptism. Once this is seen, then the thematic cohesion that Popkes observed is better established as having derived from a baptismal context and his suggestions then begin to have some force. Perdue also suggests that there is a reflection of pre-baptismal instruction: "In fact, chapter 4 recalls the language that was a part of the initial rite of passage into the community; 'submission', 'cleansing of hands', 'purifying of the heart', 'mourning', and 'humiliation.'"[66] More precision than this, however, is needed, as Perdue himself recognizes,[67] and this is what the comparative study may supply.

We begin with the reference to ἀποκύησις by means of the word. In the exhortation that follows, to be clean and to act upon the word that is being heard, we may suggest that there is continued reference to the baptismal catechesis, principally in the exhortation to put off all dirt (1:21), and in that light to see the ἔμφυτος λόγος to which reference is made as the same λόγος by which the hearers had been reborn.[68] Separating this apparently baptismal exhortation and the reference to rebirth is an exhortation to avoid anger (1:19d–20), which is certainly part of the Two Ways tradition, as well as being linked to the extension of the scope of the Decalogue at Matt 5:21–23, and on those grounds it may be said to have been part of the catechesis.[69] Such a pattern is, moreover observable else-

---

64. Wiard Popkes, *Adressaten, Situation und Form des Jakobusbriefes* (SBS 125/126; Stuttgart: Katholisches Bibelwerk, 1986), 125–56.

65. Alistair Stewart-Sykes, *From Prophecy to Preaching: A Search for the Origins of the Christian Homily* (VCSup 59; Leiden: Brill, 2001), 157. Very brief attention was given to the topic as it was incidental to the main line of the argument. Nonetheless, this is one of many parts of the book which I may wish had been better written.

66. Perdue, "Paraenesis and the Epistle of James," 251.

67. Ibid., 256.

68. So also, though on different grounds and with a less precise view of the λόγος ἀληθείας, Garleff, *Urchristliche Identität in Matthäusevangelium*, 277.

69. Wiard Popkes, *Der Brief des Jakobus* (THKNT 14; Leipzig: Evangelische Verlagsanstalt, 2001), 129, arguing that the material concerning anger is part of an extension of the

where. Thus 1 Pet 1:23–2:1 begins with a reminder of the rebirth of a Christian διὰ λόγου ζῶντος θεοῦ καὶ μένοντος and then exhorts the hearers to abandon malice, deceit, and other sins of this nature. Less immediately comparable is Col 3:8–10 in that the exhortation to lay aside anger and falsehood is not preceded but followed by a reminder of the renewal that the hearers had experienced, but the pattern nonetheless appears to be present. Finally, Eph 4:20–26 reminds the hearers of their initial catechism, and on that basis calls for the renewal of the hearers and the abandonment of falsehood and anger. James is thus reminding his hearers not only of their baptism but of the instruction received in that context.

Then looking back from the statement of the baptized status of the believer born through the word of truth we may note the significance of the statement that the Lord is "Father of lights in whom no darkness is found." Due to its context, we may suggest that this is a reference to a version of the Two Ways in which the ways are characterized as light and darkness. Moreover, it is in the light of a possible debt to the Two Ways tradition that we may accept the suggestion, advanced by Braumann, but not actually argued, that the reference to one who turns a sinner away from the πλάνη ὁδός at 5:20 is indeed a reference to pre-baptismal direction. Again, such language is not unique to James and the Didache, but is surely part of a wider and fundamental discourse of conversion, as part of which we may observe Acts 26:18, 1 Thess 5:4–5, and Eph 5:8.[70] Thus the content of this section in James may be said to have derived from a reminder of baptismal instruction.

Once the possibility of cohesion between the contents of baptismal paraenesis known from elsewhere and the contents of James is raised, the parallels between James and the Two Ways section of the Didache, as to Matt 5–7, begin to appear more readily. There is little point in enumerating them, but I note a few simply to illustrate the point. There are, for instance, the warning about the manner in which ἐπιθυμία leads on to sin, which in turn leads to death;[71] the re-enforcement and extension of the command to love one's neighbor;[72] the demand for perfection and completeness in the observance of the law;[73] and the warning against double-mindedness.[74] We cannot be sure whether material beyond that which is directly paralleled elsewhere may have derived from the catechetical tradition, and may also note the likelihood that the material has

---

material from Matt 5 suggests that the reference to the δικαιοσύνη of God is also part of the catechetical package.

70. See Edward G. Selwyn, *The First Epistle of Saint Peter* (London: Macmillan, 1946), 375–84, and the table of parallels that he presents.

71. Jas 1:15; cf. Matt 5:28; Did. 3:3.

72. Jas 2:8; cf. Matt 5:43–44; Did. 1:2.

73. Jas 2:10–11; cf. Matt 5:48 and Did. 6:2.

74. Jas 1:8; cf. Did. 2:4; 4:4.

received a fairly free treatment. Hence it is possible that 4:7–4:10 reflects a *Haustafel* of submission. Thus here one of Braumann's suggestions is shown to have some possible basis, albeit on grounds different from those that he adduced.

Thus, having seen that parts at least of Matt 5–7 and parts at least of James reflect pre-baptismal paraenesis, cohesion of other parts of their contents with Two Ways material in the Didache, which is known to function specifically (that is to say catechetically) paraenetically, indicates that some elements within James that are superficially paraenetic in the general sense, are specifically so, even if they are not framed in the context of baptismal language or explicitly linked with baptism in any way. Thus, in the light of a pre-baptismal understanding of much of James's direction, the extent to which the weight of the parallels between Matthew and James noted by Martin occur in Matt 5–7 is striking.[75]

Although this material is catechetically expressed, it is possible that it was not catechetically formed but that its genesis lay in early Judaism, not in the formation of proselytes but in the formation of disciples within inner-Jewish groups. It is thus noteworthy that the correlations between desire, sin, and death of Jas 1:14–15 and 1:19–21 is, as Huub van de Sandt notes in his essay within this collection, closely paralleled in ethos and content not only by the Matthaean antitheses and Did. 3:1–6 (the *teknon* section) but also within rabbinic literature.[76] Yet, just as the *teknon* section is secondarily included in the Two Ways found within the Didache (being absent in the version found within Barnabas) and so brought into catechetical use, so this material is already in catechetical use within the community of James. Thus Jas 1:14–15 and 1:19–21 form a frame around the exhortation not to be deceived and the reminder of the hearers' birth by the word of truth, and the whole section is concluded by an exhortation to put off all filth, a section redolent with baptismal language. Because of the catechetical framework in which the material is now found, we may suggest that these parallels denote more than a common thought-world but that the formation of those being baptized has contributed to the preservation and transmission of this material within forming Christian communities and that the communities represented by these documents had a common catechetical tradition that had incorporated material originally intended to form disciples from within Judaism.

With this in mind we may return to the theme of testing discerned by Popkes and employed by him as a rationale for seeing catechetical elements within James. Whereas we have suggested that this is of itself insufficient reason to understand James as paraenetic, other grounds for doing so have been found. So in pursuing a paraenetic basis for some of the material regarding testing we

---

75. Martin, *James*, lxxv–lxxvi. Popkes, *Adressaten, Situation und Form*, 156–76 gives a much more detailed comparison of material across the three documents.

76. See the contribution of Huub van de Sandt in this volume.

may, for instance, observe the makarism at 1:12, which Popkes observes fits closely with the makarisms of Matthew's paraenesis[77] and, on the basis of the setting of the parallel within Matthew, assign this to baptismal paraenesis. Beyond this, however, we should also note the hypothesis of Selwyn, developed from that of Carrington, that persecution and testing had called forth a "persecution catechism." Elements such as exhortations to stand firm and to be watchful had been linked by Carrington to his catechetical pattern,[78] but Selwyn had argued that these were developed later as a standard response to persecution;[79] Jas 1:2–3, 12; 4:7 and 5:8 are numbered by him among traces of this catechism. Davies' response that the Q material speaks of crisis, and thus hardly reflects regular catechism, is slightly relevant,[80] in that the formulation of a stock response is hardly a response to persecution. But Davies fails to recognize the personal crisis that is represented by the state of the catechumen turning from one way of life to another, such that material formed for catechetical purposes might well serve to strengthen a Christian faced with persecution.

We may not perceive persecution as such behind James, but there certainly is πειρασμός. It is this same "persecution catechism," observed by Selwyn, that is the basis on which Popkes observes such language as emerging from pre-baptismal direction, though rightly, with Carrington (who does not take account of James in his work) he counts it as part of a more general catechesis rather than a catechesis formed in time of trial. If then we were to ask why this familiar material is being repeated to those already baptized we may point to the πειρασμός. Having been converted and reformed through the word, the word is repeated to those in danger of reverting under testing. The persuasive force of James, therefore, derives in part from reminding the baptized hearers of the λόγος ἀληθείας of perlocutionary force, which was delivered to them at baptism. Testing and trial provide an occasion to repeat the λόγος ἀληθείας, of which traces occur throughout the document, so that it might have the same effect that it had had before.[81] It may, moreover, be significant that the epistle concludes with a mention of those who turn sinners from the path of death as here the technique of repeating the catechetical word is commended, so reflecting back on the preceding material.

It is, however, to be noted that some of these catechetical materials are found in materials beyond the three documents under consideration here, and beyond

---

77. Popkes, *Adressaten, Situation und Form*, 135–36.

78. Carrington, *Primitive Christian Catechism*, 39 and *passim*.

79. Selwyn, *The First Epistle of Saint Peter*, 439–58.

80. William D. Davies, *The Sermon on the Mount* (Cambridge: Cambridge University Press, 1966), 106–7.

81. Similarly Mussner, "Die Tauflehre des Jakobusbriefs," 66: "der Brief (ist) eine Aktualisierung des in der Taufe 'eingepflanzten Wortes' für die konkreten Gemeindeprobleme, mit denen sich Jakobus konfrontiert sieht."

documents that are conventionally termed "Jewish Christian."[82] In the case of the Didache matters are complicated as some of the parallels, particularly those with proximity to Matthew such as the demand for perfection and the material within the so-called *sectio evangelica* of Did. 1, may, by comparison to *Doctrina apostolorum*, be observed to be the work of the redactor rather than material found within a source, indicating that this redactor is closer to pharisaic circles than the writer who originated the two ways as found within the Didache. Thus although the recognition of catechetical material is notable and casts light on James's purpose and the persuasive strategy employed, it would be a mistake to employ the presence of this common material as evidence of a close relationship between the communities to which these documents are addressed. The value of this comparative study lies in the ability to place some material within a catechetical framework with far greater certainty through observing the catechetical setting of the Two Ways paraenesis but the construction of a closed relationship between the communities using these documents can only be sustained on the basis of material that is not only shared by all three but that is also unique to them. The catechetical tradition is more widespread.

That the *Sitz im Leben* for the generation of so much material may have been pre-baptismal direction should not surprise us given the central role of this activity in the emerging Christian communities. For the classical form-critics, preaching explained both the form and the preservation of a great deal of material, but, whereas missionary preaching may have occurred, our view is distorted largely by the picture of the Stoic or cynic preacher constructed by Wilamowitz-Moellendorff.[83] A more realistic picture is provided by Hock, who sees protreptic and paraenesis alike delivered on an individual and informal basis.[84] The other possible meaning of the term, preaching within the assembly, did not exist in the form in which we might recognize it, though a functionally equivalent activity occurred through the activity of the prophets.

In a concluding note, we may observe, as a final point of contact between the three documents, the emphasis that each puts on the role of the teacher.[85] Thus James warns against the dangers implicit in too ready a desire to adopt the role,[86] even as the Didache desires that teachers be supported,[87] and while Mat-

---

82. A characterization employed for the three particularly by Garleff, *Urchristliche Identität in Matthäusevangelium*, *passim* but esp. nn. 207–14.

83. Ulrich von Wilamowitz-Moellendorff, *Antigonos von Karystos* (Philologische Untersuchungen 4; Berlin: Weidmann, 1881), appendix on Teles: 292–319.

84. Ronald F. Hock, "The Workshop as a Social Setting for Paul's Missionary Preaching," *CBQ* 14 (1979): 439–50.

85. So Martin, *James*, lxxiv.

86. Jas 3:1 and much of what follows.

87. Did. 4:1; note also the direction of 15:1 that the overseers and deacons are to give financial support to the teachers alongside the prophets.

thew encourages honor to be shown to the true teacher.[88] We may, moreover, note the extent to which James in particular exhibits the style of the works identified as diatribal.[89] Whereas the *diatribē* is a subgenre of even more dubious identity than paraenesis, as a style we may nonetheless accept that it is a mark of the schoolroom.[90] Since we may envisage that the delivery of paraenesis was fundamentally a role of the teacher, in each case we may see the paraenetic role of pre-baptismal preparation leading to the creation of a circle of influence among the baptized; this in turn could be the background to the discussion of teaching that causes envy and strife at Jas 3:14–16. The significance of this, however, is the subject of another paper.

Author's Note

Wiard Popkes died in January of 2007. He had intended to give a paper at the conference and this paper was given in the stead of his. I had been looking forward to discussing these issues with him. This paper is offered as a tribute to an exemplary scholar.

---

88. Matt 13:52.

89. Thus James H. Ropes, *A Critical and Exegetical Commentary on the the Epistle of James* (ICC; Edinburgh: T&T Clark, 1916), 17: "The epistle is a diatribe." See also Stewart-Sykes, *From Prophecy to Preaching* 154–55.

90. So, in particular, Thomas Schmeller, *Paulus und die Diatribe: eine vergleichende Stilinterpretation* (NTAbh NF 19; Münster: Aschendorff, 1987).

The Presence and Absence of a Prohibition of Oath in James, Matthew, and the Didache and Its Significance for Contextualization

Martin Vahrenhorst

The Jewish character of Matthew's Gospel has been noticed from the very beginning of its reception. As early as the second century, Papias considers it to have been written in Hebrew or Aramaic (Eusebius, *Hist. Eccl.* 39.16), as many scholars have done in his footsteps. Even if we do not share Papias's opinion that the Greek Matthew is a translation of a Semitic original, we may read his ἑβραΐδι διαλέκτῳ as pointing to the "Jewishness" of this work.[1]

In twentieth-century biblical research, the voices of those who describe Matthew as an author from a Gentile background and unfamiliar with Jewish practice and traditions[2] have become more and more silent, and Ulrich Luz' monumental commentary has convinced the majority of New Testament scholars that Matthew represents a Jewish-Christian community. According to Luz, Matthew's community has only recently split from Judaism, and the sharp polemic permeating his Gospel represents the community's way of coping with this painful split.[3]

This reconstruction of Matthew's historic and social background has recently been challenged by a number of monographs from different perspectives. One of the questions raised is, What do we mean with "Judaism"? Has there ever been such a thing as a unified or organized Judaism from which Matthew's community could have split or that could have expelled it? Epigraphic, archaeological, and textual evidence all point to the fact that Judaism was by no means mono-

---

1. I thank Eric Ottenheijm who read this paper in absentia at the 2007 Tilburg conference. Peter Tomson, John Kloppenborg, and Jonathan A. Draper offered helpful comments.
   See Joseph Kürzinger, *Papias von Hierapolis und die Evangelien des Neuen Testaments* (Eichstätter Materialien 4; Regensburg: Pustet, 1983), 103.

2. See Martin Vahrenhorst, *"Ihr sollt überhaupt nicht schwören": Matthäus im halachischen Diskurs* (WMANT 95; Neukirchen-Vluyn: Neukirchener, 2002), 3–5.

3. See Ulrich Luz, *Das Evangelium nach Matthäus: Mt 1–7* (5th ed.; EKKNT 1/1; Düsseldorf: Benziger Verlag, 2002), 85–100.

lithic or uniformly organized, neither before the destruction of the Temple nor in the first centuries afterwards. Judaism can best be described as pluralistic and as resembling a kind of battlefield where different groups struggled for the hearts and minds of the Jewish people. The emerging rabbinic movement was part of that struggle, just as were different Jewish groups that confessed Jesus as God's messiah and God's special agent in the salvation history of Israel. As far as Matthew's Gospel is concerned, one should describe it as the work of a Christian *Jewish* community rather than a Jewish *Christian* one. This view, which has been promoted in the 1990s by scholars such as Andrew Overman and Anthony J. Saldarini[4] was well known to the participants of the 2003 Tilburg conference on Matthew and the Didache, where it has been embraced by several scholars.[5] It has also been adopted by two recently published commentaries on Matthew, one of which assumes that Matthew was written before 70, the other that it was written in the aftermath of the temple's destruction.[6] One can by now justly speak of a major trend in Matthean studies.

1. THE PRESENCE OF TORAH AND HALAKAH IN THE CONTEXT OF NEW TESTAMENT WRITINGS

One of the cornerstones in the debate on Matthew's attitude vis à vis Judaism, and his place inside or outside the frame of other Jewish groups, is the role he ascribes to the Torah. Matthew's strict faithfulness to the Torah, which he strongly emphasizes in Matt 5:17–20, is one of the most important arguments of those scholars who consider Matthew to be a Jewish document. In Matthew's Gospel, as with all groups that may be considered part of the diverse entity today called Judaism, the Torah is acknowledged as the all-pervasive rule that governs the group members' behavior.

To fulfill that goal, the Torah must be taken as more than a textbook that consists of the five books of Moses. The commandments of the written Torah need to be clarified and applied to present day situations. More than that, the Torah has always been held to be more than simply a written document to which commentaries or applications based on scripture have been added. In the opinion

---

4. See J. Andrew Overman, *Matthew's Gospel and Formative Judaism: The Social World of the Matthean Community* (Minneapolis: Fortress, 1990); Anthony J. Saldarini, *Matthew's Christian Jewish Community* (CSJH; Chicago, Ca.: Chicago University Press, 1994).

5. See the conference volume *Matthew and the Didache: Two Documents from the Same Jewish-Christian Milieu?* (ed. H. van de Sandt; Assen: Van Gorcum, 2005).

6. John Nolland, *The Gospel of Matthew: A Commentary on the Greek Text* (NIGTC; Grand Rapids: Eerdmans, 2005); Peter Fiedler, *Das Matthäusevangelium* (THKNT 1; Stuttgart: Kohlhammer, 2006).

of many Jews, Torah also encompasses traditions (e.g., halakic[7] decisions issued by authoritative persons)[8] that do not appear in the biblical text. Even though these teachings have no direct basis in scripture, they are considered Torah:

> [The rules about] release from vows hover in the air and have naught to support them; the rules about the Sabbath, Festal-offerings, and Sacrilege are as mountains hanging by a hair, for [teaching of] Scripture [thereon] is scanty and the rules many; the [rules about] cases [concerning property] and the [Temple-] Service, and the rules about what is clean and unclean and the forbidden degrees, they have that which supports them, and it is they that are the essentials of the Law.[9] (m. Ḥag. 1:8)

Thus, in order to clarify a given document's attitude towards the Jewish law, one has to study its use of the Pentateuch and the nonbiblical legal traditions.

The last statement, as simple as it sounds, involves a rather complicated question for New Testament research: Which non-biblical legal traditions are relevant for the understanding of the New Testament text that was composed at the end of the first century C.E.? One trend in biblical research is very strict in one respect: Rabbinic traditions are not to be taken into account when studying first-century Jewish law. This view has been expressed very strongly by Jacob Neusner and many New Testament scholars followed him in the past and still do so.[10] If Neusner were right, we would be left with the writings of the so-called intertestamental period, that is, the Dead Sea Scrolls, the works of Philo and Josephus, and the often neglected papyrological evidence.

I personally consider this view too sceptical and simplistic. Documents compiled and edited after the final redaction of a given New Testament book may still contain important evidence that sheds light on the issues that were on the agenda

---

7. In Jewish as well as biblical studies a broad understanding of the term "halakah" is increasingly accepted. My own use of this term is close to that described by Peter Tomson: "Nowadays it (the term halakah, M.V.) is used for the legal elements in such Jewish texts as the scrolls, rabbinic literature, or the writings of Philo and Josephus. There is no reason why we should not expect to find halakhah in a Christian text drawing on Jewish sources." (see "The Halakhic Evidence of Didache 8 and Matthew 6 and the Didache Community's Relationship to Judaism," in van de Sandt, ed., *Matthew and the Didache*, 132.

8. See Johann Maier, *Studien zur jüdischen Bibel und ihrer Geschichte* (SJ 28; Berlin: de Gruyter, 2004), 4–11 and 117.

9. Translation from Herbert Danby, *The Mishnah: Translated from the Hebrew with Introduction and Brief Explanatory Notes* (Oxford: Oxford University Press, 1933), 212. In order to clarify the understanding of the last sentence, the Babylonian Talmud presents a short discussion: "These are and those are not! – Say, therefore, these and those are essentials of the Torah" (b. Ḥag. 11b). Translation by I. Abrahams, in *The Babylonian Talmud, Seder Mo'ed IV* (London: Soncino Press, 1938), 58. The Hebrew of the Mishna is clearer than the English translation: הן הן גופי התורה.

10. See Vahrenhorst, *Matthäus im halachischen Diskurs*, 31–37.

in the first century, even if Jacob Neusner's famous saying, "What we cannot show we do not know," still holds true. But how can we know? In 1983 Philip S. Alexander has addressed some important methodological questions concerning the use of rabbinic literature in relation to New Testament texts.[11] He points to the diversity of the material presented by the different Jewish sources and states:

> The conclusion we should draw from this diversity is that the way forward in the study of early Judaism lies in isolating the individual systems and in describing them in their own terms. There is little to be gained at the moment from thinking globally about the teachings of early Judaism. The error of parallelomania is that it extracts elements from different systems and compares them in isolation. . . . The *elements* must be *considered within the systems to which they belong and in which they function.*[12]

Along the lines Alexander has suggested, one could proceed in the following way: In order to learn something about the state of the halakic debate in the first century we have to start with the earliest available sources. We have to find out which questions were asked concerning a given halakic issue and which answers were proposed. Then we have to move on and examine each document or group of documents with the same questions: "What are your issues, what are your interests and which answers are you proposing?" If one addresses the corpus of Tannaitic literature in the same way after having dealt with all sources prior to it, one is able to compare the results gained by examining all the material. This comparison paves the way for reconstructing the course of the halakic debates throughout the centuries around the themes dealt with in the New Testament. From a phenomenological point of view it helps to create a "map" of problems and solutions with respect to a certain halakic complex. With these data in mind one can examine related halakic passages of any New Testament writing. Do they find a place on this map or do they turn out to address absolutely different questions and pursue different aims? Where exactly are they to be positioned on this map? Do they have allies or opponents in other literary corpora?

One can easily imagine that such a method does not lead to quick results, but I am convinced that its results are fairly reliable and that it is worthwhile studying and comparing texts in such a way.

2. OATHS AND VOWS

One of the halakic issues that caused a long and widespread debate in ancient Judaism in its different facets from biblical times until the Talmudic period is the

---

11. Philip S. Alexander, "Rabbinic Judaism and the New Testament," *ZNW* 74 (1983): 237–46.

12. Alexander, "Rabbinic Judaism and the New Testament," 246.

complex of oaths and vows. Almost all Jewish sources deal with it and even non-Jewish sources reveal a strong interest in it. Thus, it may be promising to focus on this topic in order to find out how Matthew, the Didache or James is concerned with it, and if and how these writings are related to this inner-Jewish debate.

2.1. JEWISH SOURCES

In this paper I can only very briefly sketch the course of the debate on oaths and vows as it is reflected in the different Jewish sources.[13]

One very early contribution to our issue is to be found in the LXX translation of Lev 24:16. The Hebrew text proposes a punishment for cursing the name of God, while the LXX prohibits pronouncing the name of God in general. By comparing these two versions one can see that the third-century B.C.E. translators of the Pentateuch had a strong interest in protecting God's name from being profaned, a goal that could best be achieved by not using God's name at all. This intention can be traced throughout most of the debates in the following centuries.

Everybody who proposed a definition of an oath in antiquity describes it as an invocation of a deity to testify in a case where no other reliable evidence is available. A good example is Philo who explains in accordance with other Jewish and pagan voices:[14] "Our conception of an oath is an appeal to God as a witness on some disputed matter" (Philo, *Sacr.* 91).[15]

Thus, by swearing an oath, one calls God to act as a witness in a worldly debate. The danger of profanation is self-evident. I quote Philo again:

> For I know full well that there are persons who, in profane and impure places where it would not be fitting to mention either a father or mother . . . swear at length and make whole speeches consisting of a string of oaths and thus, by their misuse of the many forms of the divine name . . . show their impiety. (*Decal.* 94)

How can this impiety be avoided? Philo proposes two ways. The one he clearly prefers is: "To swear not at all is the best course" (*Decal.* 84), while "to swear truly is only, as people say, a 'second best voyage'" (*ibid.*).

What is there to be done if one cannot avoid opting for the "second-best voyage"? Philo offers a rather detailed set of rules concerning matter, time, and place and the personal disposition of the person who is going to take an oath. One factor is very important to him (and has been to other Jews before and after

---

13. For a more detailed analysis see Vahrenhorst, *Matthäus im halachischen Diskurs*, 41–214.

14. See Vahrenhorst, *Matthäus im halachischen Diskurs*, 96–97.

15. Translation of Philo's texts by Francis H. Colson, *Philo* (10 vols. and 2 suppl. vols; LCL; Cambridge, Mass: Harvard University Press, 1929–53).

him): One should not pronounce God's name or even mention God in the oath. One should rather use oath-formulas that do not mention God directly but are linked to him in an indirect way:

> And if indeed occasion should force us to swear, the oath should be by a father and mother [...]. For parents are copies and likenesses of the divine power, since they have brought the non-existent into existence (*Spec.* 2.2).

The use of such formulas has been very popular and has also been the issue of an intense debate that can be traced in Qumran writings, in pseudepigraphic writings (*L.A.E.* 19) and of course in Tannaitic literature.[16] The Damascus-document states:

> He will not swear by the Aleph and the Lamed nor by the Aleph and the Daleth, but by the oath of the youths, by the curses of the covenant. . . . And if he swears and transgresses, he would profane the name. . . . (CD XV, 1–3)[17]

Alternative oath formulas and circumscriptions of the divine name have been one solution to the problem of how God and his name could be saved from profanation. Another solution was to accept vow-formulas instead of oaths. Vows are a different form of binding speech, but they are not directly related to God. This solution is already proposed by Philo (*Spec.* 2.12) and it is also known to Josephus (*Ant.* 6.24 and *Ag. Ap.* 1.167). The rabbis rule:

> A widow may not receive the payment (of her Ketubah) from the property of the orphans unless she swears (to her claim) on oath. But when they refrained from making her swear on oath, Rabban Gamliel the Elder ordained that she would vow to the orphans . . . and receive her Ketubah (*m. Giṭ.* 4:3).

The replacement of oaths by vows had the consequence that some people used circumscriptions for vow formulas as well, which forced the rabbis to discuss which formula is a valid one and which is not. These discussions are collected in the tractate Nedarim. I quote one example: "If a man says to his fellow, *Konam* or *Konah* or *Konas*, these are substitutes for *Korban*" (*m. Ned.* 1:2). Comparable

---

16. Not every formula can be used in an oath. As we have seen, God must by definition be involved. So a valid oath formula must at least in some way be related to God. Philo defines this relationship in platonic terms: Parents are in some way images of God, thus referring to them in an oath makes the oath valid.

17. Translation by Florentino García Martínez, *The Dead Sea Scrolls Translated: The Qumran Texts in English* (Leiden: Brill, 1994): 39. "Aleph Lamed" represent an abbreviation of the word "El" (= God) while "Aleph Dalet" stands for the circumscription of God's name (= Adonai). The concern of the Damascus document is clear: the profanation of God and his name shall be avoided by all means. For this reason alternative oath formulas are proposed.

circumscriptions in discussion were "the altar," "the Temple" or "Jerusalem," terms that were also known to Matthew as we will see below. The obvious general tendency in Tannaitic sources was to avoid oaths and vows wherever possible: "honest people do not vow,"[18] and people who refrain from swearing are most praiseworthy (t. Soṭah 7:4).[19]

To summarize this brief survey: All Jewish voices participating in the discussion of oaths and vows shared the interest to protect God and his name from being profaned. Different means to achieve this aim were proposed: a) the avoidance of any oath; b) the use of circumscriptions; c) the replacement of oaths by vows.

2.2. MATTHEW

In Matthew's Gospel the material concerning oaths and vows is quite rich in both halakic and haggadic respects. Here, we find two contributions to the Jewish debate about the question how the name of God can be protected from being profaned in the process of swearing, and whether this can be done by using special oath formulas or by replacing oaths by vows (Matt 5:33–7 and 23:16–22). In addition, we have the episode of Peter denying his relation to Jesus by swearing a false oath (26:74).

The halakic material appears in two contexts that are of fundamental importance for the understanding of Matthew's view on the validity of the Torah and the community's competition with the emerging rabbinic movement. Almost no other halakic question is treated with the same intensity.

a) Matt 5:33–37 is one of the inaccurately named "antitheses" (Matt 5:21–48). Each unit begins with a quotation from the Torah, not simply in its written form but in the form in which it was interpreted. These quotations are followed by a statement of Jesus in which he does not simply reject the quotations, but points out their true intention / meaning.[20] If read in this way, the so-called "antitheses" turn out to be in perfect harmony with Matthew's introductory statement about

---

18. See Chanoch Albeck, *The Mishna. Seder Nashim* (Tel Aviv: Debir, 1988), 147 on *m. Ned.* 1:1 (כנדרי כשרים).

19. Another means to restrict swearing oaths was the introduction of the "vain oath" אשבועת שוא, which was regarded equal to a false oath. Practically, it was almost impossible to know whether an oath that seemed to be necessary was really not to be avoided, and thus a vain oath. See Vahrenhorst, *Matthäus im halachischen Diskurs*, 157–62 and 164–67.

20. The logical antithesis to "You shall not kill" would be "You shall kill," that to "You shall not commit adultery" would be "You shall commit adultery" and so on. Klaus Haacker proposed to call these units "Kommentarworte." See his "Feindesliebe kontra Nächstenliebe? Bemerkungen zu einer verbreiteten Gegenüberstellung von Christentum und Judentum" in *Dieses Volk schuf ich, daß es meinen Ruhm verkünde* (ed. F. Matheus; Schriftenreihe des Forschungsschwerpunktes Geschichte und Religion de Judentums 1; Duisburg: GEJD, 1992), 47–51.

the ongoing validity of the Torah (Matt 5:17–20). Jesus has not come to reject it, let alone abolish it, but to fulfill it. Each subsequent unit demonstrates how Jesus actually fulfills the Torah by teaching it in its true intention.[21]

The commandment "You shall not swear falsely, but carry out the vows you have made to the Lord" (Matt 5:33–37) intends to protect God and his name from being profaned,[22] which is exactly what happens if one swears a false oath or does not fulfill the vows he or she has made. Jesus is very clear about how this goal can be achieved: One should not swear at all. From the brief sketch above we have seen that Matthew's Jesus was not the first Jew who made such a recommendation and he was not to be the last one either. Compared to Philo or the Tannaitic sources, Matthew appears stricter, but his statement in any case finds its place on the map of the relevant halakic discourse.

Jesus's following argumentation further shows that God's name cannot be protected by the use of circumscriptions. As stated above, such formulae must in a way still be related to God, otherwise they are not valid. Because of this, prerequisite circumscriptions cannot achieve the goal they aim at: No matter how farfetched the link between the circumscription and God may be, God is still involved, as Jesus shows ("it is the throne of God," "it is his footstool," "it is his city").

Verse 36 follows a different logic. According to some sources, an oath is a kind of conditional self curse that comes into effect when the oath proves to be untrue or is broken. When taking the oath, one offers a kind of guaranty that will be lost as soon as the oath is broken or turns out untrue.[23] Jesus's line of argument seems to be as follows: One cannot give as a deposit something that one does not own or cannot control, since it is God who rules over a man's head and his aging process. Even such an oath involves God. There is only one consequence if one wishes to fulfill the intention of the commandment quoted at the beginning, namely, to refrain from swearing under any circumstances. Every human utterance must be true in itself.

When compared to the above-mentioned "map" of the halakah of oaths and vows Matthew's Jesus proves to be well versed in the inner logic of the system of circumscriptions. He is also honestly interested in what his "colleagues," whose statements we know from the various Jewish sources between 250 B.C.E. and 200 C.E., are interested in as well, namely, the question, How can God's holy name be

---

21. For a detailed discussion of the verb πληρόω in Matt 5:17 see Vahrenhorst, *Matthäus im halachischen Diskurs*, 236–43; Matthias Konradt, "Die vollkommene Erfüllung der Tora und der Konflikt mit den Pharisäern im Matthäusevangelium" in *Das Gesetz im frühen Judentum und im Neuen Testament* (ed. D. Sänger and M. Konradt; NTOA / SUNT 57; Göttingen: Vandenhoeck & Ruprecht, 2006), 129–52.

22. This was the intention of all participants in the ancient Jewish discourse on oaths and vows as showed in my brief sketch of the relevant Jewish sources in the preceding section.

23. Vahrenhorst, *Matthäus im halachischen Diskurs*, 267–68.

saved from profanation? His "solution" turns out to be a serious contribution to a lively Jewish debate.

b) One brief glance at Matt 23:16–22 leads to a similar result. The Matthean Jesus criticizes the representatives of his adversaries for being "blind leaders." This term is used in inner-rabbinic polemics for denouncing sages who make unfounded halakic decisions.[24] The following verses reflect discussions that can be found in Mishna and Tosefta *Nedarim*. The halakic question is: "Which formulas are binding, and which are not." The logic Matthew criticizes is: "Every formula that includes something which can be offered to God is a valid equivalent for 'Qorban'. The temple or the altar already belong to God, thus they cannot be offered. These formulas are not binding and do not constitute a valid oath. Gold and gifts can certainly be offered, so they are equivalent to 'Qorban' and can therefore introduce a binding oath." Matthew's train of thought is very much in line with his argumentation in Matt 5:33–37. Every formula, no matter whether it includes something that can be offered to God or something that already belongs to God, is related to God because he dwells above the altar that sanctifies the gift. The same holds true for circumscriptions like "heaven" or "temple," as God dwells in the temple and the heavens are his throne.

Again, Matthew knows what he is talking about and he contributes to the halakic discourse that I have described above. As all the formulas that are discussed are related to God, they cannot be used in order to protect God's sanctity. Swearing and protecting God's sanctity exclude each other, therefore the consequence must be, "Do not swear at all!"

One has to keep in mind that Matthew's Gospel is not a halakic treatise.[25] It is a gospel whose main aim is to preach Jesus and to assure the community on its way in following him. On the other hand, one of the most specific character traits of Matthew's account of the Jesus story is that it introduces Jesus as the one and only true teacher.[26] A significant portion of his teachings show a clearly halakic nature. The first audience of this teaching is the people of Israel[27] and later Gentiles are also included. The halakic orientation of Matthew's teaching

---

24. See Vahrenhorst, *Matthäus im halachischen Diskurs*, 354–57.

25. Still, Matthew can be described as a "manual for discipleship" (see Nolland, *The Gospel of Matthew*, 20).

26. See Martin Karrer, *Jesus Christus im Neuen Testament* (GNT 11; Göttingen: Vandenhoeck & Ruprecht, 1998), 230; Hans-Jürgen Becker, *Auf der Kathedra des Mose: Rabbinisch-theologisches Denken und antirabbinische Polemik in Matthäus 23,1–12* (Arbeiten zur neutestamentlichen Theologie und Zeitgeschichte 4; Berlin: Institut Kirche und Judentum, 1990), 203–4.

27. This can be shown by evaluating the frame of the Sermon. The audience of the Sermon on the Mount does not only include Jesus's disciples (i.e., Matthew's community). Matthew 5:1 and 7:28 explicitly mention the ὄχλοι that represent the people of Israel. See Peter Wick, "Volkspredigt contra Gemeinderegel? Matthäus 5–7 im Vergleich zu Matthäus 18," *Kirche und Israel* 13 (1998): 138–53; Nolland, *The Gospel of Matthew*, 191–92.

can be shown by studying Matthew's decision on oaths and vows. It can also be demonstrated by comparing his teaching on the Sabbath (Matt 12), the purity of hands (Matt 15), and legitimate reasons for divorce (Matt 19) with their Marcan parallels. In each case Matthew appears to be up to the state of the halakic debate as it is reflected in Tannaitic sources. Furthermore, Matthew is frequently proposing solutions to halakic problems that are discussed in other Jewish groups as well. His halakic teaching is in perfect harmony with Matt 5:17–20. Each single example shows the Matthean Jesus teaching Torah in a way that it leads to a life that can be described as being in accordance with the justice that exceeds that of Matthew's opponents. It paves a way of living that corresponds to the call ἔσεσθε οὖν ὑμεῖς τέλειοι (Matt 5:48). This Torah is part of what Matthew's community is to teach Israel and the Gentiles (Matt 28:19–20).[28]

What does all this tell us about Matthew's context? First of all, there is nothing in his halakic teaching or in his attitude towards the Torah that would place him outside the framework of competing Jewish groups in the aftermath of the Temple's destruction. The opposite is true: Matthew propagates a Jewish way of life in the footsteps and in the presence of Jesus, the only teacher of Israel who, according to the Gospel's message, really deserves this title (Matt 23:10).[29]

2.3. Didache

It is an open question whether the Didache reflects a similar context as Matthew. The recently published volume *Matthew and the Didache* offers an excellent survey of the state of the debate, in which the opinions, based on more or less the

---

28. Matt 28:19 has been interpreted as a hint to the fact that Matthew's community does not address Israel anymore. Its mission is limited to the Gentiles (see now Ulrich Luz' more balanced analysis in *Das Evangelium nach Matthäus: Mt 26–28* [EKKNT 1/4; Düsseldorf: Benziger, 2002], 447–52). The logic of this view is problematic. At first, Gentiles were explicitly excluded from the mission of the disciples (Matt 10:5, 6). This limitation (not the mission to Israel) is now revoked. It is not said that the Gentiles replace Israel or that the Jewish people are not to be taught anymore (see Vahrenhorst, *Matthäus im halachischen Diskurs*, 15–16; Nolland, *The Gospel of Matthew*, 1265–66). The fact that in the LXX ἔθνος is commonly used to describe the Gentiles as opposed to λαός, which is reserved for Israel, should not be used as a counterargument. In the LXX Pentateuch, Israel is called ἔθνος in Exod 19:6; 33:13; Lev 19:16; 20:3; 21:1; and Deut 4:6; 26:5.

29. The authority that Matthew ascribes to Jesus can in many ways be compared to that which the early rabbis ascribe to themselves. Matthew's insistence on Jesus as the one and only teacher who teaches in the name and authority of the God of Israel (in spite of Matt 23:2–3) and continues to do so through the halakic teaching of the community (Matt 16:19; 18:18) can be considered to be one main reason for the "parting of the ways" between Matthew's community and the emerging rabbinic movement. The latter opted for a "pluralistic" approach to authority and insisted on having more than one teacher. See Shaye J. D. Cohen, "The Significance of Yavneh. Pharisees, Rabbis, and the End of Jewish Sectarianism," *HUCA* 55 (1984): 28–53.

same observations, vary from "Jewish group" to "Gentile church."[30] In the following pages I will restrict myself to some observations relevant to the Didache's use of and attitude to the Torah.

First of all I have to ask if we can learn anything from the Didache's teaching on oaths and vows. The answer is more or less negative. There is only one saying referring to our subject, Did. 2:2, which prohibits false oaths and counts them among other vices traditionally appearing in Jewish admonitions, such as those against murder, theft, fornication, and so on.[31] In the preceding section, the presence of the discussion on oaths and vows was seen as a sign of Matthew's interest in halakic discussions and his place *inside* the first-century Jewish framework. Can the Didache's silence on this matter be interpreted as a sign of disinterest and indicate the writing's place *outside* Judaism? Arguments *e silentio* are always relatively weak and one single observation can never be decisive.

If one approaches the Didache from the Gospel of Matthew, which was interpreted as a Jewish text above, two observations meet the eye: First, every trace of an inner-Jewish debate is missing (e.g., the antithetical form of Matt 5:38–47 in its reception in Did. 1:3–6).[32] Contrary to Matthew, the didachist does not relate himself to competing Jewish opinions or halakot. Does this mean that the didachist has detached himself from the inner-Jewish discourse? Secondly, no reference to the Torah is to be found in the Didache. Contrary to Matthew, Jesus's teaching, which is authoritative for the Didache (Did. 8:2; 11:2–3),[33] is in no way linked to the Torah. Could this be due to the fact that the Torah is no longer relevant for the author of the Didache? Has its role been taken over by Jesus's and his disciples' teaching?

As is often the case in Didache studies, the same observation is open to opposing interpretations, especially if one tries to interpret it independently from the Gospel of Matthew: The Torah might not have been mentioned explicitly by

---

30. See above, n. 5. Compare also Marcello Del Verme, *Didache and Judaism: Jewish Roots of an Ancient Christian-Jewish Work* (London: T&T Clark, 2004), 74–88.

31. This passage converges with ancient Jewish ethical teachings, which are of course all based on Old Testament traditions; see Karl-Wilhelm Niebuhr, *Gesetz und Paränese: Katechismusartige Weisungsreihen in der frühjüdischen Literatur* (WUNT 2/28; Tübingen: Mohr Siebeck, 1987), 232–35.

32. The contents of the halakic teachings of the Didache are of course well rooted in Jewish traditions and mirror Jewish debates, but the Didache does not present them as such. No references to different opinions or discussions can be found. But this observation should not be overestimated as other writings of the Second Temple period, such as the community Rule of Qumran (1QS), are to a large extent written in a similar fashion.

33. See, e.g., Jens Schröter's contribution in this volume.

the didachist because he takes its authority for granted and the rules which are expressed in this work are probably considered a part of the Torah itself.[34]

It is very difficult to decide which interpretation is more plausible. With all necessary caution I suggest approaching a preliminary solution by entering into a short debate about some of the observations that led John Kloppenborg to speak of a "torahizing" of the Didache's ethical teaching.

At first, Kloppenborg compares the existing variants of the "teaching of the Two Ways" (Did. 1:1–6:2) and notices that in the Didache, Lev 19:18, and Deut 6:5 appear in a very prominent position at the beginning of the Didache (Did. 1:2).[35]

Second, he points to the fact that the Didache's teaching includes more elements of the Decalogue than any parallel tradition.[36] Even from a linguistic point of view the Didache is closer to the version as it is presented in the LXX.[37] John Kloppenborg concludes that the Didache "grounds its appeals in the Torah,"[38] which implies "that the text is edited and employed in an environment in which the authority of the Torah can be taken for granted."[39] Kloppenborg points further to other Jewish documents that operate in a similar way: the *Testament of the Twelve Patriarchs*, Jesus Sirach, Philo's *Hypothetica* and Josephus's *Against Apion*.

But if one takes a closer look at these texts, one major difference becomes immediately apparent: All of them explicitly refer to the Torah, the νόμος, on more than one occasion.[40] The Didache, however, never does. All documents Kloppenborg mentions, even the New Testament traditions (Matt 22:34–40; Rom 13:8–10) refer back to the Torah as the source of their ethical teaching.[41] The Didache does not. Even where the didachist could have easily done so, namely,

---

34. Researchers who join this position can point to the Mishna, which does not necessarily quote the written Torah in order to justify its halakic decisions (on this observation see note 40).

35. See John Kloppenborg, "The Transformation of Moral Exhortation in Didache 1–5," in *The Didache in Context. Essays on Its Text, History and Transmission* (ed. C. N. Jefford; NovTSup 77; Leiden: Brill, 1995), 98. Kloppenborg remarks that the combination of these two verses is typical of Christian documents.

36. Ibid., 99–100.

37. Ibid., 100.

38. Ibid., 101.

39. Ibid., 102.

40. Even the vast corpus of the Mishna refers to scripture more than 350 times.

41. One possible exemption to this rule is Ps.-Phocylides, which is strongly influenced by Old Testament traditions (see Pieter W. van der Horst's introduction in "Pseudo-Phocylides: A New Translation and Introduction," in *The Old Testament Pseudepigrapha* (ed. J. H. Charlesworth; 2 vols.; Garden City, N.Y.: Doubleday, 1983–85), 2:572) without making this connection explicit. But this can be understood as a part of the unknown author's endeavor to present Jewish traditions in the attire of Greek wisdom.

in Did. 11:2, which strongly resembles Matt 5:17, the object of καταλῦσαι is not the Torah[42] but the διδαχή mentioned before. The only authority the didachist explicitly points to is the διδαχή, (Did. 2:1), "the commandments of the Lord" (Did. 4:13), the "yoke of the Lord" (Did. 6:2), which equals the "way of the διδαχή" (Did. 6:1), and the only Lord the διδαχή explicitly mentions is Jesus Christ who has taught his disciples in "his gospel" (another authoritative source!)[43] how to pray (Did. 8:2).

Even though the traditions the Didache makes use of in its present form are undoubtedly taken from a Jewish environment, it is doubtful if the Didache's teaching should really be described as "torahizing." When the Didache, which does not mention the origin of its traditions, is compared to other Jewish texts that do, one might even be tempted to describe the Didache as "de-torahizing" those traditions.

Let me add one last observation to support my point. In 1939/40 Gedalyahu Alon published an important study on the halakah in the Didache. He showed that Did. 13:3, with its teaching on the ἀπαρχή,[44] mirrors actual Jewish halakah and custom.[45] Other examples can and have been added by various scholars.[46] For our purpose, Did 13:3 in its present form and context is especially interesting. It says that the ἀπαρχή is to be given to the community's prophets who are described as the community's high priests (ἀρχιερεῖς). In Jewish sources, the gifts designed as ἀπαρχή are intended to be given to the priests and Levites by the common Israelite. This rule is based on the commandments of the Torah and was respected by all Jewish groups we know of.[47] The Didache seems to break away from this consensus by establishing a new class of priests, based not on priestly

---

42. Even though some modern authors put "Torah" in square brackets in order to indicate that it is not found in the source but is added to clarify the Greek text (e.g., Jonathan A. Draper, "Do the Didache and Matthew Reflect an 'Irrevocable Parting of the Ways' with Judaism?," in van de Sandt, ed., *Matthew and the Didache*, 219, 226).

43. It seems very likely that the Didache here refers to the Gospel of Matthew.

44. See David E. Aune, "Distinct Lexical Meanings of ΑΠΑΡΧΗ in Hellenism, Judaism and Early Christianity," in *Early Christianity and Classical Culture* (ed. J. T. Fitzgerald et al.; NovTSup 110; Leiden: Brill 2003), 103–29.

45. Gedalyah Alon, "Ha-halaka ba-Torat ha-Shelihim," *Tarbiz* 11 (1939–40): 127–45. Repr.in *Studies in Jewish History in the Times of the Second Temple, the Mishna and the Talmud* (ed. G. Alon, 2 vols. 2nd. ed. Tel Aviv: Hakibutz Hameuchad, 1967–70), 1:274–94 (Hebrew) = "The Halakha in the Teaching of the Twelve Apostles," in *The Didache in Modern Research* (ed. J. Draper; trans. A. Ben-Meir; Leiden: Brill, 1996), 165–94; Huub van de Sandt and David Flusser, *The Didache: Its Jewish Sources and its Place in Early Judaism and Christianity* (CRINT 3/5 Assen: Van Gorcum, 2002), 360–64; Del Verme, *Didache and Judaism*, 189–220.

46. See, e.g., Tomson, "Halakhic Evidence of Didache 8."

47. For the early rabbinic movement see Avraham Aderet, *From Destruction to Restauration: The Mode of Yavneh in Re-Establishment of the Jewish People* (Jerusalem: Magnes Press, 1990), 367–400 (Hebrew).

offspring but on their prophetic gift. Jewish sources of the Second Temple period know of priests, especially the high priest, who possesses the gift of prophecy,[48] but never do we hear of a prophet who is considered to be a priest only because he can speak prophetically, as clearly stated by the Didache. This is not just a violation of the Torah, it also indicates that the Didache's community seems to have established a different cult with different priests.

One could object to that interpretation by stating that the community of the Dead Sea Scrolls also had established a diverging cult and yet is still considered part of the Jewish framework. But this community organized itself according to the commandments of the Torah and did not establish a new priesthood.

To conclude, the Didache in its present form formulates ethical principles for a specific group. It prescribes the way in which a given community is to function. It *implicitly* draws on Jewish traditions without mentioning their origin. Other than the Gospel of Matthew or the rabbinic writings, Didache does not seem to be interested in defining and proclaiming halakah for Israel. Maybe Didache's community does not consider itself to be struggling on the battlefield of competing Jewish groups, all teaching how Jews (and in some cases even non-Jews) should live according to the Torah. If I added the word "anymore" to the last sentence, I would also propose a date for the Didache in relation to the Gospel of Matthew. I am reluctant to do so. But if I compare those two writings, the Didache seems to be at home in a church that is no longer part of the Jewish framework.[49]

My interpretation of Did 13:3 is of crucial importance for understanding Didache as a document that is no longer part of the Jewish framework. In this light, Didache's silence on the Torah, which is in itself open to different interpretations, becomes telling. This is only one argument in an amazingly open discussion, which reminds me of the famous rabbinic saying "if a discussion is led for the sake of heaven, it will endure" (*m. 'Abot* 4:11).

---

48. See Van de Sandt and Flusser, *The Didache: Its Jewish Sources*, 363.

49. Huub van de Sandt, "Was the Didache Community a Group Within Judaism? An Assessment on the Basis of Its Eucharistic Prayers," in *A Holy People; Jewish and Christian Perspectives on Religious Communal Identity* (ed. M. Poorthuis and J. Schwartz ; Jewish and Christian Perspective Series 12; Leiden: Brill, 2006), 85–107 comes to a similar conclusion by evaluating the Didache's hope that the church "may be gathered." Didache does not include or relate itself to the hope for the gathering of Israel: "The liturgy of the Didache thus shows indications of a community which has ceased to consider itself a variety of Judaism" (ibid., 103). On the question of whether the Didache depends upon Matthew or vice versa see Alan J. P. Garrow, *The Gospel of Matthew's Dependence on the Didache* (JSNTSup 254; London: T&T Clark, 2004) and Jens Schröter's recension in *TLZ* 131 (2006): 997–1000.

2.4. JAMES

As the main focus of my paper is on the presence of law of oaths and vows in Matthew and in the Didache, my remarks on James will be very short. James 5:12 preserves a tradition that is very similar to Matt 5:33–37. The major difference between these two traditions is that James does not offer any motivation for why oaths are prohibited, and does not reflect the halakic discussion like Matthew. How are these traditions related? Hubert Frankemölle summarized the state of the debate as follows: The question if the two texts are related literally "can presently be answered negatively."[50] They seem to draw on the same tradition without depending upon each other. Matthew cast this tradition in a form that fits the halakic discourse of his time, while James seems to preserve the original form of the tradition.[51] This may even reflect Jesus's teaching.[52] We have seen that the prohibition of oaths and vows in Jewish traditions intended to protect the sanctity of God and his name. We do not know whether Jesus shared this interest, although this may very well have been the case if we take into account that the Lord's prayer is highly interested in the sanctification of God's name.[53]

How did James adopt this tradition? James is strongly concerned with speech ethics (see 1:26; 3:1–11).[54] James 3:10 links this to an even more important issue in the letter, namely, being "undivided" and "whole" (see 1:4, 6, 17). Words and deeds, faith, and works have to be in accordance with one another (1:22; 2:14–17). James 5:12 stresses the importance of what one may call "undivided speech" and thus contributes to the general message of the letter. This passage seems to be even more interested in undivided speech than in simply not swearing oaths, because it is divided speech (and not swearing) that falls under the verdict of judgement.[55]

If this interpretation is true, one can say that, on the one hand, James does not directly contribute to the Jewish halakic discourse on oaths and vows. He makes use of a tradition that may very well have done so, but he uses it for his own aims. On the other hand, "wholeness" also was a very important issue in

---

50. Hubert Frankemölle, *Der Brief des Jakobus* (ÖTK 17/1–2; Gütersloh: Gütersloher Verlagshaus, 1994), 700 (translation mine).

51. Vahrenhorst, *Matthäus im halachischen Diskurs*, 258.

52. Ibid., 259.

53. Ibid., 260.

54. See William R. Baker, *Personal Speech-Ethics in the Epistle of James* (WUNT 2/68; Tübingen: Mohr Siebeck, 1995).

55. See Udo Schnelle, *Einleitung in das Neue Testament* (5th ed.; UTB 1830; Göttingen: Vandenhoeck & Ruprecht, 2005), 440: "Man's being divided shall be overcome" (translation mine).

ancient Judaism[56] and James certainly has a lot to teach on this subject. One would perhaps not go too far in saying that James teaches a "Torah of wholeness" (see 1:25; 2:8, 12; 4:11). He does so to a Christ-believing audience (James 1:18), whose problems can be reconstructed from the letter's information.[57] James's audience is thought to have lived in the Diaspora (1:1) and is explicitly described in Jewish terms.[58] The Law and Jesus traditions are part of the same parcel as can be learned from the equation of the "law of freedom" (1:25; 2:12) and the "word of wisdom" (1:18).[59] As we have seen above, considering teachings of certain people to be Torah is not unusual in ancient Judaism or, to put it in the rabbinic terms of the Jerusalem Talmud, Scripture, Mishna, Talmud, and haggadah, "even that, which an advanced disciple will teach in the presence of this teacher, all this has already been said to Moses on Sinai" (y. Pe'ah 2, 17a) As such, the instruction is part of the Torah. Thus, the equation of Jesus's teaching and the law only strengthens the Jewish character of this letter.

Far more could be said on James's place within early Christian tradition than I can do in this paper. But if I concentrate on the role of the Torah and the halakah as an indicator for the "Jewishness" of a text and the community it represents, there is nothing that urges me to say that James is already beyond the split between Judaism and Christianity.

3. Conclusions

In this paper we have taken a brief glance at three documents that have a lot in common. We have done so from a specific point of view, the documents' relationship to the halakic discourse on oaths and vows in different Jewish groups. I hope to have shown that the examination of the way halakic issues are treated in early Christian writings can shed important light on the place of these writings within or outside the framework that is commonly called "ancient Judaism." Matthew and James turned out to belong to this "entity," which consists of various competing groups, who all relate themselves, even though in different ways,

---

56. See Vahrenhorst, *Matthäus im halachischen Diskurs*, 250–55; Martin Meiser, "Vollkommenheit in Qumran und im Matthäusevangelium," in *Kirche und Volk Gottes* (ed. M. Karrer, W. Kraus and O. Merk; Neukirchen-Vluyn: Neukirchener Verlag, 2000), 195–209; see also the contributions of Jens Schröter, Wim Weren, and Patrick Hartin in this volume.

57. Schnelle, *Einleitung in das Neue Testament*, 435. See also Oda Wischmeyer's contribution in this volume.

58. See Scott McKnight, "A Parting Within the Way: Jesus and James on Israel and Purity," in *James the Just and Christian Origins* (ed. B. Chilton and C. A. Evans; NovTSup 98; Leiden: Brill, 1999), 82–129.

59. Frankemölle, *Brief des Jakobus*, 353–55; Martin Klein, *"Ein vollkommenes Werk": Vollkommenheit, Gesetz und Gericht als theologische Themen des Jakobusbriefes* (BWANT 139; Stuttgart: Kohlhammer, 1995), 143–44.

to the Torah. As far as the Didache is concerned, I am more sceptical. But halakah is just one factor, although an important one. Other aspects might be added. May the discussion continue.

Purity in Matthew, James, and the Didache

Boris Repschinski, S.J.

Purity is a defining notion in Second Temple Judaism. It played a significant role not only in cultic circumstances such as temple or synagogue worship. Purity was influential in social relations and life in general. Thus Ed P. Sanders wrote: "Purity regulations were the most obvious and universally kept set of laws."[1] The origin of purity regulations is somewhat obscure[2] and need not detain us much longer except for the passing observation that purity regulations could be found not only in Judaism but also in many other cultures of the Middle East, and that they had no obvious hygienic or economic basis.[3] Perhaps of greater importance is the function of purity regulations to protect order and cohesion within social groups.[4]

---

1. Ed P. Sanders, *Judaism: Practice and Belief 63 BCE–66 CE* (London: SCM Press, 1992), 214. For further references on purity see Werner G. Kümmel, "Äußere und innere Reinheit des Menschen bei Jesus," in *Heilsgeschehen und Geschichte: Gesammelte Aufsätze* (2 vols.; ed. E. Grässer and O. Merk; Marburger Theologische Studien 16; Marburg: Elwert, 1978), 2:117–29; Wilfried Paschen, *Rein und Unrein: Untersuchung zur biblischen Wortgeschichte* (SANT 24; München: Kösel, 1970); Jacob Neusner, *The Idea of Purity in Ancient Judaism* (SJLA; Leiden: Brill, 1973); John K. Riches, *Jesus and the Transformation of Judaism* (London: Darton, Longman & Todd, 1980); Roger P. Booth, *Jesus and the Laws of Purity: Tradition History and Legal History in Mark 7* (JSNTSup 13; Sheffield: JSOT Press, 1986); Franz Mussner, *Die Kraft der Wurzel: Judentum – Jesus – Kirche* (Freiburg: Herder, 1987), 93–103.

2. Both religious and sociological explanations are proffered, most of them coming down to a possible function of purity to protect from strongly perceived demonic powers. See, e.g., Neusner, *Idea of Purity*, 12; Jacob Milgrom, *Leviticus 1–16: A New Translation with Introduction and Commentary* (AB 3; Garden City, N.Y.: Doubleday, 1991), 42–51.

3. Adrian Schenker, "Pureté – impureté," in *Dictionnaire critique de théologie* (ed. J.-Y. Lacoste; Paris: Presses Universitaires de France, 1998), 961–62: "L'exclusion d'animaux impurs des sacrifices et de la table est commune aux peuples du Proche-Orient ancien"; however, even though excluded species can vary, some, like pigs, are common to most of these cultures.

4. These observations go back to the comparative research of Mary Douglas, who observed purity regulations in various tribal cultures, and whose findings were subsequently adapted to the biblical purity systems. See Mary Douglas, *Purity and Danger: An Analysis of Concepts of Pollution and Taboo* (London: Routledge & Kegan Paul, 1966); ibid., *Natural Symbols Explora-*

The Jewish purity system was primarily a matter of Torah, mostly based upon legal material in Leviticus and Numbers. The classic reference is Lev 20:22–26. Canaanite behavior is revolting to God. He expels them from the land and gives it to his own people who are separated from the Canaanites. The Israelites now are to observe God's distinctions between pure and impure. To distinguish between pure and impure is to be holy as God is holy.

Consequently, the Law sets purity primarily into a cultic context. When someone, through mistake or happenstance, contracted impurity, he or she was not supposed to approach the sanctuary. Impurity erected a boundary between the place where holiness could be encountered, and the person touched by impurity. Within such a cultic reference frame, purity becomes an issue that first and foremost concerns Jewish temple worship. However, purity issues were not restricted to temple worship, but became increasingly important in Diaspora settings, even if in these contexts purity regulations underwent a curious mixture between allegorical and literal interpretation.[5] The decline of purity systems within Judaism of the rabbinic period may have one cause in the destruction of the temple.[6]

Cultic impurity is usually transmitted by touch, though not exclusively so. Sources of impurity are corpses, certain skin diseases, usually grouped under the term "leprosy," and different types of effluents like blood or genital discharges. Impurity can be removed through purification rites such as sacrifices and washing by immersion of the whole or parts of the body. Such rituals have to be performed within a defined time frame. Various types of impurities can be distinguished according to their severity, which in turn is measured by the difficulty in removing the impurity. Corpses are the source of the most serious impurity, but similarly the purification period of leprosy and menstruation is seven days. Lesser forms of impurity can be removed within a period of a day.[7] During the intertestamental period the concept of impurity was widened to include objects like food or vessels. Furthermore, the consumption of impure food has very serious

---

tions in Cosmology (New York: Pantheon Books, 1970). Douglas later revised her views at least partly, noting that the rules of defilement in Numbers and Leviticus probably do not serve to organize social categories. Mary Douglas, *In the Wilderness: The Doctrine of Defilement in the Book of Numbers* (JSOTSup 158; Sheffield: JSOT Press, 1993), 152–57.

5. Thus Sanders, *Judaism*, 214, is quite wrong when he restricts most of the impurity rules to the temple. See Aharon Oppenheimer, *The Am Ha-Aretz: A Study in the Social History of the Jewish People in the Hellenistic-Roman Period* (ALGHJ 8; Leiden: Brill, 1977), 51–62. The *Letter of Aristeas* and Philo exhibit the strange mixture of allegorical interpretation of purity regulations mixed with the admonitions to keep them literally. For the relevant discussions of these texts see Neusner, *Idea of Purity*, 44–50.

6. Judaism after the tannaitic period seems to have lost interest in purity. Thomas Kazen, *Jesus and Purity Halakha: Was Jesus Indifferent to Impurity?* (ConBNT 38; Stockholm: Almqvist & Wiksell, 2002), 6.

7. For a diagram of the various levels of impurity see ibid., 5.

consequences beyond the usual rites of purification.[8] Thus Peter's exclamation οὐδέποτε ἔφαγον πᾶν κοινὸν καὶ ἀκάθαρτον (Act 10:14) sounds like a credible concern with purity.[9]

A further source of impurity was sinful behavior (cf. Isa 1:16; Job 14:4; 15:14; Ps 51:7), sometimes also sins related to cultic actions.[10] Such impurity adds the notion of culpability of the impure person. And lastly, purity issues can be raised by genealogical questions.[11] This adds the notion of hereditary impurity, perhaps mirrored in the Johannine healing of the blind man through a rite of purification (John 9:2,6–7). Consequently, impurity as the boundary between a person and the sacred has a shifting relation to the notion of responsibility. While there are many forms of impurity that result from circumstances such as illness or disability, there are other forms of impurity that result directly from acts a person is responsible for. In such a system, impurity becomes an inescapable fact of life.

If purity was such a pervading concern in Second Temple Judaism, Jewish Christian writings would have to address this concern. They do so of course, but a look at the Gospel of Matthew, the Epistle of James, and the Didache shows that these texts do so in quite distinctive ways that set them apart not only from one another, but also from many forms of Judaism known at the time.

1. MATTHEW AND PURITY

The Gospel of Matthew describes the purpose of Jesus's life and death in terms of the forgiveness of sins. Most clearly this happens in the annunciation of Jesus's birth to Joseph, when the angel appears to Joseph in a dream and declares about Jesus: αὐτὸς γὰρ σώσει τὸν λαὸν αὐτοῦ ἀπὸ τῶν ἁμαρτιῶν αὐτῶν (Matt

---

8. Schenker, "Pureté – impureté," 961, claims: "La consommation impure ne peut être purifiée." This would explain the acceptance of martyrdom over food controversies in 2 Macc 6–7; however, the issue there seems to go beyond mere impure food by referring to sacrificial meat.

9. Further evidence for the shifting concepts of purity and for an increasing restrictiveness is found in the Dead Sea Scrolls. See Hannah K. Harrington, *The Impurity Systems of Qumran and the Rabbis: Biblical Foundations* (SBLDS 143; Atlanta: Scholars Press, 1993).

10. Schenker, "Pureté – impureté," 962. Among such sins are necromancy (Lev 19:31) or worship of foreign gods (Hos 6:10; Jer 2:23). Sinfulness amounts to infidelity to God and can lead to impurity (Isa 65:4–6). It may well be asked whether such interlacing of purity issues with moral behavior finds its roots in a prophetic critique of the cult.

11. See Christine Hayes, *Gentile Impurities and Jewish Identities: Intermarriage and Conversion from the Bible to the Talmud* (Oxford: Oxford University Press, 2002). Hayes' analysis suggests that behind genealogical issues of purity lies the idea that even though Gentiles are not intrinsically impure, since they have not entered the covenant, the mixture of Jewish and Gentile blood leads to impurity. Hence the offspring of such unions would be considered impure.

1:21). Matthew explains the meaning of the name Jesus in terms of salvation[12] and draws attention to it (γάρ) through a wordplay that becomes obvious only through the Hebrew language. It connects the name יֵשׁוּעַ through the root יָשַׁע with the Greek verb σῴζειν.[13] The careful construction of the angel's prophecy with three progressively weightier verbs in the future tense (τέξεται . . . καλέσεις . . . σώσει) and the fulfillment of the first two of these within the same pericope not only draws attention to the third verb but also heightens the expectation of the reader to its fulfillment. According to Matthew, the salvation offered through Jesus is the forgiveness of sins offered to the Jewish people.[14]

The forgiveness of sins is a christological prerogative. John the Baptist preaches repentance from sin as a way to prepare for the inevitable judgment (Matt 3:7–10), and indeed, people come to John and confess their sins (Matt 3:6). However, the purification rite John offers in his baptism[15] is not effective, and he knows so himself. His baptism is one of repentance, but it cannot wash away the sins. In Mark 1:4 John offers βάπτισμα μετανοίας εἰς ἄφεσιν ἁμαρτιῶν, but the Matthean John baptizes merely εἰς μετάνοιαν. It is going to be Jesus who will separate wheat from chaff by a baptism ἐν πνεύματι ἁγίῳ καὶ πυρί (Matt 3:11–12). John's baptism is a warning against any easy expectations of salvation: neither confession nor a purifying baptism will achieve the forgiveness of sins that is the salvation offered by Jesus.

The Matthean description of how Jesus achieves his purpose of the forgiveness of sins is couched in language of purification at the Last Supper. Matthew prepares for this in several ways. First, there is the contextualization of the forgiveness of sins in the controversy with Jesus's opponents. In Matt 9:2–8 the authority and efficaciousness of Jesus's word of forgiveness to the paralytic are at stake. Both are proven, against the evil in the hearts of the opponents (Matt 9:4),

---

12. For the connection between messianic hopes and hopes for salvation within Judaism see Lidija Novakovic, *Messiah, Healer of the Sick: A Study of Jesus as the Son of David in the Gospel of Matthew* (WUNT 2/170; Tübingen: Mohr Siebeck, 2003), 69–73.

13. The wordplay seems to have been common enough with reference to Joshua. Philo (*Mut.*121) knows of it even though his knowledge of Hebrew seems quite doubtful. See William D. Davies and Dale C. Allison, *A Critical and Exegetical Commentary on the Gospel According to St. Matthew* (3 vols.; ICC; Edinburgh: T&T Clark, 1988–97), 1:210.

14. See Boris Repschinski, "'For He Will Save His People from Their Sins' (Matt 1:21): A Christology for Christian Jews," *CBQ* 68 (2006): 248–67.

15. Immersion as a purification rite is commonly known; see Lev 16:4, 24; 15; 1 QS III, 5–9; *Sib. Or.* 4.165; Josephus *Ant.* 18.117; *Life* 11 etc. See Gerhard Delling, *Die Taufe im Neuen Testament* (Berlin: Evangelische Verlagsanstalt, 1963). John P. Meier, *A Marginal Jew: Rethinking the Historical Jesus* (ABRL; New York: Doubleday, 1992), 49–53, suggests that John's baptism is less connected to purification rites for Jews since the baptism was a once-and-for-all event. Meier thinks that it might be more legitimately connected to the purification of Gentiles received into the Jewish faith. However, there is very little evidence to show that such a rite for the reception of Gentiles was common.

through the miraculous cure.[16] The story shows that Jesus takes up the prophecy of the angel already in his ministry.

A further step towards the purification at the Last Supper concerns Matthew's attitude to the temple[17] as it is exhibited in the Jerusalem narrative of the gospel. Jesus begins his stay in the temple of Jerusalem with the cleansing, or purification, of the temple, insisting that the dealers and money changers convert the temple from a house of prayer into a den of robbers (Matt 21:12–13). Then Matthew goes on to offer a vision of the temple as a house of prayer: the blind and lame are suddenly appearing in the temple, seemingly quite oblivious to the fact that as ritually impure people they do not belong there.[18] At the same time, children acclaim Jesus as the Son of David. When the chief priests and scribes protest at this, the Matthean Jesus offers the quotation of Ps 8:3 (LXX) to explain that the acclamation of the children is indeed God's way of preparing himself praise in the temple. If the money changers are representative of the temple as a den of robbers, Jesus shows how the temple can be the house of prayer intended by Isa 56:7. The opponents of Jesus align themselves with those who prefer the temple to be a den of robbers.

This particular point is brought home when Jesus, after the Jerusalem controversies and the discourse against Pharisees and scribes, finally leaves the temple. Matthew has Jesus end his discourse in the temple with a lament over Jerusalem and the temple. Part of the lament is the allusion to Jer 22:5 with the reference to the temple's desertion in Matt 23:38: ἀφίεται ὑμῖν ὁ οἶκος ὑμῶν ἔρημος. Matthew mentions the opponents of Jesus twice in this short phrase, drawing attention to them as owners of the temple. He indicates that at the end of the Jerusalem controversies Jesus's vision of the temple has come to an end and is left to those who would make it a den of robbers. When immediately after the lament Jesus finally withdraws from the temple (Matt 24:1), God himself is leaving the temple.[19] Now it is truly deserted, and its destruction is its natural consequence. But this also means that the place where purity means most, and where lost purity can be restored, is no longer available.

---

16. Both elements are redacted to show the continuing power in the Matthean community. See Boris Repschinski, *The Controversy Stories in the Gospel of Matthew: Their Redaction, Form, and Relevance for the Relationship Between the Matthean Community and Formative Judaism* (FRLANT 189; Göttingen: Vandenhoeck & Ruprecht, 2000), 63–75.

17. See Boris Repschinski, "Re-Imagining the Presence of God: The Temple and the Messiah in the Gospel of Matthew," *ABR* 54 (2006): 37–49.

18. See Lev 21:18 for the prohibition. It is possible that Matthew contrasts the Son of David with the original David who entered Jerusalem by killing the lame and the blind (2 Sam 5:6–8), as suggested by Davies and Allison, *Critical and Exegetical Commentary on . . . Matthew*, 3:140.

19. See Repschinski, "Re-Imagining the Presence of God," 44–47, for the argument, that the withdrawal of Jesus from the temple amounts to a withdrawal of God's presence.

Into this context Matthew places his view of the salvific death of Jesus offered in the narrative of the Last Supper (Matt 26:26–29). Jesus's blood is a symbol of the covenant, and it is to be poured out for many for the forgiveness of sins (Matt 26:28). A strong cultic subtext informs Matthew's formulation. The word ἐκχυννόμενον occurs not only in connection with a violent death, but also in the sacrificial context of the Passover sacrifice of the paschal lamb.[20] Poured-out blood is a constitutive element of sacrificial rites in the temple, and those sprinkled with it are cleansed and purified.[21] Together with the mention of the covenant, Matthew alludes to Exod 24:1–11, which contains all the elements necessary for a sacrificial ritual of purification. Furthermore, the rite of Exod 24 concludes with a meal celebrating the new covenant. Thus, the Last Supper is a creative *re-lecture* of Exod 24. The reenactment of Exod 24 happens at the trial and crucifixion of Jesus when his blood is indeed poured out and all the people cry for his blood to come upon them (Matt 27:25). In a highly ironic narrative, the purpose of Jesus to save his people from their sins comes to pass as the people call for his death by asking to be sprinkled with his blood.[22]

If this is so, then the consequences for the concept of purity in Matthew are dramatic. Purification from sinfulness is no longer achieved through sacrifices offered in the temple. The whole system of purification in the temple is replaced by Jesus himself. Matthew reworks the idea of purification in the sense of forgiveness of sins in the very traditional language of sacrifice and covenant into a very untraditional statement of christological impact. Whatever the temple had to offer is replaced by Jesus. Jesus himself is priest and victim in the sacrifice of purification that is his death, sealing the new covenant.[23] In his death, Jesus replaces the cult in the temple.

If the temple cult is replaced by Jesus, one might expect a reevaluation of cultic purity in terms of christology as well. Matthew does not disappoint. The first example illustrating Matthew's attitude to cultic purity can be encountered in the healing of the leper (Matt 8:1–4). Purity is a defining issue in the peri-

---

20. See Joachim Gnilka, *Das Matthäusevangelium* (2 vols.; HTKNT 1; Freiburg: Herder, 1986), 2:402; Davies and Allison, *Critical and Exegetical Commentary on . . . Matthew*, 3:475; Repschinski, "A Christology for Christian Jews," 260–61.

21. For an overview of such rites consult Christian Eberhart, *Studien zur Bedeutung der Opfer im Alten Testament: Die Signifikanz von Blut- und Verbrennungsriten im kultischen Rahmen* (WMANT 94; Neukirchen-Vluyn: Neukirchener Verlag, 2002), 222–88.

22. See Timothy B. Cargal, "'His Blood be Upon Us and Our Children': A Matthean Double Entendre?" *NTS* 37 (1991): 101–12; D. Sullivan, "New Insights Into Matthew 27.24–5," *NBf* 73 (1992): 453–57, and for an argument from the readers' perspective Repschinski, "A Christology for Christian Jews," 263.

23. Matthew exhibits here a striking resemblance to the theology of Hebrews. See Martin Hasitschka, "Matthew and Hebrews," in *Matthew and His Christian Contemporaries* (ed. B. Repschinski and D. Sim; London: Continuum, 2008), 87–103.

cope. The leper asks to be purified (καθαρίσαι), and Jesus commands him to be purified (καθαρίσθητι), with the result that the man is purified at once (εὐθέως ἐκαθαρίσθη). The triple reference to purity puts the touching act of Jesus into even starker relief. The whole story does not just tell a story concerning a healing miracle, but makes a statement of astonishing impact. Jesus touches the leper, who is not to be touched but instead supposed to cry "unclean, unclean!" (Lev 13:45). And the leper is rendered clean. In redacting his Markan source, Matthew states that the sacrifice prescribed by Moses is no longer about the issue of purity but merely εἰς μαρτύριον αὐτοῖς (Matt 8:4). The majority of commentators sees the command to the leper as a witness to the Torah-faithfulness of Jesus, directed at those in the temple.[24] However, this is not entirely convincing. Jesus counteracts conventions regarding purity, and the encounter with Jesus is what purifies, while the ritual in the temple merely serves as testimony. Thus, it is highly plausible to take the dative in its adversative meaning,[25] as testimony against those who practice ineffective rituals of purification in the temple.

Further evidence of Matthew's christological approach to cultic purity is provided by Jesus's ease of communicating with Gentiles like the centurion of Capernaum (Matt 8:5–13) or the possessed men of Gadara (Matt 8:28–34). Particularly the last instance is telling in the description of the men as living in tombs and consequently being very dangerous (Matt 8:28). The evil spirits themselves raise the christological stakes by calling Jesus the Son of God (Matt 8:29). Interestingly, the whole story is full of agitation, first of the men and their spirits, then of the pigs, then of the herdsmen and the citizens. In the midst of all this, Jesus remains the calm eye of the storm who just once speaks to give the extraordinarily brief exorcising command ὑπάγετε (Matt 8:32). In this sense it is much more a story of reaction to Jesus than it is a story about Jesus himself. It does not raise issues of purity explicitly, but this subtext is underlying much of the account. The upshot of this story is that evil spirits cannot withstand or challenge the Son of God. Fleeing from his presence, they have no other recourse than to throw themselves into what is unclean and destroy themselves.[26] Again it is in the person of Jesus where pure and impure separate.

A further example of Matthews approach to cultic purity is the controversy concerning the eating with unwashed hands and the ensuing instruction of crowds and disciples (Matt 15:1–20). The controversy proper (Matt 15:1–9) is

---

24. See Donald A. Hagner, *Matthew 1–13* (WBC 33A; Dallas, Tex.: Word Books, 1993–1996), 1:199.

25. Stanley E. Porter, *Idioms of the Greek New Testament* (Biblical Languages: Greek 2; Sheffield: JSOT Press, 1992), 98.

26. The text does not, as Hagner, *Matthew 1–13*, 228, and many other commentators with him suggest, imply that Jesus yields to the demons' request to enter into the pigs. The Matthean ὑπάγετε (8:32) is a significant redactional change from the Markan καὶ ἐπέτρεψεν αὐτοῖς (Mark 5:13).

partly taken over from Mark 7:1–13, but heavily redacted.[27] Matthew shortens Mark's version considerably by omitting Mark's description of Jewish customs of purifications. Matthew presumes knowledge of these. Secondly, Matthew tightens the story's structure by creating three pairs of opposites: Pharisees and scribes are opposed to Jesus (Matt 15:2a.3a), the disciples transgressing the tradition of the elders oppose the Pharisees and scribes transgressing the commandments of God (Matt 15:2b.3b), and finally God's command opposes the disobedient Pharisees and scribes (Matt 15:4a.5a).[28] From the structure of the passage alone it becomes clear that Jesus, his disciples, and God all are on one side, while Pharisees and scribes are on the other side.

As the frontiers are clearly marked, Matthew keeps the issue of purity from debate with the opponents of Jesus. The Markan reference to κοιναῖς χερσίν (Mark 7:5) implying some degree of impurity[29] is replaced by οὐ νίπτονται (Matt 15:2). Matthew keeps the discussion of the opposition between the tradition of the elders and the commandments of God separate from a discussion of purity. This achieves a neat argument for Matthew, since he suddenly does not have to deal with a perceived contrast between purity and the Law as Mark's story still implies. For Matthew, God's Law (τὴν ἐντολὴν τοῦ θεοῦ) is not opposed to purity regulations, but to the misguided traditions of the opponents (τὴν παράδοσιν ὑμῶν, Matt 15:3). Consequently, Matthew's concern with purity does not touch upon the washing of hands before dinner.

However, Matthew does not ignore the underlying purity issues altogether. In the teaching of the crowds he draws out the consequences with regard to purity of the just concluded controversy (Matt 15:10–11). Suddenly it becomes clear where Matthew sees the real function of a concept of purity. It does not concern eating, but whatever leaves a person's mouth. And in the ensuing instruction of the disciples what is coming out of a person's mouth is defined in ethical terms with sinful behavior that is closely related to the second table of the Decalogue (Matt 15:19).[30] The context for the strongly ethical approach is now mentioned

---

27. Repschinski, *Controversy Stories in the Gospel of Matthew*, 154–63.

28. Daniel Patte, *The Gospel according to Matthew: A Structural Commentary on Matthew's Faith* (Philadelphia: Fortress, 1987), 216–17.

29. On κοινός and its implications of "impurity" see Walter Bauer *et al.*, *A Greek-English Lexicon of the New Testament and Other Early Christian Literature* (3rd ed.; Chicago, Ill.: University of Chicago Press, 2000), 553. Parallels for such a use include "impure": 1 Macc 1:62; Rev 21:27; Rom 14:14a; Acts 10:14; Heb 10:29; *Diogn.* 5.7b. That Matthew understood Mark's use of κοινός in terms of purity is amply evidenced by the ensuing instructions of crowds and disciples.

30. Die διαλογισμοὶ πονηροί are an introduction to a catalogue of vices all related to the Decalogue. See Davies and Allison, *Critical and Exegetical Commentary on . . . Matthew*, 2:536–37. They ask whether this might be for mnemonic or catechetical reasons. This is perhaps a possibility, but in view of the preceding controversy and the affirmation of the Law in his

five times in 15:11.18. 20 as the issue of purity. At the same time, this community instruction is put into the context of a very strong critique of the Pharisees.

Matthew seems to avoid the discussion of purity and impurity in the context of food or ablutions. In the controversy with the Pharisees he treats purity as a non-issue. On the other hand, within the community purity is quite obviously still a live issue where some sympathize with the Pharisaic position. Thus Matthew notes the way the disciples are taken aback at Jesus's strong criticism of the Pharisees (Matt 15:12). Matthew, however, gives purity a strongly ethical bend that is tied into Law observance. Yet again, Matthew does not take over Mark's clear statement that Jesus declared all foods clean (Mark 7:19). This is explainable by Matthew's Law observance. If purity issues are a legal matter, then they cannot be discarded. If Matthew takes the Law as seriously as implied by 5:17–20, then the illicitness of some foods and the purity regulations remain a live issue. On the other hand, the strongly ethical interpretation of the concept of purity ties into Matthew's willingness to interpret the observance of the Law through the prophets[31] at the authority of Jesus.

Matthew's reason for this ethical orientation of purity appears in the story immediately following the discussions of purity around the controversy of eating with unwashed hands. The story of the Canaanite woman also occurs in Mark 7:24–30. But Matthew's changes are telling. Apart from making the woman a little more unlikable,[32] Matthew also inserts a short dialogue between Jesus and the disciples, thus establishing the story more firmly as a story about the community. The problem of Gentiles asking for access to the Jewish community was a matter of lengthy deliberations, as is suggested by the imperfect ἠρώτουν in Matt 15:23. Jesus's answer to the disciples shows where the problem lies: Jesus was sent only to the lost sheep of the house of Israel (Matt 15:24), yet here an annoying Gentile intrusion into this arrangement takes place, and the woman is not to be dissuaded from her intent of worshipping (προσεκύνει, Matt 15:25) Jesus.[33] By having just directed purity concerns into an ethical direction, her inclusion into

---

Gospel it is more likely that Matthew's redactional synchronization of his list with the Decalogue has theological reasons.

31. See, e.g., Matt 5:17; 7:12; 9:13; 11:13; 12:7; 17:3; 22:40. Alexander Sand, *Das Gesetz und die Propheten: Untersuchungen zur Theologie des Evangeliums nach Matthäus* (Biblische Untersuchungen 11; Regensburg: Pustet, 1974); Klyne Snodgrass, "Matthew and the Law," in *Treasures New and Old: Recent Contributions to Matthean Studies* (ed. D.R. Bauer and M. A. Powell; Atlanta: Scholars Press, 1996), 179–96.

32. So noted by David C. Sim, *The Gospel of Matthew and Christian Judaism: The History and Social Setting of the Matthean Community* (Studies of the New Testament and Its World; Edinburgh: T&T Clark, 1998), 223.

33. At this point one has to question Sim's assertion that none of the Gentiles really become disciples of Jesus. Whatever is meant by this expression, the Canaanite woman is a worshipper of Jesus. See Sim, *Matthew and Christian Judaism*, 223.

the group of believers becomes suddenly possible, albeit under severe restrictions: As in Mark, the simile of the bread for the dogs from the table of the children is used, with the woman not at all questioning the designation "dogs." However, Matthew changes her readiness to eat not, as in Mark, the crumbs of the children, but the crumbs from the table of the masters (τῶν κυρίων, Matt 15:27). It is the recognition of the masters that lets Jesus exclaim about the greatness of her faith. Matthew's redirection of purity concerns towards ethics makes table fellowship between Jews and Gentiles possible. It is, however, a table fellowship in which the Jews are clearly the masters. Quite ingeniously Matthew uses purity as a tool of inclusiveness for his community.

The look at the cycle of stories in Matt 8 and the discussion of Matt 15 show how much purity is still an issue of concern to the Matthean community. It seems that at least some in the community had sympathies for the Pharisaic approach to purity. However, Matthew goes another way: He links purity with ethical behavior and ties it in with law observance, so that purity, law observance, and a life according to the ethical norms expressed in the Decalogue and in the great commandments become synonymous to an extent that Matthew can express the final judgment in exclusively ethical terms (Matt 25:31–46). However, this reinterpretation is not arbitrary. It depends on the authority of Jesus whose death is the purifying sacrifice that brings salvation to his people. The Son of God whose blood is sprinkled on his people is the one deciding over purity and impurity.

2. JAMES AND PURITY

It has long been recognized that there are significant parallels between Matthew and James. Mostly these concern similarities in the teaching of Jesus as presented by the Sermon on the Mount and the teaching proposed in the Letter of James.[34] However, occasionally James is considerably closer to the Lukan parallel than to Matthew, and even where James and Matthew are close, neither wording nor order of the various sayings are identical. This leads to the conclusion that Matthew and James may share a common tradition, but not necessarily knowledge of each other.[35]

However, comparing the idea of purity in James and Matthew one quickly discovers that James has but a fleeting interest in the matter, if any at all. In Jas

---

34. These are conveniently listed by Raymond E. Brown, *An Introduction to the New Testament* (ABRL; New York: Doubleday, 1997), 734–5. There are some possible parallels outside of the Sermon on the Mount: Massey H. Shepherd, "The Epistle of James and the Gospel of Matthew," *JBL* 75 (1956): 40–51.

35. This thesis is widely shared today. An example of its explication can be found in Patrick J. Hartin, *James and the Q Sayings of Jesus* (JSNTSup 47; Sheffield: JSOT Press, 1991).

1:27 there occurs a reference to θρησκεία καθαρὰ καὶ ἀμίαντος,[36] which is quite odd considering that the concept of purity usually applies to persons, not, however, to religion. In 4:8 the command καθαρίσατε χεῖρας is probably not meant literally since it parallels the command ἁγνίσατε καρδίας. Apart from these instances, one might not even guess that James knew anything about purity at all. And so it does not come as a surprise that some authors suggest that even in these instances, James does not really have traditional purity concerns in view.[37]

But such a solution seems unlikely. Even if in Jas 1:27 καθαρά would not suggest a cultic context or background, θρησκεία most certainly does so.[38] If this is so, then it is highly unlikely that the Epistle does not want to suggest traditional notions of purity. Similarly, in Jas 4:8 the command to purify one's hands stands in such close connection to the issue of drawing near to God that it is hard not to assume at least some subtext of purity. The parallel with the command to sanctify the hearts deepens this impression.

Granted that James does allude to traditional Jewish purity issues at least twice, the question of their weight and direction remains. James's purpose and train of thought are notoriously difficult to discern, particularly with regard to Jas 1.[39] However, the careful chainlinking[40] of the whole of Jas 1 through catchwords suggests that the author saw the seemingly disparate material as somehow connected.[41] Furthermore, it is also striking how the material found in Jas 1 returns in variations throughout the letter. Among these are the themes of overcoming temptations (1:2–4,12; 5:7–11), the pleading in faith (1:5–8; 4:3; 5:13–18), the reversal of rich and poor (1:9–11; 2:1–7; 4:13–5:6), the contrast between evil desires and grace (1:13–18; 3:13–4:10), the warnings against the misuse of the tongue (1:19–20; 3:1–12), and the doing of the Word (1:22–27; 2:14–26).[42] Apart from the thematic material, figures of speech in Jas 1 also return throughout

---

36. The LXX uses the verb μιαίνω occasionally to denote that someone or something is rendered impure: Lev 5:3; 11:24; 18:24; Num 5:3; Deut 21:23. The expression ἄσπιλον ἑαυτὸν τηρεῖν in the same verse is also regularly associated with ritual purity.

37. As an example of such a view see Franz Schnider, *Der Jakobusbrief* (RNT; Regensburg: Pustet, 1987), 53, 103.

38. See LSJ 806; Bauer *et al.*, *Greek-English Lexicon*, 459.

39. Thus François Vouga, *L'épître de Saint Jacques* (CNT 2/13a; Genève: Labor et Fides, 1984), 66, complains with regard to Jas 1: "Les moments de la parénèse ne se suivent pas un ordre immédiatement évident." See also Luke T. Johnson, *The Letter of James* (AB 37A; New York: Doubleday, 1995), 174.

40. For the detailed analysis of the links through keywords see ibid., 174.

41. Attempts to divide off Jas 1:2–18 as a rhetorical *exordium* are unsuccessful because of the internal links of the whole chapter, but also because 1:19–27 remains an unaccounted for fragment. For such an attempt see Hubert Frankemölle, "Das semantische Netz des Jakobusbriefes: Zur Einheit eines umstrittenen Briefes," *BZ* 34 (1990): 175–93.

42. Johnson, *Letter of James*, 175.

the letter. The most obvious of these is the use of contrasts.[43] Thus the chapter is arguably a unit that works to establish topics and figures of speech for the remainder of the Epistle. James 1 functions as an exposition to the whole work.

One further feature that gives cohesion to Jas 1 is the use of metaphors. These are ἔοικεν κλύδωνι θαλάσσης (1:6), ὡς ἄνθος χόρτου (1:10–11), ἔοικεν ἀνδρὶ κατανοοῦντι τὸ πρόσωπον τῆς γενέσεως αὐτοῦ ἐν ἐσόπτρῳ (1:23–24). All three of these metaphors are negative, and all three function as a warning against something that might go wrong with the members of the community. After the greeting in Jas 1:1, the first thing that can go wrong is the lack of patience in temptation. Patience is a work of faith, and in faith can ask God for gifts (Jas 1:5,7). Lacking faith, a person is like an ocean wave, fickle in its ways (1:6–8). The second thing that can go wrong is the reliance on earthly goods. Thus Jas 1:10–11 warns rich people with the image of a flower wilting in the heat of the sun. Against the lack of patience and the reliance on riches the author sets the grace of a God who gives πᾶσα δόσις ἀγαθὴ καὶ πᾶν δώρημα τέλειον (Jas 1:17). The gifts of God are amply proven by a reference to the creation (κτίσις) in which God gives birth to the believer (1:18). The fickleness of the ocean wave and the heat of the sun are contrasted with the God as the father of light who is without variation or change of shadow (1:17).[44]

The next section admonishes the readers to become doers of the Word planted within them (Jas 1:19–25). The metaphor contained in this section speaks of a person looking at his face τῆς γενέσεως αὐτοῦ in a mirror (Jas 1:23). The reference to γένεσις is of double importance. On the one hand, it probably refers to a person's birth, on the other hand it evokes creation as well and as such is a throwback to Jas 1:18 and the gifts of God. The mirror is like the changeable ocean wave and the wilting flower: once seen one forgets immediately what one has seen. Only the look into the perfect law of freedom that does the Word will not forget (Jas 1:25).[45] Thus the section is intimately connected to the preceding material.

---

43. Timothy B. Cargal, *Restoring the Diaspora: Discursive Structure and Purpose in the Epistle of James* (SBLDS 144; Atlanta: Scholars Press, 1993), 56–105, argues that "polar opposites" working throughout James are established in chapter 1.

44. The obvious connection of 1:17 to the two preceding images does not put to question the often proposed interpretation of παραλλαγὴ ἢ τροπῆς ἀποσκίασμα as *termini technici* of astrological phenomena. For a discussion of such possibilities see Vouga, *Jacques*, 57–58. A little more cautious, also in view of the significant textual variants, is Johnson, *Letter of James*, 196–97.

45. The confusion this metaphor creates among commentators is simply astonishing. Ralph P. Martin, *James* (WBC 48; Dallas, Tex.: Word, 1988), 49, translates Jas 1:23 as "the face that nature gave him" and misses the point; it is precisely not the face that nature gave the person, but that God gave the person as one of his good gifts. Similarly Johnson, *Letter of James*, 207, 214, argues that the mirror remains the same, but what one sees in the mirror shifts

The following two verses (Jas 1:26–27) conclude the section by drawing its suggestions together. Again James alludes to those that merely hear the Word and do not do it, thus showing themselves to be changeable waves, wilting flowers, or forgetful mirror watchers. But this time, he puts this kind of behavior into the context of worship. James now contrasts the worthless worship of the hearers with the pure and unblemished worship of the doers. Thus what the whole chapter has been leading up to is now made explicit. At the heart of the metaphors used in Jas 1 is the exhortation to a worship what is pure and undefiled and that renders a person undefiled as well.

The astonishing feature of James is, however, that the idea of pure worship is not a mere cultic procedure of ablutions, or even faithfulness to the Law. Purity of worship is achieved in acts of charity to widows and orphans. Charity is circumscribed with the word ἐπισκέπτεσθαι. In LXX usage this word refers almost exclusively to God visiting or saving his people. Widows and orphans are the "classic recipients"[46] of God's and Israel's care and take up the theme of the reversal of rich and poor alluded to in Jas 1:9–11. Thus the assistance of the needy becomes the singular way of achieving a worship that fulfills the demands of purity. James replaces rites of purification with ethical demands and puts them into the context of ritual purity.

A similar use of the purity imagery can be noted with regard to 4:8. Firstly, James puts purity into the context of approaching God, who in turn himself approaches humans. Thus the context is cultic at least in its overtones.[47] Secondly, the purification of hands and the sanctification of hearts[48] are constructed in parallelism and, consequently, are meant to signify the same fact. The reference to double mindedness (δίψυχοι) creates the bridge back to Jas 1:8.

If the readers of Jas 4:8 are exhorted to purify hands and sanctify hearts, the context of Jas 4:1–10 gives a glimpse of why purification is necessary. In 4:1–3 James speaks of wars and conflicts in the community that have their roots in desires and lead to murder and envy.[49] Obviously James uses the words in

---

from the face to the perfect law. The confusion has its origin in the misinterpretation of the parable, where both equate the natural face with the face presented by the perfect law of 1:19. However, the metaphor does not run this way. It compares not what one sees, but it compares the instrument that makes one see: κατανοοῦντι . . . ἐν ἐσόπτρῳ (1:23) and παρακύψας εἰς νόμον (1:25).

46. See Johnson, *Letter of James*, 212, with references.

47. Johnson, *Letter of James*, 284; differently Schnider, *Jakobusbrief*, 103, who sees a prophetic as opposed to a cultic tradition behind Jas 4:8.

48. Both words used here occur frequently in reference to cultic purity. For ἁγνίζειν see Exod 19:10; Num 8:21; 19:12; 31:23.

49. On the connections of this imagery with the Jewish Two Ways tradition see Huub van de Sandt, "James 4,1–4 in the Light of the Jewish Two Ways Tradition 3,1–6," *Bib* 88 (2007): 38–63.

exaggeration. But if war and murder are exaggerations, they highlight the problems behind them. In 4:4–6 it becomes obvious that the war is one that involves friendship with the world and friendship with God as polar opposites. Only one of them can be chosen, and James's call to purification and sanctification is a call to choose friendship with God over friendship with the world. To be purified and to be sanctified means that one is no longer δίψυχος, that one has taken the necessary decision to end war and conflict, the decision for friendship with God. This decision finally involves the self-humiliation before God in order to be raised by him.

In order to fill the rather abstract concept of friendship with the world with content, several solutions have been proposed.[50] But quite apart from the particular meaning given to φονεύετε or μάχεσθε καὶ πολεμεῖτε (Jas 4:2) and φιλία τοῦ κόσμου (Jas 4:4), the words evoke the world of ethics. Thus the call to purification of hands and sanctification of hearts call for a decision to be made between particular behavior towards others that James sees as springing from desires, and the behavior towards God that consists of weeping and mourning and humiliation but will finally lead to exaltation by God. The language of reversal[51] puts perspective on the wars and conflicts arising out of desires. It is reasonable to assume that with the reversal before God the reversal of the behavior among the community members is in view, where the lust for possessions gives way to humility before one another.

Again in this short allusion in Jas 4:8 it becomes clear that James is interested in the concept of purity and willing to use it as long as it illuminates the moral standards of behavior concerned with social justice. If in Jas 1 the traditional biblical appeal to widows and orphans highlights the demands of purity, here it is the war between the haves and have-nots. However, in and of itself, purity is not a concern to James.

3. The Didache and Purity

While the Didache may indeed be a document reflecting a Jewish Christian orientation,[52] it also exhibits compromises made when accommodating Gentiles

---

50. Martin, *James*, 143–44, suggests misguided faith. Johnson, *Letter of James*, 286–87, amplifies this with suggestions of a background in Jewish Wisdom literature and Hellenistic literature and suggests that a double moral standard is at issue, one for dealing with God and another for dealing with people. Matthias Konradt, *Christliche Existenz nach dem Jakobusbrief: Eine Studie zu seiner soteriologischen und ethischen Konzeption* (SUNT 22; Göttingen: Vandenhoeck & Ruprecht, 1998), 125–35, sees the issue of rich and poor in the background.

51. Johnson, *Letter of James*, 286.

52. For the state of research, see Jonathan A. Draper, "The Apostolic Fathers: The Didache," *ExpTim* 117 (2006): 177–81. For the minority opinion that the Didache is a cohesive and complete early Jewish Christian document see Aaron Milavec, *The Didache: Faith, Hope,*

into the group (Did. 1:1). Such compromises are little known to Matthew.[53] Most clearly this appears when Didache treats the concept of purity. The first instance of teaching that may be related to purity occurs at the end of the teaching on the Two Ways with a reference to ὅλον τὸν ζυγὸν τοῦ κυρίου and to τῆς βρώσεως (6:2,3).[54] Occasionally it has been speculated that this is a Jewish appendix. Consequently, the yoke would refer to the Jewish Law.[55] Even though this might fit well with the following reference to the food regulations, the context suggests much more a reference to the teaching of Jesus as explicated in the preceding chapters.[56] But if the yoke as the Law of Christ is paired with reference to food regulations, the author also suggests that the community under Law of Christ is still observing some form of food regulations, even if, as Did. 6:3 suggests, compromises are necessary.

But the reference to compromises is a telling one, because it shifts the focus to a considerable extent. If the Jewish purity system was to ensure the correct worship, the Didache emphasizes the believers and their ability or inability to keep these rules. The emphasis on purity is not to ensure proper worship, but to encourage moral behavior among the believers. But the cultic connection is not entirely lost. The severe prohibition of the εἰδωλόθυτα is legitimized with reference to λατρεία of dead deities. For the author of the Didache, purity, like the teaching of the Two Ways, is a desirable idea in order to reach perfection, but in the end the author gives in to the realities of his community and suggests an observation of both *iuxta modum*. Similar advice can be found in the baptismal instruction to use living water (7:1–3).

Thus purity in the Didache is an issue related to the practical life within the community. The only place where purity is explicitly mentioned clarifies this further. When the Didache speaks about how to achieve the necessary purity to celebrate the Eucharist (Did. 14), it speaks about the confession of sins (τὰ παραπτώματα), taking up the teaching of the Two Ways (Did. 4:14), as a pre-

---

& *Life of the Earliest Christian Communities, 50 – 70 C. E.* (New York: Newman Press, 2003); for more general arguments concerning the Jewish background of the Didache see Huub van de Sandt and David Flusser, *The Didache: Its Jewish Sources and Its Place in Early Judaism and Christianity* (CRINT 3/5; Assen: Van Gorcum, 2002), and the various essays in *Matthew and the Didache: Two Documents from the Same Jewish-Christian Milieu?* (ed. H. van de Sandt; Assen: Van Gorcum, 2005).

53. See Boris Repschinski, "Matthew and Luke," in *Matthew and His Christian Contemporaries* (ed. B. Repschinski and D. Sim; London: Continuum, 2008), 50–65.

54. Kurt Niederwimmer, *Die Didache* (2nd ed.; Kommentar zu den Apostolischen Vätern 1; Göttingen: Vandenhoeck & Ruprecht, 1993), 153, speaks of the "interpretatorischen und ergänzenden Charakter" of this appendix to the Two Ways teaching.

55. Alfred Stuiber, "'Das ganze Joch des Herrn' (Didache 6,2–3)," *StPatr* 4 (1961): 323–39.

56. See Niederwimmer, *Die Didache*, 155–56. A similar use of ζυγός is found in Matt 11:29.

requisite to guarantee the purity of the θυσία.[57] These sins are being explicated further as ἀμφιβολίαν μετὰ τοῦ ἑταίρου (Did. 14:2). Very concrete quarrels[58] within the community are the things that will render a Sunday sacrifice unclean (κοινωθῇ). In order to legitimize such a demand for purity the Didache finally quotes Mal 1:11.14, a fitting conclusion to an argument on purity that is concerned with θυσίαν καθαράν (Did. 14:3).

Yet as much as Did. 14 may be concerned with purity, it merely repeats the argument already made in Did. 10:6 about the restrictions concerning access to the Eucharist. There Didache stated: εἴ τις ἅγιός ἐστιν, ἐρχέσθω· εἴ τις οὐκ ἔστι, μετανοείτω. Again access to the Eucharist is under discussion, and again it is restricted to those who are in need of conversion, presumably because of sins that need redressing.[59] However, here the purity of the Eucharist is not mentioned, although purity concerns seem at the back of the argument in Did. 10:6 as well. Instead, the focus rests on the holiness of those having access to it.

Quite similar to Matthew, Didache takes up purity concerns and interprets them ethically. However, quite distinct from Matthew, the purity teaching in Didache concerns the community and its celebration of its liturgies. Its direction is inward. Therefore, purity becomes an issue of separation of those who are worthy from those who are not. While Matthew ingeniously uses purity to guarantee the inclusiveness of his community, Didache emphasizes the exclusivity of its liturgical celebrations.

4. Conclusion

The three texts under consideration all deal to some extent with purity. With Matthew the attention to the concept of purity is certainly greatest, and it also yields the greatest theological value. To conceive of purity in terms of christology and to declare Jesus the final and definitive sacrifice that purifies the believers is a great theological achievement. Apart from Matthew only Hebrews makes this leap in the New Testament. The consequence for the believer in Matthew's Christ is far reaching. Even though Matthew never quite says so explicitly, implicitly the whole system of purity comes to an end in Jesus. If Jesus through his death purifies the believer, there is no need for further purifications or indeed food

---

57. For our investigation, the question of whether θυσία refers to the breaking of the bread or to the eucharistic prayer is negligible. It is questionable whether the author would have intended such a fine distinction; see Niederwimmer, *Die Didache*, 237. The concepts of purity and of sacrifice are closely related, and thus the one may have provoked the other.

58. The lexical meaning of ἀμφιβολία as "being beleaguered from two sides" does not quite fit either context or use in connection with ἔχειν . . . μετά. Thus "quarrel" seems to make the most sense; LSJ, 90; Bauer *et al.*, *Greek-English Lexicon*, 55.

59. The demand for holiness seems an additional condition quite apart from the baptism mentioned in Did. 9:5.

laws. Matthew makes this point by his treatment of the earthly Jesus approaching people of varying degrees of impurity. The concept of purity is harnessed into showing how Jesus is indeed the Son of God and Messiah for a Jewish community that is ready to include Gentiles among its group.

James and Didache show less interest in the issue of purity. This may be due in part to their greater dialogue with Gentile converts within their respective communities. Purity is no longer stringently argued as a theological *topos* but becomes one of many metaphors to illustrate the right behavior in the community. What renders pure is almost entirely related to people's ethical behavior. Furthermore, when Didache speaks about purity it does not speak about people but worship. The moral behavior affects the quality of worship, and consequently immoral behavior has to be kept apart from worship. The sacrifice does not purify the believer, but the believer can render the sacrifice unclean, a belief that is popular even in today's churches.

If all three writings under discussion deal with the issue of purity, Matthew is perhaps the closest to the Jewish traditions of purity. However, there is no denying that in the last consequence, all three writings break with the traditions as well, Matthew by reinterpreting them considerably, James and Didache by mostly ignoring them. Of course one may ask why purity could be so easily dispensed with even in texts much closer to Jewish traditions than Mark's Gospel, to name but one. One reason may well be the destruction of the temple and the concomitant disappearance of many of the rituals legitimizing cultic purity. But there may be another reason for this as well, and it has to do with christology.

A belief in an earthly Jesus who touches and heals sick people, lepers, sinners, and generally unclean people, calls purity concerns into question. If this earthly Jesus is subsequently put to death but believed to have been raised by God, then even the most serious cultic impurity loses its persuasiveness. If the greatest challenge to cultic purity is the contact with a corpse, then the belief in a bodily resurrection puts not just death into question, but also severely relativizes any questions of purity associated with death and corpses. It seems to be the very nature of resurrection faith to delegitimize any notions of cultic purity. Matthew, I think, has sensed this to some extent. Consequently, he tried to save purity for coming generations in connecting it with the death of Jesus as a saving and purifying sacrifice. Others, like James and the Didache, relegate the concept of purity to a metaphor qualifying certain behavior, or just do away with it completely.

BIBLIOGRAPHY

Abrahams, Israel. *Studies in Pharisaism and the Gospels.* 2 vols. Cambridge: Cambridge University Press, 1917. Repr., New York: Ktav, 1967

Adam, Adolf. "Erwägungen zur Herkunft der Didache," *ZKG* 68 (1957): 1–47.

Adamson, James B. *The Epistle of James.* NICNT. Grand Rapids: Eerdmans, 1976.

Aderet, Avraham. *From Destruction to Restauration: The Mode of Yavneh in Re-Establishment of the Jewish People.* Jerusalem: Magnes, 1990.

Akenson, Donald H. *Saint Saul: A Skeleton Key to the Historical Jesus.* Oxford: Oxford University Press, 2000.

Albeck, Chanoch. *The Mishna: Seder Nashim.* Tel Aviv: Debir, 1988.

Aleksandrov, G. S. "The Role of ʿAqiba in the Bar Kokhba Rebellion." Pages 422–36 in *Eliezer ben Hyrcanus: The Tradition and the Man.* Edited by J. Neusner. Vol 2. SJLA 3–4. Leiden: Brill, 1973. Repr. in *REJ* 132 (1973): 65–77.

Alexander, Philip S. "Rabbinic Judaism and the New Testament." *ZNW* 74 (1983): 237–46.

Alon, Gedalyahu. "The Halaka in the Epistle of Barnabas." *Tarbiz* 11 (1939–40): 23–38, 223. Repr. as pages 295–312 in *Studies in Jewish History in the Times of the Second Temple, the Mishna and the Talmud.* 2 vols. 2nd. ed. Tel Aviv: Hakibutz Hameuchad, 1967–70 (Hebrew).

———. "The Halakha in the Teaching of the Twelve Apostles." Pages 165–94 in *The Didache in Modern Research.* Edited by J. A. Draper. Translated by A. Ben-Meir. AGJU 37. Leiden: Brill, 1996. Translation of "Ha-halaka ba-Torat 12 ha-Shelihim." *Tarbiz* 11 (1939–40): 127–45. Repr. as pages 274–94 in *Studies in Jewish History in the Times of the Second Temple, the Mishna and the Talmud.* 2 vols. 2nd. ed. Tel Aviv: Hakibutz Hameuchad, 1967–70 (Hebrew).

———. *The Jews in Their Land in the Talmudic Age.* 2 vols. Jerusalem: Magnes, 1980–84. Translation of *Toledot ha-Yehudim be-Erets-Yisrael bi-tekufat ha-Mishna weha- Talmud.* 2 vols. Tel-Aviv: Hakibbutz Hameuchad, 1967–70.

———. *Jews, Judaism, and the Classical World.* Jerusalem: Magnes, 1977.

———. "Sociological Method in the Study of the Halacha." *Tarbiz* 10 (1938–39): 241–82 (Hebrew).

———. *Studies in Jewish History in the Times of the Second Temple, the Mishna and the Talmud.* 2 vols. 2nd. ed. Tel Aviv: Hakibutz Hameuchad, 1967–70 (Hebrew).

Amélineau, Émile C. *Monuments pour servir à l'histoire de l'Égypte chrétienne aux IVe, Ve, VIe et VIIe siècles.* 2 vols. Mémoires publiés par les membres de la mission archéologique du Caire 4; Paris: Leroux, 1888–95.

Anderson, Hugh. "4 Maccabees." Pages 531–64 in *The Old Testament Pseudepigrapha.* Vol. 2. Edited by J. H. Charlesworth. Garden City, N.Y.: Doubleday, 1983–85.

Appelbaum, Shimon. *Prolegomena to the Study of the Second Jewish Revolt (A.D. 132–135)*. British Archaeological Reports. Supplementary Series 7. Oxford: British Archaeological Reports, 1976.

Assmann, Jan. "Form as Mnemonic Device: Cultural Texts and Cultural Memory." Pages 67–82 in *Performing the Gospel: Orality, Memory and Mark. Essays dedicated to Werner Kelber*. Edited by R. A. Horsley, J. A. Draper, and J. M. Foley. Minneapolis: Fortress, 2006.

Atchley, Edward G. C. F. *On the Epiclesis of the Baptismal Liturgy and in the Consecration of the Font*. London: Humphrey Milford, 1935.

Audet, Jean-Paul. *La Didachè: Instructions des Apôtres*. EBib. Paris: Gabalda, 1958.

Aune, David E. "Distinct Lexical Meanings of ΑΠΑΡΧΗ in Hellenism, Judaism and Early Christianity." Pages 103–29 in *Early Christianity and Classical Culture: Studies in Honour of Abraham J. Malherbe*. Edited by J. T. Fitzgerald, T. H. Olbricht, and L. M. White. NovTSup 105. Leiden: Brill, 2003.

———. *Prophecy in Early Christianity and the Ancient Mediterranean World*. Grand Rapids: Eerdmans, 1983.

Austin, John L. *How to do Things with Words*. 2nd ed. Oxford: Oxford University Press, 1975.

Baarda, Tjitze. "The Sentences of the Syriac Menander." Pages 583–606 in vol. 2 of *The Old Testament Pseudepigrapha*. Edited by J. H. Charlesworth. Garden City, N.Y.: Doubleday, 1983–85.

Bacher, Wilhelm. *Die exegetische Terminologie der jüdischen Traditionsliteratur*. 2 vols. Leipzig 1899–1905. Repr., Hildesheim: Olms, 1965.

Bacon, Benjamin W. *Studies in Matthew*. London: Constable, 1930.

Baer, Yizhak. "The Historical Foundations of the Halakha." *Zion* 27 (1962): 117–55 (Hebrew).

Bagatti, Bellarmino. *The Church from the Circumcision: History and Archaeology of the Judaeo-Christians*. Translated by Eugene Hoade. Publications of the Studium Biblicum Franciscanum. Smaller Series 2. Jerusalem: Franciscan Printing Press, 1971.

Baker, William R. *Personal-Speech Ethics in the Epistle of James*. WUNT 2/68. Tübingen: Mohr Siebeck, 1995.

Baldwin, Barry H. "Lucian as Social Satirist." *Classical Quarterly* NS 11 (1961): 199–208.

Bammel, Ernst. "πτωχός, πτωχεία, πτωχεύω." Pages 888–915 in vol. 6 of *Theological Dictionary of the New Testament*. Edited by G. Kittel and G. Friedrich.

Barclay, John M.G. *Jews in the Mediterranean Diaspora from Alexander to Trajan (323 BCE –117 CE)*. Edinburgh: T&T Clark, 1996.

Baron, Salo W. "Ghetto and Emancipation: Shall We Revise the Traditional View?" *The Menorah Journal* 14 (1928): 515–26.

Bauckham, Richard J. ed., *The Gospels for All Christians: Rethinking the Gospel Audiences*. Edinburgh: T&T Clark, 1998.

———. *James: Wisdom of James: Disciple of Jesus the Sage*. New Testament Readings. London: Routledge, 1999.

Baudissin, Wolf W. Graf. "Die alttestamentliche Religion und die Armen." *Preussische Jahrbücher* 149 (1912): 193–231.

Bauer, Walter. *Griechisch-deutsches Wörterbuch zu den Schriften des Neuen Testaments und der frühchristlichen Literatur*. 6th ed. Berlin: de Gruyter, 1988.

———. *Orthodoxy and Heresy in Earliest Christianity*. Edited by R. A. Kraft and G. Krodel.

Philadelphia: Fortress, 1971. Translation of *Rechtgläubigkeit und Ketzerei im ältesten Christentum*. BHT 10. Tübingen: Mohr Siebeck, 1934.

Bauer, Walter, W. F. Arndt, F. W. Gingrich, and F. Danker. *A Greek-English Lexicon of the New Testament and Other Early Christian Literature*. 3rd ed. Chicago: University of Chicago Press, 2000.

Bazzana, Giovanni B. "Early Christian Missionaries as Phyisicians: Christian Sources in the Context of Greco-Roman Medical Practice." Paper presented at the annual meeting of the Context Group, Ashton Pa., March 15–18, 2007.

Beare, Francis W. *The Gospel according to Matthew: A Commentary*. Oxford: Blackwell, 1981.

Becker, Hans-Jürgen. *Auf der Kathedra des Mose: Rabbinisch-theologisches Denken und antirabbinische Polemik in Matthäus 23,1–12*. ANTZ 4. Berlin: Institut für Kirche und Judentum, 1990.

Ben-Haim Trifon, Dalia. "Some Aspects of Internal Politics Connected with the Bar-Kokhva Revolt." Pages 13–26 in *The Bar-Kokhva Revolt: A New Approach*. Edited by A. Oppenheimer and U. Rappaport. Jerusalem: Yad Izhak Ben Zvi, 1984 (Hebrew).

Berger, Peter L., and Thomas Luckmann. *The Social Construction of Reality: A Treatise in the Sociology of Knowledge*. Garden City, N.Y.: Doubleday, 1966.

Berner, Ulrich. "Moderner und antiker Religionsbegriff." Pages 13–21 in vol. 1 of *Neues Testament und Antike Kultur*. Edited by K. Erlemann, K.L. Noethlichs, K. Scherberich and J. Zangenberg. 2nd ed. 5 vols. Neukirchen-Vluyn: Neukirchener Verlag, 2004 –2007.

Betz, Hans Dieter. *Galatians: A Commentary on Paul's Letter to the Churches in Galatia*. Philadelphia: Fortress, 1979.

———. "A Jewish-Christian Cultic *Didache* in Matt. 6:1–18: Reflections and Questions on the Problem of the Historical Jesus." Pages 55–69 in *Essays on the Sermon on the Mount*. Edited by H. D. Betz. Translated by L. L. Welborn. Philadelphia: Fortress, 1985.

———. *The Sermon on the Mount: A Commentary on the Sermon on the Mount, including the Sermon on the Plain (Matthew 5:3–7:27 and Luke 6:20–49)*. Hermeneia; Minneapolis: Fortress, 1995.

———. "The Sermon on the Mount (Matt. 5:3–7:27): Its Literary Genre and Function." Pages 1–16 in *Essays on the Sermon on the Mount*. Edited by H. D. Betz. Translated by L. L. Welborn. Philadelphia: Fortress, 1985.

Binder, Donald D. *Into the Temple Courts: The Place of the Synagogue in the Second Temple Period*. Atlanta: Society of Biblical Literature, 1999.

Bloomquist, L. Gregory. "The Rhetoric of the Historical Jesus." Pages 98–117 in *Whose Historical Jesus?* Edited by W. E. Arnal and M. Desjardins. Etudes sur le christianisme et judaïsme/Studies in Christianity and Judaism 7. Waterloo, Ont.: Wilfred Laurier University Press, 1997.

Böhl, Felix. *Gebotserschwerung und Rechtsverzicht als ethisch-religiöse Normen in der rabbinischen Literatur*. Frankfurter Judaistische Studien 1. Freiburg i. B.: Schwarz, 1971.

Booth, Roger P. *Jesus and the Laws of Purity: Tradition History and Legal History in Mark 7*. JSNTSup 13. Sheffield: JSOT Press, 1986.

Bornkamm, Günther. "Der Aufbau der Bergpredigt." *NTS* 24 (1978): 419–32.

———. "The Stilling of the Storm in Matthew." Pages 52–57 in *Tradition and Interpretation in Matthew*. Edited by G. Bornkamm, G. Barth, and H. J. Held. London: SCM, 1963.

Bradshaw, Paul F, Maxwell E. Johnson, L. Edward Phillips, and Harold W. Attridge, eds. *The Apostolic Tradition*. Hermeneia. Minneapolis: Augsburg Fortress, 2002.

Brandon, Samuel G. F. *The Fall of Jerusalem and the Christian Church: A Study of the Effects of the Jewish Overthrow of A.D. 70 on Christianity*. London: SPCK, 1951.

Braumann, Georg. "Der theologische Hintergrund des Jakobusbriefes." *TZ* 18 (1962): 401–10.

Broer, Ingo. "Anmerkungen zum Gesetzesverständnis des Matthäus." Pages 128–45 in *Das Gesetz im Neuen Testament*. Edited by K. Kertelge. QD 108. Freiburg: Herder, 1986.

———. *Freiheit vom Gesetz und Radikalisierung des Gesetzes: Ein Beitrag zur Theologie des Evangelisten Matthäus*. SBS 98. Stuttgart: Verlag Katholisches Bibelwerk, 1980.

Brown, Delwin. "Thinking About the God of the Poor: Questions for Liberation Theology from Process Thought." *JAAR* 57 (1989): 267–81.

Brown, Raymond E. *An Introduction to the New Testament*. ABRL. New York: Doubleday, 1997.

Brown, Raymond E., and John P. Meier. *Antioch and Rome: New Testament Cradles of Catholic Christianity*. New York: Paulist Press, 1983.

Bultmann, Rudolph. *Die Geschichte der synoptischen Tradition*. 8th ed. FRLANT 29. Göttingen: Vandenhoeck & Ruprecht, 1970.

———. *Die Geschichte der synoptischen Tradition*. 9th ed. Göttingen: Vandenhoeck & Ruprecht, 1979.

Burchard, Christoph. "Das doppelte Liebesgebot in der frühen christlichen Überlieferung." Pages 3–26 in *Studien zur Theologie, Sprache und Umwelt des Neuen Testaments*. Edited by D. Sänger. WUNT 107. Tübingen: Mohr Siebeck, 1998.

———. *Der Jakobusbrief*. HNT 15/1. Tübingen: Mohr Siebeck, 2000.

———. "Versuch, das Thema der Bergpredigt zu finden." Pages 27–50 in *Studien zur Theologie, Sprache und Umwelt des Neuen Testaments*. Edited by D. Sänger. WUNT 107. Tübingen: Mohr Siebeck, 1998.

———. "Zu einigen christologischen Stellen des Jakobusbriefes." Pages 353–68 in *Anfänge der Christologie*. Edited by C. Breytenbach and H. Paulsen. Göttingen: Vandenhoeck & Ruprecht, 1991

Burgess, Theodore C. "Epideictic Literature." *The University of Chicago Studies in Classical Philology* 3 (1902): 89–261.

Burridge, Kenelm. *New Heaven, New Earth: A Study of Milenarian Activities*. New York: Schocken, 1969.

Byrne, Brendan. "The Messiah in Whose Name 'The Gentiles Will Hope' (Matt 13:21): Gentile Inclusion as an Essential Element of Matthew's Christology." *ABR* 50 (2002): 55–73.

Callan, Terrance. "The Background of the Apostolic Decree (Acts 15:20, 29; 21:25)." *CBQ* 55 (1993): 284–97.

Campenhausen, Hans F. von. "Taufen in dem Namen Jesu?" *VC* 25 (1971): 1–15.

Cancik, Hubert, Burkhard Gladigow, and Matthias Laubscher, eds., *Handbuch religionswissenschaftlicher Grundbegriffe*. 5 vols. Stuttgart: Kohlhammer, 1988 –2001.

Cargal, Timothy B. " 'His Blood be Upon Us and Our Children': A Matthean Double Entendre?" *NTS* 37 (1991): 101–12.

———. *Restoring the Diaspora: Discursive Structure and Purpose in the Epistle of James*. SBLDS 144. Atlanta: Scholars Press, 1993.

Carleton Paget, James. "The Definition of the Terms *Jewish Christian* and *Jewish Christianity* in the History of Research." Pages 22–52 in *Jewish Believers in Jesus: The Early Centuries*. Edited by O. Skarsaune and R. Hvalvik. Peabody, Mass.: Hendrickson, 2007.

———. "Jewish Christianity." Pages 731–75 of vol. 3 of *The Cambridge History of Judaism*. Edited by W. Horbury, W. D. Davies, and J. Sturdy. Cambridge: Cambridge University Press, 1999.

Carrington, Philip. *The Primitive Christian Catechism: A Study in the Epistles*. Cambridge: Cambridge University Press, 1940.

Carter, Warren. *Matthew and Empire: Initial Explorations*. Harrisburg, Pa.: Trinity Press International, 2001.

———. *Matthew and the Margins: A Sociopolitical and Religious Reading*. Maryknoll, N.Y.: Orbis, 2000.

———. "Matthew and the Gentiles: Individual Conversion and/or Systemic Transformation?" *JSNT* 26 (2004): 259–82.

Causse, Antonin. *Les «Pauvres» d'Israël (Prophètes, Psalmistes, Messianistes)*. Strasbourg: Librairie Istra, 1922.

Charles, J. Daryl. "Garnishing with the 'Greater Righteousness': The Disciple's Relationship to the Law (Matthew 5:17–20)." *BBR* 12 (2002): 1–15.

Charlesworth, James H. *The Old Testament Pseudepigrapha*. 2 vols. Garden City, N.Y.: Doubleday, 1983–85.

Cheung, Luke L. *The Genre, Composition and Hermeneutics of James*. Paternoster Biblical and Theological Monographs. Carlisle: Paternoster, 2003.

Chilton, Bruce D., and Craig A. Evans eds. *James the Just and Christian Origins*. NovTSup 98. Leiden: Brill, 1999.

Cohen, Shaye J. D. "Respect for Judaism by Gentiles According to Josephus." *HTR* 80 (1987): 409–30.

———. "The Significance of Yavneh: Pharisees, Rabbis, and the End of Jewish Sectarianism." *HUCA* 55 (1984): 28–53.

Connolly, Richard H. "New Fragments of the *Didache*." *JTS* 25 (1924): 151–53.

Cooper, R. M. "Prayer: A Study in Matthew and James." *Enc* 29 (1968): 268–77.

Crosby, Michael. *House of Disciples: Church, Economics, and Justice in Matthew*. Maryknoll, N.Y.: Orbis, 1988.

Crossan, John D. *The Historical Jesus: The Life of a Mediterranean Jewish Peasant*. San Francisco: Harper & Row, 1991.

Crossley, James G. *The Date of Mark's Gospel: Insight from the Law in Earliest Christianity*. JSNTSup 266. London: T&T Clark, 2004.

Crouzel, Henri. "L'Imitation et la 'Suite' de Dieu et de Christ dans les premières siècles Chrétiens, ainsi que leurs sources Gréco-Romaines et Hébraïques." Pages 7–41 in *Jahrbuch für Antike und Christentum*. Jahrgang 21. Münster: Aschendorffsche Verlagsbuchhandlung 1978.

Daniélou, Jean. *The Theology of Jewish Christianity*. London: Darton, Longman & Todd, 1964. Translation of *Théologie du judéo-christianisme*. Tournai: Desclée, 1958.

Davids, Peter H. *The Epistle of James: A Commentary on the Greek Text*. NIGTC. Grand Rapids: Eerdmans, 1982.

———. "Palestinian Traditions in the Epistle of James." Pages 33–57 in *James the Just and Christian Origins*. Edited by B. D. Chilton and C. A. Evans. NovTSup 98. Leiden: Brill, 1999.

Davies, William D. *The Sermon on the Mount.* Cambridge: Cambridge University Press, 1966.

———. *The Setting of the Sermon on the Mount.* Cambridge, Mass.: Cambridge University Press, 1964.

Davies, William D., and Dale C. Allison Jr. *A Critical and Exegetical Commentary on the Gospel According to Saint Matthew.* 3 vols. ICC. Edinburgh: T&T Clark, 1988–97.

Deines, Roland. *Die Gerechtigkeit der Tora im Reich des Messias: Mt 5,13–20 als Schlüsseltext der matthäischen Theologie.* WUNT 177. Tübingen: Mohr Siebeck, 2004.

Delling, Gerhard. *Die Taufe im Neuen Testament.* Berlin: Evangelische Verlagsanstalt, 1963.

———. "τέλειος." Pages 68–79 in vol. 8 of *Theologisches Wörterbuch zum Neuen Testament.* Edited by G. Kittel and G. Friedrich. 10 vols. in 12. Stuttgart: Kohlhammer, 1932–79.

Del Verme, Marcello. *Didache and Judaism: Jewish Roots of an Ancient Christian–Jewish Work.* New York: T&T Clark, 2004.

Deppe, Dean B. *The Sayings of Jesus in the Epistle of James.* Ph.D. diss. Chelsea, Mich.: Bookcrafters, 1989.

Descamps, Albert. "Essai d'interprétation de Mt 5,17–48: Formgeschichte ou Redactionsgeschichte?" *SE* 1 (1959): 156–73.

Dibelius, Martin. *James: A Commentary on the Epistle of James.* Edited by H. Koester. Translated by M. A. Williams. Hermeneia. Philadelphia: Fortress, 1975. Translation of *Der Brief des Jakobus.* 11th ed. KEK 15. Rev. by H. Greeven. Göttingen: Vandenhoeck & Ruprecht, 1964.

Dibelius, Martin, and Hans Conzelmann, *The Pastoral Epistles: A Commentary on the Pastoral Epistles.* Hermeneia; Philadelphia: Fortress, 1972.

Dietzfelbinger, Christian. "Die Antithesen der Bergpredigt im Verständnis des Matthäus." *ZNW* 70 (1979): 1–15.

Donfried, Karl P. "The Allegory of the Ten Virgins (Mt 25:1–13) as a Summary of Matthean Theology." *JBL* 94 (1974): 415–28.

Douglas, Mary T. *In the Wilderness: The Doctrine of Defilement in the Book of Numbers.* JSOTSup 158. Sheffield: JSOT Press, 1993.

———. "Jokes." Pages 90–114 in *Implicit Meanings: Essays in Anthropology.* Edited by M. T. Douglas. London: Routledge & Kegan Paul, 1975.

———. *Natural Symbols Explorations in Cosmology.* New York: Pantheon Books, 1970.

———. *Purity and Danger: An Analysis of Concepts of Pollution and Taboo.* London: Routledge & Kegan Paul, 1966.

Draper, Jonathan A. "The Apostolic Fathers: The Didache." *ExpTim* 117 (2006): 177–81.

———. "Christian Self-Definition against the 'Hypocrites' in Didache VIII." Pages 223–43 in *The Didache in Modern Research.* Edited by J. A. Draper. AGJU 37. Leiden: Brill, 1996.

———. "The Didache in Modern Research: An Overview." Pages 1–42 in *The Didache in Modern Research.* Edited by J. A. Draper. AGJU 37. Leiden: Brill, 1996.

———. "Do the Didache and Matthew Reflect an 'Irrevocable Parting of the Ways' with Judaism?" Pages 217–41 in *Matthew and the Didache: Two Documents from the Same Jewish-Christian Milieu?* Edited by H. van de Sandt. Assen: Van Gorcum, 2005.

———. "First Fruits and the Support of Prophets, Teachers and the Poor in Didache 13 in Relation to New Testament Parallels." Pages 223–43 in *Trajectories through the New*

Testament and the Apostolic Fathers. Edited by A. Gregory and C. Tuckett. Oxford: Oxford University Press, 2005.

———. "The Genesis and Narrative Thrust of the Paraenesis in the Sermon on the Mount." *JSNT* 75 (1999): 25–48.

———. "The Holy Vine of David made known to the Gentiles through God's servant Jesus: 'Christian Judaism' in the Didache." Pages 257–83 in *Jewish Christianity Reconsidered: Rethinking Ancient Groups and Texts*. Edited by M. Jackson-McCabe. Minneapolis: Fortress, 2007.

———. "Jesus' 'Covenantal Discourse' on the Plain (Luke 6:12–7:17) as Oral Performance: Pointers to 'Q' as Multiple Oral Performance." Pages 71–98 in *Oral Performance, Popular Tradition, and Hidden Transcript in Q*. Edited by R. A. Horsley. SemeiaSt 60. Atlanta: Society of Biblical Literature, 2006.

———. "The Jesus Tradition in the Didache." Pages 72–91 in *The Didache in Modern Research*. Edited by J. A. Draper. AGJU 37. Leiden: Brill, 1996. Repr. from pages 269–87 in *The Jesus Tradition Outside the Gospels*. Edited by D. D. Wenham. Gospel Perspectives 5. Sheffield: JSOT Press, 1985.

———. "Ritual Process and Ritual Symbol in *Didache* 7–10," *VC* 54 (2000): 121–58.

———. "Social Ambiguity and the Production of Text: Prophets, Teachers, Bishops, and Deacons and the Development of the Jesus Tradition in the Community of the *Didache*." Pages 284–312 in *The Didache in Context: Essays on its Text, History, and Transmission*. Edited by C. N. Jefford. NovTSup 77. Leiden: Brill, 1995.

———. "Torah and Troublesome Apostles in the Didache Community." Pages 340–63 in *The Didache in Modern Research*. Edited by J. A. Draper. AGJU 37. Leiden: Brill, 1996.Repr. from *NovT* 33 (1991): 347–72.

———. "Vice Catalogues as Oral-Mnemonic Cues: A Comparative Study of the Two Ways Tradition in the Didache and Parallels from the Perspective of Oral Tradition," in *Jesus, the Voice, and the Text: Beyond the Oral and the Written Gospel*. Edited by T. Thatcher. Waco, Tex.: Baylor University Press, 2008.

———. "Wandering Radicalism or Purposeful Activity? Jesus and the Sending of Messengers in Mark 6:6–56." *Neot* 29 (1995): 187–207.

———. "Weber, Theissen, and 'Wandering Charismatics' in the Didache." *JECS* 6 (1998): 541–76.

———, ed. *The Didache in Modern Research*. AGJU 37. Leiden: Brill, 1996.

Dunn, James D. G. "The Incident at Antioch (Gal. 2:11–18)." *JSNT* 18 (1983): 3–57.

———. "Jesus Tradition in Paul." Pages 155–78 in *Studying the Historical Jesus: Evaluations of the State of Current Research*. Edited by B. Chilton and C. A. Evans. NTTS 19. Leiden: Brill, 1994.

———. *The Partings of the Ways between Christianity and Judaism and their Significance for the Character of Christianity*. Philadelphia: Trinity Press International, 1991.

Dupont, Jacques. "L'Appel à imiter Dieu en Matthieu 5,48 et Luc 6,36." *Rivista Biblica* 14 (1966): 137–58.

———. *Les Béatitudes*. 3 vols. EBib. Rev. ed. Bruges: Abbaye de Saint-André, 1969–73.

Eberhart, Christian. *Studien zur Bedeutung der Opfer im Alten Testament: die Signifikanz von Blut- und Verbrennungsriten im kultischen Rahmen*. WMANT 94. Neukirchen-Vluyn: Neukirchener Verlag, 2002.

Eckstein, Hans-Joachim. "Die Weisung Jesu Christi und die Tora des Mose nach dem Matthäusevangelium." Pages 379–403 in *Jesus Christus als die Mitte der Schrift: Studien zur Hermeneutik des Evangeliums.* Edited by C. Landmesser, H.-J. Eckstein, and H. Lichtenberger. BZNW 86. Berlin: de Gruyter, 1997.

Edgar, David H. *Has God Not Chosen the Poor? The Social Setting of the Epistle of James.* JSNTSup 206. Sheffield: Sheffield Academic Press, 2001.

Edwards, Mark J. "Ignatius and the Second Century: An Answer to R. Hübner." *ZAC* 2 (1998): 214–26.

Ehrman, Bart D. "The Didache." Pages 405–43 in *The Apostolic Fathers.* Vol. 1. LCL 24. Cambridge, Mass.: Harvard University Press, 2003.

Eichholz, Georg. *Auslegung der Bergpredigt.* 2nd ed. Neukirchen-Vluyn: Neukirchener Verlag, 1970.

Elliott, John H. "*The Epistle of James in Rhetorical and Social Scientific Perspective: Holiness-Wholeness and Patterns of Replication.*" *BTB* 23 (1993): 71–81.

Engberg-Pedersen, Troels. "The Concept of Paraenesis." Pages 47–72 in *Early Christian Paraenesis in Context.* Edited by J. Starr and T. Engberg-Pedersen. BZNW 125. Berlin: de Gruyter, 2004.

Eshel, Hanan. "The Bar Kochba Revolt, 132–135." Pages 105–27 in *The Late Roman–Rabbinic Period.* Edited by S. T. Katz. Vol. 4 of *The Cambridge History of Judaism.* Cambridge: Cambridge University Press, 2006.

Esler, Philip F. "Community and Gospel in Early Christianity: A Response to Richard Bauckham's *Gospels for All Christians.*" *SJT* 51 (1998): 235–48.

———. *Community and Gospel in Luke-Acts: The Social and Political Motivations of Lucan Theology.* Cambridge: Cambridge University Press, 1987.

———. "Making and Breaking an Agreement Mediterranean Style: A New Reading of Galatians 2:1–14." *BibInt* 3 (1995): 285–314.

Evans, Craig A. "Source, Form and Redaction Criticism: The 'Traditional' Methods of Synoptic Interpretation." Pages 17–45 in *Approaches to New Testament Study.* Edited by S. E. Porter and D. Tombs. JSNTSup 120. Sheffield: Sheffield Academic Press, 1995.

Ewherido, Anthony O. *Matthew's Gospel and Judaism in the Late First Century C.E.: The Evidence from Matthew's Chapter on Parables (Matthew 13:1–52).* SBL 91. New York: Lang, 2006.

Fiedler, Peter. *Das Matthäusevangelium.* THKNT 1. Stuttgart: Kohlhammer, 2006.

Finkelstein, Louis. *Akiba: Scholar, Saint and Martyr.* New York: Covici Friede, 1936.

———, ed. *Siphre ad Deuteronomium.* Corpus Tannaiticum 3/2. Berlin: Jüdischer Kulturbund, 1939. Repr., New York: Jewish Theological Seminary, 1969.

Fish, Stanley. *Is There a Text in This Class? The Authority of Interpretive Communities.* Cambridge, Mass.: Harvard University Press, 1980.

Fleischer, Ezra. "On the Beginnings of Obligatory Jewish Prayer." *Tarbiz* 59 (1989–90): 397–441.

Flusser, David. "'Den Alten ist gesagt': Zur Interpretation der sog. Antithesen der Bergpredigt." *Jud* 48 (1992): 35–39.

———. "Paul's Jewish-Christian Opponents in the Didache." Pages 71–90 in *Gilgul: Essays on Transformation, Revolution and Permanence in the History of Religions.* Edited by S. Shaked, et al. Leiden: Brill, 1987.

———. "A Rabbinic Parallel to the Sermon on the Mount." Pages 494–508 in *Judaism and the Origins of Christianity: Collected Articles.* Edited by D. Flusser. Jerusalem: Magnes, 1988.

———. "Die Tora in der Bergpredigt." Pages 102–13 in *Juden und Christen lesen dieselbe*

Bibel. Edited by H. Kremers. Duisburg: Braun, 1973.

Foster, Paul. *Community, Law and Mission in Matthew's Gospel.* WUNT 2/177. Tübingen: Mohr Siebeck, 2004.

France, Richard T. *Matthew: Evangelist and Teacher.* Exeter: Paternoster, 1989.

Frankemölle, Hubert. *Der Brief des Jakobus.* 2 vols. ÖTK 17/1–2. Gütersloh: Gütersloher Verlagshaus, 1994.

———. "Das semantische Netz des Jakobusbriefes: Zur Einheit eines umstrittenen Briefes." *BZ* 34 (1990): 161–97.

Freedman, David Noel, ed. *The Anchor Bible Dictionary.* 6 vols. New York: Doubleday, 1992.

Friedlander, Gerald. *The Jewish Sources of the Sermon on the Mount.* Library of Biblical Studies. New York: Ktav, 1969.

Friedmann, Meir, ed. *Seder Eliahu Rabba and Seder Eliahu Zuta.* Jerusalem: Wahrmann, 1969.

Fung, Ronald Y. K. *The Epistle to the Galatians.* Grand Rapids: Eerdmans, 1988.

Funk, Franz X. *Doctrina duodecim Apostolorum: Canones Apostolorum ecclesiastici ac reliquae doctrinae de duabus viis expositiones veteres.* Tübingen: Laupp, 1887.

Føllesdal, Dagfinn. "Hermeneutics and the Hypothetico-Deductive Method." Pages 233–45 in *Readings in the Philosophy of Social Science.* Edited by M. Martin and L. C. McIntyre. Cambridge: MIT Press, 1994.

Føllesdal, Dagfinn, Lars Walløe, and Jon Elster, *Argumentasjonsteori, språk og vitenskapsfilosofi.* 4th ed. Oslo: Universitetsforlaget, 1986.

Gafni, Isaiah. "The Status of Eretz Israel in Reality and in Jewish Consciousness following the Bar-Kokhva Uprising." Pages 224–32 in *The Bar-Kokhva Revolt: A New Approach.* Edited by A. Oppenheimer and U. Rappaport. Jerusalem: Yad Izhak Ben Zvi, 1984.

Gager, John G. *Reinventing Paul.* Oxford: Oxford University Press, 2000.

Gale, Aaron M. *Redefining Ancient Borders: The Jewish Scribal Framework of Matthew's Gospel.* London: T&T Clark, 2005.

Gammie, John G. "Paraenetic Literature: Towards the Morphology of a Secondary Genre." Pages 41–77 in *Paraenesis: Act and Form.* Edited by L. Perdue and J. G. Gammie. *Semeia* 50. Atlanta: Scholars Press, 1990.

García Martínez, Florentino. *The Dead Sea Scrolls Translated: The Qumran Texts in English.* Leiden: Brill, 1994.

García Martínez, Florentino, and Eibert J. C. Tigchelaar, *The Dead Sea Scrolls: Study Edition.* 2 vols. Leiden: Brill, 1997–98.

Garleff, Gunnar. *Urchristliche Identität in Matthäusevangelium, Didache und Jakobusbrief.* Beiträge zum Verstehen der Bibel 9. Münster: LIT, 2004.

Garrow, Alan. *The Gospel of Matthew's Dependence on the Didache.* JSNTSup 254. London: T&T Clark, 2004.

Gelin, Albert. *The Poor of Yahweh.* Collegeville, Minn.: Liturgical Press, 1963.

Gemünden, Petra von, Matthias Konradt, and Gerd Theißen, eds. *Der Jakobusbrief: Beiträge zur Rehabilitierung der "strohernen Epistel."* Beiträge zum Verstehen der Bibel 3. Münster: LIT, 2003.

George, Augustin. "Poverty in the Old Testament." Pages 5–18 in *Gospel Poverty: Essays in Biblical Theology.* Edited by A. George et al. Chicago: Franciscan Herald Press, 1977.

Giet, Stanislas. *L'Énigme de la Didachè*. PFLUS 149. Paris: Ophrys, 1970.

Gnilka, Joachim. *Das Matthäusevangelium*. 2 vols. HTKNT 1. Freiburg: Herder, 1986–88.

Goldsworthy, Adrian, *Roman Warfare*. The Cassell History of Warfare. London: Cassell, 2000. Repr., London, Phoenix, 2007.

Good, Edwin M. *Irony in the Old Testament*. Sheffield: Almond, 1981.

Goodenough, Erwin R. *An Introduction to Philo Judaeus*. 2nd ed. Oxford: Blackwell, 1962.

———. *Jewish Symbols in the Greco-Roman Period*. 13 vols. New York: Pantheon, 1953–68.

Goodman, Martin. *The Ruling Class of Judaea: The Origins of the Jewish Revolt against Rome A.D. 66–70*. Cambridge: University Press, 1987.

———. "Trajan and the Origins of the Bar Kokhba War." Pages 23–29 in *The Bar Kokhba War Reconsidered: New Perspectives on the Second Jewish Revolt against Rome*. Edited by P. Schäfer. TSAJ 100. Tübingen: Mohr Siebeck, 2003.

Goppelt, Leonhard. *Christentum und Judentum im ersten und zweiten Jahrhundert*. BFCT 2/55. Gütersloh: Bertelsmann, 1954.

———. "Das Problem der Bergpredigt." Pages 28–43 in *Christologie und Ethik*. Edited by L. Goppelt. Göttingen: Vandenhoeck & Ruprecht, 1968.

Graetz, Heinrich. *Kritischer Commentar zu den Psalmen: Nebst Text und Übersetzung*. Breslau: Schottlaender, 1882–83.

Gregory, Andrew, and Christopher Tuckett, eds. *Trajectories through the New Testament and the Apostolic Fathers*. Oxford: Oxford University Press, 2005.

Grossberg, Lawrence. "Was sind Cultural Studies?," Pages 43–83 in *Widerspenstige Kulturen: Cultural Studies als Herausforderung*. Edited by K. H. Hörning and R. Winter. Suhrkamp Taschenbuch Wissenschaft 1423. Frankfurt: Suhrkamp, 1999.

Gruen, Erich S. "Roman Perspectives on the Jews in the Age of the Great Revolt." Pages 27–42 in *The First Jewish Revolt: Archaeology, History, and Ideology*. Edited by A. Berlin and J. A. Overman. London: Routledge, 2002.

Gryglewicz, Feliks. "L'Épitre de St. Jacques et l'Évangile de St. Matthieu." *Roczniki Teologiczno-kanoniczne* 8 (1961): 33–55.

Guelich, Robert. "The Matthean Beatitudes: 'Entrance-Requirements' or Eschatological Blessings." *JBL* 95 (1976): 415–34.

———. *The Sermon on the Mount: A Foundation for Understanding*. 2nd ed. Waco, Tex.: Word, 1983.

Gundry, Robert H. "The Apostolically Johannine Pre-Papian Tradition concerning the Gospels of Mark and Matthew." Pages 49–73 in *The Old Is Better: New Testament Essays in Support of Traditional Interpretations*. Edited by R. H. Gundry. WUNT 178. Tübingen: Mohr Siebeck, 2005.

———. "In Defense of the Church in Matthew as a *Corpus Mixtum*." *ZNW* 91 (2000): 153–65.

———. *Matthew: A Commentary on His Handbook for a Mixed Community under Persecution*. 2nd ed. Grand Rapids: Eerdmans, 1994.

———. *Matthew: A Commentary on His Literary and Theological Art*. Grand Rapids: Eerdmans, 1982.

———. "A Responsive Evaluation of the Social History of the Matthean Community in Roman Syria." Pages 62–67 in *Social History of the Matthean Community: Cross-Disciplinary Approaches*. Edited by D. L. Balch. Minneapolis: Fortress, 1991.

Gussmann, Oliver. "Das Priesterverständnis des Flavius Josephus." Ph.D. diss., Universität Erlangen-Nürnberg, 2007.

Haacker, Klaus. "Feindesliebe kontra Nächstenliebe? Bemerkungen zu einer verbreiteten Gegenüberstellung von Christentum und Judentum." Pages 47–51 in *Dieses Volk schuf ich, daß es meinen Ruhm verkünde*. Edited by F. Matheus. Schriftenreihe des Forschungsschwerpunktes Geschichte und Religion des Judentums 1. Duisburg: GEJD, 1992.

Haar Romeny, Bas ter. "Hypotheses on the Development of Judaism and Christianity in Syria in the Period after 70 C.E." Pages 13–33 in *Matthew and the Didache: Two Documents from the Same Jewish-Christian Milieu?* Edited by H. van de Sandt. Assen: Van Gorcum, 2005.

Hadas, Moses. *The Stoic Philosophy of Seneca*. New York: Norton, 1958.

Hagner, Donald A. *Matthew*. 2 vols; WBC 33A-B. Dallas: Word, 1993–96.

———. "Matthew: Apostate, Reformer, Revolutionary?" *NTS* 49 (2003): 193–209.

———. "Matthew: Christian Judaism or Jewish Christianity?" Pages 263–82 in *The Face of New Testament Studies: A Survey of Recent Research*. Edited by S. McKnight and G. R. Osborne. Grand Rapids: Baker, 2004.

Hamel, Gildas H. *Poverty and Charity in Roman Palestine: First Three Centuries C.E.* University of California Publications: Near Eastern Studies 23. Berkeley and Los Angeles: University of California Press, 1990.

Hands, Arthur R. *Charities and Social Aid in Greece and Rome*. London: Thames & Hudson, 1968.

Hare, Douglas R. A. "How Jewish Is the Gospel of Matthew?" *CBQ* 62 (2000): 264–77.

Harnack, Adolf von. *Die Lehre der zwölf Apostel nebst Untersuchungen zur ältesten Geschichte der Kirchenverfassung und des Kirchenrechts*. TU 2/1–2. Leipzig: Hinrichs, 1884.

Harrington, Daniel J. *The Gospel of Matthew*. SP 1. Collegeville, Minn.: Liturgical, 1991.

———. "Matthew's Gospel: Pastoral Problems and Possibilities." Pages 62–73 in *The Gospel of Matthew in Current Study*. Edited by D. E. Aune. Grand Rapids: Eerdmans, 2001.

Harrington, Hannah K. *The Impurity Systems of Qumran and the Rabbis: Biblical Foundations*. SBLDS 143. Atlanta: Scholars Press, 1993.

Hartin, Patrick J. "Call to Be Perfect through Suffering (James 1,2–4): The Concept of Perfection in the Epistle of James and the Sermon on the Mount." *Bib* 77 (1996): 477–92.

———. *James*. SP 14. Collegeville, Minn.: Liturgical Press, 2003.

———. *James and the Q Sayings of Jesus*. JSNTSup 47. Sheffield: JSOT Press, 1991.

———. "James and the Sermon on the Mount/ Plain." Pages 440–57 in *SBLSP* 28. Edited by D. J. Lull. Atlanta: Scholars Press, 1989.

———. "The Religious Content of the Letter of James." Pages 203–31 in *Jewish Christianity Reconsidered: Rethinking Ancient Groups and Texts*. Edited by M. Jackson-McCabe. Minneapolis: Fortress, 2007.

———. *A Spirituality of Perfection: Faith in Action in the Letter of James*. Collegeville, Minn.: Liturgical Press, 1999.

———. " 'Who Is Wise and Understanding among You?' (James 3:13): An Analysis of Wisdom, Eschatology, and Apocalypticism in the Letter of James." Pages 149–68 in *Conflicted Boundaries in Wisdom and Apocalypticism*. Edited by B. G. Wright III and L. M. Wills. SBLSymS 35. Atlanta: Society of Biblical Literature, 2005.

Hartman, Lars. *Into the Name of the Lord Jesus: Baptism in the Early Church*. Studies of the New Testament and its World. Edinburgh: T&T Clark, 1997.

Harvey, A. E. "The Workman Is Worthy of His Hire: Fortunes of a Proverb in the Early Church." *NovT* 24 (1982): 209–21.

Hasitschka, Martin. "Matthew and Hebrews." Pages 87–103 in *Matthew and His Christian Contemporaries*. Edited by B. Repschinski and D. Sim. London: Continuum, 2008.

Hayes, Christine. *Gentile Impurities and Jewish Identities: Intermarriage and Conversion from the Bible to the Talmud*. Oxford: Oxford University Press, 2002.

Heinemann, Isaak. *Philo's griechische und jüdische Bildung: Kulturvergleichende Untersuchungen zu Philons Darstellung der jüdischen Gesetze*. Breslau, 1929–32. Repr., Hildesheim: Olms, 1962.

Herr, Moshe D. "Ha-hellenismus veha-Yehudim be-Erets Yisrael." *Eshkolot* NS 3–2 (1977–78): 20–27 [review of Hengel, *Judentum und Hellenismus*].

Hertig, Paul. "Geographical Marginality in the Matthean Journey of Jesus." Pages 472–89 in *SBLSP* 36. Atlanta: Society of Biblical Literature, 1999.

Hertzberg, Arthur. *The Zionist Idea: A Historical Analysis and Reader*. Repr. New York: Atheneum, 1973.

Hezser, Catherine. *The Social Structure of the Rabbinic Movement in Roman Palestine*. TSAJ 66. Tübingen: Mohr Siebeck, 1997.

Higger, Michael, ed. *Minor Tractates (Massekhtot Zeirot)*. New York 1929. Repr., Jerusalem: Makor, 1970.

———. *The Treatises Derek Erez: Masseket Derek Erez; Pirke Ben Azzai; Tosefta Derek Erez*. 2 vols. New York 1935. Repr., Jerusalem: Makor, 1970.

Hirsch-Luipold, Rainer, et al. *Die Bildtafel des Kebes: Allegorie des Lebens*. SAPERE 8. Darmstadt: Wissenschaftliche Buchgesellschaft, 2004.

Hirshman, Marc. "Rabbinic Universalism in the Second and Third Centuries." *HTR* 93 (2000): 101–15.

Hock, Ronald F. "The Workshop as a Social Setting for Paul's Missionary Preaching." *CBQ* 14 (1979): 439–50.

Hoppe, Rudolf. *Der theologische Hintergrund des Jakobusbriefes*. 2nd ed. FB 28. Würzburg: Echter, 1985.

———. "Vollkommenheit bei Matthäus als theologische Aussage." Pages 141–64 in *Salz der Erde–Licht der Welt: Exegetische Studien zum Matthäusevangelium*. Edited by L. Oberlinner and P. Fiedler. Stuttgart: Verlag Katholisches Bibelwerk, 1991.

Hübner, Reinhard M. "Thesen zur Echtheit und Datierung der sieben Briefe des Ignatius von Antiochien." *ZAC* 1 (1997): 44–72.

Hummel, Reinhart. *Die Auseinandersetzung zwischen Kirche und Judentum im Matthäusevangelium*. 2nd ed. BEvT 33. München: Kaiser, 1966.

Hurd, John C. *The Origin of 1 Corinthians*. 2nd ed. Macon, Ga.: Mercer University Press, 1983.

Ilan, Tal. "The Attraction of Aristocratic Women to Pharisaism During the Second Temple Period." *HTR* 88 (1995): 1–33.

Isaac, Benjamin, and Aharon Oppenheimer. "The Revolt of Bar Kokhba: Ideology and Modern Scholarship." *JJS* 36 (1985): 33–60.

Jackson-McCabe, Matt. *Logos and Law in the Letter of James: The Law of Nature, the Law of Moses, and the Law of Freedom*. NovTSup 100. Leiden: Brill, 2001.

———. "The Messiah Jesus in the Mythic World of James." *JBL* 122 (2003): 701–30.

———, "What's in a Name? The Problem of 'Jewish Christianity.' " Pages 7–38 in *Jewish Christianity Reconsidered: Rethinking Ancient Groups and Texts*. Edited by M. Jackson-McCabe. Minneapolis: Fortress, 2007.

———, ed. *Jewish Christianity Reconsidered: Rethinking Ancient Groups and Texts*. Minneapolis: Fortress, 2007.

Jaffé, Dan. *Le judaïsme et l'avènement du christianisme: Orthodoxie et hétérodoxie dans la littérature talmudique Ier–IIe siècle*. Patrimoines: Judaïsme. Paris: Cerf, 2005.

Jaubert, Annie. "Jésus et le calendrier de Qumrân," *NTS* 7 (1960/61): 1–30.

Jefford, Clayton N. "The Milieu of Matthew, the Didache, and Ignatius of Antioch: Agreements and Differences." Pages 35–47 in *Matthew and the Didache: Two Documents from the Same Jewish-Christian Milieu?* Edited by H. van de Sandt. Assen: Van Gorcum, 2005.

———. *The Sayings of Jesus in the Teaching of the Twelve Apostles*. VCSup 11. Leiden: Brill, 1989.

———. "Social Locators as a Bridge between the *Didache* and Matthew." Pages 245–64 in *Trajectories through the New Testament and the Apostolic Fathers*. Edited by Andrew Gregory and Christopher Tuckett. Oxford: Oxford University Press, 2005.

———, ed. *The Didache in Context. Essays on Its Text, History and Transmission*. NovTSup 77. Leiden: Brill, 1995.

Johnson, Luke T. *The Letter of James*. AB 37A. New York: Doubleday, 1995.

———. "The Use of Leviticus 19 in the Letter of James." *JBL* 101 (1982): 391–401.

Johnson, Luke T., and Wesley Wachob. "The Sayings of Jesus in the Letter of James." Pages 431–50 in *Authenticating the Words of Jesus*. Edited by B. Chilton and C. A. Evans. NTTS 28/1. Leiden: Brill, 1999. Repr. as pages 136–54 in Johnson, *Brother of Jesus, Friend of God: Studies in the Letter of James*. Grand Rapids: Eerdmans, 2004.

Jonge, Marinus de. "The Testaments of the Twelve Patriarchs and the 'Two Ways.'" Pages 179–94 in *Biblical Traditions in Transmission*. JSJSup 111. Edited by C. Hempel and J. M. Lieu. Leiden: Brill, 2006.

Jonge, Marinus de, and Johannes Tromp. "Jacob's Son Levi in the Old Testament Pseudepigrapha and Related Literature." Pages 203–36 in *Biblical Figures Outside the Bible*. Edited by M. E. Stone and T. A. Bergen. Harrisburg, Pa.: Trinity Press International, 1998.

Jónsson, Jakob. *Humour and Irony in the New Testament: Illuminated by Parallels in Talmud and Midrash*. BZRGG 28. Leiden: Brill, 1985.

Kaestli, Jean-Daniel. "Où en est le débat sur le judéo-christianisme?" Pages 243–72 in *Le déchirement: Juifs et chrétiens au premier siècle*. Edited by D. Marguerat. MdB 32. Genève: Labor et Fides, 1996.

Kaiser, Sigurd. *Krankenheilung: Untersuchungen zu Form, Sprache, traditionsgeschichtlichem Hintergrund und Aussage von Jak 5, 13–18*. WMANT 112. Neukirchen-Vluyn: Neukirchener Verlag, 2006.

Karrer, Martin. *Jesus Christus im Neuen Testament*. GNT 11. Göttingen: Vandenhoeck & Ruprecht, 1998.

Katz, Steven T. ed. *The Late Roman–Rabbinic Period*. Vol. 4 of *The Cambridge History of Judaism*. Edited by W. D. Davies and L. Finkelstein. Cambridge: Cambridge University Press, 2006.

Kazen, Thomas. *Jesus and Purity Halakha: Was Jesus Indifferent to Impurity?* ConBNT 38. Stockholm: Almqvist & Wiksell, 2002.

Keck, Leander, E. "Ethics in the Gospel according to Matthew." *The Illiff Review* 41 (1984): 39–56.

Keener, Craig S. *A Commentary on the Gospel of Matthew.* Grand Rapids: Eerdmans, 1999.

Kehrer, Günther. "Definitionen der Religion." Pages 418–25 in vol 4 of *Handbuch religionswissenschaftlicher Grundbegriffe.* Edited by H. Cancik and B. Gladigow and M. Laubscher. 5 vols. Stuttgart: Kohlhammer, 1988–2001.

Keith, P. "La citation de Lv 19,18b en Jc 2,1–13." Pages 227–47 in *The Catholic Epistles and the Tradition.* Edited by J. Schlosser. BETL 176. Leuven: Peeters, 2004.

Kellermann, Ulrich. "Der Dekalog in den Schriften des Frühjudentums: Ein Überblick." Pages 147–226 in *Weisheit, Ethos und Gebot: Weisheits- und Dekalogtraditionen in der Bibel und im frühen Judentum.* Edited by H. G. Reventlow. Biblisch-theologische Studien 43. Neukirchen-Vluyn: Neukirchener Verlag, 2001.

Kelly, Francis X. "Poor and Rich in the Epistle of James." Ph.D. diss., Temple University, 1973.

Kennard, J. Spencer. "The Place of Origin of Matthew's Gospel." *ATR* 31 (1949): 243–46.

Kilpatrick, George D. *The Origins of the Gospel according to St. Matthew.* Oxford: Clarendon, 1946.

Kimbrough, S. T. "A Non-Weberian Sociological Approach to Israelite Religion." *JNES* 31 (1972) 195–202.

Kinzig, Wolfram. "The Nazoraeans." Pages 463–87 in *Jewish Believers in Jesus: The Early Centuries.* Edited by O. Skarsaune and R. Hvalvik. Peabody, Mass.: Hendrickson, 2007.

Kittel, Gerhard. "Der geschichtliche Ort des Jakobusbriefes." *ZNW* 41 (1942): 71–105.

Kittel, Gerhard, and Gerhard Friedrich, eds. *Theological Dictionary of the New Testament.* Translated by G. W. Bromiley. 10 vols. Grand Rapids: Eerdmans, 1964–1976.

Klassen, William. *Love of Enemies: The Way to Peace.* Philadelphia: Fortress, 1984.

Klauck, Hans-Josef. *Die religiöse Umwelt des Urchristentums.* 2 vols. Stuttgart: Kohlhammer, 1995–1996.

Klawans, Jonathan. *Impurity and Sin in Ancient Judaism.* Oxford: Oxford University Press, 2000.

———. "Notions of Gentile Impurity in Ancient Judaism." *AJSR* 20 (1995): 285–312.

Klein, Gottlieb. *Der älteste christliche Katechismus und die jüdische Propaganda- Literatur.* Berlin, 1909.

Klein, Martin. *"Ein vollkommenes Werk": Vollkommenheit, Gesetz und Gericht als theologische Themen des Jakobusbriefes.* BWANT 139. Stuttgart: Kohlhammer, 1995.

Klijn, Albertus F. J., trans. "2 (Syriac Apocalypse of) Baruch." Pages 615–52 in vol. 1 of *The Old Testament Pseudepigrapha.* Edited by J. H. Charlesworth. Garden City, N.Y.: Doubleday, 1983.

———. *Jewish-Christian Gospel Tradition.* VCSup 17. Leiden: Brill, 1992.

Klijn, Albertus F.J. and Gerrit J. Reinink, eds., *Patristic Evidence for Jewish-Christian Sects.* NovTSup 36. Leiden: Brill, 1973.

Klinghardt, Matthias. *Gemeinschaftsmahl und Mahlgemeinschaft: Soziologie und Liturgie frühchristlicher Mahlfeiern.* TANZ 13. Tübingen: Francke, 1996.

Klink, Edward W. "The Gospel Community Debate: State of the Question." *Currents in Biblical Research* 3 (2004): 60–85.

Kloner, Amos. "Hideout-Complexes from the Period of Bar-Kokhva in the Judean Plain." Pages 153–71 in *The Bar-Kokhva Revolt: A New Approach.* Edited by A. Oppenheimer and U. Rappaport. Jerusalem: Yad Izhak Ben Zvi, 1984.

Kloner, Amos and Boas Zissu. "Hiding Complexes in Judaea: An Archaeological and Geographical Update on the Area of the Bar Kokhba Revolt." Pages 181–216 in *The

Bar Kokhba War Reconsidered: New Perspectives on the Second Jewish Revolt against Rome. Edited by P. Schäfer. TSAJ 100. Tübingen: Mohr Siebeck, 2003.

Kloppenborg, John S. "*Didache* 1.1–6.1: James, Matthew, and the Torah." Pages 193–221 in *Trajectories through the New Testament and the Apostolic Fathers.* Edited by Andrew Gregory and Christopher Tuckett. Oxford: Oxford University Press, 2005.

———. "Didache 16,6–8 and Special Matthean Tradition." *ZNW* 70 (1979): 54–67.

———. "Emulation of the Jesus Tradition in James." Pages 121–50 in *Reading James with New Eyes.* Edited by R. L. Webb and J. S. Kloppenborg. Library of New Testament Studies 342. London: T&T Clark, 2007.

———. "The Growth and Impact of Agricultural Tenancy in Jewish Palestine (III BCE–I CE)." *JESHO* 51 (2008): 33–60.

———. "Patronage Avoidance in the Epistle of James." *HvTSt* 55 (1999): 755–94.

———. "The Reception of the Jesus Traditions in James." Pages 93–141 in *The Catholic Epistles and the Tradition.* Edited by J. Schlosser. BETL 176. Leuven: Peeters, 2004.

———. "The Transformation of Moral Exhortation in *Didache* 1–5." Pages 88–109 in *The Didache in Context: Essays on Its Text, History and Transmission.* Edited by C. N. Jefford. NovTSup 77. Leiden: Brill, 1995.

———. "The Use of the Synoptics or Q in Did. 1:3b–2:1." Pages 105–29 in *Matthew and the Didache: Two Documents from the Same Jewish-Christian Milieu?* Edited by H. van de Sandt. Assen: Van Gorcum, 2005.

Klostermann, Erich. *Das Matthäusevangelium.* 4th ed. HNT. Tübingen: Mohr Siebeck, 1971.

Konradt, Matthias. *Christliche Existenz nach dem Jakobusbrief: Eine Studie zu seiner soteriologischen und ethischen Konzeption.* SUNT 22. Göttingen: Vandenhoeck & Ruprecht, 1998.

———. " '… damit ihr Söhne eures Vaters im Himmel werdet': Erwägungen zur 'Logik' von Gewaltverzicht und Feindesliebe in Mt 5,38–48." Pages 70–92 in *Gewalt wahrnehmen – von Gewalt heilen: Theologische und religionswissenschaftliche Perspektiven.* Edited by W. Dietrich and W. Lienemann. Stuttgart: Kohlhammer, 2004.

———. *Israel, Kirche und die Völker im Matthäusevangelium.* WUNT 215. Tübingen: Mohr Siebeck, 2007.

———. "Der Jakobusbrief als Brief des Jakobus: Erwägungen zum historischen Kontext des Jakobusbriefes im Lichte der traditionsgeschichtlichen Beziehungen zum 1. Petrusbrief und zum Hintergrund der Autorfiktion." Pages 16–53 in *Der Jakobusbrief: Beiträge zur Rehabilitierung der "strohernen Epistel."* Edited by P. von Gemünden, M. Konradt and G. Theißen. Beiträge zum Verstehen der Bibel 3. Münster: Lit, 2003.

———. "Der Jakobusbrief im frühchristlichen Kontext: Überlegungen zum traditionsgeschichtlichen Verhältnis des Jakobusbriefes zur Jesusüberlieferung, zur paulinischen Tradition und zum 1.Petrusbrief." Pages 171–212 in *The Catholic Epistles and the Tradition.* Edited by J. Schlosser. BETL 176. Leuven: Peeters, 2004.

———. "Menschen- oder Bruderliebe? Beobachtungen zum Liebesgebot in den Testamenten der Zwölf Patriarchen," *ZNW* 88 (1997): 296–310.

———. "Die vollkommene Erfüllung der Tora und der Konflikt mit den Pharisäern im Matthäusevangelium." Pages 129–52 in *Das Gesetz im frühen Judentum und im Neuen Testament.* Edited by D. Sänger, M. Konradt, and C. Burchard. NTOA/SUNT 57. Göttingen: Vandenhoeck & Ruprecht, 2006.

Kosmala, Hans. "Nachfolge und Nachahmung Gottes, II. Im Jüdischen Denken." Pages

138–231 in vol. 2 of *Studies, Essays and Reviews*. New Testament. Leiden: Brill, 1978.

Kraft, Heinrich. "Die Anfänge des geistliches Amtes." *TLZ* 100 (1975): 81–98.

Krauss, Samuel, and William Horbury, eds. *The Jewish-Christian Controversy from the Earliest Times to 1789*. TSAJ 56. Tübingen: Mohr Siebeck, 1995.

Kretschmar, Georg. "Ein Beitrag zur Frage nach dem Ursprung frühchristlicher Askese." *ZTK* 61 (1964): 27–67.

Kuhn, Heinz-Wolfgang. "Das Liebesgebot Jesu als Tora und als Evangelium: Zur Feindesliebe und zur christlichen und jüdischen Auslegung der Bergpredigt." Pages 194–230 in *Vom Urchristentum zu Jesus*. Edited by H. Frankemölle, K. Kertelge and J. Gnilka. Freiburg: Herder, 1989.

Kümmel, Werner G. "Äußere und innere Reinheit des Menschen bei Jesus." Pages 117–29 in *Heilsgeschehen und Geschichte: Gesammelte Aufsätze*. Edited by E. Grässer and O. Merk. 2 vols. Marburger Theologische Studien 16. Marburg: Elwert, 1965.

———. "Jesus und der jüdische Traditionsgedanke." *ZNW* 33 (1934): 105–30.

Künzel, Georg. *Studien zum Gemeindeverständnis des Matthäus-Evangeliums*. Calwer Theologische Monographien A/10. Stuttgart: Calwer, 1978.

Kürzinger, Joseph. *Papias von Hierapolis und die Evangelien des Neuen Testaments*. Eichstätter Materialien 4. Regensburg: Pustet, 1983.

Kuschke, Anton. "Arm und Reich im Alten Testament mit besonderer Berücksichtigung der nachexilischen Zeit." *ZAW* 57 (1939) 31–57.

Lambrecht, Jan. *The Sermon on the Mount: Proclamation and Exhortation*. Good News Studies 14. Wilmington, Del.: Glazier, 1985.

Laws, Sophie. *A Commentary on the Epistle of James*. San Francisco: Harper & Row, 1980.

———. "The Doctrinal Basis for the Ethics of James." Pages 299–305 in *Studia Evangelica*. Vol. 7. Papers Presented to the Fifth International Congress on Biblical Studies Held at Oxford, 1973. Berlin: Akademie-Verlag, 1982.

———. "Epistle of James." *ABD* 3:621–28.

Layton, Bentley. "The Sources, Date and Transmission of *Didache* 1.3b–2.1." *HTR* 61 (1968): 343–83.

Lechner, Thomas. *Ignatius Adversus Valentinianos? Chronologische und theologie-geschichtliche Studien zu den Briefen des Ignatius von Antiochen*. VC: Supplement Series 47. Leiden: Brill, 1999.

Lerner, Myron B. "The External Tractates." Pages 367–404 in *The Literature of the Sages*. Edited by S. Safrai. CRINT 2/3a. Assen: Van Gorcum, 1987.

Levine, Lee I. *The Ancient Synagogue: The First Thousand Years*. New Haven, Conn.: Yale University Press, 2000.

———. *The Rabbinic Class of Roman Palestine in Late Antiquity*. Jerusalem: Jewish Theological Seminary, 1989.

Levison, John R. "A Better Righteousness: The Character and Purpose of Matthew 5:21–48." *Studia Biblica et Theologica* 12 (1982): 171–94.

Liddell, Henry G., Robert Scott, Henry Stuart Jones, and Roderick McKenzie. *A Lexicon: With a Revised Supplement*. 9th ed. Oxford: Clarendon, 1996.

Lilje, Hanns. *Die Lehre der zwölf Apostel: Eine Kirchenordnung des ersten christlichen Jahrhunderts*. Die urchristliche Botschaft 28. Hamburg: Furche, 1956.

Lindemann, Andreas. "Antwort auf die Thesen zur Echtheit und Datierung der sieben Briefe des Ignatius von Antiochien." *ZAC* 1 (1997): 185–94.

———. Review of T. Lechner, *Ignatius Adversus Valentinianos? Chronologische und theologiegeschichtliche Studien zu den Briefen des Ignatius von Antiochen.* ZAC 6 (2002): 157–61.

Loeb, Isidore. "Les dix-huit bénédictions." *REJ* 19 (1889) 17–40.

———. "La littérature des pauvres dans la Bible." *REJ* 20 (1890): 161–98; 21 (1891): 1–42.

Lohfink, Gerhard. "Von der 'Anawim-Partei' zur 'Kirche der Armen': Die bibelwissenschaftliche Ahnentafel eines Hauptbegriffs der 'Theologie der Befreiung.'" *Bib* 67 (1986): 153–76.

Löhr, Hermut. "Jesus und der Nomos aus der Sicht des entstehenden Christentums: Zum Jesus-Bild im ersten Jahrhundert n. Chr. und zu unserem Jesus-Bild." Pages 337–54 in *Der historische Jesus: Tendenzen und Perspektiven der gegenwärtigen Forschung.* Edited by J. Schröter and R. Brucker. BZNW 114. Berlin: de Gruyter, 2002.

Lohse, Eduard. "'Ich aber sage euch.'" Pages 189–203 in *Der Ruf Jesu und die Antwort der Gemeinde. Exegetische Untersuchungen.* Edited by E. Lohse, C. Burchard, and B. Schaller. Göttingen: Vandenhoeck & Ruprecht, 1970.

Loopik, Marcus van. *The Ways of the Sages and the Way of the World.* TSAJ 26. Tübingen: Mohr Siebeck, 1991

Louw Johannes P., and Eugene A. Nida, eds. *Greek-English Lexicon of the New Testament Based on Semantic Domains.* 2 vols. 2nd ed. New York: United Bible Societies, 1989.

Ludwig, Martina. *Wort als Gesetz: Eine Untersuchung zum Verständnis von "Wort" und "Gesetz" in israelitisch-frühjüdischen und neutestamentlichen Schriften: Gleichzeitig ein Beitrag zur Theologie des Jakobusbriefes.* Europäische Hochschulschriften, Reihe 23, Theologie 502. Frankfurt: Peter Lang, 1994.

Lührmann, Dieter. "Liebet eure Feinde (Lk 6,27–36; Mt 5,39–48)." *ZTK* 69 (1972): 412–38.

Luomanen, Petri. "Corpus Mixtum: An Appropriate Description of Matthew's Community?" *JBL* 117 (1998): 469–80.

———. *Entering the Kingdom of Heaven: A Study on the Structure of Matthew's View of Salvation.* WUNT 2/101. Tübingen: Mohr Siebeck, 1998.

———. "Where Did Another Rich Man Come From? The Jewish-Christian Profile of the Story about a Rich Man in the 'Gospel of the Hebrews' (Origen, *Comm. in Matth.* 15.14)." *VC* 57 (2003): 243–75.

Luz, Ulrich. *Das Evangelium nach Matthäus.* 4 vols. EKKNT 1/1–4. Düsseldorf and Zürich: Benziger and Neukirchener, 1985–2002 = *Matthew.* 3 vols. Hermeneia. Minneapolis: Fortress, 2005–2007.

———. "The Fulfilment of the Law in Matthew (Matt. 5:17–20)." Pages 185–218 in *Studies in Matthew.* Translated by Rosemary Selle. Grand Rapids: Eerdmans, 2005. Repr. from "Die Erfüllung des Gesetzes bei Matthäus (Mt 5,17–20)." *ZTK* 75 (1978): 398–435.

———. *Matthew 1–7: A Commentary.* Trans. W. C. Linss. Minneapolis: Fortress, 1989.

———. *Matthew in History: Interpretation, Influence, and Effects.* Minneapolis: Fortress, 1994.

———. "Die Theologie des Jakobusbriefes." *ZTK* 81 (1984): 1–30.

———. "Überlegungen zum Verhältnis zwischen Liebe zu Gott und Liebe zum Nächsten (Mt 22,34–40)." Pages 135–48 in *Der lebendige Gott: Studien zur Theologie des Neuen Testaments.* Edited by T. Söding. Münster: Aschendorff, 1996.

MacMullen, Ramsay. *Christianity and Paganism in the Fourth to Eighth Centuries.* New

Haven, Conn.: Yale University Press, 1997.

———. *Christianizing the Roman Empire (A.D. 100–400)*. New Haven, Conn.: Yale University Press, 1984.

Maier, Johann. *Studien zur jüdischen Bibel und ihrer Geschichte*. SJ 28. Berlin: de Gruyter, 2004.

Malherbe, Abraham J. *Ancient Epistolary Theorists*. SBLSBS 19. Atlanta: Scholars Press, 1988.

———. "Hellenistic Moralists and the New Testament." *ANRW* 26.1:267–333.

Malina, Bruce J. *The New Testament World: Insights from Cultural Anthropology*. 3rd ed. Revised and expanded. Louisville, Ky.: Westminster John Knox, 2001.

Malina, Bruce J., and L. Rohbaugh, *Social-Science Commentary on the Synoptic Gospels*. 2nd ed. Minneapolis: Fortress, 2003.

Manns, Frédéric. *L'Israel de Dieu. Essais sur le christianisme primitif*. Studium Biblicum Franciscanum Analecta 42. Jerusalem: Franciscan Printing Press, 1996.

———. *Le Judéo-christianisme, mémoire ou prophétie?* ThH 112. Paris: Beauchesne, 2000.

Mansoor, Menahem. *The Thanksgiving Hymns: Translated and Annotated with an Introduction*. Studies on the Texts of the Desert of Judah 3. Grand Rapids: Eerdmans, 1961.

Martin, Ralph P. *James*. WBC 48. Waco, Tex.: Word, 1988.

Martin, Raymond A. *James*. Minneapolis: Augsburg, 1982.

Marxsen, Willi. *Introduction to the New Testament*. Translated by G. Buswell. Philadelphia: Fortress, 1968.

Massebieau, Louis. "L'Épitre de Jacques est-elle l'oeuvre d'un Chrétien?" *RHR* 32 (1895): 249–83.

Mathys, Hans-Peter. *Liebe deinen Nächsten wie dich selbst: Untersuchungen zum alttestamentlichen Gebot der Nächstenliebe (Lev 19,18)*. OBO 71. Göttingen: Vandenhoeck & Ruprecht, 1986.

Mayor, Joseph B. *The Epistle of St. James: The Greek Text with Introduction, Notes and Comments*. 3rd ed. London: MacMillan, 1910. Repr., Grand Rapids: Zondervan, 1954.

McCown, Chester C. "The Beatitudes in the Light of Ancient Ideals." *JBL* 46 (1927): 50–61.

McKnight, Scot. "A Parting Within the Way: Jesus and James on Israel and Purity." Pages 82–129 in *James the Just and Christian Origins*. Edited by B. Chilton and C. A. Evans. NovTSup 98. Leiden: Brill, 1999.

Meier, John P. "Antioch." Pages 12–86 in *Antioch and Rome: New Testament Cradles of Catholic Christianity*. Edited by R. E. Brown and J. P. Meier. New York: Paulist, 1983.

———. *Law and History in Matthew's Gospel: A Redactional Study of Mt. 5:17–48*. AnBib 71. Rome: Biblical Institute Press, 1976.

———. *A Marginal Jew: Rethinking the Historical Jesus*. ABRL. New York: Doubleday, 1992.

Meiser, Martin. "Vollkommenheit in Qumran und im Matthäusevangelium." Pages 195–209 in *Kirche und Volk Gottes*. Edited by M. Karrer, W. Kraus, O. Merk and J. Roloff. Neukirchen-Vluyn: Neukirchener Verlag, 2000.

Meisinger, Hubert. *Liebesgebot und Altruismusforschung: Ein exegetischer Beitrag zum Dialog zwischen Theologie und Naturwissenschaft*. NTOA 33. Göttingen: Vandenhoeck & Ruprecht, 1996.

Menken, Maarten J. J. *Matthew's Bible: The Old Testament Text of the Evangelist*. BETL 173. Leuven: Peeters, 2004.

Merklein, Helmut. *Die Gottesherrschaft als Handlungsprinzip: Untersuchung zur Ethik Jesu.* 2nd ed. FB 33. Würzburg: Echter Verlag, 1981.

Milavec, Aaron. *The Didache: Faith, Hope, and Life of the Earliest Christian Communities, 50–70 C.E.* New York: Newman, 2003.

———. "Synoptic Tradition in the *Didache* Revisited." *JECS* 11 (2003): 443–80.

———. "When, Why, and for Whom Was the Didache Created? Insights into the Social and Historical Setting of the Didache Communities." Pages 63–84 in *Matthew and the Didache: Two Documents from the Same Jewish-Christian Milieu?* Edited by H. van de Sandt. Assen: Van Gorcum, 2005.

Milgrom, Jacob. *Leviticus, 1–16: A New Translation with Introduction and Commentary.* AB 3. Garden City, N.Y.: Doubleday, 1991.

Millar, Fergus G. B. "Transformations of Judaism under Graeco-Roman Rule: Responses to Seth Schwartz's *Imperialism and Jewish Society* (2001)." *JJS* 57 (2006): 139–58.

Mimouni, Simon C. *Le judéo-christianisme ancien: Essais historiques.* Paris: Cerf, 1998.

———. "Pour une définition nouvelle du judéo-christianisme ancien." *NTS* 38 (1992): 161–86.

Mitchell, Margaret. "Patristic Counter-Evidence to the Claim that 'The Gospels Were Written for All Christians,'" *NTS* 51 (2005): 36–79.

Mitchell, Nathan. "Baptism in the *Didache*." Pages 226–55 in *The Didache in Context: Essays on its Text, History, and Transmission.* Edited by C. N. Jefford. NovTSup 77. Leiden: Brill, 1995.

Mitternacht, Dieter. "Foolish Galatians? A Recipient-Oriented Assessment of Paul's Letter." Pages 408–33 in *The Galatians Debate: Contemporary Issues in Rhetorical and Historical Interpretation.* Edited by Mark D. Nanos. Peabody, Mass.: Hendrickson, 2002.

Montefiore, Claude G. *Rabbinic Literature and Gospel Teachings.* London: MacMillan, 1930. Repr., New York: Ktav, 1970.

Moo, Douglas J. *The Epistle of James: An Introduction and Commentary.* TNTC. Grand Rapids: Eerdmans, 1985.

Moore, George F. *Judaism in the First Centuries of the Christian Era: The Age of the Tannaim.* 3 vols. Cambridge, Mass.: Harvard University Press, 1927–30.

Muecke, Douglas C. *The Compass of Irony.* London: Methuen, 1969.

Müller, Hans-Peter. *Sozialstruktur und Lebensstile: Der neuere theoretische Diskurs über soziale Ungleichheit.* Frankfurt: Suhrkamp, 1992.

Murphy, Catherine M. *Wealth in the Dead Sea Scrolls and the Qumran Community.* Studies in the Texts of the Desert of Judah 40. Leiden: Brill, 2002.

Murray, Michele. *Playing a Jewish Game: Gentile Christian Judaizing in the First and Second Centuries CE.* Waterloo, Ont.: Wilfred Laurier University Press, 2004.

Mussner, Franz. *Die Kraft der Wurzel: Judentum – Jesus – Kirche.* Freiburg: Herder, 1987.

———. "Die Tauflehre des Jakobusbriefs." Pages 61–67 in *Zeichen des Glaubens: Studien zu Taufe und Firmung.* Edited by H. Auf Der Maur and B. Kleinheyer. Freiburg: Herder, 1972.

Nanos, Mark D. *The Irony of Galatians: Paul's Letter in First Century Context.* Philadelphia: Fortress, 2001.

———. *The Mystery of Romans: The Jewish Context of Paul's Letter.* Minneapolis: Fortress, 1996.

———. "What Was at Stake in Peter's 'Eating with Gentiles' at Antioch?" Pages 282–318 in

The Galatians Debate: Contemporary Issues in Rhetorical and Historical Interpretation. Edited by Mark D. Nanos. Peabody, Mass.: Hendrickson, 2002.

Nepper-Christensen, Poul. "Die Taufe im Matthäusevangelium." *NTS* 31 (1985): 198–207.

Neusner, Jacob. *Development of a Legend: Studies on the Traditions Concerning Yohanan ben Zakkai.* StPB 16. Leiden: Brill, 1970.

———. *Eliezer ben Hyrcanus: The Tradition and the Man.* 2 vols. SJLA 3–4. Leiden: Brill, 1973.

———. "The Fellowship (חבורה) of the Second Jewish Commonwealth." *HTR* 53 (1960): 125–42.

———. "The Formation of Rabbinic Judaism: Yavneh from A.D. 70–100." *ANRW* 19.2:3–42.

———. *The Idea of Purity in Ancient Judaism.* SJLA. Leiden: Brill, 1973.

———. *A Life of Rabban Yohanan ben Zakkai c. 1–80 C.E.* StPB 6. 2nd ed. Leiden: Brill, 1970.

Nickelsburg, George W. E. "Riches, the Rich, and God's Judgment in 1 Enoch 92–105 and the Gospel According to Luke." Pages 521–46 in *George W.E. Nickelsburg in Perspective: An Ongoing Dialogue of Learning.* Edited by J. Neusner and A. J. Avery-Peck. JSJSup 80. Leiden: Brill, 2003.

Niebuhr, Karl-Wilhelm. "Die Antithesen des Matthäus: Jesus als Toralehrer und die frühjüdische weisheitlich geprägte Torarezeption." Pages 175–200 in *Gedenkt an das Wort.* Edited by C. Kähler, M. Böhm and C. Böttrich. Leipzig: Evangelische Verlagsanstalt, 1999.

———. *Gesetz und Paränese: Katechismusartige Weisungsreihen in der frühjüdischen Literatur.* WUNT 2/28. Tübingen: Mohr Siebeck, 1987.

Niederwimmer, Kurt. *Die Didache.* Kommentar zu den Apostolischen Vätern 1. Göttingen 1989.

———. *The Didache: A Commentary.* Edited by H. W. Attridge. Translation by Linda M. Maloney. Hermeneia. Minneapolis: Fortress, 1998.

———. "Der Didachist und seine Quellen." Pages 15–36 in *The Didache in Context: Essays on Its Text, History and Transmission.* Edited by C. N. Jefford. NovTSup 77. Leiden: Brill, 1995.

———. "An Examination of the Development of Itinerant Radicalism in the Environment and Tradition of the *Didache.*" Pages 321–39 in *The Didache in Modern Research.* Edited by J. A. Draper. AGJU 37. Leiden: Brill, 1996.

Nolland, John L. *The Gospel of Matthew: A Commentary on the Greek Text.* NIGTC. Grand Rapids: Eerdmans, 2005.

Novakovic, Lidija. Messiah, *Healer of the Sick: A Study of Jesus as the Son of David in the Gospel of Matthew.* WUNT 2/170. Tübingen: Mohr Siebeck, 2003.

Oppenheimer, Aharon. *The 'Am Ha-Aretz: A Study in the Social History of the Jewish People in the Hellenistic-Roman Period.* ALGHJ 8. Leiden: Brill, 1977.

———. "Bar-Kokhva and the Practice of Jewish Law." Pages 140–46 in *The Bar-Kokhva Revolt: A New Approach.* Edited by A. Oppenheimer and U. Rappaport. Jerusalem: Yad Izhak Ben Zvi, 1984.

———. Review of P. Schäfer, *Der Bar Kokhba Aufstand : Studien zum zweiten jüdischen Krieg gegen Rom, JSJ* 14 (1983): 217–20.

———, ed. *The Bar-Kokhva Revolt.* Jerusalem: Zalman Shazar Center, 1980 (Hebrew).

Oppenheimer, Aharon, and Uriel Rappaport, eds. *The Bar-Kokhva Revolt: A New Approach,* Jerusalem: Yad Izhak Ben Zvi, 1984 (Hebrew).

Osborne, Robert E. "The Provenance of Matthew's Gospel." *SR* 3 (1973): 220–35.

Overman, J. Andrew. "The First Revolt and Flavian Politics." Pages 213–20 in *The First Jewish Revolt: Achaeology, History, and Ideology*. Edited by A. M. Berlin and J. A. Overman, London: Routledge, 2002.

———. *Igreja e Comunidade em Crise: O Evangelho Segundo Mateus*. São Paulo: Paulinas, 1996.

———. *Matthew's Gospel and Formative Judaism: The Social World of the Matthean Community*. Minneapolis: Fortress, 1990.

Overman, J. Andrew, and William S. Green, "Judaism in the Greco-Roman Period," *ABD* 3:1137–54.

Overman, J. Andrew, and Robert S. MacLennan, eds. *Diaspora Jews and Judaism: Essays in Honor of and in Dialogue with A. Thomas Kraabel*. South Florida Studies in the History of Judaism 41. Atlanta: Scholars Press, 1992.

Paschen, Wilfried. *Rein und Unrein: Untersuchung zur biblischen Wortgeschichte*. SANT 24. München: Kösel, 1970.

Patte, Daniel. *The Gospel according to Matthew: A Structural Commentary on Matthew's Faith*. Philadelphia: Fortress, 1987.

Penner, Todd C. *The Epistle of James and Eschatology: Re-reading an Ancient Christian Letter*. JSNTSup 121. Sheffield: Sheffield Academic Press, 1996.

Percy, Ernst. *Die Botschaft Jesu: Eine traditionskritische und exegetische Untersuchung*. LUÅ NS 49. Lund: Gleerup, 1953.

Perdue, Leo. "Paraenesis and the Epistle of James." *ZNW* 72 (1981): 241–56.

———. "The Social Character of Paraenesis and Paraenetic Literature." Pages 5–39 in *Paraenesis: Act and Form*. Edited by L. Perdue and J. G. Gammie. *Semeia* 50. Atlanta: Scholars Press, 1990.

Perdue, L., and J. G. Gammie, eds. *Paraenesis: Act and Form*. Semeia 50. Atlanta: Scholars Press, 1990.

Piper, John. *'Love Your Enemies': Jesus' love Command in the Synoptic Gospels and in the Early Christian Paraenesis: A History of the Tradition and Interpretation of Its Uses*. SNTSMS 38. Cambridge: Cambridge University Press, 1974.

Pleins, J. David. "Poor, Poverty." *ABD* 5:402–14.

Popkes, Wiard. *Adressaten, Situation und Form des Jakobusbriefes*. SBS 125/126. Stuttgart: Katholisches Bibelwerk, 1986.

———. *Der Brief des Jakobus*. THKNT 14. Leipzig: Evangelische Verlagsanstalt, 2001.

———. "James and Paraenesis Reconsidered." Pages 535–61 in *Texts and Contexts: Biblical Texts in their Textual and Situational Contexts*. Edited by T. Fornberg and D. Hellholm. Oslo: Scandinavian University Press, 1995.

———. "Paraenesis in the New Testament: An Exercise in Conceptuality." Pages 13–46 in *Early Christian Paraenesis in Context*. Edited by J. Starr and T. Engberg- Pedersen. BZNW 125. Berlin: de Gruyter, 2004.

———. "Tradition und Traditionsbrüche im Jakobusbrief." Pages 143–70 in *The Catholic Epistles and the Tradition*. Edited by J. Schlosser. BETL 176. Leuven: Peeters, 2004.

Porter, Stanley. *Idioms of the Greek New Testament*. Biblical Languages: Greek 2. Sheffield: JSOT Press, 1992.

———. "Is *dipsychos* (James 1:8; 4:8) a 'Christian' Word?" *Bib* 71 (1990): 469–98.

Porter, Virgil V. "The Sermon on the Mount in the Book of James: Part 1." *BSac* 162 (2005): 344–60.

Prostmeier, Ferdinand R. *Der Barnabasbrief, übersetzt und erklärt.* Kommentar zu den Apostolischen Vätern 8. Göttingen: Vandenhoeck & Ruprecht, 1999.

Rahlfs, Alfred. *'anî und 'anāw in den Psalmen.* Göttingen: Dieterich, 1892.

Reinbold, Wolfgang. "Matthäus und das Gesetz: Zwei neue Studien." *BZ* 50 (2006): 244–50.

Repschinski, Boris. *The Controversy Stories in the Gospel of Matthew: Their Redaction, Form, and Relevance for the Relationship between the Matthean Community and Formative Judaism.* FRLANT 189. Göttingen: Vandenhoeck & Ruprecht, 2000.

———. "'For He Will Save His People from Their Sins' (Matt 1:21): A Christology for Christian Jews." *CBQ* 68 (2006): 248–67.

———. "Matthew and Luke." Pages 50–65 in *Matthew and His Christian Contemporaries.* Edited by D. Sim and B. Repschinski. LNTS 333. London: Continuum, 2008.

———. "Re-Imagining the Presence of God: The Temple and the Messiah in the Gospel of Matthew." *ABR* 54 (2006): 37–49.

Reventlow, Henning Graf, and Axel Graupner, eds. *Weisheit, Ethos und Gebot: Weisheits- und Dekalogtraditionen in der Bibel und im frühen Judentum.* Biblisch-theologische Studien 43. Neukirchen-Vluyn: Neukirchener Verlag, 2001.

Reydams-Schils, Gretchen J. *The Roman Stoics: Self, Responsibility, and Affection.* Chicago: University of Chicago Press, 2005.

Riches, John K. *Conflicting Mythologies: Identity Formation in the Gospels of Mark and Matthew.* Studies of the New Testament and Its World. Edinburgh: T&T Clark, 2000.

———. *Jesus and the Transformation of Judaism.* London: Darton, Longman & Todd, 1980.

Riches, John K. and David C. Sim, eds., *The Gospel of Matthew in Its Roman Imperial Context.* JSNTSup 276. London: T&T Clark, 2005.

Robinson, James M., Paul Hoffmann, and John S. Kloppenborg, eds., *The Critical Edition of Q: A Synopsis, Including the Gospels of Matthew and Luke, Mark and Thomas, with English, German and French Translations of Q and Thomas.* Hermeneia. Minneapolis: Fortress, 2000.

Roloff, Jürgen. *Der erste Brief an Timotheus.* EKKNT 15. Zürich: Benziger, 1988.

Ropes, James H. *A Critical and Exegetical Commentary on the Epistle of St. James.* ICC. Edinburgh: T&T Clark, 1916.

Rordorf, Willy. "An Aspect of the Judeo-Christian Ethic: The Two Ways." Pages 148–64 in *The Didache in Modern Research.* Edited by J. A. Draper. AGJU 37. Leiden: Brill, 1996.

———. "Does the Didache Contain Jesus Tradition Independently of the Synoptic Gospels?" Pages 394–423 in *Jesus and the Oral Gospel Tradition.* Edited by H. Wansbrough. JSNTSup 64. Sheffield: JSOT Press, 1991.

———. "Baptism according to the *Didache.*" Pages 212–22 in *The Didache in Modern Research.* Edited by J. A. Draper. AGJU 37. Leiden: Brill, 1996.

Rordorf, Willy, and André Tuilier. *La Doctrine des Douze Apôtres (Didachè).* 2nd ed. SC 248 bis. Paris: Cerf, 1998.

Rosenfeld, Ben-Zion, and Joseph Menirav. *Markets and Marketing in Roman Palestine.* JSJSup 99. Leiden: Brill, 2005.

Rosivach, Vincent J. "Class Matters in the «Dyskolos» of Menander." *Classical Quarterly* 51 (2001): 127–34.

———. "Some Athenian Presuppositions About 'The Poor.'" *Greece & Rome* 38 (1991): 189–98.

Rouwhorst, Gerard. "Didache 9–10: A Litmus Test for the Research on Early Christian Liturgy Eucharist." Pages 143–56 in *Matthew and the Didache: Two Documents from the Same Jewish-Christian Milieu?* Edited by H. van de Sandt. Assen: Van Gorcum, 2005.

Ruzer, Serge. "The Technique of composite Citation in the Sermon on the Mount (Matt 5:21–22, 33–37)." *RB* 103 (1996): 65–75.

Sänger, Dieter. "Tora für die Völker – Weisungen der Liebe: Zur Rezeption des Dekalogs im frühen Judentum und Neuen Testament." Pages 97–146 in *Weisheit, Ethos und Gebot: Weisheits- und Dekalogtraditionen in der Bibel und im frühen Judentum.* Edited by Henning Graf Reventlow. Biblisch-theologische Studien 43. Neukirchen-Vluyn: Neukirchener Verlag, 2001.

Safrai, Shmuel. "Allon, Gedalya." Pages 654–55 in vol. 2 of *Encyclopaedia Judaica.* Edited by C. Roth and G. Wigoder. 16 vols. Jerusalem: Keter, 1972.

———. "Further Observations on the Problem of the Status and Activities of Rabban Yohanan ben Zakkai after the Destruction [of the Temple]." Pages 203–26 in *Sefer zikkaron le-Gedalyahu Alon.* Edited by M. Dorman, Shmuel Safrai, and Menahem Stern. Tel-Aviv: Hakibutz Hameuchad, 1970 (Hebrew). Repr. pages 341–64 in vol. 2 of *In Times of Temple and Mishnah.* Edited by S. Safrai. Jerusalem: Magnes, 1994.

———. "Gathering in the Synagogues on Festivals, Sabbaths and Weekdays." Pages 7–15 in *Ancient Synagogues in Israel: Third–Seventh Century C.E..* Edited by Rachel Hachlili. BAR International Series 499. Oxford: B.A.R., 1989.

———. "Hasidim we-Anshei Maase." *Zion* 50 (1984–85): 133–54.

———. *In Times of Temple and Mishnah: Studies in Jewish History. Collected Studies.* (Hebrew). 2 vols. Jerusalem: Magnes Press, 1994. Repr. 1996.

———. "Jesus and the Hasidic Movement" (Hebrew). Pages 413–36 in *The Jews in the Hellenistic-Roman World: Studies in Memory of Menahem Stern.* Edited by I. M. Gafni, A. Oppenheimer and D. R. Schwartz. Jerusalem: Graphit Press, 1996.

———. "Jesus and the Hasidim." *Jerusalem Perspective* 42–44 (1994): 3–22.

———. "Martyrdom in the Teachings of the Tannaim." Pages 145–64 in *Sjaloom. Ter nagedachtenis van Mgr. Dr. A.C. Ramselaar.* Edited by Th.C. de Kruijf and H. van de Sandt. Arnhem: Folkertsma Stichting voor Talmudica, 1983. Repr. in pages 406–20 in vol. 2 of *In Times of Temple and Mishnah.* Edited by S. Safrai.

———. "Teaching of Pietists in Mishnaic Literature." *JJS* 16 (1965): 15–33.

———. "The Travels of the Sages of Yavne to Rome." Pages 151–61 in *Sefer zikkaron li-Shlomo Navon.* Edited by Ruben Bonfil *et al.* Jerusalem: Mosad Shlomo Meir / Mosad Raphael Cantoni, 1978 (Hebrew). Repr. pages 365–81 in vol. 2 of *In Times of Temple and Mishnah.* Edited by S. Safrai.

Safrai, Ze'ev. "The Bar-Kokhva Revolt and Its Effects on Settlement." Pages 182–214 in *The Bar-Kokhva Revolt: A New Approach.* Edited by A. Oppenheimer and U. Rappaport. Jerusalem: Yad Izhak Ben Zvi, 1984.

Saldarini, Anthony J. "The Gospel of Matthew and Jewish-Christian Conflict in the Galilee." Pages 23–38 in *The Galilee in Late Antiquity.* Edited by L. I. Levine. Cambridge, Mass.: Harvard University Press, 1992.

———. *Matthew's Christian-Jewish Community.* CSHJ. Chicago: University of Chicago Press, 1994.

———. *Pharisees, Scribes and Sadducees in Palestinian Society: A Sociological Approach.* Wilmington, Del.: Michael Glazier, 1988.

Sand, Alexander. *Das Evangelium nach Matthäus.* RNT. Regensburg: Pustet, 1986.

———. *Das Gesetz und die Propheten: Untersuchung zur Theologie des Evangeliums nach Matthäus.* Biblische Untersuchungen 11. Regensburg: Pustet, 1974.

Sanders, Ed P. *Judaism: Practice and Belief 63 BCE–66 CE.* London: SCM Press, 1992.

———. *Paul and Palestinian Judaism: A Comparison of Patterns of Religion.* Minneapolis: Fortress, 1977.

———. *Paul, the Law, and the Jewish People.* Minneapolis: Fortress, 1985.

Sandt, Huub van de. "'Do Not Give What Is Holy to the Dogs' (Did 9:5d and Matt 7:6a): The Eucharistic Food of the Didache in Its Jewish Purity Setting," *VC* 56 (2002): 223–46.

———. "The Egyptian Background of the 'Ointment' Prayer in the Eucharistic Rite of the Didache (10:8)." Pages 227–45 in *The Wisdom of Egypt: Jewish, Early Christian, and Gnostic Essays.* Edited by G. H. van Kooten and A. Hilhorst. Ancient Judaism and Early Christianity 59. Leiden: Brill, 2005.

———. "James 4,1–4 in the Light of the Jewish Two Ways Tradition 3,1–6." *Bib* 88 (2007) 38–63.

———. "Was the Didache Community a Group Within Judaism? An Assessment on the Basis of Its Eucharistic Prayers." Pages 85–107 in *A Holy People; Jewish and Christian Perspectives on Religious Communal Identity.* Edited by M. Poorthuis and J. Schwartz. Jewish and Christian Perspective Series 12. Leiden: Brill, 2006.

———, ed. *Matthew and the Didache: Two Documents from the Same Jewish-Christian Milieu?* Assen: Van Gorcum, 2005.

Sandt, Huub van de, and David Flusser. *The Didache: Its Jewish Sources and Its Place in Early Judaism and Christianity.* CRINT 3/5. Assen: Van Gorcum, 2002.

Satlow, Michael L. "A History of the Jews or Judaism? On Seth Schwartz's *Imperialism and Jewish Society, 200 B.C.E. to 640 C.E.*" *JQR* 95 (2005): 151–62.

Schäfer, Peter. *Der Bar Kochba-Aufstand: Studien zum zweiten jüdischen Krieg gegen Rom.* Tübingen: Mohr Siebeck, 1981.

———. "Bar Kokhba and the Rabbis." Pages 1–22 in *The Bar Kokhba War Reconsidered: New Perspectives on the Second Jewish Revolt against Rome.* Edited by P. Schäfer. TSAJ 100. Tübingen: Mohr Siebeck, 2003.

———, ed. *The Bar Kokhba War Reconsidered: New Perspectives on the Second Jewish Revolt against Rome.* TSAJ 100. Tübingen: Mohr Siebeck, 2003.

Schechter, Solomon, ed. *Aboth de Rabbi Nathan.* Vienna, 1887. Repr., New York, 1945. Rev. ed. New York: Feldheim, 1967.

Schenker, Adrian. "Pureté–impureté." Pages 961–62 in *Dictionnaire critique de théologie.* Edited by J.-Y. Lacoste. Paris: Presses Universitaires de France, 1998.

Schermann, Theodor. *Die allgemeine Kirchenordnung, frühchristliche Liturgien und kirchliche Überlieferung 1: Die allgemeine Kirchenordnung des zweiten Jahrhunderts.* Studien zur Geschichte und Kultur des Altertums, Supplement 3. Paderborn: Schöningh, 1914.

———. *Eine Elfapostelmoral oder die X-Rezension der "beiden Wege."* Veröffentlichungen aus dem Kirchenhistorischen Seminar München 2/2. München: Lentner, 1903.

Schlecht, Joseph. *Doctrina XII apostolorum, Die Apostellehre in der Liturgie der katholischen Kirche.* Freiburg i.Br.: Herder, 1901.

Schlosser, J., ed. *The Catholic Epistles and the Tradition.* BETL 176. Leuven: Peeters, 2004.

Schmeller, Thomas. *Paulus und die Diatribe: Eine vergleichende Stilinterpretation.* NTAbh

NS 19. Münster: Aschendorff, 1987.

Schnackenburg, Rudolf. "Christian Perfection according to Matthew." Pages 158–89 in *Christian* in *Existence in the New Testament*. Vol. 1. Notre Dame, Ind.: University of Notre Dame Press, 1968.

———. "Die Seligpreisung der Friedensstifter (Mt 5,9) im matthäischen Kontext." *BZ NF* 26 (1982): 161–78.

Schnelle, Ulrich. *Einleitung in das Neue Testament*. 5th ed. UTB 1830. Göttingen: Vandenhoeck & Ruprecht, 2005.

Schnider, Franz. *Der Jakobusbrief*. RNT. Regensburg: Pustet, 1987.

Schofield, Malcolm. *The Stoic Idea of the City*. Cambridge: Cambridge University Press, 1991.

Schöllgen, Georg. "Die Didache. Ein frühes Zeugnis für Landgemeinden?" *ZNW* 76 (1985): 140–43.

———. "Die Ignatianen als pseudepigraphisches Briefcorpus: Anmerkung zu den Thesen von Reinhard M. Hübner." *ZAC* 2 (1998): 16–25.

Schöllgen, Georg, and Wilhelm Geerlings. *Didache: Zwölf-Apostel-Lehre. Traditio Apostolica. Apostolische Überlieferung*. Fontes Christiani 1. Freiburg: Herder, 1991.

Schreckenberg, Heinz. "Josephus in Early Christian Literature and Medieval Christian Art." Pages 3–138 in *Jewish Historiography and Iconography in Early and Medieval Christianity*. Edited by H. Schreckenberg and K. Schubert. CRINT 3/2. Assen: Van Gorcum, 1992

Schröter, Jens. *Das Abendmahl. Frühchristliche Deutungen und Impulse für die Gegenwart*. SBS 210. Stuttgart: Katholisches Bibelwerk, 2006.

———. *Von Jesus zum Neuen Testament. Studien zur urchristlichen Theologiegeschichte und zur Entstehung des neutestamentlichen Kanons*. WUNT 204. Tübingen: Mohr Siebeck, 2007.

Schulze, Gerhard. *Die Erlebnis-Gesellschaft: Kultursoziologie der Gegenwart*. Frankfurt: Campus, 1992.

Schürmann, Heinz. "'Wer daher eines dieser geringsten Gebote auflöst...': Wo fand Matthäus das Logion Mt 5,19?" *BZ* 4 (1960): 238–50.

Schwartz, Joshua. "Judea in the Wake of the Bar-Kokhva Revolt." Pages 215–23 in *The Bar-Kokhva Revolt: A New Approach*. Edited by A. Oppenheimer and U. Rappaport. Jerusalem: Yad Izhak Ben Zvi, 1984.

Schwartz, Seth. *Imperialism and Jewish Society, 200 B.C.E. to 640 C.E.* Princeton, N.J.: Princeton University Press, 2001.

———. *Josephus and Judaean Politics*. Columbia Studies in the Classical Tradition 18. Leiden: Brill, 1990.

———. "Political, Social, and Economic Life in the Land of Israel, 66 – c. 235." Pages 23–52 in *The Late Roman–Rabbinic Period*. Edited by S. T. Katz. Vol. 4 of *The Cambridge History of Judaism*. Cambridge: Cambridge University Press, 2006.

———. "Some Types of Jewish-Christian Interaction in Late Antiquity." Pages 197–210 in *Jewish Culture and Society under the Christian Roman Empire*. Edited by R. Kalmin and S. Schwartz. Leuven: Peeters, 2002.

Segal, Alan F. "Matthew's Jewish Voice." Pages 3–37 in *Social History of the Matthean Community: Cross-Disciplinary Approaches*. Edited by D. L. Balch. Minneapolis: Fortress, 1991.

Selwyn, Edward G. *The First Epistle of Saint Peter*. London: Macmillan, 1946.

Senior, Donald. "Between Two Worlds: Gentile and Jewish Christians in Matthew's Gospel." *CBQ* 61 (1999): 1–23.

———. *The Gospel of Matthew*. Interpreting Biblical Texts. Nashville: Abingdon, 1997.

Shahar, Yuval. "The Underground Hideouts in Galilee and Their Historical Meaning." Pages 217–40 in *The Bar Kokhba War Reconsidered: New Perspectives on the Second Jewish Revolt against Rome*. Edited by P. Schäfer. TSAJ 100. Tübingen: Mohr Siebeck, 2003.

Shepherd, Massey H., Jr. "The Epistle of James and the Gospel of Matthew." *JBL* 75 (1956): 40–51.

Sim, David C. "The 'Confession' of the Soldiers in Matthew 27:54." *HeyJ* 34 (1993): 501–24.

———. "The Gospels for All Christians? A Response to Richard Bauckham." *JSNT* 24 (2001): 3–27.

———. *The Gospel of Matthew and Christian Judaism: The History and Social Setting of the Matthean Community*. Studies of the New Testament and Its World. Edinburgh: T&T Clark, 1998.

———. "The Gospel of Matthew and the Gentiles." *JSNT* 57 (1995): 19–48.

———. "The Gospel of Matthew, John the Elder and the Papias Tradition: A Response to R. H. Gundry." *Hervormde Teologiese Studies* 63 (2007): 283–99.

———. "The Magi: Gentiles or Jews?" *Hervormde Teologiese Studies* 55 (1999): 980–1000.

———. "Matthew 7.21–23: Further Evidence of Its Anti-Pauline Perspective." *NTS* 53 (2007): 325–43.

———. "Matthew and the Gentiles: A Response to Brendan Byrne." *ABR* 50 (2002): 74–79.

———. "Matthew's Anti-Paulinism: A Neglected Feature of Matthean Studies." *Hervormde Teologiese Studies* 58 (2002): 767–83.

———. "The Social Setting of the Matthean Community: New Paths for an Old Journey." *Hervormde Teologiese Studies* 57 (2001): 268–80.

Simon, Marcel. *Verus Israel: A Study of the Relations between Christians and Jews in the Roman Empire C.E. 135–425*. Oxford: Oxford University Press, 1986. Translation of *Verus Israel: Etude sur les relations entre chrétiens et juifs dans l'empire romain (135–425)*. 2nd ed. Paris: Boccard: 1983.

Skarsaune, Oskar. "The Ebionites." Pages 419–62 in *Jewish Believers in Jesus: The Early Centuries*. Edited by O. Skarsaune and R. Hvalvik. Peabody, Mass.: Hendrickson, 2007.

———. "Jewish Believers in Jesus in Antiquity: Problems of Definition, Method, and Sources." Pages 3–21 in *Jewish Believers in Jesus: The Early Centuries*. Edited by O. Skarsaune and R. Hvalvik. Peabody, Mass.: Hendrickson, 2007.

Skarsaune, Oskar, and Reidar Hvalvik, eds. *Jewish Believers in Jesus: The Early Centuries*. Peabody, Mass.: Hendrickson, 2007.

Slee, Michelle. *The Church in Antioch in the First Century C.E.: Communion and Conflict*. JSNTSup 244. London: Sheffield Academic Press, 2003.

Slingerland, H. Dixon. "The Transjordanian Origin of Matthew's Gospel." *JSNT* 3 (1979): 18–28.

Smallwood, E. Mary. *The Jews under Roman Rule: From Pompey to Diocletian. A Study in Political Relations*. SJLA 20. Leiden: Brill, 1976. Repr., 1981.

Snodgrass, Klyne. "Matthew and the Law." Pages 179–96 in *Treasures New and Old: Recent Contributions to Matthean Studies*. Edited by D. R. Bauer and M. A. Powell. Atlanta: Scholars Press, 1996.

Söding, Thomas. *Das Liebesgebot bei Paulus: Die Mahnung zur Agape im Rahmen der paulinischen Ethik.* NTAbh NF 26. Münster: Aschendorff, 1995.

Spitta, Friedrich A.W. *Der Brief des Jakobus. Studien zum Hirten des Hermas.* Vol. 2 of *Zur Geschichte und Literatur des Urchristentums.* Edited by F. A. W. Spitta. Göttingen: Vandenhoeck & Ruprecht, 1896.

Sproston North, Wendy E. "John for Readers of Mark? A Response to Richard Bauckham's Proposal." *JSNT* 25 (2003): 449–68.

Stanislawski, Michael. "Salo Wittmayer Baron: Demystifying Jewish History." No pages. Cited April 6, 2007. Online: http://www.columbia.edu/cu/alumni/Magazine/Winter2005/llbaron.html.

Stanton, Graham. "5 Ezra and Matthean Christianity in the Second Century," *JTS* 28 (1977): 67–83.

———. *A Gospel for a New People: Studies in Matthew.* Edinburgh: T&T Clark, 1992.

———. "The Origin and Purpose of Matthew's Gospel: Matthean Scholarship from 1945 to 1980." *ANRW* 25.3:1889–1951.

Starr, James. "Was Paraenesis for Beginners?" Pages 73–111 in *Early Christian Paraenesis in Context.* Edited by J. Starr and T. Engberg-Pedersen. BZNW 125. Berlin: de Gruyter, 2004.

Starr, James, and Troels Engberg-Pedersen, eds. *Early Christian Paraenesis in Context.* BZNW 125. Berlin: de Gruyter, 2004.

Stegemann, Ekkehard W., and Wolfgang Stegemann. *Urchristliche Sozialgeschichte: Die Anfänge im Judentum und die Christusgemeinden in der mediterranen Welt.* 2nd ed. Stuttgart: Kohlhammer, 1997.

Stemberger, Günter. "Der Dekalog im frühen Judentum." *Jahrbuch für biblische Theologie* 4 (1989): 91–103.

Stempel, Hermann-A. "Der Lehrer in der 'Lehre der Zwölf Apostel,'" *VC* 34 (1980): 209–17.

Stewart-Sykes, Alistair. *The Apostolic Church Order: The Greek Text with Introduction, Translation and Annotation.* Early Christian Studies 10. Strathfield, Australia: Centre for Early Christian Studies, 2006.

———. "Bread, Fish, Water and Wine: the Marcionite Menu and the Maintenance of Purity." Pages 207–20 in *Marcion und seine kirchengeschichtliche Wirkung.* Edited by G. May and K. Greschat. TU 150. Berlin: de Gruyter, 2002.

———. *From Prophecy to Preaching: A Search for the Origins of the Christian Homily.* VCSup 59. Leiden: Brill, 2001.

———. *On the Apostolic Tradition.* Crestwood, N.Y.: St. Vladimir's, 2001.

Stowers, Stanly K. *Letter-writing in Greco-Roman Antiquity.* LEC 5. Philadelphia: Westminster, 1986.

———. *A Rereading of Romans: Justice, Jews and Gentiles.* New Haven, Conn.: Yale University Press, 1994.

Strack, Hermann, L., and Paul Billerbeck, *Kommentar zum Neuen Testament aus Talmud und Midrasch.* 6 vols. Munich: Beck, 1922–61.

Strecker, Georg. "Die Antithesen der Bergpredigt (Mt 5,21–48 par)." *ZNW* 69 (1978): 36–72.

———. *Die Bergpredigt: Ein exegetischer Kommentar.* Göttingen: Vandenhoeck & Ruprecht, 1984.

———. "Judenchristentum." *TRE* 17:310–35.

———. *Der Weg der Gerechtigkeit: Untersuchung zur Theologie des Matthäus.* 3rd ed. FRLANT 82. Göttingen: Vandenhoeck & Ruprecht, 1971.

Streeter, Burnett. H. *The Four Gospels: A Study of Origins.* London: Macmillan, 1924.

Strugnell, John, Daniel J. Harrington, and Torleif Elgvin. *Qumran Cave 4. XXIV: Sapiential Texts, Part 2.* DJD 34. Oxford: Clarendon, 1999.

Stuiber, Alfred. "'Das ganze Joch des Herrn' (Didache 6,2–3)." *StPatr* 4 (1961): 323–29.

Sullivan, Desmond. "New Insights into Matthew 27.24–5." *NBf* 73 (1992): 453–57.

Syreeni, Kari. "The Sermon on the Mount and the Two Ways Teaching of the Didache." Pages 87–103 in *Matthew and the Didache: Two Documents from the Same Jewish-Christian Milieu?* Edited by H. van de Sandt. Assen: Van Gorcum, 2005.

Sysling, Harry. "De Bar-Kochba opstand, historie en legende." *Ter herkenning* 14 (1986): 165–76.

Taine, Hippolyte. *Philosophie de l'art.* 2 vols. Paris: Hachette, 1881.

Tamez, Elsa. *The Scandalous Message of James: Faith Without Works Is Dead.* Rev. ed. New York: Crossroad, 2002.

Taylor, Joan E. *Christians and Holy Places: The Myth of Jewish Christian Origins.* Oxford: Clarendon, 1993.

Taylor, Mark E. "Recent Scholarship on the Structure of James." *Currents in Biblical Research* 3 (2004): 86–115.

Taylor, Mark E., and George H. Guthrie. "The Structure of James." *CBQ* 68 (2006): 681–705.

Theissen, Gerd. "Nächstenliebe und Egalität: Jak 2,1–13 als Höhepunkt urchristlicher Ethik." Pages 120–42 in *Der Jakobusbrief: Beiträge zur Rehabilitierung der "strohernen Epistel."* Edited by P. von Gemünden, M. Konradt and G. Theißen. Beiträge zum Verstehen der Bibel 3. Münster: Lit, 2003.

———. *Die Religion der ersten Christen.* 3rd ed. Darmstadt: WBG, 2003.

———. *Sociology of Early Palestinian Christianity.* Translated by J. Bowden. Philadelphia: Fortress, 1978. Translation of *Soziologie der Jesus Bewegung. Ein Beitrag zur Entstehungsgeschichte des Urchristentums.* Theologische Existenz heute NF 194. München: Kaiser, 1977. British ed.: *The First Followers of Jesus: A Sociological Analysis of Early Christianity.* London: SCM Press, 1978.

Thiselton, Anthony C. *New Horizons in Hermeneutics: The Theory and Practice of Transforming Biblical Reading.* Grand Rapids: Zondervan, 1992.

Thornton, Stephen. "Karl Popper." *Stanford Encyclopedia of Philosophy.* No pages. Cited June 6, 2007. Online: http://plato.stanford.edu/entries/popper/.

Thyen, Hartwig. *Der Stil der jüdisch-hellenistischen Homilie.* FRLANT 65. Göttingen: Vandenhoeck & Ruprecht, 1955.

Tilborg, Sjef van. *The Jewish Leaders in Matthew.* Leiden: Brill, 1972.

Tisera, Guido. *Universalism According to the Gospel of Matthew.* European University Studies 23/482. Frankfurt: Peter Lang, 1993.

Tomson, Peter J. "The Halakhic Evidence of Didache 8 and Matthew 6 and the Didache Community's Relationship to Judaism." Pages 131–41 in *Matthew and the Didache: Two Documents from the Same Jewish-Christian Milieu?* Edited by H. van de Sandt. Assen: Van Gorcum, 2005.

———. *"If This Be from Heaven": Jesus and the New Testament Authors in Their Relationship to Judaism.* Translated by J. Dyk. The Biblical Seminar 76. Sheffield: Sheffield Academic Press, 2001.

———. "'Jews' in the Gospel of John as Compared with the Palestinian Talmud, the Synoptics and Some New Testament Apocrypha." Pages 301–40 in *Anti-Judaism and the Fourth Gospel: Papers of the Leuven Colloquium, 2000.* Edited by R. Bieringer, D. Pollefeyt and F. Vandecasteele-Vanneuville. Jewish and Christian Heritage Series 1. Assen: Van Gorcum, 2001.

———. "Das Matthäusevangelium im Wandel der Horizonte: vom »Hause Israels« (10,6) zu »allen Völkern« (28,19)." In *Judaistik und Neutestamentliche Wissenschaft.* Edited by L. Doering, H.-G. Waubke, F. Wilck. FRLANT. Göttingen: Vandenhoeck & Ruprecht, forthcoming.

———. "The New Testament Canon as the Embodiment of Evolving Christian Attitudes to the Jews." Pages 107–31 in *Canonization and De-Canonization, Papers Presented to the International Conference of the Leiden Institute for the Study of Religions (LISOR) held at Leiden 9–10 January 1997.* Edited by A. van der Kooij and K. van der Toorn. Leiden: Brill, 1998.

———. *Paul and the Jewish Law; Halakha in the Letters of the Apostle to the Gentiles.* CRINT 3/1. Assen: Van Gorcum, 1990.

———. "Paul's Practical Instruction in 1 Thess 4:1–12 Read in a Hellenistic and a Jewish Perspective." Pages 89–130 in *Not in the Word Alone: The First Epistle to the Thessalonians.* Edited by M. D. Hooker. Monographic Series of "Benedictina" 15. Rome: "Benedictina" Publishing, 2003.

———. "'Die Täter des Gesetzes werden gerechtfertigt werden' (Röm 2,13)—Zu einer adäquaten Perspektive für den Römerbrief." Pages 183–221 in *Lutherische und neue Paulusperspektive; Beiträge zu einem Schlüsselproblem der gegenwärtigen exegetischen Diskussion.* Edited by M. Bachmann. WUNT 182. Tübingen: Mohr Siebeck, 2005.

———. "The Wars against Rome, the Rise of Rabbinic Judaism and of Apostolic Gentile Christianity, and the Judaeo-Christians: Elements for a Synthesis." Pages 1–31 in *The Image of the Judaeo-Christians in Early Jewish and Christian Literature.* Edited by P. J. Tomson and D. Lambers-Petry. WUNT 158. Tübingen: Mohr Siebeck, 2003.

Tuckett, Christopher M. "Synoptic Tradition in the Didache." Pages 92–128 in *The Didache in Modern Research.* Edited by J. A. Draper. AGJU 37. Leiden: Brill, 1996.

Turner, Victor. *The Ritual Process: Structure and Anti-Structure.* Chicago: Aldine, 1969.

Un-Sok Ro, Johannes. *Die Sogennante "Armenfrömmigkeit" im Nachexilischen Israel.* BZAW 322. Berlin: de Gruyter, 2002.

Urbach, Ephraim E., *The Sages: Their Concepts and Beliefs.* Translated by Israel Abrahams. 2 vols. Jerusalem: Magnes, 1975.

Vahrenhorst, Martin. *"Ihr sollt überhaupt nicht schwören": Matthäus im halachischen Diskurs.* WMANT 95. Neukirchen-Vluyn: Neukirchener Verlag, 2002.

Verheyden, Joseph. "Epiphanius on the Ebionites." Pages 182–208 in *The Image of the Judaeo-Christians in Ancient Jewish and Christian Literature.* Edited by P. J. Tomson and D. Lambers-Petry. WUNT 158. Tübingen: Mohr Siebeck, 2003.

———. "Eschatology in the Didache and the Gospel of Matthew." Pages 193–215 in *Matthew and the Didache: Two Documents from the Same Jewish-Christian Milieu?* Edited by H. van de Sandt. Assen: Van Gorcum, 2005.

Verseput, Donald J. "Genre and Story: The Community Setting of the Epistle of James." *CBQ* 62 (2000): 96–110.

Vielhauer, Philipp. *Geschichte der urchristlichen Literatur: Einleitung in das Neue Testament, die Apokryphen und die Apostolischen Väter.* Berlin: de Gruyter, 1981.

Viviano, Benedict T. "La Loi parfaite de liberté. Jacques 1,25 et la Loi." Pages 213–26 in *The Catholic Epistles and the Tradition.* Edited by J. Schlosser. BETL 176. Leuven: Peeters, 2004.

———. "Where Was the Gospel according to St. Matthew Written?" *CBQ* 41 (1979): 533–46.

Vogt, Hermann. J. "Bemerkungen zur Echtheit der Ignatiusbriefe." *ZAC* 3 (1999): 50–63.

Vouga, François. *L'épître de Saint Jacques.* CNT 2/13a. Genève: Labor et Fides, 1984.

Vyhmeister, Nancy J. "The Rich Man in James 2: Does Ancient Patronage Illumine the Text?" *AUSS* 33 (1995): 265–83.

Wachob, Wesley H. *The Voice of Jesus in the Social Rhetoric of James.* SNTSMS 106. Cambridge, Mass.: Cambridge University Press, 2000.

Wall, Robert W. *Community of the Wise: The Letter of James. New Testament in Context.* Valley Forge, Pa.: Trinity Press International, 1997.

Wansbrough, Henry. "The New Israel: The Community of Matthew and the Community of Qumran." *SNTSU.* Serie A/25 (2000): 8–22.

Weber, Max. *Ancient Judaism.* New York: The Free Press, 1952.

———. *Economy and Society: An Outline of Interpretive Sociology.* Edited by G. Roth and C. Wittich. Translated by Ephraim Fischoff. Berkeley and Los Angeles: University of California Press, 1978. Translation of *Wirtschaft und Gesellschaft: Grundriss der verstehenden Soziologie.* Tübingen: Mohr Siebeck, 1922.

Wengst, Klaus. *Didache (Apostellehre), Barnabasbrief, Zweiter Klemensbrief, Schrift an Diognet.* Schriften des Urchristentums 2. Darmstadt: Wissenschaftliche Buchgesellschaft, 1984.

Weren, Wim J. C. *De broeders van de Mensenzoon: Mt 25,31–46 als toegang tot de eschatologie van Matteüs.* Amsterdam: Bolland, 1979.

———. "The History and Social Setting of the Matthean Community." Pages 51–62 in *Matthew and the Didache: Two Documents from the Same Jewish-Christian Milieu?* Edited by H. van de Sandt. Assen: Van Gorcum, 2005.

———. "The Use of Isaiah 5,1–7 in the Parable of the Tenants (Mark 12,1–12; Matthew 21,33–46)." *Bib* 79 (1998): 1–26.

Wettstein, Johan J. *Novum Testamentum Graecum.* Amsterdam 1752. Repr., Graz: Akademische Druck- u. Verlagsanstalt, 1962.

Wick, Peter. "Volkspredigt contra Gemeinderegel? Matthäus 5–7 im Vergleich zu Matthäus 18." *Kirche und Israel* 13 (1998): 138–53.

Wilamowitz-Moellendorff, Ulrich von. *Antigonos von Karystos.* Philologische Untersuchungen 4. Berlin: Weidmann, 1881.

Wimsatt, William K., and Monroe C. Beardsley "The Intentional Fallacy." Pages 3–18 in *The Verbal Icon.* Edited by W. K. Wimsatt. New York: Noonday, 1966.

Windisch, Hans. *Die katholischen Briefe.* 3rd ed. Revised by H. Preisker. HNT 15. Tübingen: Mohr Siebeck, 1951.

Wischmeyer, Oda, "Beobachtungen zu Kommunikation und Gliederung des Jakobusbriefes." Pages 319–27 in *Das Gesetz im frühen Judentum und im Neuen Testament.* Edited by D. Sänger and M. Konradt. NTOA 57. Göttingen: Vandenhoeck & Ruprecht, 2006.

———. "Römer 2.1–24 als Teil der Gerichtsrede des Paulus gegen die Menschheit." *NTS* 52 (2006): 356–76.

Wright, Benjamin G. "The Categories of Rich and Poor in the Qumran Sapiential Literature." Pages 101–23 in *Sapiential Perspectives: Wisdom Literature in Light of the Dead Sea Scrolls*. Edited by J. J. Collins, G. E. Sterling, and R. A. Clements. Studies in the Texts of the Desert of Judah 51. Leiden: Brill, 2004.

Wright, Benjamin G., and Claudia V. Camp, "'Who Has Been Tested by Gold and Found Perfect?' Ben Sira's Discourse of Riches and Poverty." *Henoch* 23 (2001) 153–74.

Wright, R. B., trans. "The Psalms of Solomon." Pages 639–70 in vol. 2 of *The Old Testament Pseudepigrapha*. Edited by J. H. Charlesworth. Garden City, N.Y.: Doubleday, 1985.

Yarnold, Edward. "Τέλειος in St. Matthew's Gospel." Pages 269–73 in *Studia Evangelica*. Vol. 4. Edited by F. L. Cross. TU 102. Berlin: Akademie, 1968.

Zangenberg, Jürgen. "A Conflict among Brothers. Who Were the *hypokritai* in Matthew?" in *Festschrift for Sean Freyne*. Edited by M. Daly Denton, B. McGing and Z. Rodgers. Leiden: Brill, forthcoming.

———. "Matthew and James." Pages 104–22 in *Matthew and His Contemporaries*. Edited by D. Sim and B. Repschinski. LNTS 333. London: Continuum, 2008.

———. *SAMAREIA. Antike Quellen zur Geschichte und Kultur der Samaritaner in deutscher Übersetzung*. TANZ 15. Tübingen: Francke, 1994.

Zerbe, Gordon M. *Non-Retaliation in Early Jewish and New Testament Texts: Ethical Themes in Social Contexts*. JSPSup 13. Sheffield: JSOT Press, 1993.

Zetterholm, Magnus. *The Formation of Christianity in Antioch: A Social-Scientific Approach to the Separation between Judaism and Christianity*. London: Routledge, 2003.

———. "Paul and the Missing Messiah." Pages 33–55 in *The Messiah: In Early Judaism and Christianity*. Edited by M. Zetterholm. Minneapolis: Fortress, 2007.

———. "Purity and Anger: Gentiles and Idolatry in Antioch." *Interdisciplinary Journal of Research on Religion* 1 (2005): 1–24.

Zmijewski, Josef. "Christliche 'Volkommenheit': Erwägungen zur Theologie des Jakobusbriefes." *SNTSU, Serie A/ 5* (1980): 50–78.

Zuckermandel, Moses. S., ed. *Tosephta*. Pasewalk 1881. Repr., Jerusalem: Wahrmann, 1970.

CONTRIBUTORS

Jonathan Draper is Professor of New Testament and Head of the Biblical Studies Programme at the University of KwaZulu-Natal (Pietermaritzburg Campus). Some of his publications are *Orality, Literacy and Colonialism in Antiquity*, editor (Semeia Studies 47; Society of Biblical Literature and Brill, 2004); *Performing the Gospel: Mark, Orality and Memory* (edited with R. A. Horsley and J. Miles Foley; Augsburg, 2006); *Reading the Signs of the Times: Taking the Bible into the Public Square* (edited with C. Kittredge and E. Aitken; Fortress, 2008).

Patrick John Hartin is Professor of New Testament at Gonzaga University, Spokane, Washington. His most recent publications are the Sacra Pagina commentaries on the *Letter of James* and *James of Jerusalem and Heir to Jesus of Nazareth* (both Liturgical Press).

John S. Kloppenborg is a Professor and Chair of the Department and Centre for the Study of Religion at the University of Toronto. His most recent publications are *Q, the Earliest Gospel* (Westminster John Knox, 2008) and *The Tenants in the Vineyard: Ideology, Economics, and Agrarian Conflict in Jewish Palestine* (Mohr Siebeck, 2006).

Matthias Konradt is Professor for New Testament at the University of Bern. Some of his recent publications are *Gericht und Gemeinde: Eine Studie zur Bedeutung und Funktion von Gerichtsaussagen im Rahmen der paulinischen Ekklesiologie und Ethik im 1 Thess und 1 Kor* (BZNW 117, 2003) and *Israel, Kirche und die Völker im Matthäusevangelium* (WUNT 215; Mohr Siebeck, 2007).

J. Andrew Overman is Professor of Classics at Macalester College in St. Paul, Minn. He is author of two monographs and numerous articles on Matthew's Gospel including *Matthew's Gospel and Formative Judaism: The Social World of the Matthean Community* (Fortress, 1990) and *Church and Community in Crisis: The Gospel according to Matthew* (Continuum, 1996). He is currently director of excavations at Omrit (Caesarea Phillipi) in northern Galilee under the auspices of Macalester College.

Boris Repschinski, S.J. is Professor for New Testament studies at the Leopold Franzens Universitaet Innsbruck. He has written a dissertation on "The Controversy Stories in the Gospel of Matthew" and published a number of articles on Matthew.

Jens Schroeter is Professor of New Testament Exegesis and Theology, Theological Faculty, University of Leipzig. His most recent publications are *Das Abendmahl: Frühchristliche Deutungen und Impulse für die Gegenwart* (SBS 210; Katholisches Bibelwerk, 2006), *Jesus von Nazareth. Jude aus Galiläa—Retter der Welt* (Biblische Gestalten 15, 2006; *Von Jesus zum Neuen Testament. Studien zur urchristlichen Theologiegeschichte und zur Entstehung des neutestamentlichen Kanons* (WUNT 204; Mohr Siebeck, 2007).

David C. Sim is Associate Professor in the Faculty of Theology at Australian Catholic University. He is the author of *The Gospel of Matthew and Christian Judaism: The History and Social Setting of the Matthean Community* (T&T Clark, 1998), and a co-editor of *The Gospel of Matthew in Its Roman Imperial Context* (T&T Clark, 2005), and *Matthew and His Christian Contemporaries* (T&T Clark, 2008).

Alistair Stewart-Sykes is Vicar of The Bridge Parishes, Dorset, UK. His expertise is in the formation of Christian liturgy. His most recent book is *The Didascalia apostolorum* (Brepols, 2008).

Peter J. Tomson is professor of New Testament, Rabbinics and Patristics at the Faculty of Protestant Theology in Brussels, Belgium. He co-edited *The Literature of the Sages* (1987, 2006) in the CRINT series and is general editor of the CRINT section on Jewish Traditions in early Christian Literature.

Martin Vahrenhorst is Director of the study program "Studium in Israel" at the Hebrew University Jerusalem and lecturer in New Testament exegesis at the Kirchliche Hochschule Wuppertal. His recent publications include *Ihr sollt überhaupt nicht schwören*. *Matthäus im halachischen Diskurs* (WMANT 95; Neukirchener Verlag, 2002) and *Kultische Sprache in den Paulusbriefen* (WUNT 230; Mohr Siebeck, 2008).

Huub van de Sandt is Lecturer of New Testament Studies at Tilburg University, The Netherlands. Some recent publications are *Matthew and The Didache: Two Documents from the Same Jewish-Christian Milieu?*, editor (Van Gorcum/ Fortress, 2005) and *The Didache: Its Jewish Sources and Its Place in Early Judaism and Christianity* (with D. Flusser; CRINT III/5; Van Gorcum-Fortress, 2002).

Joseph Verheyden (S.T.D.) is Professor of New Testament at the Faculty of Theology of the Catholic University of Louvain, Belgium. Recent publications include *Miracles and Imagery in Luke and John: Festschrift Ulrich Busse* (edited with G. Van Belle and J. G. van der Watt (BETL 218; Peeters, 2008).

Wim Weren is Professor of New Testament, at Tilburg University, The Netherlands. His recent publications include numerous articles and essays about Matthew.

Oda Wischmeyer holds the chair for New Testament Studies at the University of Erlangen-Nürnberg and serves as director of the Institut for New Testament Studies. Recent major publications are *Paulus: Leben-Umwelt-Werk-Briefe*, editor (UTB 2767; Francke, 2006), *Die Bibel als Text: Beiträge zu einer textbezogenen Bibelhermeneutik*, with St. Scholz (NET 14; Francke, 2008) and *Lexikon der Bibelhermeneutik*, editor (de Gruyter, 2009).

Jürgen Zangenberg is Professor of New Testament Exegesis and Early Christian Literature at the Faculty of Humanities and Professor of Archaeology at the Faculty of Archaeology of Leiden University, The Netherlands. His most recent publications are *Qumran—The Site of the Dead Sea Scrolls: Archaeological Interpretations and Debates. Proceedings of a Conference Held at Brown University November 17–19, 2002* (edited with K. Galor and J.-B. Humbert; STDJ 57; Brill, 2006), and *Religion, Ethnicity, and Identity in Ancient Galilee: A Region in Transition* (edited with H. W. Attridge and D. B. Martin; WUNT 210; Mohr Siebeck, 2007).

Magnus Zetterholm is Associate Professor of New Testament Studies at Lund University, Sweden. He is the author of *The Formation of Christianity in Antioch: A Social-Scientific Approach to the Separation between Judaism and Christianity*, (Routledge, 2003) and the editor of *The Messiah: In Early Judaism and Christianity* (Fortress Press, 2007). His forthcoming monograph, *Approaches to Paul: A Student's Guide to Recent Scholarship*, will be published by Fortress Press in 2009.

Index of Sources

Index of Subjects

Index of Ancient Personal Names

Index of Modern Authors

Printed in the United States
206346BV00001B/1-60/P

9 781589 833586